Issues in American Diplomacy

VOLUME TWO

ISSUES

IN

American Diplomacy

EDITED BY

ARMIN RAPPAPORT

University of California, Berkeley

VOLUME TWO

World Power and Leadership
Since 1895

THE MACMILLAN COMPANY · *New York*
COLLIER–MACMILLAN LIMITED · *London*

SECOND PRINTING, 1966

Library of Congress catalog card number: 65–15573

THE MACMILLAN COMPANY, New York
COLLIER–MACMILLAN CANADA, LTD., Toronto, Ontario

PRINTED IN THE UNITED STATES OF AMERICA

TO
Bernie, Jerome, and Gersten

PREFACE

THIS volume and its companion spring from fifteen years of teaching the diplomatic history of the United States to undergraduates at the University of California. During these years, I have felt the need for a book which would enable students to see that events in the past are not usually seen in the same way by different people. Often, students listening to a professor propound one point of view come to think that there is no other. They do not realize that two scholars using much the same material may emerge with two sharply conflicting interpretations.

I have, therefore, selected what I consider the most important issues in the diplomatic history of the United States and have presented two different views of each issue. The student not only has the opportunity to become aware that differences exist, but learns to exercise critical judgment in assessing the validity of each approach.

ARMIN RAPPAPORT

CONTENTS

1. *Cleveland and Venezuela*: POLITICAL PRESSURE *or*
ECONOMIC DEPRESSION?   1

   POLITICAL PRESSURE: Nelson M. Blake
      Background of Cleveland's Venezuelan Policy · 3

   ECONOMIC DEPRESSION: Walter LaFeber
      The Background of Cleveland's Venezuelan Policy:
      A Reinterpretation · 19

2. *The War with Spain*: DID THE BUSINESS COMMUNITY
WILL IT?   39

   NO: Julius W. Pratt
      The Business Point of View · 41

   YES: Walter LaFeber
      Approach to War · 51

3. *Taking the Philippines*: DESIGN *or* DRIFT?   67

   DESIGN: Ernest R. May
      American Imperialism · 69

   DRIFT: Louis J. Halle
      Dream and Reality · 81

4. *The Open Door*: BRITISH SUGGESTION *or* DOMESTIC
DEMAND?   91

   BRITISH SUGGESTION: A. Whitney Griswold
      Writing the Open Door Notes · 93

   DOMESTIC DEMAND: Charles S. Campbell, Jr.
      American Business Interests and the Open Door in China · 108

5. *Intervention in the Caribbean*: ECONOMICS *or* SECURITY?   120

   ECONOMICS: Charles A. Beard
      National Interest Formulated in Dollar Diplomacy · 122

   SECURITY: Samuel Flagg Bemis
      Safeguarding the Canal · 133

6. *The Taft-Katsura Agreement:* WAS IT A SURRENDER TO
   JAPAN?   140

   YES: Tyler Dennett
        President Roosevelt's Secret Pact with Japan · 142

   NO: Raymond A. Esthus
       The Taft-Katsura Agreement—Reality or Myth? · 148

7. *Intervention in World War I:* WAS WILSON REALLY
   NEUTRAL?   156

   NO: Edwin M. Borchard and W. P. Lage
       "Neutrality," 1914–1917 · 158

   YES: Arthur S. Link
        Wilson and Neutrality · 172

8. *Siberian Intervention:* TO AID THE CZECHS *or* TO THWART
   JAPAN?   185

   TO AID THE CZECHS: George F. Kennan
        The Decision on Siberia · 187

   TO THWART JAPAN: Pauline Tompkins
        Prelude to Intervention · 200

9. *Wilson at Versailles:* INCOMPETENT EGOTIST *or*
   PHILOSOPHER-KING?   215

   INCOMPETENT EGOTIST: John Maynard Keynes
        The Conference · 217

   PHILOSOPHER-KING: Paul Birdsall
        Wilson at Versailles · 229

10. *Good Neighbor:* HOOVER *or* ROOSEVELT?   243

   HOOVER: Alexander DeConde
        Hoover's Latin-American Policy · 245

   ROOSEVELT: Donald M. Dozer
        Roosevelt's Latin-American Policy · 262

11. *Destroyers for Bases*: DID ROOSEVELT HAVE THE
AUTHORITY?   278

    YES: Quincy Wright
    The Transfer of Destroyers to Great Britain · 280

    NO: Edwin M. Borchard
    The Attorney General's Opinion on the Exchange of Destroyers
    for Naval Bases · 288

12. *World War II*: DID ROOSEVELT PLOT WAR?   296

    YES: Charles A. Beard
    President Roosevelt and the Coming of War · 298

    NO: Basil Rauch
    Roosevelt and Japan · 318

13. *The Decision to Drop the Bomb*: WAS IT JUSTIFIED?   337

    NO: Hanson W. Baldwin
    The Atomic Bomb—The Penalty of Expediency · 339

    YES: Herbert Feis
    Comments and Conjectures on the Use of the Atomic Bomb
    against Japan · 347

14. *Yalta*: SUCCESS or FAILURE?   356

    FAILURE: William Henry Chamberlin
    The Munich Called Yalta · 358

    SUCCESS: Forest C. Pogue
    The Meaning of Yalta · 373

15. *The Communist Victory in China*: WAS CHINA BETRAYED?   387

    YES: John T. Flynn
    The Blunders That Lost a Continent · 389

    NO: John K. Fairbank
    United States Policy and the Nationalist Collapse · 402

Issues in American Diplomacy

Cleveland and Venezuela:

POLITICAL PRESSURE
or
ECONOMIC DEPRESSION?

A BOUNDARY *dispute between British Guiana and Venezuela which had been going on for half a century came to a head in 1887 when Venezuela broke off diplomatic relations with Great Britain. Venezuela demanded that the British submit the dispute to arbitration. London flatly refused to do so. Whereupon, Venezuela sought Washington's assistance. In response to the call for help President Cleveland instructed his Secretary of State, Richard Olney, to inform the British government that its action in Venezuela could be interpreted as a violation of the Monroe Doctrine and that Great Britain should accept arbitration. What astounded Britain and the world was not that a note had been sent, but rather the quality, temper, and tone of the message. It was a belligerent, bellicose, and challenging document. Olney stated, "Today, the United States is practically sovereign on this continent, and its fiat is law upon the subjects to which it confines its interposition. Why? It is not . . . because wisdom and justice and equity are invariably the characteristics of the dealings of the United States. It is because, in addition to all other grounds, its infinite resources combined with its isolated position render it master of the situation and practically invulnerable as against any or all other powers."*

Such language was not expected from the Democratic administration of Grover Cleveland. All of Cleveland's previous pronouncements on foreign affairs had been quiet, unaggressive, and modest. He had always abhorred jingoism and opposed expansionism. Why the sudden change?

For Nelson M. Blake, a professor of history at Syracuse University, the explanation lies in the political realm. In the early years of the decade of the 1890's, large segments of the Democratic party were strongly anti-British.

Irish-Americans, who constituted an important urban factor in the party, nursed an age-old animosity against England. Supporters of the free coinage of silver loathed the British, who were the leading proponents of the gold standard. It was pressure from these groups that caused Cleveland to take so firm and unexpected a stand on Venezuela. With a national election at hand he could not afford to alienate any groups in the party. Similarly, he had to "head off an almost certain political field day in foreign affairs" which the Republican opposition seemed bent on pursuing. With the Republicans virtually screaming for heroic action, Cleveland could hardly appear before the electorate as weak and pusillanimous.

Walter LaFeber of Cornell University, who has made a study of the diplomacy of the period between the end of the Civil War and the outbreak of the War with Spain (The New American Empire), admits "that Cleveland took domestic political pressures into account," but claims that his message "could not permanently have won any political enemies to his side." It is his contention that the President acted as he did because he "feared that United States interests were in jeopardy." A deep economic depression had gripped the United States in 1893. It was believed that the American economic system had reached the point of maturity with the disappearance of the frontier and that the only solution for the economic ills was expanded foreign trade, particularly in the direction of Latin America. In that area, however, the British (and to a lesser extent the French and Germans) threatened the American position of supremacy. Hence the pressing need to warn the English in positive and stentorian tones that in South America "the United States is practically sovereign." The Venezuela affair was seized upon as the occasion for the showdown.

Background of Cleveland's Venezuelan Policy

NELSON M. BLAKE

CLEVELAND'S Venezuelan policy, regarded primarily as diplomacy, seems paradoxical. Cleveland was one of the most conservative of American presidents and not in the least given to adventure in foreign affairs. Yet the Olney note on the Venezuelan issue and Cleveland's special message to Congress are among the most crudely assertive ever issued by responsible American statesmen. How did it happen that caution so abruptly became rashness? Even in the case of the rugged Cleveland it must be remembered that American foreign policy has always been exposed to many forces extraneous to diplomacy. Crosscurrents of political pressure and mobilized opinion are usually at work, and any particular step of American diplomacy may represent the resultant of many forces. Here is the clue this essay will follow in reviewing Cleveland's Venezuelan policy.

In 1895 the tide of nineteenth century imperialism was running strong. Under Harrison and the energetic Blaine it had seemed that the United States was about to join the colonial race. Cleveland, however, had set his face doggedly against this tendency. Particularly by repudiating the Republican policy in Hawaii the Democratic President had demonstrated his repugnance for his predecessor's policy.

Cleveland's natural inclination toward caution in foreign relations was supported by the two men who held the most important American diplomatic appointments. Secretary of State Walter Q. Gresham was a friendly mid-Westerner who sought to conciliate and win over by argument the foreign representatives with whom he came in contact, while Thomas F. Bayard, our ambassador to Great Britain, had a kindred preference for the smooth path of gentlemanly compromise.

The predilection of Cleveland, Gresham, and Bayard for a quiet and unassertive foreign policy had a certain amount of support. Many of the mugwumps who had been attracted to Cleveland were typical nineteenth century liberals—free traders and anti-imperialists. Notable among these were Carl Schurz, Oscar Straus, and Edward Atkinson. The New York *Evening Post* and the *Nation*, both directed by E. L. Godkin, were sounding boards for this

Nelson M. Blake, "Background of Cleveland's Venezuelan Policy," *The American Historical Review*, XLVII 1942, pp. 259–277. Reprinted by permission of The American Historical Review.

kind of opinion. Closely allied with this opposition to the diplomacy of force was a growing support for international arbitration.[1]

Among those who had no great confidence in the proximity of the era of peace through free trade and arbitration there were a few who believed that the United States should become the ally of England. The Anglo-Saxons, they asserted, were favored by Providence with a special destiny and should stand together against the world. Such sentiments were not yet safe for politicians but were thrown out with some regularity by publicists.[2] The assumption of Anglo-Saxon unity was to be met more frequently in England than in America. British isolation was already appearing dangerous, and American tourists and journalists in 1895 remarked an eagerness on the part of the English to court American sympathy.[3]

Although Americans who loved peace for peace's sake or peace with England from racial loyalty were numerous enough to raise an impressive voice in December, 1895, they were far less audible than the aggressive patriots during the early months of the year. The want of spirit in Cleveland's conduct of foreign relations was under attack from many quarters.

Republican politicians and editors led the charge. They resented deeply the rebuke to them inherent in Cleveland's Hawaiian policy; they hated Gresham as a renegade Republican.[4] Moreover, they had long ago branded the President's tariff views as subservience to Britain and free trade.[5] The brilliant and caustic Lodge was probably the most formidable critic of Democratic foreign policy, but Senators Cullom of Illinois and Chandler of New Hamushire were equally partisan and outspoken. Young Theodore Roosevelt was using all his growing influence to rout the pacifists. He paid his compliments to anti-imperialists like Edward Atkinson in these words:

These solemn prattlers strive after an ideal in which they shall happily unite the imagination of a green grocer with the heart of a Bengalese baboo. They are utterly incapable of feeling one thrill of generous emotion, or the slightest throb of that

[1] Cleveland was regarded as a friend of the arbitration movement. See numerous memorials in the 1895 and 1896 volumes of the Cleveland Papers in the Library of Congress.

[2] As illustrative see J. E. Chamberlain, "A Dream of Anglo-Saxondom", *Galaxy*, XXIV (Dec., 1877), 788–91; A. T. Mahan, "The United States Looking Outward", *Atlantic Monthly*, LXVI (Dec., 1890), 816–24; Meath, "Anglo-Saxon Unity", *Fortnightly Review*, Old Series, LV (Apr., 1891), 615–22; Andrew Carnegie, "A Look Ahead", *North American Review*, CLVI (June, 1893), 685–716.

[3] New York *Sun*, May 5, 1895; Boston *Evening Transcript*, Nov. 2, 1895.

[4] Republican bitterness toward Gresham was rebuked by the Boston *Herald*. See the *Literary Digest*, X (Dec. 29, 1894), 248.

[5] Ex-Governor Russell of Massachusetts said of these incessant Republican attacks: "Our Senators, Hoar and Lodge, are more to blame than any other men. They began upon Mr. Bayard in 1885 and have relentlessly, and most unpatriotically denounced every known movement of the State Department since." Letter to Gresham, Jan. 6, 1895, Gresham Papers, Library of Congress.

pulse which gives to the world statesmen, patriots, warriors, and poets, and which makes a nation other than a cumberer of the world's surface.[6]

If the Democrats had supported the pacific policies of the administration as vigorously as the Republicans attacked them, the State Department might have ignored its critics. But the Republicans had the satisfaction of knowing that their dislike of Clevelandism in foreign affairs was shared in important sections of the Democratic party.

The Democratic chairman of the Senate Foreign Relations Committee, John T. Morgan of Alabama, was completely out of sympathy with Cleveland and Gresham.[7] He was hostile to Cleveland's foreign policy not only because he favored the annexation of Hawaii and more activity in promoting the Isthmian canal, but because he was a silverite. All the silver enthusiasts— Democratic as well as Republican and Populist—portrayed Cleveland's monetary policies as being in the interest of English money lords. Jingoism and hostility to England were integral parts of silver oratory.[8]

The American Irish were another group disturbed by charges that the Cleveland administration was pro-British. Events during the last decade had served to make Irish dislike of England an important political factor. The long-standing alliance of the Irish-Americans with the Democratic party had been challenged throughout the eighties by a persistent effort of the Republicans to woo them away. It had required energetic organization on the Democratic side to hold the Irish in line for Cleveland in 1892.[9] Practical Democratic politicians still lived in fear that the Republicans might achieve the reputation of being the more valiant defenders of the eagle over the lion.

Peace advocates and jingoes were competing for the ear of the American public in the early months of 1895. By the testimony of all observers, whatever their own prepossession, it was the jingoes who made their appeal the more effectively. It became common opinion that there was something "un-American" about the spiritless conduct of foreign affairs by the Cleveland administration.

In almost every issue on which jingoes and anti-jingoes clashed, Anglo-American relations were involved. When American expansionists agitated for the annexation of Hawaii, it was asserted that Great Britain was about to seize it; when the same group advocated a great navy, America was menaced by British naval supremacy; when they demanded an American-controlled

[6] "American Ideals", *Forum*, XVIII (Feb., 1895), 749. See also Roosevelt's letter to Lodge, Oct. 27, 1894, *Selections from the Correspondence of Theodore Roosevelt and Henry Cabot Lodge, 1884–1918* (New York and London, 1925), I, 139.

[7] Matilda Gresham, *Life of Walter Quintin Gresham, 1832–1895* (Chicago, 1919), II, 765. For Bayard's dislike of Morgan see Bayard to Gresham, May 9, 1895, Gresham Papers.

[8] *Cf. Reminiscences of Senator William M. Stewart of Nevada*, ed. by George Rothwell Brown (New York and Washington, 1908), p. 320.

[9] See a long letter of Thos. H. Ronayne to the Democratic National Committee, May 22, 1895, Cleveland Papers.

Isthmian canal, England was intending to dominate the proposed waterway. Editorial writers, like politicians, found baiting England easy and popular. A secretary in the British embassy in Washington wrote that it would be "a comfort to go to a country where one can read the news without finding in every paper an article accusing one's country of every conceivable crime".[10]

It was in such an atmosphere that American policy on the Venezuelan question was being formulated. The situation had not caused much popular agitation until March, 1895. Neither Cleveland's advocacy of arbitration of the dispute in his annual message of December, 1894, nor the passage of a congressional resolution to the same effect in February had occasioned any considerable comment. Immediately after the adjournment of Congress, however, newspaper references to the dispute became increasingly frequent. In part this was simply a phase of the general jingo campaign against Cleveland, but ammunition for these particular volleys was supplied by active friends of Venezuela. William L. Scruggs, who had been United States minister to Venezuela under Harrison, was now a special agent of the Venezuelan government and an active propagandist. The preceding fall he had written a pamphlet entitled "British Aggressions in Venezuela, or the Monroe Doctrine on Trial". It was sold on newsstands and distributed gratis and generously to editors and politicians.[11] In March another pamphlet, prepared by E. R. Johnes "of counsel" for the Venezuelan government, was making its way into the hands of editors.[12] Other less open influences were doubtless at work. Spring Rice complained: "The South Americans are in with all the low press men and every sort of lie is propagated about British aggression." [13] Mrs. Gresham in the biography of her husband refers to the activities of speculators, and Bayard in London was alarmed at reports of the manipulations of American concessionaires.[14]

The jingo press accepted without question the Venezuelan view of the issue. To the New York *Tribune* the case was "perfectly simple". Venezuela owned the land; Great Britain coveted it and was trying to grab it—by guile if she could, by force if she must.[15] The New York *Sun* declared that, should the Venezuelans be forced to fight for their rights, it would become the duty of American citizens to support them.[16] Inaccurate accounts that Bayard had reported a refusal of the British to arbitrate were handled by even the more peaceful papers in a way likely to irritate American opinion. "None Of Our Business" was the headline summary of the British position as seen by the

[10] Spring Rice to his sisters, Mar. 12, 1895, *The Letters and Friendships of Sir Cecil Spring Rice: A Record*, ed. by Stephen Gwynn (Boston and New York, 1929), I, 175.

[11] T. D. Jervey, "William Lindsay Scruggs—A Forgotten Diplomat", *South Atlantic Quarterly*, XXVII (July, 1928), 292-309.

[12] New York *Sun*, Mar. 23, 1895.

[13] Letter to Villiers, Apr. 12, 1895, Gwynn, I, 175.

[14] Gresham, II, 794. Bayard to Gresham, Apr. 5, 1895, Cleveland Papers.

[15] May 21, 1895.

[16] Mar. 23, 1895.

Boston *Transcript*,[17] while the New York *World*, which was to win great prestige as a peacemaker in December, was indulging in extremely provocative headlines in April.[18]

The English, however, failed to heed the danger signals which warned of rising American temper. Just when the Venezuelan issue was approaching a crisis, the British foreign office proceeded to take drastic action against Nicaragua and thus arouse a new tempest of American protest. News of a British ultimatum to this Central American state became public in March, and from then on until the final settlement of the affair in May the newspapers kept the matter almost constantly on the first page under sensational headlines.

Diplomatically the "Corinto affair", as the incident came to be called, was not very important. The British government demanded reparation from Nicaragua for the seizure and expulsion from the latter's territory of several British subjects, including a consular agent. At the expiration of the three-month period set for compliance with these demands, British men-of-war proceeded to Nicaraguan waters, and on April 27 British marines occupied the port of Corinto. On May 2 a settlement was announced accepting the guarantee of Salvador for the payment of the required indemnity, and British evacuation followed promptly. The Cleveland administration handled the matter cautiously. Asked by Nicaragua to intervene against an alleged violation of the Monroe Doctrine, Gresham held that the doctrine was not involved so long as Great Britain evidenced no purpose of permanently occupying American soil. However, the good offices of the United States were used, first, in an attempt to secure a further period of grace for Nicaragua before the occupation of Corinto, and then in smoothing the way for the eventual settlement.[19]

The citizen who learned of these events through the daily press found them presented as much more exciting than they really were. Our Atlantic fleet was cruising in the Caribbean, and every movement of the ships was interpreted as being related to the Nicaraguan affair.[20] Official denials that any special significance was to be attributed to these maneuvers served only to whet popular interest.[21] News dispatches also reported great activity at the State Department, where Gresham was said to have notified the British government that coercive action against Nicaragua would be considered an infraction of the Monroe Doctrine.[22]

[17] Apr. 5, 1895.

[18] *E.g.*, New York *World*, Apr. 5, 1895.

[19] State Department Memorandum sent to Olney, Aug. 10, 1895, Olney Papers, Library of Congress.

[20] New York *Sun*, Mar. 20 and 21, 1895; New York *Tribune*, Mar. 20; Philadelphia *Public Ledger*, Mar. 21.

[21] *Ibid.*, Mar. 30, Apr. 3, 1895

[22] New York *Tribune*, Apr. 16, 1895.

Having reported that the administration's policy was much more active than it really was, the jingo press then made much of what it portrayed as a backdown by Cleveland and Gresham. "We Will Not Protest", said the New York *Sun* headlines, "England May Land Troops In Nicaragua For All Of Us." [23] The actual occupation of Corinto brought to a head all the hostile criticism of the President. Editorial writers doubted the assurances of Great Britain that no permanent acquisition of territory was contemplated. "All the world knows what a temporary occupation by Great Britain means", asserted the Boston *Post*, while the Philadelphia *Press* declared: "What is the most amazing and embittering is that this act of British aggression is consummated with the assent and sanction of the American Administration." [24]

The politicians were even more severe than the press in denunciation of Cleveland's policy. Legislative houses in Missouri, Connecticut, and New York passed resolutions condemning what the New York assembly termed "the supineness, dilatoriness and lack of National and patriotic spirit which has characterized the Administration in dealing with this complication". [25] Particularly serious for the administration were pronouncements by leading senators. Shelby Cullom, ranking Republican member of the Foreign Relations Committee, was quoted as saying: "If a plain, emphatic protest had been made by the United States Government, England would not have occupied Corinto. Now that she is there, I believe in using force, if necessary, to get her out." [26] Senator Morgan vehemently denounced British policy and asserted that Congress would deal with these aggressions in its next session. [27] A bitterly sarcastic open letter was directed to the President by Senator Stewart of Nevada. Cleveland was congratulated for his "conspicuous bravery in promoting the policy of the mother country", not only in exterminating "obnoxious bimetallists and pestiferous farmers" opposed to British financial policy but in co-operating cordially "in the policy of conquest and dominion for the mother country". [28]

The excesses of the jingoes did not pass entirely without rebuke. Senator Hill of New York warned against adventurous and unwarranted applications of the Monroe Doctrine, [29] while many newspapers denied that American interests were threatened by the events in Nicaragua. [30] The State Department itself attempted a modest bit of civic education by putting out a

[23] Apr. 25, 1895. *Cf.* the New York *Tribune*, Apr. 26.

[24] Quoted in *ibid.*, Apr. 30, 1895. For other severely critical comments see *Public Opinion*, XVIII (May 2, 1895), 468–69.

[25] Cleveland Papers; New York *Tribune*, May 1, 2, 1895.

[26] New York *World*, May 3, 1895.

[27] New York *Tribune*, May 1, 1895.

[28] Apr. 30, 1895, Cleveland Papers; New York *World*, May, 1, 1895.

[29] *Ibid.*, Apr. 22, 1895; New York *Tribune*, Apr. 29.

[30] *I.e.*, Washington *Star*, Philadelphia *Record*, Providence *Journal*. See the *Literary Digest*, XI (May 4, 1895), 1–2. For a biting criticism of the jingoism of the *Tribune* see the *Nation*, LX (May 2, 1895), 333.

pamphlet containing the exact words of President Monroe in an attempt to demonstrate the inapplicability of the famous doctrine to this controversy.[31]

The eventual withdrawal of the British seemed to the moderates proof that the administration's policy had been justified. In a note to Gresham the President wrote: "I suppose you hear how matters are straightening out in our foreign relations. Our turn to feel well is at hand and the "jingoes' are hunting for good back seats." [32] The Boston *Transcript* hailed another defeat for the "congressional blatherskites" who were attempting to excite war fever against Great Britain.[33]

Criticism of Cleveland and Gresham did not, however, abate in the least. Headlines in the *Tribune* were bitter, and the Toledo *Blade* asserted: "Had James G. Blaine been Secretary of State the past year, Americans would not now be hanging their heads in shame and humiliation." [34] Comments in the British press as quoted in American newspapers were such as to add to Cleveland's difficulties. On the one side, praise for American neutrality in a tone described as "unctuous adulation" [35] lent color to charges that the President was pro-British. On the other hand, some English comment was dangerously provocative. The London *Daily Graphic* called Nicaragua a "martyr to Monroeism" who was being given a "lesson long needed" by Latin America.[36] The London *Globe* rejoiced that a "sharp little lesson" had been given not only to Nicaragua but also to the United States, whose disposition to interfere in disputes between smaller states and Europe was as "objectionable" as it was "uncalled for." [37]

The Corinto affair, trivial as a diplomatic incident, is essential to an understanding of the background of the Venezuelan policy. Whether or not we had any right to intervene, large sections of the public did not like Great Britain's heavy-handed method in dealing with a small American state. The Cleveland administration had to take a severe drubbing, and the experience unquestionably influenced its subsequent dealings with England.

Evidences of increasing discontent with Cleveland's foreign policy were to be found in the rank and file of the Democratic party. "The Old Guard of the Democracy", said the *Sun*, "has been completely demoralized and estranged by the surrender of American interests." [38] In a meeting of the Connecticut Democratic State Committee the blunt assertion was made that the Democrats of that state did not approve the President's foreign

[31] *Extracts from the Seventh Annual Message of James Monroe, Dec. 2, 1823* (printed for the State Department, Washington, 1895); New York *Tribune*, May 2, 1895.
[32] May 4, 1895, Gresham Papers.
[33] May 6, 1895.
[34] Quoted in *Public Opinion*, XVIII (May 9, 1895), 502. *Cf.* the New York *Tribune*, May 4, 1895, and the New York *Sun*, May 4.
[35] Boston *Transcript*, Apr. 26, 1895.
[36] Quoted in the Philadelphia *Public Ledger*, Apr. 25, 1895.
[37] Quoted in the New York *Sun*, May 5, 1895.
[38] Apr. 24, 1895.

policy.[39] The principal speaker at the annual meeting of the Inter-
state Democratic Association of the District of Columbia called for the
maintenance of the Monroe Doctrine, which, it was asserted, the
British admiral at Corinto had called "an obsolete doctrine" and a
"myth".[40]

Democrats close to the administration shared this impatience with con-
servatism in diplomacy. William C. Whitney cabled from Italy to commend
Gresham for an unexpected display of vigor.[41] Before the American Society
in London our ambassador to France, James Eustis, indulged in fulsome
praise of the United States, which, he said, had great strength but never used
it for the oppression of small nations. The *Tribune* and the *Sun* contrasted
the patriotic Eustis with Bayard, who—*horribile dictu*—had proposed a toast
to Queen Victoria at the same banquet.[42]

The most notable incident, however, indicating the desire of the Cleveland
Democrats to assert their own lusty patriotism was the speech of Don M.
Dickinson on May 10. Dickinson was a close friend of Cleveland and had
been Postmaster General in his first administration. At a banquet of the
Loyal Legion in Detroit he spoke to the provocative toast, "Our Veterans:
Can They Hear the Bugle Call?" The hope that the age of wars was past, he
said, did not square with the evidence of European imperialism and militar-
ism. He called for a stronger American navy and related the history of England's long hostility to the United States, laying particular stress on Britain's
"most extraordinary claims and movements" in Nicaragua and Venezuela.[43]

Dickinson's speech was widely reported. Many papers assumed that it was
intended as a rebuke to Cleveland and Gresham. A few observed the more
suggestive fact that it was delivered directly after a trip to Washington on
which Dickinson had visited the President and that it probably reflected a
growing concern on the part of the administration with the reproaches against
its Americanism.[44]

The anxiety of Cleveland over the Venezuelan issue was further evidenced
by the fact that the President personally canvassed the field for an exceptional
man to assume the duties of minister to Venezuela.[45] The position was
offered in turn to ex-Governor Russell of Massachusetts, to G. L. Rives
of New York, and to John Bassett Moore.[46] Cleveland was apparently still
thinking in terms of a cautious policy, because all of these men were promi-

---

[39] New York *Tribune*, May 11, 1895.

[40] *Ibid.*, May 30, 1895.

[41] Gresham, II, 787.

[42] New York *Tribune*, Apr. 20, 1895; New York *Sun*, Apr. 20.

[43] Detroit *Free Press*, May 10, 1895.

[44] Philadelphia *Public Ledger*, May 13, 1895.

[45] The incumbent, Seneca Haselton, had been called home in disgrace after reports of
intemperance. New York *World*, May 14, 1895.

[46] Russell to Cleveland, Apr. 12, 1895; Rives to Cleveland, May 9, 1895; Moore to
Cleveland, May 20, 1895. All in the Cleveland Papers.

nent critics of the jingoes. Moore had just published a pamphlet on the
Monroe Doctrine in which the historic document was very conservatively
construed.[47]

Secretary Gresham, meanwhile, was working long hours over the draft of a
new note to Great Britain on the boundary dispute. According to his wife, the
Secretary was confident that the difficulty could yet be settled without friction,
that he could present such a statement of the facts that the British government
would accept arbitration.[48] It is probable, however, that not all the cabinet
were content with so cautious a policy.[49] When Gresham became seriously ill,
the persistent Scruggs went directly to the President with an appeal for strong
action.[50]

On May 28 death removed Gresham from the perplexities of the State Department. The naming of Richard Olney as his successor was interpreted at
once as evidence that the President intended to pursue a more vigorous foreign
policy. This was due in part to Olney's reputation for decisive action gained in
the Chicago strike crisis but more particularly to reports that the Attorney
General had been a conspicuous advocate of firmer diplomacy in recent Cabinet meetings.[51] Most significant of all, it was known that Olney had already
been working on the Venezuelan case before the death of Gresham.[52] The New
York *Tribune* asserted at once that a new departure in foreign policy was impending.[53] Scruggs responded to the change of personnel in the State Department by sending Olney a copy of his famous pamphlet and a fulsome letter in
which the publicist expressed "every confidence in your ability and purpose to
make the American name respected abroad".[54]

The determination to stiffen American policy, apparent when Olney took
over the State Department, must have been increased by the clear signs that
the Republicans were seeking to gain further advantage from the situation. In
June the Republican Club of New York City was giving publicity to a report
dilating on the British invasion of Nicaragua and the Monroe Doctrine.[55] In
June, also, appeared an important magazine article on the Venezuelan question
written by Senator Lodge.[56] He intended it to pave the way for a stiff declara-

---

[47] *The Monroe Doctrine: Its Origin and Meaning* (New York, 1895; reprinted from
the New York *Evening Post*). The vacant diplomatic post was eventually given to Allen
Thomas, who had been consul at La Guayra. *Dictionary of American Biography*, XVIII
(New York, 1936), 420.

[48] Gresham, II, 795.

[49] *Ibid.*, p. 798.

[50] Jervey, *South Atlantic Quar.*, XXVII, 303.

[51] New York *Tribune*, June 8, 1895. *Cf.* the Boston *Evening Transcript*, May 31.

[52] Philadelphia *Public Ledger*, June 10, 1895.

[53] A curiously accurate prediction of the whole Venezuelan policy is to be found in the
Tribune for June 11, 1895.

[54] Scruggs to Olney, June 17, 1895, Olney Paper.

[55] New York *Tribune*, June 3, 1895.

[56] "England, Venezuela, and the Monroe Doctrine," *North Am. Rev.*, CLX (June,
1895), 651–58. The tone of the article is suggested by the concluding sentence: "The

tion of the Monroe Doctrine by the next Congress. It would "make some of the brethren sit up and take notice".[57]

To Olney and Cleveland, now preparing to take a firm line, one of the most troublesome obstacles was the attitude of Ambassador Bayard. A low opinion of the Spanish-Americans,[58] a fear of the pressure of speculators, a dislike of jingoism, plus what the *Tribune* called a lack of "the superb and indispensable quality of making himself disagreeable at the proper time" [59] had made Bayard overcautious in the conduct of negotiations on the Venezuelan matter. Even a subordinate in the London embassy was grumbling about him. On June 22 J. R. Roosevelt wrote to Secretary Lamont:

Mr. Bayard has gone off for a month and I am in charge. He is as good and nice and charming as ever, but sometimes I can't help wishing that we had a little more backbone here. I try hard to get it, but of course I only get sat down upon!! He read Lodge's article and was very angry about it and of course Lodge does make himself ridiculous. But I am certain our English cousins think more of us if we hold up *well* our own end of the line, and don't pat them on the back too much.[60]

Olney's problem, then, was to strengthen American policy, to offset Bayard's lack of vigor, and also to compose a document which would, when eventually published, clear the administration of its reputation for lack of Americanism. The fruit of the Secretary's labors was the famout note of July 20. The logical and historical shortcomings in Olney's dispatch have since been laid bare by able scholars,[61] but the President was much pleased with his Secretary's handi-work.[62] It is possible that Cleveland was as enthusiastic over the prospect of scoring points over his domestic critics as over Lord Salisbury. He wrote to Dickinson: "In due time it will be found that the Administration has not been asleep. The devils that were cast out of the swine centuries ago have, I am afraid, obtained possession of some so-called Democratic leaders." [63]

Olney's dispatch was composed and sent with the utmost secrecy. Even in the State Department only a very few individuals knew what was happening, and every effort was made to keep the press in the dark.[64] Cleveland and

---

supremacy of the Monroe Doctrine should be established and at once—peacefully if we can, forcibly if we must."

[57] Lodge to Henry White, June 5, 1895. Allan Nevins, *Henry White: Thirty Years of American Diplomacy* (New York and London, 1930), p. 108.

[58] "For the U. S. to place in the control of such a set of men the virtual control of peace and war with European Powers would be simple madness." Bayard to Cleveland, May 11, 1895, Cleveland Papers.

[59] New York *Tribune*, May 3, 1895.

[60] Cleveland Papers.

[61] See especially Dexter Perkins, *The Monroe Doctrine, 1867–1907* (Baltimore, 1937), pp. 153–68.

[62] Cleveland to Olney, July 7, 1895, Olney Papers. Olney was elated with the President's letter, which he thought "astonishing for the extent of its praise". Olney to his daughter, Mrs. Minot, July 10, 1895, Olney Papers.

[63] July 31, 1895, *Letters of Grover Cleveland*, ed. by Nevins (Boston and New York, 1933), p. 402.

[64] See letters, Adee to Olney, Aug. 14, 19, 30, 1895, Olney Papers.

Olney obviously hoped that by pressing their case vigorously they would achieve something concrete which could be presented to Congress in December—thus heading off an almost certain political field day on foreign affairs. While the new policy was in gestation, there was for a time a lull in the public discussion of the boundary dispute.[65]

By October, however, a new discussion of the Venezuelan dispute had broken forth in the newspapers—much to the annoyance of Cleveland, who blamed leaks in the State Department.[66] Both English and American journalists were excited by reports that the United States had sent Great Britain a ninety-day ultimatum. The *St. James Gazette* said: "Isn't it awful? But it might be still more awful if we only knew what the blessed Monroe Doctrine was, or what on earth the United States government has got to do with a quarrel between Great Britain and another independent state." [67] The New York *World* doubted that the diplomats had sent an ultimatum, but "the people have prepared an ultimatum and are ready to enforce it. It is that England shall never control the mouth of the Orinoco or any other American river south of the Canadian line." [68] The British position seemed absurd to even conservative papers like the Boston *Evening Transcript*, which thus summarized the English case: "Great Britain, having helped herself to a large slice of Venezuelan territory, will submit to arbitration whether she shall have any more." [69]

Long before Salisbury's reply to Olney was ready, the British government took action which the press was quick to interpret as being the real answer to American intervention. First came alarming reports of military preparations being carried out in British Guiana under direct order of Joseph Chamberlain, then colonial secretary in the British government.[70] Still more inflammatory was the news that the British government was planning to repeat the tactics tried out in Nicaragua. A three-month ultimatum was being sent to Venezuela demanding an apology and compensation for the arrest of British subjects within the disputed territory.[71]

It was this cool proposal to regard the boundary dispute as a closed matter and to proceed to the punishment of Venezuela on another issue that provoked more heated comment than had yet appeared in the controversy. Front-page headlines in the New York *Tribune* characterized the ultimatum as "A

[65] The calm was only relative, however. See, for example, the speech of ex-Governor Campbell of Ohio to Tammany on July 4, New York *World*, July 5, 1895.

[66] Cleveland to Olney, Oct. 6, 1895, Nevins, ed., *Letters of Cleveland*, p. 412.

[67] Quoted in the Boston *Evening Transcript*, Oct. 3, 1895.

[68] Oct. 5, 1895.

[69] Oct. 18, 1895.

[70] New York *World*, Oct. 19, 1895; New York *Tribune*, Oct. 19, 1895; *Review of Reviews*, XXVII (Nov., 1895), 520. The English source of these alarmist reports was the *St. James Gazette*.

[71] Boston *Evening Transcript*, Oct. 19, 1895. The news was authentic. A copy of the ultimatum of Salisbury to the Venezuelan minister of foreign affairs, Oct. 14, 1895, is in the Olney Papers with certification showing that it had been sent to Olney by the Venezuelan government.

Direct Slap In The Face".[72] The New Orleans *Picayune* regarded the action of Great Britain as "nothing more than an attempt to extend her territory in South America" and asserted that "the demands of the Monroe Doctrine will receive no attention from Great Britain unless we are prepared to back up our position by a show of force".[73]

English newspaper comment was scarcely less provocative. "Lord Salisbury's ultimatum", proclaimed the *Times*, "has not come a moment too soon." [74] The *Westminster Gazette* thought that "Venezuela, like Nicaragua, after much fuss, will probably prove to be small beer." [75] The *St. James Gazette* was, as usual, the spokesman for the most offensive brand of British imperialism. After a reference to the Monroe Doctrine as a "blessed Mesopotamia" it said: "It would become the position of the United States as a great civilized Power much better to join us in bringing these Spanish-Indian barbarians to order." [76]

Politicians exploited the issue for all it was worth. Theodore Roosevelt was having "fun" making jingo speeches,[77] while in England, where he was traveling, Senator Lodge expressed strong views to both American and British reporters.[78] Senator Chandler wrote an editorial for his own Concord (New Hampshire) *Evening Monitor* entitled "Our Coming War with England— A Prediction".[79] Congressmen Joseph Wheeler of Alabama and Charles H. Grosvenor of Ohio discussed "Our Duty in the Venezuelan Crisis" in the *North American Review*,[80] while in the same magazine Lieutenant Governor Charles T. Saxton of New York wrote that the great majority of Americans felt "humiliated beyond expression" by the foreign policy of the administration.[81] Cleveland's weakness in asserting the Monroe Doctrine was further denounced by Governor D. H. Hastings, of Pennsylvania before a great Republican rally in New York City.[82]

Prominent Democrats, who were dismayed at the attempt of the Republicans to set up a monopoly in patriotism, urged Cleveland and Olney to be

[72] Oct. 22, 1895.

[73] Quoted in the New York *Tribune*, Oct. 22, 1895.

[74] Quoted in the Boston *Evening Transcript*, Oct. 22, 1895.

[75] *Ibid.*, Oct. 21, 1895.

[76] Oct. 21, 1895. This and other clippings from the English jingo press were sent to Olney by Bayard and are to be found in the Olney Papers.

[77] Roosevelt to Lodge, Oct. 29, 1895, *Roosevelt-Lodge Correspondence*, I, 195.

[78] New York *World*, Oct. 26, 1895. Reference to an interview in the London *Chronicle* in the New York *World*, Nov. 15. To Roosevelt, Lodge wrote on October 23: "The news I have seen the last day or two as to England and Venezuela has put me on pins and needles to get home. If we allow England to invade Venezuela nominally for reparation, as at Corinto, really for territory, our supremacy in the Americas is over. I am worried and angry beyond words at what I see. England is simply playing the Administration for what she can get." *Roosevelt-Lodge Correspondence*, I, 193.

[79] Summarized in the New York *Tribune*, Oct. 29, 1895.

[80] CLXI (Nov., 1895), 630.

[81] "Outlook for Republican Success", *North Am. Rev.*, CLXI; 543.

[82] New York *Tribune*, Oct. 26, 1895.

vigorous. A few state elections were being held in November, 1895, and, more important, a presidential campaign was close at hand. William C. Whitney advised Secretary Herbert that Olney was "in a position to bring himself strongly to the front if he would only take a strong stand for the Monroe Doctrine in the matter of Venezuela".[83] To Olney himself Whitney wrote: "All the State Department has needed for a long time was a strong man . . . who was not afraid to resist the encroachment of the European powers over here." [84]

From local Democratic politicians, also, came a stream of advice. Olney was assured that the rank and file of the party strongly favored a vigorous enforcement of the Monroe Doctrine.[85] A party worker in Maryland attributed Democratic defeats in that state to "the Monroe Doctrine" and appealed for ammunition to use against the jingoes.[86] An Irish officeholder in Boston begged Olney not to let a Democratic administration permit England to "steal any part of this hemisphere".[87] Congressman Ikirt of Ohio wrote that "a little Jingo" would help. in electing a friend.[88] From Wisconsin came advice to call every bluff, and the people "will see you through the woods if it takes all winter and all the surplus in the Treasury".[89] Most outspoken of all was the counsel of Congressman Thomas M. Paschal of Texas. The Venezuelan issue, he said, was a "winner" from every angle—especially to knock the pus out of the "anarchistic, socialistic & populistic boil". Furthermore, a foreign war would help in the assimilation of the "vast stream of immigration that has been pouring in and diffusing itself over the country".[90]

As November slipped away, the impatience of Cleveland and Olney with the failure of Lord Salisbury to reply to the July note increased. For months it had been apparent that the opening of Congress would force a showdown on foreign policy. Morgan, Stewart, Cullom, Chandler, and Lodge had in effect announced their intention of precipitating a bitter debate. Moreover, for months reports had been allowed to circulate unchallenged that the administration was actually taking a strong line in the Venezuelan matter. The supporters of Cleveland expected that the annual message would provide a vindication for the President's policy; his enemies anticipated a revelation of his failure.

Ambassador Bayard, however, continued to pursue extremely cautious tactics. He had not found an opportunity to deliver Olney's note to Lord Salisbury until August 7. His report of the interview referred to a previous minister's "uncertainty as to the wisdom or expediency of renewing our recommendations for a settlement by arbitration between the two Powers" and

[83] Herbert to Thurber, Aug. 25, 1895, Cleveland Papers
[84] Aug. 16, 1895, Olney Papers.
[85] Thomas Gargan to Olney, Oct. 19, 1895, *ibid.*
[86] John K. Cowan to Olney, Nov. 9, 1895, *ibid.*
[87] Joseph H. O'Neill to Olney, Oct. 31, 1895, *ibid.*
[88] Oct. 25, 1895, *ibid.*
[89] R. E. Rosenberger to Olney, Oct. 25, 1895, *ibid.*
[90] Oct. 23, 1895, *ibid.*

expressed a desire to keep such questions "in the atmosphere of serene and elevated effort".[91] Bayard's lack of enthusiasm for the Olney policy was evident also in a letter to Cleveland in which he asserted: "The principles involved are serious—and the facts complicated—as necessarily must be the case where responsibility for the acts and rights of an independent third party is assumed." [92] In October he wrote Olney that he was indisposed to express his anxiety to secure a reply from the British foreign office.[93] As late as November 23 he reported: "The circumstances which have caused delay are not doubtful and it would be unjust to suppose that it has arisen from any other than involuntary obstructions." [94] The failure of Lord Salisbury's reply to arrive in Washington before the delivery of the annual message was a most unfortunate added irritant to Anglo-American friction. Although this delay was largely caused by a stupid misunderstanding in the British foreign office as to the date of the opening of Congress, it seems probable that Bayard did little to impress the British government with the urgency of the situation.

The President could only refer in his regular message to the acute stage into which the dispute between Great Britain and Venezuela had passed and assured the legislators that the United States had taken a firm position based on the Monroe Doctrine and was waiting for a British reply.[95] There was something of anticlimax in this, and a curiously mixed response resulted from the country. On December 4 the New York *Tribune* was complimenting the President on his commitment to the "identical program which *The Tribune* first outlined", but two days later the same paper was pouring scorn on Cleveland for "Begging an Answer". Some letters coming to the President's desk praised him for asserting the Monroe Doctrine, others for resisting the tide of jingoism.[96]

It was commonly assumed that Congress would take some action. The Chicago *Inter-Ocean* declared: "The people are now more importunate in the demand for a more American foreign policy than anything else. It is the latest of popular demands and this Congress is sure to heed it." [97] It is evident

[91] Quoted in Adee to Olney, Aug. 19, 1895, *ibid*. The previous minister referred to was Phelps.

[92] Sept. 10, 1895, Cleveland Papers.

[93] Oct. 21, 1895, Olney Papers.

[94] Bayard to Olney, *ibid*.

[95] J. D. Richardson, ed., *Compilation of Messages and Papers of the Presidents* (Washington, 1907), IX, 632.

[96] The president of a Monroe Doctrine League in New York urged Cleveland to accept a third term to carry out his vigorous policy (G. W. Gibbons to Cleveland, Dec. 3, 1895); the leading congressional champion of Venezuela endorsed the President's "strong and patriotic views" (Livingston to Cleveland, Dec. 4, 1895); John Bassett Moore was so disturbed by the implications of the reference to Venezuela that he wrote a twelve-page letter of warning to a member of the Cabinet (Moore to Wilson, Dec. 10, 1895). On the other hand, two correspondents from Illinois found the message commendable because it routed the jingoes (Chester Simmons to Cleveland, Dec. 4, Lambert Tree to Cleveland, Dec. 5, 1895). All in the Cleveland Papers.

[97] Quoted in the New York *Tribune*, Dec. 14, 1895.

that Cleveland considered the legislators as the factor in the situation most likely to force action. When he left Washington for a brief hunting trip, he directed Olney to put Salisbury's reply, if it arrived, into his pocket "so that no one will know that you have it until I return. . . . If I were here, I would not be hurried in the matter even if the Congress should begin grinding again the resolution-of-inquiry mill." [98]

Not one, but several, congressional mills began to grind at once, Lodge introduced a resolution affirming the Monroe Doctrine—much to the delight of Theodore Roosevelt.[99] Senator Collom introduced a similar resolution and spoke for an hour in its support.[100] Senator Morgan attacked England in a two-hour speech reviewing the Bering Sea controversy.[101] Ambassador Bayard was raked over the coals in the House on an issue unrelated to the boundary dispute but with an animosity due in part, no doubt, to the unpopularity of his reputed Anglophilism.[102] Most interesting maneuver of all was a resolution offered by Representative Livingston of Georgia. He proposed the creation of a joint congressional committee to examine into the facts connected with the Venezuelan dispute and to recommend a course of action.[103] To reporters Livingston explained that such a committee could sit in the United States and that he had in his own possession all the necessary data for a thorough investigation. In case Great Britain refused to renounce territory held in violation of Venezuela's rights, the representative claimed that all the Democrats and two thirds of the Republicans in the House would favor declaring war.[104] Livingston may not have been a bad judge of congressional sentiment on the issue; he had been the author of the resolution on Venezuela which had passed Congress in the spring without a dissenting vote.

The leadership which Congress might have assumed was, however, taken by the administration. The sequence of events is well known. Salisbury's reply —imposing in its dialectic but very irritating in tone—at length arrived. Cleveland returned from his hunting, and the stout special message was composed and sent to Congress. The tumultuous response in Congress and in the country at large may be attributed less to the emotion-raising potency of the President's phrases than to the fact that he seemed at last to be marching in time with the martial music which had been stirring American spirits.

It would be inconsistent with the character of Cleveland to conclude that the famous message was motivated either by the demagogic seizure of a popular issue or by a surrender to political pressure. Courage, honesty, and a sense of duty were basic qualities with the President, and he challenged Eng-

[98] Cleveland to Olney, Dec. 3, 1895, Nevins, ed., *Letters of Cleveland*, p. 416.
[99] *Congressional Record*, XXVIII, 24. Roosevelt to Lodge, Dec. 6, 1895, *Roosevelt-Lodge Correspondence*, I, 199.
[100] *Congressional Record*, XXVIII, 25, 108–12.
[101] *Ibid.*, pp. 65–90.
[102] *Ibid.*, pp. 114–25.
[103] *Ibid.*, p. 27.
[104] New York *Tribune*, Dec. 4, 1895.

land on the Venezuelan issue only after he became personally convinced that
the Monroe Doctrine was at stake and that it was his duty to maintain it.

Nevertheless, no statesman, however independent, can isolate himself
from the prevailing spirit of his times. It was the agitation of the issue by
politicians and journalists which must explain both the seriousness with
which the administration came to consider a distant boundary dispute and
also the aggressive tone which the Olney note and the Cleveland message
displayed. In reality a crisis existed independently of the action of the President. It grew out of the insistent demand of influential groups that the
United States intervene in the Venezuelan situation. Had Cleveland failed to
act and had hostilities arisen between Venezuela and England, a much worse
situation than the December crisis might have resulted. Any prolonged struggle would have created a state of affairs perilously like that which involved
us in war in 1898. It is, in fact, as evidence of the rising tide of aggressive
American nationalism that the Venezuelan crisis is most interesting. A friend
of Cleveland thus described the atmosphere of 1895:

> The mere political situation need not alarm us, but we have to do with that most
> mysterious, most reasonless, yet most constant and controlling force in public
> affairs: that of periods or cycles. Not the mere wobbling from election to election,
> but something of longer range and deeper source. I note that it was just thirty
> years from the end of the Revolution to the beginning of the war of 1812, and just
> thirty years from the end of that war to the beginning of the Mexican. Neither of
> these last wars was necessary and they were repugnant to a large, respectable por-
> tion of the population. But the time had come around for a fight. It is now thirty
> years, the length of a generation, since the great Civil War. Most Americans now
> living remember nothing of it. Vaguely and uneasily that part of the beast in man
> appears to be rousing in our country. How came it in? How comes the sea in? The
> proofs are nowhere, the signs are everywhere.[105]

Despite the dangerous state of American feeling no war with England
resulted. Various factors contributed to insure a peaceful settlement. In the
first place, it should be remarked that, belligerent though Cleveland and
Olney had been, their desire and purpose was peace. It is possible that even
the wording of Olney's note and his own special message seemed less strong
to the President than to others. This was often true of the language which
Cleveland used. At all events, Cleveland's action in December furnished the
opportunity for all peace-loving elements to assert themselves. A major portion of the British public at once demanded some settlement other than
war, while in the United States pressure for a peaceful solution, although not
so nearly universal, was very strong in certain localities and among certain
influential professions—in New York and Boston, for example, and among
businessmen, educators, and the clergy. Lord Salisbury and Joseph Chamberlain were as little desirous of allowing the controversy to proceed to a violent
end as were Cleveland and Olney. Particularly after the Jameson raid and the
Kruger telegram the danger of England's isolation and the reality of Ger-

[105] A. B. Farquhar to Mrs. Cleveland, Dec. 20, 1895, Cleveland Papers.

many's hostility were patent. Step by step the British government retreated from the position taken in Lord Salisbury's note. At length the consent of all parties was obtained for the settlement of the boundary dispute by an international arbitration with the proviso that occupation of territory for fifty years by either Venezuela or Great Britain should be judged to constitute title. Although the final decision of the arbitral body failed to recognize the extreme Venezuelan claims which American editors had been championing, opinion in this country was generally satisfied. England had been successfully challenged and induced to recognize the special position of the United States in the Americas. This pleased our nationalists, who were, after all, not primarily interested in just where the vagrant Venezuelan boundary finally came to rest.

The Background of Cleveland's Venezuelan Policy: A Reinterpretation

WALTER LaFEBER

THE POLICY that Grover Cleveland's second administration formulated in the Venezuelan controversy of 1895–1896 was a direct answer to British encroachments on United States interests in Latin America. Political and business leaders believed these American interests to be economic, strategic, and political. The economic influence on the shaping of Cleveland's policy in this dispute has not received sufficient attention. After the 1893 depression paralyzed the domestic economy, United States attention focused increasingly on Latin America; indeed, it is significant that the controversy occurred during the depths of that business crisis.

American interests, both economic and strategic, were threatened during the 1893–1895 period by ominous British moves in Brazil, Nicaragua, the disputed area in Venezuela itself, and the small island of Trinidad off the Brazilian coast. During the same years Germany and France menaced United States advantages in Brazil and the Caribbean. Gravely concerned, the State Department finally forced a showdown struggle on the issue of the Vene-

Walter LaFeber, "The Background of Cleveland's Venezuelan Policy: A Reinterpretation," *The American Historical Review*, LXVI 1961, pp. 947–967. Reprinted by permission of The American Historical Review.

zuelan boundary. By successfully limiting British claims in this incident, the United States won explicit recognition of its dominant position in the Western Hemisphere.

This essay attempts to trace two developments: that international dangers motivated the Cleveland administration in formulating its Venezuelan policy; that the economic crisis arising out of the 1893 depression provided the context and played an important role in this policy formulation. This is not to say that the economic influence was the only motivating force, but that this factor, relatively overlooked by previous writers on the subject, greatly shaped the thinking of both the Cleveland administration and key segments of American society.

Five considerations should serve to establish the validity of this interpretation: timing played a key role in that the year 1895 witnessed a convergence of forces which brought the United States into the controversy (after the argument had simmered over half a century) and led it to assert control over the nations of the Western Hemisphere; the Cleveland administration and the American business community viewed foreign markets, especially those of Latin America, as providing a solution to the domestic depression; policy makers in Washington believed the Monroe Doctrine to be important primarily for what Secretary of State Richard Olney called its "practical benefits," that is, its potential strategic and economic benefits; [1] the State Department acted unilaterally in the affair, cared little for Venezuelan opinion or advice, and hoped to benefit American interests primarily, not Venezuelan; neither the political situation in the United States nor the newly discovered "psychic crisis" of the 1890's played important roles in key American decisions.

The events leading to the Venezuelan crisis were silhouetted against the somber and ominous background of the 1893–1897 depression. Economic crisis had threatened the United States since 1890 and 1891, when only unexampled American exports had averted financial trouble.[2] Despite these huge exports, American prices and wages continued their long downward swing which had begun in 1873. By late 1892 and early 1893 business observers recognized that the American economic system had reached a point

[1] Olney to Thomas F. Bayard, July 20, 1895, Department of State, Instructions to Great Britain, State Department Archives, National Archives [hereafter cited as SDA]. The note is also in *Papers Relating to the Foreign Relations of the United States* [hereafter cited as FR] (2 vols., Washington, D. C., 1896), I, 545–62.

[2] Alexander Dana Noyes, *Thirty Years of American Finance* (New York, 1898), 158–59, 200. The best accounts of the effect this depression had on the American economy are Charles Hoffman, "The Depression of the Nineties," *Journal of Economic History*, XVI (June 1956), 137–64; E. H. Phelps Brown with S. J. Handfield-Jones, "The Climacteric of the 1890's," *Oxford Economic Papers*, new ser., IV (Oct. 1952), 266–307; Frank S. Philbrick, "The Mercantile Conditions of the Crisis of 1893," *University Studies of the University of Nebraska*, II (1894–1902), 299–320; W. Jett Lauck, *The Causes of the Panic of 1893* (Boston, 1907); Gerald Taylor White, "The United States and the Problem of Recovery after 1893," doctoral dissertation, University of California, Berkeley, 1938.

of maturity which disrupted its relations with the markets of the world.[3] Panic struck the weakened nation in the spring of 1893 when the Philadelphia and Reading Railroad and the National Cordage Company collapsed.

Political and social uprisings, which were renewed and intensified by the economic breakdown, forced the Cleveland administration not only to face the problem of reviving a glutted industrial system, but to do so before radical political forces paralyzed the administration's initiative. Labor unrest manifested itself in the marches of Coxey's and Hogan's armies of the unemployed on Washington—marches which highly dramatized the fact that the great American frontier no longer attracted, but even repelled the discontented of the nation—and in the nearly successful attempt of the socialist wing of the American Federation of Labor to control that body. The threat posed by restless farmers (and many businessmen) in the West and South compounded the danger of labor dissatisfaction. Among others, James J. Hill and the assistant chairman of the Kansas State Democratic Committee warned Cleveland in 1893 that all the "isms" that had plagued society in the past were "now appearing in an organized and most formidable manner." [4]

Cleveland quickly reacted by calling a special session of Congress to repeal the Silver Purchase Act of 1890. The President hoped that the repeal would stabilize the country on a gold standard. Though this action had little immediate effect on the economy, the administration's reasons for the repeal pointed the way for further ameliorative action. Cleveland and his advisers assumed that the economic problems stemmed not from the lack of circulating medium (as the Populists and silverites charged), but from bad monetary laws and overproduction. Since a powerful Populist-silver bloc in Congress could sidetrack any legislation that would carefully regulate and restrict the amount of paper money, the administration emphasized overproduction as the causative factor of the depression. This, in turn, led to a quest for foreign markets.[5]

In a speech to the New York Chamber of Commerce in November 1893, Secretary of the Treasury John G. Carlisle explained the administration's belief that the gold standard and an expanded foreign trade went hand in hand. Carlisle declared that "our commercial interests are not confined to our own country; they extend to every quarter of the globe, and our people buy and sell in nearly every market of the civilized world. . . . Without exception these prices are fixed in the markets of countries having a gold standard."

[3] Noyes, *Thirty Years of American Finance*, 200. For a summary of the factors influenc-the new manifest destiny, see Samuel Flagg Bemis, *The Latin American Policy of the United States: An Historical Interpretation* (New York, 1943), 123–24.

[4] Hill to Cleveland, June 24, 1893, and J. B. Crouch to Cleveland, June 23, 1893, Grover Cleveland Papers, Manuscript Division, Library of Congress.

[5] Alfred Vagts believes the monetary situation directly affected Cleveland's Venezuelan policy since the policy not only silenced silverite expansionists temporarily, but also attempted to keep England away from Venezuelan gold fields which American interests had claimed. Alfred Vagts, *Deutschland und die Vereinigten Staaten in der Weltpolitik* (New York, 1935), 510, 1257.

Carlisle's *Annual Reports* and many of Cleveland's public statements emphasized the administration's belief that foreign trade provided a key to America's economic revival and that the gold standard was necessary for such trade.[6]

Two other developments motivated the Cleveland administration to view enlarged foreign trade as a means to end the depression: the withdrawal of British investments and the closing of the American frontier. American political and business leaders believed the exodus of British capital from the United States to be a basic cause of the panic.[7] When the repeal of the Silver Purchase Act failed to attract new foreign investments, the administration and the business community turned to the hope of a large foreign trade surplus as a replacement for the withdrawn capital. Such a trade balance would not only provide fresh capital to invigorate stagnant American industries, but newly found markets would revive these industries to a point where they would again be appealing to outside investors.[8]

Cleveland and others in influential positions coupled this view of foreign capital with the belief that a mature American system had finally absorbed its western frontier. They viewed this occurrence with alarm.[9] Cleveland made special mention of this in his annual message in 1893 and later attempted to reopen western lands that had been claimed by speculators.[10] Obviously, if

[6] Quoted in James A. Barnes, *John G. Carlisle: Financial Statesman* (New York, 1931), 299–302. See especially Carlisle's *Annual Report* of 1894 in which he declared that American "prosperity . . . depends largely" upon the ability of the United States to sell its "surplus products in foreign markets at remunerative prices." *Annual Report of the Secretary of the Treasury* (Washington, D. C., 1894), lxxii–lxxiii. See also Cleveland's letter to the Chicago Businessmen's Meeting, quoted in *Commercial and Financial Chronicle*, Apr. 20, 1895, 690; the President's letter to J. M. Stone, governor of Mississippi, Apr. 26, 1895, Cleveland Papers; and Carlisle's letter to Secretary of the Interior Hoke Smith, Aug. 11, 1894, *ibid.*

[7] *A Compilation of Messages and Papers of the Presidents, 1789–1897*, ed. James D. Richardson (10 vols., Washington, D. C., 1900), IX, 402; R. H. Inglis Palgrave, "An English View of Investment in the United States," *Forum*, XV (Apr. 1893), 191–200. *Banker's Magazine*, XLIX (Aug. 1894), 97–98, supplements Cleveland's and Palgrave's views.

[8] See again Carlisle's remarkable analysis in his 1894 *Annual Report*, lxxii–lxxiii; see also A. D. Noyes, "Methods and Leadership in Wall Street Since 1893," *Journal of Economic and Business History*, I (Nov. 1931), 3–4. A lack of markets for capital, not a lack of capital, caused the 1893–1897 depression in the United States. The administration paradoxically attempted to attract foreign capital at the same time American investors placed their money in foreign markets. (See the discussion of United States investments in Latin America below.) This attitude can probably be traced to such vital sections of the American economy as railroads and cotton and wheat exporters—groups that believed the London Stock Exchange to be the best indicator of economic prosperity. Also, these years marked the early stage of the transitional period when control of the international money swung from London to New York.

[9] See Lee Benson, "The Historical Background of Turner's Frontier Essay," *Agricultural History*, XXV (Apr. 1951), 59–82; Herman Clarence Nixon, "The Precursors of Turner in the Interpretation of the American Frontier," *South Atlantic Quarterly*, XXVIII (Jan. 1929), 83–89; John R. Procter, "America's Battle for Commercial Supremacy," *Forum*, XVI (Nov. 1893), 320–22.

[10] *Messages and Papers of the Presidents*, ed. Richardson, IX, 454, 661–62.

the closed frontier had been a leading cause in the glutting of the home market, the Republican protective tariff had to be revised. The Democrats thus proposed a tariff that they believed would stimulate the movement of domestic surpluses into world markets.[11]

In this desire to reinvigorate production instead of redistributing goods, Cleveland asked for a tariff bill that would include a long list of free raw materials.[12] He believed that if these industrial essentials entered the United States tariff-free, "the world [would] be open to our national ingenuity and enterprise." He related this hope of world markets to the growing labor unrest by noting that "the limited demand for . . . goods" on a "narrow market" inevitably led to industrial stagnation.[13] Carlisle expressed it more succinctly: "The demand for labor would steadily grow with the extension of trade." [14]

Cleveland's two congressional leaders, William L. Wilson of West Virginia in the House and Roger Q. Mills of Texas in the Senate, shared these opinions. Wilson introduced the tariff by observing that it had been devised "in the shadow and depression of a great commercial crisis." He declared that the free raw materials clauses would lead to "the enlargement of markets for our products in other countries, the increase in the internal commerce and in the carrying trade of our own country." All these factors would "insure a growing home market." In effect, Wilson believed that the United States had to re-build its home market by enlarging its foreign market.[15] Mills echoed Wilson's statements, then added a new note by declaring that Great Britain would have to suffer economic setbacks since she blocked the path of America's economic manifest destiny. Mills believed that the British "saw with alarm the triumph of Mr. Cleveland as the representative of commercial expansion." [16] Many other congressmen repeated these arguments during the tariff debates.[17]

A group of protectionist senators gathered support to defeat the House bill and to substitute a quasi-protectionist measure of its own. This tariff

[11] *Ibid.*, 459; *Annual Report of the Secretary of the Treasury* (Washington, D. C., 1893), lxxx–lxxxi; see also Vagts, *Deutschland und die Vereinigten Staaten*, 1257.

[12] See the excellent observations by Frank W. Taussig in "Rabbeno's American Commercial Policy," *Quarterly Journal of Economics*, X (Oct. 1895), 109.

[13] *Messages and Papers of the Presidents*, ed. Richardson, IX, 459. It is important to note that Cleveland had wagered his political life on the tariff issue in his first administration, but did not emphasize this raw materials argument as he did after the 1893 depression struck. See *ibid.*, III, 589, 776.

[14] *Annual Report of the Secretary of the Treasury*, 1893, lxxx–lxxxi.

[15] *Congressional Record*, 53 Cong., 2 sess., XXVI, pt. 9, Appendix, 193–96 (Jan. 8, 9, 1894); Frank W. Taussig, *The Tariff History of the United States* (7th ed., New York, 1923), 309; Festus P. Summers, *William L. Wilson and Tariff Reform* (New Brunswick, N. J., 1953), 172–74.

[16] Roger Q. Mills, "The Wilson Bill," *North American Review*, CLVIII (Feb. 1894), 235–44.

[17] See *Congressional Record*, 53 Cong., 2 sess., XXVI, pts. 1, 2, 945 (Jan. 17, 1894), 776 (Jan. 12, 1894), 643 (Jan. 10, 1894), 1422 (Jan. 25, 1894), and Appendix, 79 (Jan. 16, 1894).

measure resulted mainly from the lobbying of several trusts and from political and personal hatred for Cleveland. But during the congressional debate, the President continually reiterated the importance of the raw materials provisions. In disgust, he finally allowed the bill to become law without his signature, though only three free raw materials remained in the measure.[18]

The American business community followed the example of the administration in attempting to devise new means of expanding its foreign commerce. The depression reached its deepest trough in 1894-1895 as exports, especially staple agricultural products, failed to revive the economy. Business circles recognized this condition and called for drastic measures. The *Banker's Magazine* declared, "Small exports and agricultural depression are, therefore, now the chief remaining obstacles to a return of general prosperity." [19] The *Commercial and Financial Chronicle* concurred, stating that the "abnormal situation of the Treasury and of our foreign trade" had halted the growth of prosperity "several times" in 1894.[20] Perhaps Henry W. Cannon, president of the Chase National Bank, best summarized the American business community's position when he wrote in February 1895, "It is necessary, in order to restore complete prosperity, that we should compete in the markets of the world with our goods and commodities." [21] The New York correspondent of the *Economist* bluntly warned in September 1895: "Either goods or gold must go abroad to pay for our purchases there, and thus far this autumn our shipments . . . have not equalled expectations." [22] One authority explicitly prescribed the cure. A. S. Heidelbach, the senior member of a large international banking firm in New York, declared that in order to stop the gold outflow, merchandise exports would have to exceed merchandise imports by "at least" $350,000,000 per year. Some disputed his figures, but few disputed his solution.[23]

Unfortunately for the prospects of such a trade surplus, American agriculture, the main prop of the export trade, could not bear such a burden.

[18] See esp. *ibid.*, 53 Cong., 2 sess., XXVI, pt. 8, 7712 (July 19, 1894). Cleveland's letters sharply criticizing protectionist senators are in *Letters of Grover Cleveland, 1850–1908*, ed. Allan Nevins (New York, 1933), 363, 365-66.

[19] *Banker's Magazine*, XLIX (Nov. 1894), 326; see also *Bradstreet's: A Journal of Trade, Finance and Public Economy*, Feb. 16, 1895, 99. Henry L. Bryan of the State Department sent newspaper clippings to Ambassador Bayard in London (Aug. 23, 1895) which illustrated the great interest in increasing American export trade. Even some protectionist papers pointed out the need for more exports and thus opposed revising the 1894 tariff. Thomas F. Bayard Papers, Manuscript Division, Library of Congress.

[20] *Commercial and Financial Chronicle*, Jan. 5, 1895, 9.

[21] J. Sterlng Moorton, William M. Spring, and Henry W. Cannon, "The Financial Muddle," *North American Review*, CLX (Feb. 1895), 129-56, esp. 151. Another banker and merchant, A. B. Farquhar, said essentially the same thing to his good friend Cleveland (Nov. 9, 1894, Cleveland Papers).

[22] *Economist*, Sept. 21, 1895, 1244.

[23] Alfred S. Heidelbach, "Why Gold Is Exported," *Forum*, XVIII (Feb. 1895), 647-51; see also *Yale Review*, IV (Aug. 1895), 136; *Commercial and Financial Chronicle*, Mar. 30, 1895, 542-43.

Though the volume of exports for the 1894 fiscal year had been surpassed only twice before in American history, the four leading staples of the export trade—breadstuffs, provisions, cotton, and oil products—had decreased in value by almost six million dollars. This occurred because in order to find markets their producers had to accept extremely low prices, in some cases the lowest in history.[24]

Several astute observers, however, saw hope in these export tables. Worthington C. Ford, chief of the Bureau of Statistics, published an article in the summer of 1895 entitled "The Turning of the Tide." [25] Ford demonstrated that while exports of farm staples had slumped, American manufactured exports had rocketed to all-time highs. He emphasized this change by noting that the United States had imported less food in 1895, but that "more raw materials for domestic industries" had arrived.

Business journals quickly drew the lesson from such trade figures. *Banker's Magazine* and *Bradstreet's*, among others, declared that American agriculture could no longer compete with the newly exploited grain lands of Argentina and Russia.[26] The former journal foretold the consequences for the American economy: henceforth the United States must depend upon "our future manufacturing supremacy over Europe" rather than upon American "producers of food, feed, and raw materials." When this occurred, the business community's dream would be realized. There would be no more booms followed by depressions, but "slow and steady improvement . . . and our surplus manufacturing capacity turned to the production of goods we may be able to export hereafter at reduced cost and thus keep all our industries permanently employed, as England does, having the world's markets in which to unload any accumulation." [27]

In his article Ford further observed that this change in the nature of American trade had "political consequences," for it meant the United States would need markets in the underindustrialized nations of Latin America and Asia rather than in Europe. [28] Translating these words into action, the American business community began systematically opening Latin American markets. Business journals devoted much space to the promotion of a Nicaraguan canal; *Bradstreet's* called for the immediate formal abrogation of the Clayton-Bulwer Treaty.[29] American investment, composed mainly of surplus capital accumulated from the home market's collapse, flowed into Latin America in

[24] *Ibid.*, July 21, 1895, 1244.
[25] Worthington C. Ford, "The Turning of the Tide," *North American Review*, CLXI (Aug. 1895), esp. 188–95.
[26] *Banker's Magazine*, XLVIII (Mar. 1894), 649–50; *ibid.*, XLIX (Dec. 1894), 31–32; *Bradstreet's*, Apr. 27, 1895, 259; *ibid.*, Oct. 26, 1895, 674; *Economist*, Mar. 3, 1894, 273.
[27] *Banker's Magazine*, XLIX (Nov. 1894), 326–28; *ibid.* (Oct. 1894), 249. See especially the article in the Baltimore *Sun* of May 27, 1895, by Frederic Emory, a member of the State Department. Emory explained how manufactured products would have to replace raw materials as the backbone of United States exports. Copy in Bayard Papers.
[28] Ford, "Turning of the Tide," 93–95.
[29] *Economist*, Sept. 7, 1895, 1179; *Bradstreet's*, Dec. 28, 1895, 820.

increased amounts during the 1893–1898 period. New steamship lines, heavy investments in Latin American railroads, the movement of American bankers into Santo Domingo, and the expansion of the Guggenheim interests in Mexico exemplified this southward advance of the dollar.[30] The investor moved southward with a minimum of fanfare, but the manufacturer invaded Central and South America with the cheers of commercial manifest destiny ringing in his ears.[31]

James G. Blaine's intense interest in Latin American markets and tranquility, symbolized by the Pan-American Conference of 1889, had directed American commercial attention to the southern nations. But the stagnation of 1893–1895 increased and sharpened the business community's interest. Before 1893 Blaine had led, and the businessmen had willingly followed. But after 1893 the businessmen played at least an equal role in focusing attention southward and in some instances blazed paths that the State Department then followed in formulating Latin American policies.

This intensified expansion of American industrialists into Latin American markets can be illustrated by three developments: the growth of and interest in expositions held in the southern United States, the development of commercial museums, and the formation and growth of the National Association of Manufacturers. Encouraged by such business journals as *Dixie* and the Chattanooga *Tradesman*, the South held several large industrial expositions during the depression.[32] The chairman of the Atlanta Exposition of 1895 informed Secretary of State Olney that "the foreign trade idea is the basic and uppermost feature of the Exposition." [33] Olney and his predecessor in the State Department, Walter Quintin Gresham, encouraged this exposition, while President Cleveland and several members of his cabinet found time to visit it.[34]

The full bloom of the commercial museum movement appeared in the flowering of the Philadelphia Commercial Museum in 1894–1897. New York City soon followed this example. Secretaries of State Gresham and Olney again displayed much interest. Speaking at the opening of the Philadelphia

[30] Bureau of American Republics, *Special Bulletin* (Washington, D. C., Aug. 1896), 839–42; *ibid.* (May 1896), 626–27; *ibid.* (Sept. 1895), 145; James Morton Callahan, *American Foreign Policy in Mexican Relations* (New York, 1932), 508; *Bradstreet's*, Jan. 5, 1895, 14. By 1897 American investments in Cuba, the West Indies, Central and South America (excluding Mexico)·amounted to $108,000,000. Cleona Lewis, *America's Stake in International Investments* (Washington, D. C., 1938), 606; see also Hoffman, "The Depression of the Nineties," 156–57.

[31] See *Bradstreet's*, Apr. 27, 1895, 270; *Banker's Magazine*, XLIX (Mar. 1895), 498; *Public Opinion*, XVII (May 17, 1894), 159.

[32] The *Tradesman* believed that "if the South shall push her advantages . . . her ports will soon have a monopoly of many lines of trade with the West Indies, Central and South America." Quoted in *Bradstreet's*, July 7, 1894, 430.

[33] J. W. Avery to Olney, Nov. 8, 1895, Richard Olney Papers, Manuscript Division, Library of Congress.

[34] *Public Opinion*, XVIII (Apr. 25, 1895), 436–37; *Bradstreet's*, Dec. 21, 1895, 808.

museum in June 1897, Olney declared that economic solidarity in the Western Hemisphere was "inevitable." American industrialists strove to make this prediction come true, for the president of the museum, William Pepper, wrote Olney in 1895 that he was "surprised and gratified at the rapid spread of interest" shown by United States industrialists.[35]

After the panic struck, the most publicized and concerted movement for the systematic opening of Latin American markets arose from the formation of the National Association of Manufacturers in January 1895. The depression operated as a direct cause of this movement, and the association's first convention met for the avowed purpose of enlarging the Latin American trade of the United States.[36] Three themes dominated that convention: the need for foreign, especially South and Central American markets; a strong anti-British feeling, revealed in bitter references to British control of international trade and finance; and the hope that the federal government would provide favors to American businessmen which would encourage overseas economic expansion.[37] After the convention the NAM sent a group of American industrialists and financiers to inspect potential market areas in Latin America. In 1897 the association established its first sample warehouse in Caracas, Venezuela.[38]

By late 1895 a concise economic analysis had led both the American business community and the administration to the conclusion that the United States industrial system needed more Latin American markets. Such a conclusion suggested that any expansion of European (especially British) influence in the area endangered not only America's security, but also its economic and political well-being.

In 1894 and 1895 these dynamic American policies clashed with expanding European claims in Brazil, Nicaragua, and Trinidad, a small island off the Brazilian coast. A revolution erupted in Brazil in September 1893. Rebels, led by promonarchist groups, hoped to end the four-year-old republic and restore the empire. But most important for American-Brazilian commercial relations, the insurgents included elements desiring to abrogate Brazil's reciprocity treaty with the United States—the most important one the United States

[35] Pepper to Olney, Aug. 2 and Nov. 29, 1895, Olney Papers; Philadelphia Commercial Museum, *The Philadelphia Commercial Museum: What It Is, Why It Is* (Philadelphia, 1899); Olney's speech is dated June 2, 1897 (Olney Papers). For testimony to Gresham's interest in the commercial museum movement, see Pepper to Bayard, Aug. 11, 1895, Bayard Papers.

[36] See Albert Kleckner Steigerwalt, "The National Association of Manufacturers: Organization and Policies, 1895-1914," doctoral dissertation on microfilm, University of Michigan, 1953, 24-26, 381; also National Association of Manufacturers, *Purposes of the National Association of Manufacturers* (Philadelphia, 1896).

[37] For the best summary of these themes, see Steigerwalt, "The National Association of Manufacturers," 41-42, 51-53.

[38] National Association of Manufacturers, *A Commercial Tour to South America*, Apr. 25, 1896; National Association of Manufacturers, *Sample Warehouse for American Goods in Caracas, Venezuela* (2d ed., Philadelphia, 1897).

possessed.[39] The rebels planned to cut off all outside aid to the besieged government by blockading the harbor of Rio de Janeiro; indeed, they had placed all their hopes of success in this one embattled area. Secretary of State Gresham did little more in the early months of the revolution than promulgate the rule that American merchants and traders could continue their commerce with Rio harbor unless their ships crossed the line of fire.[40]

Suddenly, in December 1893, the revolutionary cause grew stronger when a key Brazilian admiral, known for his promonarchist views, defected to the insurgents. Thus reinforced, the rebels announced that they would prevent all incoming trade from unloading in Rio harbor. This meant that all foreign ships would encounter "lines of fire." When German and British business interests endorsed the new rebel stand, the State Department feared that if the insurgent policy succeeded, American trading interests would lose their favored position.[41] Influenced by urgent letters from United States exporters, especially Crossman Brothers of New York and Standard Oil President William Rockefeller, and guided by his own fervent belief that American industry needed more foreign markets, Gresham reversed his position in early January 1894.[42] Sending a strong naval force to Rio harbor, the Secretary of State instructed the commander to protect with force the landing of American goods. This was accomplished, and the revolution collapsed. American congressional leaders, applauding Gresham's policy, portrayed Great Britain as the culprit in the rebellion. The republic had not only been saved from a monarchist-inspired plot, but United States commercial interests (as the American minister to Brazil was quick to point out) had preserved intact their private inroads into the Brazilian market. The German minister to Brazil remarked, "The American dollar started to roll in order to break off the monarchist point of the revolution." [43]

Several months after the failure of this revolt, Gresham peacefully but firmly ejected British interests from the Mosquito Indian reservation in Nicaragua. This reservation occupied a crucial area, for it governed the eastern

[39] American action in the Brazilian revolt of 1893–1894 is analyzed in detail in Walter LaFeber, "American Depression Diplomacy and the Brazilian Revolution, 1893–1894," *Hispanic American Historical Review*, XL (Feb. 1960). See also James Lawrence Laughlin and H. Parker Willis, *Reciprocity* (New York, 1903), 208.

[40] Gresham to Thomas S. Thompson, American minister to Brazil, Nov. 1, 1894, Instructions to Brazil, SDA.

[41] Gresham to Bayard, Dec. 18, 1893, Instruction to Great Britain, SDA.

[42] Gresham to Isidor Straus, Jan. 6, 1894, Letterbooks, Walter Quintin Gresham Papers, Manuscript Division, Library of Congress; Rockefeller to Gresham, Jan. 4, 1894, Area 4 file, Navy Department Archives, National Archives [hereafter cited as NDA]. For Gresham's ardent belief in the need of foreign markets for the American industrial glut, see Gresham to Wayne MacVeagh, May 7, 1894, and Gresham to Judge Charles E. Dyer, May 2, 1894, both in Letterbooks, Gresham Papers; also Matilda Gresham, *Life of Walter Quintin Gresham, 1832–1895* (2 vols., Chicago, 1919)), II, 797–98. For an opposing view of Gresham, see Vagts, *Deutschland und die Vereinigten Staaten*, 1918.

[43] *Ibid.*, 1699–1700. On the effect of the American action, see *ibid.*, 1700; Lawrence F. Hill, *Diplomatic Relations between the United States and Brazil* (New York, 1932), 208.

entrance to the proposed Nicaraguan canal. During the summer of 1894 the British hesitated leaving the region as they claimed that under an 1860 treaty they had obtained rights to protect the Indians from Nicaraguan injustices. Gresham disagreed and exerted continuous pressure on the British Foreign Office; in the fall of 1894 the British surrendered their position.[44]

The American press disliked England's reluctance to leave this key area. When in the spring of 1895 British warships blockaded the Nicaraguan port of Corinto, American public and official opinion became aroused. An injury to a British citizen suffered during the 1894 trouble brought about the blockade. The State Department admitted the British right of blockade when it announced that the Monroe Doctrine had no relevance to the situation.[45] But American press and business circles, concerned over the future safety of an American-owned canal, deprecated the possibility that Great Britain would continue to rule over four million dollars worth of mushrooming American investment in bananas, timber, and inland trade in the reservation area.[46] Gresham shared this alarm, for although he disavowed the pertinence of the Monroe Doctrine, he nevertheless expressed deep concern to American Ambassador Bayard in London.[47] Then, with two strokes, the Secretary of State brought the reservation under United States control. First, Gresham implicitly agreed to protect the expanding American investments in the territory from Nicaraguan injustices. Second, he informed the British ambassador in Washington that henceforth the State Department would assume Britain's duties of guarding the rights of the mosquito Indians.[48] By doing so, Gresham replaced England's control with that of the United States.

As Venezuelan matters moved to a climax in 1895, other British actions increased American apprehension. The Foreign Office attempted to force Nicaragua to reopen the delicate reservation problem. Though the outstanding points were soon settled, Alvey A. Adee, Second Assistant Secretary of State, told Olney that this irritation was "an important indication of the drift

[44] Gresham to American minister to Nicaragua, Lewis Baker, June 13, 1894, Instructions to Central America, SDA; Gresham to Bayard, May 2, 1894, Letterbooks, Gresham Papers; Bayard to Gresham, May 28, 1894, Dispatches from Great Britain, SDA.

[45] This episode and the reaction of American policy makers is best outlined in a "memorandum" prepared for Olney dated August 10, 1895, in the Olney Papers. See also Gresham to Bayard, Apr. 24, 1895, Instructions to Great Britain, SDA.

[46] See *Review of Reviews*, XI (June 1895), 621–22; W. T. Stead, "Jingoism in America," *Contemporary Review*, LXVIII (Sept. 1895), 338; *Public Opinion*, XVIII (May 9, 1895), 502.

[47] "Memorandum" enclosed in State Department's files with cable from Baker to Gresham, Dispatches from Central America, Apr. 13, 1895, SDA.

[48] See especially Gresham's actions in restoring the rights of the Maritime Canal Company in Nicaragua and the protection he gave two American citizens who should have been dealt with by Nicaraguan law for attempting to lead a revolution in the reservation against Nicaraguan authorities: *Nicaraguan Canal . . .* (Senate Executive Documents, No. 184, 54 Cong., 2 sess., 1897), 96–97; Gresham to Baker, Aug. 4, 1894, Instructions to Central America, SDA; see also Wilfred Hardy Callcott, *The Caribbean Policy of the United States, 1890–1920* (Baltimore, 1942), 77–78.

of British policy." [49] England further worried Washington by occupying the island of Trinidad; it hoped to use this uninhabited jut of rock off the Brazilian coast as a cable station. The American press loudly supported Brazil's protests. Adee wrote Olney that "the newspaper men are wild about the Trinidad business." [50] Under scrutiny of the State Department, Brazil and England reached an agreement in 1896.

Britain's multiplying claims in the Western Hemisphere caused Adee to exclaim to Olney in August 1895 that the British were playing a "grab game" throughout North and South America.[51] But France also gave the State Department concern. In mid-1895 France and Venezuela severed relations over the French minister's alleged insult of the Venezuelan government. The United States stepped into the dispute and attempted to restore diplomatic connections. Bayard explained the State Department intervention when he wrote in August 1895 that the dispute was "of present interest" when viewed in "connection with the status of the existing Anglo-Venezuelan Boundary dispute." [52]

This situation had cooled when France attempted to occupy some 155,000 square miles of Brazil shortly after gold was discovered in the region. France had previously claimed the area, but had never forcibly tried to govern it. Olney and Bayard watched proceedings closely and even discussed the contingencies that might occur in case the United States assumed "a supervision of Brazilian boundaries, should French interests or ambitions prompt their invasion." [53] French and American interests also clashed in Santo Domingo. France demanded that the customs houses of the Caribbean nation guarantee a reparation payment which the French had demanded as a result of the murder of one of their citizens. A group of New York bankers shared the control of these customs houses and quickly asked for State Department aid. When a French naval squadron arrived at Santo Domingo, American Secretary of the Navy Hilary Herbert promptly instructed United States warships to proceed to the area and "watch carefully" over American interests. Fortunately the matter was soon adjusted.[54]

[49] Note penned by Adee on dispatch from Baker to Olney, Nov. 18, 1895, Dispatches from Central America, SDA.

[50] Adee to Olney, Aug. 2, 1895, Olney Papers.

[51] Adee to Olney, Aug. 19, 1895, *ibid.*

[52] Bayard to Olney, Aug. 8, 1895, Dispatches from Great Britain, SDA. German financiers were active in Venezuela during the 1890's (Vagts, *Deutschland und die Vereinigten Staaten*, 1525-29). Olney, Gresham, Cleveland, and key personnel in the State Department paid little attention to this infiltration, judging from their papers and diplomatic correspondence.

[53] Bayard to Olney, Oct. 25, 1895, Dispatches from Great Britain, SDA.

[54] Explanatory memorandum sent by Santo Domingo's chargé in Washington to the State Department, Feb. 5, 1894, Confidential Correspondence, NDA; Secretary of the Navy to Rear Admiral R. W. Meade, Mar. 9, 1895, *ibid.* German and American interests had clashed in Santo Domingo and Haiti before 1893. The State Department became active in pressuring Germany out of the area only after 1897. See Vagts, *Deutschland und die Vereinigten Staaten*, 1707-1709, 1788-93.

Congress and the Cleveland administration responded vigorously to these European encroachments. The character of this response can be briefly analyzed in the following incidents and personages: a congressional debate in the winter of 1894–1895 on the best means of protecting and expanding American commerce abroad; the naval appropriation debates of 1895 and 1896; a speech by Don Dickinson in May 1895; recognition by influential Americans that the Orinoco River was a vital pawn in the Venezuelan boundary dispute; Olney's concepts of American economic needs and power; statements of Cleveland and Olney during the Venezuelan boundary negotiations.

In the winter of 1894–1895 Congress became the center of an extended debate over American expansion into commercial and strategic areas and over the evolution of an anti-British policy. Henry Teller, leader of the Senate's silver bloc, sounded the keynote when he called England "our great commercial antagonist." [55] Conservative Nelson Aldrich of Rhode Island concurred as he warned that "there is a commercial warfare . . . going on among the great nations of the world for enlarged markets" and added that the United States could not "sit down silently and submissively." [56] In the House, Leonidas F. Livingston of Georgia proposed a resolution requesting Cleveland to invoke "friendly arbitration" to solve the Venezuelan-British Guiana boundary dispute. When weak opposition to the proposal appeared, William J. Coombs of New York quickly silenced it by replying, "Large American interests will be promoted by a friendly settlement of this question." Livingston added that the Orinoco River played a crucial role in the problem. Great Britain's claims endangered this waterway, which provided "the key to more than one-quarter of the South American continent." Livingston capped his argument by bluntly remarking, "This relates to a matter on our [sic] continent. Our trade and other relations with those people are involved in this settlement." [57] It is difficult to find much altruistic concern for Venezuela in this debate.

During this and the 1895–1896 session, Congress passed naval appropriation measures that provided money for the continued construction of the new American battleship fleet. The first three battleships had been authorized in 1890, and another had been added in 1892. Congress accelerated the construction program in 1895 and 1896 when it authorized the construction of five more battleships. Significantly, Congress provided money to begin building these vessels even though the Treasury suffered from an acutely depressed condition.

The cry for both commercial expansion and protection against British encroachments appeared frequently in these naval debates. Senator Orville Platt

[55] The essence of the debate is in the *Congressional Record*, 53 Cong., 3 sess., XVII, pt. 1, 157–626, *passim* (Dec. 1894–Jan. 1895).

[56] *Ibid.*, pt. 3, 1889 (Feb. 7, 1895).

[57] *Ibid.*, 1832–34. William Scruggs, former United States minister to Venezuela, had been hired by the latter country to interest the United States in the dispute. Livingston's introduction of the House resolution was one result of Scrugg's work. The interesting fact, however, is the argument used to support the resolution in debate.

of Connecticut noted the importance of the frontier's closing when he declared: "It is to the ocean that our children must look, as they have once looked to the boundless West." Senator Anthony Higgins of Delaware urged the building of more battleships with the argument that the necessity of United States commercial expansion would have serious implications for the potency of the Monroe Doctrine and "the suzerainty of the American Republic over both American hemispheres." [58] Robert Adams, Jr., of Pennsylvania, an important member of the House Foreign Affairs Committee, was more specific: he announced that the Monroe Doctrine had become not only a political principle, but a notice to all nations that the American people would brook "no foreign interference either in the political affairs or the commercial relations of this hemisphere." Adams observed that Gresham's intervention in Brazil showed how the United States would have to uphold its new interpretation of Monroe's dictum.[59] J. Fred Talbott of Maryland, chairman of the House Naval Affairs Committee, declared that the American navy had to dominate the Western Atlantic and Eastern Pacific; if anyone disagreed with this proposition, he "was not worthy to represent his people in this Congress." Talbott pointed to the enemy when he said, "Great Britain never arbitrates with anybody except one who is ready to fight her." [60] John Van Voorhis of New York added that the United States could take care of itself, but that he wanted battleships to protect Latin America from Great Britain.[61] By 1896 such arguments had silenced almost all previous opposition to the building of a battleship fleet.[62]

Perhaps a speech delivered in May 1895 by Don Dickinson, a leader of the Democratic forces in Michigan and a close friend of President Cleveland, provided the most widely publicized commercial argument for American action in the Venezuelan dispute. One student of this episode calls Dickinson's speech "the most notable incident . . . indicating the desire of the Cleveland Democrats to assert their own lusty patriotism." [63] It should be emphasized, however, that Dickinson's address was more than a reflection of internal political pressure on the Cleveland foreign policies. The speech was important because it symbolized a wide and strongly held opinion that the United States had to obtain additional foreign markets. In a flaming peroration that summarized the speech, Dickinson declared, "We need and must have open markets throughout the world to maintain and increase our prosperity." He realized that such American expansion would conflict with "the

[58] *Ibid.*, 3045, 3109; see also *ibid.*, 1950, 2259, 3043.

[59] *Ibid.*, 2307, 3106.

[60] *Ibid.*, 2310–11.

[61] *Ibid.*, 3105–3106.

[62] This is illustrated by the action of the Quaker bloc in the House. Prior to 1896 this group opposed battleship appropriations. In the 1896 debates, however, one of the Quaker leaders, John B. Robinson of Pennsylvania, rose, quoted Tennyson's vision of universal peace, and then asked for four battleships. *Ibid.*, 3249.

[63] Nelson W. Blake, "The Background of Cleveland's Venezuelan Policy," *American Historical Review*, XLVII (Jan. 1942), 267.

settled policy of Great Britain." Consequently, Dickinson asked that England's extraordinary claims and movements" be watched closely in Nicaragua and Venezuela.[64] The President applauded the speech in a personal letter to Dickinson.[65]

Cleveland had become interested in the Venezuelan dispute in early 1895, the importance of the Orinoco River especially attracting his attention. When Dickinson made a midnight call on the hard-working Chief Executive in April 1895, Cleveland displayed a large map showing the controversial boundary area. He explained that Great Britain had not previously formally included the mouth of the Orinoco in its territory, but recently the British Foreign Minister had entered such a claim. Cleveland expressed alarm since the control of the river meant the control of a rich section of the South American interior trade.[66]

The State Department shared the President's concern, for it also realized the importance of the Orinoco for American commerce. In late 1894 Venezuela closed the river in an alleged effort to end smuggling. By quickly exerting diplomatic pressure to reopen the waterway, Gresham demonstrated that the United States valued the Orinoco.[67] Venezuela took advantage of this incident to send a diplomatic note to Washington that stressed the dire consequences for American commerce if England gained control of the river's entrance. [68] Then, on April 5, 1895, the British formally claimed the Orinoco's mouth. Between this date and May 25 events moved rapidly. Cleveland told Dickinson of his concern over the control of the river; Gresham asked Venezuela to restore diplomatic relations with England in order that the United States would "be in a position" to mediate; and the President began an urgent search to find "someone . . . of a much higher grade than is usually thought good enough" to send to the vacant ministerial post in Venezuela. Gresham finally began composing a long note on the subject which he planned to send to Great Britain, but death cut short his task.[69] Olney picked up and super-

[64] Clipping in Cleveland Papers from *Detroit Free Press*, May 10, 1895.

[65] Cleveland to Dickinson, July 31, 1895, Cleveland Papers.

[66] Note that this visit occurred before Dickinson's speech in May. Allan Nevins, *Grover Cleveland: A Study in Courage* (New York, 1933), 631. Nevins is one of the few historians who have given the Orinoco River any significance in explaining American concern in the dispute. For Cleveland's anxiety over the Orinoco, see his *Presidential Problems* (New York, 1904), 182–83.

[67] See P. F. Fenton, "The Diplomatic Relations of the United States and Venezuela," *Hispanic American Historical Review*, VIII (Aug. 1938), 299–329; *Bradstreet's*, Apr. 27, 1895, 257.

[68] Seneca Haselton to Gresham, Jan. 15, 1895, Dispatches from Venezuela, SDA. William L. Scruggs also widely publicized the importance of the Orinoco in *The Monroe Doctrine on Trial* (Atlanta, Ga., 1895), 24–25.

[69] On April 5, 1895, Bayard learned from Lord Kimberley, the British Foreign Minister, that England claimed land inside the mouth of the Orinoco (Bayard to Gresham, Apr. 5, 1895, Dispatches from Great Britain, SDA). Gresham began drafting a note to England on the subject sometime during the last part of that month. There are good reasons to believe that Gresham's note would have been nearly as blunt and boastful as Olney's. As early as January 1895, Gresham told Bayard that Britain's position on the Orinoco question was

charged this growing American concern, then exploded it in the British Foreign Office with his note of July 20.

The real origins of the boundnary dispute dated from 1841, but the United States entered the controversy much later, in 1883 and 1886, and then only briefly. The State Department made the British-Venezuelan controversy a three-cornered affair only toward the close of Gresham's term of office.[70] Olney, former Attorney General, replaced Gresham upon the latter's death in May 1895. He possessed two beliefs that must be understood to comprehend American action in the dispute. First, he had a clear conception of the 1893 depression as a "labor revolution" which had resulted from the introduction of machine technology. With these new means of expanded production, more markets had to be found if Olney were to fulfill his hope of restraining this "revolution" to what he termed "peaceful and moderate channels." [71] Second, he believed that the United States had emerged from its century of internal development as a full-fledged world power. The natural corollary of this was that the United States could now exert its will almost any place in the world, particularly in the Western Hemisphere. As Olney stated this concept, "It behooves us to accept the commanding position" the United States occupies "among the powers of the earth." [72]

Olney embodied these beliefs in his July 20, 1895, note on the Venezuelan boundary question to British Prime Minister Lord Salisbury. The Secretary of State posited that American "honor and . . . interests" were involved in the controversy. He then tried to fit the Monroe Doctrine into the dispute. Historians might demonstrate that Olney made a poor fitting and that the doctrine, as defined by past use, did not apply to the question. This, however, does not lead to an understanding of either Olney's intentions or the aims of the Cleveland administration's foreign policy. Olney advanced the argument that American interests as well as Venezuelan territory were at stake. In essence, he interpreted the Monroe Doctrine as the catchall slogan that justified protecting America's self-interests. If the Monroe Doctrine had never existed, Olney's note would have been penned anyway; only the term "American self-interest" would have been substituted for the doctrine.[73]

"contradictory and palpably unjust" and that if England continued to encroach on Venezuelan territory "we will be obliged . . . to call a halt." Gresham to Bayard, Jan. 16 1895, Instructions to Great Britain, SDA. For Cleveland's reaction, see Nevins, *Grover Cleveland*, 631; *Letters of Grover Cleveland*, ed. *id.*, 392; Cleveland, *Presidential Problems*, 251–52.

[70] For the background of the boundary dispute, see Dexter Perkins, *The Monroe Doctrine, 1867–1907* (Baltimore, 1937) 44–60.

[71] Significantly, Olney changed his mind about the depression's causes between June 1893 and 1894. In 1893 he believed the panic resulted from a cyclical movement in the economy. See his remarks prepared for Harvard commencement dinner, June 28, 1893, Olney Papers; clipping from Philadelphia *Daily Evening Telegraph*, June 20, 1894, *ibid.*

[72] Richard Olney, "International Isolation of the United States," *Atlantic Monthly*, LXXXI (May 1898), 577–88; speech at national opening of the Philadelphia Commercial Museum, June 2, 1897, Olney Papers.

[73] For an opposite view of the involvement of American interests, see Perkins, *Monroe Doctrine*, 155, 180.

Declaring that the United States had political and commercial stakes in Latin America, the Secretary of State proceeded to proclaim the ideal of extending the American form of democracy to the world in sentences that resemble those of Wilson in 1917. He interrelated American interests with the Orinoco River since it controlled "the whole navigation of the interior of South America." Of vital significance is the context within which Olney placed these points, for he emphasized that the Monroe Doctrine was positive as well as negative. Not only did the doctrine formulate the rule of European abstinence from the Western Hemisphere, but "It aimed at also securing the practical benefits to result from the application of the rule." Olney then defined these benefits as "popular self-government" in Latin America, the commercial and political relationship of South and Central America to the United States, and the unencumbered use of the Orinoco. The Secretary of State climaxed this argument with the blunt assertion that if necessary these benefits could be secured and preserved by American force: "Today the United States is practically sovereign on this continent, and its fiat is law upon the subjects to which it confines its interposition." [74]

When Lord Salisbury challenged these claims, Cleveland rephrased the American argument in his special message of December 17, 1895. The President first defined the Monroe Doctrine as a statement of self-interest. He then declared that the doctrine had to be maintained since it was "essential to the integrity of our free institutions and the tranquil maintenance of our distinctive form of government." Phrasing his message candidly, Cleveland warned that if Great Britain continued its course in the boundary dispute, the United States would regard this action "as a willful aggression upon its rights and interests." [75]

The causes and intentions of the administration's policy are given in a personal letter from Cleveland to Bayard. The President emphasized two points. He wrote that the Monroe Doctrine had been invoked because of "its value and importance *to our government and welfare,* and that its defense and maintenance involve its application when a state of facts arises requiring it" [Cleveland's italics]. The President next strongly disclaimed any idea that internal political pressure, especially jingoism, had inspired the American action; such influence was "entirely irrelevant to the case and . . . had absolutely nothing to do with any action I have taken." [76]

Throughout the ensuing negotiations, the United States acted unilaterally. Venezuela did not know that Olney had penned his July note until the newspapers printed the text. Even after this, the Cleveland administration did not

[74] Olney to Bayard, July 20, 1895, Instructions to Great Britain, SDA; the note is in *FR* [1895], I, 545–62.
[75] *Messages and Papers of the Presidents,* ed. Richardson, IX, 656–58.
[76] Cleveland to Bayard, Dec. 29, 1895, Cleveland Papers; the letter is also in *Letters of Grover Cleveland,* ed. Nevins, 417–20.

consult Venezuela.[77] When, in January 1896, Great Britain proposed a court of arbitration that included a Venezuelan representative, Olney countered with an offer excluding Venezuelan membership. The Secretary of State took the same position when he opposed including the Latin American nation in the negotiations. He argued that he did not care to have Venezuela "consulted at every step." [78] Olney succeeded in including his plan for the court of arbitration in the treaty signed by England and the United States in November 1896. When the Caracas government learned of this, it demanded and obtained a representative on the tribunal. Even then Venezuela so intensely disliked both the treaty and the manner in which Olney had carried on negotiations that the legislature ratified the pact only after police ended threats of street rioting in Caracas.[79]

The United States obtained its two principal objectives: England submitted the dispute to an arbitral commission, and in the final disposition Venezuela retained control of the Orinoco River. But most important, by submitting its case to arbitration, England recognized Olney's claim of American dominance in the Western Hemisphere.

American historians have offered three interpretations to explain the Cleveland administration's policy in the boundary dispute. The most popular explanation states that domestic political attacks "must explain both the seriousness with which the administration came to consider a distant boundary dispute and also the aggressive tone which the Olney note and the Cleveland message displayed." [80] A second thesis traces the policy's roots to Olney's bellicose, stubborn temper.[81] A third interpretation declares that a "psychic crisis" struck influential segments of American opinion in the 1890's and that a new spirit of manifest destiny emerged from this "crisis." [82]

There can be little doubt that Cleveland took domestic political pressures into account, but defining these pressures as major causative elements leaves key questions unanswered and raises many others. Cleveland's bellicose policy

[77] See esp. George B. Young, "Intervention under the Monroe Doctrine: The Olney Corollary," *Political Science Quarterly*, LVII (June 1942), 251–52, 260, and Arthur P. Whitaker, *The United States and South America: The Western Republics* (Cambridge, Mass., 1948), 160–61.

[78] Olney to Bayard, Jan. 22, 1896, Olney Papers. Bayard was very bitter at Olney's exclusion of Venezuela. See Bayard's personal memorandum, undated, but written sometime during March 1896 (Bayard Papers).

[79] Young, "Intervention under the Monroe Doctrine," 276–78; London *Times*, Feb. 5, 15, 1897.

[80] Blake, "Background of Cleveland's Venezuelan Policy," 275–76. Blake acknowledges that Cleveland did not "surrender to political pressure" and that "he became personally convinced that the Monroe Doctrine was at stake and that it was his duty to maintain it." But Blake then adds the statement quoted above. Bemis, *Latin American Policy of the United States*, 119; Vagts, *Deutschland und die Vereinigten Staaten*, 510–11.

[81] Charles Callan Tansill, *The Foreign Policy of Thomas F. Bayard, 1885–1897* (New York, 1940), 776; see also Vagts, *Deutschland und die Vereinigten Staaten*, 1918.

[82] Richard Hofstadter, "Manifest Destiny and the Philippines" in *America in Crisis*, ed. Daniel Aaron (New York, 1952), 173–200, esp. 176, 178.

could not have permanently won any political enemies to his side. The Republican jingoists and the Democratic silver bloc led the cheering for the December 17 message. Neither of these groups would have agreed with Cleveland on national political objectives. The President actually alienated many of his strongest supporters, especially the eastern financiers who had once saved the gold reserve, and who, at Cleveland's request, repeated the rescue operation shortly after the December message.[83] In other words, the administration's Venezuelan policy attracted groups that were irreconcilable in domestic politics, while repelling the administration's stanchest supporters. War might have united the nation behind him, but Cleveland certainly did not want to turn the controversy into an open conflict.

No reliable proof exists which shows that Cleveland hoped to benefit personally from the episode. It is extremely doubtful that with his conservative conception of the Chief Executive's duties and responsibilities he would have broken the third term tradition even if he had possessed the support. E. C. Benedict, who handled Cleveland's investments in stocks and bonds, testified three weeks before the Venezuelan message that the President had repeatedly said that he was "impatient" to end his term in office.[84]

An interpretation that stresses Olney's bellicose character misses two important points. First, Gresham worked on a diplomatic note concerning the Venezuelan situation several months before Olney assumed the top position in the State Department. Second, Cleveland probably initiated the dispatch of the Olney note, reworked the draft, and heartily endorsed his Secretary of State's language. The President played an extremely important part in the formulation of the policy, especially during the crucial incubation period of April-July 1895.[85]

A thesis which emphasizes that Cleveland bowed to the pressure of jingoism and a mass psychological need for vicarious excitement does an injustice to Cleveland. The President's greatest assets were his courage and a strong character.[86] After all, Cleveland defied public pressures exerted for Hawaiian annexation, the application of the Monroe Doctrine in the Corinto dispute, and compromises in the silver repeal act and the 1894 tariff. There is no reason to believe that he suddenly bent to the winds of jingoism in 1895, unless he had better reasons than pleasing irreconcilable political enemies. It would be difficult, if not impossible, to put Cleveland and Olney in the social groups that supposedly were undergoing this psychological dilemma.

Olney and Cleveland acted as they did because they feared that United States interests were in jeopardy. Both men said this at the time, and there

[83] *Wall Street Journal*, Dec. 21, 1895. Two weeks before the special Venezuelan message, Henry Villard personally pleaded with the President to prevent American "arguments with Europe" until the treasury reserve was restored. Vagts, *Deutschland und die Vereinigten Staaten*, 512, 1702.

[84] *Wall Street Journal*, Nov. 27, 1895.

[85] Cleveland, *Presidential Problems*, 257–59; *Letters of Grover Cleveland*, ed. Nevins, 392; Bemis, *Latin American Policy of the United States*, 119.

[86] Nevins rightly emphasizes these traits in his *Grover Cleveland*.

is no reason to doubt their word. Such danger emanated from actual or threatened European encroachments in Latin America. This expansion not only endangered both areas held vital for American strategic purposes and existing or possible political democracies in the Western Hemisphere, but it also threatened present and potential commercial markets for American products. Both the administration and the business community proclaimed these markets to be necessary for American economic and political health. They reasoned that increased shipments of industrial products to less developed regions would have to replace faltering agricultural products as the staple of American export trade; and, as a member of the State Department observed in 1895, "It has been the task of Mr. Cleveland's foreign policy to prepare the way" for these manufactured goods.[87] One may speculate that Cleveland referred to both economic and security problems when he told a close friend late in 1896 that the Venezuelan affair was not a foreign question, but the "most distinct of home questions." [88] As Olney realized, the mature power of the United States could be used to harvest what the Secretary of State called "the practical benefits" of the Monroe Doctrine. Then these "home questions" could be solved.

[87] Unsigned article by Frederic Emory in Baltimore *Sun*, May 27, 1895, sent to Bayard, May 28, 1895, Bayard Papers.

[88] George F. Parker, *Recollections of Cleveland* (New York, 1909), 195. This conclusion differs from Vagts's belief that Cleveland's policy was one of "negative imperialism" or what Vagts describes as "eager for rule but not for gain." *Deutschland und die Vereinigten Staaten*, xi, 1416, 1701, 1702. It should be noted, however, that numerous and influential voices of the American business community applauded Cleveland's vigorous use of the Monroe Doctrine to challenge British expansion in Latin American. Many of these businessmen based their support on the hope of increased commercial expansion into Latin America once British power was weakened in the area. See Walter LaFeber, "The American Business Community and Cleveland's Venezuelan Message," *Business History Review*, XXXIV (Winter 1960), 393-402.

The War with Spain:

DID THE BUSINESS COMMUNITY WILL IT?

ONE OF THE *most popularly held and widely believed theories of historical causation is that economic considerations constitute a prime cause for wars and for territorial expansion. Manufacturers seek sources of raw materials for their factories and markets for their products, while bankers look for areas for profitable investment of capital. A successful war provides these opportunities. And while the war is in progress business, in general, booms to meet the swollen demands of the military machine.*

This view had greatest currency in the period between the two World Wars when many historians ascribed American intervention in 1917 to the influence of the business interests upon President Wilson. The Nye Committee, which in 1934 was investigating the munitions industry, came to a similar conclusion. The War with Spain and the acquisition of colonies whch resulted from it were, in the same way, ascribed by some scholars to the influence of the business community. Professor Harold Faulkner in his standard American Economic History states that "the great cause for the war" lay in the need to satisfy a nation "sufficiently advanced for financial imperialism."

Writing in 1936, Julius W. Pratt of the University of Buffalo, the leading historian of American expansionism, denies that the business communicty played any part in shaping the decision in 1898 to go to war or to acquire colonies. His view rests on an analysis of various biographies of leading industrialists and financiers, of trade and business periodicals, of proceedings of boards of trade and chambers of commerce, and of petitions and letters written to the Department of State by business people. The vast majority of the evidence leads to the inescapable conclusion that war and expansionism were considered extremely undesirable by the business community. In 1897, the American economy had begun to revive from the great depression of 1893 and, it was believed, war would impede "the march of prosperity." Peace alone was needed to complete the recovery. War "would endanger our currency stability, interrupt our trade, and threaten our costs and our commerce," says Pratt, summarizing the business points of view. In addition, more would be lost than gained by the artificial spurt of wartime prosperity. As for acquiring colonies for outlets for manufactured goods, Pratt argues that exporters did not think that their foreign trade was dependent on colonial markets. He says, "American industry had reached a point where it could meet the world on more than even terms in both the price and the quality of its products. Given a fair chance, these products could make their own way." The fair chance was a system of international free trade, not colonial monopolies.

Walter LaFeber of Cornell University finds that the most important influence on the decision to go to war came from the business community. Neither the jingo press nor a belligerent Congress affected McKinley's position. Using much of the same kind of sources as Pratt, he lays stress on those special groups which would profit or benefit from a conflict: advocates of bimetallism (silver would be needed to help pay war costs); transportation interests; steel and iron firms; and those engaged in trade or investment in Cuba. Replying to Pratt, he suggests the strong possibility "that the antiwar commercial journals in New York spoke for the less important members of the financial community" and cites a contemporary observer who said that "the steady opponents of the war among financiers were simply the life insurance men and small bankers." Indeed, the "giants"—Rockefeller, Astor, Ryan—were militant. By the end of March, 1898, the business people, LaFeber noted, strongly desired intervention and exerted enough pressure on the President to prompt his war message in April.

The Business Point of View

JULIUS W. PRATT

We may begin with a generalization, the evidence for which will be presented as the chapter proceeds. American business, in general, had strongly opposed action that would lead to war with Spain. American business had been either opposed or indifferent to the expansionist philosophy which had arisen since 1890. But almost at the moment when the war began, a large section of American business had, for reasons that will become apparent, been converted to the belief that a program of territorial expansion would serve its purposes. Hence business, in the end, welcomed the "large policy" and exerted its share of pressure for the retention of the Spanish islands and such related policies as the annexation of Hawaii and the construction of an isthmian canal.

One public man to whom the welfare of American business was of so much concern that he may almost be considered its spokesman in the Senate, was McKinley's friend, Mark Hanna. No one was more unwilling than he to see the United States drift into war with Spain. To Hanna, in the words of his biographer, "the outbreak of war seemed to imperil the whole policy of domestic economic amelioration which he placed before every other object of political action." Hanna's attitude appears to have been identical with that of leading business men. This conclusion is based not only upon the few published biographies of such men, but also upon the study of a large number of financial and trade periodicals, of the proceedings of chambers of commerce and boards of trade, and of material in the *Miscellaneous Files* of the Department of State, containing numerous letters and petitions from business men and organizations.

That business sentiment, especially in the East, was strongly anti-war at the close of 1897 and in the opening months of 1898, is hardly open to doubt. Wall Street stocks turned downward whenever the day's news seemed to presage war and climbed again with information favorable to peace. Bulls and bears on the market were those who anticipated, respectively, a peaceable and a warlike solution of the Cuban question. The "jingo," in Congress or the press, was an object of intense dislike to the editors of business and financial journals, who sought to counteract his influence by anti-war editorials in their columns. Boards of trade and chambers of commerce added their pleas for the maintenance of peace to those of the business newspapers and magazines. So marked, indeed, was the anti-war solidarity of the financial interests and their

From Julius W. Pratt, *Expansionists of 1898* (Baltimore: The Johns Hopkins Press, 1938) pp. 233–259. Reprinted by permission of The Johns Hopkins Press.

spokesmen that the jingoes fell to charging Wall Street with want of patriotism. Wall Street, declared the Sacramento *Evening Bee* (March 11, 1898),
was "the colossal and aggregate Benedict Arnold of the Union, and the syndi-
cated Judas Iscariot of humanity." Senator Thurston, of Nebraska, charged
that opposition to war was found only among the "money-changers," bringing from the editor of *The American Banker* the reply that "there is not an
intelligent, self-respecting and civilized American citizen anywhere who would
not prefer to have the existing crisis culminate in peaceful negotiations."

This anti-war attitude on the part of several leading financial journals continued up to the very beginning of hostilities. The New York *Journal of Commerce and Commercial Bulletin* declared on February 28 that the only possible
excuses for war would be (1) a finding by the naval board investigating the
"Maine" disaster that the ship had been destroyed by an official act of the
Spanish Government; or (2) a refusal by Spain to make reparation if the
board should hold that she had failed to exercise due diligence in safeguarding
the vessel. Either of these events it held to be almost inconceivable. The *Commercial and Financial Chronicle* expressed the belief on March 12 that the
opposition of the financial interests would yet prevent war; and on April 2
the same journal branded as "monstrous" the proposition to settle the Cuban
and "Maine" questions by war while the slightest chance remained for a peaceful solution. On April 16, after the House of Representatives had passed the
Cuban resolutions, the Boston *Journal of Commerce* declared: "Sober second
thought had but little to do with the deliberations. . . . The members were
carried off their feet by the war fever that had been so persistently worked up
since the Maine explosion. . . ."

The reasons for this attitude on the part of business are not far to seek. Since
the panic of 1893 American business had been in the doldrums. Tendencies
toward industrial revival had been checked, first by the Venezuela war scare
in December, 1895, and again by the free silver menace in 1896. But in 1897
began a real revival, and before the end of the year signs of prosperity appeared
on all sides. The New York *Commercial* conducted a survey of business conditions in a wide variety of trades and industries, from which it concluded
that, "after three years of waiting and of false starts, the groundswell of demand has at last begun to rise with a steadiness which leaves little doubt that
an era of prosperity has appeared." January, 1898, said the same article, is "a
supreme moment in the period of transition from depression to comparative
prosperity." This note of optimism one meets at every turn, even in such a
careful and conservative sheet as the *Commercial and Financial Chronicle*. As
early as July, 1897, this paper remarked: "We appear to be on the eve of a
revival in business"; and in December after remarking upon the healthy condition of the railroads and the iron industry, it concluded: "In brief, no one
can study the industrial conditions of today in America without a feeling of
elation. . . ." The *Wall Street Journal* found only two "blue spots" in the
entire country: Boston, which suffered from the depressed demand for cotton

goods, and New York, where senseless rate cutting by certain railroads caused uneasiness. "Throughout the west, southwest and on the Pacific coast business has never been better, nor the people more hopeful."

A potent cause for optimism was found in the striking expansion of the American export trade. A volume of exports far in excess of those of any recent year, a favorable balance of trade of $286,000,000, and an especially notable increase in exports of manufactures of iron, steel, and copper, convinced practically every business expert that the United States was on the point of capturing the markets of the world. "There is no question," said one journal, "that the world, generally, is looking more and more to the United States as the source of its supply for very many of the staple commodities of life." Especially elated were spokesmen of the iron and steel industry. Cheaper materials and improved methods were enabling the American producer to undersell his British competitior in Europe and in the British possessions, and Andrew Carnegie was talking of a great shipbuilding yard near New York to take advantage of these low costs. The *Iron Age*, in an editorial on "The Future of Business," foretold the abolition of the business cycle by means of a better planned economy, consolidation of railroads and industries, reduction of margins of profits, higher wages, and lower prices to consumers.

To this fair prospect of a great business revival the threat of war was like a spectre at the feast. A foreign complication, thought the *Commercial and Financial Chronicle* in October, 1897, would quickly mar "the trade prosperity which all are enjoying." Six months later (April 2, 1898), after a discussion of the effect of war rumors on the stock exchange, it declared: ". . . Every influence has been, and even now is, tending strongly towards a term of decided prosperity, and that the Cuban disturbance, and it alone, has arrested the movement and checked enterprise." The *Banker and Tradesman* saw in the Cuban complication the threat of a "material setback to the prosperous conditions which had just set in after five years of panic and depression." The same journal summarized a calculation made by the Boston *Transcript* showing that in February, 1898, the wave of prosperity had carried the average price of twenty-five leading stocks within 5½ points of the high for the preceding ten years and 30 points above the low of 1896, and that the Cuban trouble had, in a little over two months, caused a loss of over ten points, or more than one-third of the recent gain. "War would impede the march of prosperity and put the country back many years," said the *New Jersey Trade Review*. The *Railway Age* was of the opinion that the country was coming out of a depression and needed peace to complete its recovery. "From a commercial and mercenary standpoint," it remarked, "it seems peculiarly bitter that this war should have come when the country had already suffered so much and so needed rest and peace."

The idea that war could bring any substantial benefits to business was generally scouted. It would endanger our currency stability, interrupt our trade, and threaten our coasts and our commerce, thought the *Commercial and*

Financial Chronicle. It would "incalculably increase the loss to business interests," said the *Banker's Magazine;* while the *United States Investor* held that war was "never beneficial from a material standpoint, that is, in the long run." The *Railroad Gazette* predicted that war would result in "interruption of business enterprise of every kind, stopping new projects and diminution of the output of existing businesses and contraction of trade everywhere." Railroads would lose more than they would gain. Even arms manufacturers were not all agreed that war would be desirable. Journals speaking for the iron and steel industry also argued that war would injure business. It "would injure the iron and steel makers ten times as much as they would be benefited by the prevailing spurt in the manufacture of small arms, projectiles and steel plates for war ships," in the opinion of one of these. The *American Wool and Cotton Reporter* of New York and the *Northwestern Miller* of Minneapolis agreed that war was never materially beneficial in the long run, while trade journals in Atlanta, Chattanooga, and Portland, Oregon, saw as fruits of the approaching conflict only destruction, debt, and depressed industry.

Many conservative interests feared war for the specific reason that it might derange the currency and even revive the free-silver agitation, which had seemed happily dead. The subsidence of that agitation and the prospect of currency reform were among the hopeful factors at the close of 1897. It was not uncommonly charged that the jingoes were animated in part by the expectation that war would lead to inflation in paper or silver. The New York *Journal of Commerce,* in an editorial on "The Breeding Grounds of Jingoism," had called attention to the fact that the jingoes were generally silverites, including in their number "the financiers who desire to force bankruptcy on the country as a means of breaking down the gold standard," and had quoted with approval an editorial from another paper charging that Senator Morgan's championship of the Cuban insurgents was part of "his wild scheming in the interest of the silver standard." The *Commercial and Financial Chronicle* endorsed this view, declaring that many of the Cuban agitators "are only interested in the establishment of a free-silver standard, a plan which they think war would advance." Similar views were expressed by the *American Banker* of New, York, the *United States Investor* of Boston, and the *Rand-McNally Bankers' Monthly* of Chicago. The last-named quoted from a speech of Secretary of the Treasury Gage, delivered in Chicago in February, 1898, in which he had declared that "it would be scarcely possible for this nation to engage in war in its present condition . . . without a suspension of specie payments and a resort to further issues of Government notes." A war of any duration, in the opinion of the *United States Investor,* would certainly derange the currency and reduce business to a gambling basis.

Something of a freak among New York financial journals was the *Financial Record,* which, in November, 1897, denounced "the cowardice of our Administration in refusing the phenomenally brave Cubans the commonest rights of belligerency" as "a disgrace to the United States," and argued that war with Spain, far from depressing securities or injuring business, "would vastly increase the net earning power of every security sold on our market today." The mystery of this jingo attitude is explained when we discover that this journal had been a warm advocate of the free coinage of silver.

Business opinion in the West, especially in the Mississippi Valley, appears to have been less opposed to war and less apprehensive of its results than that of the Atlantic coast. The Kansas City Board of Trade, at the beginning of 1897, had urged recognition of Cuban independence. The Cincinnati Chamber of Commerce, at a meeting on March 29, 1898, adopted "amidst much enthusiasm" resolutions condemning Spain for cruelties to the Cubans and the destruction of the "Maine" and calling for a "firm and vigorous policy which will have for its purpose—peacefully if we can, but with force if we must—the redress of past wrongs, and the complete and unqualified independence of Cuba." The Chicago *Economist* denied that war would seriously hurt business or endanger the gold standard and asserted that the liberation of Cuba, by peace or war, would mean another star of glory for the United States and would produce "results of the highest value to mankind." The *Rand-McNally Bankers' Monthly*, of the same city, while opposing war, called attention to the fact that while the war scare had demoralized the stock market, "general business activity apparently received an impetus." Similarly the *Age of Steel* (St. Louis), while much preferring peace, "when not secured at the price of national honor," comforted its readers with the thought that although foreign trade might suffer, home trade and industries would be stimulated by war. A St. Louis bank president, Mr. Lackland, believed that war would "cause a boom in many lines of business in this country . . . and give employment to a large number of persons who are now out of work." The Chattanooga *Tradesman* stated on March 1, 1898, that a "small prospect" of war had already stimulated the iron trade in certain lines and had benefited the railroads by hurrying forward shipments of grain and other commodities in anticipation of war prices. The *Mining and Scientific Press*, of San Francisco, while holding that, in general, war "lets loose havoc and waste, and entails destructive expense," conceded that "to nearly everything related to the mining industry the war will be a stimulus."

Even in New York, business men saw some rays of light piercing the war clouds. Stock market operators, according to the *Wall Street Journal*, just after the "Maine" explosion, "did not look for any great break in the market, because actual war with Spain would be a very small affair compared with the Venezuela complication with Great Britain." Their expectation was for a drop in stocks at the beginning of hostilities, followed by a resumption of the recent advance. In fact, the first shock might well be followed by a boom. "The nation looks for peace," declared *Dun's Review*, March 5, "but knows that its sources of prosperity are quite beyond the reach of any attack that is possible." *Bradstreet's* contrasted the jumpiness of Wall Street over war news with "the calm way in which general business interests have regarded the current foreign complications," and *Dun's Review* of March 12 stated that no industry or branch of business showed any restriction, while some had been rapidly gaining, that railroads were increasing their profits while speculators sold their stocks, and that there was a growing demand for the products of all the great industries.

Despite such expressions as these, there seems little reason to question the belief that an overwhelming preponderance of the vocal business interests of the country strongly desired peace. By the middle of March, however, many organs of business opinion were admitting that a war with Spain might bring no serious disaster, and there was a growing conviction that such a war was inevitable. In the Senate on March 17, Senator Redfield Proctor, of Vermont, described, from his own observation, the terrible sufferings of the Cuban "reconcentrados." Proctor was supposedly no sensationalist, and his speech carried great weight. The *Wall Street Journal* described its effect among the denizens of the Street. "Senator Proctor's speech," it said, "converted a great many people in Wall Street, who have heretofore taken the ground that the United States had no business to interfere in a revolution on Spanish soil. These men had been among the most prominent in deploring the whole Cuban matter, but there was no question about the accuracy of Senator Proctor's statements and as many of them expressed it, they made the blood boil." The *American Banker*, hitherto a firm opponent of intervention, remarked on March 23 that Proctor's speech showed an intolerable state of things, in view of which it could not understand "how any one with a grain of human sympathy within him can dispute the propriety of a policy of intervention, so only that this outraged people might be set free!" It still hoped, however, for a peaceful solution, declaring that the United States ought to urge the Cubans to accept the Spanish offer of autonomy. That this growing conviction that something must be done about Cuba was by no means equivalent to a desire for war, was clearly revealed a few days later. Rumors circulated to the effect that Spain was willing to sell Cuba and that J. P. Morgan's return from a trip abroad was connected with plans to finance the purchase. "There is much satisfaction expressed in Wall Street," said the *Wall Street Journal*, "at the prospects of having Cuba free, because it is believed that this will take one of the most disturbing factors out of the situation. . . . Even if $200,000,000 is the indemnity demanded it is a sum which the United States could well afford to pay to get rid of the trouble." Even $250,000,000, it was thought, would be insignificant in comparison with the probable cost of a war.

It remains to examine the attitude of certain American business men and corporations having an immediate stake in Cuba, or otherwise liable to be directly affected by American intervention. Much American capital, as is well known, was invested in the Cuban sugar industry. Upon this industry the civil war fell with peculiarly devastating effect, not only cutting off profits on capital so invested, but also crippling a valuable carrying trade between Cuba and the United States. Naturally enough, some firms suffering under these conditions desired to see the United States intervene to end the war, though such intervention might lead to war between the United States and Spain. In May, 1897, a memorial on the subject bearing over three hundred signatures was presented to John Sherman, Secretary of State. The signers described themselves as "citizens of the United States, doing business as bankers, merchants, manufacturers, steamship owners and agents in the cities of Boston, New York, Philadelphia, Baltimore, Savannah, Charleston, Jacksonville, New Orleans, and other places, and also other citizens of the United States, who have been for many years engaged in the export and import trade with the Island of Cuba." They called attention to the serious losses to which their businesses had been subjected by the hostilities in Cuba and expressed the hope that, in order to prevent further loss, to reestablish American commerce, and also to secure "the blessings of peace for one and a half millions of residents of the Island of Cuba now enduring unspeakable distress and suffering," the United States Government might take steps to bring about an honorable reconciliation between the parties to the conflict.

Another memorial, signed by many of the same subscribers, was presented to President McKinley on February 9, 1898, by a committee of New York business men. It asserted that the Cuban war, which had now continued for three entire years, had caused an average loss of $100,000,000 a year, or a total loss of $300,000,000 in the import and export trade between Cuba and the United States, to which were to be added "heavy sums irretrievably lost by the destruction of American properties, or properties supported by American capital in the Island itself, such as sugar factories, railways, tobacco plantations, mines and other industrial enterprises; the loss of the United States in trade and capital by means of this war being probably far greater and more serious than that of all the other parties concerned, not excepting Spain herself."

The sugar crop of 1897–1898, continued the memorial, appeared for the most part lost like its two predecessors, and unless peace could be established before May or June of the current year, the crop of 1898–1899, with all the business dependent upon it, would likewise be lost, since the rainy season of summer and fall would be required "to prepare for next winter's crop, by repairing damaged fields, machinery, lines of railways, &c." In view of the importance to the United States of the Cuban trade and of American participation "in the ownership or management of Cuban sugar factories, railways and other entreprises," the petitioners hoped that the President would deem the situation "of sufficient importance as to warrant prompt and efficient measures by our Government, with the sole object of restoring peace . . . and with it restoring to us a most valuable commercial field."

How much weight such pressure from special interests had with the administration there is no way of knowing. But it is to be noted that the pressure from parties directly interested was not all on one side. Mr. E. F. Atkins, an American citizen who divided his time between Boston and his sugar plantation of Soledad near Cienfuegos, Cuba, which he had developed at a cost of $1,400,000, had been able, through protection received from the Spanish Government and through a corps of guards organized and paid by himself, to continue operations throughout the period of the insurrection. He was fre-

quently in Washington, where he had influential friends, during both the
Cleveland and McKinley administrations and worked consistently against the
adoption of any measures likely to provoke war.

Unlike some of the sugar plantations, American-owned iron mines in Cuba
continued to do active business despite the insurrection. Three American iron
and manganese enterprises in the single province of Santiago claimed to have
an investment of some $6,000,000 of purely American capital, a large propor-
tion of which was in property which could easily be destroyed. "We are fully
advised as to our status in case of war," wrote the representative of one company to the Assistant Secretary of State, "and that this property might be
subject to confiscation or destruction by the Spanish Government." War between Spain and the United States, wrote the president of another company,
"will very likely mean the destruction of our valuable plant and in any event
untold loss to our Company and its American stockholders." An American
cork company with large interests in Spain; a New York merchant with trade
in the Mediterranean and Black Sea; a Mobile firm which had chartered a
Spanish ship to carry a cargo of timber—these are samples of American business interests which saw in war the threat of direct damage to themselves.
They are hardly offset by the high hopes of an enterprising gentleman of Nor-
folk, "representing a party of capitalists who are enthusiastic supporters of the
Government," who applied to the State Department for a letter of marque
"to enable us to lawfully capture Spanish merchant vessels and torpedo
boats," adding: "We have secured option on a fine steam vessel, and on
receipt of proper documents will put to sea forth with."

It seems safe to conclude, from the evidence available, that the only important business interests (other than the business of sensational journalism)
which clamored for intervention in Cuba were those directly or indirectly concerned in the Cuban sugar industry; that opposed to intervention were the
influence of other parties (including at least one prominent sugar planter)
whose business would suffer direct injury from war and also the overwhelming preponderance of general business opinion. After the middle of March,
1898, some conservative editors came to think intervention inevitable on
humanitarian grounds, but many of the most influential business journals
opposed it to the end.

We can now turn to the question whether American business was imperialistic; whether, in other words, business opinion favored schemes for acquiring
foreign territory to supply it with markets, fields for capital investment, or
commercial and naval stations in distant parts of the world. American business men were not unaware of the struggle for colonies then raging among
European nations. Did they feel that the United States ought to participate
in that struggle?

We have seen above that the rising tide of prosperity was intimately connected with the increase in American exports, particularly of manufactured
articles. That the future welfare of American industry was dependent upon
the command of foreign markets was an opinion so common as to appear

almost universal. The New York *Journal of Commerce* pointed out, early in 1897, that the nation's industrial plant had been developed far beyond the needs of domestic consumption. In the wire nail industry there was said to be machinery to make four times as many nails as the American markets could consume. Rail mills, locomotive shops, and glass factories were in a similar situation. "Nature has thus destined this country for the industrial supremacy of the world," said the same paper later in the year. When the National Association of Manufacturers met in New York for its annual convention in January, 1898, "the discussion of ways and means for extending this country's trade, and more particularly its export business, was, in fact, almost the single theme of the speakers," according to *Bradstreet's*, which added the comment: "Nothing is more significant of the changed attitude toward this country's foreign trade, manifested by the American manufacturer today as compared with a few years ago, than the almost single devotion which he pays to the subject of possible export-trade extension."

But if business men believed, prior to the opening of the war with Spain, that foreign markets were to be secured through the acquisition of colonies, they were strangely silent about it. To the program of colonial expansion which for almost a decade had been urged by such men as Mahan, Albert Shaw, Lodge, Roosevelt, and Morgan, business had remained, to all appearances, either indifferent or antagonistic. To the business man, such a program was merely one form of dangerous jingoism. A large section of business opinion had, indeed, favored plans for the building of a Nicaraguan canal with governmental assistance, and some spokesmen for business had favored annexation of the Hawaiian Islands. But beyond these relatively modest projects few business men, apparently, wished to go. Two of the most important commercial journals, the New York *Journal of Commerce* and the *Commercial and Financial Chronicle*, had stoutly opposed both the canal scheme and Hawaiian annexation. The former satirized the arguments of the proponents of both schemes. "We must certainly build the canal to defend the islands, and it is quite clear that we must acquire the islands . . . in order to defend the canal." The canal was not only unnecessary, but unless fortified at each end and patrolled by two fleets, it would be a positive misfortune. Such protection—"the price of jingoism"—might "easily cost us $25,000,000 a year, besides the lump sum that will be required for the original investment, and there is absolutely no excuse whatever in our commercial or our political interests for a single step in this long procession of expenses and of complications with foreign powers." As for Hawaii and Cuba, neither was fit for self-government as a state,—and the American constitution provided no machinery for governing dependencies. The Hawaiian Islands would have no military value unless the United States were to build a great navy and take an aggressive attitude in the Pacific. The *Commercial and Financial Chronicle* saw in colonies only useless outposts which must be protected at great expense, and the St. Louis *Age of Steel* warned lest the expansion of the export trade might "lead to territorial greed, as in the case of older nations, the price of which in armaments and militarism offsets the gain made by the spindle and the forge."

Colonies were not only certain to bear a fruit of danger and expense; they were valueless from the commercial point of view. Did not the colonies of Great Britain afford us one of the most valuable of our export markets? Did we not trade as advantageously with Guiana, a British colony, as with independent Venezuela? "Most of our ideas of the commercial value of conquests, the commercial uses of navies and the commercial advantages of political control," said the New York *Journal of Commerce*, dated back to times when colonial policies were designed to monopolize colonial trade for the mother country. The *Commercial and Financial Chronicle* believed that the current European enthusiasm for colonies was based on false premises; for although trade often followed the flag, "the trade is not always with the home markets of the colonizer. England and the United States are quite as apt to slip in with their wares under the very Custom-House pennant of the French or German dependency." Outright opposition, such as this, to the idea of colonial expansion is not common in the business periodicals examined; much more common is complete silence on the subject. Positive and negative evidence together seem to warrant the conclusion that American business in general, at the opening of 1898, was either indifferent to imperialism, or definitely opposed.

Confidence in the continued expansion of the export trade was based upon faith in the working of natural forces in a world given over largely to a system of free trade. American industry had reached a point where it could meet the world on more than even terms in both the price and the quality of its products. Given a fair chance, these products would make their own way. Government could aid them, not by acquiring colonial markets but by removing or lowering the barriers that restricted imports of raw materials and exchange commodities. To one who has in mind the subsequent tariff history of the United States, it is surprising to discover the amount of free-trade sentiment which found expression in these months of 1897–1898. The preoccupation of Congress with the raising of duties in the Dingley Act was disturbing to those interested in the export trade. "It is pitiful," said the *Journal of Commerce*, "to see the national legislature bending its whole force to readjusting the trammels of a system which can only obstruct, and closing its eyes to the manifest, though unconscious, struggling of industry for a freedom that will enable it to compete successfully in any market of the world." The futility of expecting to increase exports while at the same time barring out imports was stressed by more than one writer for business journals, and a change toward free trade in American policy was freely predicted. "We are gradually losing our fear of the bugaboo of cheap foreign labor," said the *Iron Age*, "and are slowly realizing that we hold the key of the position, since there are no indications that European manufacturers will ever displace us in the van of progress." The *American Machinist* declared that the recent growth in the export trade showed that in many lines the tariff was a dead letter, that goods which could be sold under the nose of the foreign producer no longer needed protection in the home market, and that the machinery interests would in all probability bring pressure to bear on Congress "toward action which will equalize these matters." The Chattanooga *Tradesman* was convinced that the great development in the export of manufactures was certain to have upon tariff policy an effect "both broad and radical," and the president of the Baltimore Chamber of Commerce, speaking on the same theme to that body in December, 1897, predicted that "the day is not so far distant when free trade, in some measure, at least, will become part of our political faith.". . .

Approach To War

WALTER LaFEBER

ELECTIONS in 1897 had not gone well for McKinley's party, nor had more recent elections in New York and Kentucky. During the first three months of 1898 the President and other Republican leaders received many letters which drew bleak pictures of the party's future if the administration failed to deal with Cuba immediately. McKinley's letters on this point were capped with a long message from Henry Cabot Lodge on March 21. Lodge had recently returned from taking a private poll of Massachusetts opinion. The Senator first assured McKinley that the masses were firmly behind the administration. But, Lodge continued, "if the war in Cuba drags on through the summer with nothing done we should go down in the greatest defeat ever known before the cry 'Why have you not settled the Cuban question.'" Clarence Cary, who opposed a strong Cuban policy, wrote in the *Journal of Commerce* in late March that mail was pouring in "even from conservative city districts" warning of the Republican losses which would inevitably result if the Democrats could "proclaim from every stump that it was they who forced the hand of the Republican President and with the aid of a few Republicans secured the liberty of Cuba." These letters, Cary concluded, were having a "potent effect." [1]

[1] Lodge to McKinley, March 21, 1898, McKinley MSS, *Journal of Commerce*, March 30, 1898, 1:5.

Walter LaFeber, *The New American Empire* (Ithaca: Cornell University Press, 1963), 384–406.

Most of the "conservative city districts" which Cary mentioned had long opposed war with Spain.[2] There were exceptions, however. The American business community was by no means monolithic in its opposition to war. To say as a generalization that businessmen opposed war is as erroneous as saying that businessmen wanted war. It is possible to suggest, however, that by the middle of March important businessmen and spokesmen for the business community were advocating war. It is also possible to suggest that at the same time, a shift seemed to be occurring in the general business community regarding its over-all views on the desirability of war.

Financial journals which advocated bimetallism had long urged a stronger attitude toward Spain in the hope that the resulting conflict would force the Treasury to pay expenses in silver. More important, business spokesmen in such midwestern and western cities as Cincinnati, Louisville, St. Louis, Chicago, San Francisco, and especially Pittsburgh were not reluctant to admit that they would welcome war. The Louisville *Commercial* believed, "Only a few of the eastern newspapers are pessimistic as to the business outlook at the beginning of war. . . . Everywhere in the west and south there is a disposition among businessmen . . . to keep their feet, and their heads, too." This journal was not reticent in providing its own viewpoint: if war occurred, transportation lines would prosper, "other enterprises would find more profit and securities would go up all along the line. Nor would the credit of the United States be in the least impaired." The Pittsburgh *Press*, mouthpiece for that area's booming steel interests, strongly supported the Cincinnati businessmen's resolutions that asked for war. The *Press* added, "It is not to be doubted that this expresses the feeling of the real business interests of the country. . . . The mistake made in some quarters is supposing that the stock jobbers are the business interests." [3]

The Pittsburgh *Press* represented one of the special interests that would benefit from war. The Pittsburgh Chamber of Commerce also advocated the use of force, and the Chattanooga *Tradesman* suggested one reason why: the "small prospect" of conflict, the *Tradesman* noted on March 1, "has decidedly stimulated the iron trade." This journal, which did not want war, also commented, "Actual war would very decidedly enlarge the business of transportation," especially railroads. William E. Curtis wrote from Washington that the "belligerent spirit" which had infected everyone in the Navy Department, with the possible exception of Secretary Long, had been encouraged "by the contractors for projectiles, ordnance, ammunition and other supplies, who have thronged the department since the destruction of the *Maine*."

    [2] Julius Pratt discusses this opposition in detail in ch. vii of his *Expansionists of 1898*; see also Boston *Herald*, March 6, 1898, 12:13; and *Journal of Commerce*, April 1, 1898, 6:2–3.
    [3] Louisville *Commercial*, April 14, 1898, 4:1; March 5, 1898, 4:2; Cincinnati *Commercial Tribune*, March 30, 1898, 10:1; Pittsburgh *Press*, March 30, 1898, 4:1; Pratt, *Expansionists of 1898*, 243–244.

These contractors, Curtis charged, had also assisted "correspondents of sensational newspapers in manufacturing canards and scare news." [4]

A strong possibility exists that the antiwar commercial journals in New York spoke for the less important members of that financial community. Russell Sage, claiming that he spoke "not only my own views on this point, but those of other moneyed men with whom I have talked," demanded that if the "Maine" was blown up by an outside force "the time for action has come. There should be no wavering." If war did occur, "There is no question as to where the rich men stand"; they would buy government bonds as they had during the Civil War and do all in their power to bolster the nation's war resources. W. C. Beer, who attempted to make a thorough survey of leading businessmen's opinion, concluded that "the steady opponents of the war among financiers were simply the life insurance men and small bankers." Beer found such giants as John Jacob Astor, John Gates, Thomas Fortune Ryan, William Rockefeller, and Stuyvesant Fish "feeling militant." On March 28 J. Pierpont Morgan declared that further talk of arbitration would accomplish nothing.[5]

Beer's findings can be supplemented with an analysis of the membership of the Cuban League of the United States. This organization began advertising in early 1897 that it would gladly receive donations to finance its efforts to free Cuba from Spanish control. As a part of these efforts, the league sold bonds for the Cuban Junta. This organization included such militants as Theodore Roosevelt, Colonel Ethan Allen, and Charles A. Dana. But the following conservative businessmen were among the Vice-Presidents: J. Edward Simmons, former President of the New York Stock Exchange, President of the Fourth National Bank of New York; Thomas F. Gilroy, builder and real estate operator in New York City; Chauncey M. Depew, railroad president and director of numerous railway and banking corporations; Thomas L. James, Chairman of the Board of Lincoln National Bank in New York City, President of the Lincoln Safe Deposit Company; John R. Dos Passos, New York lawyer who engaged in banking, corporate and financial law and who had been active in the formation of large business amalgamations, including the sugar trust. Seated on the Board of Directors were General Daniel Butterfield, Civil War hero, bank president, and Executive Officer of the Steam Boat and Ferry Company; and Colonel John Jacob Astor.[6]

A group of interests that depended upon Cugan trade formed another category of business support which demanded that the revolution be terminated. A group of importers, exporters, bankers, manufacturers, and steamship and

[4] *Tradesman*, March 1, 1898, 58; *Journal of Commercial*, April 7, 1898, 6:3. Curtis' statement is in the Pittsburgh *Press*, March 16, 1898, 1:1.

[5] New York *Tribune*, Feb. 27, 1898, 5:1; Thomas Beer, *Hanna* (New York, 1929), 199–200.

[6] *Review of Reviews*, XV (February, 1897), 137, *Who Was Who in America*, I (1897–1942) (Chicago, 1943).

vessel owners sent McKinley a petition in February, 1898, which noted that
the fighting had created a loss of one hundred million dollars a year in business conducted directly with the island, not to mention the destruction of
American properties on the island. The petition demanded peace before the
rainy season in May; otherwise, the sugar crop of 1898 and 1899 would be
ruined. Those who signed this petition included "a large number of well-
known and influential firms" in New York City, the New York *Tribune*
noted, and also the names of businessmen in Philadelphia and Mobile.[7]

The petition noted the immense losses suffered by property owners and
merchants who had invested in the island itself. By early 1898 these persons
were becoming alarmed about something other than the day-to-day destruction of property, although this was certainly troublesome. The State Department began receiving reports that, as Fitzhugh Lee phrased the problem,
"there may be a revolution within a revolution." Conservative interests feared
that continued Spanish rule or autonomy, no matter how developed, would
result in Cuban radical forces gaining control of the government. A strong
feeling was growing which demanded American intervention to end this
threat. The American Consul in Santiago summarized this feeling on March
23, 1898: "Property holders without distinction of nationality, and with but
few exceptions, strongly desire annexation, having but little hope of a stable
government under either of the contending forces. . . . [B]ut such a move
would not be popular among the masses." These interests, the Consul reported, regretted that Americans did not favor outright, immediate annexation. McKinley learned of this sentiment from a letter written by "a gentleman of high standing, who has close personal relations with influential
Cubans who have favored the rebellion," as Levi P. Morton, former Vice-
President under Harrison and a wheelhorse of the Republican party, described
the author. This letter warned that the rebellion had to end quickly or the
radical classes would come to power. The writer believed that educated and
wealthy backers of the rebellion now wanted either annexation or autonomy
under American control. "They are most pronounced in their fears," he continued, "that independence, if obtained, would result in the troublesome,
adventurous and non-responsible class" seizing power.[8]

Many of these businessmen in Cuba hoped that annexation could be accomplished through peaceful means, but they found themselves trapped when
they realized that Spain would not surrender her sovereignty on American
terms without war. Among those who were so trapped was Edwin F. Atkins,
one of the largest American investors in Cuban plantations. He deprecated
the possibility of war on behalf of the insurgents, especially since the protection provided by Spanish troops enabled his plantations to continue their

[7] New York *Tribune*, Feb. 10, 1898, 2:3.
[8] Lee to Day, Nov. 27, 1897, Consular, Havana, and Hyatt to Day, March 23, 1898,
Consular, Santiago, NA, RG 59; enclosure in Levi P. Morton to McKinley, March 20,
1898, McKinley MSS.

harvests throughout the revolution. But as early as January, 1897, Atkins had written Lodge that the best thing that could happen would be the annexation of Cuba by the United States. Other investors, however, evaded this trap by hoping for, or openly advocating, forceful American intervention. Fitzhugh Lee wrote Day in January, 1898, "The Spanish merchants and property holders generally favor some form of intervention on the part of the United States, but are prevented from an open expression on the subject lest they be disturbed by the soldier element." The New York *Tribune* noted in a front-page story on March 14, 1898, that European, especially British, capital had been flowing into Cuba in the belief that the United States would shortly replace Spain as the sovereign power. "Large enterprises welcome peace or forcible intervention as the means of freeing them from burdens," the article continued. "The Government [of Cuba] owes everybody," the *Tribune* observed, especially the large utility and railroad companies.[9]

Perhaps the American business community exerted the most influence on the administration during the last two weeks in March when influential business spokesmen began to welcome the possibility of war in order to end the suspense which shrouded the commercial exchanges. Although other historians have touched briefly on this important change,[10] It should be noted that some important business spokesmen and President McKinley apparently arrived at this decision at approximately the same time.

During the first two months of 1898 the United States began to enjoy prosperous conditions for the first time in five years. The de Lôme and "Maine" incidents affected business conditions only in the stock exchanges, and even there the impact was slight. Business improved, especially in the West and Northwest. In early March very few business journals feared a return of depression conditions, and with the gold influx resulting from discoveries in Alaska and from the export surplus, even fewer business observers displayed anxiety over the silver threat.[11]

But in mid-March financial reporters noted that business in commodities as well as stocks had suddenly slowed. Henry Clay Frick had been optimistic in his business reports to Andrew Carnegie, who was vacationing in Scotland. But on March 24, Frick reported that "owing to uncertainty . . . of the Cuban trouble, business is rather stagnant." A Wall Street correspondent wrote on March 22 that "the last two days have been the dullest for many a month." On March 26 the *Commercial and Financial Chronicle* summarized the situation. No "sudden and violent drop in prices" had occurred. But the rapid progress in trade had stopped and now "frequent complaints are heard.

[9] Atkins' views are in Lodge to Charles Francis Adams, Jan. 22, 1897, Letterbooks, Lodge MSS; Lee to Day, Jan. 1898, Consular, Havana, NA, RG 59; New York *Tribune*, March 14, 1898, 1:6; Barrington to Salisbury, Nov. 11, 1897, Salisbury MSS.

[10] See especially Pratt, *Expansionists of 1898*, 246–247.

[11] *Bradstreet's*, March 12, 1898, 161, 170; March 19, 1898, 186; March 26, 1898, 202; *Economist*, March 5, 1898, 356; *Journal of Commerce*, March 26, 1898, 6:5.

The volume of trade undoubtedly remains large, but the reports speak of new enterprises being held in check." [12]

Businessmen had been particularly influenced by the speech of Senator Redfield Proctor of Vermont on March 17. Proctor was known for his conservative, antiwar disposition, an attitude he shared with his intimate friend, William McKinley. But the Senator had just returned from a visit to Cuba, a visit that had profoundly shocked him. Proctor discounted Spanish reforms as "too late," but he advised against going to war over the "Maine." The United States should use force, Proctor intimated, only to deliver the Cuban people from "the worst misgovernment of which I ever had knowledge." Conversations with businessmen in Cuba had provided him with most of his information; these men had declared "without exception" that it was too late for any more schemes of autonomy. They wanted an American protectorate, annexation, or a free Cuba. Although Proctor did not say so explicitly, none of these solutions was immediately possible without war with Spain. This speech deeply impressed almost all of the conservative and business journals which had opposed war. Many of these journals did not overlook Proctor's role as one of McKinley's "most trusted advisors and friends." Two weeks later the New York *Commercial Advertiser* looked back and marked this speech as the turning point in the road to war.[13]

This journal had steadily attacked the jingoes throughout January and February. But on March 10 it began to rationalize intervention not for "conquest," but for "humanity and love of freedom, and, above all, [the] desire that the commerce and industry of every part of the world shall have full freedom of development in the whole world's interest," especially "in that of nations in position to trade with it." In the week following Proctor's speech, important business opinion, tired of what the *Economist's* correspondent termed "the sudden revolutions of sentiment," began to fall into line back of the *Commercial Advertiser*. The *Wall Street Journal* noted that Proctor's speech had "converted a great many people in Wall Street" who had formerly opposed war. The *Journal of Commerce* asked for "one result or the other" to end the "present uncertainty," and wanted to present Spain with an ultimatum. The Pittsburgh *Press* noted business indecision on March 19, then remarked, "The sooner the administration executes its Cuban program the better." The Philadelphia *Press*, which was quite close to the administration, reported on March 21 that McKinley would make his final decision during the next few days. On the same day as this *Press* report, Lodge wrote McKinley a long letter assuring the President: "I talked with bankers, brokers, businessmen, editors, clergymen and others in Boston," Lynn, and Nahant, and "everybody" including "the most conservative classes" wanted the Cuban question "solved." "They said," Lodge reported, "for business one shock and

[12] Frick to Carnegie, March 24, 1898, Carnegie MSS; *Economist*, April 5, 1898, 356; *Commercial and Financial Chronicle*, March 26, 1898, 590.

[13] The speech is in *Congressional Record*, 55th Cong., 2nd Sess., 2916–2919; *Public Opinion*, March 24, 1898, 358–360; *Commercial Advertiser*, April 2, 1898.

then an end was better than a succession of spasms such as we must have if this war in Cuba went on." [14]

Perhaps the most influential note the President received that week was a telegram from W. C. Reick, a trusted political adviser in New York City and city editor of the New York *Herald.* This message arrived at the White House on March 25: "Big corporations here now believe we will have war. Believe all would welcome it as relief to suspense." On March 27, the New York *Tribune* ran a front-page article which indicated that Reick's evaluation also applied to the London Stock Exchange, a financial institution which some American investors considered of more importance than the New York Exchange. "What is wanted first of all is relief from the suspense. . . . Even a declaration of war would be preferred by bankers and stockbrokers to the continuance of a stagnant market, with hourly flurries, caused by sensational journalism and the rumors of impending hostilities," the *Tribune* reported. If war occurred, a "speculator's movement" might result in a "temporary flurry in American stocks." But other investors would hold their securities "in confident expectation that these will rise with the increased movement of railway traffic caused by war." [15]

Two days after the receipt of Reick's telegram, McKinley and Day presented an ultimatum to Spain. This move climaxed a week of hurried consultations and policy changes. Before March 20 the President had considered purchasing the island or attempting to work out a plan which would ensure American control while maintaining the trappings of Spanish sovereignty. Spain refused to sell the island, however, and the Junta and the rebels on the island would not listen to the second proposal. Now in the new climate created by Proctor's speech and the changing ideas of the business community, McKinley prepared to take more forceful steps. For the first time in the crisis the President called in a number of Democratic senators for consultations on March 22. Doubtlessly reflecting the changed attitudes of both McKinley and some business spokesmen, the war party in the Senate now claimed for the first time a majority of the forty-three Republicans, including representatives of the large corporations. These changes threatened to provoke Congress into its most belligerent outbursts on March 29 and 30.[16]

The President, however, was a week ahead of the war party on Capitol Hill. On March 20 Day instructed Woodford to ask Spain to restore peace in

[14] *Ibid.*, March 10, 1898; *Economist,* April 9, 1898, 556; Pratt, *Expanionists of 1898,* 246; *Journal of Commerce,* March 14, 1898, 6:2–3; March 23, 1898, 6:1; Pittsburgh *Press,* March 19, 1898, 1:1; Philadelphia *Press,* March 21, 1898, 6:2; Lodge to McKinley, March 21, 1898, McKinley MSS.

[15] Reick to John Russell Young, March 25, 1898, McKinley MSS; New York *Tribune,* March 27, 1898, 1:6. The *Tribune* reported on March 25, 1898, 1:1, that a movement had begun on Lombard Street to stop the war by helping Spain pay an indemnity to the United States. American bankers were reported to be organizing the drive, supposedly with help from the Rothschilds. Diplomats doubted whether the bankers would achieve any success.

[16] Leech, *Days of McKinley,* 183, 184; *Journal of Commerce,* March 30, 1898, 1:5; Washington *Evening Star,* March 23, 1898, 1:1.

Cuba promptly and make a "full reparation" for the "Maine." Noting that "feeling in the United States very acute," Day declared that "April 15th is none too early date for accomplishment of these purposes" and threatened to lay the question before Congress if Spain did not respond properly. The Spanish government asked that these demands be delayed until the Cuban parliament met, that is, until the rainy season began. Woodford replied that such a delay was not possible. When the Spanish Foreign Minister, Pio Gullón, expressed surprise "at the apparent change in the attitude of the United States," Woodford said that there had been no change; the American government had always wanted peace. The American Minister then outlined four reasons why this peace had to come immediately: first, the terrible suffering in Cuba in which "during little more than three years" the deaths "had exceeded the births by nearly four hundred thousand"; the danger of sanitary conditions breaking down and plagues and diseases threatening the United States; the American dependence upon Cuban sugar and commerce; and, finally, "the large amounts of American capital invested in Cuba." "I emphasized," Woodford reported to McKinley, "the tremendous pecuniary loss which the people of the United States suffer and must suffer until peace is restored." [17]

Despite Spain's reluctance to meet Day's demands, Woodford cabled Washington on March 25 that he believed that Spain would grant a truce which would lead to negotiations with the rebels. If these negotiations did not result in peace by mid-September, Spain and the United States would "in such event jointly compel both parties in Cuba to accept such settlement as the two Governments should then jointly advise." Woodford's comments on this offer are especially crucial in view of what was to occur on April 9 and 10. The proposition, the American Minister told McKinley, "has the advantage of immediate truce and of practical recognition by Spain of an insurgent government with which the insular congress can deal. It also admits and even invites possible intervention by the United States. It may lead to the recognition of Cuban independence during the summer." On the same day, Woodford wrote the President: "A truce once established and negotiations begun, I see but two possible results. The one will be the independence of Cuba. The other may be annexation to the United States. Truce and negotiations in Cuba mean, in my respectful judgment, that the Spanish flag is to quit Cuba." [18] At this point the Spanish government refused to put forward such an offer formally. Two weeks later, however, Spain would take the initiative in offering such an armistice, and Woodford's comments on the meaning of a truce would again be relevant.

On March 26 Day attempted to prod the Sagasta regime by demanding that Cuban independence be worked out with American mediation during an

[17] Day to Woodford, March 20, 1898, Spain, Instructions, NA, RG 59; Barclay to Salisbury, March 28, 1898, F.O. 72/2068; Woodford to McKinley, March 22 and 24, 1898, Spain, Despatches, NA, RG 59.

[18] Woodford to McKinley, March 24, March 25, Spain, Despatches, NA, RG 59.

armistice period. The following day the Assistant Secretary of State issued the first points of an ultimatum: first, an armistice until October 1 during which time the President would use his friendly offices to bring permanent peace to Cuba; second, "immediate revocation of reconcentrado order." The next day, Woodford reminded Day that under the Spanish Constitution the Ministry was powerless to recognize Cuban independence or nominal sovereignty. Only the Cortes could act on these issues, and this body would not meet until April 25. Day replied that the United States demanded the immediate promise of Cuban independence. On the 29th Day cabled that negotiations for an armistice must be concluded by March 31.[19]

The Spanish reply of March 31 renounced the *reconcentrado* orders (the Spanish further modified their position on this aspect of the negotiations on April 4 and 5), but would not promise an armistice at Spain's initiative. Woodford grieved over this last point as "a question of punctilio," forced upon the Spanish government by "Spanish pride" and the threat of revolution inside the nation. The Ministry realized, the American Minister reported, "that armistice now means certain peace next autumn." Woodford continued his efforts and on April 4 Day received a copy of the latest Spanish plan for Cuban autonomy. The Assistant Secretary tersely informed Woodford, "It is not armistice," but a Spanish appeal "urging the insurgents to lay down their arms and to join with the autonomy party. . . . The President's Message," Day concluded, "will go in Wednesday afternoon." McKinley did not send in his war message for another six days, however. He granted Fitzhugh Lee's request for time in order to remove American citizens from Havana.[20]

On April 9 Spain granted a suspension of hostilities "in order to arrange and facilitate peace on the island." Woodford cabled immediately that this move would mean "immediate and permanent peace in Cuba by negotiations" if Congress gave the President authority to conduct such discussions and full power to use the army and navy to enforce the results of the negotiations. The American Minister told McKinley that the talks would result in autonomy which the insurgents could accept, or complete independence, or cession of the islands to the United States. "I hope," Woodford asked, "that nothing will now be done to humiliate Spain as I am satisfied that the present Government is going and is loyally ready to go as fast and as far as it can." Day replied that the President "must decline to make further suggestions" to Spain, but "that in sending in his Message tomorrow the President will acquaint Congress with this latest communication." McKinley did append the Spanish offer to the end of his war message. Both the administration and Congress then proceeded to overlook the significance that Woodford attached

[19] Day to Woodford, March 26, 27, 28, 1898, Spain, Instructions, and Woodford to Day, March 28, 1898, Spain, Despatches, NA, RG 59.
[20] Woodford to McKinley, March 31, and April 1, 1898, Spain, Despatches, Day to Woodford, April 4, 1898, Spain, Instructions, and Woodford to Day, April 4, 1898, Spain, Despatches, NA, RG 59. See also comment of Leech, *Days of McKinley*, 180; and Barclay to Salisbury, March 30, 31, April 1, 1898, F.O. 72/2068.

to the offer. During the next nine days Congress debated the means, not the question, of intervention.[21]

McKinley had had the choice of three policies which would have terminated the Cuban revolution. First, he could have left the Spanish forces and the insurgents fight until one or the other fell exhausted from the bloodshed and financial strain. During the struggle the United States could have administered food and medicine to the civilian population, a privilege which the Spanish agreed to allow in March, 1898. Second, the President could have demanded an armistice and Spanish assurances that negotiations over the summer would result in some solution which would pacify American feelings. That is to say, he could have followed Woodford's ideas. Third, McKinley could have demanded both an armistice and Spanish assurances that Cuba would become independent immediately. If Spain would not grant both of these conditions, American military intervention would result. The last was the course the President followed.

Each of these policy alternatives deserves a short analysis. For American policy makers, the first choice was the least acceptable of the three, but the United States did have to deal, nevertheless, with certain aspects of this policy. If Spain hoped to win such a conflict, she had to use both the carrot of an improved and attractive autonomy scheme and the stick of an increased and effective military force. Spain could have granted no amount of autonomy, short of complete independence, which would have satisfied the rebels, and whether Americans cared to admit it or not, they were at least partially responsible for this obstinacy on the part of the insurgents. The United States did attempt to stop filibustering expeditions, but a large number nevertheless reached Cuban shores. More important, when the Spanish Minister asked Day to disband the New York Junta, the financial taproot of the insurgent organization, the Assistant Secretary replied that "this was not possible under American law and in the present state of public feeling." Woodford had given the Spanish Queen the same reply in mid-January. It was perhaps at this point that Spain saw the last hopes for a negotiated peace begin to flicker away.[22]

Seemingly unrelated actions by the United States gave boosts to the rebel cause. The sending of the "Maine," for instance, considerably heartened the rebels; they believed that the warship diverted Spanish attention and military power from insurgent forces. When the vessel exploded, the New York Junta released a statement which did not mourn the dead sailors as much as it

[21] Woodford to Day, April 9, 1898, Spain, Despatches, Day to Woodford, April 10, 1898, Spain, Instructions, "Memorandum" handed to Day from Spanish Minister on April 10, 1898, Notes from Spain, and Woodford to McKinley, April 10, 1898, Spain, Despatches, NA, RG 59.

[22] *Spanish Correspondence and Documents*, 91–92; Ernest May comments, "When even this personal appeal to McKinley produced no results, the Queen and her ministers had to face the fact that the United States would not help to bring about a negotiated peace" (*Imperial Democracy*, 162–163).

mourned the sudden disappearance of American power in Havana harbor.[23]
The Junta interpreted the passage of the $50,000,000 war appropriation meas-
ure during the first week of March as meaning either immediate war or the
preparation for war. Under such conditions, it was not odd that the rebels
were reluctant to compromise their objective of complete independence.

If the insurgents would not have accepted autonomy, no matter how liberal
or attractive, then Spain might have hoped to suppress the rebels with outright force. To have done so, however, the Spanish government would have
had to bring its army through the rainy season with few impairments, resume
to a large extent the *reconcentrado* policies, and prevent all United States aid
from reaching the rebels. The first objective would have been difficult, but
the last two, if carried out, would have meant war with the United States.
The State Department could not allow Spain to reimpose methods even
faintly resembling Weyler's techniques, nor could the Department have
allowed the searching of American vessels. McKinley and the American
people hoped that Spain would stop the revolution, but they also insisted on
taking from Spain the only tools with which that nation could deal with the
Cubans.[24]

Having found this first alternative impossible to accept, McKinley might
have chosen a second approach: demand an armistice and ultimate pacification of the island, but attempt to achieve this peacefully over several months
and with due respect for the sovereignty of Spain. This was the alternative
Woodford hoped the administration would choose. He had reported during
the two weeks before McKinley's message that the Spanish had given in time
and time again on points which he had believed they could not afford to
grant. In spite of the threat of revolution from the army, the Queen had
granted a temporary truce. The American Minister continued to ask for more
time to find a peaceful settlement. On April 11, the day the war message went
to Congress, Woodford wrote the President, "To-day it is just possible that
Moret and I have been right [in our pursuit of peace], but it is too soon to
be jubilant." [25] The American Minister sincerely believed that the negotiations during the period of truce could, with good faith on both the American
and Spanish sides, result in Spain evacuating the island. This would have to
be done slowly, however. No sovereign nation could be threatened with a time
limit and uncompromising demands without fighting back. The fact that
Spain would not grant McKinley's demand for immediate Cuban independence makes the Spanish-American War which began in April, 1898, by no
means an inevitable conflict. Any conflict is inevitable once one proud and

[23] New York *Tribune*, Feb. 17, 1898, 10:1.

[24] Chadwick denies "that the desolation of Cuba was wholly or even mainly the work of
the Spanish administration" and justifies "the right under international law" of Spain to
use the *reconcentrado* policies to stop the revolution. On the other hand, Chadwick believes American feeling correct in protesting the Spanish carelessness in feeding and caring
for the *reconcentrados* (*United States and Spain*, 486–503).

[25] Woodford to McKinley, April 11, 1898, Spain, Despatches, NA, RG 59.

sovereign power, dealing with a similar power, decides to abandon the conference table and issue an ultimatum. The historical problem remains: which power took the initiative in setting the conditions that resulted in armed conflict, and were those conditions justified?

By April 10 McKinley had assumed an inflexible position. The President abjured this second alternative and demanded not only a truce, but a truce which would lead to a guarantee of immediate Cuban independence obtained with the aid of American mediation. He moreover demanded such a guarantee of independence before the Cortes or the Cuban parliament, the two groups which had the constitutional power to grant such independence, were to gather for their formal sessions.[26]

The central question is, of course, why McKinley found himself in such a position on April 10 that only the third alternative was open to him. The President did not want war; he had been sincere and tireless in his efforts to maintain the peace. By mid-March, however, he was beginning to discover that, although he did not want war, he did want what only a war could provide: the disappearance of the terrible uncertainty in American political and economic life, and a solid basis from which to resume the building of the new American commercial empire. When the President made his demands, therefore, he made the ultimate demands; as far as he was concerned, a six-month period of negotiations would not serve to temper the political and economic problems in the United States, but only exacerbate them.

To say this is to raise another question: why did McKinley arrive at this position during mid-March? What were the factors which limited the President's freedom of choice and policies at this particular time? The standard interpretations of the war's causes emphasize the yellow journals and a belligerent Congress. These were doubtlessly crucial factors in shaping the course of American entry into the conflict, but they must be used carefully. A first observation should be that Congress and the yellow press, which had been loudly urging intervention ever since 1895, did not make a maiden appearance in March, 1898; new elements had to enter the scene at that time to act as the catalysts for McKinley's policy. Other facts should be noted regarding the yellow press specifically. In areas where this press supposedly was most important, such as New York City, no more than one-third of the press could be considered sensational. The strongest and most widespread prowar journalism apparently occurred in the Midwest. But there were few yellow journals there. The papers that advocated war in this section did so for reasons other than sensationalism; among these reasons were the influence of the Cuban Junta and, perhaps most important, the belief that the United States possessed important interests in the Caribbean area which had to be protected. Finally, the yellow press obviously did not control the levers of American foreign policy. McKinley held these, and he bitterly attacked the owners of the sensational journals as "evil disposed . . . people." An interpretation

[26] Washington *Evening Star*, April 11, 1898, 2:3, has an interesting comment from an unidentified cabinet member on the meaninglessness of the Spanish truce offer.

stressing rabid journalism as a major cause of the war should draw some link to illustrate how these journals reached the White House or the State Department. To say that this influence was exerted through public opinion proves nothing; the next problem is to demonstrate how much public opinion was governed by the yellow press, how much of this opinion was influenced by more sober factors, and which of these two branches of opinion most influenced McKinley.[27]

Congress was a hotbed of interventionist sentiment, but then it had been so since 1895. The fact was that Congress had more trouble handling McKinley than the President had handling Congress. The President had no fear of that body. He told Charles Dawes during the critical days of February and March that if Congress tried to adjourn he would call it back into session. McKinley held Congress under control until the last two days of March, when the publication of the "Maine" investigation forced Thomas B. Reed, the passionately antiwar Speaker of the House, to surrender to the onslaughts of the rapidly increasing interventionist forces. As militants in Congress forced the moderates into full retreat, McKinley and Day were waiting in the White House for Spain's reply to the American ultimatum. And after the outbreak on March 31 McKinley reassumed control. On April 5 the Secretary of War, R. A. Alger, assured the President that several important senators had just informed him that "there will be no trouble about holding the Senate." When the President postponed his war message on April 5 in order to grant Fitzhugh Lee's request for more time, prowar congressmen went into a frenzy. During the weekend of April 8 and 9, they condemned the President, ridiculed Reed's impotence to hold back war, and threatened to declare war themselves. In fact, they did nearly everything except disobey McKinley's wishes that nothing be done until the following week. Nothing was done.[28]

When the Senate threatened to overrule the President's orders that the declaration of war not include a recognition of Cuban independence, the White House whipped its supporters into line and forced the Senate to recede from its position. This was an all-out battle between the White House and a strong Senate faction. McKinley triumphed despite extremely strong pressure exerted by sincere American sentiment on behalf of immediate Cuban independence and despite the more crass material interests of the Junta's financial supporters and spokesmen. The President wanted to have a free hand in dealing with Cuba after the war, and Congress granted his wishes. Events on Capitol Hill may have been more colorful than those at the White House, but the latter, not the former, was the center of power in March and April, 1898.

[27] There is an excellent discussion of this point in Offner, "McKinley and the Origins of the Spanish-American War," 69–74; see also George W. Auxier, "Middle Western Newspapers and the Spanish-American War, 1895–1898," *Mississippi Valley Historical Review*, XXVI (March, 1940), 524, 532.

[28] Alger to McKinley, April 5, 1898, McKinley MSS; Offner, "McKinley and the Origins of the Spanish-American War," 289–300.

Influences other than the yellow press or congressional belligerence were more important in shaping McKinley's position of April 11. Perhaps most important was the transformation of the opinion of many spokesmen for the business community who had formerly opposed war. If, as one journal declared, the McKinley administration, "more than any that have preceded it, sustains . . . close relations to the business interests of the country," then this change of business sentiment should not be discounted.[29] This transformation brought important financial spokesmen, especially from the Northeast, into much the same position that had long been occupied by prointerventionist business groups and journals in the trans-Appalachian area. McKinley's decision to intervene placated many of the same business spokesmen whom he had satisfied throughout 1897 and January and February of 1898 by his refusal to declare war.

Five factors may be delineated which shaped this interventionist sentiment of the business community. First, some business journals emphasized the material advantages to be gained should Cuba become a part of the world in which the United States would enjoy, in the words of the New York *Commercial Advertiser*, "full freedom of development in the whole world's interest." The *Banker's Magazine* noted that "so many of our citizens are so involved in the commerce and productions of the island, that to protect these interests . . . the United States will have eventually to force the establishment of fair and reasonable government." The material damage suffered by investors in Cuba and by many merchants, manufacturers, exporters, and importers, as, for example, the groups which presented the February 10 petition to McKinley, forced these interests to advocate a solution which could be obtained only through force.[30]

A second reason was the uncertainty that plagued the business community in mid-March. This uncertainty was increased by Proctor's powerful and influential speech and by the news that a Spanish torpedo-boat flotilla was sailing from Cadiz to Cuba. The uncertainty was exemplified by the sudden stagnation of trade on the New York Stock Exchange after March 17. Such an unpredictable economic basis could not provide the springboard for the type of overseas commercial empire that McKinley and numerous business spokesmen envisioned.

Third, by March many businessmen who had deprecated war on the ground that the United States Treasury did not possess adequate gold reserves began

[29] Chicago *Times-Herald* quoted in Cincinnati *Commercial Tribune*, Dec. 28, 1897, 6:2. The Chicago paper was particularly close to the administration through its publisher's friendship with McKinley. The publisher was H. H. Kohlsaat. Ernest May remarks, regarding McKinley's antiwar position in 1897 and early 1898, "It was simply out of the question for him [McKinley] to embark on a policy unless virtually certain that Republican businessmen would back him" (*Imperial Democracy*, 118). The same comment doubtlessly applies also to McKinley's actions in March and April.

[30] *Commercial Advertiser*, March 10, 1898, 6:3; *Bankers' Magazine*, LVI (April, 1898), 519–520.

to realize that they had been arguing from false assumptions. The heavy exports of 1897 and the discoveries of gold in Alaska and Australia brought the yellow metal into the country in an ever widening stream. Private bankers had been preparing for war since 1897. *Banker's Magazine* summarized these developments: "Therefore, while not desiring war, it is apparent that the country now has an ample coin basis for sustaining the credit operations which a conflict would probably make necessary. In such a crisis the gold standard will prove a bulwark of confidence." [31]

Fourth, antiwar sentiment lost much strength when the nation realized that it had nothing to fear from European intervention on the side of Spain. France and Russia, who were most sympathetic to the Spanish monarchy, were forced to devote their attention to the Far East. Neither of these nations wished to alienate the United States on the Cuban issue. More important, Americans happily realized that they had the support of Great Britain. The *rapprochement* which had occurred since the Venezuelan incident now paid dividends. On an official level, the British Foreign Office assured the State Department that nothing would be accomplished in the way of European intervention unless the United States requested such intervention. The British attitude made it easy for McKinley to deal with a joint European note of April 6 which asked for American moderation toward Spain. The President brushed off the request firmly but politely. On an unofficial level, American periodicals expressed appreciation of the British policy on Cuba, and some of the journals noted that a common Anglo-American approach was also desirable in Asia.[32] The European reaction is interesting insofar as it evinces the continental powers' growing realization that the United States was rapidly becoming a major force in the world. But the European governments set no limits on American dealings with Spain. McKinley could take the initiative and make his demands with little concern for European reactions.

Finally, opposition to war melted away in some degree when the administration began to emphasize that the United States enjoyed military power much superior to that of Spain. One possible reason for McKinley's policies during the first two months of 1898 might have been his fear that the nation was not adequately prepared. As late as the weekend of March 25 the President worried over this inadequacy. But in late February and early March, especially after the $50,000,000 appropriation by Congress, the country's military strength developed rapidly. On March 13 the Philadelphia *Press* proclaimed that American naval power greatly exceeded that of the Spanish forces. By early April those who feared a Spanish bombardment of New York City were in the small minority. More representative were the views of Win-

[31] *Bankers' Magazine*, LVI (March, 1898), 347–348; LVI (April, 1898), 520; Pittsburgh *Press*, April 8, 1898, 4:1; *Commercial and Financial Chronicle*, April 23, 1898, 786.

[32] Dugdale, *German Documents*, II, 500–502; Porter to Sherman, April 8, 1898, France, Despatches, and Hay to Sherman, March 26, 28, 29, April 1, Great Britain, Despatches, NA, RG 59; *Public Opinion*, March 24, 1898, 360–361.

throp Chanler who wrote Lodge that if Spanish troops invaded New York "they would all be absorbed in the population . . . and engaged in selling oranges before they got as far as 14th Street." [33]

As the words of McKinley's war message flew across the wires to Madrid, many business spokesmen who had opposed war had recently changed their minds, American military forces were rapidly growing more powerful, banks and the United States Treasury had secured themselves against the initial shocks of war, and the European powers were divided among themselves and preoccupied in the Far East. Business boomed after McKinley signed the declaration of war. "With a hesitation so slight as to amount almost to indifference," *Bradstreet's* reported on April 30, "the business community, relieved from the tension caused by the incubus of doubt and uncertainty which so long controlled it, has stepped confidently forward to accept the situation confronting it oweing to the changed conditions." "Unfavorable circumstances . . . have hardly excited remark, while the stimulating effects have been so numerous and important as to surprise all but the most optimistic," this journal concluded.[34] A new type of American empire, temporarily clothed in armor, stepped out on the international stage after a half century of preparation to make its claim as one of the great world powers.

[33] Leech, *Days of McKinley*, 176; Philadelphia *Press*, March 13, 1898, 8:3; Garraty, *Lodge*, 191.

[34] *Bradstreet's*, April 9, 1898, 234, also April 30, 1898, 272, 282.

3

Taking the Philippines:

DESIGN *or* DRIFT*?*

HOSTILITIES *between the United States and Spain came to an end on August 12, 1898. The preliminaries of peace included Spanish withdrawal from Cuba, the cession of Puerto Rico and an island in the Marianas to the United States, and American occupation of Manila pending a definitive treaty of peace. The American government had not yet decided on the future of the Philippine Islands. That vast area lying on the opposite side of the world from the United States, comprising 115,600 square miles and consisting of over 7000 islands, had not figured in the origins of the conflict with Spain. But as soon as war broke out, Admiral George Dewey was ordered from Hong Kong to Manila to destroy the Spanish fleet, and on May 1 he did just that. Shortly thereafter in August, an American army landed at Manila and took possession of the city. Meanwhile Washington prepared instructions for the peace delegation which was scheduled to meet in Paris on October 1. The instructions relating to the Asiatic islands were vague, saying only that the Philippines were commercially useful and that the United States would retain Luzon, the largest of the islands. On October 25, 1898, the American commissioners asked President McKinley for specific instructions. He replied that the United States would annex all of the Philippine Islands. Why had the President decided on the entire archipelago? What factors had intervened to crystallize McKinley's ideas on the territory? Was it design or drift? Did he, in fact, know what he was doing?*

Ernest R. May, a professor of history at Harvard and author of a standard work on World War I, as well as a work on the coming of the war with Spain from which the following selection is taken, believes that the President was fully aware of what he was doing as he moved from a position of uncertainty on acquiring the islands to the decision to annex them. The aura of ineptitude which accompanies McKinley's well-known comment, "I could not have told where those darned islands were within 2000 miles," is unfortunate. His re-

mark to the visiting Methodist clergymen that "I walked the floor of the White House night after night until midnight; . . . went down on my knees and prayed to Almighty God for light and guidance . . . and one night late it came to me . . ." is also misleading. May claims that from the outset of the war there was the possibility that McKinley wanted Spanish possessions. McKinley followed Dewey's military operations, he anticipated victory, and after victory did not discourage imperialist thoughts. After carefully assessing the situation—that the Filipino rebels could not govern themselves, that the islands would fall to a foreign power if the United States did not annex them, that there was popular sentiment to keep the territory as compensation for the American military and naval effort, and that missionary and business interests were favorable to American ownership—the President came to the deliberate and thoughtful decision to annex all the islands.

From Louis J. Halle's account of the War an entirely different picture emerges. Formerly a member of the Policy Planning Staff of the Department of State and a teacher of international relations at the University of Virginia, and at Geneva, Halle characterizes American policy as one of drift. At the outset of the war, he writes, "virtually no one in the United States had any notion of acquiring an Asiatic empire. It was an exceptional American who knew where the Philippine Islands were . . . those whom we identify today with their acquisition appear to have had no thought, as yet, of acquiring them." No positive decision to attack the islands was ever formulated. The order went to Dewey, in part, since it was necessary, in any case, that he leave Hong Kong because of Britain's declared neutrality in the war. Too, the order to attack was a naval measure without any thought of political consequences. The decision to occupy the islands was made without any idea of keeping them, and, after the landing of American troops, no one had a clear view of the army's mission. The President did not know what to do and finally, "unhappily deciding at last that we had no choice," gave the order to demand the entire archipelago of Spain.

American Imperialism

ERNEST R. MAY

THE WAR appeared to change McKinley. He came out for Hawaiian annexation. He resolved to keep some foothold in the Philippines. Eventually he decided to take the whole archipelago, Guam, and Puerto Rico. He seemed to become an imperialist.

In the case of Hawaii, his conversion came at the last moment. Though he had submitted an annexation treaty to the Senate in 1897, he had not pressed it. Indeed, he assured opponents that it would not pass. When annexationists resorted to a joint resolution, needing only majorities in both chambers rather than two-thirds in the Senate, he still gave them no open encouragement. The project appeared hopeless, for Speaker Reed, who opposed annexation, had proved powerful enough in the past to prevent the House's even discussing measures distasteful to him. But the war and especially Dewey's victory persuaded many congressmen that Hawaii was really needed.

The New York *Tribune* declared on April 23 that the islands might have to be seized. Annexationists demonstrated that they could collect the 219 signatures required for a petition to override the Speaker. Paul Dana of the *Sun*, who helped round up signers, wrote to General Wilson, "I think we are dealing with [Reed] as effectively as if we pointed a gun straight at his head." After Reed caved in, it seemed certain that a resolution would pass, and at that stage McKinley took a stand. On June 4, 1898, the New York *Tribune* announced that he wished annexation.

As when he asked for intervention in Cuba, the President appeared to be jumping aboard a vehicle he could not brake. The resolution was to pass the House by a vote of 209–91, the Senate by 42–21. Except for starchy mugwump sheets like the New York *Evening Post* and the Springfield *Republican*, the press acclaimed annexation. Religious and business journals that had drawn back after Cleveland's revelations in 1893 either took the view that five years had erased moral stains or interpreted Dewey's triumph as a sign from Providence. Reed, who had remained in opposition, was pictured by the sympathetic *Nation* as "standing alone, so far as party friends are concerned, and as one of a feeble minority, mostly Democrats." McKinley had certainly taken the more popular position. But, significantly, he had also convinced himself that he was right. In the hearing of one of his private secre-

From *Imperial Democracy*, © 1961, by Ernest R. May. Reprinted by permission of Harcourt, Brace & World, Inc. Pp. 243–259.

taries he declared, "We need Hawaii just as much and a good deal more than we did California. It is manifest destiny."

This does not mean that he had experienced a complete change of mind. Many who spoke for annexing Hawaii said in the same breath that they would oppose other colonies. The *Catholic World* and the Protestant *Independent* did so. Representative Francis Newlands of Nevada, who had introduced the joint resolution, defended it as establishing "scientific boundaries" for America. McKinley could have spoken as he did about Hawaii and still doubted that imperialism offered the best policy for the future. On the other hand, it is certainly worth notice that, despite his stated conviction, he appeared even more circumspect with regard to Hawaii than he was to seem with regard to the Philippines.

There is a faint possibility that from the very outset of the war the President nurtured in his mind the hope of taking from Spain some part of her Pacific empire. He was later to tell his friend, H. H. Kohlsaat, that Dewey's victory had surprised him completely and that he had to search out the Philippines on his office globe: "I could not have told where those darned islands were within 2,000 miles!" Probably, however, the President was stretching the truth, for he had been told as early as September, 1897, that the navy planned to strike Manila. The Secretary of the Navy twice discussed with him the orders to be given Dewey, and McKinley himself approved the directive sent on April 24, reading, "War has commenced. . . . Proceed at once to the Philippine Islands. Commence operations at once, particularly against the Spanish fleet. You must capture vessels or destroy. Use utmost endeavors." On Friday, April 29, two days before the battle, Comptroller Charles G. Dawes wrote in his diary: "An engagement is expected by Sunday in the Pacific between our Asiatic Squadron and the Spanish ships at Manila." The President could not, of course, anticipate a complete triumph. But he did know that Dewey had the Spaniards outgunned; he could expect some kind of victory; and he may have hoped that it would give the United States a claim to territory beyond Hawaii.

After learning of Dewey's victory, McKinley certainly made no move to discourage others from thinking imperialist thoughts. In its resolution for intervention in Cuba, Congress had declared explicitly against taking or keeping Cuba, and the President could have proclaimed that this self-denying ordinance applied to the Philippines as well. Instead, the White House allowed the New York *Tribune* to report on May 4: "it is held by the President and his political and military advisers that it will be time enough to discuss the sale, barter or retention of the islands when Spain has been driven to abandon Cuba and sue for conditions of a general peace."

The thought of retaining the islands occurred to the President as soon as to any imperialist. Even Lodge was slow to grasp that an opportunity existed. He wrote to Henry White on May 5, "The victory at Manila was at first so overwhelming I did not take in all its possibilities." He had needed "a day's reflection" before realizing "that we must on no account let the Islands go.

. . . We hold the other side of the Pacific and the value to this country is almost beyond imagination." Despite the excitement created by the naval victory, few voices spoke for conquering and keeping the islands. Lodge did not disclose his views in public. Neither did Chandler or Cullom. Though the New York *Sun* came out for keeping the Stars and Stripes over Manila, few other jingo papers did so. Hearst's San Francisco *Examiner* said the colony had been "a source of corruption and weakness to Spain" and might be so for America. The St. Louis *Republic* reported a straw poll among members of the House and Senate yielding only one vote unequivocally for annexation, that of Representative Joel P. Heatwole of Minnesota who said, "On general principles, I believe we should hold fast to all that we can get." Frye of Maine, a longtime champion of imperialist causes, refused to comment at all. At the time when the New York *Tribune* reported the White House considering possible retention of the islands, there was no evident public movement for such a course, even among avowed imperialists.

Nor was there any such movement when the President authorized an expeditionary force to take Manila. Another of Kohlsaat's recollections was of McKinley's saying, "If old Dewey had just sailed away when he smashed that Spanish fleet, what a lot of trouble he would have saved us." At the time, however, the President showed no misgivings. According to Secretary of War Alger, indeed, he made his decision even before Dewey's victory. Owing to technical disagreements between the commanding general of the army and the officer designated to captain the expedition, the order was not given until May 16. In the meantime, McKinley was warned against committing troops to the islands. Oscar S. Straus wrote him that "nothing but entanglement and embarrassment" could result; "I fear we will not be able afterwards to withdraw our troops without turning over the islands to anarchy and slaughter." But McKinley was not deterred. He let the expedition depart as soon as the two generals reached a compromise. The President seemed untroubled by the prospect of having to decide, not whether to take the islands, but whether to keep them or give them back.

The explanation need not be that McKinley's mind was already teased by imperialist thoughts. Nearly everyone seemed to regard Dewey's victory as putting a finish to Spanish sovereignty. The vehemently anti-imperialist Springfield *Republican* declared on May 5 that the Philippines were in America's hands and that it would be immoral to return them to "a dominion hated, crushed, and unregenerate." The *Republican* urged their transfer to some other power. The Boston *Herald* and the New York *Evening Post* favored granting independence. According to the French ambassador, congressmen talked of nothing but possible sale, partition, or transfer. It seemed to be generally assumed that the islands were America's to dispose of as she would. The President may just have shared this popular belief.

Whatever McKinley may have meditated before the war or just after Dewey's victory, it was not in any case the acquisition of all the Philippines, for at the beginning of June he sketched peace terms that would have given the

United States nothing but a naval base in the islands. Ambassador Hay reported a semiofficial inquiry about conditions for an armistice. The Secretary of State replied that the President would ask evacuation of Cuba, surrender of Puerto Rico, cession of a coaling station in the Ladrones, and the "Philippine Islands to be allowed to remain with Spain except a port and necessary appurtenances, to be selected by the United States." Hay was cautioned, "These terms will be acceptable to the President at the present juncture, saving further sacrifice and loss of life. Prolongation of the war may change this materially." But there can be little doubt that the President meant them seriously, for he also stipulated that there should be no indemnity and that the United States would assume payment of American claims in Cuba. Had his intention been to seem conciliatory but to prevent negotiations, he would have included some financial clause that bankrupt Spain could not accept. At this stage, he almost certainly had no aim beyond the acquisition of Manila.

Had Spain accepted his terms at once, he might even have been ready to give up all claim on the Philippines. He may have wanted a naval base and trading station in the Far East, but his mind was busier with immediate preoccupations. As he studied preparations for a campaign in Cuba, he must have remembered how murderous the climate and terrain had proved to Spanish regular troops. He knew the volunteers assembling in American army camps to be enthusiastic but undisciplined and short of artillery, shells, transport, rifles, cartridges, and even uniforms. He must have wanted, if at all possible, to escape sending raw troops against Spanish veterans or against the mosquitoes and miasmata of Cuba. Foreseeing campaigns that could well be long, costly, and bitter, he may have thought of the Philippines merely as a pressure point. He may have hoped that Spain, fearing loss of her richest colony, would agree to a quick settlement. He may have believed that acquisition of Puerto Rico would be ample salve for imperialists.

Abruptly, however, he abandoned such thoughts. When Hay described Salisbury as willing to communicate McKinley's terms to Madrid, the Secretary of State cabled back almost immediately, "The President cannot make proposals for peace. My confidential message to you indicated his state of mind at that time and was only intended to advise you of it. . . . It has seemed to the President that any action on our part at this time would be premature and be liable to misinterpretation. . . . If proposal comes from Spain on the basis of my telegram . . . before situation changes, President will consider it."

One reason for this *volte-face* was undoubtedly increased concern for the Philippine rebels. When first reports came to Washington of an impending conference between Dewey and the rebel leader, Emilio Aguinaldo, the admiral had been cautioned, "It is desirable, as far as possible, and consistent for your success and safety, not to have political alliance with the insurgents or any faction in the islands that would incur liability to maintain their cause in the future." Dewey had nevertheless met with Aguinaldo. While he denied having entered into any alliance, press dispatches reported the rebels preparing arsenals for the American invaders and Aguinaldo calling for a republic under American protectorate. The Secretary of State explained to Hay that the President had drawn back from his original peace proposal because the insurgents had "become an important factor in the situation and must have just consideration in any terms of settlement."

Another, more important reason for the President's swift retreat was mounting evidence of public interest in the Philippines. Among the few newspapers that had begun to call for annexation were the Washington *Silver Knight* and the silverite Denver *Rocky Mountain News*. More important, the news columns of eastern and midwestern newspapers reported annexationism bubbling up among some of the very groups that had clamored for intervention in Cuba. On May 16, for example, the New York *Tribune* described a branch of the Sons of the American Revolution exulting that Dewey had "paralyzed the . . . oppressor's hand, deprived her of her richest colony," while an adjoining column quoted a sermon in Calvary Baptist Church by the Reverend Dr. MacArthur. "The Philippines Islands . . . should be made the garden of the universe," he declared. ". . . We will fill them with school houses and missionaries." On May 21 the Newark *Advertiser* printed a resolution by local Daughters of the American Revolution predicting "that our country at the close of this war will enter upon a new career, grander and more imposing than anything that had distinguished her in the past." This language was vague, but no more so than that of earlier resolutions and sermons on the Cuban problem.

Even weak signals from the groups that had brought on the crises of March and April could cause nerves to flutter. The *Tribune* quoted on May 17 a speech made by Chauncey Depew before the Republican Club of New York: "in my daily business I have clipped out for me reports in the papers from all over this country. Every morning they are placed before me, so that I may see how things that may have some bearing on the railroad business are going. I can't help seeing what a strong feeling is spreading over the whole land in favor of colonial expansion. The people are infatuated with the idea. . . . This feeling is getting so strong that it will mean the political death of any man to oppose it pretty soon." In Chicago the editor of the Baptist *Standard* wrote on May 21 of a developing "popular craze" for annexations.

The President must have heard similar warnings, and, just after he had sent off his proposed peace terms, he discovered that this incipient movement might have strong leadership. The *North American Review* appeared with two articles, one by Truxtun Beale, contending that the United States should take the Philippines in order to win the trade of China, the other by Senator Morgan, arguing against keeping the islands on account of the Filipinos' racial inferiority and the danger of conflict with other powers. Beale was a California Republican who had held a diplomatic post under President Harrison. Morgan had, of course, been a conspicuous jingo and imperialist.

The litmus-sensitive New York *Tribune* on June 6 published an editorial attacking Morgan and, in effect, endorsing Beale. Other Republican journals followed suit. When debate opened in the House on the Hawaiian question, Republicans from New England, New York, Pennsylvania, Illinois, Iowa, Michigan, and California advanced arguments that would also justify annexing the Philippines. The President could see that there was danger of his own party's taking up the imperialist cause.

McKinley began to feel that the United States might need more than just a harbor or naval base. William M. Laffan, publisher of the New York, *Sun*, talked with him on July 13 and wrote Lodge that he had heard the President say, "we will first take the Philippines [*sic*], the Ladrones, the Carolines and Porto Rico. Then when we have possession, undisputed, we will look them all over at our leisure and do what seems wisest. Personally I am in favor now of keeping Luzon and fortifying Manila. . . . I think the United States possessed of all of Spain's colonies would do well to act with great magnanimity and show European governments the lofty spirit that guides us. Apart from that idea I favor the general principle of holding on to what we get." Lodge himself assured Chandler on July 23 that he had just seen McKinley and that "in the Pacific [he] means to go much farther than anyone I think guesses."

Just how far, the President himself did not seem to know. On the afternoon of July 26, Jules Cambon, the French ambassador, brought to the White House a message from the Spanish Foreign Minister, inviting negotiations for peace. At the moment, though Spain's naval power had been utterly broken, American ground forces occupied only the eastern tip of Cuba, a beachhead on Puerto Rico, and the outskirts of Manila. Of the islands that McKinley had mentioned to Laffan, the United States held a close grasp only on Guam. General Shafter, commanding at Santiago, had just reported cases of fever among the troops mounting at a rate of five hundred a day. General Anderson at Cavite had intimated that all was not going well in relations with the Philippine insurgents, and Dewey was to cable on July 30 that Aguinaldo had "become aggressive and even threatening toward our Army." Though press dispatches described Spain as bankrupt and demoralized, the President could not feel sure that she would accept any terms he imposed. He jotted on a scrap of paper:

As a condition to entering upon negotiations looking to peace, Spain must withdraw from Cuba and Porto Rico and such adjacent islands as are under her dominion. This requirement will admit of no negotiations.

As to the Philippines, I am of the opinion, that with propriety and advantage they can be the subject of negotiation and whenever the Spanish gov't desire it, I will appoint Commissioners to that end.

For four days he discussed the matter with individual advisers and eventually with his full cabinet. Secretary of State Day took the view that the government ought not to assume responsibility for "eight or nine millions of absolutely ignorant and many degraded people." As the President summarized it, Day wanted to keep only "a hitching-post" in the islands. The Secretary of the Treasury and the Secretary of the Navy agreed, while the Secretary of the

Interior and the Attorney General argued for keeping the entire archipelago on account of its prospective commercial value, and the Secretary of Agriculture contended that there was a great opportunity to Christianize the natives. The Naval War Board, which included Captain Mahan, advised retention on strategic grounds. Secretary of War Alger evidently warned that it might be politically unsafe to do anything else.

McKinley held his foggy middle ground. After innumerable drafts of a protocol had been exchanged, discussed, revised, and rewritten, the final terms stipulated that Spain surrender Cuba and Puerto Rico and leave "the control, disposition, and government of the Philippines" to be determined by later negotiations.

When picking the five commissioners to represent him in Paris, McKinley selected three who favored outright annexation. That may have been accident, for his principal object was to make the eventual treaty acceptable to the Senate and the public, and his original slate had been made up of men who were not publicly committed. Only after several refusals did the President end up with Secretary Day and Democratic Senator George Gray of Delaware, both of whom opposed annexation, Senators Davis and Frye, who were known to favor it, and, as a fifth member, Whitelaw Reid, whose New York *Tribune* had come out editorially for taking the islands. But, since Reid and Day could both be counted on to vote as the President asked, McKinley retained the power to make any decision he chose.

By the second week in September, when the commission left for Paris, the President had decided that he must ask for all of Luzon. Otherwise, his parting directions to the commissioners remained delphic. He said:

It is believed that the true glory and the enduring interests of the country will most surely be served if an unselfish duty conscientiously accepted and a signal triumph honorably achieved shall be crowned by such an example of moderation, restraint, and reason in victory as best comports with the traditions and character of our enlightened Republic. . . . It is none the less true, however, that, without any original thought of complete or even partial acquisition, the presence and success of our arms at Manila imposes upon us obligations which we can not disregard. The march of events rules and overrules human action.

As sessions opened in Paris, the President set off on a midwestern speaking tour. When questions came in by cable, he answered that the commissioners should adhere to the armistice protocol and his instructions.

Not until late October did he finally have to make up his mind. The Spanish negotiators tried to tempt the Americans with the thought of keeping Cuba instead of making it independent. Though some of the commissioners and McKinley's new Secretary of State, John Hay, found this notion attractive, the President did not. He cabled tersely, "We must carry out the spirit and letter of the resolution of Congress." But the Spanish proposition had also involved the issue of the Cuban debt, and McKinley had to instruct his commissioners in no circumstances to assume responsibility for any part of it. By taking this stand, he obliged himself to decide the Philippine issue, for, as he was warned, the Spanish commissioners were certain then to ask if Spain would be responsible for the Philippine debt. He could not long defer the precise instructions which his commissioners repeatedly begged.

He sat down and wrote out in pencil a cablegram. Before it could be sent out, he received a message detailing the antiannexationist views of Day and Gray. The Secretary of State drafted a revised cablegram. The President added to it in order to meet some of Day's and Gray's arguments. The final text dispatched on October 26 read:

The information which had come to the President since your departure convinces him that the acceptance of the cession of Luzon alone, leaving the rest of the islands subject to Spanish rule, or to be the subject of future contention, can not be justified on political, commercial, or humanitarian grounds. The cession must be of the whole archipelago or none. The latter is wholly inadmissible, and the former must therefore be required.

In a famous interview with a delegation of Methodist clergymen in 1899, McKinley explained that this conclusion had come to him almost in a flash of revelation:

I walked the floor of the White House night after night until midnight; and I am not ashamed to tell you, gentlemen, that I went down on my knees and prayed Almighty God for light and guidance more than one night. And one night late it came to me this way—I don't know how it was, but it came: (1) That we could not give them back to Spain—that would be cowardly and dishonorable; (2) that we could not turn them over to France or Germany—our commercial rivals in the Orient—that would be bad business and discreditable; (3) that we could not leave them to themselves—they were unfit for self-government—and they would soon have anarchy and misrule over there worse than Spain's was; and (4) that there was nothing left for us to do but to take them all, and to educate the Filipinos, and uplift and Christianize them, and by God's grace do the very best we could by them, as our fellow-men for whom Christ also died.

There can be little doubt that these thoughts actually did come to the President. As early as July 27, they came to him through the mail. His old friend, Spencer Borden, wrote him a letter that merits quotation because of its resemblance to what McKinley said later:

It would be cowardly and pusillanimous for us to turn the islands back to Spain, giving them the power again to misrule the natives. . . . We would be equally despicable to ask Great Britain to take and care for them—which would make a greater row—and we must never permit the three bullying nations that deprived Japan of the fruits of her victory over China, to play the same game with us.

There is only one logical course to pursue. Spain has shown herself unfit to rule her colonies, and those that have come into our possession as the result of war, must be held, if we are to fulfill our duties as a nation . . . , giving them the benefits of a christian civilization which has reached its highest development [sic] under our republican institutions.

The President must have recognized at a very early date that he could not simply return to Spain ground that had been occupied by American troops. No voice in the land had spoken except against such a course. Lodge commented to Henry White, "I have never seen such a universal feeling as there is against handing the islands back to Spain." Nearly all evidence filtering back to the White House pictured Spanish rule as worse in the Philippines than in Cuba. The American who had been McKinley's consul in Manila declared every week of his service to have been "a history of barbarities by Spaniards." Another, who had represented Cleveland, wrote in *Scribner's* of "Spanish misrule and oppression." Hardly a popular magazine in either the United States or England failed to print someone's reminiscence or comment on Spanish iniquity. From the time when he gave up his initial idea of negotiated peace, McKinley must have known that he could not return the Philippines to Spain.

Nor could he have believed for long that sale or transfer was a feasible alternative. While the war was still in progress, the British and Japanese governments both said that if the United States did not want the islands, they did. The German ambassador in London told Hay of Germany's desire for at least a base or coaling station. The New York *Herald* reported on July 3 a rumor that France and Russia had agreed to support Germany if she sought the whole archipelago. For the United States to offer the islands to any one power would surely bring protests, if nothing worse, from the rest. At home, the Germans and Irish would fight transfer to England, while others would oppose sale to anyone else. Moreover, as McKinley later observed, any such transaction might prove "bad business." The Philippines were reputed not only to offer advantageous bases for trade and navigation but also to possess rich resources, including quantities of gold. Weighing possible trouble with the powers, the likelihood of Senate failure to ratify a bargain, and the danger that the abandoned territory might prove a new California or Transvaal, McKinley could scarcely have given serious consideration to this possibility.

His one real option was to insist on independence for the islands, and he may have postponed final decision partly in order to collect information on the character and disposition of the natives. Early data painted a depressing picture. John Foreman, an Englishman regarded as the foremost expert on the islands, wrote in the July *Contemporary Review*, "The Philippine Islands . . . would not remain one year peaceful under an independent native government. It is an utter impossibility." McKinley saw this article, for he obtained a copy from his private secretary. Though complaining of eyestrain, he may also have read other similar writings, of which magazines and newspapers were full. At any rate, he saw little to contradict Foreman; hardly anyone claiming first hand knowledge disputed his conclusions. And before the armistice had been signed McKinley was advised officially by the Japanese Foreign Minister that the Filipinos were incapable of governing themselves.

Yet McKinley did continue to ask for reports on the natives. He requested opinions from Dewey and American generals who had been in the Philippines, and he waited until the commissioners could hear testimony from the admiral, General Merritt, and Foreman himself. When telling the commissioners of his decision, McKinley mentioned information that had reached him after their departure, and he may have been referring to this expert testimony. Perhaps it should have been obvious to him that few authorities would credit the Filipinos with capacity for self-government, yet he may actually have regarded independence as a feasible alternative down to the last moment.

But if doubt lingered in his mind, it was because his thoughts were not really on rational alternatives. His advisers talked of what would be wise, statesmanlike, and in the national interest. He did not.

In his explanation to the French ambassador of why he could not offer precise armistice terms, the President said, "The American people would not accept it if we did not obtain some advantage from our great victories at Manila and from the sacrifices we have made in sending to the Philippines a large body of troops." When Oscar Straus advised him early in August not to take the islands, "he seemed," Straus noted in his diary, "to fear public opinion would not approve such a course." When McKinley first drafted a final directive to his commissioners, he did not mention information newly come or any other such consideration. He wrote simply, "There is a very general feeling that the United States, whatever it might prefer as to the Philippines, is in a situation where it can not let go . . . , and it is my judgment that the well-considered opinion of the majority would be that duty requires we should take the archipelago." The sole concern of the President was with the mood and whim of public opinion.

He had observed how the press gradually swung toward annexation. Shortly after the New York *Tribune* attacked Senator Morgan's *North American Review* article, Cleveland and Bryan came out almost simultaneously against taking the Philippines, and a large part of the Republican press immediately became raucously imperialist. The *Literary Digest* published a survey on July 9, quoting editorials of more or less imperialist tone from the leading Republican dailies of New York, Philadelphia, Baltimore, Chicago, Milwaukee, Minneapolis, Topeka, St. Louis, Louisville, and San Francisco. The *Digest* reported even more significantly that Cleveland had been criticized by conservative Democratic papers and Bryan by silver Democratic organs. On August 4 *Public Opinion* listed twenty-eight major dailies as unreservedly for annexation and many others wavering. By September 10 the *Literary Digest* reported eighty-four papers favoring annexation of the whole archipelago, among them many of the best known and most widely circulated journals in the country.

This evidence suggested that a majority of city and town newspaper editors saw local opinion leaning toward annexation. There were relatively few organization meetings, resolutions, or public rallies to bear this judgment out. From the fastness of the White House, McKinley probably wondered whether the press spoke for the multitude or not.

The President could see that church and business leaders, like newspaper editors, were taking no chance on being ridden down by a mass movement

like that which had followed the sinking of the *Maine.* Churchmen may have
been caught, of course, by the dream of converting several million Visayas
and Tagalogs. McKinley's Presbyterian Secretary of Agriculture was affected
by such a fancy, and so, it was said, was the President's invalid wife. But the
early and ardent annexationists within the churches were not in the missionary
societies, where this motive would have been expected to flourish. Indeed, the
Presbyterian, Baptist, and Congregational mission boards held conventions
in which the Philippine question was scarcely discussed, and the monthly
Methodist Review of Missions refrained from any comment at all until after
the President reached his decision. Some clergymen and laymen connected
with these associations or with the American Bible Society actually joined the
Anti-Imperialist League.

Religious periodicals other than those published by mission boards did cite
missionary opportunities as one argument for annexation, but few that came
out for taking the islands made this the primary justification for their stand.
Their tone was rather one of resignation. The widely read nondenominational
New York *Outlook,* for example, observed that return of the islands to Spain
would "not be tolerated by the American people." As early as May 28 it
declared, "The devout man . . . will always seek to ascertain what God's
will is, and always endeavor to conform his action to it. The events of the past
four months have made that will plain." The *Outlook* was one of those journals that had opposed war and then backed down in fright after seeing the
hysteria of the public, and its other editorials laid constant stress on the need
for clergymen to "achieve a healthful and needed influence in the time of
perilous excitement." Though never saying so publicly, the *Outlook's* editors
evidently believed that would-be leaders who opposed annexation, like those
who had opposed war, would simply not be followed.

The Boston *Congregationalist* spoke of "responsibilities which God lays
on" and the *Catholic World* of a "logic of events" compelling America to
keep the Philippines. Though some of these writers may have been hypocriti-
cally masking imperialist convictions, many would seem to have been voicing
the feeling that Mr. Dooley put less reverently when he wrote, "We've got
the Ph'lippeens, Hinnissy; we've got thim the way Casey got the bulldog—be
th' teeth. . . . As Hogan an' McKinley both says: 'Th' natio's in th' hands iv
the Lord, an'll give Him what assistance it can spare fr'm its other jooties.'
. . . We're a gr-reat civilizein' agent, Hinnissy, an' as Father Kelly says, 'so's
th' steam roller.' An' bein' a quiet man, I'd rather be behind thin in fr-ront
when th' shtreet has to be improved."

Though some businessmen and business journals took up the cause of annexation joyfully, it may be that many of them were also trying to keep ahead
of the steamroller. When thirty prominent men gathered in late August at
Saratoga, New York, to debate the Philippine issue, one who spoke for imperialism was Eugene V. Smalley of St. Paul, Minnesota, editor of the *Northwest Magazine* and secretary of the National Sound Money League. He said,
"I believe that a nation cannot safely absorb itself in its own affairs. . . . It

breeds strange and dangerous disorders. The most wholesome influences upon our home politics will be exerted by getting interested in questions that concern the whole world." Henry Watterson wrote in the Louisville *Courier-Journal*, "We risk Caesarism certainly, but even Caesarism is preferable to anarchism." According to the New York *Journal of Commerce*, most businessmen actually kept a "deathlike silence." James Ford Rhodes, the historian, wrote McKinley that "the higher intelligence and the business interests" and "practically all the preachers and the religious folk" wanted simply to be led by the President.

Many varied considerations undoubtedly entered into the conscious and unconscious thoughts of those who in the name of religion or business advocated imperialism, among them piety, superstition, patriotism, and greed. Teachings from social Darwinists and Mahan had their effect. But the apparent conversion of churchmen and businessmen came so quickly that it is hard to explain in terms of impulses or ideas that had long been present or afloat. Something had shaken these people. While it may have been Dewey's triumph or the sheer sense of being in battle, more likely it was the shocking, terrifying experience of the previous spring, when a nameless, formless, and seemingly leaderless public opinion rode the country into war. Church and business leaders spoke like men determined not to be left behind again.

McKinley could not look to these groups, as he had before April, 1898, to tell him what he should do. Not only was the smell of fear on them, but the very event that had frightened them had proved how impotent they were to subdue and direct the people. The President had to establish his own rapport with the public.

In order to do so, he arranged a speaking tour that would carry him through Indiana, Illinois, and Iowa, three states whose electoral votes had made the difference between victory and defeat in 1896, and through Nebraska and Missouri, where he had lost narrowly to Bryan. Considered either in terms of the contest for the House of Representatives or the approaching 1900 campaign, these were the areas that mattered.

In the course of each speech, McKinley said something that could be interpreted as referring to the Philippines. At Tama, Iowa, on October 11, he asserted, "We want to preserve carefully all the old life of the nation,—the dear old life of the nation and our cherished institutions—"; there was scattered clapping. He went on, "but we do not want to shirk a single responsibility that has been put upon us by the results of the war"; and there was great applause. Yet at Arcola, Illinois, on October 15, he won a similar rousing response with these words: "We have had great glory out of the war, and in its settlements we must be guided only by the demands of right and conscience and duty."

He tried imperialism out at Ames, Iowa, from whence had come innumerable petitions to Congress in favor of pacifist causes. He experimented with anti-imperialism in Denison, the home of the state's war-hawk governor, Leslie M. Shaw. On each occasion, a stenographer made careful notes on the intensity and duration of applause. McKinley's own ears presumably registered the more subtle sounds.

By the time he had circled to Omaha, Nebraska, and started back through Iowa, the President had found his answer. At the Trans-Mississippi Exposition in Omaha, he asked, "Shall we deny to ourselves what the rest of the world so freely and so justly accords to us?" From the audience came a loud cry of "No!" He went on amid great applause to speak of "a peace whose great gain to civilization is yet unknown and unwritten" and to declare, "The war was not more invited by us than were the questions which are laid at our door by its results. Now as then we will do our duty."

After the reception given these words, he virtually ceased to sound the cautious note. At Chariton, Iowa, on the return trip, he said, "Territory sometimes comes to us when we go to war in a holy cause, and whenever it does the banner of liberty will float over it and bring, I trust, blessings and benefits to all the people." [Great applause.] At Columbus, Ohio, he proclaimed, "We know what our country is now in its territory, but we do not know what it may be in the near future. [Applause.] But whatever it is, whatever obligation shall justly come from this strife for humanity, we must take up and perform and as free, strong, brave people, accept the trust which civilization puts upon us." [Enthusiastic cheers and applause.]

The President had heard the voice of the people.

There can be no doubt that this was what he had waited for. He may have wanted it so, or he may have spoken the truth when he later told John G. Schurman, "I didn't want the Philippine Islands . . . and . . . I left myself free not to take them; but in the end there was no alternative.". . .

Dream and Reality

LOUIS J. HALLE

THE MODERN history of American foreign policy, as distinct from its ancient history, begins in 1898. Up to 1898 the United States had cultivated and enjoyed the isolation implicit in the geographical concept of two hemispheres. In 1898 it lost or gave up that isolation by assuming commitments overseas. It entered the arena of European rivalries as a newly arrived world power. All this, as we shall see, was implicit in its acquisition of the Philippine Islands as a piece of real estate outside the New World, on the other side of interplanetary space.

This engagement in overseas imperialism was so abrupt and unpremeditated, however, and we were so little prepared for it, that our thinking could not adjust itself. We could not grasp what it meant for our isolation and, consequently, our isolationism. For almost half a century after our isolation was gone we still clung to the isolationist policy. Only a nation with such vast reserves of strength as we had could have survived this failure of understanding to keep up with change. As it was, the price we had to pay was high. We are still paying it today in many ways, including the present weakness of our diplomatic and strategic position in the Far East. But all this will come out in what follows.

One might say that the nineteenth century ends in the 1890's with a period of transition leading to the birth of the twentieth century in 1914. Up through the 1890's the *Pax Britannica* had dominated the world. Britain held the balance of power in Europe. She protected the independence of the American hemisphere. And in the competition for empire around the rim of Asia—a competition that represented an extension of the power contests in Europe— she had the chief role.

But a fundamental change took place in the 1890's with the appearance on the world scene of three new powers: Germany, Japan, and the United States. All three were suddenly realizing their potential strength; all three were being tempted by dreams of what that strength might gain for them; all three were unseasoned, like children who have grown up suddenly to possess an adult strength beyond their wisdom and experience.

Both Germany and Japan, in a sort of ecstasy of power, embarked on a course of empire that was to lead to the crashing collisions of the twentieth century. The United States, in the 1890's, briefly felt the same impulse, tentatively embarked on the same course, made commitments that would plague her, and then subsided again under the overriding sway of her liberal and isolationist traditions alike. After her one brief adventure in empire she retired. She emerged from her retirement and her strength became available to check that of Germany and Japan only when disaster was already upon the world. One might say that Germany and Japan used their newly found strength to disrupt world order, while the United States withheld its newly found strength from the maintenance of world order.

Quite aside from the overseas commitment which we Americans acquired in 1898, the ending of the *Pax Britannica* was bound, in itself, to end our putative isolation. When our surrounding oceans were no longer securely dominated by a power that was well disposed to us we would find ourselves vitally dependent on the outcome of political and military contests across those oceans. Our own security would require us to pursue an active diplomacy designed to prevent any hostile or potentially hostile power on the other side from dominating them.

For the moment, however, I am not concerned with this larger picture. I am concerned with what appears to have been a deliberately assumed commitment on the far side of the Pacific, a commitment which could not have been brought into any logical or practical correspondence with the continuation of an isolationism based on independence of Old World politics. This inconsistency would have been obvious if we had acquired Ireland as a colonial possession which we had to defend. Immediately we would have become, unmistakably, a power in the Old World, deep in its politics. In our acquisition of the Philippines this may have been less obvious, but it was no less true. The Philippines were at the heart of a distant area in which the rival European powers and Japan, greedy for empire, deployed substantially more strength than we did. If we were to defend the Philippines, we would have to muster some military strength of our own in the area and we would have to enter upon the diplomatic game of playing the other powers off against one another. Because we did not see this, the historical record reveals a direct line of causation from our acquisition of the Philippine commitment in 1898 to the Japanese attack on Pearl Harbor in 1941, an attack that coincided with the temporary Japanese capture of the Philippines. Perhaps that same line of causation can be traced even to the Korean War and our conflict with Communist China.

Virtually everyone would agree, today, that it was a mistake to acquire the Philippines and, at the same time, seek to continue our isolationist policy. Most students of the subject, I think, would also agree that, whatever our policy, it was still a mistake to acquire the Philippines. Their possession served no strategic interest but was, rather, a strategic liability, especially as, with the passage of time, it came to represent a challenge to Japan. And what we got from the Philippines in markets and trade was far less than what it cost us to administer and defend them. The Philippines would have been useful to us only if, as a handful of American imperialists in 1898 wanted us to do, we had set out to dominate the world. In fact, however, they were pure burden from start to finish, and we had to recognize them as such. But, once the fateful mistake of acquiring them was made, we were stuck with them, and it is clear that even today, when they have at last become independent, their defense is still a charge upon us. In meeting that charge we have added the defense of Japan, Korea, and Formosa to the burden we already bore.

I am interested in the particular question of how we came, in 1898, to make this strategic misstep. And I mean to explore the question, in this and the following two chapters, not for its own sake but because it seems to me to epitomize the limitations under which statesmen everywhere labor and the compulsion of circumstance that tends to shape the policy of every nation. In other words, such an examination should suggest how history actually is made, and that is its real value.

What I have to say here is the product of an extended investigation of the source materials and the historical interpretations that bear on the question. I started this investigation with the common view that a quite avoidable blunder had been made by the administration of President McKinley in acquiring the Philippines. I wanted to find out at what particular point in the sequence of events the mistake had been made, and by whom, and on the basis of what thinking. I supposed that there was one day and one hour and one place where one man or a group of men had decided that we should take the Philippines, when he or they were quite free to decide that we should not take them. By the time I finished my investigation, however, I had concluded instead that, given the total situation at the time, it would have been virtually impossible for the McKinley administration to have avoided the acquisition of the Philippines. I never did find the single point in the drift of events where its tendency could have been stopped or turned back, where the administration, consequently, really had a choice in the matter—even when it thought that it did have such a choice and was exercising it. If we understand this, in the particular case under scrutiny, we shall understand much better how foreign policy in general develops and is determined—today no less than in the past.

Having presented my conclusion in advance, let me add that it does not necessarily imply historical predestination. I assume, still, that history is made by men who have a certain freedom of choice. But I am impressed by the heavy compulsions that drive them to make one choice rather than another, so that the freedom they enjoy is to oppose forces that are generally too great for them.

Most of us Americans remember, from our history lessons, the Spanish-American War of 1898. This was the first display of that strength which made us a world power. On this occasion we used that strength, as became our liberal tradition, for the liberation of the long-suffering Cubans from the tyranny of Spain. This we all remember. What few of us remember is the Philippine War, which began two days before the formal conclusion of the Spanish-American War, which lasted some four years, and which was substantially more costly in blood and treasure alike. In this second and much heavier war we Americans, to our horror, found ourselves engaged in desperate combat with the distant Filipinos who were resisting our attempt to subjugate them. We have good reason for not wanting to remember this war, in which we became engaged without any intention and essentially against our own will. How was it, then, that we found ourselves fighting to conquer a land off the shores of Asia which, as was widely apparent, we would have done well to refuse as a gift?

When we went to war with Spain on April 25, 1898, virtually no one in the United States had any notion of acquiring an Asiatic empire. It was an exceptional American who knew where the Philippine Islands were, or, perhaps, had even heard of them. Those whom we identify today with their acquisition appear to have had no thought, as yet, of acquiring them. Apparently it was not in the mind of Theodore Roosevelt, then Assistant Secretary of the Navy, when he made the arrangements for Commodore Dewey's attack on the Spanish squadron at Manila; it had not occurred to the Commodore; and Captain Mahan, the philosopher of expansionism, experienced misgivings when it first appeared that we might be committed to their acquisition.

Not only did we have no thought of acquiring the Philippines before we entered upon the course of action by which they became ours, their acquisition, if it had been proposed, would have been regarded as repugnant to our national policy. We believed that a nation like ours, dedicated to representative government with the consent of the governed, could not include within its jurisdiction some seven million distant subjects, unqualified for citizenship, over which it exercised the kind of colonial rule against which it had declared its own independence. Many Americans questioned whether our Constitution, with its guarantees of human rights, would allow it. Even if these bars had not existed, our people had shown before, as they have shown since, their aversion for the kind of empire which the European great powers had been establishing among the "lesser breeds." Yet the fact remains that, early in 1899, we found ourselves already committed to the prosecution of a long and painful war for the subjugation of the Philippines. Our virtually unquestioned policy was one thing; our action was the opposite. How could this be?

The Spanish-American War was not made by statesmen acting with deliberation, weighing their responsibilities, and taking the requirements of national policy as their guide. In 1898 our nation, for the moment, lost its sobriety and abandoned itself to glory. This was a people's war into which our government was swept by public opinion.

What does it mean to say this? Who were the people? What was public opinion?

Public opinion, as far as governments are concerned, is not the spontaneous expression of the population as a statistical total. It is, rather, the opinion expressed by those who can influence significant parts of that population to a degree which might be politically decisive. In 1898 this meant, most notably, newspaper publishers. The yellow press, competing in sensationalism, deliberately embarked on a campaign against Spanish treatment of the Cubans as a means of increasing its circulation. It elaborated atrocity stories to arouse alike the animal passion and the self-righteousness of its readers. For this and other reasons public pressures were developed, emotional pressures of a nature hard for any government to deal with; since to those who do not share their sobriety the reasons of the sober sound like the counsels of cowardice.

Historians generally recognize today that we had no legitimate *casus belli* against Spain. Her inherited position in Cuba and Puerto Rico, a last remnant of her empire in the New World, had become obsolete and increasingly untenable by the end of the nineteenth century. It would have to be adjusted. But the Spanish government recognized this, and there was no reason to doubt that, given time, patience, and the absence of public excitement in either country, the adjustment could be accomplished without war. It had, in fact, almost been accomplished before the war broke out. The Spanish government, moving as fast as an impassioned public opinion in its own country allowed, was co-operating earnestly with our government to achieve a diplomatic solution. Twenty days before we actually went to war our essential demands had already been met.

By this time, however, the yellow press had another case for incitement to war, in the explosion which had sunk our battleship, *The Maine*, in Havana harbor. This disaster was laid at the door of Spain, even though it had almost surely not been caused by Spain. The press howled for war to avenge the national honor.

The administration of President McKinley bowed, at last, to a basic rule of politics: where you cannot lead you had better follow. It had tried, like its predecessor, to calm public opinion and to achieve a diplomatic settlement with Spain before too late. Now it saw an excited Congress, moved by the mass emotion, preparing to act on its own to have a war. It fell into step and, two days after the Spanish capitulation to our demands, the President sent his war message to Congress.

Historians and statesmen since Thucydides have recognized, as a prime danger inherent in war, that states which embark on it tend to lose control of their own destiny. A typical manifestation of this danger is the repeated inability of states to keep to the limited objectives for which they have gone to war, once victory comes within their reach. Our war with Spain had the sole objective of liberating Cuba. This objective was made explicit in a joint Congressional resolution which disclaimed territorial greed by forswearing any disposition to acquire Cuba for ourselves.

As we now know, Spain did not have the military means to defend Cuba. We might therefore have confined our military effort to the vicinity of Cuba, making the military objective the same as the political objective, that of pulling Cuba out of the Spanish grasp. There was really no more necessity of attacking Spain's islands in the Pacific than of attacking her islands in the Mediterranean. Military orthodoxy since Clausewitz, however, has held that the prime military objective in warfare (or in warfare at its best) is not the capture of territory, but the destruction of the enemy's power and will to fight. Since our military had been brought up on this doctrine it did not occur to them to limit or localize the military effort. It would surely have been hard to show them any reason for doing so.

For many decades we had maintained a small naval squadron in the western Pacific, apparently to support our commerce and "show the flag." Commodore Dewey's predecessor in command of that squadron, seeing the likelihood of war with Spain and knowing that a Spanish naval squadron was roosting in the Philippines, made plans for an attack on that squadron, plans which Commodore Dewey inherited from him. Such action by a naval officer in such a position is less noteworthy, perhaps, than would have been its omission.

In a real sense, no positive decision ever was taken to adopt a policy calling for an attack on the Philippines. The President merely found that this was the naval policy that the navy had in mind, and he seems to have assumed that it must be right. "While we remained at war with Spain," Dewey later wrote, "our purpose must be to strike at the power of Spain wherever possible." This implication of unlimited war, which might have given a Bismarck pause, was unquestioned among us at the time. The *political* objective of the war was to liberate Cuba; but the *military* objective must be to hurt Spain wherever we could until she cried quits. The western Pacific was one of the principal places where we could hurt her. Given these premises, the naval officers were right in assuming that we would strike at the Philippines in case of war. A special policy decision would have been needed rather to exempt them from the area of our military operations than to include them.

The outbreak of war did not, in itself, occasion the dispatch of any orders whatever to Commodore Dewey, who lay in Britain's colony of Hong Kong with our Far Eastern squadron. Action to instruct him on what he should do was taken only in response to an urgent cable from him, reporting that the British declaration of neutrality forced him to leave Hong Kong immediately and requesting instructions. At a meeting in the White House an order to Dewey was drafted and the President approved it. It read: "War has commenced. . . . Proceed at once to Philippine Islands. Commerce operations particularly against the Spanish fleet. You must capture vessels or destroy. Use utmost endeavor." No one thought of this order in terms of the significance that it might have for the general position of the United States in the Far East. It represented merely the implementation of a war strategy that had never been questioned.

Dewey carried out his mission with punctilio and daring. He proceeded to the Bay of Manila, where the Spanish squadron lay, and destroyed it at its anchorage without the loss of a single American life.

The American people had been showing increasing frustration at the lack of any heroic military action coincident with the outbreak of war, and the government in Washington had been coming under mounting criticism for timidity. Dewey's departure from Hong Kong and his destination were front-page news on April 25. For five tense days nothing more was heard. Then, on May 2 the news of the victory came. The relief and rejoicing were universal, but no place more so, I suspect, than in the corridors of Washington where the public pressure for action had been so keenly felt. A *New York Times* dispatch reporting this added: "The victory has scarcely been fully reported before the fact flashes upon the Administration, as it has upon the European diplomatic circles, that the United States Government has suddenly acquired a status in the East that was not at all looked for, and that may greatly change the discussion of Eastern problems." This is not the last time, in the course of these chapters, that we shall have occasion to note how implications of an event that become obvious immediately after it takes place remain unforeseen throughout the period in which it is anticipated only.

Until this moment, no one in Washington had concerned himself with the implications and consequences of Dewey's mission. No one had asked: What next? Consequently, when the Spanish squadron had been destroyed Dewey found himself without those landing forces which he would need to carry out the "offensive operations in Philippines" that he had been instructed to undertake after dealing with the squadron. This omission also became obvious to Washington in the moment of victory.

Although Dewey himself was not heard from until May 7, on May 3 the Commanding General of the Army recommended to the Secretary of War that General Thomas M. Anderson be sent "to occupy the Philippine Islands," in command of certain specified troops; and on May 4 the President ordered that these troops be assembled at San Francisco. This represented the decision, made without forethought, to take the Philippines, whether temporarily or permanently.

Still, no one was clear on the mission of these landing forces. The general chosen to command them, having had an interview with the President on May 12, wrote him on the 15th: "I do not yet know whether it is your desire to subdue and hold all of the Spanish territory in the islands, or merely to seize and hold the capital." The President didn't know either. Finally, however, on May 19 he defined the mission of the expeditionary force in a letter to the Secretary of War. He wrote that: "The destruction of the Spanish fleet at Manila, followed by the taking of the naval station at Cavite, the paroling of the garrisons, and acquisition of the control of the bay, have rendered it necessary, in the further prosecution of the measures adopted by this Government for the purpose of bringing about an honorable and durable peace with Spain, to send an army of occupation to the Philippines for the two-fold purpose of completing the reduction of the Spanish power in that quarter and of giving order and security to the islands while in the possession of the United States. . . .

"The first effect of the military occupation of the enemy's territory is the severance of the former political relations of the inhabitants and the establishment of a new political power. . . ."

Without looking forward as far as the postwar future, but merely trying to stay abreast of the present, the government had concluded that events "rendered it necessary" to take possession of the Philippine Islands.

At this time the American people had shown themselves thoroughly opposed to the acquisition of overseas territory even as close in as the Hawaiian Islands. Consequently, no one, at first, contemplated the possibility that the Philippines might be kept in our possession. To some it seemed that we should hold them as collateral for a Spanish indemnity at the war's end, returning them to Spain upon its payment. To others it seemed logical that we should grant them their independence, as we intended to do with Cuba.

The mental uncertainty and agony which the *New York Times* displayed on its editorial page is representative. On May 3 it found it unthinkable that we should ever return the islands to Spain. Exploring alternatives, it added that "nobody pretends that the natives of the Philippines are fit for self-government, as we believe the Cubans to be. On the other hand, all the arguments against the annexation of Hawaii are available, with even greater force, against our retention of the Philippines for ourselves." It concluded that we had already incurred a responsibility in seizing them which could be discharged only by having Great Britain take them off our hands.

The following day, in one and the same editorial, the *Times* was saying that "we could not in any event take the islands for ourselves," and also that if Britain "declines to take them on reasonable terms we must even retain them for ourselves," since we could neither return them to Spain nor hand them over to their primitive inhabitants. It was thus foreseeing the possibility of a dilemma in which every possible alternative was impossible to contemplate—such a dilemma as is not unique in the conduct of foreign affairs.

Finally, by May 9, the *Times* had at last brought itself to contemplate what could not be contemplated at first. "It is becoming plainer every day," it said, "that paramount necessity will compel us to assume for a time of which we cannot now see the end the duty of governing and controlling the Philippine Islands."

The President, too, was still behind the march of events, trying to catch up with them. Being at a loss to know what we should do with the Philippines, now that they were at our disposal, he postponed decision. One of the conditions that he made for a truce with beaten Spain, on July 30, was that we should continue to occupy "the city, bay and harbor of Manila pending the conclusion of a treaty of peace which shall determine the control, disposition, and the government of the Philippines."

At last, on September 16, in his instructions to the American commissioners appointed to negotiate the peace with Spain, the President wrote: "Without any original thought of complete or even partial acquisition, the presence and success of our arms at Manila imposes upon us obligations which we cannot disregard. The march of events rules and overrules human action. . . . we cannot be unmindful that without any desire or design on our part the war has brought us new duties and responsibilities which we must meet and discharge as becomes a great nation on whose growth and career from the beginning the Ruler of Nations has plainly written the high command and pledge of civilization."

We may not doubt that President McKinley, who sought divine guidance for his decision on the Philippines, wrote this with sincerity. But it confronts us with a paradox that goes to the root of this inquiry. It virtually states, in its first two sentences, that "the presence and success of our arms at Manila" does not belong in the category of "human action" but in some other category that "overrules human action." This other category is identified with "the march of events." Here the government of the United States discounts its own authority over the march of events, conceding the sway of destiny.

President McKinley, unhappily deciding at last that we had no choice but to make the Philippines ours, concluded that destiny must have predetermined an outcome so far from our intentions. This immediately became the view of all who faced the unexpected consequence of Dewey's famous victory at Manila Bay. Captain Alfred Thayer Mahan, who had participated notably in the development of the strategy which led to Dewey's victory, wrote: ". . . the preparation made for us, rather than by us, in the unwilling acquisition of the Philippines, is so obvious as to embolden even the least presumptuous to see in it the hand of Providence."

Surely, however, it was by actions of our own free choice that we at last found ourselves holding the Philippines. Surely we had been free to shape our policy so that we would not acquire them. Surely it was by our own decision that the Philippines came into our hands.

In point of fact, there never was a decision to attach the Philippines to us until it was found that they virtually were attached already. By the time the issue was full-blown, the question which presented itself for decision was not whether we should *take* them. It was whether we should *keep* them. And by this time there was no acceptable alternative to keeping them.

The Open Door:

BRITISH SUGGESTION
or
DOMESTIC DEMAND?

THE POLICY which came to be known as the "Open Door" was expressed in the form of two notes, one on September 6, 1899, and the other on July 3, 1900, which Secretary of State John Hay dispatched to all the great powers interested in China. In the notes Hay urged the powers to support equality of commercial opportunity in China for all nations and to help maintain the territorial integrity and administrative entity of the Chinese empire. What prompted the enunciation of this policy at that time? The immediate cause for the first note was the seizing, in 1898 and 1899, of parts of China by European powers for European exploitation—Germany in Shantung, Russia in Manchuria, and France in Hainan. The second note was caused by the events surrounding the Boxer Rebellion. A Chinese secret society known as the Boxers rose in 1900 to eliminate all foreign influences from China. During the course of the uprising they attacked Peking and threatened the lives of foreign diplomats and missionaries living there. To relieve the city the great powers prepared an international expeditionary force which Hay feared might result in the permanent occupation of Chinese territory. But why should these two situations, so distant from the United States, have prompted American intercession? Two different interpretations have been suggested.

The first, proposed by Alfred Whitney Griswold who died in 1962 after having served Yale University both as president and professor of history, is based on the proposition that the Open Door was "to a large extent influenced by forces extraneous to both the United States and the Far East." It was his view that the policy was suggested and instigated by Great Britain. At the end of the century the international balance of power was being upset by Britain's three rivals, Germany, France, and Russia. Those three nations were threatening British power in every part of the world. In China, where Britain had been virtually supreme both commercially and politically since the 1840's, the danger was greatest. Each exclusive concession held by a European power diminished England's favorable position. The best solution for Britain was to gain the help of the United States to aid in keeping the door open in China. Prominent Britons influenced John Hay, who was an ardent Anglophile, and other officials in the administration to enunciate the policy which England felt would save its stake.

Charles S. Campbell, Jr., a professor of history at Claremont Graduate School and an authority on Anglo-American relations of the nineteenth and twentieth centuries, presents another view. He maintains that the Open Door policy resulted from the insistent pressure of the American business community on the Department of State to protect the American market in China. When the great powers began to carve out exclusive areas in China, American businessmen—coton exporters, investment bankers, railroad builders, industrialists—feared the possible loss of outlets for their goods and capital. Immediately, they organized into associations and launched a campaign to influence the government (through letters, telegrams, and personal visits to policy makers) and the public (by means of articles and reports published in a magazine founded exclusively for that purpose). For them an open door in China was essential, and the government responded to their pressures by dispatching the two notes.

Writing the Open Door Notes

A. WHITNEY GRISWOLD

THE PHILIPPINES had been called the key to the markets of Asia. Now
the key had to be fitted to the lock, and turned. Would the United States
emulate Great Britain and turn Manila into a *bona fide* Hongkong, from
which by displays of naval power to challenge its competitors in China? Or
would the precarious situation of the new colony dictate a more cautious
decision? First answers to these questions came in the two great declarations
of policy embodied in the open door notes of September 6, 1899, and the
Hay circular of July 3, 1900.

Like the annexation of the Philippines, the famous notes were to a large
extent influenced by forces extraneous to both the United States and the Far
East. Chief among these were Great Britain's attempts to restore the balance
of world power recently upset by her three great rivals. In Europe, Germany
was building alliances and a fleet with which to assert her own continental
supremacy and break down the British colonial monopoly. In Africa, German
colonies were being founded, and diplomatic fences erected against British
conquest of the Boers. The Anglo-French struggle for the Nile Valley nearly
resulted in the outbreak of war at Fashoda in 1898. All Asia was feeling the
impact of Russian imperialism which threatened to overrun British spheres
of influence in China and perhaps even the Indian frontier itself. In America
the Venezuela boundary crisis of 1895–1896 had shown that the determination of the United States to resist any European intrusions into the affairs
of the Western Hemisphere was stronger than ever. For a moment England
stood alone, friendless, amid the ruins of her once "splendid" isolation. Then,
in a characteristically pragmatic fashion, her diplomats began a search for
allies on three continents, and a systematic effort to re-establish the balance
of power wherever British interests demanded it. One by one overtures for
alliances or understandings were made to Russia, the United States, Japan,
Germany and France, ultimately resulting in the Anglo-Japanese Alliance of
1902 and the *Entente Cordiale* with France in 1904. . . . Meanwhile, conditions in the Far East called for immediate attention. . . .

Since 1840 England had played the leading part in the economic exploitation of China. Now her trade with China amounted to 65 per cent of China's
total foreign trade, 85 per cent of which was carried in British vessels. To
protect her lucrative Chinese markets from the closing pincers of France in
the south and Russia in the north (allies since 1894), England took a new

From *The Far Eastern Policy of the United States*, by A. Whitney Griswold, copyright,
1938, by Harcourt, Brace & World, Inc.; and reprinted with their permission. Pp. 36–37,
39–65, 67–72.

interest in the territorial integrity of China. She opposed any further economic or territorial concessions to France in the south, and as against Russia, actively supported Chinese suzerainty over Korea. The two policies proved complete failures. China was powerless to halt the extension of the French sphere of influence; while Chinese claims to sovereignty over Korea merely ran afoul of Japanese ambitions, precipitating the Sino-Japanese War (1894–1895). As part of her winnings Japan secured Formosa and the Liaotung Peninsula, a long-coveted foothold on the continent. But Russia, assisted by her ally, France, and her erstwhile partner, Germany, intervened to compel the retrocession of the Liaotung Peninsula to China. The net result of the war, therefore, was to remove the last barrier to Russia's penetration from the north, leaving her free to overrun Korea, as she speedily attempted to do. England was thus surrounded in the Far East, as elsewhere, by political rivals and economic competitors.

British diplomacy thereupon underwent a speedy reorientation. With Japan, whether by chance or by design, the way had already been paved for an understanding. Since 1890 Britain had profited as much by the ineptitude of Secretary Blaine's diplomacy as by her own preponderant share of Japanese trade to build up a growing influence over that country. By shrewdly abstaining from the triple intervention she had earned rich dividends of Japanese gratitude.

A period of watchful waiting followed during 1896 and 1897. The cabinet was agreed that British interests in China must be defended, but seemed to have lost faith in attempting single-handed to uphold the integrity of China as a means to that end. It was determined, as Curzon put it, "to pounce the moment anyone else pounces." When, at length, news arrived that a Russian squadron had occupied Port Arthur, Lord Salisbury opined to Chamberlain "that 'the public' will require some territorial or cartographic consolation in China. It will not be useful and will be expensive; but as a matter of pure sentiment, we shall have to do it." No further evidence is needed to show that England perfectly realized the true relation of China to Europe as that of a pawn to the kings, castles and bishops nearer home. Her only motives were to stay the advance of Russia and protect her own economic stake in the Far East by whatever means seemed most practicable, and in company with whatever nation might be induced to come to her assistance.

As the situation now reduced itself, "cartographic consolation"—which meant joining in the scramble for concessions—could not accomplish England's purpose. Further territorial concessions would be costly to defend and of dubious value in checking economic competition. Of the vast British sphere of interest in the Yangtse Valley, approximately one-third of China proper, neither Britain herself nor any other power could hope to make an exclusive territorial concession. To maintain her advantageous position there and to guard against exclusion from other parts of China scarcely less important to her commerce, Great Britain was casting about for a new and more efficacious method of upholding China's territorial integrity. The alternatives that presented themselves were an alliance or, in keeping with balance of power tactics, an international stalemate that would have the same result. Still another faint possibility was that her competitors might be persuaded to open their spheres and leaseholds to British commerce on the most-favored-nation, or open door principle. But even this meager benefit could not be secured without the help of some other nation to weight the scales in England's favor. The problem, which preoccupied the British cabinet during the winter and spring of 1898, was solved at last by cautious moves toward each of the suggested objectives. While the cabinet secretly discussed taking part in the dismemberment of China, its members publicly frowned on that policy and proclaimed their faith in the open door, their determination to defend British interests in China, and, on January 17, extended the first feeler for an alliance —with Russia. When this failed to produce results, they turned to the United States.

As we have seen, a dramatic improvement in Anglo-American relations during the War with Spain resulted. It began early in the year. American traditions against foreign alliances were well known to Downing Street, but the United States seemed to be undergoing a change of heart. Mahan was widely read in England. The enthusiasm of Roosevelt, Lodge, Hay, Whitelaw Reid and Henry White for closer Anglo-American co-operation was remarkable. Then there was Mr. Olney's communication on the subject of the Armenian atrocities, which Chamberlain could scarcely have forgotten. It was not surprising, therefore, that while England dickered for understandings with Russia, and later with Japan and Germany, all kinds of overtures, official and unofficial, were made to the United States for any arrangement that would bring the United States to England's aid in the region of the Far East.

In the process, Chamberlain played a persuasive role. Of all the cabinet he appears to have been the most sanguine of obtaining an alliance with the United States. In any case, he was directly responsible for the first official step toward it. On February 3, 1898, he addressed the following memorandum to the Acting Foreign Secretary:

Secret

Highbury,
Birmingham.
Feb. 3. 98.

My dear Balfour,

I wish that you read all the papers just now. If you did, you would, I think, agree with me that grave trouble is impending upon the Govt. if we do not adopt a more decided attitude in regard to China.

What are the facts? We have a permanent interest in the trade, and have gained much credit both at home and in America by insisting that while we do not intend to oppose the occupation by Germany and Russia, we are determined that their ports shall be Treaty Ports, or subject to regulations, and that our influence shall be maintained.

The Germans appear to have accepted our terms, although we have not got, as we ought to get, a definite assurance that Kiao Chau will be a Treaty Port. But the Russians have done us at every point.

They have induced us to let our ships leave Port Arthur, while they have reciprocated our friendly attitude by opposing our loan proposals. They have forced us to withdraw our proposals to make Talien Wan a Free Port.

They are placing Russian officers in control of railways, &c., to the exclusion of English.

They are ousting us from influence in Corea.

They pretend that their occupation is temporary and not in restraint of trade. We all believe that this is false, and that they will transform the occupation into a permanent one, and will exclude us altogether from the Liao Tung peninsula.

We pretend to rely on our treaty rights; but if they declare an annexation these rights disappear, and in any case they will know how to make the position intolerable for our merchants. All this is known to our friends and to our enemies. If matters remain as they are, our prestige will be gone and our trade will follow. I would not give a year's life to the Government under such conditions.

The question is, what can we do, and it is most difficult of course for any of us outsiders to frame a policy. If only Lord Salisbury sees the peril and is prepared to meet it I would rather leave to him the methods than rush in with what may be impossible suggestions. But, as the matter now appears to me, I should propose:

1. To approach the United States officially, and to ask an immediate reply from them to the question—Will you stand in with us in our Chinese policy?

2. To approach Germany at the same time with the same definite questions.

3. Our Chinese policy to be a declaration that any port occupied by a foreign nation shall be, *ipso facto*, a Treaty Port open to all on precisely similar conditions.

That this applies to Talien Wan, Port Arthur and Kiao Chau, and to any other further acquisition of land or ports by any European nation, or by the Japanese.

Further that they should join with us in putting pressure on the Chinese—loan or no loan—to open Nanking and other Ports suggested by us and to give freedom of internal navigation.

That if Russia refuses these terms, we should summon her fleet to leave Port Arthur and make her go if necessary.

I dare say this line is much too strong for the Cabinet, but if we do not do something and that quickly we shall have a bad quarter of an hour when Parliament meets.

yours very truly,

J. CHAMBERLAIN.

This document is remarkable, not only because it shows Anglo-Russian antagonism to have been the very axis of Far Eastern politics. It also reveals that eighteen months before the despatch of the Hay notes, and well over a year before the idea of collective action to guarantee the open door appears to have entered the head of an American diplomat, it had been introduced into practical diplomacy by the Colonial Secretary of Great Britain.

The approach to the United States followed soon afterwards. On March 8 Pauncefote addressed a "very confidential" inquiry to Secretary of State Sherman. "There are two methods," Sir Julian wrote, "by which foreign Powers may restrict the opening of China to the commerce of all nations, either by procuring the lease of portions of the Chinese coast under conditions which would ensure preferential treatment to the Power acquiring such lease, or by obtaining the actual cession of the Chinese littoral. Her Majesty's Government are anxious to know whether they could count on the co-operation of the United States in opposing such action by foreign Powers and whether the United States would be prepared to join with Great Britain in opposing such measures should the contingency arise."

Sherman and McKinley, preoccupied with the imminent hostilities with Spain, rejected the proposal with the blunt statement that, although they were "not . . . unmindful of the situation in China and its possible effect upon American trade interests" all their "advices up to the present time indicate no foreign occupation which interferes with that trade or aims at exclusive commercial privileges." They could see no reason, therefore, of departing from "our traditional policy of [sic] respecting foreign alliances and so far as practicable avoiding interference or connection with European complications." But in this first British overture (that may very well have been encouraged by Ambassador Hay) was the kernel of a doctrine to which the Department of State was soon to be converted. Vague as was Sir Julian's note, its implications were plain enough. How were foreign powers to be prevented from securing cessions or leaseholds save by defending, in some way, the feeble object of their depredations? For such a venture, in March, 1898, the United States was not prepared. The Battle of Manila had yet to be fought, the national conversion to imperialism yet to be accomplished.

Rebuffed by Russia and the United States, England next approached Japan, then Germany, with like results. Meantime Weihaiwei was taken as "consolation" for Port Arthur. As matters stood when the United States went to war with Spain, British policy had failed of its first and second objectives in the Far East, and had been forced to content itself with a poor third. Neither a collective guarantee of the territorial integrity of China nor an alliance had been secured. The lease of Weihaiwei was more of a stimulus than a deterrent to the partitioning of China. That it would have the desired effect of halting Russia few Englishmen appeared to have believed. Its value to England was to be measured in the abstract terms of *amour propre*.

Accordingly, British attention veered back to the United States. Efforts were renewed to promote Anglo-American friendship and, in spite of Pauncefote's early failure, to devise some means whereby the United States might be brought into the Far Eastern balance. Systematic encouragement was given to American retention of the Philippines. The press in England and in the Dominions outspokenly expressed its sympathy for the United States, and its approval of closer Anglo-American co-operation. Chamberlain virtually took the stump for an Anglo-American alliance. Anglo-American leagues and committees were organized in London and New York to promote the idea which, impractical though it may have been, symbolized the unprecedented friendliness of Anglo-American relations. Concurrently the open door policy was proclaimed so loudly and so consistently by cabinet officers, members of Parliament and journalists as to suggest the desire to impress it on other countries than England. During the winter of 1898–1899, Lord Charles Beresford made his celebrated barnstorming tour of China and Japan, returning to England *via* the United States. It was one long after-dinner speech in favor of the open door. He consulted Hay before leaving London, wrote him letters reporting the enthusiasm of Americans in the Orient for closer co-operation with England, and called on him at the State Department on the way home. As Hay was advised in advance, Beresford had "based all his hopes of keeping the open door by enlisting the sympathies of America during his trip across the Continent." Soon after his return, Beresford published *The Break-up of China*, written as much for Americans as for Englishmen, and further exploiting the theme he had so pointedly advertised in his travels.

Before Beresford reached America, England had made two more efforts to secure the co-operation of the United States in the Far East. In the fall of 1898 the French decided to extend their concession at Shanghai. The plan was immediately opposed by the British, whose minister approached Mr. Conger, the American Minister at Peking, on December 22 with the idea of entering a joint protest against it. Conger wired Hay for instructions, receiving the ambiguous reply: "Protest French extension if against American interest." Mr. Conger protested, though independently rather than in company with the British. He was persuaded to do so, he explained, by the "protests of the American landowners, merchants, and missionaries at Shanghai against having their property included in the extension" and not by the importunities of the British minister. He himself could "see no good reason for this objection to the extension of the French settlement." He thought the British opposition was "mainly political, that it came principally from London" and that it was "directed against any increase of French power or holdings in the Yangtse Valley."

In Washington, meanwhile, acting under instructions from London, Pauncefote again attempted to secure from the President a formal undertaking to co-operate with England in the Far East. "I am aware," he wrote (January 8, 1899), "that it would be a departure from the usual practice of your government . . . who, I believe, adopt the form of identic representations in preference to conjoint action, but the departure in the present instance might be justified by the special community of interest arising out of the new condition of affairs in China." Again the British Ambassador was turned down.

By the summer of 1899 the most England had to show for her troubles was Weihaiwei, an extension of her holdings at Hongkong, and a railway agreement with Russia. By the terms of the latter (concluded April 28) the great wall of China was mutually recognized as the southern boundary of the Russian sphere of railway construction and the northern boundary of the English. The agreement did not mention the open door for commerce. The dismemberment of China now seemed more likely than ever as, indeed, the decision to take Weihaiwei and the agreement with Russia implied. The Boer War was only a few months off. Unremitting pressure on America had elicited nothing more definite than expressions of esteem and a few independent and rather non-committal statements in favor of the open door. As Pauncefote made clear, his country desired something more than sympathy and identic action. It wanted a formal understanding—a deposit of American political support in Eastern Asia on which England could draw, whenever necessary, to protect her interests there.

The influence on the United States of nations other than Great Britain was less direct. For the most part, it was brought to bear through British diplomacy. Russia and Germany played their parts in calling forth the open door notes as catalytic agents whose hostile *Weltpolitik* and whose overt acts in the Far East spurred Britain to seek American aid. To a lesser degree, so did France. Japan's influence must be counted as relatively negligible, while China's, though considerable, was of a negative character. To perceive the working of these various international forces it is necessary to turn back for a moment and consider the parallel development of an American Far Eastern policy which ultimately met the British halfway.

The United States was far from being an unwilling recipient of British attention. If Chamberlain made speeches in favor of an Anglo-American alliance, so did John Hay. An ardent Anglophile, he did all in his power as Ambassador to abet the British quest for American assistance. "Chamberlain's startling speech," he wrote Lodge, "was partly due to a conversation I had with him, in which I hoped he would not let the opposition have a monopoly of expressions of good-will to America." In a personal letter to President McKinley in June he re-opened the subject of Pauncefote's unsuccessful proposal of the previous March. When Hay became Secretary of State he had lost none of his sympathy for his many friends and his *beau ideal* in England. It was a mood shared by many of Hay's American acquaintances as well. "If I had my way," Lodge had written him early in 1898, "I should be glad to have the United States say to England that we would stand by her in her declaration that the ports of China must be opened to all nations equally or to none, and if England takes that attitude firmly I am in hopes this may come about, although our foreign policy is always more haphazard than I like to see it." The American press reciprocated the sentiments emanating from British and Dominion pens. Small wonder Downing Street was encouraged to keep trying for an Anglo-American accord, no matter how many failures beset its efforts.

What gave the British policy still greater pertinency was the growing American apprehension of England's enemies in Eastern Asia. Here were four great European nations at daggers drawn over the moribund Chinese Empire. The French, constantly expanding northward from Indo-China into the southern Chinese provinces of Yunnan, Kwangsi and Kwangtung, extorted railway and mining concessions from Peking at the point of the sword. The British were similarly exploiting the enormous Yangtse Valley, as the Germans were Shantung and the Russians Manchuria and Korea. The tendency of the businessmen and diplomats of each nation was, quite naturally, to seek exclusive commercial and financial privileges within their respective spheres. This was as true of the British as it was of all the others, especially in the field of capital investment. Lord Salisbury himself defined a sphere of influence as "a sort of an 'ear mark' upon territory which in case of a break up England did not wish any other power to have." There could be little doubt that the collapse of China would mean the pre-emption of most of its vast territories by England, France, Germany and Russia.

Since the two nations first came on the scene, commercial rivalry between England and the United States had been sharp, and often acrimonious. Now England was as determined to preserve the Yangtse Valley for her own bankers and railroad builders as Russia was Manchuria. It is difficult to discern in England's Far Eastern policy any motive essentially different from those of her rivals. "In spite of the immense amount of sentimentality that England and the U.S. have been engaged recently in expressing," Mr. Denby wrote from Peking (April 2, 1897), "the stern fact remains that in the Far East, and I believe elsewhere, England looks on all questions in the light of her own interest. Here in China her people are our rivals in every branch of trade and commerce and industry. Our worst antagonists in the building of railroads or furnishing supplies therefore are the English. I venture to state that there is not an English railroad man in China who does not attack, denounce and belittle American locomotives and the American railroad system." The American Minister's appraisal of the situation was entirely accurate. Nevertheless, compared to her rivals, England was a sated nation, more anxious to keep what she had in China than to acquire more. Her unique position as money-lender and exporter to the world enabled her to profit more by the application of the free-trade—or open door—principle to China than by preferential tariffs and trade wars. For these reasons, rather than because of any supposed tendency to welcome American commerce and capital to her concessions and sphere of influence, her policy seemed more congenial to the United States than did the policies of Germany, France and Russia. Her sedulous courting of American favor during the War with Spain strengthened the belief that British and American interests in the Far East were identical, Germany and Russia their common enemies.

The French sphere was so far south that it escaped the direct line of American competition. Insofar as France affected American policy at all it was *via* her alliance with Russia and opposition to England, as in the case of the Shanghai extension. Germany's open hostility to the United States in South and Central America, her part in the Samoan controversy and the alleged activities of Diederichs in Manila Bay had, as we have seen, thoroughly aroused American suspicions of the Kaiser's *Realpolitik*. These were only intensified by the seizure of Kiaochow. British insinuations to the too susceptible Hay and Henry White must be held partially to account for the poor state of German-American relations; but a material foundation made the propaganda of Chamberlain and Salisbury all the more effective. To the United States Germany was a suspicious character.

The case of Russia is less clear. Russo-American relations had been extremely cordial since the days of the American Civil War. In 1870 the Russian Empress had actually led one of her ministers to believe that a Russo-American Alliance against England was in the making. Even after the Sino-Japanese War, and the launching of the Czar's ambitious program of absorbing Manchuria and Korea, the two nations remained on excellent terms. In the same despatch that impunged British intentions toward American commerce in the Far East, Denby had concluded that "in the interests of our manufacturers, our friendly relations with Russia should be enhanced." The Russians, on their part, made heroic efforts to cultivate American good will and to prevent England from drawing the United States into her anti-Russian orbit. They held out prospects of large purchases of American raw materials and industrial products essential to the railway building and general economic development of Manchuria.

The American ambassadors to Russia, Hitchcock and Tower, were convinced of Russia's good faith. They repeatedly urged the Department of State not to adopt any policy that would jeopardize American trade with Russia or Manchuria. Hitchcock was a man of considerable influence in Republican circles (he eventually became Secretary of the Interior) and for a while it is safe to say his advice carried more weight than Denby's and Conger's, from Peking. On the very eve of the despatch of the Hay notes an imperial ukase (August 15, 1899) opened Talienwan as a free port, an act hailed by Ambassador Tower as being, "insofar as Russia is concerned . . . the open door to China . . . a great step forward in the progress of the world," one that opened the way "to the future development of American trade and the certain increase of American mercantile prosperity." William W. Rockhill, Hay's closest adviser on the Far East, was more alarmed by France and Germany than he was by Russia. But John Hay's mistrust of Russia was deep. Nor was it unfounded. The whole world knew that in spite of his gestures of amity the Czar's ultimate goal was to extend his empire over as much of Eastern Asia as his armies and diplomats could hold in their grasp.

Japan, while resentful of all parties to the triple intervention of 1895, singled out Russia as her obvious antagonist. Already Japanese statesmen were preparing for the inevitable war for mastery of Korea and Manchuria. In the interim any project that hampered the Russians, or helped to keep them north of the great wall, served Japan well. She could not take the initiative in such schemes, or allow them to infringe upon the sphere which she, too, had staked out for herself in China. Her plans for the future differed from Russia's only in their immaturity. At the time, her power was not great enough to inspire much trepidation in Washington or much hope in London. In the chain of circumstances that produced the open door notes, Japanese links were few and far between.

In the United States itself the "large policy" of 1898 had its commercial counterpart. The annual report of the Department of State's Bureau of Foreign Commerce for 1896–1897 had spoken hopefully of "what may be termed an American invasion of the markets of the world," of which it considered China "one of the most promising." For the United States to secure equality of opportunity in that vast Empire "would doubtless result in immense gains to our manufacturers in the demand, sure to follow, for lines of supplies and goods of various descriptions that we are pre-eminently fitted to provide." The seizures of Kiaochow and Port Arthur started the first memorials to Washington from apprehensive boards of trade and chambers of commerce. Under their pressure, Secretary Sherman promptly inquired the intentions of the German and Russian governments toward American trade and treaty rights in the neighborhood of the new leaseholds. The replies he received apparently allayed the Secretary's own apprehensions and, for the time being, undoubtedly blunted the point of the intermittent British overtures to the McKinley Administration.

German assurances (if such they may be called) were oral, and somewhat evasive in character. Russia's were hardly more definite. Each consisted in perfunctory statements of respect for existing treaty rights in China, and of the intention to admit foreign commerce to Kiaochow and Talienwan, respectively. That they satisfied Sherman indicates nothing so much as the plain lack of national interest impelling him to seek more binding commitments. Moreover, Sherman appears to have discerned political motives in England's overtures to the United States, and to have feared the involvement in European rivalries into which they might lead. He could see no reason why the United States should "view with any jealousy the southward movement of Russia," he wrote, the year after his retirement. "Russia is our very good friend and has been so for many years. England would like to enlist us in all the controversies that she has on her hands in Eastern Asia. She would then make sure of us as an ally. But it is not to our interest to act in that manner."

During the summer and autumn of 1898 the McKinley Administration was too preoccupied with the Spanish War to give much further attention to events in the Far East. Twice the President expressed concern for the open door; in his instructions to the peace commissioners (September 16) and in his annual message to Congress (December 5). . . .

The President, apparently, was no less willing to accept the German and Russian assurances at face value than Secretary Sherman had been. He was determined to avoid any commitment that might make the United States "an actor in the scene" of European intrigue and aggression then being enacted in China. A month later (January 8, 1899) he proved his determination with a second rebuff to Pauncefote.

With Dewey's victory, the McKinley Administration underwent a change of heart. The first impulse of Mr. Conger (who succeeded Mr. Denby at Peking July 11, 1898) was to combat the concessions-scramble by taking part in it. He deplored his countrymen's lack of interest in the great financial and commercial opportunities in China, an interest which he took it upon himself to promote by urging, first the retention of Manila, then a more aggressive American competition for railway contracts, and finally the acquisition of a port in China itself. . . . A few months later he asked Hay outright if he might not seek for the United States a "strong foothold" in China from which it would be possible "to keep permanently open doors for our commerce."

During the winter of 1899 the pressure of business groups for a more spirited Far Eastern policy increased. American industries (especially the textile) were becoming engrossed in the markets of Northern China and Manchuria, the very regions most affected by German and Russian imperialism. The diplomats of these two nations duly noted the "new and brilliantly successful imperialism" of the United States, which they took for granted would direct its energies toward Eastern Asia. "The United States," wrote Cassini, the Russian ambassador in Washington, soon after the Battle of Manila, "has definitely started on a policy . . . whose horizons are much broader than the traditional ones held heretofore." Mouravieff, the Russian Foreign Minister, spoke of the United States as having "acquired a new view of its mission in this world." It was true: American politicians and diplomats, the statesmen of the expansionist school, had turned promoters on a large scale, and were doing what they could to push American commerce and capital into the Far East. The few business groups already active there were encouraged to seek the support of Washington. Hay responded to their petitions with further soundings of Mouravieff, the reassuring results of which did not mitigate the Secretary's British-fed mistrust of all things Russian.

Business and diplomacy were not the only forces impelling Hay toward his fateful decision. American missionaries in the Far East had also been thrilled by the conquest of the Philippines. In 1899 there were between one thousand and fifteen hundred of them in China where they, and their predecessors, had early assumed a political importance out of all proportion to their numbers. Now their situation was very comparable to that of American businessmen in China. Just as they were rejoicing in the annexation of the Philippines for the aid and comfort they thought it would give their cause, they found themselves confronted by an anti-foreign movement stirred up partly by the concessions-scramble, partly by their own proselytizing, that was to culminate in the Boxer Rebellion. In 1899 they, too, wished the United States to show a strong hand in China.

So far the McKinley Administration had adhered strictly to precedent in the Far East. It had kept free of alliances or understandings with foreign powers. It had called the attention of Europe to the long-established interest of the United States in the open door and the preservation of existing treaty rights. From the two particular nations that caused it most alarm it had obtained assurances. The President had declared himself satisfied with these, and proved it by rejecting Pauncefote for the second time within a year. In spite of the concessions-scramble, American trade with China, small though it was, was actually increasing. If it appeared likely to certain business groups that Russia would some day close them out of Northern China, others contemplated great profit in the sale of products essential to Russia in the development of that region. As yet Germany had been no less hospitable to American trade and capital in Shantung than England had been in the

Yangtse Valley. American fears of exclusion, like American hopes of gain, were all in the future. Up to the summer of 1899 neither had been strong enough to cause a departure from the diplomatic traditions and precedents of the past hundred years.

Then, in July and August, through informal, personal channels, the British influence was once more turned on Hay, this time with success.

Like most Secretaries of State, John Hay had only a superficial knowledge of conditions in the Far East. To advise him on this complicated subject he had chosen a friend and, as it happened, one of the best-informed authorities on China of his generation, William W. Rockhill. Born in Philadelphia in 1854, Rockhill's early youth was spent in France, where he completed his education at the military school at Saint Cyr, and where he acquired an interest in the Chinese language and literature. After three years of service as lieutenant in the French Foreign Legion in Algeria, he returned to the United States, and in 1884 procured an appointment as Second Secretary of the Peking Legation. The next year he was promoted to First Secretary. During the winter of 1886–1887 he served as Chargé d'Affaires at Seoul, Korea. He had entered the diplomatic service as a means of pursuing his Chinese studies. He resigned because of personal incompatibility with Denby. After two famous journeys of exploration through Mongolia and Tibet (1888–1889 and 1891–1892) he returned to the diplomatic service as Chief Clerk of the State Department in 1893. From February 14, 1896, to May 10, 1897, he served as Assistant Secretary of State under Olney, during part of which period (March 4 to May 10, 1897) he filled the gap between Olney and Sherman as Acting Secretary.

By this time Rockhill's scholarly writings and explorations had brought him membership in learned Oriental societies and scientific institutes all over the world. His wide experience in the Far East and in the Department of State had established his reputation as an expert on China and earned him the friendship and admiration of influential Republicans including Roosevelt, Lodge and Hay. When it became evident that Denby was to be replaced, Rockhill's friends urged McKinley to appoint him Minister to China, a post his training pre-eminently qualified him to fill. They were disappointed. Rockhill was sent to Athens as Minister to Greece, Roumania and Servia. It was from this post that Adee and Hay rescued him in April, 1899, by helping to secure his appointment as Director of the Bureau of American Republics in Washington, presumably in order to have the benefit of his counsel on affairs in Eastern Asia. In any event, Rockhill had no sooner assumed his new office (May 22) than the Secretary of State began to solicit his advice.

Rockhill, too, had his confidential adviser in Alfred E. Hippisley, a British subject and a member of the Chinese Imperial Maritime Customs Service. Hippisley was an old China hand. It should be recalled that the Chinese customs service was administered by the British, a privilege ultimately sanctioned by treaty in 1898 for as long as England's share of China's foreign trade should exceed that of any other nation. A member of this service since 1867,

Hippisley had long followed political affairs in China with a sharp, intelligent eye. His acquaintance with Rockhill dated from the autumn of 1884 when the latter first joined the staff of the American legation in Peking. "In a small community such as that of Peking," wrote Hippisley many years later, "acquaintance quickly ripens into intimacy between persons who have similar tastes, and both Rockhill and I were deeply interested in China and Chinese politics, and in my case the intimacy was made the closer by my marriage in the following year with Miss Howard, a friend of long standing of Mrs. Rockhill's, who had accompanied the latter and her husband from Baltimore." What Rockhill was to Hay, Hippisley was to Rockhill: an old friend and trusted adviser on the Far East.

Mutual friendship—and fate—drew the three men together in the early summer of 1899. Simultaneously with Rockhill's inauguration as Director General of the Bureau of American Republics, a periodic leave of absence brought Hippisley to the United States on his way home to England. From about the middle of June to the end of July the Englishman visited his wife's family in Baltimore. He was pleased to renew his acquaintance with Rockhill, whom he had not seen for over ten years. "Naturally," he remembers, "I went over as frequently as I could to Washington to discuss the conditions in China with him and especially what could be done to maintain the 'open door' or equality of opportunity for all nations in that country." On one of these occasions Rockhill, deeply impressed by his friend's ideas, introduced him to the Secretary of State. Hay heard him expound, in outline, the scheme ultimately comprehended by the open door notes.

Throughout the informal negotiations of that summer, Hippisley was clearly the prime mover. Hay, though disposed to co-operate with England, was waiting for Rockhill to find a way to do it. Rockhill, who had been absent from China for seven years, was rusty on China. Hippisley came fresh from the scene, his mind brimming with images and theories of the concessions-scramble and how to deal with it. It was he who took the intiative, who supplied the concrete plans; nor did he lack encouragement. "China is, and will remain, the one absorbing subject," Rockhill told him, "so I am awfully anxious to have all the data you can give me on the subject, that I may not make any mistake, and that my conclusions shall be practicable."

When, about August first, Hay left Washington for his summer home in New Hampshire, and Hippisley departed Baltimore on a leisurely journey, *via* Lenox and Bar Harbor to Quebec (whence he would sail for England September seventh), Hippisley opened an active correspondence with Rockhill. "As I shall not now have an opportunity of seeing you before we start for Europe," he wrote July 25, "I write these lines to ask you to use your influence towards, if possible, inducing the govt. to do what it can to maintain the open door for ordinary commerce in China.". . .

Rockhill passed Hippisley's recommendations on to Hay after adding to their weight his own authoritative *imprimatur*. The same day he replied to Hippisley:

You know what my views are about the position the United States should take in China; I would like to see it make a declaration in some form or other, which would be understood by China as a pledge on our part to assist in maintaining the integrity of the Empire. I fear, however, that home politics and next year's elections will interfere with this, for it might be interpreted by a large part of the voting population of the United States, especially the Irish and the Germans, as an adoption of the policy advocated by England, and any leaning towards England on the part of the administration would, at this time and for the next year to come, be dangerous, and might lose the President his nomination. I consequently fear that he will do absolutely nothing either on the lines you indicate, and which are clearly those most beneficial to our interests in China, or in any other which will commit us. We will simply continue drifting along.

Hay confirmed these doubts. "I thank you for your letter inclosing Mr. Hippisley's," he wrote, August 7. "I am fully awake to the great importance of what you say, and am more than ready to act. But the senseless prejudices in certain sections of the 'Senate and people' compel us to move with great caution."

Hippisley did not give up hope. His reason for "urging *prompt* action" along the lines of his last note was, he explained, "precisely to forestall any suggestion likely to prove injurious to the Administration that it was following the lead of or leaning towards England by inducing it to take the initiative itself; then if England took similar action, she would follow America's lead." The Englishman had developed a remarkable solicitude for the welfare of the United States. "I think it would be suicidal for America to drift and do nothing for another year," he warned. . . .

This time Rockhill's response was more encouraging. He had received "today," he wrote on the eighteenth, "pretty clear assurances from the State Department that it may take some action sooner than could be anticipated from the position it held until within a few weeks and which I gave you in my last letter." But Rockhill was not over-sanguine. Once more he showed himself to be in advance of Hippisley: he favored securing "tangible" assurances from the powers "as to their desire to maintain and insure the integrity of the Chinese Empire. . . ." This, he still believed the Administration was unwilling to consider; the best he and Hippisley could do was to "keep pegging away at it." The next day he submitted to Adee long extracts from Hippisley's last two letters.

Meanwhile two things had come to Hippisley's support. Almost simultaneously came the news of the return to the United States of Dr. Jacob Gould Schurman, Chairman of the President's Philippine Commission, and the Czar's ukase of August 15 declaring Talienwan a free port. All that restrained Hay from embarking on the policy advocated by Hippisley, apparently, was the opposition to it of the President himself. Whatever the true source of this opposition—respect for tradition, the lingering influence of Sherman, sincere conviction or mere partisan expediency—it had tied the Secretary's hands since his assumption of office. Undoubtedly Hay had been converted as early as June, 1898, when he had written McKinley a personal letter from the London embassy, urging him to reconsider the first Paunce-fote overture. More lately he had professed to be "more than ready to act" and lamented the "senseless prejudices" that restrained him. It is probable that, for the past year, whenever the occasion had offered, he had urged on the President some such policy as that now in the making. Dr. Schurman and the Czar seem to have knocked the last props from under McKinley's resistance.

To post himself on the mysterious Philippines, McKinley had appointed a Commission which sailed for Manila early in February, 1899, under the lead-ership of Dr. Jacob Gould Schurman, President of Cornell University, to investigate and report exhaustively on conditions in the islands. Academic duties brought Schurman home in advance of his colleagues. He arrived in San Francisco August 14, the day before the Czar issued his ukase. The Presi-dent had reposed great trust in Schurman, his personal representative, to whom he looked for advice on the Far East as Hay looked to Rockhill. There could be no doubt the Schurman's opinions would carry weight with the White House. It was therefore much to the satisfaction of Rockhill and Hip-pisley that the chief Philippine commissioner told reporters:

As I said . . . to one of the great statesmen of Japan, after I had seen some-thing of the Orient, it seems to me that the great question there is not Formosa nor the Philippines, but China. . . . It is feared, now that Russia has taken Man-churia, it will try to encroach gradually on some or all of the other eighteen prov-inces of China, and when it gets them it will do as that country has done hitherto —put a duty on all foreign goods. . . . Englishmen and Japan [sic] feel that America should stand with them in preventing the dismemberment of China. . . . Everywhere and at all times . . . it was recognized that the future of China was the one overshadowing question. China, it was agreed, should maintain its independent position, but its doors should be kept open. It means much to Eng-land and Japan and not less to America.

While apparently belying Schurman's fears of Russia (and substantiating the judgment of Hitchcock and Tower) the Czar's ukase nevertheless had the same effect as Schurman's interview. Hippisley describes it vividly:

"I received last night your interesting letter of the 18th," he wrote Rockhill, August 21. "I am so encouraged by the possibility of the govt. taking action with regard to China that I send you a memo. on the 'open door' I drew up so soon as I read the Czar's ukase declaring Talien-wan an open port *for the whole period of the treaty*, i.e., for the next 23 years. This is most satisfactory. It gives a natural opportunity for opening negotiations to settle the conditions that are to hold in China for, at least, the immediate future, & it seems to promise cooperation on Russia's part in the direction we hope for. Let the Admin. then act at once, say I, and so forestall any advance on the part of Gt. Britain; and if it does, I foretell success. Proposals from England would be viewed with suspicion; proposals from the U. S. would not—on the contrary, they would be received in a friendly spirit. And I would earnestly suggest that negotiations be opened before Beresford arrives, for, bluff, garrulous, and unrestrained by any sense of responsibility as he is, and already committed to impossible proposals, he will, I fear, do much more harm than good by his speeches. . . .

This crucial letter was accompanied by a "Memorandum on the 'Open Door' in China," drawn up by Hippisley on August 17, the substance of which was to be incorporated in the open door notes. Hippisley had fired his last telling shot. Though his letters continued, both frequent and hortatory, long after he had returned to England, the wrting of the open door notes was now in the hands of Rockhill. . . .

American Business Interests and the Open Door in China

CHARLES S. CAMPBELL, JR.

ONE OF the basic aims of American foreign policy has been to maintain the right of all countries to trade with China on an equal basis. The first formal declaration of this aim came with the sending of the Open Door notes in September, 1899. The origin of these notes has received much attention from historians in recent years, and certain aspects of their origin, particularly the part played by W. W. Rockhill and the Englishman, Alfred Hippisley, have become very well known. At least one aspect, however, has been entirely overlooked: namely, that special business interests in the United States were concerned over the possible loss of the Chinese market; were eager to have the government take just the sort of action which it did take; and were active in bringing pressure to bear on the government. It is the thesis of this article that they were partly responsible for the sending of the notes and, consequently, for America's Open Door policy.

It should be emphatically stated, however, that this article does not pretend to give a complete account of the origins of the Open Door policy. Not only does the author not believe that such an account can be given merely in terms of business pressure on Washington, but the article does not even consider business in general; it is limited almost exclusively to two groups of

Charles S. Campbell, Jr., "American Business Interests and the Open Door," *The Far Eastern Quarterly*, I, 1949, pp. 43-58. Reprinted by permission of The Journal of Asian Studies.

special interests, which might, indeed, be called one, so closely did they over-lap. The almost complete absence of reference to many of the well-known aspects of the origin of the policy does not mean that the author considers these factors unimportant, but simply that he is confining himself to what has not been elaborated elsewhere. Numerous writers have attempted to give a rounded account of the matter; a very few have gone deeply into the part played by business; but no writer has dealt specifically with the special in-terests here under consideration. Yet the influence of these interests appears to have been so great that any complete history of the origins of the Open Door policy should include some mention of them.

One of these special interests was the American-China Development Com-pany, a corporation founded in 1895 for the purpose of getting railroad con-cessions in China. Its sixty shares of stock were held by forty-nine shareholders, of whom the best known were the following: the Carnegie Steel Company; Thomas C. Platt, Senator from New York; Levi P. Morton, vice-president of the United States under President Harrison; Frederick P. Olcott, president of the Central Trust Company of New York; John I. Waterbury, president of the Manhattan Trust Company; James Stillman, president of the National City Bank; George F. Baker, president of the First National Bank of New York; Charles Coster, member of J. P. Morgan and Company; Jacob Schiff, member of Kuhn, Loeb, and Company; E. H. Harriman, chairman of the ex-ecutive committee of the Union Pacific Railway; and G. R. Hegeman, presi-dent of the Metropolitan Life Insurance Company. Three officials of the Development Company were also important shareholders: A. W. Bash, its representative in China; General William Barclay Parsons, its chief engineer; and Clarence Cary, its legal adviser. With seven shares of stock, Cary was the company's chief shareholder.

Shortly after the formation of the American-China Development Company, Bash was sent to China to try to get a concession. In May, 1895, he called on Charles Denby, the American minister in Peking, and asked for his assistance. Since Denby had for years been trying to persuade Americans to do business in China, he was anxious to do what he could for Bash; but in view of the State Department's traditional caution about supporting private business in-terests, he thought it prudent to ask for instructions from Washington.

About this time Richard Olney became Secretary of State. As an advocate of more vigorous support for American enterprise in foreign countries than most of his predecessors, it is not surprising to find him advising Denby "to em-ploy all proper methods for the extension of American commercial interests." It was perhaps as a result of this note that Bash secured shortly afterwards a preliminary contract for a railway concession between Peking and Hankow. But Bash was not empowered to conclude the contract; it was, therefore, necessary to wait until authorized agents of the company should arrive in China. When the agents, one of whom was Clarence Cary, did arrive, they found the Chinese refusing to continue negotiations. Accordingly, they com-plained to Denby. The minister called on the Chinese foreign office and told the officials that it would be "a breach of good faith" not to go through with the contract. Taking a strong line, he succeeded in persuading the Chinese to resume negotiations.

Meanwhile Olney had been succeeded by John Sherman, a man who did not believe in government support for such ventures as the Development Company. When the new Secretary of State read Denby's official report about the above incident, he was not pleased. "You should be cautious," he warned the minister, "in giving what might be understood as this Government's indorsement of the financial standing of the persons seeking contracts with that of China." It is not wholly surprising, therefore, that two months later a Belgian syndicate, instead of the American-China Development Company, was awarded the contract.

Despite the turn of events the Americans continued their efforts to obtain a concession somewhere in China; but the year closed with no success to report. Did the officials and the powerful shareholders of the Development Company know of Sherman's warning to Denby? Whether they did or not, they must have found little to their liking in the negative policy of the State Department under its new Secretary; and some of them took part in the organized attempt, as will be noted in what follows, to persuade the government to adopt a different policy.

A second group of special interests was the American exporters of cotton goods. Cotton goods were America's chief export to China, and that country provided by far the largest market for American cotton mills. In 1899 this country exported $24,852,691 worth of cotton goods, of which almost half, $10,290,981, went to China alone. No other country came close to this, the second largest importer taking only about one-fourth as much.

At that time England was the leading exporter of cotton goods to China, the United States was second, and far in the rear were Japan and the Netherlands. Although the annual value of the American exports was only about half that of the English, it had increased over 120 per cent from 1887 to 1897; while English exports had declined almost 14 per cent. Americans attached considerable importance to this rapid growth of exports. They believed that the United States was capturing the Chinese market and that it was a market well worth acquiring. Even those with little or no business in China were impressed, for they had great hopes for the future. In those times, as still today, China was considered in wide circles to be potentially the greatest market in the world.

We have, then, in the case of cotton, an American industry vitally concerned with the Chinese market. As many members of the industry were almost altogether dependent on that market, anything which the government might do to preserve it would be to their direct interest. The same, of course, was true of the American-China Development Company. The men connected with this company, along with the cotton exporters, were those who had the greatest financial interest in China, and it was they who were most active in bringing pressure to bear on the American government. Of course, business anxiety over the Chinese market was by no means limited to these two groups, but as they had so much more at stake than any other group, it would be misleading not to give them special treatment.

The first step taken by these special interests occurred at the beginning of 1898. At that time considerable anxiety arose out of developments in China. The previous March, France had made the island of Hainan a sphere of influence; in November, German troops had landed at Kiaochow; and shortly afterwards a Russian fleet had dropped anchor at Port Arthur. It looked to many businessmen as though something which they had been fearing for several years—the partition of China—might be on the verge of realization. The threat to Port Arthur was particularly disturbing to Americans, for it was a key city of Manchuria, which, together with the adjoining provinces of China proper, was the chief market for American cotton goods. It was widely expected that, should Russia get control, discriminatory tariffs would be introduced, and an important market would be lost to the United States.

Business opinion was also aroused by the attitude of the State Department. Despite what seemed to be so obviously a dangerous situation in China, responsible officials were giving no sign of alarm; in fact, they seemed almost to welcome the situation. Interviewed by the Philadelphia *Press*, Secretary Sherman stated that he did not see any likelihood of partition—at least, not for some time. Even if China should be partitioned, he said, "the powers would gladly seize the opportunity to trade with us. Our commercial interests would not suffer, as far as I can see, in the least—quite the contrary."

This expression of opinion was most disturbing to those with financial interests in China. In an article which he wrote apparently just after Sherman's statement, Clarence Cary, back from his unsuccessful trip to China in behalf of the American-China Development Company, denounced what he termed the Secretary's "quaint and dangerous view that the interests of the citizens of the United States are not threatened by a possible partition of China." In a similar vein, the New York *Journal of commerce and commercial bulletin*, a newspaper which often expressed the point of view of many cotton exporters, spoke in a strongly worded editorial of the "generally admitted necessity of prompting the Administration to give notice to the world that the United States will suffer no interference with the commercial rights it now possesses in China."

This combination of encroachment on Chinese soil and evidence of what they took to be disinterestedness on the part of the State Department so alarmed some of those with financial interests in China that they determined to take action. On January 6, 1898, three days after Sherman's statement to the *Press*, they held a meeting in the office of Clarence Cary in New York City. At the meeting a "Committee on American Interests in China" was founded. It was instructed to confer, first with the New York Chamber of Commerce, and then, if it should seem desirable, with other commercial organizations throughout the country, regarding "the methods to be adopted to conserve the rights of citizens of the United States in the Chinese Empire."

There were five members of the Committee: Clarence Cary, Everett Frazer, S. D. Brewster, John Foord, and E. L. Zalinski. Cary has been mentioned before; Frazer was the head of an American firm in Shanghai; Brewster, a partner in one of the large firms handling the export of cotton to China; Foord, a contributing editor of the *Journal of commerce and commercial bulletin*; and Zalinski, a member of the Bethlehem Iron Company. It should be noted that men connected both with the American-China Development Company and with the cotton interests were on the committee. The committee became the channel through which men like Cary, interested in China as a field of investment, and others, anxious to preserve a market for their cotton, could and did attempt to divert the government from the negative attitude characteristic of it while Sherman was Secretary of State. Through it they were able to organize and co-ordinate their efforts to bring about a new policy.

Just a week after its founding the committee submitted to the New York Chamber of Commerce a petition signed by a large number of important firms. The petition urged the chamber to take such action as would direct the attention of the government to the threatening situation in China and would ensure "that the important commercial interests of the United States" be safeguarded. As a result of the petition the chamber adopted the following memorial on February 3 and forwarded it to President McKinley the same day:

That there are important changes now going on in the relations of European powers to the Empire of China . . . affecting the privileges enjoyed under existing treaty rights by American citizens trading in and with China. That the trade of the United States to China is now rapidly increasing, and is destined, with the further opening of that country, to assume large proportions unless arbitrarily debarred by the action of foreign governments. . . . That, in view of the changes threatening to future trade development of the United States in China, the Chamber of Commerce . . . respectfully and earnestly urge that such proper steps be taken as will commend themselves to your wisdom for the prompt and energetic defence of the existing treaty rights of our citizens in China, and for the preservation and protection of their important commercial interests in that Empire.

Secretary Sherman, to whom the President had referred the memorial, informed the New York Chamber that the matter was being given the "most careful consideration." As a matter of fact, the same day that he wrote to the chamber he instructed the ambassador in Berlin to inform the authorities in that country of "the interest which this Government must necessarily feel in conserving and expanding the volume of trade which it has built up with China." If, as seems probable, this step was in part the result of the above memorial, it was the first success of the special interests in influencing the policy of the government.

During the first four months of 1898 there were several further developments which originated in the Committee on American Interests in China. The committee had communicated with the commercial organizations of Philadelphia, Boston, San Francisco, and Cleveland, as well as with that of New York, and during this period all except the Cleveland Chamber sent to Washington memorials similar to the one quoted above. Not quite so directly attributable to the committee were memorials received by the government from the Chambers of Commerce of Baltimore and Seattle. That they were inspired, at least indirectly, by the Committee on American Interests is evident in the fact that they were almost identical in wording with the memorial from the New York Chamber. It might also be mentioned that a number of American businessmen in China sent a telegram to the New York body, endorsing its memorial and stating that "immediate action" was necessary for the protection of American interests. This message was forwarded to the State Department.

The adoption of these memorials of early 1898 is doubtless to be attributed not only to the Committee on American Interests but also to events taking place in China during these same months. In February, China was forced to promise Great Britain that the rich Yangtze provinces would never be alienated to another power. This came as something of a shock to Americans, for Britain was commonly regarded as one of the bulwarks of the Open Door in China. Two months later a similar agreement regarding some of the southern provinces was made with France. Most alarming of all were the settlements with Germany and Russia in March—settlements which wound up the Kiaochow and Port Arthur affairs, the beginnings of which have been referred to. Germany succeeded in obtaining a ninety-nine-year lease of the land around Kiaochow Bay, along with extensive economic rights in Shantung province. Russia, after an acute crisis which almost led to war with Great Britain, secured a twenty-five-year lease of the southern tip of the Liaotung peninsula, with the right of building a railway to its principal city, Port Arthur. A more direct threat to the North China market could hardly have been imagined.

Despite both the ominous developments in the Far East and the memorials urging action, the State Department was not pursuing a forceful line. Apart from the mild warning to Germany mentioned above, the only positive step taken during the first part of 1898 was the sending of a telegram by the Secretary of State to Ambassador Hitchcock in St. Petersburg. Hitchcock was instructed to sound out Russia's intentions and to inform the Russian government that the United States was anxious to "maintain open trade in China." Although it was not at all the strong kind of move desired by the special interests, this *démarche* represented a further step in the evolution of the State Department away from the extreme indifference of Sherman earlier in the year. Together with the telegram to Germany it suggests that the memorials originating in the Committee on American Interests were having some effect in Washington.

Not only the government, but also the public in general, was becoming more conscious of the China market; and here too, part of the change must be attributed to the Committee on American Interests in China. Since the memorials inspired by it had been widely discussed in the press, they had reached a larger audience than government circles, and they had not been without effect on public opinion. Evidence for this is to be found in an article by John Foord, stating that because of the memorials the whole question of American business interests in China "began to assume a position of national prominence." As a member of the Committee on American Interests and as an editor of the *Journal of commerce*, Foord, it would seem, was in a position to assess the situation accurately.

The war with Spain, which began in April, 1898, brought with it a rising tide of imperialistic sentiment in the United States. Caught up in this tide and modified by it was the American attitude toward the complex situation in China. To be sure, there was no widespread thought of China as a possible colony, or even of a sphere-of-influence there, but, as Professor Pratt has shown, the foothold which the triumph at Manila Bay gave us in the Philippines was considered by many to be important chiefly because it might help us to hold open the door in the Far East. Then too the fact that America seemed to be suddenly growing up into a great power probably had the effect of making Americans more insistent that treaty rights, including those in China, be upheld.

During the war one of the most important developments in the history of the origins of the Open Door policy took place. The Committee on American Interests had come to the decision that a more permanent form of organization was needed, and to meet that need the committee was transformed in June, 1898, into the American Asiatic Association. The association had the same general aim as its predecessor. As stated in its constitution, this was "to secure the advantage of sustained watchfulness and readiness for action . . . in respect of . . . Asiatic trade, as well as in matters of legislation, or treaties affecting the same." All the members of the original committee became members of the Asiatic Association, and four of them became leading officials. Everett Frazer was the president; S. D. Brewster, the vice-president; John Foord, the secretary; and Clarence Cary, a member of the executive committee.

The reader will have noticed how often the names of two of these officials, Clarence Cary and John Foord, have occurred in the above pages. Both of them were intimately associated with the campaign to influence the policy of the government. Consider the strategic position of each: Cary, counsel for the American-China Development Company and member of the executive committee of the American Asiatic Association; Foord, secretary of the Asiatic Association, editor of its magazine, *Asia*, and contributing editor of the *Journal of commerce*. Although these men were influential only in indirect ways, it is entirely possible that they had as much to do with the sending of the September notes as had such well-known figures as W. W. Rockhill and Alfred Hippisley.

Four days after its founding the Association had just under fifty members. Among them were the General Electric Company; the Guaranty Trust Company; the New York Central and Hudson River Railroad Company; Charles Denby; W. W. Rockhill; Calvin Brice and W. D. Washburn, both officials of the American-China Development Company; and a large number of men in the cotton business.

In order to reach as wide an audience as possible, the association undertook the publication of a periodical entitled *Asia: journal of the American Asiatic association,* the editor of which, as has been said, was John Foord. But propaganda by the association did not become particularly widespread at this time; for, like its predecessor, the association devoted its attention chiefly to the State Department.

The American Asiatic Association was the principal channel through which the special interests made their influence felt in Washington and in the country at large. It was strongly supported by the *Journal of commerce and commercial bulletin,* which devoted an extraordinary amount of editorial and news space to questions of the Chinese market and consistently advocated energetic action by the government to safeguard that market. Co-operation between the association and the journal was doubtless facilitated by the fact that John Foord occupied an important position in each of these guardians of American interests in the Far East.

The founding of the Asiatic Association was the chief event concerned with the origins of the Open Door policy which took place during the war with Spain. However, a few other developments of the same time, though of comparatively minor importance, may also be mentioned.

Perhaps the outstanding of these was a recommendation to Congress by Sherman's successor in the State Department, William R. Day, that a trade commission be sent to China to investigate possibilities for greater exports to that part of the world. Although Congress took no action at the time, the incident has some significance as marking a further step in the evolution of the government toward the point of view of the special interests.

Also of significance was the appointment of John Hay to the position of Secretary of State. In view of the memorials of the early part of the year and such a further indication of the opinion of influential businessmen as the establishment of the Asiatic Association, it is quite possible that Hay's well-known propensity for the Open Door in China was one of the reasons for his appointment. Hardly had he assumed office when the new Secretary showed that his Far Eastern policy was going to be stronger than that of his two predecessors. Perhaps as a result of a memorial from one of the American establishments in China, stating that there was a "probability of serious interference [by Russia] with America's important trade in cotton . . . unless immediate steps are taken in Pekin to insist that our treaty rights with China be maintained", Hay ordered two gunboats to proceed to North China. The New York Chamber of Commerce, incidentally, expressed its "high appreciation" of the act. For the time being, however, nothing further came of the Russian threat.

The last event we need mention which occurred during the war was the annual message to Congress of President McKinley. Repeating Day's recommendation of a trade commission, the President stated that the United States was not an "indifferent spectator" of what was going on in China but that it would preserve its "large interests in that quarter by all means appropriate to the constant policy of our Government." This strong declaration was naturally hailed with delight by those with business interests in China.

When the war with Spain formally came to an end early in 1899 with the ratification of the peace treaty by the Senate, the government was able to turn its attention from military matters to such peacetime considerations as trade with China. In January it received an important memorial. Coming from a large number of cotton manufacturers, the memorial stated that the Chinese market would be lost to American cotton exporters "unless a vigorous policy is pursued on the part of the . . . Government"; it requested that the American diplomatic representatives at Peking and St. Petersburg "be instructed to give special attention to the subject". This memorial seems to have impressed Secretary Hay even more than the memorial of the preceding January had impressed Sherman. Referring to the "high character and standing of the signers", he ordered the envoys to give the "special attention" requested of them; and about a month later, apparently afraid he had not been sufficiently emphatic, he wrote a second time to the ambassador to Russia, asking him to continue "to act energetically in the sense desired by the numerous and influential signers of the petition."

Another episode of early 1899 worth mentioning was the Asiatic Association's strong support of a protest by the United States against an attempt by France to extend her concession in Shanghai. The association wrote to McKinley and Hay, urging that "all available means" be used "towards preserving for the world's commerce an 'open door' in the Far East". In sharp contrast with this was the association's viewpoint regarding an attempt to obtain an extension of the combined British and American concession. Negotiations with China had been going on for some time but without success. Angered and alarmed, the association informed Secretary Hay of "the necessity of . . . vigorous action . . . in order to obtain a definite solution". Sending a copy of this letter to the minister to China, Hay instructed him to devote his efforts to obtaining the extension. Two months later China gave way.

In March the campaign for the Open Door took a more decisive turn. It became known at that time that Italy was endeavoring to secure from the Chinese government a lease of Sanmen Bay, a bay located not far from Shanghai, the center of foreign business in China. Fears of partition once again rose quickly to the surface. There was widespread suspicion that Italy had the backing of Great Britain; if true, it would mean that the only remaining great power opposed to the partition of China was the United States.

The situation disturbed the American Asiatic Association to an extent which might seem surprising today. Today we know that the Sanmen Bay affair turned out to be a comparatively insignificant incident. But to those who lived at the time of the crisis itself this knowledge was lacking, and to them, fearful as they were that it would take very little indeed to start off the process of dismembering China, the spring of 1899 was a time of grave anxiety. So disturbing was the situation to the officials of the Asiatic Association that they held a series of meetings in order to discuss the possibility of a fundamental modification of the policy they had been pursuing.

As has been shown, this policy was to concentrate on the Department of State. True, there had been a certain amount of propaganda directed at the public in general through the periodical, *Asia: Journal of the American Asiatic association,* and true it is also that this propaganda had been meeting with some success. As early as January the *Journal of commerce,* that close observer of anything pertaining to the Open Door, had pointed to the "new attitude of this country towards its commercial interests in China" and had stated that it was "partly the result of the American Asiatic Association." Nevertheless, greater success had been gained with the State Department. Secretary Sherman and Secretary Day had moved closer to the viewpoint of businessmen who were eager to see the Chinese market safeguarded. John Hay had not once failed to carry out any formal request regarding Far Eastern policy, and, indeed, the department under Hay had shown itself so willing to co-operate that there could be no doubt about its desire to maintain the Open Door in China.

Because of these facts the *Journal of commerce* and the Asiatic Association appear to have realized that pressure upon the State Department had become much less necessary than before. But this did not suggest to them that their usefulness was at an end. For although it was clear that many of the high officials in Washington were convinced that the Chinese market was of considerable value to the United States, it was equally clear that the general public was not convinced. Consequently, what had become desirable in place of so much attention to the State Department was, as the journal said, "education of the people, the press, and the politicians by those who see the vital necessity of the Chinese market"—in short, "active propaganda in the country at large." The Asiatic Association, as a faithful ally of the journal, came to the same conclusion. At the series of meetings which its officials were holding it was decided to embark upon "a campaign of public education in regard to the magnitude of the commercial interests of the United States in China." A committee to take charge of the campaign was appointed.

The writer has not been able to discover many details about the ensuing campaign. It is known that it was carried on in the press—the *Journal of commerce* presumably being the chief organ—and in publications of the association itself. It is also known that by the end of 1899 the association had at its disposal a fund for propaganda purposes amounting to several thousand dollars and that among the contributors to this fund were many of the exporters of cotton goods. Not much additional material, however, is available.

Did the campaign have any success in persuading the public of the importance of the market in China? No conclusive answer can be given to this
question; for not only is it foolish to make too definite claims about the
effects of any bit of propaganda, no matter how much one may know of its
nature, but also we have here a propaganda campaign concerning which
relatively little is known.

It is worth while, however, to point out that both the American Asiatic
Association and the *Journal of commerce* were convinced that their propaganda did have very considerable success. The statement of the journal in
January, 1899, regarding the influence of the Asiatic Association in moulding
public opinion has been mentioned above. Ten months later, in November,
the propaganda of the Association had had more time to make itself felt.
At that time the *Journal of commerce* reported that "there has never been a
more remarkable advance of public sentiment in this country than that which
has taken place . . . in regard to the responsibilities to be faced by our Government in the Far East." The journal boasted that "to the stage of public
education which has been reached on this subject [the necessity of the Open
Door to the United States] this journal may fairly claim to have largely contributed." The vice-president of the Asiatic Association said that the work
of his organization would "take its place in history as part of one of the most
memorable chapters in the annals of the American people. . . . You have
only to compare", he said, "the state of public sentiment which we found
existing in regard to the responsibilities of our country in Eastern Asia with
the feeling which exists on that subject to-day to appreciate what the influence of the Association has been."

Moreover, at least one contemporary observer supported their claims. James
S. Fearon, one of the leading exporters of cotton to China and for years
chairman of the Shanghai Municipal Council—presumably a man whose
opinions regarding American relations with China are worthy of respect—
stated that much of the credit for the changed attitude of the American
people toward the Chinese market was due to the American Asiatic Association and to the *Journal of commerce*.

The propaganda campaign was the outstanding feature of the months just
before the sending of the Open Door notes, but this period was also marked
by further pressure brought to bear on the State Department by the special
interests. Although they initiated no more memorials at this time, the officials
of the Asiatic Association are known to have corresponded with Secretary
Hay and to have called upon him frequently regarding the country's Far
Eastern policy.

The activity of the special interests during these months of 1899 was of
such a nature as to make it extremely difficult to evaluate its significance. It
is, of course, quite understandable that no records exist stating explicitly
whether or not the administration was influenced by the propaganda campaign, and it is equally understandable that Secretary Hay never wrote down

anything which would enable us to judge whether or not his thinking was affected by the letters from the officials of the Asiatic Association and by the visits these men paid him. It is far easier to trace the effects of the memorials of 1898 than of the propaganda and informal contacts of 1899.

But it would be a great mistake to overlook the possibility that these later activities too were of considerable importance. It may well have been that the *Journal of commerce* and the Asiatic Association were quite correct in their belief that the propaganda campaign was successful. If it was successful, if it did in fact make the public more conscious of America's stake in the Far East, it doubtless made it easier for the administration to take action designed to preserve the Chinese market. As for the letters and visits from the Asiatic Association to Hay, it is highly probable that such frequent reminders of the desires of certain businessmen had at least the effect of bolstering up the Secretary's own inclinations with respect to China. At any rate, it is clear that these activities of the special interests during the spring and summer of 1899 must have, along with the memorials of 1898, a place in any complete history of the origins of the Open Door policy.

On September 6, 1899, the first group of Open Door notes was dispatched. This was just the kind of step for which the special interests had been hoping and for which they had been working. To the cotton exporters the notes meant that their market appeared to be far more secure; and to the American-China Development Company they meant that there was much to be hoped for from a grateful China—and, indeed, a few months later the company at last secured the contract which it had so long been seeking. . . .

Intervention in the Caribbean:

ECONOMICS *or* SECURITY ?

FROM THE end of the Spanish-American War to the time of American intervention in World War I, the United States pursued an aggressive and expansionist policy in the Caribbean and in Central America. Chiefly by means of direct military intervention, but also by purchase and non-military coercion, Washington extended its influence and power over the area so that by 1916 the Caribbean was an American lake—a mare nostrum. By that date the United States had acquired two colonies (Puerto Rico and the Virgin Islands), five protectorates (Cuba, Haiti, the Dominican Republic, Panama, and Nicaragua), and a number of naval bases in some of the protectorates. Americans dominated the political and economic life of the area: political life by having marines in occupation and by supervising elections; economic life by means of loans floated by American bankers and by supervising the collection of customs. In every instance the American position was legalized by bilateral treaty. Each of the three presidents of the period—Roosevelt, Taft, and Wilson—pursued the same positive policy, although Democratic Wilson engaged in more interventions than his two Republican predecessors. Why did successive governments find it necessary to intervene in the internal affairs of the republics in the Caribbean and Central America? Two widely opposing points of view have been advanced by historians in answer to the question of motivation. One is economic; the other is strategic.

Charles Austin Beard, one of America's most distinguished historians, author of numerous works on United States history, and a principal exponent of the economic determinist school of historical interpretation, advances the economic viewpoint. He believes that "Modern diplomacy is commercial. Its chief concern is with the promotion of economic interests abroad." It seeks to gain sources of raw material, markets for manufactured goods, and opportunities for capital investment. "Dollar diplomacy," for Beard, is the term which describes the uses which financial and industrial interests make of the government. *Those interests sway government policy to the extent that the government will intervene in the affairs of other nations to provide advantages for those interests. As a typical example of "dollar diplomacy" he cites American policy in Nicaragua. There, he notes, important American economic interests were threatened by a dictator who refused to satisfy legitimate claims. American military intervention followed, the dictator was overthrown, a new American-supported leader was recognized, a treaty was made with the "pliant president," and American economic interests were secured. This, for Beard, is "dollar diplomacy."*

Samuel Flagg Bemis, an equally distinguished and prolific historian, and for many years professor of diplomatic history at Yale, espouses the strategic interpretation. "Dollar diplomacy" describes the uses made by the government of the financial interests. For strategic reasons the government desires stability in the various republics. It sends marines to end revolutions and provides financial aid to end economic chaos. The dollar was used by Taft in Nicaragua not "to profit private interests. It was intended rather to support the foreign policy of the United States". Bemis goes on to demonstrate that Wilson pursued an identical policy, although clothed in idealistic garment, for exactly the same reason—defense strategy. To substantiate his position Bemis quotes a part of a speech by Adolph A. Berle, a prominent diplomatist and jurist.

National Interest Formulated in Dollar Diplomacy

CHARLES A. BEARD

THROUGHOUT his administration, President Taft, duly instructed by the State Department, emphasized the fact that "modern diplomacy is commercial." It was accompanied, to be sure, by "idealistic humanitarian sentiments" and moral obligations, but there was no doubt about the main business in hand. "The diplomacy of the present administration," he said in his message of December 3, 1912, "has sought to respond to modern ideas of commercial intercourse. This policy has been characterized as substituting dollars for bullets. . . . It is an effort frankly directed to the increase of American trade upon the axiomatic principle that the Government of the United States shall extend all proper support to every legitimate and beneficial American enterprise abroad. How great have been the benefits of this diplomacy, coupled with the maximum and minimum provision of the tariff law, will be seen by some consideration of the wonderful increase in the export trade of the United States."

In the realization of this policy, the State Department was reorganized to handle more effectively the "mass of intricate business vital to American interests in every country of the world." Through the establishment of regional divisions in the Department, "American interests in every quarter of the globe are being cultivated with equal assiduity." Foreign trade advisers were added to "coöperate with the diplomatic and consular bureaus and the politico-geographical divisions in innumerable matters where commercial diplomacy or consular work calls for such special knowledge." The merit system was strengthened in the State Department to guarantee continuity of service and greater technical competence; and "in order to assure to the business and other interests of the United States a continuance of the resulting benefits of this reform," additional legislation was requested from Congress.

Much had been done to advance American interests abroad, the message continued; but a greater consolidation of forces and more ingenuity were necessary: "If this Government is really to preserve to the American people that free opportunity in foreign markets which will soon be indispensable to our prosperity, even greater efforts must be made. Otherwise the American merchant, manufacturer, and exporter will find many a field in which Ameri-

Quoted by permission, from Beard, Charles A., and Smith, George H. E., *The Idea of National Interest; an Analytical Study in American Foreign Policy*, The Macmillan Company, 1934. Copyright 1934 by Charles A. Beard. Copyright renewed 1962 by William Beard and Mrs. Miriam B. Vagts.

can trade should logically predominate preëmpted through the more energetic efforts of other governments and other commercial nations. There are
many ways in which through hearty coöperation the legislative and executive
branches of this Government can do much. The absolute essential is the spirit
of united effort and singleness of purpose. I will allude only to a very few
specific examples of action which ought then to result. America cannot take
its proper place in the most important fields for its commercial activity and
enterprise unless we have a merchant marine. American commerce and enterprise cannot be effectively fostered in those fields unless we have good American banks in the countries referred to. We need American newspapers in those
countries and proper means for public information about them. We need to
assure the permanency of a trained foreign service. We need legislation en-
abling the members of the foreign service to be systematically brought into
direct contact with the industrial, manufacturing, and exporting interests of
this country in order that American business men may enter the foreign field
with a clear perception of the exact conditions to be dealt with and the officers themselves may prosecute their work with a clear idea of what American
industrial and manufacturing interests may require."

In other words, President Taft believed he saw the dawn of a "new age" in
American diplomacy; although what he beheld seemed very much like the
fires of Federalist *Machtpolitik* kept glowing through the years, especially by
the navy, and fanned into flame by the economic intensities of the twentieth
century. "We have emerged full grown as a peer in the great concourse of
nations. We have passed through various formative periods. We have been
self-centered in the struggle to develop our domestic resources and deal with
our domestic questions. The Nation is now too mature to continue in its
foreign relations those temporary expedients natural to a people whose domestic affairs are the sole concern. In the past our diplomacy has often consisted,
in normal times, in a mere assertion of the right to international existence.
We are now in a larger relation with broader rights of our own and obligations to others than ourselves. . . . The successful conduct of our foreign
relations demands a broad and modern view. We cannot meet new questions
nor build for the future if we confine ourselves to outworn dogmas of the past
and to the perspective appropriate to our emergence from colonial times and
conditions. . . . We must not wait for events to overtake us unawares." To
this conclusion the President had come, and now "Congress should fully realize the conditions which obtain in the world as we find ourselves at the
threshold of our middle age as a Nation." By 1912, the Executive Department
of the Federal Government had taken on the doctrines of *Realpolitik* which
Germany had already begun to pursue in an effort to secure "free opportunity
in foreign markets," to push "legitimate economic interest," and to find "a
place in the sun"; but American policy was accompanied by a special emphasis on moral obligations and "idealistic humanitarian sentiments."

Here, then, is the "new" *Realpolitik*. A free opportunity for expansion in
foreign markets is indispensable to the prosperity of American business. Mod-

ern diplomacy is commercial. Its chief concern is with the promotion of economic interests abroad. Possession or control of the sources of raw materials and freedom to trade in the existing old markets and to exploit the new are essential to the progress of the country. These things must be actively fostered by the Government and the preëmption of them by competitors under the protection of rival governments must be prevented. The Government of the United States can do much in this direction and must have the united support of the country in such foreign relations. These objectives and the process by which they are to be obtained require a large navy, a merchant marine, American banking houses in foreign countries, American newspapers abroad to convey information and counter the propaganda of rival sheets, a larger and more efficient consular and commercial service, and systematic efforts to establish direct and intimate connections between the government officials engaged in commercial promotion on the one side, and industrial, manufacturing, and exporting interests in the United States on the other. Such were the instrumentalities and implications of dollar diplomacy by which the national interest was to be actively fostered and achieved. . . .

ILLUSTRATIONS OF NATIONAL INTEREST IN ACTION

The broad outlines of national interest in commercial expansion previously drawn, even if accurate and precise, do not go far in presenting the actualities of policy or the mechcanics of its execution. Here as elsewhere generalizations have meaning only when they are illuminated by reference to concrete events embedded in their underlying content. In a strict sense, therefore, it is only when the ultimate realities of the particular cases constituting the sum of national interest in official practice are brought within the circle of minute examination and viewed in the order of their inherent relations that the nature of the dogma can be discovered and made to stand forth as objective occurrence and experience. This much may be said with safety, even though Berkeley's denial of abstractions be rejected by philosophers.

Yet the task here suggested is obviously impossible of practical performance. The pursuit of national interest has involved innumerable private activities —negotiations for concessions, commercial privileges, investment opportunities, and other economic advantages. It has likewise included innumerable official conversations, promises, demands, and orders. The influence of an immense number and variety of forces of a kind difficult to perceive, impossible to measure or describe, and soon obliterated by time, enters into the relevant situations and shapes the course of events. Of many operations, even those highly important in nature, no record was made and little or nothing can be known about them. Where documentary evidence of specific events has been kept, it is seldom complete and by no means always open to the scrutiny of a mere scientific inquirer, whether in private or public archives. It is an old story: all the relevant data of the whole problem or any partial aspect cannot be assembled or known. Obviously, then, the only recourse left open is the illustration of national interest as officially conceived by a minute description of some narrow area or areas of operations concerning which authentic and plentiful material is available.

THE DIPLOMACY OF NATIONAL INTEREST IN NICARAGUA (1909–1912)

Of all such limited areas perhaps the best for purposes of illustration is that of American procedure in, and with reference to, Nicaragua from 1909 to 1912. Voluminous papers bearing on the subject have been published by the Department of State. Contests in Congress over executive and naval actions have led to investigations and have developed detailed testimony respecting the primary things and occurrences of the total situation in the chosen area of time and space. In other words, it is possible to secure a minute and fairly accurate picture of the realities of national interests as pursued by citizens and the Government of the United States in Nicaragua during this particular period.

The background of the scene is Nicaragua in 1909. It was at that time an independent country about the size of the state of New York, inhabited mainly by Indians, Negroes, and mixed races, with a white population amounting to approximately one-eighth of the total. Primitive in economy, its immigration from Europe and the United States was almost negligible. Most of its roads were mere trails, and communication between the different sections was slow and hazardous. Managua, the capital city, had an estimated population slightly in excess of 30,000. The population of Bluefields, one of the principal Atlantic (or Caribbean) seaports, was placed at 5,000. Its industries were few in number and unimportant. Mineral and timber resources, though abundant, were in a low state of development. Agriculture was the chief occupation of the people, and while for the most part primitive in character it supplied coffee, sugar, cocoa, and fruits for which the United States provided a favorable market. In effect, the government of Nicaragua, if nominally constitutional, was a dictatorship under the direction of José Santos Zelaya who, as a student of Caribbean affairs has said, sold concessions "for almost any privilege, which international-gambler investors would buy, censored the press, and imposed heavy and oppressive taxes on both exports and imports," thus interfering arbitraily with the course of foreign trade.

AMERICAN INTEREST IN NICARAGUA

In 1909 the American private economic interests in Nicaragua fell into certain broad classes.

The first included individuals and concerns engaged in operating plantations. In the field of industry and commerce there were a number of American concerns actively interested in Nicaraguan affairs. Prominent among them was the George D. Emery Company which had secured from Zelaya a lumber concession. According to the specifications of the original contract the Company paid $30,000 flat for its rights, and agreed to pay $10,000 a year plus additional sums in the nature of a royalty of $1.00 for each log cut in the course of its operations. In addition, it obligated itself to plant two trees for every one cut within its area of exploitation. After the Company had been under way for some time it fell into a dispute with Zelaya. He claimed that it was not planting trees as required by the contract, and it insisted that its obligations in that respect were being duly observed. After some controversy, the government of Nicaragua cancelled the concession and the Company, which had been making an annual profit ranging from $170,000 to $180,000, filed claims for damages amounting, it appears, to $100,000.

On the assumption of national interest, the Government of the United States took up the claim of the Emery Company against Nicaragua and pressed for a settlement. After prolix negotiations, the Secretary of State, Philander C. Knox, secured a treaty with Nicaragua on May 25, 1909, in which an agreement was reached to submit the dispute to arbitration by a special tribunal, the expenses of which were to be equally shared by the two governments. The tribunal was duly appointed and rendered a verdict on September 18, 1909, awarding to the United States of America "for and in behalf of the George D. Emery Company" the sum of $600,000 gold, to be paid in installments, in return for a complete release of all its claims against Nicaragua. But before the transaction was completed by payment, revolution broke out in Nicaragua, leaving this claim as one of the vested interests considered in the diplomacy which accompanied and followed the upheaval.

A second American interest in Nicaragua was "the United States-Nicaragua Concession," held by a Pittsburgh concern. So far as later claims against Nicaragua were concerned this seems to have been the most important American interest in that country. It was a mining concession covering 6,000 square miles and operated on a royalty basis. Important American citizens were connected with it, including the Fletcher family; and Philander C. Knox, in his capacity as a lawyer, had formerly served as counsel for the Company and had passed upon the validity of the original agreement. Like the Emery Company, the United States-Nicaragua concern became involved in difficulties with Zelaya who insisted that the grant was objectionable and wished to cancel it, in the hope, it was asserted, of re-selling the concession on more favorable terms. This dispute was also pending when the revolution against Zelaya broke out and the American rights asserted under the concession constituted the largest claim to be settled after Zelaya was overthrown by arms. In fact, the American consul at Bluefields during the disturbance, Thomas P. Moffat, declared at a Senate committee hearing that this claim was "the cause of the desire to eliminate Zelaya."

A closely related American interest in Nicaragua was the La Luz and Los Angeles Mining Company (engaged in operating the United States-Nicaragua concession). If the testimony of the United States consul in Bluefields at the time is to be accepted, the Company was "under the control of the

Fletcher family" and the Knox "interests.",At all events, John Martin, the husband of the former Miss Fletcher, was resident manager of the Company in Bluefields. During the revolution in Nicaragua, he advised installing the local secretary of the Company, Adolfo Diaz, in the presidency of the Republic, and told the American consul that his future promotion would be assured if he would "put Adolfo over the line there."

Such was the situation in Nicaragua in 1909 when diplomacy in defense of American interests was put into active operation by the Secretary of State, Philander C. Knox. American citizens and business concerns had large outstanding claims against the Nicaraguan government; their operations were subjected to adverse interference on the part of Zelaya; losses had been incurred, and prospective profits had been seriously endangered. No satisfactory headway could be made while he remained in power. Here were substantial, measurable reasons why American interests desired a change in political affairs and the establishment of a government in Nacaragua more compliant with American claims and demands. And as constantly happens in certain Latin-American regions, there was a great deal of discontent among the natives, civilian and military, which furnished the fuel for a quick revolutionary outburst.

In October, 1909, the revolution came. Early in the month the American consul at Bluefields informed the State Department in Washington that he had received secret information on the subject, that in his opinion a revolution would start in Bluefields on the 8th, that a provisional government would be set up, and that appeal for recognition would be made immediately to Washington. A few days later the consul announced the revolution as a fact and stated that the new government was "friendly to American interests," that the tariff was to be reduced, that all concessions not owned by foreigners were to be cancelled, and that "the foreign business interests are jubilant."

During the struggle which ensued between President Zelaya and the revolutionary government set up at Bluefields under the provisional presidency of Juan J. Estrada, Secretary Knox wrote a sharp note on Zelaya's policy and terminated official relations with his diplomatic representative in Washington. In this attack on the President of Nicaragua, Secretary Knox accused him of keeping Central America in turmoil, putting an end to republican institutions in his own country, throttling the press and public opinion, rewarding with prison "any tendency to real patriotism," placing a blot on the history of his people, executing two American citizens in a barbarous manner, menacing the American consulate in Managua, and offering no promise of protection for "American interests." "The Government of the United States," the note asserted, "is convinced that the revolution represents the ideals and the will of a majority of the Nicaraguan people more faithfully than does the Government of President Zelaya, and that its peaceable control is well-nigh as extensive as that hitherto so sternly attempted by the government at Managua." Having disposed of Zelaya in this summary fashion, Secretary Knox severed formal relations with his government. At the same time he informed the government of Nicaragua, as well as the leaders of the revolution, that the United States would hold it strictly accountable "for the protection of American life and property" and would take such steps as it deemed "wise and proper to protect American interest."

Long afterward the curtain was raised, by a Senate investigation and the publication of state papers, on the inner history of the revolution, and it was made known that American citizens and officials in Nicaragua had aided in fomenting and carrying through the uprising against President Zelaya. A former official of Nicaragua testified before the Senate committee that "this revolution was supplied with money and arms by Americans." Pressed for details, he named Bellanger and Company as one of the participants in the transaction, and declared that Adolfo Diaz, an employee of the La Luz and Los Angeles Company, an American concern, filed a claim for $600,000 against the Nicaraguan government for money furnished by himself to the revolution, when "in fact everybody knows in Nicaragua that it was supplied by American interests in the United States."

This statement, which may be discounted as *ex parte* testimony in behalf of Nicaragua, is supplemented by other evidence. A number of diplomatic documents show that two American citizens, Le Roy Cannon and Leonard Groce, were active among the revolutionists as "dynamiters," and were captured and shot by Zelaya's forces. The American consul at Bluefields, Thomas P. Moffat, later testified at a Senate investigation that shortly after his arrival at his post he heard intimations that American officials before him and naval officers had been suggesting to the people that they "get up and get rid of Zelaya" and had been making promises of some kind to them. He added that he had noticed Adolfo Diaz engaged in the conferences and discussions which preceded the uprising. Two revolutionary leaders, Estrada and Diaz, told Mr. Moffat "that some of our [American] naval officers had said, 'Now, some of the Americans at home are not satisfied with some of the concessions that are being interfered with, and Zelaya, they think, ought to be put out. They would be very glad to see him go out.' And Estrada said he asked, 'Well, what would be the attitude of the American Government? Would it [revolution] be supported or not?' They told him to go ahead: 'You will get the support.'"

Whether these promises were made or not, official support for the revolution was certainly afforded by the Government of the United States soon after the uprising was started. When Zelaya's army approached Bluefields for the purpose of suppressing the insurrection there, General Estrada, in charge of the revolution in the city, told the American consul, Mr. Moffat, that he was unable to overcome the advancing troops with the forces at his command, and that they would loot the town, in case they entered it, because they "feel that the Americans have started this revolution." The consul replied that this would mean an enormous loss to the foreign interests, the Americans alone having about $2,000,000 worth of supplies in Bluefield, and that protection should be provided. Accordingly, the consul cabled the State Department and consulted "with different businessmen and they said, yes." In due course American forces under Major Smedley Butler arrived on the scene and "the situation cleared up in Bluefields," that is, Zelaya's efforts to put down the revolution were checked by the appearance of American troops. In these circumstances the uprising was successful at the point of inception.

Stripped of authority in Bluefields, President Zelaya issued a manifesto to the National Assembly at Managua and tendered his resignation. In this message he ascribed the chief responsibility for the revolution to "the hostile attitude of a powerful nation which, against all right, intervened in our political affairs and publicly furnished the rebels with all the aid which they have asked for"—to employ his phrasing of the case. Expressing a desire to contribute to the good of Nicaragua and the establishment of peace and to end "the hostility manifested by the American Government," he deposited his power with the Assembly and proposed the designation of a successor in conformity with the terms of the constitution. Without any express objection on the part of the United States—a position which, President Taft declared, "equally implied no approval or acquiescence"—Zelaya found refuge on board a Mexican war vessel and was taken out of the country.

Zelaya's successor, Dr. José Madriz, unanimously designated by the Nicaraguan Congress, now proposed a truce with the revolutionary leaders and sought a settlement by conference; but the latter refused to abide by the action of the Congress and insisted on treating Madriz as a "usurper of the rights of the people." Defeated in this attempt at pacification, Madriz for a time continued the unequal struggle. His government purchased at New Orleans a British vessel, loaded it with guns and ammunition, and, after fitting it out as a war ship at San Juan del Norte, tried to blockade the port of Bluefields with the design of preventing, as President Madriz put the case, "the revolution from continuing to receive, as before, arms, supplies, and funds from New Orleans." After the troops of Madriz stormed the Bluff commanding Bluefields and his new war vessel prepared to blockade the harbor, the Government of the United States intervened, forbade fighting in Bluefields, kept the port open for supplies destined to the revolutionists, compelled the payment of customs to the latter, and informed the Madriz commander that a shot fired by his ship at any incoming American vessels would mean a declaration of war against the United States. In other respects the Government of the United States took a position of neutrality in the conflict between the contending factions.

In such circumstances, Dr. Madriz was unable to make headway, and late in the summer of 1910 he too fled from Managua, while the troops which had been supporting him crumbled before the army of the revolution. Thereupon a provisional government headed by General Estrada was established at the capital, and the Secretary of State at Washington was informed that a general election would be held, a new constitution adopted, the aid of the Department of State sought in securing a loan to rehabilitate finances, and reparations made for the death of the two Americans shot as revolutionists by Zelaya. Replying to such overtures, the Department of State ordered Thomas P. Dawson, minister to Panama, to proceed to Managua and, with the aid of the two American consuls, Moffat and Olivares, to facilitate a settlement. In its instructions to Mr. Dawson it suggested the following program as the basis for action: the election of a president at the earliest practicable date, the establishment of a liberal constitution containing "suitable guarantees for foreigners" and affirming the "inhibitions of commercial monopolies," the re-habilitation of finances, a loan to pay claims secured by customs receipts according to an agreement to be reached between the governments of the United States and Nicaragua, payment of claims already determined, adjust-ment of other claims arising out of the revolution by a commission created by convention to be drawn by the two governments, and reparation for the death of the two Americans executed by the Zelaya government.

After extended negotiations with the revolutionary leaders, the minister of the United States was able to bring them into agreement on the principles proposed by the Department of State and the documents were signed on October 27, 1910. An understanding was reached respecting the candidates—Estrada for president and Diaz for vice president; the Zelayistas were excluded from the government; elections were held late in November, 1910; the candi-dates suggested were unanimously elected; and the American consul reported "intense enthusiasm."

But the program was soon disturbed by events. In February, 1911, the new American Minister, Elliott Northcott, stated that Estrada saw no hope for Nicaragua except in "close alliance with the United States," that opinion in Central America was against such a step, that "the natural sentiment of an overwhelming majority of Nicaraguans is antagonistic to the United States," that even in Estrada's cabinet there was distrust of American motives, and that the Zelayistas were again active in stirring up opposition to the settle-ment. A month later, the American minister added: "As the matter now looks to me, President Estrada is being maintained solely by the moral effect of our support and the belief that he would unquestionably have that support in case of trouble."

Despite the apparent settlement, things were not running smoothly in fact. The American minister, therefore, informed President Estrada: "You have got to turn over the power and leave the country; otherwise my Gov-ernment will not further recognize you." So Estrada, unsatisfactory to the American Government and yet attacked by the Nicaraguan National Assem-bly for his compliance with American requests, passed from the scene, and at last Adolfo Diaz, who had evidently been the principal American candidate from the beginning of the revolution, was installed in the presidency. Then the American minister announced the news to the State Department and added that "a war vessel is necessary for the moral effect." Acting Secretary Huntington Wilson replied: "Make suitable expression of this Government's satisfaction with the Diaz Government's assurance of its desire to continue with the program." The American war vessel *Yorktown* was ordered from Panama to intercept a filibustering movement against Diaz engineered by an "anti-American party." By way of supplement Secretary Knox instructed the American minister in Nicaragua to inform Diaz that the United States "renews assurances of support in assisting his government in so far as it properly may," and to warn the principal rival of Diaz, General Mena, that "since Diaz is the constitutional President, recognized by this Government as such," the General "must see it to be indispensable to his own interest that Diaz remain in office." The minister was also to let Diaz know that the *Yorktown* had been ordered from Panama "to watch for the reported filibuster."

With a pliant President installed in Nicaragua the Department of State drew up a convention determining the issues of national interest at stake in the country. Although it deferred action on a proposal from Diaz that a treaty should be made, or the Nicaraguan constitution amended, with a view to permitting the United States to "intervene in our [Nicaragua's] internal affairs in order to maintain peace and the existence of lawful government," it took steps to put the affairs of that country on a positive basis. In the convention signed on June 6, 1911, Nicaragua agreed to make a contract providing for the refunding of the external debt, to settle all claims, and to establish its finances on "a sound and stable basis." It promised to make the refunding loan a first lien on its customs duties and not to alter charges affecting the import and export of goods without the approval of the Government of the United States. Full and detailed statements respecting fiscal operations under the contract were to be made periodically to the Department of State in Washington and at other times on request. The manager of the customs, "who need not be a Nicaraguan," was to be chosen with the approval of the President of the United States and afforded full protection in the discharge of his functions. As a precaution it was added: "The Government of the United States, should the circumstances require, will in turn afford such protection as it may find requisite."

The program, of course, was realized largely through private operations. Owing to the failure of the treaty to receive the consent of the Senate, Brown Bros. and Co. and J. & W. Seligman and Co., the bankers who were to lend $15,000,000 to Nicaragua upon the ratification of the treaty, entered into the Treasury Bills Agreement of September 1, 1911 with the Nicaraguan Government. Under this agreement the bankers obtained virtual control over the fiscal structure of the country. The bills issued under the agreement were to be a lien and charge upon the customs duties which were not to be altered without the agreement of the bankers. The collector general was to be nominated by the bankers, approved by the Secretary of State of the United States, and "appointed by the President of Nicaragua." Notwithstanding the fact that they had in President Diaz a man of their own choosing, the American interests were taking no chances. Mr. Clifford D. Ham, an American citizen, was for this reason chosen to serve as Collector General of Customs. He served in that capacity from December, 1911, until June, 1928. His successor, Mr. Irving A. Lindberg, had been Deputy Collector General since 1912. The bankers also were given an option to secure at par 51 per cent of the shares of a National Bank which was to be established under the Treasury Bills Agreement and the supplementary monetary law, enacted at the suggestion and under the supervision of the bankers in March, 1912. The bank, with a paid-in capital of $100,000, all subscribed by the Nicaraguan Government, was incorporated under the laws of Connecticut as the Banco Nacional de Nicaragua. It opened for business in August, 1912, with its management under the supervision of the bankers. How intimately associated this bank was with the fiscal structure of Nicaragua may be seen in the powers possessed by the bank. It had the exclusive right to issue notes which were legal tender; and it was made the fiscal and disbursing agent for the government and the depository of government funds.

The bankers also became the authorized agents of Nicaragua for the purpose of reaching a settlement with the Ethelburga Syndicate, prior creditors of the government; and under their authority settlements with the English and French bondholders were effected in June, 1912. Among other provisions of a supplementary loan agreement of March 26, 1912, the bankers secured further liens on customs duties, and an option to purchase 51 per cent of the stock of the Pacific Railway, together with its steamship lines, which was to be reorganized and incorporated in the United States with the management under the control of the bankers. Bankers' commissions and the customary interest charges were charged against all funds advanced.

Thus the foundations for the security of American interests in Nicaragua were firmly laid by diplomatic and naval action on the part of the United States Government. An official of an American mining company was established as President of Nicaragua. A constitution incorporating economic principles common to the conduct of business enterprise in the United States and appropriate legal methods for securing enforcement were adopted with the counsel and supervision of the State Department. Provisions were made for stabilizing Nicaraguan finances, introducing American investment bankers into the financial scene, guaranteeing the payment of American claims against the government of Nicaragua, and affording security for American citizens operating in Nicaragua. Customs duties on exports and imports were subjected to the control of the State Department. A tribunal, composed of one Nicaraguan and two Americans, was instituted to pass upon claims lodged against the government of Nicaragua by foreigners, including American citizens and concerns. Finally, the armed forces of the United States were employed on executive order to facilitate the transactions which led to the settlement satisfactory to the State Department. The fact that the Senate of the United States three times rejected the Loan Convention and refused to accept the final adjustment did not prevent the State Department and the President from realizing the major and more substantial portion of their program, in spite of many vicissitudes. Thus in a single case, relatively detailed but actually given in bare outline and limited to a brief time, is presented a concrete picture of national interest in commercial expansion, as conceived by the Department of State, and a description of the technique employed in its realization. . . .

Safeguarding the Canal

SAMUEL FLAGG BEMIS

DISCERNING students have blamed Taft and more particularly his Secretary of State, Philander C. Knox, for carrying the Roosevelt Corollary toward a more active and less disinterested intervention, notably in Nicaragua. They have stigmatized this action with the derogatory phrase of "dollar diplomacy," taking their cue from some frank avowals of the President that he considered it a most useful function of government to advance and protect the legitimate trade and investments of United States citizens in foreign countries, particularly in areas of competition like China, where they served to chaperon or neutralize imperialistic designs. In the course of this study we shall have more to say of dollar diplomacy. It was not designed to profit private interests. It was intended rather to support the foreign policy of the United States; in the instance of Latin America, to support the Roosevelt Corollary to the Monroe Doctrine. In these interventions in Central America and the Caribbean there was also a certain characteristic missionary impulse to help the people themselves, willy-nilly, by stabilizing their governments and economies.

Zelaya resented the diplomatic intrusion of the United States and Mexico because it interfered with his own ambition to unify all Central America under his mastery by overturning governments in the neighboring states and putting in his puppets. He had consistently opposed the whole movement toward Central American solidarity by diplomatic and by constitutional processes. In his resentment he had also been very hostile to American private capital legally invested in Nicaragua. For example, he wished to cancel the United States-Nicaragua Concession, a mining property owned by a Pittsburgh corporation which represented the principal American private capital in the Isthmian republic. He wanted to take back this concession and sell it

From *The Latin American Policy of the United States,* copyright, 1943, by Samuel Flagg Bemis. Reprinted by permission of Harcourt, Brace & World, Inc.

over again to somebody else for better terms. As a Pennsylvania lawyer and counsel to the corporation, Philander C. Knox, before he became Secretary of State, had himself passed upon the validity of the contract. It became clear that the Nicaraguan dictator was the greatest single menace to the whole treaty structure, as well as to American private contracts; that the Washington conventions would have little effect in stabilizing and uniting the five republics as long as Zelaya remained President of Nicaragua. There is no evidence to show that President Taft and Secretary Knox were more charitable toward the ambitious Isthmian general because of the latter's high-handed violation of these concessions, like Castro in Venezuela; on the contrary! Nor did reports of Zelaya's plans to make secret advances to Japan for a canal treaty ingratiate the dictator with the United States Government.

United States intervention in Nicaragua followed a revolution which broke out in 1909 against Zelaya in Bluefields and had at least the sympathy of the company which operated the United States-Nicaragua Concession. Zelaya's forces captured two United States citizens, named Cannon and Groce, professional dynamiters, who were laying mines in the San Juan River for the revolutionists, and executed them after court martial. They held commissions in the revolutionary army and considered themselves prisoners of war. President Taft made this the occasion for dismissing Zelaya's representative at Washington and landing marines to protect foreign nationals and property at Bluefields. Secretary Knox declared that the United States was convinced "that the revolution represented the ideals and will of a majority of the Nicaraguan people more truthfully than does the government of President Zelaya." As a result of this intervention Zelaya was overthrown. President Porfirio Díaz of Mexico, who had cooperated throughout with the United States to bring stability to Central America, advised Zelaya to quit. Soon a revolution in Mexico dethroned Díaz himself and left the United States as the sole sponsor of the precarious regional peace structure.

After a confusing interlude of shifting personnel in the revolutionary Nicaraguan government, Adolfo Díaz, who had been secretary of the United States-Nicaragua Concession emerged in 1911 with the assistance of American diplomacy as "constitutional" President, recognized by the United States. Secretary Knox negotiated with the new Government a treaty (the Knox-Castrillo convention), signed June 6, 1911, generally similar to the treaty of 1907 with the Dominican Republic, and identical to one that had just been signed with Honduras (January 10, 1911), for the purpose of refunding the debt of Nicaragua through new loans from New York bankers (Brown Brothers, J. and W. Seligman & Co.). This would have taken the old debt entirely out of the hands of an English syndicate, and put the new loan in a schedule of payment under an American receivership like that in the Dominican Republic. A separate executive agreement provided for a mixed commission to arbitrate the claims of American citizens against Nicaragua.

The Senate of the United States rejected both of these treaties, but the bankers, at the request of the Department of State and with its assistance, put through private contracts with Nicaragua which set up much the same sort of regime without treaty guaranties. On this basis they made a much smaller loan, $1,500,000 instead of $15,000,000, upon condition of securing control of the contemporaneously established National Bank of Nicaragua and the Nicaraguan state railways. Knox may have felt that he had the precedent behind him of Theodore Roosevelt's *modus vivendi* with the Dominican Republic after the Senate had first rejected the "protocol" of 1905; but unlike the Dominican example, the Senate never ratified the Knox treaties.

A new revolution against Adolfo Díaz's regime threatened to drift into the control of Zelaya's followers. If they should have gained control of the government, "all of the efforts of the State Department [says an historian of Central America] to place Nicaragua on her feet politically and financially would have been useless, and the interests of the New York bankers, who had undertaken their operations in the country at the express request of the United States Government, would be seriously imperiled." Accordingly, at the request of the Díaz Government the United States landed some 2,700 marines in 1912 and occupied the principal cities of the interior after a sharp engagement at Leon. From 1912 to 1933 (except for a brief interval following a trial withdrawal in 1925) a small force of United States marines maintained the Government of Nicaragua in office, supervised and policed elections, and trained up a Nicaraguan constabulary.

Thus fortified the government kept up payments on the old loans by the London bankers and the new loans of the New York bankers. Meanwhile, continued political agitation, crime, periodic revolts, disease, grasshopper plagues, and earthquakes worried, robbed, harassed, ravaged, devoured, and shook the already impoverished country and its people. The intervention of the United States was barely adequate to maintain elected governments in power and thus keep the pledged finances in order; it was not enough to regenerate Nicaragua as an effective protectorate had done in Cuba. Light as the intervention was, it was sufficient to arouse the animosity of other Latin American countries to whom Nicaraguan dissidents made their appeal. A full protectorate would not have been more hateful, and could have benefited the people much more.

After the failure of his financial treaties, Secretary Knox, alarmed at rumors of German interest in the Nicaraguan waterway, signed another treaty agreeing to pay Nicaragua $3,000,000 for an exclusive right of way for a canal, a naval base on the Gulf of Fonseca, and a ninety-nine-year lease of Great Corn and Little Corn Islands in the Caribbean near the Atlantic terminus of the route. This treaty was submitted to the Senate too late to get ratification before the end of the Taft Administration, but President Wilson took up the idea, with some modifications, and put it through, as we shall see in a later chapter.

It was one thing to build up, by cooperative measures short of actual military intervention, a structure of preventive diplomacy, designed to remove any justification for intervention by a non-American power in the Caribbean region. So Roosevelt and Root had done in Cuba and the Dominican Republic, in the latter instance with the implied mandate of the European powers, and this Roosevelt had rested on his famous Corollary. It was another step that Taft had taken under Knox's legal guidance: outright military intervention to safeguard the strategical interest of the United States in the Isthmian region. This smacked more of Roosevelt's intervention in Panama than it did of his diplomatic intervention in the Dominican Republic carried through under Root's guidance. By the same token, and other appearances (that of serving private interests), it created greater resentment both in Latin America and at home than did the Dominican receivership.

Intervention in Nicaragua and the occupation of that republic were certainly high-handed, uncalled for by any immediate exigency of foreign policy or national security, and actually contrary to the principles of the Washington conventions of 1907. Its effect, after the Senate rejected the Knox treaties of 1911, was to place the finances of that Isthmian country in the hands of private bankers for the next eight years. Their strict measures, alleviated by the Bryan-Chamorro Treaty ratified in 1916, and terminated by the Financial Plan of 1917, achieved the fiscal redemption of the country, but it is doubtful whether the local governments thus supported by United States marines furthered the concept of Central American confederation and union.

Knox would have imposed financial receiverships on Honduras and Guatemala too, if the Senate would have stood for it.

The Taft Administration took great pains to justify the Nicaraguan intervention constitutionally before Congress. Mr. J. Reuben Clark, Jr., Solicitor of the Department of State, compiled a long memorandum on *The Right to Protect Citizens in Foreign Countries by Landing Forces*, as established in international law and by United States precedent. Even after these arguments, the candid historian may be critical of the whole episode, but it certainly would be most unjust to attribute even the occupation of Nicaragua —cited so profusely as the standard illustration of the evils of dollar diplomacy—to the controlling power of private vested interests over the United States Government. Back of that intervention was an honest intent, at least, to stabilize and strengthen the international relations of Central America by substituting for Zelaya's focus of revolution and wars a truly representative and independent government and to further a union of all the Central American states on the foundation of the Washington conventions. The United States was interested in promoting this regional peace structure principally in order to remove any conceivable danger, even a remote one, of ultimate foreign intervention that might give military lodgment in the neighborhood of the Panama Canal, then advancing toward completion, or any possibility of a rival canal route falling under non-American influence.

Unfriendly foreign critics quickly used the phrase "dollar diplomacy" to suggest a deliberate design by the United States to dominate the nearest Latin American republics, even the whole Western Hemisphere, for the private profit of "Wall Street." While not losing sight for one moment of the

mistakes of foreign policy in the hands of the blundering Knox and Taft—
and it is fortunate that the United States did not have to confront under their
leadership any major crisis of diplomacy during the years 1909–1913—it is
only fair to say that dollar diplomacy was more an easily misusable journalistic
alliteration, alliterative unfortunately in all the principal languages of the
New World and western Europe, that easily lent itself to hateful propaganda
and exaggerated Yankeephobia, than it was a truthful characterization of the
protective foreign policy of the United States.

In their own uniquely inept way Taft and Knox were also following the
instinct and traditions of continental security rather than the lead of selfish
private interests. Nicaragua, like the Dominican Republic, like Panama, like
Haiti (where Woodrow Wilson was soon to send marines as well as to Santo
Domingo), was one of the states of the New World, indeed of the entire
world, where the least American capital was invested. It is a well-known fact
that before the First World War indigenous capital found more lucrative
employment in the United States than outside of its boundaries, that it was
only with difficulty that the Department of State was able to persuade bankers
to invest their funds for political purposes in foreign countries. The larger
holdings of capital invested abroad in the New World were in Cuba, where
"big business" had opposed intervention in 1898; in Mexico, where the
United States Government and public opinion have certainly been averse to
intervention for nearly a century; in Canada, and in the larger and more
stable republics of South America.

It seems to be an historical fact that the more capital a country of the New
World has accepted from private investors in the United States the less danger there has been of intervention. Such investments have brought a
wealth of good to Latin American countries, but in the large it is doubtful
whether they have been profitable to the economy of the United States, not
to mention the investors. This is because they have not been wholly safe.
They represented an overflow of luxury that the United States, unlike the
great powers of the Old World, had not been willing, with it deep continental instincts of nonintervention, to guarantee and to secure by the use of
force. But American diplomacy has always been sensitive to the strategical
requirements of continental security. This, and not selfish private interests,
really explains both the Roosevelt Corollary and the dollar diplomacy of Taft.
It also explains in large measure the Latin American policy of Woodrow
Wilson.

ADOLPH A. BERLE, JR., ON CARIBBEAN INTERVENTIONS

"Many of our own major mistakes, indeed, in this hemisphere have been due
more to the fear of European domination than to any desire to increase the area
of our territory. Conspicuous among these were the interventions beginning at the
time of the Panama Canal incident, the Nicaraguan occupation, and the occupations of Haiti and Santo Domingo. It has been customary, particularly among
students who hold the Marxist view of history, to ascribe these to desire to protect

American capital, which thus became the forerunner of imperialism. Yet as the history becomes increasingly clear, and as the documents are more completely available, the Marxian student finds that the facts do not bear him out. In many cases the intervention of American capital in Central America and in the West Indian republics was undertaken not at the instance of American capitalists seeking outlet for their funds. It was undertaken at the direct instance of the American Government; and the motive appears to have been the fear lest European capital, affected with European politics, might find foothold on this side of the Atlantic. An example may be found in the occupations of Haiti and Santo Domingo. In each case American banks had purchased the control of the banks previously serving those island countries; but the documents today make it clear that the American financiers did so rather unwillingly, at the direct urging of the Department of State; and that the Department of State urged the American financial moves as a means of eliminating European financial moves. It may also be noted that alone among the great powers of the world, having accomplished that objective, public sentiment in the United States swiftly mobilized against the continuance of the occupations, they were withdrawn freely and without reserve, largely in consequence, first, of the continuous urging of the present Under Secretary, Mr. Sumner Welles, then a staff member of the Department of State, and finally, as a part of the broad policy laid out and executed by Secretary Hull. The final result has been the firmer establishment of independent nations who owe their safety not to their military force but to the strength of the pan-American idea." From Address of Assistant Secretary of State Adolph Berle, Jr., on "The Policy of the United States in Latin America," delivered at the Academy of Political Science, New York City, May 3, 1939. Department of State, *Press Releases*, XX, No. 501, Publication 1328, p. 378.

Since the turn of the century and the appearance of the new order of sea power the Caribbean and Central American areas had become increasingly important as primary concerns of American defensive strategy, expressed in what I have been designating as the Panama Policy of the United States. In that policy, itself a major chapter of Latin American policy, the Roosevelt Corollary now held a paramount place. Wilson and Bryan had no idea of repudiating it; rather they strove to strengthen influence and control in these regions in order to remove further than ever justification for any European intervention. All this they covered with a sincere Wilsonian zeal for saving the people from bad government, tyranny, and economic exploitation in order that they might be made fit and stable for self-government, liberty, and the pursuit of happiness under protection of the United States, as in the case of Cuba. All this the missionaries of Democracy desired in order that "benighted" peoples might be saved from themselves for themselves.

The new missionaries professed to be more jealous of the power of special interests over national interests, of the baleful "dollar diplomacy" which they imputed to their less moral predecessors; but their pious endeavors were never in conflict with strategic demands for defense of the Continental Republic which always boxed the compass of the Latin American policy of the United

States. In pursuing their idealistic and strategic purposes they traveled farther along the pathway of protective imperialism than did their precursors.

William Jennings Bryan had a homeopathic cure for the ills of dollar diplomacy, a putative remedy which was a quarter of a century in advance of his time, like so many of Bryan's ideas good and bad. Doubtless he did not know about proposals of his predecessors Seward, Fish, and Blaine pointing in the same direction. He proposed that the United States Government be a "modern good Samaritan" and loan enough money to Nicaragua, or indeed to any Latin American republic that was in serious trouble with private foreign creditors, to free them from their debts.

"They [the Latin American republics] are now compelled to pay a high rate of interest and to sell their bonds at a discount. . . . If the United States offers to loan them its credit to the extent that such a loan is safe, the bonds could be made to draw four and a half per cent, which would be an immediate saving to them in the way of interest and the difference of a [per] cent and a half between their bonds and ours could go into a sinking fund which would, in a reasonable time, at compound interest, pay off their debts and leave them free. We could, in this way, relieve them of the debts which embarrass them, and enable them to construct such railroads as are imperatively necessary for the development of their countries.

"The second advantage would be that *the plan would give our country such an increased influence . . . that we could prevent revolutions, promote education, and advance stable and just government. . . .*

". . . We would in the end profit, negatively, by not having to incur expense in guarding our own and other foreign interests there, and, positively, by the increase of trade that would come from development and from the friendship which would follow the conferring of the benefits named."

6

The Taft-Katsura Agreement:

WAS IT A SURRENDER TO JAPAN?

IN THE summer of 1905, Secretary of War William H. Taft, while en route to the Philippines, stopped in Tokyo where he talked to Count Katsura, the Japanese Prime Minister. Their conversation was incorporated in an "agreed memorandum" which Taft sent to President Roosevelt who promptly and enthusiastically gave it his approval. The whole matter was kept secret and did not become public knowledge until almost twenty years later. Three items were touched upon by Taft and Katsura. In the first "Count Katsura . . . positively stated that Japan does not harbor any aggressive designs whatever on the Philippines;" in the second he suggested that the best way to preserve peace in eastern Asia was by "an understanding between the three governments of Japan, the United States, and Great Britain" and that American support could be expected since "the people of the United States were as fully in accord with the policy of Japan and Great Britain;" and in the third "Secretary Taft fully admitted . . . that, in his personal opinion, the establishment by Japanese troops of a suzerainty over Korea . . . wes the logical result of the present [Russo-Japanese] war and would directly contribute to permanent peace in the East." What was the meaning of this agreement? Why did the Roosevelt administration approve it? Was it a part of a specific Far Eastern policy?

The earliest interpretation, which has since become the one most generally accepted, was advanced by Tyler Dennett in the article which appears below. It was Dennett, a professor of history at Johns Hopkins University and at Williams College and subsequently the president of Williams, who first discovered the document in the Roosevelt papers. According to Dennett, the agreement was an essential part of Roosevelt's Far Eastern policy. It was in the nature of a quid pro quo. In return for American acquiescence in Japanese hegemony over Korea, Japan pledged that she would not interfere in the Philippines. Only in this way could Roosevelt safeguard the islands. His mili-

tary and naval forces were inadequate for the islands' defense and, more importantly, the American people would not support a war in Asia even if it was to defend an American possession. His only alternative was to seek the good will of the nation most likely to attack the Philippines by acquiescing in that nation's expansion.

Raymond A. Esthus, who teaches history at Tulane University, disagrees with Dennett's interpretation. He does not consider the agreement as part of a broader policy, nor does he see Taft as an emissary of Roosevelt sent to arrange a quid pro quo. Historians, he claims, have mistaken the term "agreed memorandum" for "agreement." No agreement was reached or intended. The conversation revolved around Korea and the Philippines not by preconceived designed but most naturally. Korea was at that time Japan's chief problem; Taft, a former Governor General of the Philippines, was, at the time of the conversation, Secretary of the War Department which administered the islands. Indeed, Taft mentioned specifically that he had no mandate from the President to discuss Far Eastern affairs. He was acting entirely on his own. The President did, of course, approve Taft's position. Roosevelt himself believed that Japanese possession of Korea would be better for Korea and for all of Asia, and he welcomed the statement by Japan that she did not covet the Philippines.

President Roosevelt's Secret Pact with Japan

TYLER DENNETT

On July 29, 1905, Count Katsura, Prime Minister of Japan and temporarily in charge of the Ministry of Foreign Affairs in the place of Baron Komura, who was on his way to the Portsmouth Peace Conference, effected an exchange of opinion with a personal representative of President Roosevelt relative to the cooperation of the United States with Great Britain and Japan in the Far East. At the request of Katsura the nature of the agreement was regarded as so secret that it was not disclosed even to Lloyd C. Griscom, the American Minister in Tokio. An "agreed memorandum" of the understanding was drawn up and submitted to President Roosevelt, who on July 31 replied: "Your conversation with Count Katsura absolutely correct in every respect. Wish you would state to Katsura that I confirm every word you said." We have therefore in this memorandum the text of perhaps the most remarkable "executive agreement" in the history of the foreign relations of the United States.

The following is the text, after necessary deletions had been made . . .

July 29, 1905.

From Tokio,
    To *****
        Washington.
The following is agreed memorandum of conversation between Prime Minister of Japan and myself:

"Count Katsura and [Taft] had a long and confidential conversation on the morning of July 27. Among other topics of conversation the following views were exchanged regarding the question of the Philippine Islands, of Korea and of the maintenance of general peace in the Far East.

"First, in speaking of some pro-Russians in America who would have the public believe that the victory of Japan would be a certain prelude to her aggression in the direction of the Philippine Islands, [Taft] observed that Japan's only interest in the Philippines would be, in his opinion, to have these islands governed by a strong and friendly nation like the United States, and not have them placed either under the misrule of the natives, yet unfit for self-government, or in the hands of some unfriendly European power. Count Katsura confirmed in the strongest terms the correctness of his views on the point and positively stated that Japan does not harbor any aggressive designs whatever on the Philippines; adding that all the in-

Tyler Dennett, "President Roosevelt's Secret Pact with Japan," Current History, XXI, 1924, pp. 15–21. Reprinted by permission of Current History.

sinuations of the yellow peril type are nothing more or less than malicious and clumsy slanders calculated to do mischief to Japan.

"Second, Count Katsura observed that the maintenance of general peace in the extreme East forms the fundamental principle of Japan's international policy. Such being the case, he was very anxious to exchange views with [Taft] as to the most effective means for insuring this principle. In his own opinion, the best, and in fact the only, means for accomplishing the above object would be to form good understanding between the three Governments of Japan, the United States and Great Britain, which have common interest in upholding the principle of eminence. The Count well understands the traditional policy of the United States in this respect and perceives fully the impossibilities of their entering into a formal alliance of such nature with any foreign nation, but in view of our common interests he couldn't see why some good understanding or an alliance in practice, if not in name, should not be made between those three nations in so far as respects the affairs in the Far East. With such understanding firmly formed, general peace in these regions would be easily maintained, to the great benefit of all powers concerned. [Taft] said that it was difficult, indeed impossible, for the President of the United States of America to enter even to any understanding amounting in effect to a confidential informal agreement, without the consent of the Senate, but that he felt sure that without any agreement at all the people of the United States were so fully in accord with the policy of Japan and Great Britain in the maintenance of peace in the Far East that, whatever occasion arose, appropriate action of the Government of the United States, in conjunction with Japan and Great Britain, for such a purpose could be counted on by them quite as confidently as if the United States were under treaty obligations to take.

"Third, in regard to the Korean question Count Katsura observed that Korea being the direct cause of our war with Russia, it is a matter of absolute importance to Japan that a complete solution of the peninsula question should be made as the logical consequence of the war. If left to herself after the war, Korea will certainly draw back to her habit of improvidently entering into any agreements or treaties with other powers, thus resuscitating the same international complications as existed before the war. In view of the foregoing circumstances, Japan feels absolutely constrained to take some definite step with a view to precluding the possibility of Korea falling back into her former condition and of placing us again under the necessity of entering upon another foreign war. [Taft] fully admitted the justness of the Count's observations and remarked to the effect that, in his personal opinion, the establishment by Japanese troops of a suzerainty over Korea to the extent of requiring that Korea enter into no foreign treaties without the consent of Japan was the logical result of the present war and would directly contribute to permanent peace in the East. His judgment was that President Roosevelt would concur in his views in this regard, although he had no authority to give assurance of this. Indeed, [Taft] added that he felt much delicacy in advancing the views he did, for he had no mandate for the purpose from the President, * * *. He could not, however, in view of Count Katsura's courteous desire to discuss the questions, decline to express his opinions * * *, and he would forward to Mr. Root and the President a memorandum of the conversation. Count Katsura said that he would transmit the same, confidentially, to Baron Komura."

Prime Minister quite anxious for interview. If I have spoken too freely or inaccurately or unwittingly, I know you can and will correct it. Do not want to "butt in," but, under the circumstances, difficult to avoid statement, and so told truth as I believe it. Count Katsura especially requested that our conversation be confined to you and the President, so have not advised Griscom. Is there any objection? If necessary, under your direction, Foreign Office can give him a copy.

[Taft]

Since the announcement by the writer of the terms of this understanding at the Institute of Politics at Williamstown in August it has been argued that this document did not constitute a "secret agreement." That it was secret is evident from the fact that it was concealed even from Griscom at the time and that its existence was unknown not only in the officially published records of the Department of State, but also unknown to more than half a dozen people in the United States until the recent disclosure. That it was an agreement is clear from the text itself. This text, a photostat of which is given herewith, was found in the Roosevelt private papers which are deposited for safekeeping, subject to the control of the Roosevelt family, in the Library of Congress. The writer knows of at least two other copies of the memorandum. There can be no possible question as to its authenticity. The text reproduced with this article appears to have been a copy of the first translation from the cipher dispatch, and it is possible that two or three words were mangled in either transmission or in decoding. It would appear, however, that certain awkward or unidiomatic expressions in the text were due to the fact that the memorandum was probably drawn up by a Japanese.

The document contains three important paragraphs to which are added some sentences of explanation indicating not only that Katsura wished the agreement to be kept very secret, but also that he took the initiative in effecting the conversation. So insistent, in fact, was the Japanese Prime Minister that, though President Roosevelt's agent was reluctant to enter the conversation, it seemed less awkward to do so than not to do so.

In the first paragraph Count Katsura is made to state: "Japan does not harbor any aggressive designs whatever on the Philippines." This assurance was of importance to the United States Government at that time. The Roosevelt papers clearly reveal that Japanese intentions with respect to the Philippines had given the President no little concern in the course of the preceding six months. This alarm had also extended to Hawaii, since a few months before the President had even gone so far as to suggest to the War Department that additional troops ought to be sent to Honolulu. Roosevelt, while consistently preferring a Japanese to a Russian victory in the existing war, repeatedly expressed the fear that the astonishing triumphs of Japanese arms might turn the heads of the Japanese Government and lead to subsequent alarming aggressions. He felt, on the other hand, that a Russian victory would be the certain prelude to the dismemberment of China and, after weighing the probabilities, concluded that Japan was both more reliable and less to be feared than the discredited Czarist Government. Count Katsura's statement therefore tended to confirm Roosevelt's previous conclusions and to justify his support of Japan. This self-denying declaration by Katsura also doubtless had an important influence upon Roosevelt's action three weeks later at Portsmouth. It will be recalled that when the Portsmouth Conference reached a deadlock the President stepped in and became the mediator of the settlement. Without the assurances which Katsura had so formally given, the President's action at Portsmouth might have been different.

THE ANGLO-JAPANESE ALLIANCE

The terms of the second Anglo-Japanese Alliance were announced about two weeks after the date of this conversation. Probably the terms of the alliance were in process of negotiation in London at the same time. This fact is important, because in the second paragraph of the memorandum Katsura specifically asks for "a good understanding or an alliance in practice if not in name" of the United States, Great Britain and Japan. In other words, the United States Government was invited to become a secret member of the second Anglo-Japanese alliance. To this invitation the American replied, and the reply was fully endorsed by Roosevelt, that

he felt sure that without any agreement at all the people of the United States were so fully in accord with the policy of Japan and Great Britain in the maintenance of peace in the Far East that whenever the occasion arose appropriate action of the Government of the United States, in conjunction with Japan and Great Britain, for such a purpose could be counted on by them quite as confidently as if the United States were under treaty obligation to take [it].

The preamble of the second Anglo-Japanese alliance declared that the compact was designed for the maintenance of the peace of the Far East. The inference is fairly conclusive that President Roosevelt was prepared to give and did give his personal pledge that the United States Government during his administration would act, so far as he could lead, as an unsigned member of this alliance. At least we may say that, if a treaty to that effect, to expire on March 4, 1909, had been formally negotiated and ratified by the Senate, the result would have been no different.

There is ample evidence that President Roosevelt did not share the traditional fear of entangling alliances. Indeed there is documentary evidence that Roosevelt was in favor of a triple alliance of Great Britain, Japan and the United States. Throughout the Russo-Japanese War he had acted in close cooperation with Great Britain and Japan, though independently, and there is reason to believe that he had assumed, so far as he was able, the same obligations to aid Japan that Great Britain had assumed in the first Anglo-Japanese alliance. The evidence for this assertion is in the process of preparation and will be published within a few months.

During the Russo-Japanese War the late George Kennan was in Japan as a correspondent. He was on particularly intimate and confidential terms with the highest Japanese officials. Early in 1905 he wrote to Roosevelt, with whom he was accustomed to correspond, and proposed that the United States ought to enter an alliance with Great Britain and Japan. Kennan was merely voicing an opinion which had been current in London and Tokio for at least six years. I do not find it difficult to suppose that his letter to Roosevelt was written with the knowledge of Count Katsura. Under date of May 6, 1905, Roosevelt replied:

> As to what you say about the alliance, the trouble is, my dear Mr. Kennan, that you are talking academically. Have you followed some of my experiences in endeavoring to get treaties through the Senate? I might just as well strive for the moon as for such a policy as you indicate. Mind you, I personally entirely agree with you. But if you have followed the difficulty I have had even in getting such obvious things done as those connected with Panama and Santo Domingo, you would get some faint idea of the absolute impossibility of carrying out any such policy as you indicate in your letter.

Again I have no difficulty in supposing that the contents of the above paragraph was known to Katsura, so that, when he asked for the conversation at the end of July, he was fairly sure of his ground.

THE KOREAN QUESTION

The third paragraph of the memorandum related to Korea. When invited by Katsura to express an opinion as to what policy Japan ought to pursue in the peninsula, the American is made to state that "in his personal opinion, the establishment by Japanese troops of a suzerainty over Korea to the extent of requiring that Korea enter into no foreign treaties without the consent of Japan was the logical result of the present war and would directly contribute to permanent peace in the East." This opinion was also endorsed by the President.

This statement had been prefaced by one in which the American was led to assent to the Japanese claims that "Korea was the direct cause of the war." This is a very broad claim which has usually been accepted, but which does not appear to have been supported by the facts. We should prefer to say that the direct cause of the war was the control of Manchuria and that the indirect cause was the control of China. This very generous and uncritical assent to the Japanese claim would appear to have been phrased by Katsura, and the phrasing is one of the reasons for inferring that the document itself is the product of Japanese diplomatic craftsmanship.

The discussion of the paragraph about Korea might easily lead into a detailed investigation of the Korean question. Indeed, unless we are familiar with these details we are almost sure to reach an unsound conclusion about the rightness or wisdom of this official acquiescence of Roosevelt in the Japanese policy in Korea. The writer of the memorandum again reveals himself as a rather clever diplomat. He separated in the text the two paragraphs which are related in thought. Perhaps it was felt that the document would read better if the exchange of opinion in regard to Korea was not made to follow immediately after the conversation about the Philippines. That there was in the mind of the Japanese statesman a quid pro quo is fairly evident. Indeed the assertion was made in the Japanese newspaper Kokumin on Oct. 4, 1905, that there was such an exchange and that in return for the Japanese declaration in regard to the Philippines, the United States Government had agreed to allow Japan a free hand in Korea. Speaking of the agreement as a whole the Kokumin, which was regarded as the mouthpiece of the Japanese Government, continued:

In fact, it is a Japanese-Anglo-American alliance. We may be sure that when once England became our ally America also became a party to the agreement. Owing to the peculiar national conditions, America cannot make any open alliance, but we should bear in mind that America is our ally, though bound by no formal treaty; we firmly believe that America, under the leadership of the world statesman, President Roosevelt, will deal with her Oriental problems in cooperation with Japan and Great Britain.

This editorial, in the light of the facts now known, has rather an unpleasant sound and suggests that Japan felt that she had in fact outstepped the American diplomats. It may be said in explanation of the American position that there is no evidence whatever that President Roosevelt supposed that as the agent of the United States he was trading Korea for the Philippines. About six months before he had reached his conclusion about Korea. In a note to Secretary Hay at the end of January we find a postscript in the President's own handwriting in which he remarked: "We cannot possibly interfere for the Koreans against Japan. They could not strike one blow in their own defense." This characteristic conclusion about Korea was fully in accord with American policy for twenty-five years. If there was a quid pro quo in the agreement of July 29, it was merely that in return for a statement of a conclusion which had been reached six months earlier and purely on the merits of the case the Japanese Government had been led to make the most formal declaration that it would not interfere in the Philippines.

THE RUSSIAN DANGER

On the other hand, we may say this: President Roosevelt felt that a quick reconciliation between Japan and Russia was possible. Indeed, he foresaw the possibility of an alliance. A Russo-Japanese alliance appeared to him something to be dreaded. It was therefore a cardinal point in his policy to treat Japan so well that she would find it preferable to associate herself with Great Britain and the United States rather than with Russia. The wisdom of this policy, from an American point of view, can hardly be challenged. It is a significant fact that within a few months after the agreement of Aug. 29, 1905, was clumsily repudiated or abrogated by Secretary Knox in 1910, when he put forward the proposal for the neutralization of the Manchurian railways, Japan actually entered into a secret treaty with Russia which appears to have been directed against the United States. Such a treaty between Japan and Russia would have been extremely unlikely if the Roosevelt policy had been continued.

Unquestionably the Roosevelt agreement is exposed to serious criticism. Yet, if it overlooks the attendant circumstances and fails to consider what would have been their alternative choices, such criticism goes wide of the mark. President Roosevelt believed that when Russia was defeated in the Far East Japan conferred a benefit upon American interests. The distinctive feature of Roosevelt's Far Eastern policy was that he did not ignore the implied obligation. He was prepared, in return, to help Japan—he was prepared to have the United States make some payment for the advantages which Americans enjoyed in Eastern Asia. It has been rare to find American statesmen who would follow President Roosevelt in this very honorable principle. Perhaps the most conspicuous characteristic of American policy in the Far East, viewed in the large, has been the desire to get something for nothing. Possibly in assenting to the agreed memorandum he displayed a willingness to pay too much. He really assented to something like a blank check, for he did not have the foresight to require a bill of particulars as to the measures which would be taken under the second Anglo-Japanese Alliance to maintain the peace of the Far East—measures which turned out to be inimical to American interests. However, the fact that the diplomacy was bungled does not affect the fact that the principle of statesmanship was sound.

The Taft-Katsura Agreement—
Reality or Myth?

RAYMOND A. ESTHUS

In August 1924, Tyler Dennett revealed, before a meeting of the Institute of Politics at Williamstown, Massachusetts, what appeared to be still another example of that "old diplomacy" which had lately come into considerable disrepute. While searching in the Roosevelt papers at the Library of Congress, Dennett had come across an "agreed memorandum" of a conversation of July 27, 1905, between the secretary of war, William Howard Taft, and the Japanese premier, Tarō Katsura. Dennett was so sure that he had uncovered

Raymond A. Esthus, "The Taft-Katsura Agreement—Reality or Myth?" *Journal of Modern History*, XXXI, 1959, pp. 46–51. Reprinted by permission of the University of Chicago Press.

something of first-rate significance that he had asked permission from the secretary of state, Charles Evans Hughes, to make the document public. Hughes had thereupon asked Taft, who raised no objection to the publication of the text. It was shortly thereafter that Dennett read the document to the Institute of Politics. In the same year he published it in an article in *Current History* entitled "President Roosevelt's Secret Pact with Japan."

The interpretation which Dennett gave the "agreed memorandum"—and the interpretation which has been generally accepted since—is that it represented a secret bargain in *Realpolitik*. The terms were simple, yet fraught with all that cynical *sang-froid* which presumably characterized pre-war European diplomacy: Japan renounced any aggressive designs on the Philippine Islands in return for America's acquiescence in Japan's subjugation of Korea. The fact that Dennett deleted the names of sender and recipient from the memorandum added to the impression that it was a mysterious bargain conceived *sub rosa*. Here, it seemed, was a salient example of that shrewd realism which characterized Theodore Roosevelt's thrust into world politics.

Those scholars who have studied Roosevelt would probably agree that his diplomacy contained a strong element of realism which could have easily encompassed such a secret pact. Furthermore, at the time Taft visited Japan the atmosphere in the Far East was heavy with international intrigue. The stage was well set for a typical Rooseveltian diplomatic maneuver. It is all the more perplexing to the historian, therefore, to find evidence indicating that perhaps there was no such "secret pact" or "Taft-Katsura agreement." Such evidence does exist in the "agreed memorandum" itself, in the Roosevelt papers, and in the records of the department of state. Since the "Taft-Katsura agreement" has become a standard item in the history textbooks of the day, it seems worthwhile to re-examine the validity of Dennett's interpretation.

The Taft-Katsura conversation took place against the backdrop of world-shaking developments in the Far East. Just two months before the secretary's arrival in Tokyo the Japanese navy had sent the Russian Baltic fleet to the bottom of the sea, and in the subsequent weeks Roosevelt had taken steps to bring the belligerents to the peace table. While the president was thus engaged, Taft visited Japan on his way to the Philippine Islands. Japanese leaders were at that time wrestling with the difficult problem of Korea. The conflicting interests of Japan and Russia in the Hermit Kingdom had been one of the major causes of the war, and the Katsura ministry was anxious to regularize some measure of control over Korea, at least to the point of establishing a protectorate. It was not unusual, therefore, that Katsura took the occasion of Taft's visit to gain reassurance regarding the policy of the United States. The fact that Taft headed the war department rather than the state department doubtless did not trouble Japanese leaders. In the land of the samurai tradition a war minister's views on questions of foreign relations were considered of no mean importance.

During the long—and now famous—conversation between Taft and Katsura on July 27, it was but natural that one of the topics of discussion was the Philippine Islands. Taft had won distinction there as governor general, the islands were then under his administration as secretary of war, and indeed the primary purpose of his journey to the Far East was to visit the Philippines. It appears from the text of the agreed memorandum that Taft brought up the subject, remarking that some pro-Russians in the United States would have the public believe that the victory of Japan would be a certain prelude to her aggression in the direction of the Philippines. Taft ventured his opinion—doubtless hoping that Katsura would concur—that Japan's only interest in the Philippines would be to have the islands governed by a strong and friendly nation like the United States. Katsura did not disappoint him. The premier said he would confirm in the strongest terms the correctness of Taft's views and stated categorically that Japan did not harbor any aggressive designs whatever on the Philippines.

The text of the memorandum does not indicate that the question of Japan's policy *vis-à-vis* the Philippines was discussed in connection with the policy of the United States regarding Korea. After giving his assurances to Taft regarding the islands, Katsura turned the discussion to a general consideration of means to insure peace in the Far East following the conclusion of the war. In his opinion, he said, the only effective way to accomplish that would be to form a good understanding between the governments of Japan, the United States, and Great Britain. Katsura said that he understood that the traditional policy of the United States made it impossible for it to enter a formal alliance, but he thought "an alliance in practice if not in name" should be made between the three nations concerning the affairs of the Far East. To this Taft replied that the people of the United States were so fully in accord with the policy of Japan and Great Britain in the maintenance of peace in the Far East that co-operation could be counted on by those nations quite as confidently as if the United States were under treaty obligations.

Finally the discussion turned to the question of Korea. Katsura stated that it was of absolute importance to Japan that a complete solution of the peninsular question should be made as the logical consequence of the war. If left to herself after the war, Korea would certainly draw back to her old habit of entering into agreements with other powers, thus confronting Japan with the same complications that existed before the war. In view of this, he said, Japan felt constrained to take some definite steps to preclude that possibility. Katsura was doubtless trying to draw Taft out on the question, and his efforts met with success. The secretary stated that it was his personal opinion that the establishment by Japanese troops of a suzerainty over Korea to the extent of requiring that Korea enter into no foreign treaties without the consent of Japan was the logical result of the war and would contribute to the permanent peace of the Far East. Taft said further that he believed President Roosevelt would concur in his views, though he added that he had no authority to give assurance of this. He then went on to explain that he felt much delicacy in advancing the views he did, for he had no mandate for the purpose from the president. Furthermore, since his departure from Washington Elihu Root had been appointed secretary of state, and he might thus be trespassing on another's department.

Following the conversation an "agreed memorandum" was drawn up, presumably by Katsura, embodying the views exchanged. There was apparently nothing unusual about the writing of such a memorandum. When Taft visited Japan again in 1907 a similar memorandum was drawn up of the conversation he had with Premier Kimmochi Saionji. On that occasion Saionji gave the same assurances to Taft regarding the Philippines that had been forthcoming from Katsura in 1905. It has never been alleged, however, that a secret pact was concluded in 1907. In form the documents are essentially the same. Neither was signed by the parties and neither gives any indication that it represents a binding instrument. Internal evidence alone would seem to show that the memoranda were simply records of conversations. In his report to Root, Taft referred to the memorandum of 1905 as an "agreed memorandum of conversation." This did not mean that the memorandum was an "agreement," but that the parties "agreed" that the memorandum accurately recorded the conversation. The text itself states nothing about commitments, but merely says "the following views were exchanged."

Taft's reports to Root and Roosevelt make it clear that he had not gone to Japan with any instructions to make a secret agreement, nor even with any instructions regarding entering into conversations with Japanese leaders. On the contrary, it appears that Taft was somewhat reluctantly pushed into an exchange of views by Katsura. In his report to Root, after giving the text of the memorandum, he explained:

Prime Minister quite anxious for interview. If I have spoken too freely or inaccurately or unwittingly, I know you can and will correct it. Do not want to "butt in," but under the circumstances, difficult to avoid statement and so told truth as I believe it.

To Roosevelt he wrote:

I sent Mr. Root from Tokio a long cable concerning a conversation which I had with Count Katsura. They were anxious that it should be sent and I did not know but it might help you in your conference with Komura. They sought the interview.

These reports show that there is no basis in fact for the assumption that is frequently made that in July 1905 Taft was "Roosevelt's emissary" and that he was sent to Japan to negotiate an agreement. Moreover, nothing in the reports suggests the conclusion of any pact, agreement, or any other form of binding commitment.

It is, of course, true that Roosevelt concurred in Taft's views and so informed the Japanese. When the reports arrived in Washington, Root was away from the capital; but Roosevelt promptly cabled: "Your conversation with Count Katsura absolutely correct in every respect. Wish you would state to Katsura that I confirm every word you have said." In giving this assurance to Katsura, however, the president was not necessarily responding to the premier's offer of nonaggression. He was reiterating a policy which had been decided upon definitively many months previously. Within a fortnight of the sinking of the Russian fleet at Port Arthur, Roosevelt's foremost adviser on Far Eastern affairs, W. W. Rockhill, had stated accurately the policy of the Roosevelt administration. "I cannot see any possibility of this Government using its influence 'to bolster up the Empire of Korea in its independence,'" Rockhill wrote to Minister Horace N. Allen at Seoul. Furthermore, said Rockhill, the annexation of Korea by Japan "will be better for the Korean people and also for the peace in the Far East." A few months later Roosevelt himself told the German ambassador, Speck von Sternberg, that the United States would make no objection to Japan's taking control of Korea. Then in January 1905 he wrote Secretary of State John Hay that much-quoted note: "We can not possibly interfere for the Koreans against Japan. They couldn't strike one blow in their own defense."

Despite the facts that Taft expressed, with Roosevelt's concurrence, merely what for months had been established policy, and that Katsura expressed merely what had been said previously by Japanese leaders and was to be said subsequently on many occasions, there remains the suspicion of a "secret pact"—first, because the memorandum was kept secret; and second, because of the apparent element of *quid pro quo* in the document. Dennett's interpretation ultimately rests on these two factors. Regarding the matter of secrecy, Taft's report to Roosevelt indicates that the memorandum was kept secret at the request of Katsura. The premier did not even want Taft to give a copy to the minister, Lloyd C. Griscom. The injunction for secrecy was hardly unusual, however, in view of the fact that the document contained rather definite information regarding steps Japan proposed to take in Korea. During 1905 Japan pursued a consistent policy of keeping the Korean court in doubt until she was ready to act. As it turned out, when Marquis Hirobumi Itō went to Korea in November 1905 to establish a protectorate, the Koreans had not yet been given any information as to what would be their fate. Katsura's request that the conversation be confined to Root and Roosevelt may have been due to the fact that Griscom was known to be somewhat sympathetic to the Koreans.

Regarding the seeming element of *quid pro quo* in the memorandum, the records indicate that Dennett was not the first to suspect that the conversation represented a bargain. Indeed, such a charge was made only a few months after the conversation took place. On October 4, 1905, Griscom reported by cable that rumors of an agreement were circulating in the Japanese press. According to the press reports, an understanding had been concluded wherein Japan disavowed any design on the Philippines and the United States signified her unequivocal support in the matter of Japan's protectorate over Korea. When Griscom's report reached Roosevelt, he immediately took exception to the suggestion that his Korean policy was a result of any bargain with Japan. Obviously irritated about the matter, he wrote to Taft:

I think that a sufficient answer would be that we neither ask nor give any favor to anyone as a reward for not meddling with any American territory. We are entirely competent to prevent such meddling, and require no guaranty of assistance to preserve our territorial integrity.

After reading the "agreed memorandum" again, Roosevelt was even more sure of his interpretation. "The statement about the Philippines," he wrote to Taft,

was merely to clear up Japan's attitude, which had been purposely misrepresented by pro-Russian sympathizers and is shown to have been entirely apart from your statements—that is, our statements—in reference to Korea and in reference to our having the same interests with Japan and Great Britain in preserving the peace of the Orient.

Roosevelt apparently took the matter up with the Japanese minister at Washington, for within a few days a cable came from Katsura stating as follows:

You are hereby instructed to assure the President at the first favorable opportunity that the [*Kokumin*] although friendly [to] is in no sense of the word organ of the Japanese Government and that the article to which the President referred, was not inspired by the Government nor based on information supplied by the Government. You will add that the Japanese Government were unaware of the currency in Tokio of the rumor to which U.S. Minister referred in his telegram. . . . Japanese Government fully recognize and cordially appreciate friendly attitude of U.S. regarding problems which confront them in Corea, they are well aware that that attitude is entirely spontaneous and they agree with the President that any suggestion absolutely contrary to fact. That the attitude of U.S. was the result of a bargain or understanding would place U.S. in a false position and lessen the value of her support. You will say to the President finally that the Japanese Government will endeavor as fully as possible to make the actual position of U.S. completely and accurately understood.

It is difficult to conceive of a denial that could have been any more unequivocal. It was by no means the usual official denial that emanates from governments when secrets leak to the press. It was a categorical statement to Roosevelt by the Japanese premier agreeing with the president's interpretation of the Taft-Katsura conversation.

Whether Katsura was telling the truth when he denied official inspiration of the press rumors remains uncertain. The *Kokumin*, which first printed the story, was undoubtedly a pro-government organ in close touch with Japanese leaders. It is possible that the ministry was attempting to make the conversation into something more than it was. In October 1905, when the rumors first appeared in Tokyo, the ministry was under fierce attack for the alleged diplomatic failure at Portsmouth. Perhaps the news of the Taft-Katsura "bargain" —a bargain that could be interpreted as something of a diplomatic *coup*— was leaked to the press in an effort to counteract the criticism of the ministry for its failures in the diplomatic field. If this were the case, Katsura knew he was on weak ground, for he promptly backed down from this interpretation when Roosevelt called his hand.

Roosevelt's policy regarding the Korean question in 1905, as he himself viewed it, was neither based upon nor accompanied by a "secret pact" or "agreement" with Japan. Rather, it was based upon a realistic consideration of the power relationships in the Far East. He viewed Japanese control of Korea as a good thing in itself, good for the balance of power in the Far East and therefore good for the United States. A *quid pro quo* in the nature of a guarantee of the Philippines was neither asked for nor apparently desired by Roosevelt in 1905. Such an assurance was in substance a guarantee not to make war on the United States and was therefore considered by Roosevelt to be superfluous. The time soon came when Roosevelt was by no means so confident that the United States was "entirely competent to prevent such meddling," and indeed in 1907 he became very much concerned over the possibilities of war with Japan. Yet throughout the war scarce of 1907 and during the subsequent period of Roosevelt's administration, he never laid claim, either to his close associates or to the Japanese, to the existence of a pact, agreement, or bargain with Japan. If the alleged "secret pact" had any reality, it is strange indeed that not even passing reference to it is found in the records of the department of state or the voluminous private papers of Roosevelt, Taft, and Root during the years 1906–09.

To characterize the Taft-Katsura conversation and accompanying memorandum as a "secret pact" or "agreement" is therefore to stretch the meaning of those terms beyond their generally accepted use in international relations. It would be more accurate to describe the incident simply as an honest exchange of views, as it is described in the memorandum itself. It was by no means a meaningless conversation. The Japanese doubtless put great value on the assurances regarding American policy. But even here it would be easy to overestimate the importance of the exchange of views, for, many months before, Katsura had already been given assurances on the Korean question. As early as February 1905 Roosevelt undertook to inform Japanese leaders through an informal channel that he favored their taking Korea. This information was conveyed through Richard Barry and George Kennan. Barry interviewed Roosevelt at the White House, and, as Barry wrote to Kennan, then in Tokyo, "the President's expressions to me were in the nature of messages to yourself." Kennan was then to pass the president's views on to "a few men of influence in Japan." The views had the usual Roosevelt directness: "Japan must hold Port Arthur and she must hold Korea. Those two points are already settled." In March 1905 Kennan read a verbatim account of Roosevelt's interview to Katsura. Thus, at least four months before the Taft-Katsura conversation, the premier had been given definite information regarding the policy of the Roosevelt administration *vis-à-vis* Korea. In the following month, April 1905, Roosevelt personally told the Japanese minister, Kogorō Takahira, that though he reserved judgment on the question of indemnity, he approved of Japan taking over Korea, Port Arthur, Dalny (after 1906, Dairen), and the Harbin-Port Arthur railway. The statement which Katsura elicited from Taft three months later was, therefore, only a reiteration of assurances which had already been communicated to Japanese leaders through both formal and informal channels. The conversation was certainly a helpful exchange of views, but it was nothing more. It would be safe, therefore, to relegate such terms as "Taft-Katsura agreement" and "Roosevelt's secret pact" to the realm of things that did not happen.

7

Intervention in World War I:

WAS WILSON REALLY NEUTRAL?

WHEN WAR *broke out in Europe in 1914, the vast majority of the American people wanted no part of it. Wholeheartedly, they wished to remain neutral. They appreciated, as never before, the wide expanse of ocean which insulated them from strife-ridden Europe. A Chicago newspaper reflected popular opinion when it gave "thanks to Columbus for having discovered America." Even those hyphenate Americans who could not avoid sympathizing with their mother countries did not wish to get involved. President Wilson shared the sentiments of his countrymen. He called the conflict "a war with which we have nothing to do, whose causes cannot touch us." Immediately, he issued a proclamation of neutrality and made known his determination to keep the United States out of war. Two years and eight months later, in April, 1917, he appeared before the Congress and asked for a declaration of war against Imperial Germany. Congress voted overwhelmingly for war.*

What had happened to change the President's mind and the public's temper? This question has generated a large body of historical work on the subject which falls into one or the other of two groups. One group maintains that Wilson was unneutral from the very beginning; that he favored the Allied cause; that he got the nation emotionally and financially involved in Allied fortunes to the point that intervention was finally necessary. The other group claims that the President tried desperately to remain impartial, but that German submarine warfare, cruel and inhumane in his point of view, finally forced him to ask for the defense of American rights.

The first group is represented here by one of America's most distinguished professors of international law, a professor who taught his subject to a generation of Yale students. It is Edwin Borchard's contention that "the conduct of the American Government during that period [1914–1917] was a negation of nearly all the requirements of neutrality both in thought and action." He cites numerous examples of pro-Allied statements made by Wilson or his advisors and describes unneutral conduct which the President engaged in. The crux of his argument is that Wilson's "refusal to hold Great Britain to account and his inability to win a single concession from her were compensated by a determined and unyielding attitude toward Germany." The President "was inveigled from one misstep to the next and . . . the end of the trail was intervention." The basis for his conduct was an affinity for the British cause.

Representing the other group is Arthur S. Link, a professor of history at Princeton, author of a biography of Wilson and the editor of Wilson's papers. Link admits that the President was "to a degree pro-British; [and] on two, perhaps three, occasions . . . avowed to close friends his personal sympathy for the Allied cause. But it would be a difficult task to prove that Wilson's pro-British sympathies were ever controlling or indeed even very strong." He further admits that the policies pursued by the President favored the Allies, but he denies that those policies were pursued in order to benefit the Allied cause. Wilson's failure to break the British blockade can be ascribed to the way England conducted the blockade and to the fact that to have destroyed it would have led to "the wrecking of American friendship with the two great European democracies . . . without a single compensating gain for . . . the United States." Link concludes with a consideration of the submarine issue which was, in his viewpoint, the cause for intervention.

"Neutrality," 1914–1917

EDWIN M. BORCHARD and W. P. LAGE

IT IS NOT a grateful task to record the diplomacy of the United States during the period 1914–17. Although President Wilson had enjoined on the nation the necessity for remaining neutral "in thought as well as in action," unfortunately he soon found himself entangled in an emotional drift toward intervention in the war. It is possible that he did not realize the extent to which he was committing himself. With little if any useful aid from Secretary Lansing, who seems to have fumbled nearly every legal issue, with an Ambassador in London who was less interested in his own country than in the success of what he supposed to be a crusade for civilization, and with a most adroit and effective propaganda operating to persuade the United States into seeing only one side of the issue, it required a strong, sophisticated, and detached mind, with a philosophical view of history, to resist the pressure and allurements to which President Wilson was subjected. Volumes have already been written, and more are likely to be written, analyzing the various factors which served to propel the United States into the European war. In this book no detailed examination of the diplomatic history of the time can be attempted; but it is possible to say that the conduct of the American Government during that period was a negation of nearly all the requirements of neutrality both in thought and in action. The difficulty was not decreased by the profession that we were acting as neutrals, for neutrality and unneutrality became inextricably confused. There is no doubt that the administration desired to see the Allies win and declined to take any action even in defense of American neutral rights which would seriously interfere with that objective. Perhaps the objective is understandable—this is not the place to discuss that question—but to suggest that the objective was consistent with the maintenance of American neutrality is a travesty of the truth. We were unneutral and we paid the price.

Our unneutrality began as early as August, 1914. If neutrality was to be the national policy, the struggle to attain it, if such it was, did not last long. As we shall observe, the effort to obtain British adherence to the Declaration of London disclosed an obsequiousness on the part of Ambassador Page, Colonel House and Mr. Lansing which must have forfeited British respect for the American case and for the capacity of America's representatives to defend it. As Ray Stannard Baker says, "By October [1914], perhaps earlier, our case was lost."

From Edwin M. Borchard and W. P. Lage, *Neutrality for the United States* (New Haven: Yale University Press, 1937) pp. 33–43; 113–117; 164–175. Reprinted by permission of Yale University Press.

Again, in the protest against the British "measures of blockade" which grad-ually exposed all American trade with the neutrals of Europe to British and Allied control, the United States as early as December, 1914, practically gave away the American case against Allied impositions with the pathetic admis-sion that such trade could not be interfered with "unless such interference is manifestly an imperative necessity to protect their [Allied] national safety, and then only to the extent that it is a necessity." The note appealed to "the deep sense of justice of the British nation" in requesting it to "refrain from all unnecessary interference with the freedom of trade" and to "conform more closely" to the rules of international law. But as long as the belligerents were to be the judges of "imperative neceessity," this friendly admonition had the effect of acquiescing in their illegal measures. The British seem so to have construed it. Baker remarks:

". . . One cannot avoid the impression, after a careful study of this document, that the Administration's defense of American policy was in reality a defense of the British blockade, and furnished the British government with a whole arsenal of arguments against our own criticism of that blockade."

Although on August 18, 1914, President Wilson had solemnly urged "every man who really loves America" to "act and speak in the true spirit of neu-trality, which is the spirit of impartiality . . . and friendliness to all con-cerned," and had warned against "partisanship" and "taking sides," on August 30, 1914, only twelve days later, he is recorded as telling Colonel House "that if Germany won, it would change the course of our civilization and make the United States a military nation."

The submarine campaign initiated by Germany in February, 1915, seems to have deeply offended President Wilson and to have fixed his attachment to the Allied cause. This influenced both the tone and contents of his notes to Germany and he began to talk about "strict accountability." Even before the *Lusitania* sinking in May, 1915, Attorney General Gregory attended a Cabinet meeting which he described as follows:

While these conditions existed [i.e., the sinking of ships before the *Lusitania*] a cabinet meeting was held, at which several of Mr. Wilson's advisers expressed great indignation at what they considered violation [by Britain] of our international rights, and urged a more vigorous policy on our part.

After patiently listening, Mr. Wilson said, in that quiet way of his, that the ordinary rules of conduct had no application to the situation; that the Allies were standing with their backs to the wall, fighting wild beasts; that he would permit nothing to be done by our country to hinder or embarrass them in the prosecution of the war unless admitted rights were grossly violated, and that this policy must be understood as settled.

Like all true-hearted Americans, he hoped that the United States would not be drawn into the war; but he was of Scotch and English blood, and by inheritance, tradition and rearing at all times the friend of the Allies.

On September 22, 1915, Colonel House records Wilson's views as follows: "Much to my surprise, he [Wilson] said he had never been sure that we ought not to take part in the conflict, and, if it seemed evident that Germany and her militaristic ideas were to win, the obligation upon us was greater than ever."

Mr. Tumulty, the President's Secretary, reports the President as believing that the public demand that he keep England within legal bounds was actuated by a "sinister political purpose." The President is reported to have approved Sir Edward Grey's statement that "of course many of the restrictions that we have laid down and which seriously interfere with your trade are unreasonable, but America must remember that we are fighting her fight as well as our own to save the civilization of the world." The President thereupon adopted this idea as his own, stating, according to Mr. Tumulty: "England is fighting our fight and you may well understand that I shall not, in the present state of affairs, place obstacles in her way." He declined to take any action to embarrass England when she "is fighting for her life and the life of the world."

Secretary Lansing admits in his *Memoirs* that as early as July, 1915, he had concluded that "the German Government is utterly hostile to all nations with democratic institutions" and that "Germany must not be permitted to win this war or to break even, though to prevent it this country is forced to take an active part. This ultimate necessity must be constantly in our minds in all our controversies with the belligerents. American public opinion must be prepared for the time, which may come, when we will have to cast aside our neutrality and become one of the champions of democracy."

We shall have occasion to see that the legal positions of the United States in its controversies with the belligerents were highly colored by this view, to which Mr. Lansing gave repeated expression. Describing his notes to England, Mr. Lansing says:

The notes that were sent were long and exhaustive treatises which opened up new subjects of discussion rather than closing those in controversy. Short and emphatic notes were dangerous. Everything was submerged in verbosity. It was done with deliberate purpose. It insured continuance of the controversies and left the questions unsettled, which was necessary in order to leave this country free to act and even to act illegally when it entered the war.

On October 6, 1915, Colonel House wrote to Mr. Page: "We have given the Allies our sympathy and we have given them, too, the more substantial help that we could not offer Germany even were we so disposed—and that is an unrestricted amount of munitions of war and money. In addition to that, we have forced Germany to discontinue her submarine warfare . . ." In 1915, Mr. Lansing wrote to Colonel House: "In no event should we take a course that would seriously endanger our friendly relations with Great Britain, France, or Russia, for, as you say, our friendship with Germany is a thing of the past."

On January 11, 1916, Colonel House records a conference he held with British leaders in which they had asked "what the United States wished Great Britain to do." To this the neutral Colonel replied: "The United States would like Great Britain to do those things which would enable the United States to help Great Britain win the war." Page admired this "cleverness."

And Mr. Lansing discloses at least one reason for his insincere defense of American neutrality, by stating: "in dealing with the British Government there was always in my mind the conviction that we would ultimately become an ally of Great Britain." His point of view being that of a prospective ally, his conduct was in reasonable accord.

No wonder that Sir Cecil Spring-Rice's biographer could say of him: "As to his value in negotiation, it cannot be overlooked that during the period while America was neutral, all the issues in dispute between England and America were decided as England wished." And Lord Reading adds: "I believe it to be the case that the Allied governments were never forced to recede from their position in any important question owing to American opposition."

The American surrender was, unfortunately, not merely a betrayal of neutrality, of which Lansing declared we were to be the "champions"; it was a surrender of the independence of the United States and of American self-respect. Furthermore, it must have forfeited the respect of Great Britain and her Allies. The surrender was not made through malevolence but through shortsighted emotionalism, a confusion of ideas as to where America's interest lay. It set the mood for that partiality and that incapacity to take and stand upon correct legal positions which ultimately made of the United States an instrument of the foreign policy of certain European belligerents.

We need only refer to the agreement between Colonel House and Sir Edward Grey on February 22, 1916 (of all days!), for the contingent intervention of the United States on behalf of the Allies if the Central Powers failed to accept terms of peace suitable to the Allies. Such an agreement is unique in the history of "neutrality."

Nor need more than passing reference be made to the "Sunrise Breakfast Conference" in April, 1916, in which President Wilson sought to find out from Speaker Clark, Floor Leader Kitchin, and Chairman Flood of the Foreign Affairs Committee of the House whether Congress could be persuaded to approve war against Germany.

It is now established that the British Ambassador was often notified in advance that important notes of protest against British violations of American rights were merely formal and not to be taken too seriously. In connection with the American note of October 21, 1915, Ambassador Spring-Rice was requested to send Sir Edward Grey a cable preparing him for a protest. Spring-Rice assured his government that the note was due to the fact that "the United States must defend their rights and they must make a good showing before Congress meets, but that the correspondence should not take a hostile character but should be in the nature of a juridical discussion."

An entirely different attitude distinguishes the correspondence of the United States with Great Britain from that with Germany. Had there been no fundamental prejudice in favor of one group of belligerents, the legal questions might have been approached with greater felicity and understanding.

On the armed merchantmen question, the unsustainable position was taken that, notwithstanding the ability of a single shot to sink a submarine and notwithstanding the British Admiralty orders to ram or fire on submarines at sight, nevertheless the submarine had no right to fire on and sink an armed belligerent merchantman which had Amercan citizens on board. Thus, the neutral United States undertook to defend British merchantmen from attack by their enemy, a practice new in history. The real legal issues involved in the *Lusitania* case—her naval status, her cargo, her course in the war zone, the risks the passengers assumed—were not carefully examined, but ultimata were sent to Germany which were not and have not since been justified. The administration declined to inform American citizens, notwithstanding Secretary Bryan's importunities, that they took passage on belligerent vessels at their own risk. It fought the Gore-McLemore Resolutions of 1916 which merely sought to declare this elementary rule of law.

No more than casual reference needs to be made to one of the more egregious lurches into unneutrality, whereby the United States and its people were led into financing the munitions supply of one set of the belligerents, the Allies. In August, 1914, the administration had announced that the flotation of loans for the belligerents was "inconsistent with the spirit of neutrality." In October, 1914, as the munitions traffic developed, a plausible argument was advanced by Mr. Lansing that bank credits for the purchase of supplies were not public loans and hence should not be banned. The President agreed, but was not willing to let the public know that he had approved this qualification of his original position. By August, 1915, this trade had developed to such proportions that the credits needed to be funded and, it was argued, the Allied governments had to have new money to buy their enormous supplies. The 1914 prohibition and its reasons stood in the way. The Secretary of the Treasury made an eloquent plea to the President for authority to permit the Federal Reserve banks to discount bills, and acceptances, a flagrantly unneutral act of the United States Government, and to permit the Allied governments to float loans in the United States. Again the President yielded, but again not publicly. He thus committed himself to a policy which could have but one end, for as the need for Allied credit continued—the argument was that American prosperity could not be permitted to decline—and private lenders became reluctant, only public lending could meet the need, and that meant war. Like the impressment issue to the "War Hawks" of 1812, the German submarine note of January 31, 1917, must have been a godsend to the interventionists. The way to the public Treasury was now open. The subsequent record is current history.

The strange thing is that President Wilson apparently failed to perceive that he was inveigled from one misstep to the next and that the end of the trail was intervention. Perhaps his mental attitude in August, 1915, was already such that he conceived it legitimate to reverse Secretary Bryan's and his own sensible position of August, 1914. Those members of the Federal Reserve Board who in August, 1915, were reluctant to permit the Federal Reserve banks' participation in this violation of neutrality were denounced by Secretary McAdoo as "pro-German," then as later a form of psychological terrorism to discourage the well-balanced, the thoughtful, the really neutral devotees of America, its traditions and its independence. The remarkable fact is that under the impact of the mighty forces making for American involvement, including the consistently unneutral attitude of mind and action of the leaders of the administration, American intervention was nevertheless delayed for more than two years. That fact alone attests the fundamental detachment of the American people and their aversion to participation in European wars.

No wonder that the belated effort of President Wilson in December, 1916, to end the war fell in England on unresponsive ears. The British Government had no reason to believe that the United States would exert pressure on England or that it would even act impartially. The mediatory or constructive influence of the United States had been frittered away; only its physical power as a belligerent was now sought. That ultimate seduction was not difficult.

Great Britain, well aware of the situation in Washington, timed its replies so as to conceal the downright refusal of practically every American protest; they were almost invariably delivered when the administration was engrossed in the clouds of controversy incidental to American protests against the German submarine. Thus, the American note of October 21, 1915, was answered on April 19, 1916, when the *Sussex* controversy was at its height. This was excellent strategy, like the release of the Bryce reports on German atrocities in Belgium at the time of the *Lusitania* controversy. In like manner, Great Britain made cotton absolute contraband on August 20, 1915, the day following the sinking of the British steamer *Arabic*.

It is not necessary to extend the demonstration of American unneutrality by a discussion of the feeble protest at the seizure of American mails and the diversion of all northern transatlantic shipping into British ports for examination. Nor is it necessary to discuss the forcible removal of passengers from American ships on the high seas if they were thought to be German reservists.

President Wilson thought the "national honor" required him to fight for the right of American citizens to take passage unmolested on British merchant ships. As John Bassett Moore stated to the Senate Foreign Relations Committee in 1936: "We became involved in war directly as the result of our undertaking to guarantee the safety of belligerent merchantmen and our taking the position that armed belligerent merchantmen were to be considered as peaceful vessels." It is not necessary to emphasize the fact that scarcely a ton of cargo left an American port from 1915 to 1917 without the control of a British agent. And we need merely call attention to the submission of the United States to the impositions of the British black list which prevented an American citizen from trading with Germans or even Chileans in Chile if their names had been placed on the British black lists—this at a time when Canada refused to submit to such a black list and freely sent shipments to those very firms! . . .

THE GORE–MCLEMORE RESOLUTIONS

The momentary effort to restore American neutrality by retracting an error, the consternation this aroused in interventionist circles, and the successful campaign to induce the return to error, had produced a confusion of counsels not altogether without its amusing features. In spite of the arguments employed by Lansing to prove the inconsistency between the American position of 1914, on armed merchantmen, and the further insistence on their immunity from submarine attack, President Wilson nevertheless declined to draw the natural inference that if armed merchantmen were subject to submarine attack, American citizens on such vessels were obviously exposed to the same danger. At Topeka on February 2, 1916, in the Preparedness Campaign, the President had urged the need to protect and safeguard "the rights of Americans no matter where they might be in the world." In a letter of February 24, 1916, to Senator Stone, Wilson pictured the right of American citizens to travel unmolested on armed belligerent merchantmen as a matter of national "honor," fundamental "principle," and "of the very essence of the things that have made America a sovereign nation." To yield on that point he regarded as a confession of "impotency as a Nation" and a "surrender" of American independence.

The introduction of the Gore-McLemore Resolutions in February, 1916, warning American citizens against taking passage on armed belligerent merchantmen, although approved, according to Speaker Clark's statement to the President, by a majority in Congress, was firmly opposed by the administration. The President summoned the Congressional leaders on February 21 and made the defeat of the resolutions a matter of personal prestige. Many members became convinced that the President would insist on the right of American citizens to travel unmolested on armed belligerent merchantmen, even at the risk of war. To clarify the issue Senator Stone wrote the President on February 24, giving his version of the conference of the twenty-first:

I have stated my understanding of your attitude to be substantially as follows:

That while you would deeply regret the rejection by Great Britain of Mr. Lansing's proposal . . . you were of the opinion that if Great Britain and her allies rejected the proposal and insisted upon arming her merchant ships she would be within her right under international law.

Also that you would feel disposed to allow armed vessels to be cleared from our ports; also that you are not favorably disposed to the idea of this Government taking any definite steps toward preventing American citizens from embarking upon armed merchant vessels.

Furthermore that you would consider it your duty, if a German warship should fire upon an armed merchant vessel of the enemy upon which American citizens were passengers, to hold Germany to strict account.

* * *

I find it difficult for my sense of duty and responsibility to consent to plunge this Nation into the vortex of this world war because of the unreasonable obstinacy of any one of the powers upon the one hand, or, on the other hand, of foolhardiness, amounting to a sort of moral treason against the Republic, of our people recklessly risking their lives on armed belligerent ships. I can not escape the convictions that such would be so monstrous as to be indefensible.

To this letter, the President immediately replied, in part, as follows:

. . . . But in any event our duty is clear. No nation, no group of nations, has the right, while war is in progress, to alter or disregard the principles which all nations have agreed upon in mitigation of the horrors and sufferings of war; and if the clear rights of American citizens should very unhappily be abridged or denied by any such action, we should, it seems to me, have in honor no choice as to what our own course should be.

For my own part, I cannot consent to any abridgment of the rights of American citizens in any respect. The honor and self-respect of the Nation is involved. We covet peace, and shall preserve it at any cost but the loss of honor. To forbid our people to exercise their rights for fear we might be called upon to vindicate them would be a deep humiliation indeed. It would be an implicit, all but an explicit, acquiescence in the violation of the rights of mankind everywhere and of whatever nation or allegiance. It would be a deliberate abdication of our hitherto proud position as spokesman, even amid the turmoil of war, for the law and the right. It would make everything this Government has attempted and everything that it has accomplished during this terrible struggle of nations meaningless and futile.

It is important to reflect that if in this instance we allowed expediency to take the place of principle the door would inevitably be opened to still further concessions. Once accept a single abatement of right, and many other humiliations would certainly follow, and the whole fine fabric of international law might crumble under our hands piece by piece. What we are contending for in this matter is of the very essence of the things that have made America a sovereign nation. She cannot yield them without conceding her own impotency as a Nation and making virtual surrender of her independent position among the nations of the world.

The Gore-McLemore Resolutions were duly defeated, a result which was hailed in Washington and London as a vindication of the President's position. But it meant war. There is something tragic in making a moral issue out of a fundamental mistake. Wilson, of course, thought he was legally right and standing on solid ground. It exemplifies the tricks that emotionalism can play on intelligence. The solemnity of the avowal was inappropriate. Solemnity may well be evoked, however, by the painful consciousness that the President of the United States had by very poor advice been led into a blunder as preposterous as it was fatal.

Had the President been really interested in the law and sought competent advice, he would have been told that Congress needed no legislation to accomplish its object; it was elementary law, as we shall see, that a person sailing under a foreign flag takes his legal position and protection from that flag and cannot look to his own country to protect him from the risks of his location on belligerent "territory." Contrary to Mr. Lansing's view that there was no legal authority in the President to issue such a warning, the President merely had to announce the elementary rule of law, which requires no legislation to confirm it. Indeed, the only objection there is to legislation prohibiting or warning American citizens against taking passage on belligerent merchantmen or treating armed merchantmen as warships in our ports is that such legislation implies that this is not already established law.

The public as represented in Congress was for the most part really desirous of avoiding opportunities to enlist in a foreign war, and the Gore-McLemore Resolutions were a response to this demand. The objections, however, to the Lansing proposal of January 18, 1916, and President Wilson's determination to repudiate that proposal, caused the administration to concentrate all its pressure to bring about the defeat of the Gore-McLemore Resolutions which its own policy of January, 1918, had invited. The Congress tried to be neutral. The administration would not permit it. . . .

AFTER THE LUSITANIA

While there were no major passenger sinkings between May 7 when the *Lusitania* went down and July 21 when the last *Lusitania* note was dispatched by the United States, the respite was temporary only. Without acknowledging the change in policy to foreign countries, it seems that the German civil authorities had induced the naval authorities to avoid the sinking without warning of large passenger vessels. Yet on August 19, 1915, the British White Star Liner *Arabic* was sunk without warning. This was contrary to orders, the Germans claimed. Two American lives were lost. Lansing had informed Bernstorff on July 21, 1915, that war would eventuate if any more American lives were lost. Bernstorff now feared an immediate rupture and advised a conciliatory response to the American protest. House wished to sever relations immediately. The cause of the *Arabic's* sinking was not at once clear, but Bernstorff stated that the loss of American lives was contrary to German intentions and, in advance of an investigation of the facts, expressed his sympathy.

In Germany the dispute between civil and naval authorities continued, unabated, the former claiming that American intervention must be avoided, the latter that restraints on the submarine were preventing them from ending the war.

The issue had been so framed by the American *Lusitania* note of July 21, 1915, that a failure to restrain the submarine, even against enemy vessels, would doubtless have caused a break with the United States. However, public opinion in the United States at that time—a period marked by further inva-

sions of neutral rights by Great Britain, such as making cotton absolute contraband—was not, in spite of the propaganda, as yet conditioned for war. The
Germans were thus in an acute dilemma and so was the Wilson administration. The situation was saved by assurances that the submarine would continue to be restrained. On September 1 Bernstorff announced to Lansing that
liners would not be sunk without warning and without providing for the
safety of the lives of noncombatants, providing the vessels did not resist or
try to escape. The recurrence of an *Arabic* incident was considered out of the
question. It was stated that the submarine commander who sank the *Arabic*
was convinced that the ship intended to r~m the submarine, and indemnity
was offered for the American lives lost.

But sinkings of the British steamship *Persia* and the Italian steamship
Ancona in the fall of 1915, the one by German and the other by Austrian
submarines, again intensified the situation. In January, 1916, came the Lansing
proposal to the Allies for the disarmament of merchantmen as a condition of
further protest against submarine warfare. The President's subsequent withdrawal from that sound position has already been noted.

With things in this state of suspension, the submarine issue was actively
revived by the torpedoing, without warning, on March 24, of the unarmed
French Channel steamer *Sussex*. Again Colonel House announced that war
was inevitable. No American lives were lost, but a few Americans were injured. Lansing advised an immediate severance of diplomatic relations. Several of Wilson's ambassadors prepared to come home.

A very sharp note was thereupon sent to Germany which pointed the course
of future events. It took the categorical position that submarine attacks on an
enemy's commerce are "utterly incompatible with the principles of humanity,
the long established and incontrovertible rights of neutrals and the sacred
immunities of non-combatants." In this respect it reiterated the pronouncements of earlier notes but hardly improved their legal correctness. The note
ended with another ultimatum stating that unless the German Government
should immediately abandon its methods of submarine warfare against passenger and freight ships, the United States would sever diplomatic relations.

The tension was temporarily relieved by the German reluctance to risk
drawing America in. They made a new and far-reaching commitment to restrain the use of the submarine as a commerce destroyer. The Germans even
asked Ambassador Gerard whether they might reserve the right to sink armed
merchantmen at sight. They were given to understand, however, that the
President demanded that submarines conform entirely to the rules governing
surface vessels. They acquiesced, expressing the hope that the President would
exert his efforts to bring about peace. They promised in the note of May 4,
1916, that "in accordance with the general principles of visit and search and
destruction of merchant vessels recognized by international law, such vessels,
both within and without the area declared as naval war zone, shall not be
sunk without warning and without saving human lives, unless these ships
attempt to escape or offer resistance." The note added, however, that if the

United States should be unable to obtain from Great Britain a respect for "the rules of international law universally recognized before the war," as laid down by the United States in notes to the British Government of December 28, 1914, and November 5, 1915, so that "the laws of humanity might be followed by all belligerent nations, . . . the German Government would then be facing a new situation in which it must reserve [to] itself complete liberty of decision."

While this was regarded as a complete victory by Colonel House and the President, Mr. Wilson declined to accept the qualification at the end of the German note that Germany would reserve its freedom of action if the United States could not persuade the British to modify their illegalities. Reasserting the position taken in the note of February 10, 1915, and in the *Lusitania* note of May 13, 1915, he stated that he

cannot for a moment entertain, much less discuss, a suggestion that respect by German naval authorities for the rights of citizens of the United States upon the high seas should in any way or in the slightest degree be made contingent upon the conduct of any other government affecting the rights of neutrals and non-combatants.. Responsibility in such matters is single, not joint; absolute, not relative.

This persistent refusal of President Wilson to see that there was a relation between the British irregularities and the German submarine warfare is probably the crux of American involvement. The position taken was obviously unsustainable, for it is a neutral's duty to hold the scales even and to favor neither side. No one had more strongly insisted upon this than President Wilson himself in his proclamation of neutrality and in his speeches at the beginning of the war. Yet his actions took a different course. His refusal to hold Great Britain to account and his inability to win a single concession from her were compensated by a determined and unyielding attitude toward Germany. That hostility was not pressed to the point of war, however, even though it was contemplated by the administration as early as 1915, until American public opinion in the Middle and Far West could be prepared for that final step.

Although Germany had on several occasions claimed that it was sacrificing its right to conduct submarine warfare against enemy shipping, in accordance with its notice of February 4, 1915, and that it was yielding its rights in order to conciliate the United States, the unmistakable promise to conduct submarine warfare according to the rules governing surface vessels, as the President had demanded, doubtless served to convince Mr. Wilson that his peremptory demand was legally flawless. But it was not. At this time Allied merchant vessels were arming with increasing frequency and a regular warfare against submarines with armed and disguised merchantmen was under way. Under such circumstances, to demand that passengers and crew be saved before merchantmen could be sunk was to invite the submarine to commit suicide or at the very least to impair greatly its utility as a weapon against British commerce. It is not surprising, then, that Colonel House had called Grey's attention to this service which the United States was rendering to Britain.

Germany's agreement to continue the restrictions on the submarine, on condition that the United States succeed in getting Great Britain to abide by the rules of international law and enable Germany to trade with neutrals in foodstuffs and raw materials, merely repeated the position taken in earlier notes. The President's refusal to accept the condition reflected the administration's policy to make no further demands in this direction upon Great Britain —the last protest had been sent on October 21, 1915, after cotton was made contraband—and acceptance would have conflicted with the President's unfortunate view that the violations by each belligerent of neutral rights were distinct affairs and that this country was privileged to take a different attitude toward each without thereby impairing American neutrality. A tacit acknowledgment of this error may be found in the fact that he rested the discrimination between the two belligerents on the difference between the loss of life and the loss of property. But even here the distinction is less convincing than it seems. The loss of life occurred primarily among American seamen or passengers on British or Allied merchantmen, where they were under the protection of the British or Allied flag under which they voluntarily sailed, and not under the protection of the United States. So far as concerns the loss of property, we know that subsequent administrations failed to collect substantial damages from Great Britain, and have placed serious obstacles in the path of claimants to the limited funds left in American hands under the Executive agreement of May 19, 1927, to compensate the sufferers. So the last justification for the discrimination disappears, leaving the bare and all too perceptible fact that the administration did not really desire to remain neutral after the middle of 1915. Various influences gradually converged to produce that policy, and in September, 1916, two months before the November election with its slogan, "He kept us out of war," we find the President saying, "The business of neutrality is over."

All parties doubtless realized that the precarious submarine truce could hardly last. In May, 1916, Colonel House had informed Bernstorff that the United States could do nothing to mitigate the British "blockade." Germany placed its entire hopes on an early peace which might avoid the showdown, and made several tentative moves for peace through President Wilson and then, on December 12, 1916, directly. But Great Britain was adamant, doubtless comprehending that the German demands were due to the relentless pressure exerted by the "measures of blockade" and the war of attrition, which the Allies could stand much better than Germany.

The President's own efforts at mediation in December, 1916, postponed until then owing to the November election, fell on barren soil in England, for his influence now was limited, as Page had earlier suggested, to his expected aid as a belligerent. His helpfulness as a mediator was hardly desired.

Notwithstanding the election slogan, the country was subjected to unremitting Allied and home propaganda for intervention. Only the necessary occasion was lacking to set off the dynamite. Yet the President continued to speak as if he were a mediator and would not engage in the war, for on January 22, 1917, he made his famous "Peace without victory" speech.

On January 31, 1917, the bombshell burst. Germany, unsuccessful in bringing the belligerents to a discussion of peace, and with her population demanding a cutting of the Gordian knot by drastic action, took the desperate step of announcing that the Allies' insistence on the continuation of the war gave back to Germany her "freedom of action" reserved in the *Sussex* note of May 4, 1916. After February 1, 1917, "all navigation, that of neutrals included," was forbidden in the war zone around the British Isles, with certain exceptions, which she was willing to negotiate, for passenger vessels. The whole series of American ultimata was put to the test. It had either to be backed up or withdrawn. On February 3, 1917, diplomatic relations with Germany were severed.

On that day the President went before Congress and reviewed the diplomatic correspondence which had led to the break. He emphasized again his reply to the German condition attached to the *Sussex* note: that the United States "cannot for a moment entertain, much less discuss, a suggestion that respect by German naval authorities for the rights of citizens of the United States upon the high seas should in any way or in the slightest degree be made contingent upon the conduct of any other Government affecting the rights of neutrals and non-combatants." Although he informed Congress that diplomatic relations were severed, he still gave the impression that he thought hostilities might be avoided. The justification for this hope is not easy to perceive.

On February 26, 1917, the President hit upon the idea of arming American merchant vessels as had been done in 1798 against French depredations on American commerce. Possibly realizing that this might immediately result in war, and advised that Congress must give the authority for such arming, he informed Congress that two American vessels had been sunk, one carrying foodstuffs consigned to a London firm, the other carrying lemon box staves to Palermo; that American shipping had been tied up by the war zone decree and the promise of ruthless submarine warfare. He therefore requested authority to arm our neutral vessels. Yet, strangely, he expressed the devout hope that it would not be necessary to put armed forces into action on the ground that the "American people do not desire it." He still maintained that he was "the friend of peace" and stated his determination "to preserve it for America so long as I am able. I am not now proposing or contemplating war or any steps that need lead to it."

Congress declined to give him the power requested because of a Senate filibuster in which twelve Senators participated. These were the Twelve Wilful Men who, for venturing to exercise their constitutional privilege to oppose the President, were pilloried by the administration. But their effort to resist war was futile. Denied the power by Congress, the President decided to proceed without it, and stated in his Inaugural Address of March 5, "we have been obliged to arm ourselves. . . . We stand firm in armed neutrality." But he now admitted that "we may even be drawn on, by circumstances, not by our own purpose or desire, to a more active assertion of our rights as we see them and a more immediate association with the great struggle itself." In that speech he again expressed his devotion to the freedom of the seas "for the use of all peoples, under rules set up by common agreement and consent."

At first, arms were provided for American neutral vessels but no United States naval officers were placed in charge. Here, the President was running a great risk. These neutral vessels were undertaking to fire on belligerents, a privilege not open to neutrals. The bedlam of the times, and the belief that submarine warfare as then conducted was without legal justification, possibly tempered the thoroughness with which the question of legality was examined. But on advice from competent authority that the arming of neutral ships under such circumstances constituted piracy and left the neutral without a recognized place in law, the United States Government on March 20, 1917, assumed official responsibility for the firing of guns and put naval men in charge of them. Under these circumstances firing would be a public act and to that extent regular. But it would be an act of war.

On April 2, 1917, the President appeared before Congress and demanded recognition of the state of war thrust upon the United States by the acts of Germany. He rejected the German plea of retaliation and claimed that submarines were "impossible to employ as it [Germany] is employing them without throwing to the winds all scruples of humanity or of respect for the understandings that were supposed to underlie the intercourse of the world. . . . The present German submarine warfare against commerce is a warfare against mankind . . . a war against all nations." He added that the ships of other and friendly neutral nations had likewise been sunk. "The challenge is to all mankind. Each nation must decide for itself how it will meet it. . . . Our motive will not be revenge or the victorious assertion of the physical might of the nation, but only the vindication of right, of human right, of which we are only a single champion. . . . Armed neutrality, it now appears, is impracticable." Submarines as commerce destroyers "are in effect outlaws," apparently because "it is impossible to defend ships against their attacks as the law of nations has assumed that merchantmen would defend themselves against privateers or cruisers, visible craft giving chase upon the open sea." That is, because submarines were different from surface vessels and because armed merchantmen could not defend themselves against them as they could against privateers or surface cruisers—the antithesis of Lansing's argument of January 18, 1916—submarines were outlaws. This is a legal proposition somewhat difficult to defend. The defense is made even more difficult by the President's statement, reiterating the British position, that "it is common prudence in such circumstances, grim necessity indeed, to endeavor to destroy them before they have shown their own intention. They must be dealt with upon sight, if dealt with at all." He added that "the wrongs against which we now array ourselves are no common wrongs.. They cut to the very roots of human life."

After pointing out that full coöperation, military and financial, with the Allied governments was necessary, including the "extension to those Governments of the most liberal financial credits, in order that our resources may so far as possible be added to theirs," he pictured the great adventure as a crusade for peace. He said:

Our object now, as then, is to vindicate the principles of peace and justice in the life of the world as against selfish and autocratic power and to set up amongst the really free and self-governed peoples of the world such a concert of purpose and of action as will henceforth insure the observance of those principles. Neutrality is no longer feasible or desirable where the peace of the world is involved . . . We have seen the last of neutrality in such circumstances. We are at the beginning of an age in which it will be insisted that the same standards of conduct and of responsibility for wrong done shall be observed among nations and their governments that are observed among the individual citizens of civilized states.

Thus neutrality ended for the United States.

Wilson and Neutrality

ARTHUR S. LINK

. . . Wilson struggled hard and on the whole successfully to be impartial in thought as well as in deed, as he had asked the American people at the outbreak of the war to do. In fact, he succeeded in this impossible undertaking far better than most of his contemporaries and his historical critics. His method was to rely upon the general assumptions that he was sure were sound and then virtually to seal himself off from the passionate arguments and indictments of partisans of either alliance, by simply refusing to listen to them. "I recall," Secretary Lansing afterward wrote, for example, "that . . . his attitude toward evidence of German atrocities in Belgium and toward accounts of the horrors of submarine warfare . . . [was that] he would not read of them and showed anger if the details were called to his attention."

This does not mean that Wilson was able completely to subordinate emo-

From Arthur S. Link, *Wilson the Diplomatist* (Baltimore: The Johns Hopkins Press, 1957) pp. 34-46; 51-60. Reprinted by permission of The Johns Hopkins Press.

tional reactions and personal feelings. Like the majority of Americans, he was to a degree pro-British; on two, perhaps three, occasions during the two and a half years of American neutrality he avowed to close friends his personal sympathy for the Allied cause. But it would be a difficult task to prove that Wilson's pro-British sympathies were ever controlling or indeed even very strong. At no time did he act like a man willing to take measures merely to help his supposed friends. On the contrary, all his policies were aimed either at averting American participation on Britain's side or at ending the war on terms that would have denied the spoils of victory to Britain and her allies. If this is too big an assertion to be taken on faith, then perhaps the reasons for making it will become apparent as we see the way in which Wilson executed policies toward the two leading antagonists.

All authorities, whether friendly or hostile to Wilson, would agree that the acid tests of his neutrality were the policies that he worked out and applied vis-à-vis the British from 1914 to 1917. He has been most condemned by that group of historians highly censorious of his policies, generally known as re- visionists, on this score—for becoming the captive of pro-Allied influencies within his administration, for condoning such sweeping British control of neutral commerce that the Germans were forced to resort to drastic counter- measures, for permitting American prosperity to become dependent upon loans and exports to the Allies, in short, for permitting a situation to develop that made it inevitable that the United States would go to war if the success of Allied arms was ever seriously threatened.

Like most fallacious arguments, this one contains a certain element of plausibility. Wilson did condone a far-reaching British maritime system. American neutrality did work greatly to the benefit of the Allies. The error arises in saying that these things occurred because Wilson and his advisers necessarily wanted them to occur.

Perhaps the best way to gain a clear understanding of why Anglo-American relations developed as they did from 1914 to 1917 is to see how the policies that decisively shaped those relations emerged in several stages in response to certain pressures, events, and forces. The first stage, lasting from August, 1914, to about August, 1915, was in many ways the most critical, because the basic American response to the war and to the British maritime system was formulated then. That response was governed in the first instance by two domestic realities: the overwhelming, virtually unanimous, American desire to be neutral, and the pressures in the United States for a large measure of free trade with Britain's enemies.

In view of the prevailing American sentiment at the outbreak of the war, a policy of strict official neutrality was the only possible course for the United States government. This fact prompted the President's official proclamations of neutrality, supplemented by his appeal to the American people for impar- tiality in thought; the subsequent working out by the State Department of the elaborate technical rules to preserve American neutrality; and the establishment of a Joint State and Navy Neutrality Board to advise the various departments upon the correct interpretation of international law.

One cannot read the records revealing how these policies were formulated without being convinced that their authors were high-minded in their determination to be fair to both sides. Indeed, Wilson and the man who chiefly influenced him in the formulation of the rules of neutrality, Secretary of State Bryan, were so intent upon being fair to the Germans that they adopted policies during the first months of the war that were highly disadvantageous to the British, if not unneutral. One was to prevent the sale of submarine parts, and hence parts for any naval craft, by a private American firm to the British government, on the ground that such a sale would be "contrary to . . . strict neutrality." Wilson persisted in supporting Bryan in this matter, in spite of advice from Counselor Lansing and the Joint Neutrality Board to the effect that their position was contrary to international law.

Infinitely more damaging to the Allies was the administration's second effort to lean over backward in being "strictly" neutral—the ban of loans by American bankers to the belligerent governments that the President permitted Bryan to impose in August, 1914. From a technical viewpoint, the ban was not unneutral, but it was highly prejudicial to the Allies because its effect was potentially to deny them their otherwise legal right to purchase supplies in the American market. These two incidents are not to be understood as revealing any anti-British bias on the part of Wilson and Bryan, although British officials at the time were convinced that they did. I mention them only to show what an important role the administration's desire to be impartial played in the formation of policies vis-à-vis the British during the early period of American neutrality.

The other pressure shaping American policies at this time was the force of combined demands at home for the virtually free transit of American ships and goods to the European neutrals and the belligerent Central Powers. So powerful were these demands, especially from cotton growers and exporters and their spokesmen in Congress, that Wilson personally sponsored two measures highly disadvantageous to the British and unneutral in fact as well as in spirit. One was a change in the ship registry law, put into effect by an act approved August 18, 1914, which made it easy for German or other foreign shipping firms to take out American registry for their vessels. The other was a plan to establish a federal corporation to purchase German ships in American ports and to use them to carry supplies to the belligerents, particularly to Germany. Wilson applied heavy pressure to obtain congressional approval of this, the so-called ship-purchase bill, during the short term from December, 1914, to March, 1915; he failed only because of a stout senatorial filibuster.

In negotiations with the British government during the early months of the war, Wilson fought hard in response to domestic pressures to keep the channels of international commerce open to American ships and goods. He did not go as far in defense of neutral rights as some of his predecessors, but he did suggest a code so sweeping that an enforcement of it would have meant almost total destruction of the British system of maritime controls. Specifically, the President first proposed on August 6, 1914, that the belligerents adopt the rules of naval warfare laid down in the Declaration of London of 1909, a convention never ratified by Great Britain or the United States, which permitted the free transit of all goods except those obviously contraband. When the British rejected this suggestion, the President came back on October 16, proposing a compromise that would have still seriously impaired the effectiveness of British sea power. When this effort also failed, Wilson then announced that his government would assert and defend all its rights under international law and treaties.

I have described these policies and proposals because they so clearly reveal Wilson's neutral intentions and what he would have done in matters of trade had he been able to make the rules himself. But he obviously could not follow his personal preferences alone or respond only to domestic pressures. In seeking to assert and defend American neutral rights he ran head-on into a reality as important as the reality of the pressures at home. It was the British determination to use sea power to prevent American ships and goods from going to the sustenance of the German economy and military forces.

British assumption of a nearly absolute control of the seas washing western Europe began with relatively mild measures in August, 1914, and culminated in the suppression of virtually all commerce to the Central Powers in March, 1915. For the British, this was not a question of adhering to the laws of blockade or of violating them, or of doing things merely to be nice to American friends. It was a question of achieving their supreme objective, to deprive their enemies of vital raw materials and goods, without risking the alienation of the United States. The controlling fact for the British was the necessity of preserving American friendship, in order to assure the uninterrupted rhythm of the North Atlantic trade. As the British Foreign Secretary at the time frankly put it:

> Blockade of Germany was essential to the victory of the Allies, but the ill-will of the United States meant their certain defeat. . . . It was better therefore to carry on the war without blockade, if need be, than to incur a break with the United States about contraband and thereby deprive the Allies of the resources necessary to carry on the war at all or with any chance of success. The object of diplomacy, therefore, was to secure the maximum of blockade that could be enforced without a rupture with the United States.

The crucial question all along, therefore, was whether the United States, the only neutral power strong enough successfully to challenge the British measures, would acquiesce or resist to the point of threatening or using force. The American response during the formative period of neutrality was, in brief, to accept the British system and to limit action against it to a vigorous assertion of American legal rights for future adjudication. All this is too well known to require any further exposition. What is not so well understood are the reasons why Wilson and his advisers acquiesced in a solution that denied the objectives that they and a large segment of the American public demanded. These reasons may be briefly summarized, as follows:

First, the British maritime system, in spite of American allegations to the contrary, enjoyed the advantage of being legitimate and usually legal, or nearly so, by traditional criteria. It was legitimate rather than fraudulent, and legal rather than capricious or terroristic, in its major aspects because the British did in fact hold undisputed sea supremacy and were therefore able to execute their controls in an orderly fashion. In asserting their own rights, the Americans could not well deny the advantages that accrued to the British by virtue of their sea power. The British, for example, had an undoubted right to establish a blockade of the Central Powers, and the American attempt to persuade the London government to use techcniques effective only in the days of the sailing ship did not have much cogency in the twentieth century.

Second, much of the success of the British in establishing their control depended upon the way in which they went about it. Had they instituted their total blockade at the outset of the war, the American reaction would undoubtedly have been violent. Instead, the British applied their controls gradually, with a careful eye upon American opinion, using the opportunities provided by recurrent crises in German-American relations to institute their severest measures.

Third, the British were careful never to offend so many American interests at one time that retaliation would have been inevitable, or any single interest powerful enough by itself to compel retaliation. There was the case of cotton, which the officials in London were determined to prevent from going to Germany because it was an ingredient of gunpowder. Not until a year after the war began did they put cotton on the list of absolute contraband; even then they went to the extraordinary length of underwriting the entire American cotton market in order to avert an irresistible southern pressure in Congress for retaliation. In addition, although they were ruthless in enforcing their blockade, the British took careful pains to avoid any serious injury to American property interests. They confiscated only the most obvious contraband; in all doubtful cases they paid full value for cargoes or ships seized. Their objective was to control, not to destroy, American commerce.

Fourth, there was great significance in the language and symbolism that the British Foreign Office used in defending the measures of the Admiralty and Ministry of Blockade. By justifying their maritime system in terms of international law and the right of retaliation, and (at least before the summer of 1916) by making an honest effort to meet American objections half way when possible, the British made it almost inevitable that the Washington authorities would have to reply in the same language, thus giving a purely *legal* character to the issues involved and for the most part avoiding raising the issues of sovereignty and inherent national rights. The significance of this achievement can be seen in the conviction of Wilson and the majority of Americans that the Anglo-American disputes did involve only property rights, which should be vindicated only by an appeal to much-controverted international law. Moreover, by appealing to the American government and people in the name of friendship and by always professing their devotion to the cause of humanity, the British succeeded in evoking strong feelings of sympathy and understanding on the other side of the water.

Finally, the British were able partially to justify their own blockade measures as legitimate adaptations to a changing technology by pointing to precedents established by the Washington government itself during the American Civil War. To be sure, the British drew some incorrect analogies (as Lansing pointed out) between American and British practice; even so, their main contention—that the American government had also stretched the rules of blockade to allow for technological changes—was essentially correct.

Wilson's refusal to challenge the British maritime system, in short, to break the British blockade, was almost inevitable in view of the facts we have just reviewed, *if the President's objective was simply to maintain as best he could the neutral position of the United States.* An absolute neutrality was in any event impossible because of the total character of the war and America's importance in the world economy. It often happened that any action by the United States inevitably conferred a benefit on one side and thereby injured the other, at least indirectly. In these circumstances, neutrality often consisted of doing the things that would give the least unwarranted or undeserved advantages.

By this standard, it would have been more unneutral than neutral for Wilson to have broken the British maritime system by enforcing highly doubtful technical rights under international law. Judged by practical standards rather than by the often conflicting criteria of neutrality, Wilson's acceptance of the British system seems realistic and wise—indeed, the only choice that he could have made in the circumstances. This is true because the results of destroying the British blockade would have been the wrecking of American friendship with the two great European democracies and the probable victory of the Central Powers, without a single compensating gain for the interests and security of the United States. Only the sure achievement of some great political objective like a secure peace settlement, certainly not the winning of a commercial advantage or the defense of doubtful neutral rights, would have justified Wilson in undertaking a determined challenge to British sea power.

The second stage in Anglo-American relations, lasting from the summer of 1915 to the late spring of 1916, saw the development of the natural economic consequence of the American adjustment to tightening British control of the seas. That consequence was the burgeoning of an enormous war trade between the United States and the Allies. The United States became the storehouse and armory of the Allies neither because there was any conspiracy on the part of certain pro-Allied leaders in Washington to make American prosperity dependent upon an Allied victory, nor because American businessmen and bankers were willing to incur the risks of war in order to increase their profits. The United States became the storehouse of the Allies for the simple reason that Great Britain and not Germany controlled the seas.

The war trade itself was entirely neutral. Indeed, any action by the United States government to impede it, unless undertaken for overriding political motives, would have been grossly prejudicial and unneutral. If it had been permitted to develop in a normal way, this commerce would have raised no important problems in the relations of the United States with the Allies. A problem of the first magnitude did arise, however, because the President, in the summer of 1914, had permitted Secretary Bryan to enforce his own private moral views by imposing a ban on loans by American bankers to the belligerents.

There was no difficulty so long as the British and French governments could find gold and dollars to settle their adverse trade balances. By the summer of 1915, however, Allied gold and dollar resources were near the point of exhaustion; and American insistence upon a continuation of cash payments could result only in gravely damaging the Allied economies and ending the North Atlantic trade altogether. Credit could be found only in the United States, but credit meant floating loans, and loans to the belligerents were as much a political as an economic question because of the existence of Bryan's ban.

It is well known that the State Department under Bryan's direction substantially relaxed its credit embargo during the spring of 1915 and that Wilson and Bryan's successor, Lansing, lifted the ban altogether a few months later, at a time when the credit needs of the Allied governments were demonstrably acute. Even though the full facts bearing upon this matter have been available to scholars for more than twenty years, the reasons for the administration's reversal are still not properly understood.

Bryan's ban could not survive the development of the war trade on a large scale because, in the first place, it (like the Embargo of 1808) was potentially nearly as disastrous to the United States as to the Allies. American material well-being was in large measure dependent upon foreign trade, and particularly upon trade with the Allied world. Such trade was possible during wartime only if American businessmen were willing to do for the Allies what they always did for solvent customers in temporary straits, namely, sell them goods on credit.

The most important reason that Bryan's embargo could not survive, however, was that it was an essentially unneutral policy that impeded the growth of the chief economic consequence of American neutrality, the legitimate war trade. The credit embargo and the war trade could not both survive. The former gave way because Wilson finally realized that it would be as unneutral to interfere with the extension of credit as it would be to stop the flow of goods. Bryan's ban was in a sense, therefore, a casualty chiefly of American neutrality.

The historian can talk himself blue in the face without really convincing his listeners that these simple facts are true. He can point out that Britain's existence depended upon her ability to use sea power to keep the channels of trade and credit open, just as Germany's existence depended upon the use of superior land power. He can demonstrate that the sale of goods and the extension of credit to belligerents by private parties were neutral in theory, tradition, and practice. He can show that the effect of unwarranted interference with such intercourse would have been seriously to penalize sea power to the advantage of land power. But a historian arguing this way makes little impression upon an American audience, because the issue is still too supercharged with emotionalism and is still resolved within a framework of economic determinism, of hostility to the business and financial classes, and of moralistic pacifism. . . .

So long as the British controlled the seas and the Germans commanded the strategic territories and resources of Europe, the American task of neutrality was the relatively easy one of accepting a *de facto* situation and of pursuing the most impartial policies possible within this framework of power. Thus Wilson permitted the German invasion of Belgium to pass without protest, even though some Americans contended that he was morally obliged to denounce such a gross violation of international law; thus he accepted the British maritime system. In this situation of actual stalemate, there was little likelihood of an Anglo-American rupture and no possibility of a German-American conflict, because there were no points of friction between the two governments. But the German decision to attempt to break the stalemate by using an untried weapon, the submarine, created a situation of great peril for the United States because it raised the issue of fundamental national rights and made it exceedingly difficult for the President to continue to steer a neutral course. Before we see how he struggled to find some adjustment to this new situation, let us consider for a moment some of the underlying factors that helped to govern German submarine policy and Wilson's response.

First, German decisions regarding the use of the submarine were determined almost exclusively by internal and objective considerations—the number of submarines on hand and their calculated effectiveness, the military situation in Europe and how it might be affected by American intervention, and the like—and in no essential way by American policies vis-à-vis the British, or by the rules of international law for cruiser warfare. Many historians have assumed that stern American resistance to the British maritime system, resulting in opening the channels of trade in noncontraband materials to the Central Powers, would have rendered the so-called submarine blockade unnecessary. This conclusion assumes that the Germans used the submarine only to force the British to abandon their own blockade. Actually, the chief and in the final showdown the only reason the Germans used the submarine was to cut Britain off from her indispensable sources of supply and thereby to win the war. To put the proposition in its strongest form, the Germans would have used the submarine to knock England out of the war when they had enough U-boats to accomplish this goal, even if the British had long since given up their maritime system altogether. That is to say, calculations of sheer military advantage or disadvantage and not American or even British maritime policies dictated the way in which the Germans would prosecute their underseas campaign.

Second, the submarine was in 1915 a new weapon of naval warfare. This was an important fact, for it meant that there was no special international law to govern its use when the rights of neutrals were involved. The only laws that could be applied were the rules of cruiser warfare, which required attacking warships to warn merchant ships before sinking them and to make provision for the safety of passengers and crew. The trouble was that the submarine was not a cruiser, but a frail craft that had to rely upon deception and quick striking power for safety and effectiveness. If its use had been an issue only between the belligerents, then international law would not have been much involved. But international law was directly involved, because its provisions defined not only the rights of neutrals, but their obligations to the belligerent powers as well. Having chosen a course of neutrality under international law, Wilson had to work within accepted rules in formulating his response to the submarine challenge insofar as American rights were concerned. The Allies, understandably, would not consent to modifications to permit enemy submarines to operate at their peak deadly efficiency; their refusal made it difficult for Wilson to insist upon changing the rules without seeming to be unneutral in spirit and without in fact conferring enormous advantages upon the Germans.

Third, all questions of international law aside, a great power like the United States could not view the submarine blockade as a legitimate weapon, one that should be considered and perhaps accepted on grounds of expediency or necessity. This was true because at the time of its inauguration in February, 1915, the submarine blockade was actually a sham, since the Germans were then able to keep at most only seven U-boats at one time in all the waters surrounding the British Isles. The Germans, in fact, inaugurated the "blockade" with four submarines in service in the area. A year later, at the time of the *Sussex* crisis, the German Admiralty could send only eleven or twelve submarines into western waters at one time. Knowledge of these facts decisively influenced the way in which Wilson and his advisers viewed the so-called blockade and formulated policies regarding it, for it was one of the oldest and most generally recognized rules of international law that a blockade must be effective in order to be legal.

Fourth, unlike the Anglo-American disputes over trading rights, which involved only property interests, the German submarine campaign as it was often prosecuted raised an issue which no great power should ever evade or arbitrate—the safety and welfare of its people in pursuits and areas where they have a right to be. It is almost inconceivable that Wilson and the American people could have thought of going to war with the British over issues of search and seizure or of blockade. It is also inconceivable that they would not have been willing to think in terms of war with a government that permitted, indeed, instructed, its naval commanders to slaughter Americans indiscriminately upon the high seas.

It would, however, be a mistake of almost fatal magnitude to conclude, as so many writers have done, that Wilson's response to the submarine challenge was a simple and automatic reaction governed entirely by these factors. Although they played an important role, Wilson actually formed and executed, not a single consistent submarine policy, but a series of policies in response to changing issues and circumstances and in response to his own larger diplomatic objectives.

His first policy was formed in answer to the original German proclamation of submarine warfare. Avoiding the more difficult issue raised, the one involving the right of Americans to travel in safety on belligerent ships, Wilson replied by simply but strongly affirming the right of American vessels to use the seas subject to limitations permitted by international law, and by warning that the United States would hold Germany to a "strict accountability" (Counselor Lansing's words) for lives and property lost as a consequence of illegal submarine attacks against *American neutral* shipping. It was the only position that the President could have taken without abandoning the pretense of neutrality and national dignity, and the Germans soon retreated and gave such sweeping guarantees regarding American ships that this issue was never again a point of conflict between the two governments before 1917.

There still remained the necessity of devising a policy to deal with the more controversial issue of the right of American citizens to travel and work on *belligerent* merchant ships under conditions of safety specified by international law. When a German submarine sank the British liner *Falaba* without warning in March, 1915, killing an American citizen, Wilson's advisers in the State Department squared off in a momentous debate over the formulation of a proper response. One group, headed by Secretary Bryan, argued that American interests were not sufficiently involved to warrant a stern protest against submarine attacks on Allied ships, even when Americans were traveling on them, and that the spirit of neutrality demanded that the United States condone German violations of international law as it had done with British violations. The other group, headed by Counselor Lansing, replied that the attack on the *Falaba* had been such a flagrant infraction of international law that the United States must protest uncompromisingly in order to defend its neutrality and honor.

The records reveal that Wilson would have preferred to avoid any involvement while the two giant belligerents fought it out on the seas. In legal theory he agreed with Lansing, but he was so strongly moved by Bryan's pleading that he had apparently decided by the end of the debate over a *Falaba* note to make no protest at all. This is the course that he would probably have followed in the future if the Germans, by confining their underseas campaign to attacks against Allied cargo ships and by showing a desire to avoid the loss of American life, had made it possible for him to find a means of adjusting to the new situation.

A policy of noninvolvement, however, became impossible when a German U-boat sank the British passenger liner *Lusitania* without warning on May 7, 1915, with the loss of almost 1,200 civilians, including 128 Americans, men, women, and children. Wilson had to make some positive response now, so atrocious was the deed in the eyes of the American people, so flagrant was the violation of elemental national rights, so unneutral and degrading would be an acceptance of the terror campaign against the North Atlantic passenger liners.

The strategic facts of the situation—the German inability to maintain any effective blockade of the British Isles and the consequent serious dangers to Germany from a break with the United States—would have justified the President in peremptorily demanding prompt disavowal and guarantees. Wilson's response, however, reflected his own desire and that of the majority of Americans to preserve neutrality and to avoid taking any position short of yielding essential rights that might lead to hostilities with Germany. Thus all during the summer of 1915 Wilson pounded out notes on his typewriter, for the sole purpose of persuading the German government to disavow the sinking of the *Lusitania* and to abandon its campaign against unarmed passenger vessels. Threatening to break relations after a U-boat sank the liner *Arabic* on August 19, 1915, Wilson finally won the promise that he demanded.

By the end of the summer of 1915 the President had thus worked through two stages of policy and had won immunity from ruthless submarine attacks on American neutral ships and unarmed belligerent passenger liners. Up to this time, at any rate, Wilson had been patient, conciliatory, and firm only in his demand that the Germans give up measures that had already taken American lives and threatened untold others.

The third stage in the formulation of Wilson's policies toward the submarine, lasting from the early autumn of 1915 through the *Sussex* crisis in the spring of 1916, saw the President attempting to reach a definitive understanding with the Berlin authorities over all phases of submarine warfare against merchant shipping. The issue was daily becoming more difficult to solve by the application of traditional law, because the Allies since March, 1915, had been arming some passenger and cargo ships and ordering them to attack submarines that showed "hostile intent." But Wilson and Lansing persisted in trying to find a solution in spite of the obstacles because they (or Wilson, at any rate) and the majority of Americans still earnestly desired to avoid conflict over merely technical issues.

By patient negotiation Lansing finally won something resembling a German apology for the loss of American lives on the *Lusitania* and an implicit reaffirmation of the *Arabic* pledge. In order to hasten this German concession and to avert even the possibility of future contention, Lansing proposed his *modus vivendi* of January 18, 1916 (already mentioned), designed to provide a new code to govern the German underseas campaign against maritime commerce. This was the proposal that the Allies disarm their merchant ships and that the German submarines observe the rules of cruiser warfare in attacking them.

Adoption of the proposal by the opposing belligerents, or by the United States and Germany alone, would have achieved Wilson's objective of a comprehensive settlement of the submarine issue. And yet, for reasons that we have already seen, Wilson jettisoned the *modus vivendi* in order to save the House-Grey Agreement. Soon afterward, during the *Sussex* controversy (as we have also seen), he launched a new campaign to force the German government to conduct submarine operations against all merchant ships, armed and unarmed, within the rules of cruiser warfare.

Wilson's rejection of the opportunity to come to a seemingly definitive understanding with Germany seems altogether logical and wise when we remember his objectives and the circumstances in which he made these decisions during the third stage in German-American relations. Wilson's supreme objective now was peace through his own mediation. Mediation seemed possible at this time only through the co-operation of the British government. But the British would co-operate only if they believed that the President was genuinely neutral, and certainly not if he insisted upon a code of submarine warfare that minimized the risks to Americans at the expense of British sea power to the advantage of an essentially illegitimate weapon.

Mediation was a noble objective with such great benefits to the United States that it justified taking a few risks to achieve. But Wilson could have followed no other course than the one he followed during the crises over armed merchantmen and the *Sussex*, even if his objective had been merely to maintain American neutrality. In the circumstances prevailing in the late winter of 1916, Wilson had to choose between continuing to accept the British maritime system, mooted by American Civil War precedents, or acquiescing in the challenge to that system, the German submarine blockade. The first was legitimate because it was based upon *de facto* power as well as legal precedent; the second was not legitimate because it was still a paper blockade without any power of effective enforcement. By insisting upon adherence to traditional rules insofar as the rights of Americans were concerned, Wilson was not at this time depriving the Germans of a weapon essential for their survival or one the free use of which would bring them victory at this time. This, essentially, was the reason that they yielded (for the time being) to Wilson's demands in the *Sussex* crisis. By insisting upon the adoption of Lansing's *modus vivendi*, on the other hand, Wilson in effect would have changed the traditional rules and aimed a heavy blow at the British maritime system, and only for the illusory purpose of averting the possibility of a conflict with Germany.

The final test of any foreign policy is whether it serves the national interest. If it was to the interest of the United States to avoid participation in the war at any cost, regardless of its outcome, and if implementing the *modus vivendi* would have averted all possibility of American involvement, then

Wilson's policies at this time were unwise. This generalization, however, is faulty in all its assumptions. To begin with, American interests would be best served by a stalemate and by a peace of reconciliation through Wilson's mediation, not by driving the Allies into sullen opposition, thereby making mediation impossible, and not by promoting a German victory. More important was the fact that implementing the *modus vivendi* would not have prevented the conflict with Germany that Wilson wished to avoid. As we now know, and as Wilson did not know, conflict would come inevitably when the Germans had enough submarines to institute an effective blockade. In that event neither right nor law nor concessions by the United States would dissuade the Germans from making an all-out bid for victory through a devastating attack upon all maritime commerce to the Allied nations.

With the conclusion of the *Sussex* crisis, Wilson's task of erecting a solid structure of neutral policies to govern relations with Britain and Germany was complete, and the next great effort of American foreign policy would be aimed at the higher goal of peace. Operating within the limitations imposed by American public opinion, external realities, and his own conception of the right role for the United States to play, Wilson had made the only kind of adjustments possible in view of American rights and duties as the leading neutral power. He was now in a position from which he could launch his peace campaign. Thus by virtue of Wilson's leadership, American neutrality was not merely a fact in the spring of 1916, but the most important and the most hopeful fact of international life at the time.

There remains only the question whether it was wise. Some critics have argued that Wilson's great failure lay actually in being too neutral, in failing to see that conflict with Germany was inevitable, in failing to prepare the American people emotionally and physically to meet the test of war, and in failing to throw American resources and influence behind the Allies early in the war, in the same way that Franklin D. Roosevelt did in 1940 and 1941.

If one remembers the domestic circumstances and realities that helped to govern the formation of the policy of neutrality, and if one recalls that war with Germany did not *seem* inevitable at any time before 1917, then this criticism seems positively unreal. If one remembers Wilson's strenuous efforts to force a reluctant Congress to expand the nation's military and naval forces, and how he succeeded only partially because of popular opposition, then the criticism seems unfair. If one agrees that American interests, indeed, the interests of mankind, would have been best served by a peace based upon the inability of either side to impose sweeping terms, then the criticism seems also shallow.

Siberian Intervention:

TO AID THE CZECHS
or
TO THWART JAPAN?

WHEN REVOLUTION *broke out in Russia in March, 1917, the Allies welcomed it as the prelude to an increased and improved war effort. The Tsarist
military machine had become so ineffective that its contribution amounted
virtually to nothing. But Allied hopes came to nought. In November the
moderate provisional government was overthrown by the Bolsheviks who immediately suspended military operations and entered into peace negotiations
with Germany. On March 3, 1918, the Treaty of Brest-Litovsk was signed and
Russia retired from the war. With the eastern front closed, Germany was able
to direct her undivided attention to the west. For the Allies the great problem
was how to ease the pressure on the western front and to divert the Germans
once again to the east. One way was to assist anti-Bolshevik forces in Siberia
to regain control of Russia and bring that nation back into the war. It was
decided, therefore, to land troops in the Siberian port of Vladivostok. These
troops would be valuable in a number of ways. They would guard a vast storehouse of war materiel in that city and thus prevent it from falling into German hands; they would keep the Trans-Siberian Railway open and thereby
facilitate the shipment of supplies to anti-Bolshevik forces operating in the
Ukraine; and, they would assist a large body of Czechoslovakian troops
stranded in eastern Siberia to move westward to join other Czech units, in
western Siberia, from which they had been separated. American cooperation
to land the troops was considered essential by the Allies. President Wilson
would not, however, approve United States participation, and for many
months he resisted Allied requests. Finally, in July, he changed his mind and
authorized the dispatch of American troops to Vladivostok from the Philippines. What had caused the President to alter his position?*

George F. Kennan, diplomat and Pulitizer Prize-winning historian, traces the steps by which Wilson came to his decision to join in the intervention in Siberia in one chapter of his study The Decision To Intervene. The Allies were "desperate and slightly hysterical" because of tremendous German pressure on their western front, and constantly apprised the President that the expedition to Siberia was essential for military victory. But Wilson was unmoved by their arguments. What did move him, however, were the reports in June, 1918, that the Czechoslovakian troops had requested aid in their efforts to join their western units. They needed Allied protection of their rear as they moved westward from Vladivostok. This was the precise reason the President gave in an official statement in which he said, "that the present situation of the Czecho-Slovaks requires this Government and other governments to make an effort to aid those at Vladivostok in forming a junction with their compatriots in western Siberia; and that this Government on sentimental grounds and because of the effect upon the friendly Slavs everywhere would be subject to criticism if it did not make this effort . . ."

An entirely different interpretation is presented by Pauline Tompkins, a political scientist at Wellesley College. She sees Wilson's Siberian expedition as a facet of "the compulsions of American Far Eastern policy." It was Japanese ambition in Siberia which caused the President to change his mind. Throughout April, 1918, Japan's intentions to extend its influence further into Russian territory were becoming clear. Japanese occupation of Vladivostok (following the murder of a Japanese by Russians) and support of an anti-Bolshevik uprising were two important manifestations of Japan's intentions. Subsequently, Wilson was informed by the Allies that Japan planned a large-scale, unilateral intervention. This news made the President realize that only by participating in the intervention could Japan's ambitions be curbed.

The Decision on Siberia

GEORGE F. KENNAN

THE BEGINNING of June found the senior officials in Washington, for the first time, somewhat divided in their feelings about the various proposals for action in Siberia.

The War Department, in the persons of General March and Secretary Baker, remained consistently scornful of the Anglo-French schemes. "Intervention via Vladivostok," Baker wired to Bliss on May 28,

is deemed impracticable because of the vast distances involved and the size of the force necessary to be effective. The expedition could serve no military purpose . . .

In the State Department, at the level just under the Secretary, opinion had swung—to the indignation of the War Department—in the direction of acceptance of the Anglo-French pressures. Lansing himself had been considerably affected by this prevailing sentiment. He went to some lengths, in late May and early June, to explore the availability of shipping, both Japanese and American, for a possible Siberian expedition; but the results of this exploration were so negative that he came away from the inquiry as frustrated as ever, convinced only that *something* ought to be done.

This last was also, in increasing degree, the feeling of House. Now officially vacationing at his home in Magnolia, Massachusetts, House nevertheless kept in close touch, by mail, telegraph, and telephone, with developments in Washington, and received a steady stream of visitors who made the pilgrimage to Magnolia to gain his ear for their views on the Russian problem. As the month of June progressed, and particularly the first fortnight with its alarming reports of the situation on the western front, House's conviction that *some* action must be taken, if only for action's sake, became overpowering.

As for Wilson, he continued to vacillate between conflicting impulses. He accepted entirely the views of his military advisers on the military absurdity of the Anglo-French schemes. Yet he, too, as was seen above, had at last been persuaded of the need for some sort of action. He took no one fully into his confidence; but there is every indication that his mind was incessantly occupied at this time by the anxious search for some expedient that would demonstrate America's friendship for the Russian people, give them the needed reassurance, and strengthen the anti-German forces in Russia, without committing the United States to pretentious military adventures or linking it to the ulterior political designs of the other Allies. His correspondence contains repeated reflections of the anguish of this quest for the correct solution.

In this month of June the reports, stimuli, suggestions, and pressures coming to the Administration in connection with the Russian question assumed formidable proportions. The matter had now become the dominant problem of American foreign policy. The heavy German pressure on the western front had thrown all hopes to the east; and Washington's long vacillation in its Russian policy had now drawn down upon its head the multitudionous pleas and pressures of a desperate and slightly hysterical Allied world. The telegraph tapes in the State and War Departments poured out a bewildering plenthora of reports, information, misinformation, and recommendations about Russia—from Vologda, Moscow, Stockholm, Paris, London, Tokyo, Peking, Harbin, and Vladivostok. Along with this there came a veritable inundation of influential visitors, endeavoring to accomplish by personal suasion what could not be accomplished by the cables and letters. "We have been literally beset," Baker complained in early July, "with the Russian question in its various forms." More people had come from Russia in that one month, he thought, than in the entire previous year. "Each one's solution is dictated by the occurrences which he saw in the little corner of Russia in which he happened to be stationed." Former officials of the Tsarist and Provisional Governments were now beginning to appear in numbers. Masaryk was in full circulation. To these were added a bevy of unofficial envoys whom the French—in their desperation—had sent over. General H. M. Berthelot, former head of the French Military Mission in Rumania, who had passed through Moscow and Murmansk on his way home, was despatched to Washington in the evident hope that his prestige and authority in the technical-military field could shake the obdurate skepticism of the President and his military advisers as to the strategic merits of a possible Siberian expedition. Professor Henri Bergson, noted philosopher and world figure, was also despatched—presumably to exploit Wilson's known weakness for the academic world. The newly appointed French Ambassador to Japan, Marcel Delanney, appeared en route to his new post, obviously instructed not to hasten on to his new job but to see as many influential people as he could in the United States and thus to support the efforts of his colleague, Jusserand, on behalf of Siberian intervention. He came armed with a desperate personal plea to Wilson from Clemenceau. On the British side, the incessant efforts of [Lord] Reading continued to be supplemented by those of Sir William Wiseman, now back from England and in close touch, as always, with House and other influential figures.

The historian might wish that time and space permitted him to disentangle the turmoil that resulted from the workings of these manifold influences, and to trace to their precise origins, in impulse and informational background, the various steps that led, during the month of June, to America's ultimate involvement in the Siberian venture. Unfortunately, this is not possible within the limits of a study intended to hold meaning for the general public as well as for the specialist. One encounters, at this point, the problem that is bound to beset diplomatic historians in increasing measure as they move into the effort to recount the course of the international life of the present century: the huge number and complexity of contacts between the bloated governmental bureaucracies and the stupendous volume of the written record to which they have given rise. In these circumstances it becomes simply unfeasible to attempt to permit the sources to tell their own story. The historian has no choice but to simplify, to generalize, and to ask the reader to lean on his judgment. This means, in the present instance, that the processes by which the United States government finally clarified its attitude in the Siberian question in June and July 1918 can be only roughly summarized here. A great many individual communications, visits, and other events, each no doubt of some importance, must be left without specific mention.

When the Supreme War Council met on June 3 at Versailles, the sound of the German guns could be heard in the distance. Preparations, as noted above, were under way for the possible evacuation of Paris. Siberia appeared as almost the only hope. But Wilson was still the stumbling block. Considering that the chances for overcoming his opposition might be best if the Japanese could be induced first to give the necessary assurances, the three Allied Foreign Ministers decided at Versailles to ask the Japanese whether, in the event that the President's consent was forthcoming, Japan would be prepared to intervene under the following conditions:

(a) that she should promise to respect the territorial integrity of Russia;

(b) that she should take no side in the internal politics of Russia; and

(c) that she should advance as far west as possible "for the purpose of encountering the Germans."

In the ensuing days a joint note was drawn up accordingly and despatched to Tokyo. There it unleashed a new and lively debate in governmental circles over the course Japan should take. The prospect of being pressed into an involvement with the western powers in a joint Siberian venture was always an alarming one to many Japanese. The new Allied step must surely have aroused the feelings of those who wished to see Japan, relying on the agreement recently concluded with the Chinese, "go it alone" in an effort to gain exclusive control not only of eastern Siberia but of northern Manchuria as well.

Washington, promptly informed of this Allied step, viewed it with a skepticism bordering on contempt, and awaited without inordinate anxiety the Japanese reply. The minds of the men around Wilson were preoccupied, just in those days, with a sudden flurry of discussion and maneuvering over the question of a possible Russian commission. What brought this question to the fore just at that time is not wholly clear; presumably it was the combined impact of a report written (June 4) by Mr. Thomas D. Thacher, who had just reached Washington and had seen Lansing on May 28, and of the findings of the three-man committee appointed by the War Trade Board to look into the problem of the resumption of economic relations with Russia. Thacher, stressing vigorously the need for working through the Soviet government, urged the establishment of "a commission equipped with financial support and personnel sufficient to render assistance to the Russian people," to be sent to Russia at once. Thacher's well-written and effective report was given circulation among a number of influential people. The War Trade Board committee recommended (June 5) that the President appoint a "Russian Commissioner" whose function it would be to "take charge of all matters pertaining to Russia." The Commissioner, it was suggested, should enter Russia via Siberia and should coordinate his work with the activities of the Russian cooperatives. In addition to these recommendations, the activity of Carpenter, engaged in just those days in the effort to extract from the President an official blessing for the League to Aid and Cooperate with Russia, may have contributed to the agitation of this question.

The suggestion of a Russian commission, in any case, set a number of wheels to spinning furiously. The Department of State was naturally worried at the danger, now threatening from several quarters, to its control of Russian affairs. A rivalry was immediately stimulated, as between the Red Cross faction headed by Thompson and the more conservative entourage of the Root Commission, supported by the Russian Embassy, for control of any commission that might be established. Finally, most important of all, the matter threatened, for a moment, to become the subject of partisan politics. At some time in the first week of June, ex-President William Howard Taft published in the Philadelphia *Public Ledger* an article calling for immediate action in Russia, along lines to be agreed with the Allies. On June 6, Senator James W. Wadsworth, speaking at a Republican Party dinner in New York (Theodore Roosevelt was also a speaker) voiced similar sentiments.

These developments caused consternation in the Administration. There was a general feeling that some initiative must be taken immediately if the Republicans were to be headed off from a partisan exploitation of the intervention issue. The ensuing days, particularly the 12th and 13th, witnessed a crescendo of high-level communication over the question of a commission for Russia and who should head it. Communications on this topic flew thick and fast between the State Department, the White House, the British Embassy, Wiseman in New York, and Colonel House in Magnolia. Although Mott's name had previously been mentioned in this connection (on June 4, by William Phillips to Lansing) it was now Herbert Hoover on whom all hopes centered. His appointment in this capacity commended itself to everyone as an answer to the Republican threat. The suggestion apparently originated with House, or in his entourage. It met with the enthusiastic approval of House, Auchincloss, Polk, Reading, and Wiseman. Lansing wrote personally to the President on the 13th, warmly urging the establishment of a commission "along the same lines as the 'Commission for the Relief of

Belgium,' " to be headed by Hoover. The move, he thought, "would, for the time being, dispose of the proposal for armed intervention." His letter was supported by one from House, of the same date.

Through Auchincloss, House sounded out Hoover. The latter responded favorably, but left it up to the President to decide. At some point, Wilson talked to Hoover about it. "I informed the President," Hoover relates in his memoirs,

that I would serve anywhere, any time, but that to send an army to attack the Bolshevists' Eastern Front while extending kindness on their Western Front was not quite logical. In any event, our ideas of industrial organization would scarcely fit into the philosophy of Messrs. Lenin and Trotsky, even if they did not reject the plan utterly as an Allied Trojan horse. I heard nothing more of the matter.

This passage leaves room for question as to whether Hoover understood—or remembered—very well the proposal at issue. But it makes it clear that Wilson never definitely asked him to serve. The reason for this hesitation remains a matter of conjecture. It may have been that he felt that Hoover was still more needed as Food Commissioner. It seems more likely that he realized that Hoover's appointment would mean that the Russian question would be, from that time forth, effectively out of his hands. For this, surely, he was not yet ready.

While not appointing Hoover, Wilson did not reject entirely the idea of a commission. On the contrary, he instructed the Secretary of Commerce to explore further the economic problems with which such a commission would have to cope, thus setting the wheels of government busily in motion. But plainly, the suggestion of a commission did not seem to him, even now, the entire solution of the problem. There was, after all, still the question as to how a commission could enter Siberia and function there without some sort of armed support and protection. The point Kennan had just recently raised (May 22)—that one must reckon with the existence of Soviet power—was an inexorable one; and however reluctant Wilson may have been to recognize it in his public statements, it is doubtful that it escaped his attention entirely. All of eastern Siberia, from and including Irkutsk to Vladivostok, was, after all, still in Soviet hands; and the reaction of the Soviet authorities to the Japanese landing of April 5 had shown that they would not take kindly to any Allied incursion, be it even by a peaceful commission, on which they had not been consulted.

Thus Wilson, in principle not at all disinclined toward the idea of economic aid to Russia and prepared to see preliminary work along this line go forward, still could not find in the idea of a commission the answer to his problem. Aside from the fact that the staffing of such a body obviously involved awkward domestic-political problems, there was the unanswered question as to how it could function on territory held by the Bolsheviki.

The way out of these perplexities was then suddenly provided—or seemed to be provided—by the reports coming into Washington about the position and aspirations of the Czechs in Siberia. News of the Czech uprising reached Washington belatedly and in confusing driblets throughout the month of June. It was not until after the middle of the month that there was any reasonably intelligible picture of what had occurred, and even this was spotty and in many respects confusing. But in Washington, as in the Allied community in Russia, the dawning realization that the Czechs were in possession of a large portion of Siberia aroused a host of speculations as to their possible role in solving the dilemmas of Allied policy. Lansing's senior aides, notably Basil Miles and Butler Wright (himself recently back from a passage through Siberia), immediately became greatly excited over the possibility of using the Czechs on the spot. Their reaction was precisely that of Poole, in Moscow. And even the President, on reading (June 17) a telegram from Reinsch in Peking, urging that the Czechs be left in Siberia to "control" the region against the Germans, suddenly thought he saw in this suggestion "the shadow of a plan that might be worked, with Japanese and other assistance." The Czechs, after all, he observed to Lansing, were the cousins of the Russians.

From this moment, things moved rapidly to a conclusion. Wilson had now found an approach that seemed to him really hopeful, although the outlines of the possible action were not yet wholly clear. The day after reading Reinsch's telegram (June 18) he told Delanney, who had come in to transmit Clemenceau's message, that he was "considering anew the entire situation" and would express his conclusions within ten days. Through Delanney this startling news was at once circulated throughout the entire Allied community. Encouraging as it was in some respects to the British and the French, it also had disturbing possibilities from their standpoint; for the President's words were still wholly non-committal with relation to the Anglo-French proposals for a military intervention deep into Siberia. The possibility had to be faced that his decision might not be at all what was desired in London and Paris.

Consideration of the project for a commission, meanwhile, moved apace in the President's entourage. Washington buzzed with schemes and plans. The British and French received the impression that this was definitely the direction in which American policy was moving. House continued to press for a commission, with Hoover at its head. Robins' arrival, in mid-June, added to the intensity of the discussion. On the 25th Wilson met, in an unprecedented night session, with five of his Cabinet members: Lansing, Baker, Secretary of Commerce William C. Redfield, Secretary of Agriculture David F. Houston, and Secretary of Labor William B. Wilson. The course of the preparatory work on the economic side, embracing both economic assistance and revival of commercial exchanges, was reviewed, and the President encouraged the others to press ahead vigorously with these studies.

All this had, from Wilson's standpoint, the advantage that it gave the others something to keep them busy, relieved him of the incessant pressure to "do something," and permitted him to address himself in privacy to the real decision which, under State Department encouragement, was ripening in his mind. The abundant documentation concerning the treatment of the

Russian problem in Washington in June 1918 cannot—in fact—be understood unless it is realized that throughout the latter part of the month two things were happening simultaneously: almost everyone involved in the treatment of this problem, except the President himself, was busy working out schemes for the creation of some sort of high-powered commission, on the Belgian pattern; whereas the President himself, content that it should be this way, was pursuing in the quiet of his own mind a parallel, but wholly different, line of thought.

On or about June 25, the Japanese reply was made to the French-British-Italian approach. Although the full text is not available, it is evident that the Japanese, while agreeing to respect Russia's territorial integrity and to refrain from interfering in her internal affairs, would make no promise to go beyond Irkutsk. And they clung to their insistence that they would take no action unless America joined in the request.

Something—not all—of this reply was revealed to the United States government by Ishii on June 26, when he handed Lansing a three-sentence telegram from his government on this subject. It was indicated here that the Japanese had told the Allies that they

. . . could not feel at liberty to express their decision before a complete and satisfactory understanding on the question was reached between the three Powers and the United States.

Wilson was delighted. He had read Ishii's communication, he told Lansing, "with genuine pleasure." The Japanese reaction took care of the Anglo-French initiative of early June and relieved him of the necessity of rejecting the proposal himself. In his relief, Wilson made the mistake of supposing that the Japanese reply reflected the same delicate sympathy in Tokyo for the American view that Ishii had manifested in Washington. The President failed to realize the depths of the differences within the Japanese government on these matters and the extent to which Japanese calculations were now coming to be influenced by the desire to pursue in Siberia an independent policy, having nothing to do either with American aspirations or with those of the French and British.

To the British, the Japanese reply brought consternation. They knew that the President had made up his mind to take some action. They had received no encouragement to believe that there had yet been any change of heart in the White House or the War Department about the military merits of the proposed expedition. The Japanese reaction, involving as it did a refusal to go beyond Irkutsk, was hardly likely to overcome the American inhibitions. The British now had all the more reason to fear that the President's mind might be moving in a direction undesirable from their standpoint.

The next meeting of the Supreme War Council was now only a few days off. It was decided in London to use this meeting for a last powerful effort to swing the President into line. A message was therefore sent to him (de-

livered personally by Reading on the 28th) from Lloyd George and the War
Cabinet, saying that the British government would lay before the Supreme
War Council at its coming meeting on July 2nd, "proposals for the assistance
of the Russian people in their present unhappy situation," and expressing
the hope that the President would refrain from a decision until the Supreme
War Council's view had been communicated to him. This was supported by
an eloquent message from Foch (June 27) approving the despatch of American troops to Russia and stating that

. . . in the interests of military success in Europe, I consider the expedition to
Siberia as a very important factor for victory, provided action be immediate, on
account of the season being already advanced. I take the liberty of insisting on
this last point.

With these approaches, the French and British had introduced their
largest guns. But it was now too late. It was the reports concerning the
Czechoslovaks, not the arguments of the Allied chanceries, that were now
determining Wilson's decision.

From the moment of Masaryk's meeting with the President on the 19th,
the American intimacy with the Czechoslovak cause grew apace. On the 23rd,
the British Embassy sent over a paraphrase of a message from Lockhart,
expressing apprehension over the possibility of a seizure of Moscow by the
Germans and adding:

. . . if we leave the Czechs to their fate and if we fail to intervene now we shall
suffer a blow to our prestige in Russia from which it will take us years to recover.

Lansing at once sent this message to the President with an accompanying
letter in which he wrote:

The situation of the Czecho-Slovak forces in western Siberia seems to me to
create a new condition which should receive careful consideration. Prof. Masaryk
assured me that these rebels against Austria-Hungary, collected from the Russian
prison camps and from deserters, would not fight against the Russians, but only
sought to pass via Vladivostok to the western front.
Now it appears that their efforts to reach Vladivostok being opposed by the
Bolsheviks they are fighting the Red Guards along the Siberian line with more or
less success. As these troops are most loyal to our cause and have been unjustly
treated by the various Soviets ought we not to consider whether something cannot
be done to support them?
. . . Is it not possible that in this body of capable and loyal troops may be
found a nucleus for military occupation of the Siberian Railway?

The following day there was received from Admiral Knight at Vladivostok
the first of three messages concerning the Czechs which had a decisive influence on the thinking of the senior State Department officials and, directly or
indirectly, of the President as well. After describing the military position of
the Czechs, Knight reported the "seizure" of Irkutsk by German war pris-

oners, and ascribed the obstruction of the Czech passage through Siberia to German influences. "It is believed," he stated,

that the Czech is now ready to cooperate with the Allied movements against German activities in Siberia and for reestablishment [of an] Eastern front . . . Czech situation and future movements have become dominating factor in Siberia and perhaps Russian situation.

Knight's telegram was received with enthusiasm by the senior State Department officials, whose hopes had already been aroused by Lansing's letter to the President. "This is a 'God-send!' " Wright said to Miles, on a chit accompanying the message. "It is just the news we want. Masaryk is in town! Let's concentrate on this with all our power at once."

And concentrate they did, with no small success. The following day (June 25) the State Department forwarded for Masaryk, through its official facilities, a long communication to Chicherin protesting the Soviet attitude toward the Czechs and reproaching the Soviet government for its failure to live up to the guarantee it had once given of free and unmolested passage of the Corps to France. The transmission of this message by the Department was a most unusual procedure. On the same day the Department wired Caldwell asking for a full report on the military situation of the Czechs.

On the 26th, a telegram was received from Caldwell, relaying a request from the representatives of the Czechoslovak National Council in Vladivostok for military support. They had decided, the Czech representatives said, that the 15,000 Czech troops who had reached Vladivostok in early May, prior to the uprising, would have to turn westward once more and mount an operation to break through to Irkutsk and to reestablish communication with their compatriots in western Siberia. The Allied consuls agreed that this action was necessary; they recommended that both supplies and arms be sent and that an Allied armed force also be despatched to assist this Czech action. The Czech request was also transmitted through Admiral Knight, whose report contained many more details, and also plainly favored acquiescence.

The final determinant of the American decision was added when the Czechs, on the 29th, after delivery of an ultimatum to the local Soviet authorities, took armed action and seized the city of Vladivostok. This action was the culminating point of a long series of frictions between the Czechs and the local Soviet, in which the Czech hand was strengthened by encouragement from the local Allied representatives. But the action flowed automatically from the decision of the Vladivostok Czechs to move to the aid of their compatriots farther westward. This decision made it impossible for them to remain further in a state of nominal peace with the local Soviet authorities.

The Czech action was followed immediately by the landing of additional Japanese and British forces. Admiral Knight, too, now landed a small detachment of marines to guard the American Consulate. Caldwell reported that the entire development had been welcomed by the majority of the population.

In this way, by a curious coincidence, the power of the central Soviet gov-

ernment came to an end in Vladivostok at precisely the same moment that
the last vestiges of central Soviet authority similarly disappeared in Murmansk. Just at the time when Wilson was on the verge of decision with respect to the American action at both points, his problem was simplified, and
his decision facilitated, by the fact that the respective ports suddenly gravi-
tated into the hands of forces friendly to the Allies and eager for their intervention.

Official reports of the Czech seizure of Vladivostok began to come into the
State Department on July 2nd, but it was not until the following morning that
Lansing had a clear enough picture of what had happened to warrant his
picking up the telephone and communicating this important news to the
President.

Meanwhile, the Supreme War Council had met in Paris and approved a
long document, prepared in advance by the British, going through the intervention question, once more, from beginning to end. All the familiar arguments were repeated, in the light of the new situation, and the position of the
Czechs was also brought in. A plan for an Allied military move into Siberia,
to be accompanied—this time—by "relief expeditions under American direction and control to supply the wants and alleviate the sufferings of the Russian
people," was then elaborated in detail. The necessity of American support
and encouragement for the militay expedition was stressed. It was stated
as the unanimous opinion of Foch and the military advisers that the immediate despatch of such an expedition was essential for the victory of the Allied
army. In conclusion, the Council appealed to President Wilson "to approve
the policy here recommended and thus to enable it to be carried into effect
before it is too late."

This final appeal from the Supreme War Council reached Washington, and
was handed by Reading to the President, on the afternoon of July 3, shortly
before Lansing's phone call about the Czech seizure of Vladivostok. The time
of decision had now finally arrived. The choice—to the President, at least—
now seemed reasonably clear.

The next day was the Fourth of July, and one of the hottest. There was an
excursion to Mount Vernon on the Presidential yacht, *The Mayflower*. Both
the President and Lansing were aboard. The other guests included a number
of representatives of various foreign language groups in the United States. It
was understood that the President would make a speech at Mount Vernon;
and it was thought by many that he might use this as an occasion for announcing his decision with respect to Russia.

Wilson was courteous enough to his guests, and tried to make them feel at
home in the face of the sweltering heat. But we may assume that both he and
Lansing had their minds rather on Siberian matters than on the steaming
banks of the Potomac past which they moved. At some time during the course
of that day, whether before or after the excursion, Lansing found the leisure
to draw up a memorandum for the President on the Siberian question. It was
to prove a decisive recommendation. The seizure of Vladivostok by the

Czechs, and their success in western Siberia, had "materially changed the situation," Lansing wrote, "by introducing a sentimental element into the question of our duty." There was now an American responsibility to aid them. He proposed that a supply of arms be sent to the Czech contingent in Vladivostok, and that "some" troops be sent to assist them in policing the railroad and in "disarming and dispersing" the German and Austrian prisoners-of-war who, he understood, were opposing them. Aiding the Czechs was, after all, an entirely different thing from intervening on other grounds. Even though some American forces were sent, one would have to rely on Japan to supply the bulk of the requisite forces. The announcement of the intention, and the readiness to refrain from interfering in Russian internal affairs, should be made at once. A peaceful commission of representatives of various phases of society, "to-wit, moral, industrial, commercial, financial and agricultural," should be sent and should "proceed westward from Vladivostok following as closely as possible, with due regard to safety, the Czech-Slovaks." Its final destination and function should depend on its reception by the Russian people and on the military resistance encountered.

Lansing's memorandum was presumably sent to the President on the morning of Friday, the 5th. Later that day the President phoned and said he wished to see Lansing, Baker, Secretary of Navy Josephus Daniels, and General March at two o'clock on the 6th. The meeting took place that Saturday afternoon, as scheduled, in an upper room of the White House, with Admiral W. S. Benson (Chief of Naval Operations) also attending. "After we had . . . seated ourselves, somewhat in order of rank," General March later recorded, "the President entered the room with a pad in his hand, and taking a position standing and facing us, . . . read from his pad his views on the matter at issue."

The views which the President set forth emerged, substantially unchanged, as the official record of the consensus of the gathering. Here is the text:

. . . After debating the whole subject of the present conditions in Siberia as affected by the taking of Vladivostok by the Czecho-Slovaks, the landing of American, British, French, and Japanese forces from the naval vessels in that port, and the occupation of the railroad through western Siberia by other Czecho-Slovaks with the reported taking of Irkutsk by these troops; and after reading and discussing the communication of the Supreme War Council favoring an attempt to restore an eastern front against the Central powers; and also a memorandum by the Secretary of State—

The following propositions and program were decided upon:

(1) That the establishment of an eastern front through a military expedition, even if it was wise to employ a large Japanese force, is physically impossible though the front was established east of the Ural Mountains;

(2) That under present conditions any advance westward of Irkutsk does not seem possible and needs no further consideration;

(3) That the present situation of the Czecho-Slovaks requires this Government and other governments to make an effort to aid those at Vladivostok in forming a junction with their compatriots in western Siberia; and that this

Government on sentimental grounds and because of the effect upon the friendly Slavs everywhere would be subject to criticism if it did not make this effort and would doubtless be held responsible if they were defeated by lack of such effort;

(4) That in view of the inability of the United States to furnish any considerable force within a short time to assist the Czecho-Slovaks the following plan of operations should be adopted, provided the Japanese Government agrees to cooperate;

   (a) The furnishing of small arms, machine guns, and ammunition to the Czecho-Slovaks at Vladivostok by the Japanese Government; this Government to share the expense and to supplement the supplies as rapidly as possible;

   (b) The assembling of a military force at Vladivostok composed of approximately 7,000 Americans and 7,000 Japanese to guard the line of communication of the Czecho-Slovaks proceeding toward Irkutsk; the Japanese to send troops at once;

   (c) The landing of available forces from the American and Allied naval vessels to hold possession of Vladivostok and cooperate with the Czecho-Slovaks;

   (d) The public announcement by this and Japanese Governments that the purpose of landing troops is to aid Czecho-Slovaks against German and Austrian prisoners, that there is no purpose to interfere with internal affairs of Russia, and that they guarantee not to impair the the political or territorial sovereignty of Russia; and

   (e) To await further developments before taking further steps.

When the President had finished reading the paper, General March recalled,

. . . he turned to Secretary Lansing, who agreed and commended the paper, Secretary Daniels also approved, and Secretary Baker nodded. Turning to me and finding me shaking my head vigorously, he said with some asperity, "Why are you shaking your head, General?" and instantly went on, "You are opposed to this because you do not think Japan will limit herself to 7,000 men, and that this decision will further her schemes for territorial aggrandizement." I have never been a "yes-yes" man, so I said in reply, "Just that, and for other military reasons which I have already told you." He replied, "Well, we will have to take that chance."

The President's decision was subsequently restated, in his own words, in an *aide-mémoire* presented on July 17 to the Allied envoys in Washington. This was the only detailed statement Wilson ever made of his rationale for the actions undertaken in Siberia and the northern ports, and its importance for this study is basic. The document is too long for incorporation in the narrative in its entirety; the full text will be found in the Appendix. But it is necessary to take note here of those passages which deal specifically with the Siberian action; for Wilson's decision found expression in all three of these documents —Lansing's memorandum of July 4, the record of the decisions arrived at in the July 6 meeting, and the President's *aide-mémoire* of July 17. None of the documents suffices, alone, as an adequate basis for judgment.

The *aide-mémoire* included the following passages bearing on the Siberian action:

It is the clear and fixed judgment of the Government of the United States . . . that miltary intervention [in Russia] would add to the present sad confusion . . . rather than cure it, . . . It can not, therefore, take part in such intervention or sanction it in principle. . . . Military action is admissible in Russia . . . only to help the Czecho-Slovaks consolidate their forces and get into successful coopera- tion with their Slavic kinsmen and to steady any efforts at self-government or self- defense in which the Russians themselves may be willing to accept assistance. . . . the only legitimate object for which American or Allied troops can be employed, it submits, is to guard military stores which may subsequently be needed by Rus- sian forces and to render such aid as may be acceptable to the Russians in the organization of their own self-defense. For helping the Czecho-Slovaks there is immediate necessity and sufficient justification. Recent developments have made it evident that that is in the interest of what the Russian people themselves desire, and the Government of the United States is glad to contribute the small force at its disposal for that purpose. . . . But it . . . can go no further. . . . It is not in a position, and has no expectation of being in a position, to take part in organ- ized intervention in adequate force from . . . Vladivostok. . . . It . . . will feel at liberty to use the few troops it can spare only for the purposes here stated and shall feel obliged to withdraw those forces, . . . if the plans . . . should develop into others inconsistent with [this] policy. . . .

It hopes to carry out the plans for safeguarding the rear of the Czecho-Slovaks operating from Vladivostok in a way that will place it and keep it in close coopera- tion with a small military force like its own from Japan, and if necessary from the other Allies, and that will assure it of the cordial accord of all of the Allied pow- ers . . .

It is the hope and purpose of the Government of the United States to take advantage of the earliest opportunity to send to Siberia a commission of merchants, agricultural experts, labor advisers, Red Cross representatives, and agents of the Young Men's Christian Association accustomed to organizing the best methods of spreading useful information and rendering educational help of a modest sort, in order . . . to relieve the immediate economic necessities of the people there. . . . The execution of this plan will follow and will not be permitted to embarrass the military assistance rendered in the rear of the westward-moving forces of the Czecho-Slovaks.

The nature of the President's decision flows plainly from these documents, and needs no extensive recapitulation. Small American and Japanese forces were to enter Siberia to facilitate the effecting of the junction of the Czech forces in Vladivostok with those west of Irkutsk. Later there might be an economic commission. This was all. . . .

Prelude to Intervention

PAULINE TOMPKINS

THE OVERTHROW of the Provisional Government came as a tremendous shock to the Allied nations, particularly as the willful blindness of those closest to the scene had prevented any real comprehension of the Russian picture from sifting into the battle-wearied minds of the statesmen at home. Initial incredulity (matched by a woeful underestimation of the holding power of the Bolsheviks) gave place to keen anger at the audacious suggestion of Foreign Commissar Trotsky that all the warring states cease fighting and conclude a general peace. The antiwar slogan of the Bolsheviks (no victory, no annexations) was a sharp knife cutting at the morale of tired peoples throughout the world and, although it rallied support for the Communists within Russia, it was hardly a boon to the victory-pledged leaders of the Allied powers. The United States hastily assured Ambassador Bakhmetev that the Soviet Government would receive no comfort from America (although both the Red Cross and the railroad missions remained in Russia, as did the American and Allied diplomatic representatives).

In January 1918, following the publication by the Bolsheviks of the network of secret treaties among the Allies, the Soviet leaders issued a decree repudiating Russia's international financial obligations. Earlier in the month [American Ambassador] Francis began to hint of the inevitability of a separate peace with Germany; negotiations between representatives of the two powers had been opened on December 22, 1917, and after a fortnight's recess were again continued. Finally, on March 3, 1918, the treaty of Brest-Litovsk was signed. A few days later, in answer to a Japanese query regarding Russia's status as far as the Allies were concerned, the American position was enunciated in what, on the surface at least, could best be described as an equivocal statement. The United States did "not feel justified in regarding Russia either as a neutral or as an enemy, but . . . as an ally," the note declared. However, because of its policy of nonrecognition of the Bolshevik regime, the State Department denied that there was, at present, any Russian Government to deal with. Nevertheless, it still behooved the powers "to treat with Russians as in all respects our friends and allies against the common enemy."

The possibility of Russian defection from the European war had plagued the Allies ever since the March Revolution, and the American declaration was manifestly an indirect plea to the Russians to continue their resistance to the Central powers. This was not the only motive, however, nor was it of

---

greatest importance. For more than three months the question of intervention in Siberia had spasmodically raised its head and the Washington pronouncement in March was aimed obliquely at those nations which favored
such a policy. The explanation of the American opposition was to be found
not primarily in terms of the requirements of the European war, although
these were frequently mentioned and exerted some influence, but rather in
the compulsions of American Far Eastern policy. The State Department
viewed with alarm a potential invasion of Siberian soil by an Allied force which
of necessity would have to consist predominantly of Japanese troops. As a
result the United States was forced into the awkward and contradictory role
of protector of Russian sovereignty, while its loathing of the Russian political
system increased. Beginning in December 1917 and continuing through 1922,
the old American principle of "the territorial integrity of China" was broad-
ened to include Soviet Asia and, indeed, in a very real sense the United States
went further in its efforts to safeguard Russian sovereignty than it had ever
done for the traditionally beleaguered Chinese.

In contrast to the consistent refusal of Washington to countenance intervention prior to July 1918, the Allied powers began to commit themselves
favorably as early as the previous summer, and in the months pursuant to the
November Revolution the United States was subjected to a recurrent diplomatic pressure which eventually caused it to fall in line, however reluctantly.
In their efforts to gain American sanction the Allies employed a variety of
motives, real and assumed, to rationalize their projected invasion. Included
among them might be listed: the re-creation of an Eastern front against the
German army; the oft-repeated fear of German control of Siberia, which
would include the Allied stocks located there; the alleged danger arising from
the existence of Austrian and German prisoners of war in Siberia; the moral
necessity to "rescue" the Czechoslovakian legions in their long trek across
Russia to Vladivostok; the admitted terror evoked by the menace of bolshevism.

Behind these motives lay others of a less publicized nature, but equally
forceful—if not more so—in explaining the Allied attitude. On the part of
France an anathema to communism was inextricably associated with the
Soviet repudiation of debts, the vast percentage of which were owed to French
stockholders. Moreover, the danger to the Third Republic resulting from
Russian withdrawal from the war was more immediate and serious than to
any of its colleagues, and French statesmen were therefore less sober in their
appraisal of the need for intervention than they might otherwise have been.
At the same time France and Britain together feared the probable expropriation of their Russian industrial and commercial properties by a surviving
Communist government. Empire was a major motivating factor to the British:
reports of a potential German-Turkish invasion of India, coupled with rumors
of a German-Japanese rapprochement which would likewise spell disaster for
England's imperial holdings, disposed Downing Street to support the interventionist schemes.

For Japan, anxiety over a possible threat to existent colonial possessions was not so great as the desire to take advantage of the sudden Russian weakness by further expanding Japanese holdings on the Asiatic mainland. While the proponents of this frankly aggressive policy eventually won out, they were opposed in Japan by a more moderate, less militaristic element composed mainly of liberal business men and the enlightened intelligentsia, who seized every opportunity to soften the harsh ambitions of the general staff. Nevertheless, the army was aided immeasurably by the genuine Japanese suspicion of communism, a factor which can doubtless be better appreciated by Americans of the present generation than by those of three decades ago.

The motives, genuine and fabricated, of the Allies in proposing intervention, together with the evolving American position, arose from and were peripheral to Russia's weakened condition. Here was a radical and unproved government exercising unrecognized jurisdiction. Beyond the limited radius of effective Soviet rule Russia consisted of a political vacuum and this drew the powers with the force of a magnet. An irresistible desire to fill the political empty spaces made intervention of some sort inevitable; the rivalry of nations paradoxically lent to the intervention its Allied character.

In the summer and autumn of 1917 the press in the United States and Japan began to feel its way around the still unofficial subject of intervention in Siberia. It was believed by contemporary authors that this newspaper propaganda originated in the Japanese Embassy in London; whether or not this conviction was justified, the fact remained that the press spoke of Japan as the power to which France and Britain would turn if the worsening conditions in Siberia demanded Allied action. In view of Tokyo's geographical propinquity to Siberia and the military situation on the Western front this was a logical inference and, moreover, one borne out by the diplomatic record beginning a few months later.

Apparently trial balloons on the subject of intervention were first sent up almost simultaneously by France and Britain in late November and December 1917. In the instance of France, Clemenceau specifically named Japan as the nation which should supply an expeditionary force; the British Ambassador at Tokyo used a more general approach in discussions with the Japanese Government, but this did not represent any opposition to a unilateral Japanese occupation.

The immediate negative reaction of Tokyo, which recurred periodically throughout the winter and spring of 1918, was motivated primarily by the basic desire that military intervention in Siberia should redound to Japan's imperialist advantage. This desire was forthrightly and unequivocally stated by the Japanese Ambassador in Washington: if America and England "claim certain rights in countries not belonging to them," they "must allow Japan to claim similar rights." This attitude was behind the long efforts of Tokyo to forestall intervention of an inter-Allied character which would perforce circumscribe Japan's freedom of action. For if Britain and France could be prevailed upon to sanction a Japanese intervention, it was certain that Washington could not. But it was not diplomatically feasible so early in the game to veto an international army in favor of a lone Japanese expedition. Consequently, in December 1917 Tokyo went on record as being opposed to any intervention while simultaneously hinting that for security purposes Japan might be compelled to send a token force to Siberia. The result of this double-edged diplomacy was, initially, to endow Japanese policy toward intervention with a "now we're for it, now we're not" quality which was strongly disconcerting to the Allies. The discrepancies between the various Japanese statements rankled Cecil, who wrote Balfour that the Japanese would not inform Britain of their plans, and were irritated by the suggestions of others.

By the end of 1917 the American position with regard to intervention had crystallized into approximately the form it was to maintain until the following summer. Despite the suggestion of Ambassador Francis in November that troops be sent via Vladivostok and Siberia to aid European Russia in the lingering struggle against Germany; despite his forebodings concerning the alleged pro-German attitude of Lenin and Trotsky; and notwithstanding the anti-bolshevism of the American Secretary of State, the general opposition of Washington to Siberian intervention remained intact. This was partially explained by the uncompromising resistance of the War Department. At the same time, Wilson's close friend and adviser, Colonel Edward M. House, urged a noninterventionist policy, on his return from Europe at the close of 1917. Moreover, the absorption of the government in the war needs of the Western front, the general mistrust of any policy which would sanction the presence of Japanese troops on the mainland of Asia, and an historic aversion to foreign intervention seemed to eliminate any alternatives to the policy adhered to by the State Department. With the passage of time the Allies were able to soften the American attitude somewhat, but with few exceptions Washington's position was undeviating.

Early in January a French suggestion that a military mission (composed predominantly of French troops) be sent to Harbin and Irkutsk evoked a negative rejoinder from Tokyo, which for the first time pressed openly its campaign for a unilateral Japanese intervention. Following a notice that a cruiser would shortly be dispatched to Vladivostok, Japan asked that the occupation of that city and of the Chinese Eastern and Amur Railroads be left to her if such action were necessary. And at the end of January the Foreign Minister "rather intimated" that the landing of American troops would not please the Japanese people.

President Wilson had already enunciated the guiding principles of United States policy toward Russia in his message to Congress on January 8.

Whether their present leaders believe it or not, it is our heartfelt desire and hope that some way may be opened whereby we may be privileged to assist the people of Russia to attain their utmost hope of liberty and ordered peace . . . The treatment accorded to Russia by her sister nations in the months to come will be the acid test of their good will, of their comprehension of her needs as distinguished from their own interests, and of their intelligent and unselfish sympathy.

This was reinforced by Lansing's rejection, a week later, of the French-proposed mission to Siberia, and by an American statement to the Japanese Government on January 20. . . .

Meantime the British Foreign Office launched a new offensive to win Washington's consent to intervention. Instead of pressing for a solitary Japanese force the British took their cue from the Soviet attitude and in one move catered to the anti-Japanese sentiment of both Russia and America by suggesting a joint intervention in which United States troops would participate in sizable numbers. In view of the numerous evidences of Bolshevik interest in such a project it is not inconceivable that an American acquiescence at this time would have been followed by some sort of *modus vivendi* with the Soviet Government. However, Wilson was still undecided, and before he had finally cast his lot with the interventionists, Russia and the Allies had become hopelessly alienated.

An event early in April had repercussions which ultimately were more influential in turning the American Government to intervention than all the verbose arguments of the Anglo-French diplomats. Seizing upon an old guise dearly familiar to the imperialistic powers of the West, Tokyo took advantage of the slaying by armed Russians of a Japanese national in Vladivostok and expeditiously occupied the city. Twenty-four hours later (on April 5) the British followed suit, although with fewer troops involved and a semi-apologetic gesture to Trotsky. Both powers were sufficiently adept at this game to assure each other (and thus the world at large) immediately of the disinterestedness of their motives, and the British Government took the extra precaution of urging the United States to join the party.

The reaction in Moscow was spontaneous, bitter, and aimed mainly at Tokyo, with a few pertinent questions directed to London. Nor could the American Government escape the inquisition of the Soviet; on April 7 Foreign Commissar Chicherin, in a note addressed to Raymond Robins, referred to "the highly unfavorable influence" which the Anglo-Japanese landing might have "upon the relations between the Soviet republic" and the United States (a curious statement in view of the absence of formalized contact between the two governments). In concluding, the Foreign Minister demanded "a full and definite immediate statement of the [American] attitude toward the occurrence." Such a report was not forthcoming for a long time, however. A clue to Washington's reticence was given by the President in mid-April. "Unfortunately," he wrote, "the whole state of sentiment in Russia is so confused and even problematical that I have found nothing more difficult than determining what course would be the best to pursue."

One of the major elements to complicate the picture for Washington was the gathering strength of indigenous anti-Soviet factions in Siberia throughout the late winter and early spring of 1918. The existence of these groups was significant to the State Department both for their avowed opposition to communism and for the rumored intrigue of England and Japan with certain of their leaders. Early in February the British interest in Captain Semenov had been acknowledged. A month later the American chargé at Harbin had reported a proposal to restore a Far Eastern army and government in Siberia under Admiral Kolchak. And on April 4 the American consul at Harbin sent a cable to Washington which quoted an alleged telegram from General Tanaka to Horvat. The Japanese general, after expressing his inability to assist the Russians prior to the establishment of a local Siberian Government, stated that following the formation of such a government Japan would be in a position to render aid. In return, Tokyo's "compensation" included:

(1) dismantling of all fortifications at Vladivostok, which should be an open port;

(2) full fishing rights in all Siberia;

(3) open navigation of the Amur River;

(4) preferential forest and mining concessions similar to those demanded of China.

The cable also contained a message from Horvat to the State Department: "Can we secure the support of the United States at all and if so would it continue to the point [of] standing by in case of dispute [with] Japan, or would we be abandoned for commercial reasons?" No sooner had Washington received the Horvat message than a telegram arrived from the Prime Minister of the newly formed autonomous Siberian Government. In tone and language the incipient Russian state echoed the democratic united front promises of the deceased Kerensky regime, and to these pledges it added a vociferous denunciation of all things Bolshevik and an invitation to the Allies to intervene in Russia.

Regardless of the growing distaste with which the American Government viewed the Soviet leaders, President Wilson could not bring himself to encourage "any of the movements for a government of Siberia." Combined with a traditional respect for the right of peoples to self-determination were, on the one hand, an acute suspicion of the control which the Japanese might exert over any Far Eastern Russian government which Washington supported and, on the other hand, the contradictory information in the possession of the State Department concerning the need for Allied intervention.

For several weeks the advocates of a Siberian expedition had been concentrating on the threat posed by German and Austrian prisoners of war who, released following the Brest-Litovsk Treaty, were supposedly about to seize control of Siberia in the interests of the Central powers. Depending on their personal attitudes toward intervention, the German threat was respectively highlighted or discredited by American observers in their reports to Washington, and the consequent discrepancies in these reports made policy-forming uncommonly difficult. In March, Admiral Knight, aboard the U.S.S. *Brooklyn* outside Vladivostok, termed "preposterous" Japanese newspaper statements anticipating the arrival of German forces in eastern Siberia. But early the following month word from Harbin stressed that the only way to save Siberia from the Central powers was through "complete control of the railroad with ample military support." This unqualified opinion was substantiated by the "anti-Bolsheviks" in the United States Foreign Service, including Messrs. Macgowan, Jenkins, Thomson, and Neilsen. Conversely, Paul Reinsch declared emphatically that there was "no evidence of a concerted plan on the part of the Germans to control Siberia through the prisoners, nor could such an attempt succeed"; and in answer to a request from Washington, Professor Thomas G. Masaryk, distinguished leader of the embryonic Czechoslovakian movement, further disparaged the German danger in Siberia and urged closer relations with the Soviet authorities. After sifting the contrary evidences the State Department temporarily acquiesced in the "pro-Soviet" view of the problem:

> The reports of German influence in Siberia appear to have been greatly exaggerated . . . prisoners are for the most part Austro-Hungarian subjects—not German—and . . . who . . . are joining the Bolsheviki in order to fight capitalistic governments. . . . So long as the Bolsheviki are not antagonized by the Allies they and their Austrian confederates may be regarded as co-belligerents with us against the autocracy.

This attitude, with its concomitant of nonintervention, was maintained for the next six weeks despite the resurgence of fresh Anglo-French arguments, supplemented in turn by American consular reports and the pressure of various Russian groups. The chief weapon employed by Paris statesmen to batter down American resistance was the suggestion that independent Japanese action was probable—a contingency which had become all the more plausible since the Japanese landings at Vladivostok on April 4. This approach was also adopted by the Italian Ambassador to Russia, and although Francis wired from Vologda that he "did not believe . . . Japan would intervene against our wishes," he was forced to admit the existence of a "situation which gives a grasping nation a magnificent opportunity."

Only too clearly aware of Tokyo's capacity for infiltration on the mainland of Asia, and stung into further skepticism by the forthright Communist efforts to sow dissension between Japan and America, Secretary Lansing had a long discussion with the newly appointed Japanese Ambassador on April 29. The 1918 version of the Lansing-Ishii conversations produced no executive agreement, but the Secretary of State was nevertheless able to record his gratification that the Japanese agreed "fully" with the American viewpoint, and "do not see at present the military compensation for the danger of uniting the Russian factions to resist intervention and of throwing them into the arms of Germany." On the basis of these reassurances Washington became more emphatic in its opposition to a Siberian expedition.

Meanwhile both France and Britain were stressing the imperative need for intervention to offset the critical situation on the Western front. Toward the end of April, Balfour suggested that London and Washington simultaneously approach the Soviet Government with an offer of Allied intervention and a guarantee of withdrawal at the end of the war, that the American Government agree to participate in the expedition, that the military command be left in Japanese hands. The American response showed the influence of military as well as diplomatic considerations on the Department of State. Regarding the latter, Lansing's political wariness of any cooperative policy with Trotsky had been revealed almost as a reflex immediately after the receipt of the British proposal; moreover, the American statesman was anxious to avoid the alienation of the anti-Soviet forces in Siberia and this would hardly be possible if Washington entered into formal agreements with the Moscow Government. On the military side, the Secretary of State told Lord Reading, the British Ambassador, on May 11 that the United States had thus far been unable "to find any advantages in sending troops to Siberia."

As far as pure strategy was concerned, the American General Staff was pursuing a course of iron logic in its resistance to intervention. In contrast, the Japanese military were of the opinion that something very "effective" would result from an armed expedition into Asiatic Russia, and beginning the middle of May all reports pointed to the rising supremacy of the army group in Tokyo's ruling circles. In over three and a half years of participation in the World War, the Japanese had never been noted for their solicitude regarding the Allied struggle, nor had they been receptive to any suggestions that Japanese troops be sent to the European fighting fronts. Consequently the eager persistence with which Tokyo now pressed for intervention could be explained only on three possible grounds: a genuine fear of a German-controlled Siberia, a similar terror of a Communist regime in the Russia Far East, or an overriding desire to extend the Japanese empire at a crucial moment. That the last of these alternatives was the determining one, and that the other two were employed largely to rationalize an imperialistic policy, was the final verdict of Washington and, indeed, of later history. So that although Ambassador Morris cabled on May 16 that Tokyo was emphasizing "the necessity of establishing order, supporting more moderate elements and repressing Bolshevik movement," its soldier-diplomats were busily taking steps to advance the power position of Japan in Siberia. On one side this was illustrated in the policy adopted toward Kolchak and Semenov, whereby promises of support were offered in turn for questionable "compensation," and in which the two leaders were unscrupulously played off against each other to their common detriment. Thus, following the split between Kolchak and Semenov in mid-May, Tokyo's General Nakajima declared that he would "continue to support with arms and ammunition both factions." In the light of later events, this was an open invitation to fratricide.

Another aspect of Japan's policy was demonstrated in its relations with China. As early as February, Reinsch had been informed of Tokyo's confidential advances to Peking regarding the "disorder" in Siberia, and in March and May respectively the two countries exchanged notes providing for armed collaboration against the enemy, the March agreement in particular being focused on China's northern frontier where the activities of the "Reds" in

Siberia were allegedly endangering the interests of Peking and Tokyo. American skepticism of the usual Japanese variant of "joint cooperation" and American anxiety lest Japan, under the pretext of a possible Siberian intervention, occupy and eventually annex Manchurian territory were added factors in the diplomatic relations of the two countries in the ensuing months.

A third illustration which emphasized the imperialistic basis of Japanese policy was found in the purposeful press campaign by which the suspicions of the peoples of both Siberia and Japan were aroused as to ulterior American intentions in Asiatic Russia. In the main the activities ascribed to the United States were economic, and the following news dispatch, which appeared in papers throughout Japan on May 18, was typical of Tokyo's method:

The United States is making steady progress in its activity in Siberia and it is now reported that the Washington government, as a result of recent agreement with the Bolshevik government, has obtained an exclusive control of the Siberian Railway and Emerson and several other engineers now believed soon to start from Vladivostok for Moscow.

The press in Vladivostok and northern Manchurian cities were fed variations of this, including charges that Washington "means to share with Germany in despoiling Russia."

Official disclaimers from Tokyo sought to blind the State Department to the origin of these sniping news dispatches as well as to Japan's esoteric motives in Siberia. However, unlike previous instances when the proponents of Japanese aggrandizement had been temporarily defeated by the nonmilitary groups, the tacking and weaving of Nippon's policy from May onward represented mere feints to cover an undeviating ambition to intervene in the Russian Far East. At the same time, and notwithstanding Japan's efforts at deception, far more was being perceived than was admitted in Washington, and this gradually led to an about-face in the Wilson policy. Diplomatic etiquette prohibited the two powers from acknowledging their rivalry or the relation of their mutual antagonism to their respective Siberian policies and, ironically, it was left for the blunt-spoken Soviet leaders to forecast the future with cynical realism. On May 14 Lenin prophesied that an "inevitable conflict will arise between Japan and America for supremacy of [the] Pacific and its coasts," and pointed to "the conflicting interests" of the two "imperialistic countries" which, "screened by an alliance against Germany," checked "the movement of Japanese imperialism against Russia."

On June 1 in Paris a special Allied conference considered afresh the Siberian question. A very important factor in the decision to call this meeting was the official interest manifested in intervention by the new Japanese Government under the premiership of Baron Goto. At the Paris session the prime ministers of the European Allies, in conjunction with the Supreme War Council, elaborated three conditions subject to which they would approve Japanese intervention. Japan "should promise to respect the territorial integrity of Russia," to "take no side in the internal politics of the country," to "advance as far west as possible for the purpose of encountering the Germans." According to the advices forwarded to Washington, on the receipt of a satisfactory Japanese response the American Government would be approached "as it was well known that the Japanese Government would not act" without United States approval and consent. . . .

. . . On June 18 Wilson informed the French Ambassador to Japan that he "was considering anew the entire situation, and would express his conclusions within the next ten days." Commenting on this statement afterwards, the French Ambassador to Russia remarked that Wilson's protestations revealed his hostility to an expedition which "by the nature of things would have to be executed by the Japanese." This, of course, was the crux of the whole issue as far as Washington was concerned. Aside from Ambassador Francis, whose naïveté regarding power politics was demonstrated in this, as in frequent other instances, the State Department had little faith in Japanese declarations, no matter how eloquently phrased. Thus the official reply of Tokyo to the Allied communication in early June, in which the "conditions" of Japanese intervention had been outlined, was only partially satisfactory to the Wilson Government. After reiterating its disinclination to consider intervention without American sanction, and its willingness, in the event that such a sanction were obtained, to abide by the first two Allied condtions, the Japanese note stated:

With regard to the third condition, requiring the Allied expedition to advance as far West as possible, the Japanese Government regret that they should find it impossible for them to engage to extend Westward their military activities beyond the limits of Eastern Siberia, in view of the grave difficulties with which such operations will be practically confronted.

The utility of such limited intervention in terms of reestablishing the Eastern front, capturing the majority of escaped prisoners of war, and protecting the sizable Allied stocks between Lake Baikal and the Urals was highly doubtful to Washington, and therefore the motives of Tokyo were once again questioned. But by the end of June there were indications that intervention in Siberia would eventuate in the not-distant future, with or without American approval; and given the myriad pressures on the State Department, the Czechoslovakian "justification," the admitted dislike for the Bolsheviks, and the implications for America's Far Eastern position in a Japanese-sponsored expedition, the United States had little latitude in formulating its policy. Accordingly, President Wilson summoned to the White House on July 6 the Secretaries of State, War, and Navy, General March, and Admiral Benson. The conferees discussed in detail the ramifications of the Siberian issue, and emerged with a document which was a tribute to the confusion surrounding the problem and which anticipated the public statement of American policy a few weeks later. In brief, the imploring Allied appeals for the establishment of an Eastern front were repudiated as a valid cause for intervention; evacuation of the Czechs from Russia was unhappily omitted in the numerous references which stressed solely the need to protect these exiles in their march to join their compatriots in the *interior* of Siberia; and the inter-Allied expedition to accomplish this was to consist of seven thousand Americans and an equal number of Japanese, armed with weapons of war and promises of non-interference.

From a memorandum on July 8 Lansing appeared to be convinced that Viscount Ishii shared the American point of view as to the purposes of intervention and the numerical strength to be employed. The underlying discordance between the two countries was sufficiently manifested in the next ten days, however, to belie the outward aura of calm and mutual trustfulness. In the first place, information relating to the newly formed Horvat Government in Siberia, reputedly monarchist in sentiment and backed by Tokyo, was extremely disquieting to the State Department. Although the Japanese Foreign Minister, in response to an American note, promptly assured Ambassador Morris that "Japan would pledge herself not to support any group or interfere in the internal politics of Siberia," other points of irritation persisted. In the main these were centered on Japanese activities in Manchuria and along the Chinese Eastern Railroad, where it was apparent that Tokyo was seeking to infiltrate under spurious pretenses. For example, Washington had been notified by China three months previously that Japan was opposed to any arrangement whereby American assistance would be used on the railroad in northern Manchuria. And in May the Horvat faction, always associated with Japan in the Washington mind, had reached an agreement with China which reorganized the board of directors of the C.E.R. with the result that the legal connection with the Russian Government, dating back to the treaty of 1896, was dissolved "until [the] complete restoration of order in Russia." In reply to the report in July that China was contemplating action to regain control of the line—a control which, once again, was inalterably linked to Japanese maneuvers, by the State Department—the American Government felt compelled to defend the rights of the State of Russia and to protest any untoward step by Peking. Moreover, a similar démarche was sent to Tokyo on July 19 after Morris had telegraphed: "The General Staff is urging upon the Cabinet the immediate occupation of Manchuria by Japanese troops . . . The plan submitted includes taking over the control of the Chinese Eastern Railroad." While the twin problems of Manchuria and the C.E.R. continued to worry the United States long after American troops had entered Siberia, they were simultaneously additional factors in precipitating the decision to intervene.

On July 17 the Secretary of State dispatched an *aide-mémoire* to the Allies and Japan which proposed that America and Japan each send seven thousand troops to "assist the Czechoslovaks in Siberia." Surrounding the core of the declaration were successive layers of platitudes and inconsistencies which were intended to soothe Russian feelings, delimit by inference Japanese activity, and outline broadly America's motives. . . .

On July 24 the Japanese Ambassador conferred with Acting Secretary Polk and stated quite frankly that "his government for political reasons could not bind itself to limit the force to 7,000," as this would be regarded by the opposition as an Allied vote of no confidence in Tokyo's motives. Therefore Japan would dispatch an initial force of "about 12,000 men," but with the implicit understanding that the total number of troops to be sent "would depend on the amount of resistance that they met from the Bolsheviks, Austrian and German prisoners." "I tried to argue with him as to limiting the number to 7,000," wrote Polk to the President, "but without success." In the official declaration left by Ishii at the Department on the same day Japan emphasized its solicitude for the Russian people, its concern over the fate of the Czechs, and, of paramount importance, its "special position" vis-à-vis Asia.

The Japanese counter-proposal was received in Washington with undisguised consternation. On the 26th Polk told Ishii: "The acceptance of the Japanese Government was not an acceptance of our proposal but a new proposal."

We felt that by sending troops in not only without any limitation as to number, but even indicating that more troops would be sent if the occasion demanded, the natural impression would be created in the Russian mind that this was an expedition which had more in view than merely assisting the Czechs. We felt . . . that the number should be limited, and if later it appeared that this force was not adequate, the question could be discussed and this Government would then . . . decide whether they would continue or . . . withdraw, leaving the Japanese and the other Governments to proceed if they saw fit.

I also called his attention to the words "having regard at the same time to the special position of Japan," and said that it hardly seemed necessary to put that in, as the Lansing-Ishii agreement very clearly indicated our attitude toward Japan . . . but putting it in might create difficulties in Russia . . .

Nor was the Japanese declaration the only source of American anxiety. On July 24 MacMurray telegraphed from Peking that China had been notified of the Japanese plan, and that Tokyo expected automatic Chinese approval of the establishment of Japanese railroad patrols along the Chinese Eastern Railroad in Manchuria, on the basis of the Sino-Japanese military convention. Two days later Assistant Secretary of State Long sought to counteract Tokyo's move by informing Chinese Minister Koo that in the event of a Siberian intervention the United States felt it would "be advisable" for China to control "alone . . . that part of the Chinese Eastern Railroad which lies within Chinese territory." This advice was passed along to Japan on July 29. The receipt of word at the end of the month that Tokyo had ordered "a number of torpedo boats to Nicolaievsk to protect Japanese interests," added to the above instances of Japan's policy toward intervention, caused Wilson to complain bitterly that "the Japanese Government is trying to alter the whole plan in a way to which we cannot consent and for the time being . . . the whole matter is in suspense."

This atmosphere did not prevail for long, however. On August 1 and 2 Japan yielded sufficiently to the American position to win final approval for the Siberian expedition. In the first place the Minister for Foreign Affairs let it be known that while the situation concerning the Chinese Eastern was a difficult one, Tokyo would doubtless agree to Washington's suggestion that only Chinese troops be utilized to guard the railroad "simply because . . . [the Japanese minister] and his colleagues desired to act in full accord with our views." In regard to the Siberian intervention in particular, Viscount Ishii presented the State Department with an undated memorandum on August 2 which omitted the most disturbing features of the July 24 pronouncement. Although Tokyo still balked at committing itself to round numbers in describing its military contingent, the Wilson Government was apparently satisfied with the oral explanations of the Japanese Ambassador and on the afternoon of August 3 the official American declaration on intervention was given to the Allies and the press. In every important respect the August statement was almost identical with that which had been circulated among the Entente powers on July 17; in other words, the criticisms of the Allies were not incorporated in the final American draft and the latter was as replete with contradictions as the initial proposal: Washington consented to an intervention of which it heartily disapproved; it sought to limit the action of the Allies by freeing them of its own self-imposed restrictions; and it renounced political interference by offering assistance to those Russians who desired it.

Wherein lay the explanation for this bundle of diplomatic inconsistencies which, through its ambiguity, provided a platform on which the Principal Allied and Associated Powers could stand in superficial agreement, the while they clung to their respective, and frequently antithetical, motives for intervention?

In the preceding eight months Britain and France had gradually swung to an espousal of a large-scale intervention; one in which a million or more Allied troops, predominantly Japanese, would invade Siberia and march west through Russia in order to halt the movement of German forces from the Eastern front to France. The growing terror of a German victory and the accompanying dread of the loss of the Anglo-French colonies in southeast Asia were mainly responsible for the Allied position, and these factors had relegated to the background the pardonable fear of Japanese entrenchment in Siberia after the war.

In contrast, Tokyo was opposed to the creation of a "second front" in the Russian Far East. To the general staff the German danger was as incidental to Japanese policy as it had been for the past three years, and accordingly Japan was explicit in its unwillingness to dispatch troops west of Irkutsk—a point too many hundreds of miles from the European battle lines to have any important bearing on the struggle. At the same time, Tokyo was equally adamant in its refusal to countenance a "small" intervention, reserving ultimate freedom of action in determining the number of troops it would send to Eastern Siberia.

The American high command, averse on grounds of strategy to *any* intervention, large or small, had provided the Wilson Administration with one of its most convincing arguments for many weeks. Secretary Baker recounted some years later that the President had told him of his satisfaction "with the soundness of the War Department's view but that, *for other than military reasons, he felt obliged to cooperate* in a limited way in both proposed expeditions." The sense of obligation which moved Wilson to participate in an intervention which he believed to be unjustified from a military standpoint could have stemmed only from political considerations. To what extent, it may then be asked, did these considerations of high policy emanate from a hatred of communism, and to what extent from a fear of Japan?

The anti-bolshevism of the American press and people was unqualifiedly articulate throughout the spring and summer of 1918, and the President expressed his own feeling for the Soviet when he wrote: "I don't think you need fear any consequences of our dealing with the Bolsheviki, because we do not intend to deal with them." With this in mind, the August declaration that the United States desired "to steady any efforts at self-government . . . in which the Russians themselves may be willing to accept assistance" could not have been intended to console the Soviet rulers. This was confirmed by the sharp reproof cast upon American motives by the Bolsheviks a few weeks later. Nevertheless, logic required that anti-communism be dismissed as the guiding motive in the American policy. In the first place, it in no wise explained the unremitting attempts of the State Department to forestall intervention from December 1917 through June of the following year; and secondly, an expedition limited by American insistence to a few thousand men could not conceivably have unseated the Soviet Government. Once the decision to intervene had been made, the emotional antipathy of the American people to bolshevism played the role of an accessory, a role which was overemphasized simply because the principal motive behind the American intervention was never openly revealed. The closest which Washington came to such a revelation was in that part of the August statement which solemnly assured the Russian people that the United States contemplated no action which would in any way impinge on Russia's sovereignty and territorial integrity. In view of the historic aloofness of America to foreign conquest this pledge was intended to tie other hands than its own, specifically those of Japan.

In essence, the United States consented to intervene after a policy-duel of several months had failed to turn the Japanese from their desire to send an army to Siberia, a desire in which Tokyo had received support and encouragement from London and Paris. Having witnessed the penetration of Japanese imperialism on the mainland of Asia between 1914 and 1917, Washington had no illusions concerning the true intentions of Tokyo in Siberia. Similarly, the State Department was at last fully cognizant of the impotence of diplomatic protests unaccompanied by physical commitments. Viewed from the perspective of history, the August pronouncement on the purposes and goals of the Siberian expedition was therefore an integral part of American Far Eastern policy: Czechs, Germans, the war in Europe, and the interests of the Russian people provided a moral rationalization for what was basically a political struggle between Japan and the United States. In the summer of 1918 the scales of power in Asia were weighted heavily on the side of Tokyo, and the twin principles by which America had traditionally sought to protect its interests—the open-door and the preservation of the territorial integrity of Asiatic states—were in danger of lasting effacement. The necessity to stop the Japanese drive for empire was accordingly imperative. By virtue of war and revolution Soviet Russia became the scene of the battle, and the United States emerged as the defender of Russian sovereignty in the Far East.

9

Wilson at Versailles:

INCOMPETENT EGOTIST
or
PHILOSOPHER–KING?

As the war drew to a close, President Wilson turned his mind to thoughts of peace. He was determined that the peace would be just and lasting, honorable and fair—a "peace without victory." In a series of speeches in 1918, he laid down various proposals for such a peace. The most comprehensive blueprint, however, appeared in his famous address to Congress on January 8, 1918, the Fourteen Points. He called for the end of secret diplomacy, freedom of the seas, removal of trade barriers, reduction in armament, adjustment of colonial claims, settlement of territorial boundaries consistent with ethnographic justice, and the creation of a League of Nations. These principles were accepted by the Germans on October 13, 1918, and by the Allies on November 4, and they thus became the bases for the peace negotiations.

Wilson himself journeyed to Europe to insure the adoption of his program at the peace conference. He landed at Brest on December 13, 1918, and after a triumphant four-week tour of Great Britain, Italy, and France, during which millions of Europeans hailed him a modern Messiah, he settled down in Paris with the other Allied leaders to draft the treaty. The Treaty of Versailles which was signed on June 28, 1919, after more than five months of deliberation, violated many of Wilson's ideas. To be sure, a League of Nations was included and many of the territorial settlements were just, but Japan's retaining of Shantung and the assignment of Southern Tyrol to Italy betrayed the principle of national self-determination. And the economic sections of the treaty saddled Germany with a cruel and unrealistic financial burden. Why did the President fail to have all of his proposals incorporated in the treaty? Who was responsible for violating the promises to adhere to the Fourteen Points?

One of the most influential books of the post-World War I period was written by J. M. Keynes, the eminent British economist, from which a chapter is reproduced below. It is a severe and harsh indictment of the Treaty of Versailles, particularly its economic sections. He considers the treaty a failure and blames Woodrow Wilson. He ascribes the President's inability to negotiate a just and honorable treaty based on the Fourteen Points to Wilson's debilities—"one of the decisive moral events of history." The President, according to Keynes, was unsuited by qualities of mind, character, and temperament to overcome the guiles of the experienced European statesmen who demanded a vindictive peace. He lacked sufficient intellectual equipment, was insensitive to his surroundings, had come to Paris without detailed proposals, demonstrated incompetence in the "agilities of the council chamber," possessed a slow mind, and had an arrogant, egotistical, and obstinate character. This "blind and deaf Don Quixote" who before the treaty had appeared to the world as the savior of mankind simply did not measure up to the challenge. The Presbyterian theocrat was "bamboozled" by Clemenceau and Lloyd George.

Paul Birdsall, a historian at Williams College, sees the circumstances differently. Keynes's account he calls "caricature not history." He does not agree that Wilson failed completely. After all, the League of Nations must be counted a victory for Wilsonianism, and equally successful, although in a negative sense, was the President's moderating influence on Clemenceau and Lloyd George. Had that influence been removed, the treaty could, indeed, have been Carthaginian. Birdsall admits that the settlement contained many unfortunate provisions, but they must be considered in the light of certain conditions over which Wilson had no control. The Congressional elections of 1918 placed a Republican majority in the House and the Senate, thereby impairing the President's prestige at home. Within his own delegation he lacked support—Lansing did not want the League of Nations and Colonel House wanted one so badly that he was willing to give France and Britain anything they desired in exchange for their support. As for the cession of Shantung to Japan, that country's diplomatic and political position was unassailable. Wilson appears in Birdsall's portrait not as arrogant and obdurate, but shy and sensitive—a great leader who was simply too idealistic for the harsh and realistic climate of Paris.

The Conference

JOHN MAYNARD KEYNES

In Chapters IV. and V. [of *The Economic Consequences of the Peace*] I shall study in some detail the economic and financial provisions of the Treaty of Peace with Germany. But it will be easier to appreciate the true origin of many of these terms if we examine here some of the personal factors which influenced their preparation. In attempting this task, I touch, inevitably, questions of motive, on which spectators are liable to error and are not entitled to take on themselves the responsibilities of final judgment. Yet, if I seem in this chapter to assume sometimes the liberties which are habitual to historians, but which, in spite of the greater knowledge with which we speak, we generally hesitate to assume towards contemporaries, let the reader excuse me when he remembers how greatly, if it is to understand its destiny, the world needs light, even if it is partial and uncertain, on the complex struggle of human will and purpose, not yet finished, which, concentrated in the persons of four individuals in a manner never paralleled, made them, in the first months of 1919, the microcosm of mankind.

In those parts of the Treaty with which I am here concerned, the lead was taken by the French, in the sense that it was generally they who made in the first instance the most definite and the most extreme proposals. This was partly a matter of tactics. When the final result is expected to be a compromise, it is often prudent to start from an extreme position; and the French anticipated at the outset—like most other persons—a double process of compromise, first of all to suit the ideas of their allies and associates, and secondly in the course of the Peace Conference proper with the Germans themselves. These tactics were justified by the event. Clemenceau gained a reputation for moderation with his colleagues in Council by sometimes throwing over with an air of intellectual impartiality the more extreme proposals of his ministers; and much went through where the American and British critics were naturally a little ignorant of the true point at issue, or where too persistent criticism by France's allies put them in a position which they felt as invidious,

---

of always appearing to take the enemy's part and to argue his case. Where, therefore, British and American interests were not seriously involved their criticism grew slack, and some provisions were thus passed which the French themselves did not take very seriously, and for which the eleventh hour decision to allow no discussion with the Germans removed the opportunity of remedy.

But, apart from tactics, the French had a policy. Although Clemenceau might curtly abandon the claims of a Klotz or a Loucheur, or close his eyes with an air of fatigue when French interests were no longer involved in the discussion, he knew which points were vital, and these he abated little. In so far as the main economic lines of the Treaty represent an intellectual idea, it is the idea of France and of Clemenceau.

Clemenceau was by far the most eminent member of the Council of Four, and he had taken the measure of his colleagues. He alone both had an idea and had considered it in all its consequences. His age, his character, his wit, and his appearance joined to give him objectivity and a defined outline in an environment of confusion. One could not despise Clemenceau or dislike him, but only take a different view as to the nature of civilized man, or indulge, at least, a different hope.

The figure and bearing of Clemenceau are universally familiar. At the Council of Four he wore a square-tailed coat of very good, thick black broadcloth, and on his hands, which were never uncovered, gray suède gloves; his boots were of thick black leather, very good, but of a country style, and sometimes fastened in front, curiously, by a buckle instead of laces. His seat in the room in the President's house, where the regular meetings of the Council of Four were held (as distinguished from their private and unattended conferences in a smaller chamber below) was on a square brocaded chair in the middle of the semicircle facing the fireplace, with Signor Orlando on his left, the President next by the fireplace, and the Prime Minister opposite on the other side of the fireplace on his right. He carried no papers and no portfolio, and was unattended by any personal secretary, though several French ministers and officials appropriate to the particular matter in hand would be present round him. His walk, his hand, and his voice were not lacking in vigor, but he bore, nevertheless, especially after the attempt upon him, the aspect of a very old man conserving his strength for important occasions. He spoke seldom, leaving the initial statement of the French case to his ministers or officials; he closed his eyes often and sat back in his chair with an impassive face of parchment, his gray gloved hands clasped in front of him. A short sentence, decisive or cynical, was generally sufficient, a question, an unqualified abandonment of his ministers, whose face would not be saved, or a display of obstinacy reinforced by a few words in a piquantly delivered English. But speech and passion were not lacking when they were wanted, and the sudden outburst of words, often followed by a fit of deep coughing from the chest, produced their impression rather by force and surprise than by persuasion.

Not infrequently Mr. Lloyd George, after delivering a speech in English, would, during the period of its interpretation into French, cross the hearthrug to the President to reinforce his case by some *ad hominem* argument in private conversation, or to sound the ground for a compromise,—and this would sometimes be the signal for a general upheaval and disorder. The President's advisers would press round him, a moment later the British experts would dribble across to learn the result or see that all was well, and next the French would be there, a little suspicious lest the others were arranging something behind them, until all the room were on their feet and conversation was general in both languages. My last and most vivid impression is of such a scene—the President and the Prime Minister as the center of a surging mob and a babel of sound, a welter of eager, impromptu compromises and counter-compromises, all sound and fury signifying nothing, on what was an unreal question anyhow, the great issues of the morning's meeting forgotten and neglected; and Clemenceau silent and aloof on the outskirts—for nothing which touched the security of France was forward—throned, in his gray gloves, on the brocade chair, dry in soul and empty of hope, very old and tired, but surveying the scene with a cynical and almost impish air; and when at last silence was restored and the company had returned to their places, it was to discover that he had disappeared.

He felt about France what Pericles felt of Athens—unique value in her, nothing else mattering; but his theory of politics was Bismarck's. He had one illusion—France; and one disillusion—mankind, including Frenchmen, and his colleagues not least. His principles for the peace can be expressed simply. In the first place, he was a foremost believer in the view of German psychology, that the German understands and can understand nothing but intimidation, that he is without generosity or remorse in negotiation, that there is no advantage he will not take of you, and no extent to which he will not demean himself for profit, that he is without honor, pride, or mercy. Therefore you must never negotiate with a German or conciliate him; you must dictate to him. On no other terms will he respect you, or will you prevent him from cheating you. But it is doubtful how far he thought these characteristics peculiar to Germany, or whether his candid view of some other nations was fundamentally different. His philosophy had, therefore, no place for "sentimentaility" in international relations. Nations are real things, of whom you love one and feel for the rest indifference—or hatred. The glory of the nation you love is a desirable end,—but generally to be obtained at your neighbor's expense. The politics of power are inevitable, and there is nothing very new to learn about this war or the end it was fought for; England had destroyed, as in each preceding century, a trade rival; a mighty chapter had been closed in the secular struggle between the glories of Germany and of France. Prudence required some measure of lip service to the "ideals" of foolish Americans and hypocritical Englishmen; but it would be stupid to believe that there is much room in the world, as it really is, for such affairs as the League of Nations, or any sense in the principle of self-determination except as an ingenious formula for rearranging the balance of power in one's own interests.

These, however, are generalities. In tracing the practical details of the Peace which he thought necessary for the power and the security of France, we must go back to the historical causes which had operated during his lifetime. Before the Franco-German war the populations of France and Germany were approximately equal; but the coal and iron and shipping of Germany were in their infancy, and the wealth of France was greatly superior. Even after the loss of Alsace-Lorraine there was no great discrepancy between the real resources of the two countries. But in the intervening period the relative position had changed completely. By 1914 the population of Germany was nearly seventy per cent in excess of that of France; she had become one of the first manufacturing and trading nations of the world; her technical skill and her means for the production of future wealth were unequaled. France on the other hand had a stationary or declining population, and, relatively to others, had fallen seriously·behind in wealth and in the power to produce it.

In spite, therefore, of France's victorious issue from the present struggle (with the aid, this time, of England and America), her future position remained precarious in the eyes of one who took the view that European civil war is to be regarded as a normal, or at least a recurrent, state of affairs for the future, and that the sort of conflicts between organized great powers which have occupied the past hundred years will also engage the next. According to this vision of the future, European history is to be a perpetual prize-fight, of which France has won this round, but of which this round is certainly not the last. From the belief that essentially the old order does not change, being based on human nature which is always the same, and from a consequent skepticism of all that class of doctrine which the League of Nations stands for, the policy of France and of Clemenceau followed logically. For a Peace of magnanimity or of fair and equal treatment, based on such "ideology" as the Fourteen Points of the President, could only have the effect of shortening the interval of Germany's recovery and hastening the day when she will once again hurl at France her greater numbers and her superior resources and technical skill. Hence the necessity of "guarantees"; and each guarantee that was taken, by increasing irritation and thus the probability of a subsequent *revanche* by Germany, made necessary yet further provisions to crush. Thus, as soon as this view of the world is adopted and the other discarded, a demand for a Carthaginian Peace is inevitable, to the full extent of the momentary power to impose it. For Clemenceau made no pretense of considering himself bound by the Fourteen Points and left chiefly to others such concoctions as were necessary from time to time to save the scruples or the face of the President.

So far as possible, therefore, it was the policy of France to set the clock back and to undo what, since 1870, the progress of Germany had accomplished. By loss of territory and other measures her population was to be curtailed; but chiefly the economic system, upon which she depended for her new strength, the vast fabric built upon iron, coal, and transport must be destroyed. If France could seize, even in part, what Germany was compelled to drop, the inequality of strength between the two rivals for European hegemony might be remedied for many generations.

Hence sprang those cumulative provisions for the destruction of highly organized economic life which we shall examine in the next chapter.

This is the policy of an old man, whose most vivid impressions and most lively imagination are of the past and not of the future. He sees the issue in terms of France and Germany, not of humanity and of European civilization sturggling forwards to a new order. The war has bitten into his consciousness somewhat differently from ours, and he neither expects nor hopes that we are at the threshold of a new age.

It happens, however, that it is not only an ideal question that is at issue. My purpose in this book is to show that the Carthaginian Peace is not *practically* right or possible. Although the school of thought from which it springs is aware of the economic factor, it overlooks, nevertheless, the deeper economic tendencies which are to govern the future. The clock cannot be set back. You cannot restore Central Europe to 1870 without setting up such strains in the European structure and letting loose such human and spiritual forces as, pushing beyond frontiers and races, will overwhelm not only you and your "guarantees," but your institutions, and the existing order of your society.

By what legerdemain was this policy substituted for the Fourteen Points, and how did the President come to accept it? The answer to these questions is difficult and depends on elements of character and psychology and on the subtle influence of surroundings, which are hard to detect and harder still to describe. But, if ever the action of a single individual matters, the collapse of the President has been one of the decisive moral events of history; and I must make an attempt to explain it. What a place the President held in the hearts and hopes of the world when he sailed to us in the *George Washington!* What a great man came to Europe in those early days of our victory!

In November, 1918, the armies of Foch and the words of Wilson had brought us sudden escape from what was swallowing up all we cared for. The conditions seemed favorable beyond any expectation. The victory was so complete that fear need play no part in the settlement. The enemy had laid down his arms in reliance on a solemn compact as to the general character of the Peace, the terms of which seemed to assure a settlement of justice and magnanimity and a fair hope for a restoration of the broken current of life. To make assurance certain the President was coming himself to set the seal on his work.

When President Wilson left Washington he enjoyed a prestige and a moral influence throughout the world unequaled in history. His bold and measured words carried to the peoples of Europe above and beyond the voices of their own politicians. The enemy peoples trusted him to carry out the compact he had made with them; and the allied peoples acknowledged him not as a victor only but almost as a prophet. In addition to this moral influence the realities of power were in his hands. The American armies were at the height of their numbers, discipline, and equipment. Europe was in complete dependence on the food supplies of the United States; and financially she was even more absolutely at their mercy. Europe not only already owed the United States more than she could pay; but only a large measure of further assistance could save her from starvation and bankruptcy. Never had a philosopher held such weapons wherewith to bind the princes of this world. How the crowds of the European capitals pressed about the carriage of the President! With what curiosity, anxiety, and hope we sought a glimpse of the features and bearing of the man of destiny who, coming from the West, was to bring healing to the wounds of the ancient parent of his civilization and lay for us the foundations of the future.

The disillusion was so complete, that some of those who had trusted most hardly dared speak of it. Could it be true? they asked of those who returned from Paris. Was the Treaty really as bad as it seemed? What had happened to the President? What weakness or what misfortune had led to so extraordinary, so unlooked-for a betrayal?

Yet the causes were very ordinary and human. The President was not a hero or a prophet; he was not even a philosopher; but a generously intentioned man, with many of the weaknesses of other human beings, and lacking that dominating intellectual equipment which would have been necessary to cope with the subtle and dangerous spellbinders whom a tremendous clash of forces and personalities had brought to the top as triumphant masters in the swift game of give and take, face to face in Council,—a game of which he had no experience at all.

We had indeed quite a wrong idea of the President. We knew him to be solitary and aloof, and believed him very strong-willed and obstinate. We did not figure him as a man of detail, but the clearness with which he had taken hold of certain main ideas would, we thought, in combination with his tenacity, enable him to sweep through cobwebs. Besides these qualities he would have the objectivity, the cultivation, and the wide knowledge of the student. The great distinction of language which had marked his famous Notes seemed to indicate a man of lofty and powerful imagination. His portraits indicated a fine presence and commanding delivery. With all this he had attained and held with increasing authority the first position in a country where the arts of the politician are not neglected. All of which, without expecting the impossible, seemed a fine combination of qualities for the matter in hand.

The first impression of Mr. Wilson at close quarters was to impair some but not all of these illusions. His head and features were finely cut and exactly like his photographs, and the muscles of his neck and the carriage of his head were distinguished. But, like Odysseus, the President looked wiser when he was seated; and his hands, though capable and fairly strong, were wanting in sensitiveness and finesse. The first glance at the President suggested not only that, whatever else he might be, his temperament was not primarily that of the student or the scholar, but that he had not much even of that culture of the world which marks M. Clemenceau and Mr. Balfour as exquisitely cultivated gentlemen of their class and generation. But more serious than this, he was not only insensitive to his surroundings in the external sense, he was not sensitive to his environment at all. What chance could such a man have against Mr. Lloyd George's unerring, almost medium-like, sensibility to every one immediately round him? To see the British Prime Minister watching the company, with six or seven senses not available to ordinary men, judging character, motive, and subconscious impulse, perceiving what each was thinking and even what each was going to say next, and compounding with telepathic instinct the argument or appeal best suited to the vanity, weakness, or self-interest of his immediate auditor, was to realize that the poor President would be playing blind man's buff in that party. Never could a man have stepped into the parlor a more perfect and predestined victim to the finished accomplishments of the Prime Minister. The Old World was tough in wickedness anyhow; the Old World's heart of stone might blunt the sharpest blade of the bravest knight-errant. But this blind and deaf Don Quixote was entering a cavern where the swift and glittering blade was in the hands of the adversary.

But if the President was not the philosopher-king, what was he? After all, he was a man who had spent much of his life at a University. He was by no means a business man or an ordinary party politician, but a man of force, personality, and importance. What, then, was his temperament?

The clue once found was illuminating. The President was like a Nonconformist minister, perhaps a Presbyterian. His thought and his temperament were essentially theological not intellectual, with all the strength and the weakness of that manner of thought, feeling, and expression. It is a type of which there are not now in England and Scotland such magnificent specimens as formerly; but this description, nevertheless, will give the ordinary Englishman the distinctest impression of the President.

With this picture of him in mind, we can return to the actual course of events. The President's program for the World, as set forth in his speeches and his Notes, had displayed a spirit and a purpose so admirable that the last desire of his sympathizers was to criticize details,—the details, they felt, were quite rightly not filled in at present, but would be in due course. It was commonly believed at the commencement of the Paris Conference that the President had thought out, with the aid of a large body of advisers, a comprehensive scheme not only for the League of Nations, but for the embodiment of the Fourteen Points in an actual Treaty of Peace. But in fact the President had thought out nothing; when it came to practice his ideas were nebulous and incomplete. He had no plan, no scheme, no constructive ideas whatever for clothing with the flesh of life the commandments which he had thundered from the White House. He could have preached a sermon on any of them or have addressed a stately prayer to the Almighty for their fulfilment; but he could not frame their concrete application to the actual state of Europe.

He not only had no proposals in detail, but he was in many respects, perhaps inevitably, ill-informed as to European conditions. And not only was he ill-informed—that was true of Mr. Lloyd George also—but his mind was slow and unadaptable. The President's slowness amongst the Europeans was noteworthy. He could not, all in a minute, take in what the rest were saying, size up the situation with a glance, frame a reply, and meet the case by a slight change of ground; and he was liable, therefore, to defeat by the mere swiftness, apprehension, and agility of a Lloyd George. There can seldom have been a statesman of the first rank more incompetent than the President in the agilities of the council chamber. A moment often arrives when substantial victory is yours if by some slight appearance of a concession you can save the face of the opposition or conciliate them by a restatement of your proposal helpful to them and not injurious to anything essential to yourself. The President was not equipped with this simple and usual artfulness. His mind was too slow and unresourceful to be ready with *any* alternatives. The President was capable of digging his toes in and refusing to budge, as he did over Fiume. But he had no other mode of defense, and it needed as a rule but little manœuvering by his opponents to prevent matters from coming to such a head until it was too late. By pleasantness and an appearance of conciliation, the President would be manœuvred off his ground, would miss the moment for digging his toes in, and, before he knew where he had been got to, it was too late. Besides, it is impossible month after month in intimate and ostensibly friendly converse between close associates, to be digging the toes in all the time. Victory would only have been possible to one who had always a sufficiently lively apprehension of the position as a whole to reserve his fire and know for certain the rare exact moments for decisive action. And for that the President was far too slow-minded and bewildered.

He did not remedy these defects by seeking aid from the collective wisdom of his lieutenants. He had gathered round him for the economic chapters of the Treaty a very able group of business men; but they were inexperienced in public affairs, and knew (with one or two exceptions) as little of Europe as he did, and they were only called in irregularly as he might need them for a particular purpose. Thus the aloofness which had been found effective in Washington was maintained, and the abnormal reserve of his nature did not allow near him any one who aspired to moral equality or the continuous exercise of influence. His fellow-plenipotentiaries were dummies; and even the trusted Colonel House, with vastly more knowledge of men and of Europe than the President, from whose sensitiveness the President's dullness had gained so much, fell into the background as time went on. All this was encouraged by his colleagues on the Council of Four, who, by the break-up of the Council of Ten, completed the isolation which the President's own temperament had initiated. Thus day after day and week after week, he allowed himself to be closeted, unsupported, unadvised, and alone, with men much sharper than himself, in situations of supreme difficulty, where he needed for success every description of resource, fertility, and knowledge. He allowed himself to be drugged by their atmosphere, to discuss on the basis of their plans and of their data, and to be led along their paths.

These and other various causes combined to produce the following situation. The reader must remember that the processes which are here compressed into a few pages took place slowly, gradually, insidiously, over a period of about five months.

As the President had thought nothing out, the Council was generally working on the basis of a French or British draft. He had to take up, therefore, a persistent attitude of obstruction, criticism, and negation, if the draft was to become at all in line with his own ideas and purpose. If he was met on some points with apparent generosity (for there was always a safe margin of quite preposterous suggestions which no one took seriously), it was difficult for him not to yield on others. Compromise was inevitable, and never to compromise on the essential, very difficult. Besides, he was soon made to appear to be taking the German part and laid himself open to the suggestion (to which he was foolishly and unfortunately sensitive) of being "pro-German."

After a display of much principle and dignity in the early days of the Council of Ten, he discovered that there were certain very important points in the program, of his French, British, or Italian colleague, as the case might be, of which he was incapable of securing the surrender by the methods of secret diplomacy. What then was he to do in the last resort? He could let the Conference drag on an endless length by the exercise of sheer obstinacy. He could break it up and return to America in a rage with nothing settled. Or he could attempt an appeal to the world over the heads of the Conference. These were wretched alternatives, against each of which a great deal could be said. They were also very risky,—especially for a politician. The President's mistaken policy over the Congressional election had weakened his personal position in his own country, and it was by no means certain that the American public would support him in a position of intransigeancy. It would mean a campaign in which the issues would be clouded by every sort of personal and party consideration, and who could say if right would triumph in a struggle which would certainly not be decided on its merits. Besides, any open rupture with his colleagues would certainly bring upon his head the blind passions of "anti-German" resentment with which the public of all allied countries were still inspired. They would not listen to his arguments. They would not be cool enough to treat the issue as one of international morality or of the right governance of Europe. The cry would simply be that, for various sinister and selfish reasons, the President wished "to let the Hun off." The almost unanimous voice of the French and British press could be anticipated. Thus, if he threw down the gage publicly he might be defeated. And if he were defeated, would not the final Peace be far worse than if he were to retain his prestige and endeavor to make it as good as the limiting conditions of European politics would allow him? But above all, if he were defeated, would he not lose the League of Nations? And was not this, after all, by far the most important issue for the future happiness of the world? The Treaty would be altered and softened by time. Much in it which now seemed so vital would become trifling, and much which was impracticable would for that very reason never happen. But the League, even in an imperfect form, was permanent; it was the first commencement of a new principle in the government of the world; Truth and Justice in international relations could not be established in a few months, —they must be born in due course by the slow gestation of the League. Clemenceau had been clever enough to let it be seen that he would swallow the League at a price.

At the crisis of his fortunes the President was a lonely man. Caught up in the toils of the Old World, he stood in great need of sympathy, of moral support, of the enthusiasm of masses. But buried in the Conference, stifled in the hot and poisoned atmosphere of Paris, no echo reached him from the outer world, and no throb of passion, sympathy, or encouragement from his silent constituents in all countries. He felt that the blaze of popularity which had greeted his arrival in Europe was already dimmed; the Paris Press jeered at him openly; his political opponents at home were taking advantage of his absence to create an atmosphere against him; England was cold, critical, and unresponsive. He had so formed his *entourage* that he did not receive through private channels the current of faith and enthusiasm of which the public sources seemed dammed up. He needed, but lacked, the added strength of collective faith. The German terror still overhung us, and even the sympathetic public was very cautious; the enemy must not be encouraged, our friends must be supported, this was not the time for discord or agitations, the President must be trusted to do his best. And in this drought the flower of the President's faith withered and dried up.

Thus it came to pass that the President countermanded the *George Washington*, which, in a moment of well-founded rage, he had ordered to be in readiness to carry him from the treacherous halls of Paris back to the seat of his authority, where he could have felt himself again. But as soon, alas, as he had taken the road of compromise, the defects, already indicated, of his temperament and of his equipment, were fatally apparent. He could take the high line; he could practise obstinacy; he could write Notes from Sinai or Olympus; he could remain unapproachable in the White House or even in the Council of Ten and be safe. But if he once stepped down to the intimate equality of the Four, the game was evidently up.

Now it was that what I have called his theological or Presbyterian temperament became dangerous. Having decided that some concessions were unavoidable, he might have sought by firmness and address and the use of the financial power of the United States to secure as much as he could of the substance, even at some sacrifice of the letter. But the President was not capable of so clear an understanding with himself as this implied. He was too conscientious. Although compromises were now necessary, he remained a man of principle and the Fourteen Points a contract absolutely binding upon him.

He would do nothing that was not honorable; he would do nothing that was not just and right; he would do nothing that was contrary to his great profession of faith. Thus, without any abatement of the verbal inspiration of the Fourteen Points, they became a document for gloss and interpretation and for all the intellectual apparatus of self-deception, by which, I dare say, the President's forefathers had persuaded themselves that the course they thought it necessary to take was consistent with every syllable of the Pentateuch.

The President's attitude to his colleagues had now become: I want to meet you so far as I can; I see your difficulties and I should like to be able to agree to what you propose; but I can do nothing that is not just and right, and you must first of all show me that what you want does really fall within the words of the pronouncements which are binding on me. Then began the weaving of that web of sophistry and Jesuitical exegesis that was finally to clothe with insincerity the language and substance of the whole Treaty. The word was issued to the witches of all Paris:

> Fair is foul, and foul is fair,
> Hover through the fog and filthy air.

The subtlest sophisters and most hypocritical draftsmen were set to work, and produced many ingenious exercises which might have deceived for more than an hour a cleverer man than the President.

Thus instead of saying that German-Austria is prohibited from uniting with Germany except by leave of France (which would be inconsistent with the principle of self-determination), the Treaty, with delicate draftsmanship, states that "Germany acknowledges and will respect strictly the independence of Austria, within the frontiers which may be fixed in a Treaty between that State and the Principal Allied and Associated Powers; she agrees that this independence shall be inalienable, except with the consent of the Council of the League of Nations," which sounds, but is not, quite different. And who knows but that the President forgot that another part of the Treaty provides that for this purpose the Council of the League must be *unanimous*.

Instead of giving Danzig to Poland, the Treaty establishes Danzig as a "Free" City, but includes this "Free" City within the Polish Customs frontier, intrusts to Poland the control of the river and railway system, and provides that "the Polish Government shall undertake the conduct of the foreign relations of the Free City of Danzig as well as the diplomatic protection of citizens of that city when abroad."

In placing the river system of Germany under foreign control, the Treaty speaks of declaring international those "river systems which naturally provide more than one State with access to the sea, with or without transhipment from one vessel to another."

Such instances could be multiplied. The honest and intelligible purpose of French policy, to limit the population of Germany and weaken her economic system, is clothed, for the President's sake, in the august language of freedom and international equality.

But perhaps the most decisive moment, in the disintegration of the President's moral position and the clouding of his mind, was when at last, to the dismay of his advisers, he allowed himself to be persuaded that the expenditure of the Allied Governments on pensions and separation allowances could be fairly regarded as "damage done to the civilian population of the Allied and Associated Powers by German aggression by land, by sea, and from the air," in a sense in which the other expenses of the war could not be so regarded. It was a long theological struggle in which, after the rejection of many different arguments, the President finally capitulated before a masterpiece of the sophist's art.

At last the work was finished; and the President's conscience was still intact. In spite of everything, I believe that his temperament allowed him to leave Paris a really sincere man; and it is probable that to this day he is genuinely convinced that the Treaty contains practically nothing inconsistent with his former professions.

But the work was too complete, and to this was due the last tragic episode of the drama. The reply of Brockdorff-Rantzau inevitably took the line that Germany had laid down her arms on the basis of certain assurances, and that the Treaty in many particulars was not consistent with these assurances. But this was exactly what the President could not admit; in the sweat of solitary contemplation and with prayers to God he had done *nothing* that was not just and right; for the President to admit that the German reply had force in it was to destroy his self-respect and to disrupt the inner equipoise of his soul; and every instinct of his stubborn nature rose in self-protection. In the language of medical psychology, to suggest to the President that the Treaty was an abandonment of his professions was to touch on the raw a Freudian complex. It was a subject intolerable to discuss, and every subconscious instinct plotted to defeat its further exploration.

Thus it was that Clemenceau brought to success, what had seemed to be, a few months before, the extraordinary and impossible proposal that the Germans should not be heard. If only the President had not been so conscientious, if only he had not concealed from himself what he had been doing, even at the last moment he was in a position to have recovered lost ground and to have achieved some very considerable successes. But the President was set. His arms and legs had been spliced by the surgeons to a certain posture, and they must be broken again before they could be altered. To his horror, Mr. Lloyd George, desiring at the last moment all the moderation he dared, discovered that he could not in five days persuade the President of error in what it had taken five months to prove to him to be just and right. After all, it was harder to de-bamboozle this old Presbyterian than it had been to bamboozle him; for the former involved his belief in and respect for himself.

Thus in the last act the President stood for stubbornness and a refusal of conciliations.

Wilson at Versailles

PAUL BIRDSALL

I F THE first World War taught us anything, it taught us that after four years of bloodshed democracies become thoroughly vindicative toward the enemy who has caused them to suffer. The peoples of England and France were in a mood to "hang the Kaiser" and to "squeeze the orange until the pips squeak." It is by now a commonplace that a hysterical populace in Allied countries called for punishment and destruction of Germany, and Allied leaders, true to the principles of democracy, bowed to the storm. Belief in the unique guilt of the Kaiser for the horrors of the World War was unanimous. Can the peoples of Great Britain and France entertain many doubts about the guilt of Hitler? If they could regard the people of Imperial Germany as "Huns" and barbarians, how will they think of their Nazi enemies?

How can such passions be controlled? They must be controlled if democracy is to solve the problem of a stable peace and of a durable world order. Only in a stable world can democracy survive. Those who decry idealism and justice as sentimental and unrealistic terms in world politics miss the point. For idealism and justice are the very rudiments of common sense. They amount to a practical realization of what the traffic will reasonably bear. They require the sacrifice of immediate vengeance for the sake of long-term enlightened self-interest.

Woodrow Wilson symbolized the forces of reason in the fight for a peace of justice. He spoke too much the language of idealism and self-sacrifice and too little the plain language of a genuine community of interest, and to that extent he brought upon himself the misrepresentation which obscured his real rôle in the Paris Peace Conference and contributed to the defeat of his program in the United States. A hard-boiled and disillusioned age is quick to gibe about cant and hypocrisy, and Keynes' characterization of the Presbyterian theocrat who was "bamboozled" by Clemenceau and Lloyd George and could not be "debamboozled" has found recent echoes in Harold Nicolson's references to the "arid revivalism" of the "American Prophet," in whose pronouncements Nicolson observed "a slight tinge of revivalism, a touch of Methodist arrogance, more than a touch of Presbyterian vanity."

The simple thesis of such writers is that the doctrinaire and unrealistic program of Wilson collapsed under the impact of the power politics of Europe. Nationalist aims triumphed over his principles. There was division of the spoils of war, "bartering about of peoples and provinces from sovereignty to sovereignty as if they were chattels or pawns in a game," in defiance of his principle of self-determination. Worst of all, there had to be pretense. The Allied governments had accepted Wilson's program. While violating it, still they must pay it lip-service and hence, according to Keynes, they joined with Wilson in weaving "that web of sophistry and Jesuitical exegesis that was finally to clothe with insincerity the language and substance of the whole Treaty." Keynes in his disillusionment has fixed the legend of a Carthaginian Peace in Wilsonian disguise.

This is caricature, not history, but like most successful caricature it has enough verisimilitude to be plausible. Scarcely as much can be said for Lloyd George's recent *Apologia*, which present the exactly opposite thesis that Versailles was a purely Wilsonian peace. Only he does not call it Wilsonian because it was he, Lloyd George himself, who achieved the peace of justice practically single-handed. Always adept at sleight of hand, in his latest masterpiece he demonstrates that he achieved Wilson's program in spite of Wilson. Like most commentators, he deplores the choice of war-worn Paris as the seat of the Peace Conference, but hastily adds, "I cannot point out that in the sequel the purely Parisian influence made any serious impression on the actual stipulations of the document finally agreed to, since *I cannot discover a single particular in which it has departed from the terms of peace laid down by the Allies before the War came to an end.*" That statement acquires a peculiarly fine flavor of irony from the fact that Lloyd George himself bears major responsibility for the most egregious breach of faith contained in the entire treaty. The "Reparation" chapter of the Treaty of Versailles, besides being a clear violation of the Pre-Armistice Agreement with Germany, proved in the outcome to be the most disastrous section of the treaty. Keynes spoke with authority and even with clairvoyance on that subject.

The prosaic truth is that elements of good and bad were combined in the treaties. There were Carthaginian features like the Reparation settlement and Wilsonian features like the League of Nations. There was actually a distribution of colonial spoils of war, but only after the valuable principle had been established that colonial powers administered their new estates under specified conditions and subject to review and correction by an international tribunal, the League of Nations. The territorial settlement in Europe was by no means the wholesale, iniquitous, and cynical perversion of Wilson's principle of self-determination which has been pictured.

Harold Nicolson has explained many of the worst boundary decisions as resulting from sheer lack of coördination between the various expert commissions charged with a supremely difficult task. Yet most critics of the settlement forget the difficulties of that task. One of the commonest criticisms is directed against the shattering of the former Dual Monarchy of Austria-Hungary into those fragments called the Succession States. In this view the negotiators at Paris should have foreseen the economic and political need of a Danubian Confederation to combine the fragments. Yet Austria-Hungary had fallen apart before the Peace Conference convened and *de facto* national governments ruled the pieces. British and American delegates in Paris actually proposed a customs union for the area, only to encounter Italian objection, based on the principle of "divide and rule."

The populations of central Europe are hopelessly mixed, and therefore Simon-pure self-determination is impossible. Any boundary will leave national minorities on one side or the other. Moreover, the history of the past few years has certainly justified the commissioners in taking account of strategic factors in the award of boundaries to the new states of Europe. The aftermath of the Munich settlement proved that Czechoslovakia could not exist without possession of its historic and strategic boundaries in the Bohemian mountains, even if that area is inhabited by 3,000,000 Germans. It is equally clear that a special status for the purely German city of Danzig, involving segregation from the political structure of the German Reich, is essential to the security of the Polish Corridor, which on the basis of pre-war German statistics is "indisputably" Polish territory. Hitler's demand for the reincorporation of Danzig in the German Reich was accompanied by a demand for territory across the Corridor itself. To have granted the demand for Danzig would have left the way open for the "fourth and final partition of Poland," even without the formality of war. If the Allies should ever conquer Germany again, the negotiators of the new Versailles will face precisely the same dilemma. They can simply accept the traditional German thesis that Slavic peoples as an inferior racial breed have no right to independent national existence and permit Germany to rule Poland, Bohemia, Moravia, and Slovakia, or, if they acknowledge any right of self-determination to these peoples, they must inevitably violate in some degree the rights of German minorities. Hard as it is to visualize in 1941, it would not be surprising if the negotiators of the new Versailles were to recreate Poland and Czechoslovakia within something like the original Versailles boundaries.

In any case, it is well to be reminded by Professor Seton-Watson that it was not directly the Great Powers which profited from the partition of former German and Austro-Hungarian territory, but those new Slavic states which had themselves been partitioned and dominated for centuries. If their sense of injury was deep and their territorial appetite greedy in 1919, those sentiments are not likely to be extinguished by their present plight. If they received an unduly large measure of sympathy from the victorious Great Powers at that time, they would again secure at least their due share.

Finally, the territorial settlement contained in the various treaties negotiated at Paris is still, with all its faults, the closest approximation to an ethnographic map of Europe that has ever been achieved. If the next Peace Conference does better, it will be because of the achievements as well as the mistakes of Versailles. It can scarcely hope to do better unless some leading figure is prepared to undertake the rôle of Woodrow Wilson in restraining the forces of extravagant nationalism. It will take a brave man to assume that rôle.

AMERICAN PROPHET

President Wilson's own claims were modest. When the rough and tumble of negotiation was over in early June, 1919, he said to the entire American Delegation, "though we did not keep them [the British and French] from putting irrational things in the treaty, we got very serious modifications out of them. If we had written the treaty the way they wanted it, the Germans would have gone home the minute they read it. Well, the Lord be with us."

Unfortunately, purely negative accomplishments, the prevention of positive harm, rarely attract public attention. Yet the record of what Wilson prevented is just as important as his one great positive achievement, the League of Nations, which, however dead at this moment, is certain to be revived in some form in the event of another Allied victory over Germany. The story of Wilson's struggle to restrain nationalist demands is equally important for an understanding of the problems of the next Peace Conference. Unless his successor is even better equipped to cope with the forces of reaction, the second chapter of the League of Nations can hardly have any happier ending than the first. An understanding of Wilson's difficulties will be the beginning of wisdom for anyone bold enough to reënact his part.

The difficulties began before Wilson sailed for Paris, reactionary nationalism being equally at home on both sides of the Atlantic. To Wilson it seemed particularly strong in the ranks of the Republican Party. Naturally, though unwisely, he invited the American electorate to return only faithful Democrats to Congress, on the assumption that they alone could be counted upon to support his program. This purge, like a more recent one in American history, failed to come off. Republicans captured control of both branches of the legislature in the elections of November, 1918, and the most conspicuous and bitter opponent of Wilson's program—Henry Cabot Lodge—became chairman of the Senate Committee on Foreign Relations. Lodge's lifelong friend, Theodore Roosevelt, interpreted the election for the benefit of the nationalists of Europe:

Our allies and our enemies and Mr. Wilson himself should all understand that Mr. Wilson has no authority whatever to speak for the American people at this time. His leadership has just been emphatically repudiated by them. The newly elected Congress comes far nearer than Mr. Wilson to having a right to speak the purposes of the American people at this moment. Mr. Wilson and his Fourteen Points and his Four Supplementary Points and his Five Complementary Points and all his utterances every which way, have ceased to have any shadow of right to be accepted as expressive of the will of the American people. . . .

Acceptance of the Wilsonian principles referred to had become a contract between the Allied and Associated Powers on the one hand and Germany on the other, as a condition for the granting of an armistice and the convening of a Peace Conference. In effect, Roosevelt was inviting the Allied governments to repudiate their pledges to both President Wilson and the German Government. Though noisy, Theodore Roosevelt was only a private citizen. It was one thing for him to announce that the American people had themselves rejected the whole contractual basis for peace. It was quite another for his friend Henry Cabot Lodge, as Chairman of the Senate Committee on

Foreign Affairs, to indulge in similar pronouncements. On December 21, 1918, less than a week after Wilson's arrival in Paris, the *Congressional Record* published the substance of Lodge's speech to the Senate, in which he advised Europe that what it did to Germany was no concern of the United States. Let the Allies administer a severe peace to leave Germany disabled and helpless, and exact heavy indemnities. No attention need be paid to Wilson's principles with regard to new boundaries in Europe, for that was none of his business. Above all, postpone all plans for the construction of a League of Nations until Germany had been summarily disposed of.

The alliance of reactionary nationalisms in Europe and America undermined Wilson's position from the start. The alliance was tacit but real. Colonel House records that "the elections of last November have been a deterrent to free action by our delegates," and Lloyd George is smugness itself in describing the contrast between his own and Wilson's position. Lloyd George enjoyed an overwhelming popular mandate, and knowing the weakness of Wilson's position, could be nonchalant about Wilson's threats to appeal to public opinion. "His occasional threats to appeal to American opinion, when he did not get his way at the Conference, convey no real menace. There was no assurance that his country would support him in a break with the Allies on any issue."

Many writers have commented on this initial handicap, but few have bothered to analyze the more subtle and complicated difficulties created by the behavior of the American Delegation at the Peace Conference. It is notorious that Secretary of State Lansing was hostile to the whole idea of a League of Nations as contrary to American traditions of isolation, and that he logically joined forces, at a later date, with the Republican "Irreconcilables" to wreck the peace settlement. Wilson, at least, knew where Lansing stood and therefore excluded him from any appreciable part in the peace negotiations. The rôle of Colonel House, the President's closest friend and most intimate adviser, is so difficult to estimate that it is still clouded by controversy. This much, at least, is clear. He was so devoted to one part of the President's program—the establishment of a League of Nations—that he was willing to sacrifice almost any amount of the rest of that program to reach his goal. He was so afraid that Italy, or Japan, or France, or even Great Britain, would refuse to join the League of Nations, that he was ready to satisfy their nationalist ambitions for territory or indemnities in order to be assured of their support. He would "satisfy the greedy ones by giving them what they want." House was, moreover, a genial man with a flair for human relations, and much too adroit for either his own or Wilson's good. He got on with Europe's leaders far better than the President, and they formed the habit of using him as their intermediary when Wilson proved stiff and difficult. They constantly explained to him that, unlike the President, he was a diplomat to his finger-tips, and the Colonel's diary for this period shows that he was not wholly immune to this form of flattery. Indeed, one of his colleagues among the American Commissioners, the professional diplomat Henry White, goes so far as to suggest that House became the unwitting ally of European nationalism. White's letter to Lansing of November 8, 1919, deserves fairly full quotation:

I was not aware until recently of the extent to which intrigue went on "upstairs" during the earlier months of the Conference, with a view to preventing any of the views of our experts, which happened to be contrary to those held there, from reaching the President. Still less had I any idea of the attempts made to get some of the experts to change their views and adopt those advocated in the small upper chamber previously mentioned.

Since your departure I have realized more and more how grievously misled the Italians and others were by the tendency to compromise and by the assurances of friendship and sympathy, of a general nature at least, if not actually with their particular views, expressed during their interviews upstairs: and there is no doubt in my mind that Fiume and other questions would have been settled while the President was still here, if they had been left in your hands or kept in the President's, and had not been hampered by a feeling upstairs that no decision should be attempted, much less reached, which would in any way be likely to cause jeopardy to the adoption of the League of Nations Covenant. . . .

Under these circumstances and in view of the undue influence which I cannot but think our British friends exercise over our late colleague, I cannot help feeling anxious . . . about participation in the League of Nations if we are to be represented there by a man . . . given to compromise and not strong enough and willing to make a fight in which our interests (which besides being commercial are those of world peace as against special national interests such as land-grabbing and sphere-of-influence capturing, now rife in Europe) are likely to be overridden unless carefully guarded and defended. . . .

It is only fair to add that, in part, the Colonel's behavior is to be explained by a deep and entirely natural sympathy with the sufferings of France and the other victims of German arms. It was a sympathy widely shared by the American experts of the Peace Delegation, and however chivalrous its basis, it greatly complicated Wilson's task by making him seem ungenerous. Clemenceau openly accused the President of being pro-German on one issue where even Wilson's own experts were against him. One of the most usual complaints against Wilson made by European writers is this same lack of sympathetic understanding, in contrast to the greater warmth of other members of the American Delegation. In case after case he held out against concessions urged upon him by the experts and Colonel House.

What, then, is the true picture of the man who tried against such odds to maintain his principles? Undermined at home, imperfectly supported by his own colleagues in Paris, his frequent refusals to compromise may well have seemed the inflexible rigidity of an arid revivalist or the arrogance of a prophet. The harsh lines of the caricature fade out in the kindlier and more realistic portraiture of Henry White, and White's portrayal is all the more convincing because of the absence of any natural bonds of affinity between himself and Wilson. A professional diplomat with thirty years' experience of old-world diplomacy, he was scarcely an eager disciple of any prophet of a new world order. Republican Party affiliations and a lifelong friendship with Senator

Lodge ought to have kept him immune from too much sympathy for Wilson. Yet this is what he wrote his friend, Representative Rogers, from Paris on April 7, 1919:

I have discovered since knowing him that he is really shy, and in an atmosphere which he does not feel to be entirely sympathetic, much more in one which is antagonistic, his reserve increases in proportion to the absence of sympathy. That he has a very human side there is no doubt, and I have also found him at various times attractive. . . . I have also noticed that he is much more "get-at-able" in conversation with one other person: whether on account of his natural shyness or what, I do not know . . . certainly when we talk to him as a Delegation, he is apt to do most of the talking, whereas when I see him alone, I have found him a very good listener and apparently appreciative of what is said to him. I suppose it is for that reason that he deals so much with and through Colonel House, rather than taking advantage of the collective information of all those by whom he is immediately surrounded; whether it be the Peace Conference or his own Cabinet at home.

When one considers the deplorable lack of understanding available in Paris, the President's reputation for stiffness is more readily understood. It was not the stiffness of prophet or revivalist, but the protective covering for the sensitiveness of an academic temperament. Lloyd George is, therefore, much nearer the mark when he abandons talk of the missionary and the theocrat, and contrasts the toughness of his own hide with Wilson's sensitiveness, because the President's nerves had not been "hardened for the stinging and scorching arrows that burn and fester in the ruthless conflicts of a political career." It is clear why Lloyd George did not regard Wilson as "comparable to his great rival, Theodore Roosevelt."

For all the weaknesses of the academic temperament, Wilson remained a man of courage in the face of almost insuperable obstacles. White admitted that he became more and more impressed with the greatness of that quality, and he repeatedly sought to impress upon Senator Lodge that "dignity and distinction" characterized everything which Wilson did in Europe. He tried in vain to convince Lodge of the soundness of the President's program and begged him not to wreck it. He maintained that Wilson's activity in Europe had vastly increased American prestige.

WHAT PRICE A LEAGUE OF NATIONS?

The cardinal point of Wilson's program was its most vulnerable spot. The Allied premiers well knew Wilson's determination to establish a League of Nations in the treaties themselves as the corner stone of a new world system, and they were not scrupulous in exploiting that determination to extract concessions from him. Henry White suggests that Colonel House was responsible personally for fatal concessions to nationalist greed in order to purchase support for the League, but he has said more generally of Wilson:

The fact is that the League of Nations in which he has been more deeply interested than anything else from the beginning . . . has been played to the limit by the French and Japanese in extracting concessions from him; to a certain extent by the British too, and the Treaty as it stands is the result. The Italians overshot the mark.

That remark is the most valuable clue to the labyrinthine maze of Peace Conference negotiations that has yet been offered. It may be true, as Harold Nicolson has said, that there was no recognizable pattern of negotiation, that in the confusion and fog of Paris there was "amazing inconsequence, the complete absence of any consecutive method of negotiation or even of imposition." Yet it is extraordinary what a clear scheme of diplomatic strategy emerges from the fog, once the major territorial and other problems are studied in relation to the contemporaneous negotiations in the League of Nations Commission.

It was one thing to secure acceptance of the principle that there should be a League of Nations in the treaty. It was quite another to expect the states of Europe to adopt any particular constitution of a League that Wilson might formulate. Indeed, he was wise enough to avoid the presentation of any cut-and-dried proposition of his own. The actual construction of a League was bound to raise fundamental questions affecting the sovereign rights of all nations, and the Great Powers, at least, had the right to decide as to what provisions should or should not be embodied in the charter to which they were invited to subscribe. The negotiations which dealt with the actual text of the Covenant in the League of Nations Commission were a magnificent opportunity for obstruction. French, Japanese, or even British representatives in the Commission could press their own proposals, or withhold assent to Wilson's, not necessarily on the merits of the proposals themselves, but for the sake of "nuisance value" or bargaining advantage.

Wilson's dilemma was serious enough without such complications. He must devise a Covenant which would genuinely assure America's support to a system of collective security, without at the same time too patently violating American traditions of isolation. A small group of Senate "Irreconcilables" led by Senator Lodge was determined to reject any League of Nations which Wilson could devise, and he must at all costs avoid giving them the ammunition with which to compass that destruction. He must, therefore, resist French and Japanese proposals which would seem to endow the League with the authority of a superstate to restrain the exercise of sovereign rights by member states. He must equally secure the adoption of American provisions explicitly safeguarding certain distinctively American rights, like the Monroe Doctrine, as sacred and inviolable.

On both fronts the President was in a peculiarly vulnerable position. Too much restraint on the authority of the League, either from resistance to French and Japanese proposals or from insistence on American reservations, would justify the foreigner in saying that such a League afforded him no security and that he must, therefore, look to more tangible guarantees. Since these tangible guarantees usually involved an annexationist scheme totally at variance with the rest of Wilson's program, the horns of his dilemma were particularly sharp. This dilemma is the clue to the maze of Peace Conference diplomacy, and it determines the structure of the present book.

DESIGN FOR DIPLOMACY

Nationalist aims of territorial aggrandizement in Europe and Africa and Asia took shape before Wilson formulated his Fourteen Points, and Chapter Two of this book is a study of the conflict between the real intentions of the Allied governments and their professions of loyalty to Wilson's principles.

The main body of the book is organized to show the diplomatic strategy of the British, Japanese, and French delegations in the attainment of their nationalist ambitions. It is arranged to indicate the relation between the different items of the nationalist program of each of these states. It is particularly designed to reveal how each of the delegations conducted its negotiations in the League of Nations Commission with a view to the achievement of more tangible aims.

First, chronologically and logically, came the claims of certain of the British Dominions—supported by the British Delegation—to annex former German colonies in Africa and in the Pacific. Such claims were a direct challenge to Wilson's proposal that all the former German colonies become the property of the League of Nations, to be administered by mandatory powers chosen by the League and subject to its supervision. There was as yet no League and there was certainly no code for Wilson's mandatory principle that could be regarded as binding the Dominions. Their acceptance of the mandatory principle was necessarily contingent upon some concession to their demand for direct and unconditional control of former German territory. They were willing to sell their support to a League of Nations Covenant including the mandates principle—at a price.

Next, logically, appeared the Japanese program. It included annexationist aims in the Pacific, which had to be accorded the same consideration which the Dominions claims received. More serious were the extensive ambitions of Japan on the mainland of China. Her claims to rights formerly exercised by Germany in the Shantung province raised grave problems about the place of China in a new world order. They constituted a direct challenge to Wilson's program. Yet, at the same time, Japan presented a perfectly reasonable request for explicit recognition of the equality of races in the League of Nations Covenant. While reasonable enough in the abstract, this proposal was defeated by the practical consideration that it might possibly endow the League of Nations with authority to dictate to member states about their immigration legislation in cases where it discriminated against particular races. Could Japan be expected to submit to defeat on both the racial question and Shantung? No account of the Shantung settlement is complete without attention to the concurrent negotiations of the Japanese delegates in the League of Nations Commission.

Most important of all was the French program, since it was the most extensive, the most clearly articulated, and by far the most dangerous challenge to Wilson's program. The French program envisaged the permanent disruption and subjugation of the German Reich. It comprised a variety of individual items which, taken together, form a remarkably consistent pattern, and the separate items gained additional coherence from the directing genius of Clemenceau who personally coördinated the negotiations of the French delegates by a single strategic plan. The essence of that plan was to press for amendments to the League of Nations Covenant which Wilson was bound to oppose, and to oppose American amendments which Wilson was bound to press—ostensibly for the sake of French security, actually to create bargaining power. The chapter which deals with the policy of Bourgeois and Larnaude in the League of Nations Commission is not only essential to a understanding of the deep divergence between Anglo-American and French mentality; it also forms a necessary introduction to the study of individual aspects of the French program. Succeeding chapters deal with French proposals for the disarmament of Germany; for the endowment of Poland with maximum territories at the expense of Germany in the east; for the creation of a buffer state out of Germany's Rhineland provinces in the west; for the annexation of the Saar Valley; for the exaction of the entire cost of the war from Germany.

In every phase of these negotiations—with the British concerning colonies and mandates, with the Japanese concerning Shantung, above all with the French in every particular of their national demands—Colonel House was active and conciliatory. His concern for the League, sharpened by his experience in the League of Nations Commission, his anxiety about protracted negotiation in a chaotic world, his intimacy with the Allied premiers, especially Clemenceau, led him to adopt an "appeasement" philosophy. On every major issue he advocated compromise and concession at the expense of the accepted principles of peace, and in every case beyond definite limits set by Wilson. To this extent he assisted the strategy of the British, Japanese, and French in extracting concessions from Wilson, although in every instance except that of the Reparation Settlement Wilson successfully stopped short of the extremes of compromise to which the Colonel was urging him. Yet in both substance and method Colonel House's negotiations with the Italian Delegation proved a climax of appeasement philosophy. They revealed a rift within the American delegation, cutting deep to roots of philosophy and method; they led to an open break with the Italian Delegation; and they apparently ended the Colonel's own relations of mutual trust and confidence with President Wilson. Fiume and its consequences are symbolic of the deeper reasons for the failure of a new world order to emerge from Versailles. The Fiume episode, though distinct from the Versailles negotiations, forms an appropriate conclusion for any analysis of the diplomatic factors which shaped the general character of the treaties at the end of the first World War. . . .

WHO WERE THE REALISTS?

The intellectual nihilism of the twenty years since Versailles has destroyed faith in the Wilsonian program at Paris. By misrepresenting the character of the treaty, the motives that inspired it, above all by denial of any genuine American stake in European settlement, it has provided the strongest moral force by which Hitler "softens" his victims before striking them down with physical force. The disillusioned liberal has been the unwitting ally of the cynical advocate of physical force as the only conceivable basis for world politics.

In such an atmosphere, any constructive effort like Wilson's is bound to appear silly and unrealistic. The romantic liberal must see the immediate realization of his hopes or turn on the author of his hopes with charges of betrayal, and those who have thoroughly cynical reasons for opposing a new order will welcome the charges. The statesman who labors for the best constructive results obtainable in a chaotic world starts under the terrible handicap of a war on two fronts: against cynical opposition, and equally against his sentimental and perfectionist supporters. At Paris the situation was complicated by the fact that the American Delegation contained not merely representatives of the Simon-pure liberal school, but advocates of the opposition itself, not in any cynical sense, but because they were so profoundly impressed with political realities as they existed that intinctively they thought in terms of compromise beyond the limits of any real necessity.

In this welter of conflicting viewpoints it has recently become fashionable to eschew all standards of judgment and to resort to the methods of social psychology in describing the mêlée. The result has the pleasingly remote, detached, and scientific atmosphere of a study in anthropology. It becomes a study in abstraction and determinism, and involves no issues or principles with which any reader need concern himself. It is both the realistic and the scientific method applied to the writing of history, and it reinforces the intellectual nihilism of the disillusioned liberal.

Is it really scientific in taking account of all the data within the particular field of its concern? The only thing this method leaves out is the set of standards and principles which men themselves accepted as the basis upon which they agreed to work, and thereby accepted as the standards by which they might legitimately be judged. The only element which gives coherence and significance to the study of the Paris Peace Conference is the set of principles with reference to which it acted, the degree to which it embodied them in the treaties, the extent to which it departed from them, and the reasons—personal and political—for the result. No account which ignores or prejudges that frame of reference can claim to be scientific.

To assume at the outset that the Fourteen Points were unreal and impractical, incapable of being translated into concrete terms of peace, ignores the simple fact that they constituted a legal contract between the Allied and Associated Powers and Germany to govern the terms of peace. It is just as unrealistic to impugn the intelligence and integrity of the Peace Commissioners who took the contract seriously in the first place as to denounce them all indiscriminately as hypocrites who systematically violated principles in which they never believed, or as fools who could not recognize the violation of a principle when they committed it. The contract was there as the basis of all their efforts. It was a reasonably ascertainable contract, the details of application admittedly difficult, but by no means so impossible as many writers have alleged. It is quite as possible to distinguish between the degrees of good faith and intelligence brought to the task by the different national delegations at Paris, as it is possible to distinguish the degrees of intelligence and good faith within the personnel of any one of these delegations. Such treatment must, obviously, take account of the real political pressures upon men by national tradition and public opinion. To ignore the necessity of reasonable compromise in political affairs is just as fatal to realism as to assume that, all politics being of the essence of compromise, there are no rules at all and no standards of judgment but those of immediate political success.

It is an extraordinary fact that as yet there has been no balanced interpretation of Peace Conference diplomacy to take the measure of all the factors involved. When a penetrating critic like Harold Nicolson undertakes to recall the discussion to a firm basis of reality by emphasizing the fundamental conflict of principle, he does so only to go off the deep end of romantic-liberal disillusionment, and produces a spiritual autobiography of his loss of faith in Wilson. In his reaction against the prophets and dreamers of the world, he embraces the realists who at least know the rules of the balance of power in Europe—for example, Eyre Crowe of the British Foreign Office and Colonel House, "the best diplomatic brain America has yet produced."

The issue of realism at Paris is mainly the question of the short-term as against the long-range view. The pressures of national demands, made effective and menacing through diplomatic strategy in the League of Nations Commission, made immediate and pressing by the danger of delay in pacifying a turbulent and disintegrating Europe, necessitated a degree of compromise. The realists of the American Delegation lost their perspective under such pressure and were ready to throw away all their cargo in the scramble for the lifeboats. The cargo consisted of the Fourteen Points, the substance of the Pre-Armistice Agreement, the contract with Germany. Colonel House felt that if the boat were lightened sufficiently, it would still carry the League of Nations, but Harold Nicolson's description of a general *sauve qui peut* attitude in the later phases of the Peace Conference applies well to elements within the American delegation. In this atmosphere, one concession was an argument for the next.

Mezes could not see why the American delegation should "stand up so much straighter" on the Fiume question against the Italians than in other questions involving other Powers; Colonel House advocated extreme concession to the Japanese on the ground that, although clearly a violation of principle, it was no worse than many other concessions which had already been made. There was little attempt to discriminate between detail and principle, between the relative merits of national demands, between the varying degrees of diplomatic strength which supported the demands. Above all, there was no thought save for the immediate future—make peace quickly and start the League of Nations. The realism of these men consisted in an abdication of sheer nerve and intelligence.

Naturally, President Wilson looked stiff and unrealistic when viewed through the eyes of such men, at the very time when William Bullitt was resigning from the American Delegation in protest at Wilson's sacrifice of principle, and others were grumbling that the treaty was thoroughly bad. To the former group he seemed rigid and uncompromising, to the latter weak and uncertain in his stand on principle. A careful study of the record reveals an extraordinary consistency in Wilson's fight for his program under over-whelming difficulties, as well as a high degree of political intelligence in trans-lating the abstract principle of his program into concrete details of application.

The President's understanding of the real issues involved in the Saar case was superior to that of his own experts, and that was the only issue where he stood completely alone against everyone in Paris. In the Polish case, he was convinced by the arguments of Lloyd George as to the long-term results of a settlement based on the Polish Commission's report and loyally supported Lloyd George's efforts to modify that settlement in the face of the Polish sympathies of the American experts. He withstood steadfastly Colonel House's pressure to compromise on the Colonial question, the Rhineland, the Saar, the Adriatic. His worst defeats were the Reparation settlement and Shantung; the first occurred while Wilson was ill, when Colonel House abandoned the American program; the second, because of an impregnable political and diplo-matic position held by the Japanese.

Throughout the conference Wilson maintained his stand on principle as the only safe guide in a welter of conflicting interests, as the sole safeguard against laying foundations for future conflict. That was the meaning of his attempt to force an admission from Colonel House that the pro-French pro-posals of the American experts for the Saar valley were a violation of the Four-teen Points. The record for the crucial April period is eloquent testimony to the President's perspective and force, and Fiume is the final symbol. In the nature of the case, Wilson's rôle—aside from the arduous work in the League of Nations Commission—had to be negative rather than constructive, to con-cern itself with prevention rather than cure. Consequently the failure of his curative and constructive work, as the result primarily of American refusal to ratify the treaty and enter the League of Nations, has obscured the real nature of his achievement at Paris. It is so much easier to record failures than to carry through the laborious task of assessing a man's work by careful meas-urement of what he prevented, as well as by study of positive achievements.

Perhaps the most general criticism President Wilson has encountered, at the time and since, has been on the score of his decision to attend the Peace Conference in person. The decision itself was attributed to excessive vanity, and the effect has generally been described as the degradation of the remote and lofty, almost godlike arbiter to a bloody and battered contestant in the European prize ring. The assumption is that Wilson in Washington could

have retained his detachment with an ultimate power of decision while dele-
gating the rough-and-tumble of negotiation to Colonel House in Paris. It is
interesting that Secretary Lansing and Colonel House, who agreed upon practically nothing else, should have consistently concurred on the unwisdom of
the President's coming to Paris. Independently, they tried in advance to prevent it; subsequently, they communed over the misfortune of the event. Yet,
in view of Lansing's attitude toward Colonel House, it is difficult to imagine
his acquiescing in the Colonel's primacy in Paris. It is possible that each man
in the assurance of his own superior wisdom felt confident of exercising greater
influence in Wilson's absence.

The present book affords the most positive answer on this point. The record clearly shows that on every major question but that of Reparation, the
Treaty of Versailles would have been a worse treaty had Wilson remained in
Washington. With all his mistakes, he emerges as the only man of real stature
at Paris.

His fight for ratification—when he returned to the United States—is another story and another Wilson. The strain of his intensive speaking campaign on behalf of ratification super-added to the long strain of the struggle
in Paris, brought a physical collapse. After the stroke of paralysis, in October
1919, he became readier prey to the tactics of the Senate Irreconcilables,
whose game was so to amend and denature the League Covenant that the
author himself would reject his own handiwork. At the very moment when
French and British officials indicated their willingness to accept the denatur-
ing amendments for the sake of continued American collaboration in Europe,
Wilson gave the fateful order of rejection:

I shall consent to nothing. The Senate must take its own medicine.

10

Good Neighbor:

HOOVER *or* ROOSEVELT ?

By the end of World War I, relations between the United States and the Latin-American republics were strained and unpleasant. A decade and a half of intervention and interference by the "Colossus of the North" in the internal affairs of its southern neighbors had left a legacy of rancor and hostility. In magazines and newspapers, poems and essays, books and articles, those Latin Americans who were writing in the period between 1900 and 1920 branded the United States as an aggressive and predatory nation, and they looked upon the Monroe Doctrine as a vehicle of oppression. The refusal of the United States to join the League of Nations provided additional proof of Washington's evil course of conduct. The League had been considered by the South Americans as a means of achieving equality with the United States in international affairs, since all nations—big and small—would have but one vote in the Assembly and small nations would be represented on the Council. In 1921, when Harding came to the Presidency, there was no hemispheric solidarity or amicability.

By the beginning of World War II, the situation had changed completely. As soon as war broke out in Europe in 1939, the American republics joined in common agreement to defend the hemisphere. Their foreign ministers met in Panama three weeks after Hitler invaded Poland and adopted a declaration warning the belligerents to steer clear of this hemisphere. Meeting in Havana in 1940, they declared that a foreign attack on an American state would be considered an act of aggression against all the Americas. The attack on Pearl Harbor persuaded nine American countries to declare war against Japan and Germany and for four others to sever relations with the Axis. A conference in Rio de Janeiro early in 1942 convened to coordinate the war effort in the hemisphere. What happened in the period between the two wars to change the Latin American attitude toward the United States? What caused the nations to be cordial and cooperative? When had the transition been made from bad to good neighbor?

Alexander DeConde of the University of California at Santa Barbara believes that the Good Neighbor policy began in Herbert Hoover's administration. He says, "With the advent of Herbert Hoover to the White House there came a marked and deliberate change in the Latin American policy of the United States," and goes on to note, ". . . in its main essentials, the good neighbor policy had its roots in the Hoover Administration; Roosevelt only adopted and expanded it." The evidence he supplies to substantiate his position is impressive: Hoover's inaugural address and subsequent speeches in which he indicated his policy of conciliation; the publication of the Clark Memorandum; the refusal to intervene in the affairs of certain republics; the disinclination to protect American private financial investments; and the withdrawal of marines from some of the republics.

Donald M. Dozer, also of the University of California at Santa Barbara, gives Franklin D. Roosevelt the credit for transforming hemispheric relations. He admits that many of Roosevelt's predecessors used the term "good neighbor," but they seldom followed it. It was Roosevelt who took the major steps which caused Latin America to alter its view of the United States. As important milestones he cites the three conferences at Montevideo, Buenos Aires, and Lima; the abrogation of the Platt Amendment; the withdrawal of the remaining United States marines from Haiti and the Dominican Republic; and the reciprocal trade agreements which permitted Latin America to increase its exports to the United States. He emphasizes, too, that the social aspect of the New Deal greatly aided in changing the image of the United States. Roosevelt's social legislation was viewed as the acts of a nation which was no longer interested in imperialism and expansion. Dozer depends heavily on writings in the Latin-American press for his interpretation. It is there he finds most of the evidence to support his contention that Franklin Roosevelt is responsible for the Good Neighbor policy.

Hoover's Latin-American Policy

ALEXANDER DeCONDE

WITH THE advent of Herbert Hoover to the White House there came a marked and deliberate change in the Latin-American policy of the United States. The change is evident in the words and tone of his inaugural address of March 4, 1929, in which he devoted a paragraph specifically to inter-American relations. He referred to the southern continent and his recent trip there in friendly and understanding terms, and assured the southern nations that he wished "only the maintenance of their independence, the growth of their stability, and their prosperity." He also indicated that the Latin-American policy of his administration was to be an integral part of a foreign policy predicated on peace. . . .

Although in the last two years of the Hoover administration inter-American affairs were overshadowed by portentous events in Europe and Asia and by the great depression at home, "the fundamental purposes and philosophy" of the administration in foreign affairs were to be found in its Latin-American policy. Basic to this policy was the Monroe Doctrine, a pillar of American foreign policy since it was first announced by President James Monroe and his astute Secretary of State, John Quincy Adams. Another essential principle of Latin-American relations, inherited by Hoover, was the *de facto* domination of the Central American and Caribbean area by the United States. In this danger zone the United States has been extremely sensitive to any actual or attempted intervention by any other first-rate power. The region has formed a vital link in American defense strategy for over a century, and since the building of the Panama Canal it has been considered the jugular vein of the American defense system.

The Caribbean area had not been difficult to dominate, as the independent republics in it were small, quarrelsome, and impotent in a world of power politics. As a consequence, the United States had taken every action which seemed consonant with its own national interest and which would prevent other powerful nations from intervening in the affairs of these countries. At times American intervention was pursued in terms of self-interest, but quite often it was carried on under the guise of the Monroe Doctrine—especially since 1904, when Theodore Roosevelt added his famous corollary to this historic document. The interventions and the unilateral interpretation of Monroe's words by the United States stirred up a strong fear and hatred of the northern giant in Latin America. This feeling of resentment was buttressed by the thoughtless attitude of many Americans toward the doctrine, as evidenced by a senator who declared that "it was given us in Providence to state and interpret the Monroe Docctrine." From previous experience, the people of Latin America had little faith in providence; they looked upon the Monroe Doctrine as a beacon of *yanqui* imperialism. . . .

When Hoover took up the reins of government, the Monroe Doctrine had become a barrier to cordial inter-American relations, and the United States was involved directly or indirectly in the internal affairs of about a half-dozen Caribbean countries. In order to carry out his shift in the nation's Latin-American policy. and to demonstrate his friendship for the peoples to the south, it was necessary for Hoover to remove from the Monroe Doctrine the onus of the Roosevelt corollary and, particularly, the stigma of its being used as a camouflage for American intervention. Hoover did this by adopting as his own, and issuing as a public document, a comprehensive *Memorandum on the Monroe Doctrine*, which was prepared by an eminent international lawyer and a former Undersecretary of State, J. Reuben Clark.

This interpretation of the formula of 1823 was written near the end of the Coolidge administration at the request of Secretary of State Kellogg and submitted to him under the date of December 17, 1928. It was based on state papers and the pronouncement of statesmen and authorities. The study was devoted primarily to stripping Monroe's original message of its various excrescences and corollaries. It struck directly at the Roosevelt corollary, which proclaimed the principle that inasmuch as the United States would permit no European nation to intervene in the affairs of Latin-American countries, it must therefore act as an international policeman and assume the responsibility of preserving order and protecting life and property in these countries. Clark denounced the use of the doctrine for such purposes, by declaring that "it is not believed that this corollary is justified by the terms of the Monroe Doctrine, however much it may be justified by the application of the doctrine of self-preservation." Clark did not denounce all intervention, but mainly that which was practiced under the mantle of the Monroe Doctrine; nor did he renounce the right of unilateral interpretation of the doctrine by the United States.

The former Undersecretary of State concluded his study by reassuring the Latin-American countries that they had nothing to fear from the Monroe Doctrine, as it was not "an instrument of violence and oppression" but "a wholly effective guaranty of their freedom, independence, and territorial integrity against the imperialistic designs of Europe." Originally the Clark document was not intended for public consumption, as President Coolidge was not in accord with its principles, and for some time after it was composed it remained, without having been used, in the files of the State Department. Hoover knew of its existence, and since his ideas were in line with those expressed by the memorandum, he adopted it when he became President as a means of implementing his good-neighbor policy. In the early part of 1930 he had it published as a public document, and thereby indicated to the governments of Latin America that his administration would be guided to a large extent by its principles—though by this time Hoover had gone much further than the document suggested. He had committed himself to a policy of nonintervention, regardless of the form under which it might be practiced. . . .

The publication of the Clark document met with a favorable reception in general, both at home and abroad. The idea that the Monroe Doctrine was to be used "for the defense rather than the domination of Latin America" aided considerably in dispelling fear of the "colossus of the north" harbored by many of the southern nations. The reaction of press opinion in the United States was favorable. This was indicated by two separate analyses of the editorial comment concerning the Clark memorandum in the newspapers of the United States. Editorial comment was overwhelmingly friendly to the pronouncement, but revealed a wide variance in the interpretation of it. . . .

The Department of State continued placating the fears of the sensitive American republics by often assuring them that the Monroe Doctrine was to be used only for their protection, not their destruction. Undersecretary of State William R. Castle, Jr., stressed this principle a year later by declaring that "the Monroe Doctrine confers no superior position on the United States." He made his point clear to all when he exclaimed that "in the protection of American interests in Latin-American countries, the Monroe Doctrine has no more place than in the protection of those interests in the Orient." At the same time another official denied that the Monroe thesis implied tutelage. In all these ways it was brought home to the peoples of Latin America that the Hoover policy was one of peace and nonintervention. . . .

RENUNCIATION OF INTERVENTION AND DOLLAR DIPLOMACY

Long before he became President, Hoover was known to be opposed to United States intervention in Latin America. As early as 1922, when he was Secretary of Commerce, it was intimated that he was in favor of withdrawing the Marines from Haiti and Santo Domingo. On his good-will tour one of the most important contributions he made was to stress that intervention would not be the policy of the United States in the future. In his address delivered at Guayaquil, Ecuador, he expressed his attitude toward intervention with the concise statement that "true democracy is not and cannot be imperialistic. The brotherhood of this faith is the guarantee of good will."

Early in the second month of his administration, Hoover chose the occasion of a Gridiron Club dinner to emphasize his aversion to dollar diplomacy and to intervention in the internal affairs of Latin-American countries. After expressing his appreciation for the courtesy and good will shown him on his visit to Latin America, he declared:

And in this connection of the relations of great and little nations may I mention one sinister notion, fear of which I detect in some sections of the press, as to policies of the United States bearing basically upon our relationships with our Latin-American Neighbors? That is, fear of an era of the mistakenly called dollar diplomacy. The implications that have been colored by that expression are not a part of my conception of international relations. I can say at once that it never has been and ought not to be the policy of the United States to intervene by force to secure or maintain contracts between our citizens and foreign States or their citizens. Confidence in that attitude is the only basis upon which the economic co-operation of our citizens can be welcomed abroad. It is the only basis that prevents cupidity encroaching upon the weakness of nations—but, far more than this, it is the true expression of the moral rectitude of the United States.

This pronouncement constituted a pointed intimation that the attitude of the giant northern republic toward its Latin neighbors was changing. Not only was the new President against political and military intervention in the internal affairs of the Latin-American countries, but he was also strongly opposed to intervention for the purpose of protecting private American investments.

How much the Latin-American policy of the United States had changed in the four years of the Hoover regime is shown by the action of the administration during its last days. At the meeting of the governing board of the Pan American Union, on January 4, 1933, Assistant Secretary of State Francis White, representing Stimson, agreed without exception to Argentina's proposition to place on the agenda of the forthcoming Pan-American conference at Montevideo the draft of an antiwar treaty prepared by its Foreign Minister, Dr. Carlos Saavedra Lamas. The proposed antiwar objectives were already covered by the Kellogg-Briand peace pact; the real essence of the Argentine plan was the rejection of intervention in any form. This was in actuality a maneuver to throw the subject of intervention into the arena of debate at Montevideo and there, in the presence of the assembled delegates, spearhead an attack against the past policies of the United States. The attitude of the Washington government was significant, because it revealed that Hoover and Stimson were not only opposed to the practice of intervention but were even ready to relinquish the legal "right" of intervention. They were thus prepared to go beyond the limits of international law in their renunciation of intervention. The Latin-American policy of the nation had traveled far on the road to good-neighborliness since the Havana conference of 1928, where Hughes had ably defended the legal "right" of intervention.

Probably the most striking phase of the Latin-American policy of the Hoover administration was "its deliberate pursuit of nonintervention in the sensitive Central American and Caribbean area." An example of this was Hoover's outright avoidance of intervention at the outbreak of a seven-hour revolution in the Isthmian republic of Panama. This uprising swept the administration of President Florencio Harmodio Arosemena from power in the early morning hours of January 2, 1931. The United States carefully refrained from interfering in any way in the progress of the revolt, although at least one American citizen was killed. The attitude of the Hoover administration was noteworthy, as the preceding administration had indicated that the people of Panama would not be allowed any revolutionary privileges. Thus, the first revolution in the tiny republic of Panama was made possible by a definite reversal of policy by the United States. That a Washington government would allow a revolution to take place near its vital canal and not exercise treaty rights to intervene was a significant break with the past. The administration maintained its policy of restraint. It did not interfere in Panamanian affairs when in May 1931 a clash between United States military police and Panama police in Colón aroused hostile feelings between the two countries.

The same policy of restraint was exercised by the Hoover administration when an insurrection broke out in another Central American republic. In April 1931, the Indian general and professional revolutionist, Gregorio Ferrera, who had a large following among the Indian workers of the American-owned fruit plantations, led a revolt against the existing government of Honduras. During the course of hostilities, American property, primarily that of the United Fruit Company, was attacked and looted, and the lives of American citizens were endangered. In consequence, the United States sent several warships to Honduran waters, confining their activities, however, "to making provision for the safety of American lives and property in the coast towns." Except for evacuation by these warships of several hundred Americans employed by the American fruit companies, there was no intervention by the United States. Secretary Stimson stressed the American policy of nonintervention by maintaining that the revolutionary movement was an internal matter, to be handled solely by the Honduran government, and that the United States would not participate in any way. This pronouncement was later published by the Honduran press and was highly praised. Several diplomatic incidents occurred during the course of the uprising, which involved the United States; but they had no serious consequences. With the death of Ferrera, early in June 1931, the revolt automatically collapsed, and the United States recalled its warships.

After the 1932 elections in Honduras, another rebellion broke out. Despite the repeated appeals for aid from the Honduran government, and the evident aid given the insurgents by El Salvador, the United States scrupulously maintained its policy of noninterference. By the end of December, the Honduran government had decisively defeated the rebel forces and reasserted its authority.

In line with the administration's policy of respecting the independence and integrity of all nations of the American continent, Secretary of State Stimson delivered a nationwide broadcast on May 9, 1931, in which he explained to the American people the purpose of the government's Latin-American policy. He characterized certain difficulties and misunderstandings in Latin-American –United States relations as "sore spots," and stated that they "have damaged our good name, our credit, and our trade far beyond the apprehension of our own people. The State Department is addressing itself seriously and successfully toward the removal of these sore spots." He then enumerated some of the ways in which the United States had sought "to eradicate the sore spots of Latin-American diplomacy," and added that the press comments throughout the Western continent "have indicated that the effort has not been unsuccessful."

Stimson served notice that intervention was being abandoned, and that the Hoover administration was adhering to the principle, enunciated by Elihu Root when he was Secretary of State, that the Army and Navy would not be used to collect debts from weaker powers. Stimson stressed the intention that the people of Latin America should be left alone to manage their own affairs. He spoke of Pan-American solidarity, of trying to promote a policy of good will and mutual trust, and maintained that good relations with Latin America "constitute one of the cardinal tenets of our foreign policy." He concluded the address by tying together the Latin-American and general foreign policies of the administration and emphasizing the good-neighbor approach in the Western Hemisphere. Public reaction to Stimson's words was varied but generally favorable throughout the United States.

Hoover's reluctance to use military intervention in Panama, Honduras, and El Salvador, and his steps toward the liquidation of imperialism in Nicaragua and Haiti were a vital part of his Pan-American program. This was aimed at the removal of the suspicion with which Latin America had viewed United States motives in inter-American relations. In another Gridiron Club speech in April 1930, the President underscored this objective of his Latin-American policy by warning that "there began to pervade the world a jealousy, a suspicion, and an ill will toward the United States, such as never before existed in peace history. Therefore, it became the first duty of the American officials responsible for the foreign policies of the Government to realign this sentiment and this public opinion in the world back to the true actualities of American aspirations." He referred to the fear with which many Latin-American countries viewed United States economic expansion; an expansion that some characterized as a species of national arrogance. He asserted that "a large part of the world had come to believe that they were in the presence of the birth of a new imperial power intent upon dominating the destinies and freedom of other peoples." He repudiated this viewpoint, which he labeled a misconception, and then enumerated the various measures taken by his administration to supplant the patent animosity with good will and amity. He concluded by declaring that the United States was aiming for progress "by the creation of good will and human advancement and not by exploitation."

The Hoover administration's financial policy toward Latin America was based on the abandonment of "dollar diplomacy." It had often made clear its intention to enforce no private concessions entered into by Americans and Latin-American governments, and to collect no debts by military threats. The Washington government took the stand that American citizens should not seek official support in their private transactions in Latin America, unless their claims were reasonable in themselves and they sought redress after exhausting the usual legal facilities of the country in which they had a griev- ance. If such a procedure were followed, then the United States required only that its nationals be accorded treatment equal to that given to other for- eigners, and that it not fall below the minimum standard set by international practice.

This policy was carried still further when, in April 1931, Nicaraguan in- surgents under General Sandino attacked and killed about nine Americans near the town of Puerto Cabezas on the east coast of Nicaragua. Upon learning of the attack, the State Department at once had war vessels ordered to the scene of action. Then, on April 16, 1931, Secretary Stimson sent a telegram to the American foreign-service officials in Nicaragua, announcing a new protection policy to be followed by the Hoover administration. He indicated that American citizens who carried on business in Latin America did so at their own risk, and that they could not expect to be protected by United States forces, even though their lives as well as their property might be in danger. This was a complete reversal of President Coolidge's position that Americans and their property were to be protected by the government "wherever they may be."

Stimson made known that the "government cannot undertake general pro- tection of Americans throughout that country with American forces." To have assumed such protection would have led the government into difficulties and commitments which Stimson made clear the government did not pro- pose to undertake. He then laid down the policy that Americans who did not feel secure in the interior should withdraw from the country or go to the coast towns where the United States government would give them protection or evacuate them.

Although this was an innovation in Latin-American relations, the principle of extending protection to American citizens only in coastal areas was not new in United States foreign affairs. This policy was adopted by the State Department in 1927 in connection with disorders in China. But it was strik- ingly important in Central America because, if the old policy had been followed, active intervention by American forces would have been almost certain.

Public reaction to Stimson's declaration was instantaneous, and the press generally favored it, although a large section expressed hostility to the new policy. Answering the vociferous attacks of the newspapers which did not favor the policy, particularly the Hearst chain, Stimson amplified and justified it in a formal statement on April 18, 1931. He conveyed the opinion that the outbreak was "a problem with which the sovereign Government of Nicaragua is primarily concerned, and a problem which it is primarily the right and duty of that Government to solve." Stimson then went on to assert that there had been "no change in the determination of the American Gov- ernment not to send American troops into the interior." In this he was vigorously supported by President Hoover.

This same policy of coastal protection only was extended to American citizens in Honduras during the April 1931 rebellion there. At home and abroad, the policy was widely interpreted as a marked change in the attitude of the United States toward Central America, and was heralded as additional evidence of a nonintervention policy in the vital Caribbean area. . . .

RETREAT FROM IMPERIALISM

One of the most serious and delicate problems in the nation's foreign relations when Hoover became President was the forcible occupation of Nicaragua and Haiti by United States military forces. To Latin America this was the *cause célèbre* of inter-American relations, and to alarmists it furnished tangible evidence of the imperialistic propensities of the northern colossus. Shortly after assuming office, Hoover made it apparent that he intended to liquidate United States commitments in the two Caribbean republics. In his first annual message to Congress, on December 3, 1929, he stated that approximately "1,600 marines remain in Nicaragua" and "about 700 marines" in Haiti, and that these forces were already materially reduced, but that he was "anxious to withdraw them further as the situation warrants." He maintained that the problem of Haiti was the more difficult, "the solution of which is still obscure." His intentions were made clear when he avowed in the same message that "in the large sense we do not wish to [be] represented abroad in such manner."

United States armed intervention in Nicaragua had its beginnings in the palmy days of Taft's "dollar diplomacy." In August 1912, American troops were stationed in the "banana republic" to aid the Conservative government against revolutionary anti-American Liberals and to protect the lives of United States nationals. The troops remained on Nicaraguan soil until August 1925, when they were withdrawn by the Coolidge administration. The withdrawal was not for long, however, as revolution promptly upset the country's equilibrium, and the next year, at the request of the Conservative faction, Coolidge poured the American forces back into the troubled land. This marked the beginning of Coolidge's differences with Mexico, and his "private war" in Nicaragua. In view of the increasingly difficult situation, Coolidge sent Henry L. Stimson to Nicaragua as his personal "trouble shooter," with full power to find a solution for the devastating civil war. In consequence of the Tipitapa agreements of May 1927, negotiated by Colonel Stimson, a semblance of order was restored to the country, and American occupation continued with the understanding that it was to "guarantee order, liberty, and property." This was the basis for the occupation when Hoover came to office.

The pacification of the republic, as called for by the Stimson negotiations, was retarded by the depradations of the guerrilla chieftain Sandino, who baffled both the Marines and the American-trained Nicaraguan national guard in their efforts to capture him or his forces. The Sandinistas carried on a campaign of defiance and destruction by attacking Americans and their property, and they resisted all efforts at conciliation. Sandino insisted that all United States armed forces should leave the country before he would discontinue his guerrilla activities.

Soon after Hoover's inauguration, Sandino temporarily left Nicaragua for a haven in Mexico, where he remained in retirement for little less than a year. In a farewell gesture of defiance he issued a call to the peoples of Central America to discuss the Nicaraguan problem at a conference to be held in Buenos Aires, which was undoubtedly an effort to make use of Argentina's coolness toward the United States. In the meanwhile, the Hoover administration followed the practice of leaving the country's internal troubles to the *guardia nacional* under its American officers. In July 1929, after Sandino's retreat to Mexico, Hoover accelerated the evacuation of the Marines, begun earlier in the year, by ordering the withdrawal of about one third of them. More withdrawals followed, and by June 1930, only a little over a thousand Marines remained in the country.

In the latter part of November 1929, Stimson announced in Washington that it was the government's policy to withdraw the American forces from Nicaragua as rapidly as conditions permitted. The Marines who remained in the country were being used to train the *guardia nacional* who were to take over the task of maintaining order when the United States evacuation was complete. The Marines were also used to supervise elections and to assist United States officials in the supervision of the republic's finances. In the early part of 1930 Sandino returned to Nicaragua, where the fighting had continued during his absence. With his presence on the scene the tempo of the warfare increased. In order to cope with Sandino's depredations, the Nicaraguan government increased the personnel of the *guardia* threefold, but there was no increase in the American forces.

The Hoover administration's policy of relaxed control continued, and in the latter part of 1930 Stimson considered that conditions in the country were improved to such an extent that plans should be made for the full evacuation of the American forces after the Nicaraguan presidential elections of 1932. On February 13, 1931, Stimson made a public announcement of this. He also stated that by June all the Marines, except a small detachment on noncombatant duty, were to be withdrawn, and he intimated that the practice of supervising elections and of furnishing officers for the native constabulary would be discontinued. This declaration came despite repeated anti-United States outbreaks under Sandino's banner, and it was not revised when in the following April a new surge of fighting cost several American nationals their lives. About this time a devastating earthquake also added to Nicaragua's misery. American aid to the stricken was gratefully received.

The preliminary withdrawal program was effected by June 3, 1931. From that date there were no Marine combatant patrols in the field; the fighting was left entirely to the *guardia*. The criticism which American intervention in Nicaragua had long drawn, both in the United States and in Latin America, probably had some influence on the Hoover administration's determination to withdraw the Marines at that time. This criticism took concrete form when the United States Senate on January 5, 1931, passed a resolution—introduced by the fiery Hiram Johnson—calling upon the Department of State for full information on the course and conduct of the Nicaraguan occupation since 1924. An additional resolution was introduced, declaring it to be "the sense of the Senate that the President should immediately withdraw" the American armed forces from Nicaragua.

Another important factor was the leading position of the United States in bringing about the Kellogg-Briand Anti-War Pact of Paris. It would have been strangely inconsistent if one of the most insistent advocates of the 1928 peace pact did not put its own house in order in accordance with the principles enunciated by the treaty. As a leading sponsor of the pact, and as the country most emphatic in its protests over Russian and Japanese encroachments in Manchuria, the United States was embarrassed over its own Caribbean activities. The State Department's labors on behalf of peace and nonaggression smacked too much of the pot calling the kettle black. If the United States used troops to force its interests in Nicaragua, how could it remonstrate successfully against Japanese aggression in Manchuria? The State Department's hand could be strengthened considerably in its policy toward Japan if it had no Manchuria of its own. Whatever the reasons prompting it, Stimson's February announcement was highly effective. It was hailed with approval both north and south of the Rio Grande and by liberal spokesmen in Congress.

The restraint shown by the administration toward Sandino was well in line with this policy, and was part of Hoover's campaign to win friends among his southern neighbors. In his annual message to Congress on December 10, 1931, he showed his determination to end the American occupation of the Central American republic by reiterating Stimson's words. He made known that the "armed forces of the United States" were "reduced to the minimum deemed necessary to the training of the Nicaraguan Constabulary." He "proposed to withdraw completely American armed forces from Nicaragua after their presidential election in 1932."

There was considerable skepticism in Nicaragua over the promised withdrawal. In the summer of 1932, Dr. Juan B. Sacasa, one of the presidential candidates, sent a special emissary to Washington to inquire if the Marines might not be left in Nicaragua for some time after the new president took office. If this were done, the new president might be firmly in the saddle before he would have to rely on the *guardia nacional* officered by Nicaraguans. Stimson refused to entertain this request as well as a similar suggestion by the American director of the *guardia*. He averred that it was essential to adhere to the plan of withdrawing the Marines as scheduled.

After the Nicaraguan presidential elections of November 6, 1932—which were supervised by a high-ranking American naval officer—the Hoover administration's promise was carried to its complete fulfillment. The defeated candidate, Adolfo Diaz, had at one time received the support of the United States.

The victory of Dr. Sacasa, the Liberal candidate, was thus an indication that American supervision had not influenced the result of the election. Virtually all of the Marines were out of Nicaragua by the end of December. The last detachment left on January 2, 1933. On this occasion the Department of State issued a statement declaring that "no American armed forces will remain in that country, either as instructors in the constabulary, as a legation guard, or in any other capacity whatsoever."

This final evacuation terminated an intervention which, save for a short period in 1925–1926, had lasted continuously for twenty years. The responsibilities of the United States in Nicaragua after evacuation was limited to the exercise of supervision over Nicaraguan finances. The United States also retained certain rights it had acquired to a canal route across Nicaraguan territory. Acting upon a congressional resolution authorizing an investigation and survey of the proposed Nicaraguan canal, President Hoover appointed a five-man Interoceanic Canal Board in June 1929 to carry out its terms. Nicaragua and Costa Rica gave their consent to the investigation and to a survey by a battalion of United States Army engineers. Both countries, for obvious reasons, greeted the idea of the new canal with great enthusiasm, but nothing came of the proposal. The board, which reported in December 1931, did not recommend any action in connection with the proposed canal.

The administration's retreat from imperialism in Nicaragua justified itself, for in the following month Sandino signed a peace agreement with President Sacasa. By its terms, Sandino agreed to disarm his men and cease hostilities. In return he received an amnesty, a grant of public lands for settlement, and a program of public works to give employment to his followers for one year.

The other troublesome United States occupation, that of Haiti, had its beginnings in the Wilson administration. United States Marines landed at Port au Prince in the latter part of July 1915, just a few hours after a frenzied mob had dragged the Negro republic's president, Vilbrun Guillaume Sam, from the sanctuary of the French legation and had torn him bodily apart in the streets. The mob's fury was in retribution for Sam's responsibility in the brutal bayoneting of some one hundred sixty-seven political prisoners held captive in the city's jail. The Marines restored order, and later that year, under pressure from Washington, the Haitian government agreed to a treaty. The terms of the agreement gave the United States almost complete control of the country. The United States was to assist the republic in the rehabilitation of its finances, the organization of an efficient police force, and the development of its natural resources. The powers conferred on the United States were exercised by a high commissioner and five other treaty officials who were American citizens.

Originally, the treaty was to run for ten years, but it was extended to twenty in 1917. This placed its terminal date in May 1936. The duties of the Marines on the island republic were many. They supervised elections, trained a native constabulary, and helped administer the country's finances. Despite the Marines and their "pacification" of the country, sporadic outbreaks against American rule were not uncommon. With the passing of the years the occupation created major problems of policy, which became more perplexing as the expiration date of the treaty approached. The Haitians had many grievances, but most of all they hated being subjected once again to the foreign domination of the whites. They resented the imposition of a culture alien to their French traditions. In the minds of many Haitians these grievances far outweighed any material benefits that may have been conferred upon them by the American occupation such as new highways, modern hospitals, free clinics, etc. This was the situation that Hoover inherited on March 4, 1929.

President Hoover was acutely aware of conditions in the Negro republic and desired a clarification. On September 25, 1929, he sent a letter to his Secretary of State, suggesting the use of an investigating commission to study the situation. He stated gravely that he was "in great doubt as to whether this Administration wants to pledge itself to undertake to take on the indefinite policies of the last Administration in connection with this island." In his reply Secretary Stimson concurred with the President's idea and informed him that he had given the matter considerable thought "as it is one of the major and difficult problems we are confronted with in our foreign relations."

Hoover immediately followed this up by incorporating in his first annual message to Congress on December 3, 1929, a proposal to "dispatch a commission to Haiti to review and study the matter in an endeavor to arrive at some more definite policy than at present," if Congress approved. A few days after he made the proposal, events in Haiti showed the necessity for a more definite policy. Anti-American outbreaks resulted in the declaration of martial law on the island by the United States military forces stationed there. Clashes between Haitians and United States Marines occurred on December 5 and 6, and at Aux Cayes a Haitian mob of about fifteen hundred encountered an armed Marine patrol, with the result of a score or more of wounded and dead Haitians. Reinforcements were rushed to the island the following day. But within a few days the situation quieted, so that Hoover ordered the additional Marine reinforcements that were en route to the island diverted to Guantánamo.

The disturbances in the Negro nation caused Hoover to accelerate his plans. On December 7, 1929, upon receipt of the news of the bloody encounter at Aux Cayes, he sent a special message to Congress, requesting authority to send a commission to Haiti immediately, and also for a large appropriation to finance it. The House of Representatives promptly passed a joint resolution, giving the President the necessary authority. It was amended by the Senate, and finally approved by both Houses early in February. In a press conference on February 4, 1930, the President discussed the purpose and task of the commission he intended sending to Haiti. He pointed out that "the primary question which is to be investigated is when and how we are to withdraw from Haiti. The second question is what we shall do in the meantime." He emphasized his peaceful intentions by reiterating that "I have no desire for representation of the American Government abroad through our military forces."

Considerable political pressure was manifested by numerous individuals and groups, such as the National Association for the Advancement of Colored People, and on February 7, 1930, Hoover appointed a five-man commission "for the Study and Review of Conditions in the Republic of Haiti." A former governor-general of the Philippines, W. Cameron Forbes, was appointed chairman. An independent Negro commission, which was to undertake an exhaustive investigation of the educational system in Haiti, was also sent to the island by Hoover. It was headed by Dr. Robert E. Moton, president of Tuskegee Institute.

The Forbes commission visited Haiti at the beginning of March 1930 and was later followed by the Moton commission. During the Forbes commission's stay on the island, considerable political unrest was apparent throughout the country. This commission began its inquiry without delay, by holding daily public sessions before which all Haitians were allowed to appear, and it granted private audiences to those who desired to give their evidence in that manner. It also allowed the presentation of a case by eight antiadministration groups, organized into a committee called "The Federated Committee of the Associated Groups of the Opposition."

After a trip to the northern section of the country, the commission returned to Port au Prince and resumed its hearings there. "The commission found the situation in regard to the election of a new president critical." The tension was so great that the commission recommended that the matter of the coming elections be settled by the Haitians themselves. "After protracted negotiations" with both the opposition and the administration in power, a definite electoral plan "was drawn up which was approved by President Hoover."

In the middle of the month, the commission left the island republic, and on March 26, 1930, it submitted its report to the President. The report was thorough and penetrating. It praised some of the work of the United States occupation officials but did not fail to expose wrongs uncovered. The report admitted candidly that "the high hopes of our good works in this land have not been realized," and gave as reasons "the failure of the Occupation to understand the social problems of Haiti, its brusque attempt to plant democracy there by drill and harrow." The commission made recommendations for the future policy of the United States toward Haiti. In regard to the termination of the occupation "the commission found the immediate withdrawal of the Marines inadvisable, it recommends their gradual withdrawal in accordance with arrangements to be made in future agreement between the two Governments." The various recommendations offered suggestions as to how the dangerous situation in the Negro land could be eased and the steps to be followed. Two days after receiving the report, President Hoover announced that he had adopted the recommendations of the commission as the future policy of the United States toward Haiti.

The Moton commission arrived in Haiti in the middle of June 1930 and remained there for about three weeks, after which it returned to the United States. In the following October it submitted a final report to the President. The report summarized social and economic conditions, explained the educational needs of the country, examined the existing educational system, and made sixty-one specific recommendations. The commission's most prominent recommendation was that the vocational schools set up by the occupation should be articulated with the national school system of Haiti and that financial and administrative aid should be contributed by the United States toward developing an adequate system of education in the island republic. In its appraisal of the educational facilities, the commission contended that from the viewpoint of finances education in the republic was worse off under American occupation than it had been when it was exclusively under Haitian control.

Largely as a result of the steps taken in accordance with the recommendations of the Forbes commission, relations with the island republic improved considerably. In compliance with the commission's recommendation that the military office of high commissioner be abolished and its duties be taken over by a civilian, who would also act as a diplomatic representative, Hoover appointed Dr. Dana G. Munro, then chief of the Latin-American Division of the States Department, minister to Haiti. The Forbes commission had suggested "increasingly rapid Haitianization" of the various treaty services. Accordingly, Munro began at once to return to Haitian control most of the important public functions that had been assumed by the Americans. This relaxed control followed the October 1930 congressional elections in Haiti, in which the United States followed a strictly "hands off" policy.

The way was thus paved for the Haitianization agreement of August 5, 1931, which terminated United States control of most of the departments of the Haitian administration, except the country's finances and a few services, such as the *garde d'Haiti*. At the same time the military authorities withdrew the proclamation of martial law and technically put an end to the American occupation. After reconciling some differences over American control of Haiti's finances, a treaty of friendship and two protocols were signed on September 3, 1932, calling for the termination of the American occupation by December 31, 1934—about two years earlier than called for by the previous treaty. The 1932 treaty envisaged the complete Haitianization of the *garde*, but allowed the United States still to retain some financial control over the country. As a result, the Haitian national assembly, after a tumultuous session, unanimously rejected not only the treaty but even "the principle" of such a treaty. Despite the nonratification of the treaty, the Haitianization program of the Hoover administration did not slacken, and the retreat from imperialism continued unabated.

The withdrawal planned and started by Hoover was later completed by his successor. The 1932 treaty formed the ground work of an executive agreement with Haiti, entered into by the Roosevelt administration. Thus, in October 1934, the termination of the long-lasting occupation was completed by the man who had reputedly written Haiti's 1918 constitution and was in accordance with plans laid earlier in the Hoover administration. . . .

CONCLUSION

In retrospect it is evident that Hoover's foreign policy was essentially predicated on a desire to maintain peace and had as one of its main objectives the creation of a policy of good will and neighborly understanding toward the southern Americas. Even before he entered the White House, Hoover indicated that he was determined to better the relationship of the United States with our Latin-American neighbors. In accordance with this objective, Hoover constructed a definite Latin-American policy for his administration. He made it a positive part of the government's program to cultivate the friendship of the southern nations and to practice the ideal of the "good neighbor." In summarizing the policy of the Hoover administration toward the Latin-American nations, Henry L. Stimson declared that "we have sought to make our policy towards them so clear in its implications of justice and good will, in its avoidance of anything which could be even misconstrued into a policy of forceful intervention or a desire for exploitation of those republics and their citizens, as to reassure the most timid or suspicious among them." These efforts were not in vain, for it is evident from the results of Hoover's Latin-American policy that good will between the Americas improved considerably during his administration.

It should be clear that Hoover's policy contributed to a favorable transformation in our relations with Latin America, as it should also be clear that inter-American relations prior to the Hoover administration were at a dangerously low ebb. . . .

The 1928 Havana conference marked a turning point in inter-American relations. It was the last Pan-American gathering in which American imperialism was defended. [Secretary of State] Hughes impressed upon the southern nations that the United States was interested in improving relations with them; and the conference thus laid the ground for a trend of better understanding. Hoover helped make this trend a reality. On his preinauguration trip Hoover explained his good-neighbor ideal, which he later put into practice, to the peoples of the southern republics. Through the deeds of his administration he overcame many of their fears of United States imperialism and of the Monroe Doctrine, and he allayed their Yankeephobia. He sought to substitute neighborly interest and understanding in the place of "police diplomacy." During his four years in the White House, he probably traveled farther along the road of Pan-American solidarity than any previous President.

If Hoover's Latin-American policy was to have any lasting value it had to be a national policy, not the policy of the Republican party. This apparently was recognized by his administration, and the policy followed was avowedly nonpartisan. As such, it was adopted and expanded by his Democratic successor, President Franklin D. Roosevelt. Hoover's Undersecretary of State, William R. Castle, Jr., succinctly expressed the nonpartisan qualities of the government's Latin-American policy in the following manner:

Our relations with Latin America are, above all, not in any way partisan. It is the United States which has duties and responsibilities, not the party. To be sure, the party in power has to carry out those duties and responsibilities, but no government would dare to stray far from the national policy. That is, and must always be, a policy of frank and friendly co-operation with our friends in Latin America.

This was intended as an assurance to the nations of the Western Hemisphere that the friendly and neighborly interest of the United States would not change with the ever whirling wheel of political fortune.

As Hoover's Latin-American policy was admittedly nonpartisan and was adopted by his Democratic successor, it was in many ways the real beginning of what has come to be popularly known as the good-neighbor policy. The entrance of Roosevelt into the White House did not result in any marked charge in the Latin-American policy which the country had been following in the previous four years. If there was any noticeable change in the policy, it was primarily in the increased tempo of the program, especially in the mid-thirties, when unsettled world conditions gave a strong impetus to inter-American solidarity. Probably the weakest link in Hoover's Latin-American policy was his administration's tariff policy, which to many Latin Americans was anathema. In this regard, the Roosevelt administration made a significant change by putting in effect a program of reciprocal trade agreements, championed by Secretary of State Cordell Hull. This apparently operated to reduce the tariff, and to increase Latin-American good will. But in its main essentials, the good-neighbor policy had its roots in the Hoover administration; Roosevelt only adopted and expanded it.

In December 1943, the United Press made a survey of prominent Republican leaders, who were asked to comment on United States–Latin-American relations in connection with the charges of Republican Senator Hugh A. Butler. The senator, on the basis of a hasty tour of the southern continent, condemned the New Deal's good-neighbor policy. Thomas E. Dewey, at that time a hopeful presidential prospect, stated that there "was no partisanship in the United States regarding the good-neighbor policy," and that it had been established during Republican administrations. America's senior statesman and former President, Herbert Hoover, commented on the same subject by reviewing his accomplishments in the field of inter-American relations, his use of the term "good neighbor," and his reversal of the nation's practice of intervention. He pointed out that he had emphasized nonintervention throughout his administration and that he had given proof of his intentions by withdrawing the Marines from Nicaragua and the occupation troops from Haiti. He concluded by stating that he "was happy to say that it was the last of these interventions and the last of the policy of American interference in the domestic policies of the Latin-American States."

Sumner Welles, who was one of the principal architects of Franklin D. Roosevelt's Latin-American policy, took exception to Hoover's claims "for the paternity of the good-neighbor policy." He contended that Hoover's policies were well-intentioned and were steps in the right direction, but that they failed for two reasons. The first was that Hoover had served for eight years in the cabinets of Harding and Coolidge, which, Latin Americans felt, tinged him with interventionist relationships. The second was that "only a year after Mr. Hoover assumed office he signed the Smoot-Hawley Tariff Act." Even though Hoover's good-neighbor policy might well lay claim to being non-partisan, its results have been subject to debate in the political arena.

As to the origin of the term "good neighbor," there should be little ground for dispute. It is a phrase which has undoubtedly been used by many states-men on numerous occasions. As early as the year 1815, prior to complete Latin-American independence, the term or its equivalent was used in refer-ence to Western Hemisphere relations. The term "good neighborliness" (*buena vecindad*) as applied to international relations was a common one in the Spanish correspondence of the early 1800's. The Spanish minister to the United States of that period, Don Luis de Onís, used the phrase in reference to the attitude of the United States toward the struggling and estranged colonies of Spain.

In its modern sense, Elihu Root had used the phrase as far back as 1907 in relation to Santo Domingo. Hoover applied the term to Latin-American affairs in several of his addresses while on his good-will tour in 1928. President Franklin D. Roosevelt first availed himself of the phrase in his inaugural address and made it applicable to the foreign relations of the United States throughout the world. It was not at first intended to apply solely to inter-American relations, but "more by chance than by deliberate intent" it came to mean the policy pursued by the United States government in its dealings with the twenty other republics of the Western Hemisphere. In the course of time its broader meaning was lost, and it was applied only to inter-American relations. From this, it can be seen that the concept of the "good neighbor" was not original with either Hoover or Roosevelt. Hoover even before he was inaugurated applied the good-neighbor ideal specifically to Latin America, whereas Roosevelt appropriated the same concept and gave it world-wide application. As such things happen, the term has become popularly associated with Roosevelt and inter-American relations.

From the day he accepted the Republican party's nomination for President to the day he left the White House, the Quaker statesman's words and actions reflected his avowed objections of peace and good will and his en-deavor to fulfill the good-neighbor ideal in regard to Latin America. His good-neighbor policy did much to bring the Americas closer together; it contributed to the elimination of some of the "sore spots" in inter-American relations; it helped to overcome some of the fears and hates aroused by the policies of previous administrations; and it laid the foundation for a Latin-American policy that paid rich dividends in the crisis of World War II. Thus, in any study of the building of the modern Latin-American policy of the United States, Hoover justly merits recognition as one of its important architects.

Roosevelt's Latin-American Policy

DONALD M. DOZER

A NATION blighted as was the United States after 1929 by a devastating economic depression unparalleled in its history was deemed in Latin America to be ready for a change in its political leadership. It was thought to have largely created its own plight by raising ever higher barriers against the importation of foreign products and at the same time endeavoring to find wider outlets for the products of its own vast industrial machine. The presidential election of 1932, conducted in time of national crisis and resulting in a victory for the Democratic candidate, Franklin D. Roosevelt, was acclaimed in Latin America as a "beautiful episode" in democracy, and the triumph of his party was generally interpreted as evidence that the United States was bent upon "a policy of democratic and liberal action." The Republicans, observed *O Jornal* of Rio de Janeiro, Brazil (November 11, 1932), "are always inclined to accentuate national aspects and to lean toward isolation, which forms a part of the traditional psychology of the Nation." Hoover's campaign, explained *La República* of La Paz (November 16, 1932), had been "supported by the great capitalist forces." The Democrats, on the other hand, observed *Excelsior* of Mexico City (November 10, 1932), "have always represented themselves in the political and social fields as the champions of the oppressed, of the immigrants, of the disabled, and, in general, of those dissatisfied with conditions. Their tendencies toward the betterment of the lower classes, however, have not a revolutionary origin but are mainly conservative." This same newspaper (November 9, 1932) regarded it as quite significant that although the United States had seven or eight million persons out of work "the good sense of the American public" rejected Communist and Socialist candidates, thus "maintaining itself faithful to its traditional good judgment, moderation, and

From Donald M. Dozer, *Are We Good Neighbors?* (Gainesville: University of Florida Press, 1959) pp. 16–37. Reprinted by permission of the University of Florida Press.

devotion to the established order." "It is probable that Mr. Roosevelt will be a great president," predicted *La Razón* of La Paz, Bolivia (November 11, 1932), a few days after his election.

But some apprehension was expressed that the new President might follow the same course toward Latin America as had his Democratic predecessor, Woodrow Wilson, whose interventionist actions had created bitter resentment south of the border. Had not Roosevelt admitted, even boasted, that while Assistant Secretary of the Navy he had written the new constitution for Haiti in 1918? Latin America's forebodings were allayed, however, by the new President's inaugural address on March 4, 1933, which was interpreted as showing that a profound transformation had taken place in the outlook and policy of the United States. "The weak nations now have no reason to fear the gigantic Republic of the North," exulted *El Orden*, an independent newspaper of Asunción, Paraguay (May 31, 1933). "This same nation," it added, "is abandoning its unsociable seclusion in order to constitute itself into an immense force at the service of humanity and of the peace and welfare of the world."

In particular, the international policy which Roosevelt announced in his first inaugural address seemed to augur new cooperative attitudes toward the peoples and governments of Latin America. This policy had been foreshadowed in the Democratic platform of 1932, which had called for "no interference in the internal affairs of other nations" and for "cooperation with nations of the Western Hemisphere to maintain the spirit of the Monroe Doctrine." The methods by which this might be worked out for Latin America had been embodied in a memorandum of suggestions to the president-elect from Sumner Welles. In that memorandum this intimate friend of Roosevelt, who was soon to become Assistant Secretary of State in charge of relations with Latin America, had proposed that "the creation and maintenance of the most cordial and intimate friendship between the United States and the other republics of the American Continent must be regarded as a keystone of our foreign policy." To establish this relationship the United States must abolish the impression that its policies involved "a threat to the sovereignty or to the national well-being of any republic of the Western Hemisphere." In particular the application of these policies "should never again result in armed intervention by the United States in a sister republic." In addition Welles went on to suggest the improvement of the procedure and machinery of consultation among all the American nations and the abolition of the "barriers and restrictions which now hamper the healthy flow of commerce between their respective nations."

This policy, it is easy to recall, was set forth by Roosevelt in his inaugural address as the "policy of the good neighbor—the neighbor who resolutely respects himself and, because he does so, respects the rights of others—the neighbor who respects his agreements in and with a world of neighbors." A similar policy had been announced repeatedly by many of Roosevelt's predecessors and their associates in government but had been seldom followed. Secretary of State Henry Clay had characterized his policy toward Latin America with this phrase over a century before. Secretary of State John Forsyth had referred to "the obligations of good neighborhood" in discussing the relations of his government with Latin America in 1835. President Tyler in his message to Congress on December 7, 1841, had declared it to be "the ardent desire of the United States . . . to fulfill all the duties of good neighborhood toward those who possess territories adjoining their own." The treaty of Guadalupe Hidalgo of 1848 ending the war between the United States and Mexico mentioned "the spirit of . . . good neighborship" (Article XX). President Abraham Lincoln had advocated a policy of "strengthening our ties of goodwill and good neighborhood" with the republics of this hemisphere in a message to the Senate on May 30, 1862. Senator Charles Sumner of Massachusetts, in his "Naboth's Vineyard" speech in the Senate on December 21, 1870, urged that the United States follow a policy of "good neighborhood" toward the independent countries of the Caribbean Sea. The phrase was also used by Secretary of State Thomas F. Bayard in the late 1880's. It had formed the basis for policy and pronouncements on Latin American affairs by at least two later secretaries of state, James G. Blaine and Elihu Root, the latter having used the phrase "good neighborhood" in describing the relationship of the United States with Santo Domingo in 1907. And President-elect Hoover on his goodwill tour through Latin America in 1928–1929 repeatedly characterized both his own attitude and the future policy of his administration toward Latin America as that of the "good neighbor."

If now this policy of "live and let live," as President Roosevelt described it in his speech at Cartagena, Colombia, in July, 1934, could be properly implemented it might conceivably transform Caliban into an angel of light. Roosevelt himself disarmingly admitted in a speech at the Woodrow Wilson Foundation on December 28, 1933, that if he had been engaged in a political campaign as a citizen of some other American republic he might have been strongly tempted to play upon the fears of his compatriots "by charging the United States of North America with some form of imperialistic desire for selfish aggrandizement. As a citizen of some other republic," he said, "I might have found it difficult to believe fully in the altruism of the richest American republic. . . . I might have found it hard to approve of the occupation of the territory of other republics, even as a temporary measure." He explicitly pledged that "the definite policy of the United States from now on is one opposed to armed intervention" and thus recognized the primary responsibility of each nation for "the maintenance of law and the orderly processes of government in this hemisphere." In that same month Secretary of State Cordell Hull signed an inter-American pledge to this effect at the Seventh International Conference of American States at Montevideo, declaring unequivocally that "No state has the right to intervene in the internal or external affairs of another."

Such heart-warming sentiments as these, particularly when confirmed by actions, gave Latin America a new conception of the United States. Here was a nation transformed into an altruistic, anti-imperialist, peace-loving neighbor, whom the Latin Americans could admire and love. As the Good Neighbor Policy was put into execution by the Roosevelt administration through the repudiation of unilateral armed intervention, the abrogation of the Platt Amendment with Cuba, the final withdrawal of United States troops from Haiti and the Dominican Republic, the negotiation of a new canal treaty favorable to Panama, the abandonment by the United States of earlier rights of free transit across the Isthmus of Tehuantepec in Mexico, and the signing of many bilateral trade agreements, Latin Americans were persuaded to soften their harsh attitudes toward the United States and to accept their powerful neighbor as a winsome and trustworthy friend. As a result of such acts as these implementing the Good Neighbor Policy, jubilated *La Nación* of Buenos Aires (July 12, 1934), "a current of frank and sincere friendship is bringing together Anglo-Saxons and Latin Americans," and the previous "colonial policy" of the United States toward Latin America was being transformed into the policy of the "good neighbor." "The policy of the 'Big Stick' and the later 'policy of the Dollar' have passed into history," it concluded. "There is in the White House," declared José Manuel Puig Casauranc, Mexican delegate to the Montevideo Conference in 1933, "an admirable, noble, and good man—a courageous man who knows the errors of the past but who feels that the errors really belong to the past."

The changed attitude toward the United States was reflected generally in the Latin American press. . . . [and] was largely due, as Sumner Welles later observed, to the Roosevelt administration's pledge and policy of nonintervention, to its demonstrated lack of aggressive designs against its weaker neighbors.

A few commentators south of the border continued, however, to view with jaundiced eyes this relatively sudden conversion of the United States into a good neighbor of the Latin American peoples. They insisted that its policy of good neighborliness was dictated mainly by considerations of self-interest. To the Roman Catholic newspaper *La Palabra* of Mexico City (February 26, 1935) the Good Neighbor Policy was the new method which the United States had chosen for making its economic, political, and cultural influence felt in Latin America. According to *La Opinión* of Ciudad Trujillo (March 30, 1936), "the ruling classes" in the United States had "come to recognize after many years that it is more profitable for them to have friendly and satisfied peoples south of the Rio Grande than people who are discontented and full of old rancors and whose sentiments might possibly take a dangerous form in some emergency in which the United States might find itself involved in the future." United States offenses against Nicaragua were recapitulated in a pamphlet of diatribe entitled *La Garra Yanqui (The Yankee Claw)* written by Agenor Argüello and published in El Salvador in late 1934. So persistent was the fear of a revival of the interventionist spirit that in 1935 there was a general feeling in Nicaragua, as reported by the United States minister there, that the next president of that country would be chosen by the United States. *Listín Diario* of Santo Domingo (June 2, 1933) cynically suggested that the United States had withdrawn its troops from Nicaragua only in order to be in a better position "to formulate accusations against the imperialistic policy of Japan in the Far East." According to an influential Guatemalan journalist, Carlos Bauer Aviles, the primary reason for the efforts of the Roosevelt administration to develop more cordial relations with Latin America was to relieve the economic depression in the United States by increasing its export trade to Latin America and also to further Pan-American solidarity as a measure of security to the United States in readiness for possible conflicts in the Far East. He cautioned that Roosevelt's promises of nonintervention committed only his administration and did not completely renounce intervention since they left open the possibility of resort to it in cases of absolute necessity.

This possibility seemed to present itself when Roosevelt declared in an address at Chautauqua, New York, in August, 1936, that "if there are any distant nations which do not wish us well . . . we shall protect ourselves and we shall protect our neighbors." The independent *Ultimas Noticias* of Mexico City (August 15, 1936) spurned this pronouncement in an editorial entitled "Don't Protect Us, Old Chap!" Here was evidence, it felt, that "under the allurements of the good neighbor and despite its solicitude and flattery, the imperialism of the United States though transformed still persists." As late as 1936, Haya de la Torre was writing that the Good Neighbor Policy was only "transitory and precarious," and that "what it boils down to is a political maneuver." He expected that the United States, under the compulsion of inexorable economic laws, eventually would resume its policy of loans, interventions, and political domination. In the event of "war between the United States and any other rival power," predicted Haya de la Torre, "the imperialist pressure on the governments of our countries . . . would attempt to involve us in the conflict to profit by our blood and our resources. . . . It would invoke, also in this case, as a dominant principle 'the defense of the interests of North American citizens' and in its name would give an honest appearance to the excesses of power of the stronger."

Complementary to, and perhaps equally influential with, the Good Neighbor Policy in creating a favorable conception of the United States in Latin America was the New Deal. To "liberal" elements the policies of a "controlled economy" were particularly appealing, since they proclaimed, in the words of *El Diario* of Montevideo (November 9, 1934), "the predominance of the community over the individual, collective welfare over personal prerogative." Roosevelt's New Deal was characterized by *El Nacional* of Mexico City (August 25, 1935) as "one of the greatest efforts ever made to establish a system of social justice within the procedures of a reformist system." And Latin Americans early perceived that the "internal policy" of the New Deal was sister to the "continental policy" of the Good Neighbor. Only when "the more democratic sentiment of that great republic began to overcome the mammon power of the millionaire trusts," observed *El Uruguay* of Montevideo (June 7, 1936), did "the imperialism of the Dollar and the tyranny of Wall Street" fade into the background and allow a more enlightened policy to be followed toward Latin America. The most "redoubtable" hindrance to "the free flow of confidence among all the nations of the continent" was removed, the Mexican political leader Ezequiel Padilla later wrote, when "the trusts and monopolies—as an all-powerful force controlling international and domestic policies"—were brought under the power of the people of the United States by means of the New Deal program. Plutocracy beaten at home was also forced to desist from its exploitation abroad. Latin America felt that Roosevelt's "policy of moderate radicalism," as a writer in *El Hombre Libre* of Mexico City (June 11, 1936) called it, was directed not only at promoting recovery in the United States but also at stimulating commercial interchange between his nation and the rest of the world. That increased interchange meant economic advantage for the peoples of Latin America.

The Latin American policy of the United States, as set forth by Secretary Hull in a radio address on February 28, 1936, was "(1) to promote better understanding among our sister republics of this hemisphere; (2) to lend every assistance for the maintenance of peace and the perfection of peace machinery on this continent; and (3) to eliminate excessive artificial barriers to inter-American trade." The assumption underlying the policy and conduct of the Roosevelt administration toward Latin America was that the general welfare of the United States was linked with that of the other American nations. For this reason it behooved the people and government of the United States to have well-disposed neighbors in the Western Hemisphere, who would develop with them a mutually advantageous commerce and who would support them in international affairs. The object of the United States was declared to be "the maintenance of relations of complete trust and friendship among the American Republics." If the previous use of force as a method of extending the influence of the United States in the Western Hemisphere had been self-defeating, perhaps sincere words, acts of friendship, and increased commercial interchange would be effective.

The execution of this policy was deemed to call for more frequent inter-American consultation and collaboration. With the active concurrence of the United States all the American nations, as noted above, repudiated the practice of unilateral armed intervention by one state in the affairs of another at the Seventh International Conference of American States at Montevideo in 1933. At subsequent conferences held at Buenos Aires in 1936 and Lima in 1938 plans for closer economic cooperation and for mutual exchange in the fields of science, technology, literature, and the arts among all the peoples of the Americas were worked out. Under the leadership of the United States the American nations subscribed to certain high principles of conduct including the recognition of the juridical equality of states, the proscription of territorial conquest, respect for international law and treaty obligations, racial and religious tolerance, and the settlement of all international differences by peaceful means, which they consecrated in the "Declaration of American Principles" signed at Lima in 1938. In all this the American nations, under the inspiration of the United States and with its full cooperation, emphasized the essentially moral basis of the revitalized inter-American system of interdependence and cooperation.

At the same time an important catalytic agent in changing Latin America's unfavorable opinion of the United States after 1933 was the trade policy of the Roosevelt administration. In the year before Roosevelt's inauguration the value of United States trade with Latin America sank to less than $575 million, its lowest point in twenty-three years. The new administration, therefore, undertook as one of its prime objects the task of correcting this situation which was so obviously unprofitable to both the United States and Latin America. At the Montevideo conference in 1933 Secretary Hull secured the adoption of a resolution that the American nations would promptly undertake "to reduce high trade barriers through the negotiation of comprehensive bilateral reciprocity treaties based upon mutual concessions," a resolution which was reaffirmed at the Buenos Aires conference in 1936 and the Lima conference in 1938. In accordance with this principle of liberalized trade relations the United States between 1934 and 1938 concluded trade agreements with ten Latin American nations—Cuba (1934), Brazil (1935), Haiti (1935), Colombia (1935), Honduras (1935), Nicaragua (1936), Guatemala (1936), Costa Rica (1936), El Salvador (1937), and Ecuador (1938).

The gradual drying up of Latin American markets in Europe under the system of economic nationalism rampant there made Latin Americans particularly receptive to overtures which promised them enlarged outlets for their products in the Western Hemisphere. Their esteem for the United States heightened after 1933 generally in proportion to the increase in the prices received and the expansion of their markets in the United States for Cuban sugar, Uruguayan meat, Chilean wines, and other products of their countries. In this trade program, declared Agustín Edwards, proprietor of *El Mercurio* of Santiago, Chile (March 4, 1935), the North American nation, "which is essentially practical, is not seeking to impose itself politically or militarily but rather it is seeking economic understandings of reciprocal benefit." The people of the United States were motivated by the simple purpose, as it seemed to him, "of procuring the products which they do not have in sufficient quantity and of sending us in return the material resulting from their fertile and inexhaustible mechanical genius." Partly as a result, Latin America came to assume a much more important place in the commercial relations of the United States than ever before. The trade benefits to the United States, so desperately needed in the depression era and so skillfully worked out by the reciprocal trade agreements program, were immediate and considerable. Between 1933 and 1937 United States imports from Latin America jumped from $329.4 million to $705 million, or over 114 per cent; during the same period its exports to Latin America increased from $240.4 million to over $639.4 million, or more than 166 per cent. At the same time, by way of contrast, its imports from Europe increased by only 82 per cent and its exports to Europe by only 60 per cent. In other words, by 1937 the general trade relationship of the United States with Latin America, expressed in terms of foreign trade statistics, was 236 per cent better than it had been in 1933, whereas its general trade relationship with Europe had improved by only 167 per cent. To cite specific examples of these economic gains in Latin America, United States trade with Chile, Cuba, Mexico, and Peru doubled between 1934 and 1937, and with certain other countries it even trebled in either exports or imports. Trade with Argentina, in particular, showed a phenomenal gain increasing from $72.1 million to $233.1 million, or 223 per cent, during that period. Whereas between 1929 and 1932 the United States had accounted for 35 per cent of the total foreign trade of Latin America as a whole, by 1938 it was responsible for 45 per cent of the total foreign trade of that area. During the years before the outbreak of the European war the Good Neighbor Policy paid off in dollars and cents, as it was later to pay off in strategic materials furnished and lives saved from the holocaust of war. As early as 1934 this policy was characterized by *La Prensa* of Buenos Aires (June 17, 1934) as a policy of "practical Americanism."

To Latin Americans, the contrasts and stresses in the United States were sharply accentuated as the presidential election of 1936 approached. Since Woodrow Wilson's administration they had had a predilection for the Democratic Party in the United States as being less directly involved in a policy of intervention in their affairs than the Republican Party, as the more Roman Catholic of the two major parties, and as being generally opposed to the raising of high tariff barriers against their products. In 1936 the Republican Party, declared *La Nación* of Buenos Aires (June 13, 1936), was contending for a "policy of economic isolation which, six years ago, brought about the most prejudicial effects of the world crisis; it has taken no warning whatever from the terrible catastrophe that has befallen trade since the erection of the Chinese wall of protectionist duties, dividing the world into watertight reservoirs and compelling other nations to protect themselves by similar means in order not to be absorbed by the formidable financial power of a nation which buys nothing and wants to sell everything." Moreover, as *El Cronista* of Tegucigalpa (January 16, 1936) explained, Latin America considered that former "Republican rulers" of the United States had undertaken "to oppress various countries of the South, to impose on them standards of living, to set at naught the determination of their sovereignty, to seize their sources of production for the profit of North American capitalism." Since all these hateful operations might be re-enacted "with the ascent to power of the Republican Party and of a chief with imperial tendencies," many Latin American newspapers frankly advocated President Roosevelt's re-election.

By reason of both the Good Neighbor and the New Deal policies, President Roosevelt had already become to Latin America a symbol of high achievement and of roseate hope for the future. On his visit to Cartagena, Colombia,

in July, 1934, the first visit of a President of the United States to a South
American country, he was effusively praised by Latin Americans as "the
courageous initiator of the new era of understanding and of mutual support
which has to be the basis of continental progress." According to the official
report of his visit by the United States minister to Colombia, "the President's
personality made a splendid effect on all who saw him" and "will have a
beneficial effect on our relations with Colombia."

Evidence of Roosevelt's popularity throughout Latin America was overwhelming. *El Panamá-América* of Panama (April 20, 1936) considered him
"a real democrat" because of the New Deal, which served the interests of
labor, and the Good Neighbor Policy. Asked to name the president among
"those rulers who have occupied the White House in Washington whose
policy has been most beneficial for Hispano-American countries," its "categorical answer" was "Franklin Delano Roosevelt." Under Roosevelt's leadership, declared the editor of a Guatemalan newspaper, *Diario de Centro-
América* (September 8, 1936), "the former threatening shadow of the White
House has been changed into the friendly beam of a lighthouse which points
out not only to the United States but also to the other countries of America
and of the world the directions of new policy." The conservative *Diario de
la Marina* of Havana (January 22, 1936) was impressed with the admirable
results of Roosevelt's program including "the policy of farsighted intervention
in agriculture and industry, the policy of interchange, that of the 'New Deal,'
that of the relations of good neighbor with the American countries and of
reciprocity with as many of them as possible." "Mr. Roosevelt governs a
Democracy," declared *La Nación* of Buenos Aires (August 16 and 20, 1936),
and "personifies its ideals of welfare and tranquillity, which are the ideals of
the whole of America." His vigorous personality exuding the quality of confident leadership appealed to Latin Americans. "An admirable example of the
great men of North America," generalized *Diario de la Marina* (January 22,
1936), "in him are combined both idealism and the faculty of action." To
La Epoca of Tegucigalpa (June 26, 1936) it appeared that "All the America
of Columbus renders him its homage of admiration."

Whether Roosevelt won re-election or not, however, Latin Americans
hoped that his policy toward Latin America would, in the words of *Listín
Diario* of Ciudad Trujillo (March 25, 1936), "be declared a national policy,
without being subject to changes of interpretation by the Democrats or Republicans that alternate in power." *La Opinión* (March 30, 1936) of the
same capital explained that "it is only fair to recognize that this policy had
Presidents Coolidge and Hoover as its precursors," that "it was President
Coolidge who, through his instructions to Secretary of State Charles Evans
Hughes, ordered the cessation of intervention in our country," and that "it
was President Hoover who arranged for the evacuation of Nicaragua by
American forces and took the first steps (Forbes Commission) toward the
evacuation of the Republic of Haiti." Mindful of the mutually beneficial
effects of the Good Neighbor Policy, *El Imparcial* of Santiago, Chile (No-

vember 7, 1936), forecast that even in the event of a Republican victory the government at Washington could not and would not abandon that policy.

The United States which re-elected Roosevelt by a greater majority than any of his predecessors was a nation that seemed to Latin America to have vindicated democracy. According to *Diario Latino* of San Salvador (November 7, 1936), the "GREAT DEMOCRACY" had re-elected the "GREAT DEMOCRAT." His victory, said *El País* of Montevideo (November 4, 1936), represented a triumph for "the ideal of democracy, of liberty, and of peace." In an extraordinary action the Cuban Senate voted unanimously to send a message of congratulations to the United States Senate on his re-election. "Here," enthusiastically declared *Noticias Gráficas* of Buenos Aires (November 3, 1936), "is the United States giving the world the example of its extraordinary civic faith and its devotion to order and respect for the law." The North Americans, observed *Diario de la Marina* of Havana (November 5, 1936), "possess in high degree the virtue which Salvador de Madariaga described with the English expression 'fairplay.' . . . For the citizens of North America elections are much the same as a sporting event. Before the 'match' factions are irreconcilable and they fight bravely using all the instruments which the law allows. After the 'match' both teams shake hands and even give each other enthusiastic 'cheers.' The loser is the first to recognize the legitimate triumph of his opponent. The winner, on the other hand, applauds the courage and the decorum with which his adversary has fought." Not only the fair play but also the orderliness of the election of 1936 appeared to give the lie to the criticisms of democracy which were being increasingly spread by Nazi-Fascist propagandists. Latin Americans considered it especially significant that neither the Socialist nor Communist parties nor the Constitutional Union Party led by Congressman William Lemke attained any measure of success. "Under the Democratic regime," observed *Avance* of Havana (November 4, 1936), "the Union does not appear to be threatened by the dangers which are rising in other nations of the world. The red phantom is not in the house of Uncle Sam, as in European lands, a sinister spectre which haunts the dream of those who are fond of the present system."

For this situation Latin Americans gave considerable credit to Roosevelt's New Deal. That program, representing "the solution of social problems by normal and legitimate means," made Roosevelt, according to *El Diario* of Buenos Aires (November 4, 1936), "the greatest obstacle to local Fascism and . . . as well the sure preventive against Communism because of his careful, serene, and unprejudiced consideration of social ills." His New Deal, said *Diario de la Marina* of Havana (November 5, 1936), "has revealed to the New Continent an interesting formula by which it is possible to cure completely the frantic 'isms,' not by abandoning democratic procedure but by making it more flexible and by adjusting it to the times." In this way, Senator José Manuel Casanova of Cuba declared, "the great American people openly identifies itself with the work of social renovation, oriented toward the improvement of the conditions of the poorer classes and directed toward the attainment of a more equitable and useful distribution of wealth." The result was that in this election "all the power of the strongest plutocracy of our times and of history," as *El Universal* of Mexico City (November 5, 1936) declared, "was obliged to surrender, to yield to the irresistible will of the people. All the apparatus of economic royalty, the crushing weight of its money, the eighty-five per cent of the press which served as its mouthpiece, Wall Street and Heart [Hearst] . . . were swept away by the largest torrent of votes that has ever been seen in the United States." It was, according to *Avance* of Havana (November 4, 1936), this "frank and sincere policy" of achieving "a better standard of living for the man who works and fights—a thing which is equivalent in these troubled times to guaranteeing internal peace—which is the reason for the greatness of the great northern people."

Here was a nation which, to the delight of Latin America, had purged itself of its offensive habits and was now practicing "democracy" at home and good neighborliness in its international relations. It had made itself, as *Noticias Gráficas* of Buenos Aires (November 3, 1936) declared, "a model for the other nations of the continent." It had become, said *El Uruguay* of Montevideo (November 7, 1936), "as it was in the eighteenth century, the victorious emblem around which may rally the multitudes thirsting for social justice and human fraternity." In particular, Roosevelt's victory meant for Latin America "the consecration of the 'Good Neighbor' policy." Under Roosevelt's leadership the North American people had, in the words of *El País* of Montevideo (November 2, 1936), "demonstrated, by a sustained action over a period of four years, their purpose to become good neighbors in fact, to act in a democratic spirit and on a basis of equal footing." Their government had abandoned "dollar diplomacy" and was no longer acting as "the agent of the bankers of Wall Street." To *Diario de Hoy* of San Salvador Roosevelt represented "the tendency to conciliation in the American family." This was especially demonstrated when at his suggestion representatives of all the American nations assembled at Buenos Aires in December, 1936, "to determine how the maintenance of peace among the American republics may best be safeguarded." At that conference a greater degree of unanimity among the American republics was manifested than at any previous conference for many years back.

Roosevelt himself attended the Buenos Aires conference and took advantage of his trip to pay brief visits also to Rio de Janeiro and Montevideo. At Rio de Janeiro the day of his visit was declared a national holiday. As he disembarked from his ship he was greeted by thousands of school children, who waved red, white, and blue banners and sang the national anthem of the United States. He then made a triumphal tour of the city with President Getúlio Vargas. For his visit Vargas' Itamaraty Palace was lavishly decorated with orchids, some of which had been furnished by generous citizens who stripped their own plants of blossoms for this occasion, and others had been supplied by florists at a total cost of approximately $2,100, an extraordinary expense in a country where orchids were cheap.

During his visit Roosevelt addressed a special joint session of the Brazilian Congress and Supreme Court. After his address he was hailed by the spokesman of the Brazilian Congress, amidst applause, as "the *Man*—the fearless and generous man who is accomplishing and living the most thrilling political experience of modern times." "The President completely captivated the officials of the Brazilian Government, as well as the press and people," reported the United States embassy in Rio de Janeiro. "His tremendous personal charm and great dignity were commented [on] widely and there has not been a single discordant note in the voluminous editorial and news comment which filled the Brazilian press during the days immediately preceding and succeeding the President's visit. . . . The newspapers, many of which had special commemorative editions on the day of his arrival, termed him the outstanding world figure in public life today."

The same outpourings of popular acclamation occurred when Roosevelt reached Buenos Aires. Again the day of his arrival was declared a national holiday. "The charm of his manners and his personality completely captured the Latin mentality and imagination of his hosts," reported the United States ambassador in Buenos Aires. Again in Montevideo, where Roosevelt stopped briefly after leaving Buenos Aires to return to the United States, he received tremendous acclaim. "No word of anything but friendliness toward him appeared in any section of the press," reported the United States minister in Montevideo. Even the normally anti-"Yanqui" *El Debate* (December 3, 1936) welcomed him as a "worthy successor of President Monroe!"

The sentiments in favor of peace and democracy which Roosevelt expressed in his speech opening the Buenos Aires conference were applauded by Latin American public opinion. Now, jubilantly proclaimed *Diario de Costa Rica* of San José (December 24, 1936), the Monroe Doctrine was being given a "continental character." According to *Diario de Hoy* of San Salvador (December 1, 1936), the Latin American countries "will not have to fight against the strategy of Nordic imperialism but will be able to devote all their strength to enthusiastic and loyal collaboration with the United States for the maintenance of continental peace." Roosevelt's warm reception in Rio de Janeiro could perhaps have been expected by reason of long United States-Brazilian amity, but his complete acceptance in Argentina, where antipathy to the United States was traditional, impressed Latin Americans as something of a phenomenon. There, as also in Uruguay, the emphasis which Roosevelt placed upon democracy was seized upon by the opposition as a weapon with which to belabor the existing governments of their own countries, that of President Augustín P. Justo of Argentina and President Gabriel Terra of Uruguay, as antidemocratic. In both countries attention was called to the need for the United States to follow up Roosevelt's visit by relaxing its tariff barriers and its sanitary restrictions against their products.

The new attitudes of the United States toward Latin America and the affinity of the Good Neighbor Policy with the New Deal were clearly demonstrated in the reaction of the Roosevelt administration to the expropriation policy of the Lázaro Cárdenas government in Mexico in 1938. When that government, in pursuance of its program of recovery of the resources of the Mexican nation and the distribution of land to the landless, expropriated agricultural and petroleum lands, some of which were owned by citizens of the United States, the Roosevelt government did not resort to intervention or threats of intervention. Instead, Secretary of State Hull assured Mexico that the United States did not question the right of that government "in the exercise of its sovereign power to expropriate properties within its jurisdiction." The Roosevelt government, Hull informed the Mexican ambassador, "has frequently asserted the right of all countries freely to determine their own social, agrarian and industrial problems. This right includes the sovereign right of any government to expropriate private property within its borders in furtherance of public purposes." Hull adverted to the fact that "The Government of the United States has itself been very actively pursuing a program of social betterment . . . in short, it is carrying out the most far-reaching program for the improvement of the general standard of living that this country has ever seen. Under this program it has expropriated from foreigners as well as its own citizens properties of various kinds, such as submarginal and eroded lands to be retired from farming, slums to be cleared for housing projects, land for power dams, lands containing resources to be preserved for government use." The United States therefore obviously could not complain against the policy of the Mexican government so similar to its own. But Hull insisted that, in accordance with international law, the owners of these expropriated properties must receive prompt, adequate, and effective compensation. In the ensuing negotiations the United States concerned itself, therefore, not with the Mexican government's policy of expropriation as such but only, in general, with the amount of compensation and the arrangements for its satisfactory payment.

This self-restraint toward Mexico was hailed by President Cárdenas in a message to the United States ambassador in Mexico City on March 31, 1938, as a new "proof of friendship" which the Mexican people would carry in their hearts. He paid tribute to the United States which "through its President continues to support the policy of friendship and respect of each nation, a policy which is winning for your country the affection of many peoples of the world."

Not only in Mexico but in other Latin American countries as well public opinion responded favorably to the position taken in Washington. Peruvian newspapers expressed praise for "the admirable calmness of the Secretary of State." El Telégrafo of Guayaquil declared that the United States was quite right in its attitude, "which could not be more moderate and conciliatory." Other newspapers, including El Relator of Cali, Colombia, and El Sur of Concepción, Chile, warmly commended the temperate action of the United States.

Under Roosevelt's Good Neighbor Policy, then, the United States had frankly laid the Big Stick on the shelf and was relying upon the development of a community of interests in the Western Hemisphere to produce common attitudes and unity of action. It had withdrawn its forces of occupation from Latin American countries, had renounced the use of armed force in its future dealings with them, had assumed treaty obligations not to intervene in their affairs, and had reversed its restrictive trade policy to their advantage. Roosevelt even assured Argentina during his visit to Buenos Aires in 1936 that he would work for the removal of restrictions upon the importation of Argentine meat into the United States. As a result, little by little the distrust of the United States, built up in Latin America by previous pressures, had abated and confidence had been slowly re-established. Chile and Argentina invited the United States in April, 1935, to join them in the mediation of the Chaco War between Paraguay and Bolivia—a mediation which resulted in the establishment of peace in that troubled area three years later.

This changed inter-American relationship—largely the result of the United States policy of self-restraint, international decency, and cooperation—was reflected in the Latin American press. The United States through President Roosevelt, concluded *La Nación* of Santiago, Chile (October 7, 1937), was "directing its expressions of goodwill toward the American nations, with whom it feels itself logically bound by the closest bonds of mutual understanding and interest." Roosevelt and his Secretary of State, Cordell Hull, said *O Jornal* of Rio de Janeiro (March 19, 1938), "have given to American relations the practical character of good neighborliness, which consists in the defense of common interests and in the solidarity of all, in safeguarding the integrity and independence of the nations of this continent, in augmenting commercial interchange, and in the harmony of the republics of this hemisphere." President Roosevelt's Good Neighbor Policy, concluded *El Liberal Progresista* of Guatemala City (May 10, 1937), "has already brought about a complete change in the relations between the United States and the American countries and a flourishing intercourse in matters relating to continental commerce." This powerful northern nation, according to *La Crónica* of Lima (March 8, 1938), was no longer "the big brother, the tutor, and the caretaker of the patrimony of all America, through the development of an imperialistic policy." A radical change had taken place in its policy and attitudes. As *El Liberal* of Bogotá (October 14, 1938) generalized, "From the 'Big Stick' to the 'Good Neighbor' policy was not only an evolution but a revolution. The people presided over by the second Roosevelt has really been a good neighbor to Latin Americans." The distrust and fear of the United States formerly so prevalent in Latin America, declared *La Prensa* of Buenos Aires (November 17, 1940), "have been dissipated and replaced by an atmosphere of friendship." In this new atmosphere "an unlimited horizon" opened up, said *La Nación* of Santiago (October 7, 1937), "for the hopes of the people of America for a near future built upon solidarity, cooperation and unity of outlook for the countries of the continent."

For "this new atmosphere," this changed orientation of the United States, Latin Americans were inclined to give credit to the leadership of the Democratic Party and President Roosevelt. In a formal resolution unanimously adopted by the Colombian Senate "the figure of the North American statesman" was declared to be "one of the greatest and most noble of our epoch. . . . With respect to the American republics," the Senate resolution continued, "the policy called that of the good neighbor, which President Roosevelt preaches and practices with firm loyalty as the application of democratic principles internationally, has completely eliminated the justifiable resentments produced by the opposite policy." The idea grew up, and was encouraged by the Roosevelt administration, that the United States, under previous Republican administrations, had been committed, in the words of *El País* of Montevideo (October 7, 1937), to a "policy of intervention, protectionism *à outrance*, and economic imperialism" and that a return to these policies would make "impossible the march toward a true solidarity of the two Americas in defense of their liberty and their peace." Only the Democratic Party favored *rapprochement* with Latin America and fair treatment of its peoples, it was said. According to *Ahora* of Caracas (November 10, 1938), the Good Neighbor Policy was entirely a policy of the Democratic Party and the replacement of that party by the Republicans would mean an "intensification and extension of the imperialism that would swallow up countries in Central and South America."

To others it seemed that this unhappy result was to be anticipated not only from the Republicans but also from other administrations in Washington of whatever political complexion. The Mexican nationalist José Vasconcelos repeatedly argued that there was a basic incompatibility between "Bolivarism" and "Monroism" which rendered a durable good neighbor policy impossible. The Good Neighbor Policy could not be accepted at its face value, argued the Chilean government newspaper, *La Nación* (May 20, 1939), because it might be altered by Roosevelt's successors in the White House and also because strong nations can always evade their obligations to weaker countries.

But in general it was said in Latin America that greater progress had been made toward the attainment of inter-American harmony in this brief period of Roosevelt's Good Neighbor Policy than during the entire previous century of inter-American relations. International tensions which had embittered the feelings of the American peoples had been relieved. Official relations which had often been characterized only by formal amity had become genuinely cordial. New techniques of inter-American cooperation had been applied in a system of joint consultation and multilateral action based upon mutual trust and respect for agreements. The Pan-Hispanic movement had been largely disarmed and the cause of Pan-Americanism saved. Even if some of the Latin paeans of praise for the Roosevelt administration are discounted as mere flattery or only characteristic Latin American effusiveness, it was clear at the beginning of his second term as President that responsible opinion in Latin America had been largely won over to the United States and was disposed to cooperate with him in the programs of his administration. His strong personal leadership, his aggressive use of the national powers of the presidency, and his left-of-center domestic program coincided generally with the ideas and expectations of Latin Americans in the 1930's. . . .

11

Destroyers for Bases:

DID ROOSEVELT HAVE THE AUTHORITY?

THE REMARKABLE *success of the German military machine in Poland in September 1939, was clearly a harbinger of assaults elsewhere. Anticipating an attack on the western democracies, President Roosevelt asked Congress to lift the American embargo on arms and other war materials. Congress approved the changes in the neutrality laws in November, 1939, thus permitting the democracies to purchase supplies in the United States. In the spring of 1940, the Nazis began their campaigns against the west. First Norway and Denmark fell; then Belgium and the Netherlands; and finally in June, 1940, France. Great Britain alone was left to withstand the forces of Hitler. To soften England for an invasion, the German air force began a tremendous air offensive over the island. This Battle of Britain lasted all through the summer of 1940. The destruction of life and property was great and Britain had been weakened, but the invasion never came off.*

Meanwhile, British forces were battling in North Africa to keep the Germans away from the oil fields of the Middle East. Supplies were desperately needed for this campaign as well as for stockpiling in England should there be a German invasion. As important as the supplies were, fast warships to protect the cargo vessels transporting the supplies across the Atlantic were also needed. To fill this demand President Roosevelt, by an exchange of notes in September, 1940, traded fifty overage World War I destroyers for lease rights to a number of naval bases in the Caribbean and Bahama Islands. He did not ask for Congressional authority, but acted on his own. Did he have the authority? The Attorney General delivered an opinion, at the President's request, stating that he had the right. Authorities disagree on the question.

Quincy Wright, a distinguished authority on international law and for many years a professor at the University of Chicago, deals with the matter in relation to domestic law and to international law. Of the former, Wright maintains that the President acted perfectly legally. He had the right to enter into an executive agreement which in its execution disposed of public vessels and acquired bases. No law prohibits such an action. As for its relation to international law, such an act by a neutral state would be illegal, but Wright suggests that the United States was not a neutral at the time but rather "a supporting state . . . one which assists a defending state without armed force." Any state has the right to assist another state against a third one acting contrary to a treaty. Hence the transfer, under international law, is legal.

Edwin M. Borchard, who taught international law at Yale, disagrees with Wright's position. His principal contention is that the President does not have the right to "conclude and bind the nation in fundamental matters." He may, indeed, negotiate executive agreements, but only on relatively minor matters. But even if he had the authority, he nevertheless transgressed a domestic statute which makes it "unlawful to send out . . . any vessel . . . to a belligerent nation." And international law was violated, too, because it does not permit a neutral government (as distinguished from neutral citizens) to sell war goods to a belligerent. He dismisses the allegation that the action was justified because Germany was an aggressor. There are not, he says, two rules of law—"one for lawful war and one for aggression." He finds the destroyer transfer inconsistent "with neutrality, with United States statutes, or with international law."

The Transfer of Destroyers to Great Britain

QUINCY WRIGHT

ON SEPTEMBER 3 President Roosevelt announced to Congress that the United States had received from Great Britain ninety-nine year leases on certain naval bases in the Caribbean in exchange for fifty over-age destroyers. The transaction has aroused some controversy in and out of Congress on grounds both of municipal law and international law. An opinion by the Attorney General dealing with these questions accompanied the President's message.

So far as the municipal law of the United States is concerned, the Attorney General's opinion appears to be conclusive, although on one point his reasons may not be entirely satisfactory. The President has ample statutory authority to dispose of destroyers under the conditions which existed [1] and he has ample authority under the Constitution to acquire naval bases by the method of executive agreement. Executive agreements have been utilized in practice for

---

[1] "No vessel of the navy shall hereafter be sold in any other manner than herein provided, or for less than such appraised value, unless the President of the United States shall otherwise direct in writing." (Act of March 3, 1883, Sec. 5, U. S. Code, Tit. 34, Sec. 492.) "The word 'unless' qualifies both the requirements of the concluding clause." (Levinson v. United States, 258 U. S. 198, 201.) "Notwithstanding the provision of any other law, no military or naval weapon, ship, boat, aircraft, munitions, supplies or equipment, to which the United States has title, in whole or in part, or which have been contracted for, shall hereafter be transferred, exchanged, sold, or otherwise disposed of in any manner whatsoever unless the Chief of Naval Operations in the case of naval material, and the Chief of Staff of the Army in the case of military material, shall first certify that such material is not essential to the defense of the United States." (Act of June 28, 1940, Sec. 14 (a).) "Thus to prohibit action by the constitutionally created Commander in Chief except upon authorization of a statutory officer subordinate in rank is of questionable constitutionality." Waiving this question, and in view of the legislative history of the act, "It is my opinion that in proceeding under Section 14 (a) appropriate staff officers may and should consider remaining useful life, strategic importance, obsolescence and all other factors affecting defense value, not only with respect to what the Government of the United States gives up in any exchange or transfer, but also with respect to what the Government receives. In this situation good business sense is good legal sense." (Opinion of Attorney General Jackson, Aug. 27, 1940.)

Quincy Wright, "The Transfer of Destroyers to Great Britain," *American Journal of International Law*, XXXIV, 1940, pp. 680–689. Reprinted by permission of the American Journal of International Law.

transactions of the type in question,[2] and the broad independent powers of the President in foreign affairs have been sustained by the Supreme Court.[3] While there is no clear line between the subjects on which the President can enter into agreements under his constitutional powers to conduct foreign relations and those on which he must ask the advice and consent of the Senate, it appears that the prime consideration is whether the agreement imposes legal obligations upon the United States beyond the independent power of the President to fulfill. If the aid of Congress is necessary for fulfillment, the President should, before finally approving the instrument, either get the advice and consent of the Senate, thus making it a treaty in the constitutional sense, or he should get an authorizing act from Congress making appropriations or enacting legislation to fulfill such obligations. Since the present agreement imposed no such obligation requiring Congressional action, neither of these procedures was necessary.[4]

The Attorney General dealt with the Act of June 15, 1917,[5] which was

[2] President Fillmore authorized an executive agreement with Great Britain for acquiring Horseshoe Reef near the outlet of Lake Erie, on condition that the United States would not fortify it and would erect a lighthouse on it. Congress had made a provisional appropriation for the lighthouse in 1849 and subsequently made an additional appropriation. (Miller, Treaties, etc., of the United States, Vol. 5, p. 905 ff.) President Theodore Roosevelt acquired a naval base at Guantanamo by executive agreement with Cuba in 1903, in pursuance of a general provision in the Platt Amendment of 1901 and the United States-Cuba Treaty of 1903. (Crandall, Treaties, Their Making and Enforcement, Washington, 1916, p. 139.) Texas and Hawaii were annexed by exchanges of notes in 1845 and 1898, transmitting acts of the respective legislative bodies. (Miller, *op. cit.*, Vol. 4, p. 689 ff.; Crandall, *op. cit.*, p. 135 ff.)

[3] United States v. Curtiss-Wright Export *Corporation* (1936), 299 U. S. 304. . . .

[4] The purpose of the agreement cannot, of course, be fulfilled unless Congress makes appropriations to develop the bases. There is, however, no international obligation to do so.

[5] "Sec. 2. During a war in which the United States is a neutral nation, the President, or any person thereunto authorized by him, may detain any armed vessel owned wholly or in part by American citizens, or any vessel, domestic or foreign (other than one which has entered the ports of the United States as a public vessel), which is manifestly built for warlike purposes or has been converted or adapted from a private vessel to one suitable for warlike use, until the owner or master, or person having charge of such vessel, shall furnish proof satisfactory to the President, or to the person duly authorized by him, that the vessel will not be employed by the said owners or master, or person having charge thereof, to cruise against or commit or attempt to commit hostilities upon the subjects, citizens, or property of any foreign prince or state, or of any colony, district, or people with which the United States is at peace, and that the said vessel will not be sold or delivered to any belligerent nation, or to an agent, officer, or citizen of such nation, by them or any of them, within the jurisdiction of the United States, or, having left that jurisdiction, upon the high seas.

"Sec. 3. During a war in which the United States is a neutral nation, it shall be unlawful to send out of the jurisdiction of the United States any vessel built, armed, or equipped as a vessel of war, or converted from a private vessel into a vessel of war, with any intent or under any agreement or contract, written or oral, that such vessel shall be delivered to a belligerent nation, or to an agent, officer, or citizen of such nation, or with reasonable cause to believe that the said vessel shall or will be employed in the service of any such belligerent nation after its departure from the jurisdiction of the United States." (Act of June 15, passed in order to fulfill the obligations of the United States as a neutral under the principles of the Alabama award and the Thirteenth Hague Convention of 1907, and which was alleged to prevent the dispatch of the over-age destroyers to Great Britain. He held that Sec. 3 applied only to vessels which had been "built, armed or equipped as a vessel of war, or converted from a private vessel into a vessel of war," with intent that the vessel should be delivered to a belligerent or employed in its service. As the destroyers were not built, armed, equipped or converted with the intent of trading them to Great Britain, he held that the Act did not apply.

The natural construction of this section of the Act of 1917 would read the "with any intent" clause as modifying not "built, armed or equipped as a vessel of war," but "to send out of the jurisdiction of the United States." There is a comma before the "with," and the final phrase "after its departure from the jurisdiction of the United States" would more naturally qualify an intent related to "sending out of the jurisdiction of the United States" than an intent related to "building, arming or equipping a vessel as a vessel of war" or "converting from a private vessel into a vessel of war." It cannot be said, however, that this natural construction is conclusive, and the Attorney General rejected it on the grounds that it would make the preceding section of the Act meaningless, and that it would go beyond the obligations of international law.

The preceding section of the Act of 1917 apparently authorizes the President to permit the departure from the United States of armed vessels for sale or delivery to a belligerent in *foreign territory* (not within the jurisdiction of the United States nor upon the high seas). It was argued that if Section 3 were given its natural interpretation, American citizens would be deprived of the opportunity to build war vessels in the United States for sale to a belligerent in foreign territory as a commercial transaction, an opportunity to which the Attorney General considered them entitled under international law, subject only to the risk of seizure as contraband by the opposing belligerent. "The difference between selling armed vessels to belligerents and building them to order" was supported by citations from Oppenheim's *International Law:*

An armed ship, being contraband of war, is in no wise different from other kinds of contraband, provided that she is not manned in a neutral port, so that she can commit hostilities at once after having reached the open sea. A subject of a neutral who builds an armed ship, or arms a merchantman, not to the order of a belligerent, but intending to sell her to a belligerent, does not differ from a manufacturer of arms who intends to sell them to a belligerent. There is nothing to prevent a neutral from allowing his subjects to sell armed vessels, and to deliver them to belligerents, either in a neutral port or in a belligerent port.

The Attorney General's construction of the statute is by no means convincing. Section 2 of the Act of 1917 would naturally be construed as in-

1917, 40 U. S. Stat. 221; U. S. Code, Tit. 18, Secs, 32, 33; Deák and Jessup, Neutrality Laws, Regulations and Treaties, Washington, 1939, Vol. 2, p. 1092.)

tended to cover the case of a war vessel built or converted abroad and transiently in an American port. In this case the President's duty is limited to obtaining guaranties that such vessel shall not be used for war purposes until it has reached its foreign destination. Article 3, on the other hand, would naturally be construed to apply to the different case of a war vessel built or converted in the United States. The President in this case has the broader duty of preventing its departure altogether if there is any reason to believe it is destined to a belligerent or to be used in a belligerent's service.

This construction would conform the statute to the usual interpretation of the Rules of the Treaty of Washington, the Alabama award, the Hague Convention, and the requirements of the present law of neutrality. The Hague Convention (Article 8) requires a neutral government:

(1) To employ the means at its disposal to prevent the fitting out or arming of any vessel within its jurisdiction which it has reason to believe is intended to cruise, or engage in hostile operations, against a Power with which that government is at peace;

and

(2) To display the same vigilance to prevent the departure from its jurisdiction of any vessel intended to cruise, or engaged in hostile operations which has been adapted entirely or partly within the said jurisdiction for use in war.[6]

[6] The first rule of the Treaty of Washington was the same except that "to use due diligence" appears in place of "to employ the means at its disposal." The duty under the first sentence of this article was adequately met by Secs. 3 and 4 of the United States Act of 1794 which, with a few amendments, has been incorporated in Secs. 23 and 24 of the United States Code, Tit. 18. . . . Oppenheim paraphrased the second sentence in the Hague convention "the neutral is bound . . . to prevent the departure from his jurisdiction of any vessel which *by order of either belligerent* has been adapted to warlike use" . . . obviously changing its meaning. While there was at first doubt whether the rules of the Treaty of Washington could be regarded as declaratory of customary international law (see Moore's Digest of International Law, Vol. 7, pp. 1064 ff., 1068 ff.), and while some writers, like Oppenheim, following W. Beach Lawrence and Wharton (Criminal Law, 8th ed., Philadelphia, 1880, Vol. 2, p. 626 ff.), have attempted to read the old distinction between commercial and belligerent intent into them, the overwhelming opinion and practice have ignored this distinction in the case of warships and have considered that a warship, built or outfitted in neutral territory, and proceeding on its own keel, is not merely contraband (its inclusion in that category in the Declaration of London (Art. 22) was to assure the belligerents' right of capture in case the neutral failed in its duty), but cannot be allowed to leave neutral territory for belligerent use. . . . During the Spanish American War, Great Britain refused to allow the departure until the war was over of two war vessels under construction in British shipyards for Brazil, but purchased by the United States from Brazil before the war began. (Moore's Digest, Vol. 7, p. 861.) . . . The North German Lloyd and the Hamburg American Line sold to Russia during the Russo-Japanese War, four of their merchant vessels designed to be converted into war vessels in time of war. Germany made no effort to prevent the transaction and apparently Japan did not protest. (Moore's Digest, Vol. 7, p. 863.) . . . During the World War it was contended that neutrals must prevent the sale even of merchant vessels to belligerents from their territory. (Hyde, *op. cit.*, Vol. 2, p. 762 ff.) While this is not an established rule of law, unless the merchant vessel

The natural interpretation of Article 3 of the Act of 1917 conforms to the
second requirement, while the Attorney General's construction does not.
Furthermore, there is nothing in Article 8 of the Hague Convention which
requires a neutral to detain a ship built abroad for war purposes and transiently within its jurisdiction. The neutral is, however, bound to prevent
its territory being made use of as a base of naval operations under Article 5
of the Hague Convention, and Section 2 of the Act of 1917, with its natural
construction, would seem to meet this obligation.[7]

But whether or not the Attorney General's construction of the Act of 1917
is correct, that Act seems irrelevant to the case in hand. The destroyers were
sent out of the United States by the United States Government itself. The
Act of 1917 is a criminal statute presumably dealing with acts of individuals,
not of the government. In spite of the general terms used in Section 3 ("it
shall be unlawful to send out") it cannot have been intended to interfere
with the President's disposition of vessels of the Navy. That subject is dealt
with in other statutes. Furthermore, the Act applies only "during a war in
which the United States is a neutral nation." It may be doubted whether the
United States has that status in relation to the hostilities against Germany.
It should be added, however, that since presidential proclamations have invoked the general neutrality legislation of the United States as a matter of
municipal law, private persons would be well advised to be guided by that
legislation unless further proclamation is made. The destroyer transfer, however, was not a transaction by private persons, the Act of 1917 was not applicable, and the President had ample authority to effect the transaction by the
procedure adopted under the law of the United States.

With respect to international law, the duties of the United States depend
upon its status *vis-à-vis* the European hostilities. If it were a neutral, the
transfer of the destroyers to Great Britain would be difficult to justify, but
not on the ground that it violated the principle of the Alabama award and
Articles 5 and 8 of the Hague Convention. These provisions deal with a
neutral government's duty to prevent certain acts by private persons within
its jurisdiction. Critics should rather refer to Article 6 of the Hague Convention which deals with the neutral government's duty itself to abstain
from certain acts: "The supply in any manner, directly or indirectly, by a
neutral Power to a belligerent Power of warships, ammunition or war material of any kind whatever is forbidden." This rule is so well established that
reference seems superfluous. The Harvard Draft on Neutrality states the rule:
"A neutral state shall abstain from supplying to a belligerent assistance for

---

is in condition to be immediately converted at sea, it is believed that the rules of the Hague
Convention are. Consequently the fact that at least one state engaged in the present hostilities (Poland) is not a party to this convention is unimportant. If the situation were one
of war and neutrality, and the facts were pertinent, the rules quoted would be applicable.

[7] The commentary to the Harvard Research Draft Convention on Neutrality cites "operating against enemy craft from neutral refuges" as among acts constituting neutral territory
a "base of operations."

the prosecution of the war" (Article 5). It is true certain cases of indirect aid are referred to in the commentary as exceptions: for instance, the use of neutral ports for twenty-four hour sojourn or for asylum by belligerent war-ships, the use of neutral pilots by belligerent warships, and the use of neutral postal facilities, but none of these cover the case of the destroyers. On October 15, 1914, a United States Department of State circular said: "For the Government of the United States itself to sell to a belligerent nation would be an unneutral act." The fact that the transfer of the destroyers was made for valuable political considerations would not affect the application of this rule. If anything, it would make the breach of neutrality more serious.

In the writer's opinion, however, the United States is not a neutral in relation to the European hostilities. It has, instead, the status of "a supporting state," to use the terminology of the Harvard Draft on Rights and Duties of States in Case of Aggression. A supporting state is defined as one "which assists a defending state without armed force."

By becoming a supporting state, a state acquires the right to discriminate against the aggressor, but it may not do any act to the detriment of states other than the aggressor unless such act would be lawful if done by a defending or co-defending state. Against an aggressor, a supporting state has the rights which, if it were neutral, it would have against a belligerent.

It is true the Harvard Draft is in the form of a proposal for a treaty rather than in the form of a statement of existing international law. In the writer's opinion, however, it does state substantially existing international law binding parties to the Pact of Paris. This view was taken by the International Law Association in the Budapest Articles of Interpretation which declared among other things:

Whereas the Pact is a multilateral lawmaking treaty whereby each of the high contracting parties makes binding agreements with each other and all of the other high contracting parties, and

Whereas by their participation in the Pact sixty-three states have abolished the conception of war as a legitimate means of exercising pressure on another state in the pursuit of national policy and have also renounced any recourse to armed force for the solution of international disputes or conflicts:

(1) A signatory state cannot, by denunciation or nonobservance of the Pact, release itself from its obligations thereunder.

(2) A signatory state which threatens to resort to armed force for the solution of an international dispute or conflict is guilty of a violation of the Pact.

(3) A signatory state which aids a violating state thereby itself violates the Pact.

(4) In the event of a violation of the Pact by a resort to armed force or war by one signatory state against another, the other states may, without thereby committing a breach of the Pact or of any rule of international law, do all or any of the following things:

(a) Refuse to admit the exercise by the state violating the Pact of belligerent rights, such as visit and search, or blockade, etc.;

(b) Decline to observe toward the state violating the Pact the duties prescribed by international law, apart from the Pact, for a neutral in relation to a belligerent;

   (e) Supply the state attacked with financial or material assistance including munitions of war;

   (d) Assist with armed forces the state attacked.

These articles were in general regarded by the British Government as the proper construction of the Pact, and they conform to Secretary of State Stimson's construction of the Pact in 1932.

This interpretation holds that a state which has initiated hostilities in violation of its obligations under the Pact of Paris is not a lawful belligerent and that third states are under no obligation to observe toward it the duties of neutrals. This distinction is thus stated in the introductory comment upon the Harvard Draft on Aggression:

This Draft Convention on rights and duties of states in case of aggression is based upon the assumption that a distinction in law is to be drawn between war on the one hand and, on the other hand, certain forceful acts determined to constitute a violation of a particular type of legal obligation. In the case of war which is dealt with in the Convention on Rights and Duties of Neutral States, the legality, illegality or extra-legality of the action of the state in commencing the war is not a matter of concern. However, where the resort to armed force is in violation of a specific legal obligation not to resort to such measures, it is possible to speak in terms of the illegality of the state's action. The illegal use of armed force may amount to "war" in the material sense of the term, but under this Draft Convention, which does not deal in terms of the traditional rights of belligerents and neutrals, war in the technical legal sense never results.

This position was accepted by the United States and other governments in the cases of the Japanese invasions of China, and the Russian invasion of Finland. It was also accepted by members of the League of Nations in the Italian invasion of Ethiopia. These cases were not regarded as involving formal duties of neutrality.

Germany and Italy are parties to the Pact of Paris, as are all the countries they have invaded, and the United States. The invasion of Poland by Germany was regarded by the British and French Governments as an act of aggression requiring them to give the assistance they had pledged to Poland in that event. The British Dominions, except Ireland, soon accepted this position. While other states, including the United States, proclaimed neutrality, this has not precluded them from subsequently recognizing the situation as one of aggression. The successive victims of Germany's aggressions have done so, as have the American states.[8]

[8] "The text of the joint declaration by the American Republics with regard to the invasion of Belgium, Holland, and Luxemburg proposed by the Uruguayan Government and agreed to by the other American Republics was released, May 19, 1940, by the President of Panama and reads as follows:

"The American Republics in accord with the principles of international law and in application of the resolutions adopted in their inter-American conferences, consider unjustifiable the ruthless violation by Germany of the neutrality and sovereignty of Belgium, Holland and Luxemburg.

It is believed that the various public declarations by the President and Secretary of State that Germany and Italy are aggressors, that international law and the Pact of Paris have been violated, that acts of the violating states professing to change the status of occupied territories will not be recognized, and that forms of aid incompatible with a status of neutrality will be extended to the victims of aggression,[9] are adequate to indicate that the United States is no longer a neutral from the point of view of international law.

There has, it is true, been no repeal of the President's proclamations of September 5, 1939, and subsequently, which recognized a "state of war" and invoked the general neutrality laws of the United States, nor of those of November 4, 1939, and subsequently, which "proclaimed that a state of war unhappily exists" and invoked the act of November 4, 1939. These proclamations, however, and the acts to which they refer, are measures of municipal law. Their invocation and application are not conclusive as to the status under international law which the United States now has in relation to the European hostilities. Even though the United States regards the European hostilities as a situation of aggression and its own position as, not that of a neutral, but that of a "non-belligerent" or a "supporting state," it might still wish to apply its domestic "neutrality" regulations, and there is nothing in international law to prevent it from doing so. On the other hand, there is nothing in international law to prevent it from modifying these regulations as it sees fit.[10]

"In paragraphs four and five of the Ninth Resolution of the Meeting of Foreign Ministers held at Panama in 1939, entitled 'Maintenance of International Activities in accordance with Christian Morality,' it was established that the violation of the neutrality or the invasion of weaker nations as a measure in the conduct and success of war, warrants the American Republics in protesting against this infraction of international law and the requirements of justice.

"The American Republics therefore resolve to protest against the military attacks directed against Belgium, Holland and Luxemburg, at the same time making an appeal for the restablishment of law and justice in the relations between countries." (Department of State Bulletin, May 25, 1940, Vol. II, p. 568.)

[9] "Making every possible effort under present conditions, the Government of the United States has made it possible for the Allied armies to obtain during the weeks that have just passed airplanes, artillery and munitions of many kinds and this Government so long as the Allied governments continue to resist will redouble its efforts in this direction. I believe it is possible to say that every week that goes by will see additional matériel on its way to the Allied nations. . . . So long as the French people continue in defense of their liberty which constitutes the cause of popular institutions throughout the world, so long will they rest assured that matériel and supplies will be sent to them from the United States in ever-increasing quantities and kinds. I know that you will understand that these statements carry with them no implication of military commitments. Only the Congress can make such commitments." (President's letter to French Premier Reynaud, June 15, 1940, *ibid.*, Vol. II, p. 639.)

[10] The situation has some analogy to that of insurgency in which states have exercised a certain discretion in applying neutrality regulations. (Moore's Digest, Vol. 7, p. 1077 ff.; G. G. Wilson, Naval War College, International Law Situations, 1904, pp. 41–51; N. J. Padelford, "International Law and the Spanish Civil War," this JOURNAL, Vol. 31 (1937), p. 230 ff.)

It is believed that the United States has a complete answer to any challenge to the propriety of the destroyer transaction under international law. The states of the world have generally recognized that Germany has initiated hostilities in violation of its international obligations under the Pact of Paris and other instruments.[11] Consequently Germany is not a lawful belligerent, and parties to these instruments are not obliged under international law to observe toward Germany and her allies the duties of a neutral.[12]

The Attorney General's Opinion on the Exchange of Destroyers for Naval Bases

EDWIN M. BORCHARD

THE Attorney General's opinion of August 27, 1940,[1] on the exchange of destroyers for naval bases is a veritable *tour de force*. The arrangement was concluded by executive agreement. As Professor Briggs points out in his article

[11] These include Germany's non-aggression agreements with Poland, Jan. 26, 1934, Belgium, Oct. 13, 1937, and Denmark, May 31, 1939.

[12] The Harvard Research draft does not permit a state to be treated as an aggressor until its resort to armed force "has been duly determined by a means which that state is bound to accept, to constitute a violation of an obligation." . . . It appears, however, that general recognition constitutes such a method under customary international law. . . . It is believed that at least 35 parties to the Pact of Paris and four other states have recognized Germany as an aggressor in recent hostilities. These include Great Britain, France, Canada, Australia, New Zealand, South Africa, India, Egypt, Poland, Denmark, Norway, Iceland, Belgium, Netherlands, Luxemburg, Ethiopia, Czechoslovakia, Portugal and the 21 American Republics (*supra*, note 23), four of which, however (Argentina, Bolivia, El Salvador, and Uruguay), are not parties to the Pact. Of the remaining 28 parties to the Pact, four are, or recently have been, engaged in aggressions (Germany, Italy, Japan, Russia); ten, as present or recent victims of aggression (Austria, Albania, Spain, Danzig, China, Finland, Latvia, Lithuania, Estonia, Rumania), and seven as small states in close proximity to the aggressors (Bulgaria, Greece, Hungary, Sweden, Switzerland, Turkey, Yugoslavia), are not in a position to take any independent action. The position of the seven remaining parties to the Pact (Afghanistan, Iran, Iraq, Ireland, Liberia, Saudi Arabia, Siam) is not clear.

[1] Dept. of State Bulletin, Sept. 7, 1940, p. 201. . . .

Edwin M. Borchard, "The Attorney General's Opinion on the Exchange of Destroyers for Naval Bases," *American Journal of International Law*, XXXIV, 1940, pp. 690–697. Reprinted by permission of the American Journal of International Law.

in this issue,[2] the transaction was sustained under statutes which hardly bear the construction placed upon them. It is significant that the Attorney General limited his research and opinion to "the questions of constitutional and statutory authority, with which alone I am concerned." He thus, evidently intentionally, omitted all reference to international law, without which the opinion could hardly be complete. So far as the record shows, no one expressed an opinion on the question whether the transaction was privileged under international law, although Mr. James W. Ryan[3] thinks that it was. The Attorney General postulates his conclusion, however, on the assumption that the transaction is justified under the rules of neutrality. Others appear to conclude[4] that because Germany is an "aggressor," the United States under League of Nations theories and the Kellogg Pact is not obliged to maintain neutrality, and therefore may presumably exert sanctions. Inasmuch as international law does have something to say about this matter, it is well to inquire what it tells us and what the country's legal status now is. Without attempting here to pass on the question of policy, we may assume that the transaction itself meets with popular approval. Yet because it is so portentous in its facts and implications, it may be suggested that the transaction be regularized so far as and soon as possible by act or resolution of Congress.

Without going over the ground so convincingly covered by Professor Briggs, there are certain matters in the Attorney General's opinion which deserve examination.

(1) The Attorney General starts from the assumption that the assumed plenary powers of the President to deal with foreign affairs, his powers as Commander in Chief to safeguard the national defense, and his statutory power through the Secretary of the Navy to dispose of "naval vessels" which have been "found unfit for further use and stricken from the naval registry" justify the executive agreement. In support of the supposedly plenary power in foreign affairs, a dictum of Justice Sutherland in the case of United States *v.* Curtiss-Wright Export Corporation is relied upon. The Curtiss-Wright case involved a criminal prosecution for the violation of an arms embargo in the Chaco War. The embargo was imposed by the President under a Joint Resolution of Congress of May 28, 1934, which specifically authorized the President to impose the arms embargo if he finds that it "may contribute to the re-establishment of peace" between the belligerents. The defendants contended that this delegation of power to make a determination that the embargo may "contribute to the re-establishment of peace" was not adequately controlled by criteria. Judge Byers in the District Court agreed with that view, but the Supreme Court reversed on the ground that in the matter of *"negotiation and inquiry"* Congressional legislation "must often accord to the President a degree of discretion and freedom from statutory restriction which would not be admissible were domestic affairs alone involved." This

2 *Supra,* p. 569.
3 Appendix to Congressional Record, Sept. 11, 1940, pp. 18, 110.
4 Quincy Wright in this issue of the JOURNAL, p. 680 at p. 685.

does not give the President *carte blanche* to do anything he pleases in foreign affairs, for it is limited to "negotiation and inquiry." Certainly the President is the "sole organ of the nation in its external relations and its sole representative with foreign nations," as Marshall said in 1800. This speaks merely of agency, but not of power to *conclude and bind* the nation in fundamental matters. He necessarily must make all kinds of provisional agreements and *modi vivendi*, but it has been the usual practice, aside from executive agreements on minor matters or under Congressional authority, to submit important matters to Congress or the Senate for approval. When Justice Sutherland speaks of the "very delicate plenary and exclusive power of the President," he adds that it "must be exercised in subordination to the applicable provisions of the Constitution." But apart from these provisions, there are constitutional understandings which require that agreements of great importance, particularly involving the question of war and peace, shall not be concluded by Executive authority alone. The somewhat loose dicta of Justice Sutherland ought not to be permitted to break down constitutional safeguards. As in the case of the Rush-Bagot Agreement of 1817 limiting armaments on the Great Lakes, it would have been and is now perfectly possible to submit the arrangement to Congress for its approval, and this indeed would be a protection to the Executive against future recriminations and trouble. Indeed, it is doubtful how far future governments of Great Britain would consider themselves bound by the executory character of the options given to the United States by the agreement, and even though the United States' obligation may be executed by the delivery of the destroyers, future American administrations may take a different attitude toward the agreement. Naval bases in the territory of another country carry far-reaching implications.

Some of the supposed precedents cited by the Attorney General are not in point, such as executive agreements concluded under authority of a Congressional statute. (Congress did not authorize the present transaction.) For example, the agreements of February 16 and July 2, 1903, for the lease of naval and coaling stations in Cuba were concluded under the Platt Amendment of the Act of March 2, 1901, providing for such bases "at certain specified points to be agreed upon with the President of the United States." So with the reciprocal trade agreements. Horseshoe Reef was not acquired from a belligerent government, and, as the Attorney General points out, its acquisition was submitted to Congress for the appropriation of the necessary funds to build the lighthouse. Louisiana was purchased not in time of war but in time of peace, some time before the Treaty of Amiens was broken by the renewed outbreak of the war in 1803. A real precedent might have been cited in the Lansing-Ishii Agreement of 1918. But this agreement exemplifies the temptations and dangers involved in political executive agreements because it included a secret clause which, while relatively unimportant, was not disclosed until the agreement was abrogated by the Washington Treaties of 1923. The treaty-making power could easily be circumvented if it were to become customary to make important matters affecting the fate of the country the subject of executive agreements.

(2) The Attorney General invokes a statute of 1883 which authorized the Secretary of the Navy to dispose of vessels unfit for further use and stricken from the naval register after an appraisal and an offer to sell to the highest bidder above the appraised value "unless the President of the United States shall otherwise direct in writing." In the case of Levinson v. United States, in connection with the disposal of an unneeded yacht, the President availed himself of this power to authorize the acceptance of a bid lower than the highest and dispensed with advertising and other unimportant details. That deal the Supreme Court under the circumstances approved. To use this statute and this case as a support for the disposal by executive agreement of fifty over-age destroyers whose usefulness had been attested by naval officers appearing before the Senate Committee on Naval Affairs, seems a little unusual. It had never heretofore been supposed that the President as Commander in Chief of the Army and Navy could transfer a part of the Navy to a foreign Power. If this can be done, a dangerous power is vested in the President for, according to the Attorney General, there is no limitation as to the transferee, individual, corporate or government, belligerent or neutral, nor any limitation on the consideration which may be obtained.

Congress, however, fearing an Executive transfer of certain naval vessels to Great Britain, enacted a statute on June 28, 1940, seeking to limit such disposition by requiring a certificate from the Chief of Naval Operations in the case of naval material "that such material is not essential to the defense of the United States." The Attorney General doubts the constitutionality of this limitation but pretermits the question by a construction which, to say the least, is novel. The Attorney General concludes that the naval bases would, as compared with the destroyers, add so much to the defensive position of the United States that the Chief of Naval Operations not only may but "should certify under Section 14 (a) that the destroyers involved are not essential to the defense of the United States, if in his judgment the exchange of such destroyers for such naval and air bases will strengthen rather than impair the total defense of the United States." Admiral Stark in presenting his certificate invokes in each paragraph this construction of the Attorney General, throwing upon him the responsibility for the certificate that he rendered. It is fair to assume that the draftsmen of Section 14 (a) hardly contemplated such a construction of the section.

But another difficulty presents itself. In justifying an executive agreement instead of a treaty to cover the transaction, the Attorney General emphasizes the fact that the President was not incurring future obligations by acquiring naval bases but was taking only an option or privilege of which the United States might or might not take advantage. He says: "The acquisitions which you are proposing to accept are without express or implied promises on the part of the United States to be performed in the future."

If such promises had been implied and the Congress committed, the inference is that a treaty would be necessary, as in the treaty of 1903 with Cuba. Yet unless such promises are implied, or, at least, unless the naval bases are actually acquired, the transfer of the destroyers could hardly be deemed to strengthen "the total defense of the United States."

(3) It has been observed that the Attorney General confines himself to constitutional power and statutes and omits the questions of international law involved. His opinion can therefore be considered as a partial opinion only, for the legality of the issue involves all aspects of the law and not merely some. In construing Sections 2 and 3 of the Act of June 15, 1917, the Attorney General falls into the error which Professor Briggs has pointed out. Section 3, as reproduced by the Attorney General, provides:

During a war in which the United States is a neutral nation, it shall be unlawful to send out of the jurisdiction of the United States any vessel [,] built, armed, or equipped as a vessel of war, or converted from a private vessel into a vessel of war, with any intent or under any agreement or contract, written or oral, that such vessel shall be delivered to a belligerent nation or . . . that the said vessel shall or will be employed in the service of any such belligerent nation after its departure from the jurisdiction of the United States. (Brackets supplied.)

Apart from the fact that the original Statutes at Large print *no* comma between the word "vessel" and the word "built" and thus leave the meaning free from ambiguity, the history of this statute clearly shows that the words "with any intent" relate back to the words "it shall be unlawful to *send*" any vessel out of the jurisdiction of the United States with intent that it shall be used in belligerent service. The Attorney General, however, reaches his conclusion that the destroyers may be sent to Great Britain by construing the statute as if the words "with any intent" relate back to the words "built, armed or equipped as a vessel of war . . . with any intent" that such vessel shall be used in belligerent service. He concludes that the destroyers were not *built*, armed or equipped with that intent, but with the intent that they should be used by the United States Navy. Hence he approves the transaction. He fortifies his conclusion by the statement that unless Section 3 is construed as he misconstrues it, Section 2, which provides for the detention in port of any armed vessel owned by American citizens, manifestly built or converted for warlike purposes, until the owner shall prove that it will not be employed in the service of a belligerent, is meaningless. As Professor Briggs points out, Section 2 has applications quite different from those of Section 3, and Section 3 has a history in the Rules of Washington which fully explain it. The second clause of Rule 1 makes it the duty of the neutral "to prevent the departure from its jurisdiction of any vessel intended to cruise or carry on war . . . such vessel having been specially adapted in whole or in part within such jurisdiction to warlike use." Attorney General Gregory in 1917 felt it important to incorporate this obligation of international law into our municipal statues. He called it "despatching," as do the British. The first clause prohibits "fitting out or arming or equipping," each a complete offense.

Mr. Ryan would escape the inhibitions of Section 3 by maintaining that it does not apply to the United States, but only to individuals. But the section is a response to an obligation resting upon the United States not only itself to refrain from supplying warships, but to prevent its citizens from so doing.[5] Article 6 of Hague Convention XIII provides: "The supply in any manner directly or indirectly by a neutral Power to a belligerent Power of warships, ammunition or war material of any kind whatever is forbidden"; and if it is answered, as Mr. Ryan does, that the Hague Convention *qua* convention is not binding because Great Britain did not subscribe to it—because the convention as a whole did not go far enough—it may be answered that Article 6 presents a rule of law which has been generally accepted law since 1793 and has not been dissented from by any country.[6]

To justify his opinion that only ships "built, armed or equipped" for a belligerent may not be sent out of the United States, the Attorney General invokes the authority of the English writer, Oppenheim, who does contend that a private merchant may deal in warships. But Oppenheim stands practically alone in that opinion, which is not supported by his own government.[7] Oppenheim also gratuitously interpolates the words "by order of a belligerent," a qualification which is not to be found either in the Rules of Washington or in Article 8 of Hague Convention XIII, or in the British Foreign Enlistment Act of 1870, which punishes any person who "despatches or causes or allows to be despatched, any ship with intent or knowledge or having reasonable cause to believe that the same shall or will be employed in the military or naval service of any foreign state at war with any friendly state." When the United States Government through Admiral, then Lieutenant, Sims, sought to recover the deposit money on two vessels purchased in England just before the outbreak of the war with Spain, but not delivered by the sellers because of the war, the Queen's Bench Division decided that the delivery of the ships contracted for had become illegal after the outbreak of the war. Rivier has stated that it is a universal rule.[8] While it is true that in the early part of the century private trade in warships, though rare, was not prohibited, and Story in a dictum in the *Santissima Trinidad* so affirmed, Mr. J. C. Ban-

[5] John Bassett Moore has well said: "It is a self-evident proposition that if a government may by legislation fix the measure of what it owes to other states, there is no such thing as international law or international obligation." Moore's Arbitrations, I, 677.

[6] The circular of the Dept. of State, Oct. 15, 1914, reads: "For the Government of the United States itself to sell to a belligerent nation would be an unneutral act . . ." Woodrow Wilson (Jan. 1915) opposed the sale of government-owned *Krag* rifles "to *any* one during the progress of the present war," and felt "it is really our duty (in the *spirit*, at any rate, of the *Alabama* decision) to prevent submarines being shipped from this country, even in parts." . . .

[7] In 1914, it was said by the British Embassy at Washington that "the Rules (of Washington) may be said to have acquired the force of generally recognized rules of international law." American White Book, 1914, II, 37, quoted in Hyde, International Law, II, 713.

[8] "No State would dream of contesting the principle they (the Rules of Washington) contain." Moore's Arb., I, 674.

croft Davis for the United States repudiated Story's view in the Alabama arbitration.[9]

It is unfortunate that the Attorney General's research became diverted to the obligation of private individuals with respect to trading in warships, for the case submitted involved a trade by the United States Government. International law could therefore hardly be avoided, if the rules of law constituted the object of investigation. A more appropriate quotation from Oppenheim, Section 321, would have been the following:

If a State remains neutral it violates its impartiality by furnishing a belligerent with troops or men of war; and it matters not whether it renders such assistance to one of the belligerents or to both alike.[10]

As Professor Hyde says, "In fitting out, arming and removal from neutral territory of a vessel which becomes attached to the service of a belligerent and engages in hostilities in its behalf, this principle (the territorial source of the aid) finds simple application and wide recognition. Such conduct constitutes participation in the conflict, a result which is due to the removal of an instrument of war from neutral territory."

There was therefore no sound basis for distinguishing the "mosquito" boats from the destroyers on the ground that the former required completion in American shipyards. Both types were in the same legal category—public vessels of the United States—and subject to the same rules of law.

Finally, it has been suggested, that in view of the fact that Germany is an "aggressor," the rules of neutrality have no application and that Germany has exposed herself to the discriminatory treatment contemplated in the privately proposed Draft Convention on Rights and Duties of States in Case of Aggression. That draft "does not deal in terms of the traditional rights of belligerents and neutrals," for, under its hypotheses, "war in the technical legal sense never results" when an aggressor resorts to armed force "in violation of a specific legal obligation not to resort to such measures." This provision of two rules of law, one for lawful war and one for aggression, one rule for one belligerent and one for another, seems, with entire respect, like a prescription for more or less perpetual war and a counsel of anarchy. By what right are nations permitted to pass judgment upon each other's political morals and take discriminatory action accordingly? Needless to say, unanimity on such issues is impossible of achievement, and while a theoretical argument might be made

[9] "If that eminent jurist had said that a vessel of war was to be regarded in public law as an article which might be legitimately constructed, fitted out, armed, equipped, or dealt in by a person in the territory of a neutral, with the intent that it should enter the service of a belligerent, subject only to a liability to capture as contraband of war by the other belligerent, the United States would have been forced, with great regret, to ask this tribunal to disregard an opinion so at variance with common sense, and with the whole current of the action of nations." Moore's Dig., VII, 895.

[10] Oppenheim sustains the sale of Hamburg American and North German Lloyd unarmed merchant vessels to Russia in the Russo-Japanese War because he considers them not to be auxiliary naval vessels. Were they to be so considered, their sale would be and has been subject to serious criticism, as Professor Briggs points out.

for an objective tribunal of all the nations reaching a unanimous decision on the point, nothing can be said for individual national judgments made, as such judgments are necessarily made, not on objective criteria but as the result of self-interest, prejudice, prior commitments, and alliances. The "draft convention" on "aggression" is an evangelical expression of moral convictions which will not bear the brunt of practical application and, for this uneasy world, is non-legal in its connotations.

To the writer there is no possibility of reconciling the destroyer deal with neutrality, with United States statutes, or with international law. It can only be explained by the legal fact that the United States is now, and it is submitted, has been for some time, in a state of limited war, analogous to but not identical with that which prevailed between the United States and France in the period between May, 1798, and May, 1800, when the ships of the United States, under authority of an Act of Congress, made attacks upon and captured French vessels which had been spoliating American commerce. The concept of "non-belligerency" like that of "measures short of war" has no legal status. It is apparently designed to justify breaches of neutrality or acts of war, perhaps with the hope that they will not result in a state of war. With full deference, it is not easy to justify that part of the President's message informing Congress of the destroyer-bases exchange reading: "This is not inconsistent in any sense with our state of peace." It will be interesting to see whether "measures short of war" can long avert a state of war. But it would have been a more grateful task for the Attorney General had he not sought to reconcile the transaction with a state of peace and neutrality.

12

World War II:

DID ROOSEVELT PLOT WAR?

As the war clouds gathered in Europe and in Asia in the 1930's, the vast majority of the American people were determined on a policy of noninterference. As the Japanese moved into Manchuria and then Shanghai and Peking, as Italy attacked Ethiopia, as Germany re-armed in defiance of the Treaty of Versailles and marched into the demilitarized Rhineland and expanded into Czechoslovakia and Austria, the American people began to feel uneasy. They were disturbed and distressed at the thought that brute force was replacing the rule of law and that the western democracies might be attacked by the mighty German military machine. But they refused to permit their sympathies to ensnare them in any conflict. To insure neutrality in any war the Congress passed, by large majorities, a series of laws between 1935 and 1937 designed to make involvement impossible. Generally, these laws prohibited loans and the exporting of war goods to belligerents, forbade Americans to travel on belligerent merchant ships, prevented American merchant ships from sailing into designated war zones, and ruled against the arming of merchant ships. President Roosevelt signed these acts into law, thus indicating his own desire to steer clear of involvement. Yet, in December, 1941, America was at war with Japan and Germany, and found itself fighting both in Asia and in Europe. What had caused the United States to become involved? Historians disagree on the interpretation of the course to war. Some maintain that the war was a result of a diabolical plot foisted on the American people by President Roosevelt. While promising the people that he would keep them out of war, he conducted affairs in a way that made war inevitable. Others reject the "devil theory," and see the war as an unavoidable and inevitable consequence of the unfolding of events.

The eminent historian Charles A. Beard is the leading exponent of the "plot" theory. In his opinion, President Roosevelt's actions become part of a preconceived plan to fight the Japanese. Further, each of the President's actions was either deliberately kept from the public or given out in garbled form. Beard sees American policy as being unremittingly hostile to Japan. Japan was given no opportunity to present its case. When Ambassador Grew, in Tokyo, urged the President to accept the Japanese offer to negotiate outstanding differences Roosevelt and Hull delayed their reply and finally rejected the offer. When once again Tokyo made an offer to open conversations, it was similarly rebuffed. The implication is clear that Roosevelt wanted war and got it.

In opposition to the "plot" hypothesis is Basil Rauch, a professor of history at Barnard College. Not only did Roosevelt not engender war with Japan, he sought positively to avoid it. Roosevelt's primary concern was with Germany, which he considered the chief enemy. The President's actions and statements must not be viewed, as Beard viewed them, as parts of a preconceived and diabolical plan, but rather as responses to immediate situations. Roosevelt's rejection of the Japanese offer to negotiate was not because Roosevelt and Hull did not wish the conference to succeed, but because the "Japanese proposals were unacceptable as a basis for agreement." Rauch does not believe that Japan sincerely sought peace, as Beard does. He is convinced that the island empire was determined on war if it could not get a free hand in Asia, and that the United States, to avoid that contingency, had no choice but to fight.

President Roosevelt and the Coming of the War

CHARLES A. BEARD

THERE IS also now available sufficient evidence respecting two primary questions with which my inquiry is particularly concerned: (1) How did the secret actions of the Roosevelt Administration bearing on relations with Japan from August 17 to December 7, 1941, as described in official documents now available, square with official representations of the Administration to the American people at the time—realities with appearances? (2) Do these official documents sustain the official thesis respecting relations with Japan presented to Congress and the people by President Roosevelt's message to Congress on December 8, 1941?

On that occasion, the President said—to repeat, for convenience—that on December 7, 1941, the United States was at peace with Japan, that at the solicitation of Japan it was still in conversation with the Japanese Government and Emperor, looking toward the maintenance of peace in the Pacific, and that on that day Japan had undertaken a planned "surprise offensive," of which the attack on Pearl Harbor was a phase. Did the course of American-Japanese affairs as conducted during the months preceding Pearl Harbor, however it "looked," actually point in the direction of peace with Japan? Were those affairs in such a state at any time during this period that the President actually expected them to eventuate in the maintenance of peace in the Pacific? Did the Japanese Government make any proposals during this period which looked to the possibility of maintaining peace in the Pacific? And, if so how did Secretary Hull and President Roosevelt treat these proposals with a view to the maintenance of peace? Did the President think that the Japanese final memorandum delivered to Secretary Hull on December 7 actually constituted no threat or hint of an armed attack? Was the Japanese offensive really a surprise to the Administration? With reference to these questions there are some answers in the documents now available.

As early as October 8, 1940, during the campaign of that year while he was still making peace pledges to the country, President Roosevelt had become convinced that Japan would make a mistake and that the United States would enter a war in the Pacific. He expressed this conviction to Admiral J. O. Richardson, Commander in Chief of the Fleet in the Pacific, whose duty it

---

From Charles A. Beard, *President Roosevelt and the Coming of the War*, 1941 (New Haven: Yale University Press, 1948) pp. 484–516. Reprinted by permission of Yale University Press.

was to prepare plans for the war thus foretold by the President. The development of an American war plan, based on arrangements made with the British Commonwealth and the Netherlands in the spring of 1941, contemplated a general war in which the United States would participate when and if it came—a plan which President Roosevelt approved, "except officially," to use Admiral's Stark's ingenious phrase.

On December 14, 1940, the American Ambassador in Tokyo, Joseph Grew, wrote a long letter to President Roosevelt on American-Japanese relations, in the course of which he said that, unless the United States was prepared to withdraw bag and baggage from the entire sphere of Greater East Asia and the South Seas, "(which God forbid), we are bound eventually to come to a head-on clash with Japan." President Roosevelt replied, January 21, 1941, "I find myself in decided agreement with your conclusions"; and went on to say that "our strategy of self-defense must be a global strategy which takes account of every front and takes advantage of every opportunity to contribute to our total security." In other words, in January, 1941, President Roosevelt envisaged a head-on clash with Japan as a phase of assistance to Great Britain in a world of inseparable spheres of interest. This conclusion squared with the conviction he had expressed to Admiral Richardson on October 8, 1940: Japan will make a mistake and we will enter the war.

Concerning the course of specific transactions in official relations between the United States and Japan from the opening of the Atlantic Conference until December 7, 1941, the American people knew little at the time. Those who read the newspapers learned from reports of the President's meetings with representatives of the press that, at the Atlantic Conference, no new commitments had been made, that the country was no closer to war, that arrangements for operations under the Lend-Lease Act had been developed, that a list of grand principles, soon known as the Atlantic Charter, expressing hopes for a better world, had been promulgated over the names of the President and the Prime Minister, and that relations with Japan were dangerously strained. From the President's quip that he and Mr. Churchill had discussed affairs in all the continents of the earth, newspaper readers possessed of the slightest imagination could conclude that affairs in the Far East had in some manner been reviewed at the Atlantic Conference.

PRESIDENT ROOSEVELT'S WARNING NOTE TO JAPAN
ON AUGUST 17, 1941

But the American people had no official information until 1945 that Japanese affairs had come up first in the proceedings of the Atlantic Conference, that there the President made a definite commitment to Mr. Churchill's proposal for joint action in respect of Japan. It is true that after the United States had been involved in war for several months, two journalists, Forrest Davis and Ernest K. Lindley, permitted to make a "scoop" from secret information which had been conveyed to them by the White House and the State Department, published a story that approached a correct, if in many respects inadequate, account of the transactions relative to Japan at the Atlantic Conference. Yet, after all, Davis and Lindley were simply journalists whose report could be repudiated as unofficial or unreliable by any defender of the Roosevelt Administration, if their allegations made trouble for its high officials. Hence, it is proper to say that nothing like the real truth about the discussions of Japanese affairs at the Atlantic Conference in August, 1941, was revealed to the American people until December, 1945, when an official record of certain proceedings at the conference made by the Undersecretary of State, Sumner Welles, was placed among the exhibits in the documentation of the Congressional Committee on Pearl Harbor. What does that record show?

Japanese affairs, it was learned from the Welles' memoranda, were taken up by the principal parties to the Atlantic Conference on the evening of August 9 and they received close attention subsequently until agreement was reached on a program of parallel warnings to Japan. President Roosevelt rejected Mr. Churchill's proposal that he strengthen his warning to the Japanese Government by adding a declaration of his intention to seek authority from Congress to aid any power attacked by Japan in the Southwestern Pacific. But the President agreed to send a stiff note to Japan—a note in the nature of an ultimatum—after he had returned to Washington.

Although Mr. Churchill said that, as a result of the warning agreed upon, there was a reasonable chance of avoiding war in the Pacific, President Roosevelt expressed no such hope. On the contrary, he remarked that by taking this course "any further move of aggression on the part of Japan which might result in war could be held off for at least thirty days." Hence, it now appears, President Roosevelt did not think, on August 11, 1941, that the warning he was about to give to Japan would go very far in the direction of the "maintenance of peace in the Pacific."

On August 17, 1941, after his return from the Atlantic Conference, President Roosevelt called the Japanese Ambassador to the White House and told him point-blank, among other things:

. . . this Government now finds it necessary to say to the Government of Japan that if the Japanese Government takes any further steps in pursuance of a policy or program of military domination by force or threat of force of neighboring countries, the Government of the United States will be compelled to take immediately any and all steps which it may deem necessary toward safeguarding the legitimate rights and interests of the United States and American nationals and toward insuring the safety and security of the United States.

Such was the formula of the President's warning as recorded in the State Department's *Peace and War*, published in July, 1943 (p. 714).

To the Japanese Ambassador, familiar with the language of diplomacy, the statement could have had only one meaning. Although the President did not even hint that he would appeal to Congress for a declaration of war if the Japanese Government failed to heed his warning, he did indicate that if that government took any further steps in the direction of dominating neighboring countries, by force or threat of force, the United States would do something besides send another diplomatic memorandum to Tokyo.

Long historical practice justified this interpretation of his note on August 17. When on July 31, 1914, for instance, the German Ambassador in Paris asked the French Foreign Minister what France would do in case of a war between Germany and Russia, the latter replied: "France will have regard to her interests"; and that meant France would fight. When President Roosevelt informed Japan on August 17, 1941, that, in case of any more aggressive moves on her part against her neighbors, the United States would safeguard its interest, he meant that the United States would, sooner or later, take effective action to stop such moves. This interpretation of the President's intention is supported by evidence produced by the Congressional Committee on Pearl Harbor.

At a hearing of the Congressional Committee on November 23, 1945, when the former Undersecretary Welles appeared as a witness, the Assistant Counsel, Mr. Gesell, first offered as Exhibit 22, two telegrams and a draft of a proposed communication to the Japanese Ambassador brought to the State Department by Mr. Welles after the Atlantic Conference. After the documents had been put on record, Mr. Gesell asked Mr. Welles to indicate briefly his position in the State Department during the years 1940 and 1941. The following dialogue ensued:

MR. WELLES. During those years my time and attention were primarily given to relations between the United States and the other American republics and, to a considerable extent, to our relations with European governments. I had no participation in the diplomatic discussions which went on between Secretary Hull and the Japanese Government representatives and only at certain times, when the Secretary was away on a much needed vacation or was not in the Department and I had to act as Acting Secretary of State did I take any active part.

MR. GESELL. You were present, were you not, during the meeting in the Atlantic between President Roosevelt and Prime Minister Churchill?

MR. WELLES. I was.

MR. GESELL. *Did you at that time participate in any discussion between President Roosevelt and Prime Minister Churchill concerning Japan or developments in the Far East?*

MR. WELLES. No. *During the meeting at Argentia the President delegated to me the work which had to with the drafting of the Atlantic Charter. My conversations were almost entirely taken up with talks with the British Under Secretary of State for Foreign Affairs, Alexander Cadogan, and those conversations related solely to the drafting of the Atlantic Charter text* and to one of the diplomatic negotiations, *none of which had to do with Japan.* (Italics supplied.)

MR. GESELL. Did you receive any information at that meeting as to any agreement or arrangement or understanding that had been arrived at, if there was any, between President Roosevelt and Prime Minister Churchill concerning joint action of the United States and Great Britain in the Pacific?

MR. WELLES. When I left the President, since he was due to return to Washington before myself, he told me that he had had a conversation, or several conversations, with Mr. Churchill with regard to the Japanese situation and the increasing dangers in the Far East; that Mr. Churchill had suggested to him that the two Governments, as a means which might be of some effect, should take parallel action in issuing a warning to the government of Japan.

As I recall it, the President stated that what Mr. Churchill had suggested was that the Government of the United States should state to the Government of Japan that if Japan persisted in her policy of conquest and aggression the United States, in the protection of its legitimate interests and in order to provide for its own security, would have to take such acts as were necessary in its own judgment.

The President also asked me to tell Secretary Hull that he wished to see the Japanese Ambassador immediately upon his return and that warning which had been suggested as a parallel action by Mr. Churchill was communicated to the Japanese Ambassador by the President on August 17 of that year.

MR. GESELL. Were you present at the meeting?

MR. WELLES. I was not. You mean the meeting between the President and the Japanese Ambassador?

MR. GESELL. Yes.

MR. WELLES. No.

MR. GESELL. Now, the Exhibit 22 which has just been introduced includes as the first document a document dated August 10, 1941, reading as follows:

DRAFT OF PARALLEL COMMUNICATIONS TO THE JAPANESE GOVERNMENT

Declaration by United States Government that:
"1. Any further encroachment by Japan in the South West Pacific would produce a situation in which the United States Government would be compelled to take counter measures even though these might lead to war between the United States and Japan.

"2. If any third Power becomes the object of aggression by Japan in consequence of such counter measures or of their support of them, the President would have the intention to seek authority from Congress to give aid to such Power."

Declaration by H. M. G.
"Same as above, mutatis mutandis, the last phrase reading:
'. . . their support of them H. M. G. would give all possible aid to such Power.'"

Declaration by Dutch Government.
"Same as that by H. M. G.

"Keep the Soviet Government informed. It will be for consideration whether they should be pressed to make a parallel declaration."

Do you recall ever having seen this document?

MR. WELLES. I do not remember having seen that document. I remember seeing the draft, however, which I took from Argentia to Washington and which is one of the exhibits itself in this collection.

MR. GESELL. Well, now, did you prepare that draft or do you know who prepared it?

MR. WELLES. As I recall it that was prepared after discussions between the President and myself the last day of the Argentia meeting.

MR. GESELL. The last paragraph of that draft reads:

"The Government of the United States, therefore, finds it necessary to state to the Government of Japan that if the Japanese Government undertakes any further steps in pursuance of the policy of military domination through force or conquest in the Pacific region upon which it has apparently embarked, the United States Government will be forced to take immediately any and all steps of whatsoever character it deems necessary in its own security notwithstanding the possibility that such further steps on its part may result in conflict between the two countries."

Was that, in essence, your understanding of the agreement between President Roosevelt and Prime Minister Churchill concerning the notice or threat which should be given to the Japanese?

MR. WELLES. That is correct.

MR. GESELL. Now, referring to Volume 2, Foreign Relations of the United States with Japan 1931–1941, where the conversations between President Roosevelt and the Japanese Ambassador on August 17, 1941 is reported.

At page 556 I find in the paragraph beginning at said page what appears to be a somewhat different statement. This is the oral statement handed by the President to the Japanese Ambassador. It reads:

"Such being the case, this Government now finds it necessary to say to the Government of Japan that if the Japanese Government takes any further steps in pursuance of a policy or program of military domination by force or threat of force of neighboring countries, the Government of the United States will be compelled to take immediately any and all steps which it may deem necessary toward safe-guarding the legitimate rights and interests of the United States and American nationals and toward insuring the safety and security of the United States."

That statement that I have just read is a somewhat watered down version of the one you brought back, is it not, Mr. Welles?

MR. WELLES. That is correct.

MR. GESELL. Is it your opinion that the statement that I have just read from Volume II is, in fact, the statement which was made at this meeting rather than the statement that you brought back?

MR. WELLES. The statement was handed by the President, I understood, to the Japanese Ambassador in writing, as an aide-mémoire, and that is the statement to which you refer.

MR. GESELL. Have you any information as to what accounted for the watering down process?

MR. WELLES. I am not informed on that point, beyond the fact that the papers I brought back were given to Secretary Hull and he discussed them with the President before the President handed them to the Ambassador.

So much for Mr. Welles' accounting to the Congressional Committee on what happened at the Atlantic Conference with regard to the warning message handed to the Japanese Ambassador on August 17, 1941. At its hearing on December 18, 1945, about three weeks after the examination of Mr. Welles, Mr. Gesell placed in the records of the Congressional Committee three documents which had been secured from the State Department. These documents, entered as Exhibits 22-B, 22-C, and 22-D, were memoranda, dated August 10–11, 1941, of conversations at the Atlantic Conference. These memoranda set down by Mr. Welles' own hand put in a curious perspective his sworn statements to the Congressional Committee in November. Either Mr. Welles' memory had been faulty on November 23, 1945, or his understanding of the English language differed from that which generally prevails among persons less experienced in diplomatic usages.

Mr. Welles, on November 23, 1945, had said "No," when asked whether he had participated in any discussions between President Roosevelt and Mr. Churchill concerning Japan or developments in the Far East. But, according to Mr. Welles' memorandum for August 10, 1941, a conversation on the subject of a warning to Japan actually was held by President Roosevelt, Mr. Churchill, Sir Alexander Cadogan, and Sumner Welles at dinner on the evening of August 9. Sir Alexander made tentative drafts of proposed parallel and simultaneous declarations by the British and the United States Governments relating to Japanese policy in the Pacific, to be presented to Japan by the President and the Prime Minister at the close of the Atlantic meeting. The next day, August 10, Sir Alexander handed drafts of the proposed declarations to Mr. Welles; and on August 11, the subject was taken up at a meeting attended by the President, Mr. Churchill, Sir Alexander, Harry Hopkins, and Sumner Welles, and discussed. As a result, a general formula was agreed upon, to be finally shaped up by Sir Alexander and Mr. Welles.

Out of the conversations and arrangements at the Atlantic Conference, with Mr. Welles acting as the President's agent in draftsmanship, emerged a text or draft of a warning note to Japan. This text or draft Mr. Welles took to the State Department on his return. It represented in substance the formula upon which the President and the Prime Minister had agreed at the conference. That formula as outlined by the President at the conference had met the approval of Mr. Churchill, who said that "it had in it an element of 'face saving' for the Japanese and yet, at the same time would constitute a flat United States warning to Japan of the consequences involved in a continuation by Japan of her present course." The text or draft dated August 15, 1941, taken by Mr. Welles to the State Department was sharper than the note of August 17 delivered to the Japanese Ambassador by the President. The draft of August 15 read:

The Government of the United States, therefore, finds it necessary to state to the Government of Japan, that if the Japanese Government undertakes any further steps in pursuance of the policy of military domination through force or conquest in the Pacific region upon which it has apparently embarked, the United States Government will be forced to take immediately any and all steps of whatsoever character it deems necessary in its own security notwithstanding the possibility that such further steps on its part *may result in conflict between the two countries.*

In the memoranda made by Mr. Welles on the meetings at the Atlantic Conference it is patent that the notice given by President Roosevelt to the

Japanese Ambassador on August 17, 1941, was intended to be in the nature of a war warning. It is true that in the final form given to the notice, two points brought up at the Atlantic Conference had been eliminated or softened. Mr. Churchill's suggestion that the President inform Japan that he intended to seek authority from Congress to implement his notice was rejected. Also eliminated from the draft dated August 15, 1941, were the words: "notwithstanding the possibility that such further steps on its [Japan's] part may result in conflict between the two countries"; for these words were substituted a formula more veiled, but scarcely any less meaningful to Ambassador Nomura and the Government of Japan.

Nevertheless, Secretary Hull, who was present when President Roosevelt delivered this warning to the Japanese Ambassador on August 17, 1941, refused to concede in 1946 that the President's statement implied warlike action if Japan refused to heed. In May, 1946, Senator Ferguson, as a member of the Congressional Committee on Pearl Harbor, directed a written question to Secretary Hull, inquiring whether the Japanese warlike movements between November 30 and December 6, 1941, in the Southeastern Pacific, constituted a challenge to the United States to implement the position it had taken in its note of August 17, 1941, to Japan. Secretary Hull replied in a statement that looks queer when put beside Undersecretary Welles' account of the agreement concerning action against Japan reached by President Roosevelt and Mr. Churchill at the Atlantic Conference.

Secretary Hull's statement of May, 1946, read:

The purpose of the United States in making the statement of August 17 under reference was to tell Japan *in a friendly* way that if she kept encroaching upon *our rights and interests, we would defend ourselves.* This Government at that time was acutely concerned over Japan's refusal to agree to our proposal for the neutralization of Indochina, to abandon her jumping-off place there, and otherwise to desist from the menace she was creating to us and other peace-minded nations. It *wholly misrepresents the attitude of the United States* in the period after August 17 *to allege that this Government was planning any step other than that of pure defense in the event the Japanese should attack. Other aspects of this question,* for example, where, when, and how we would resist the Japanese, *were essentially a military matter.*

THE JAPANESE GOVERNMENT'S PROPOSAL FOR A PACIFIC CONFERENCE REJECTED

While the Japanese Government was considering President Roosevelt's stern warning of August 17, with a diplomatic postulate of implementation, it was seeking to develop a proposal to the President, which, at least on its surface, looked in the direction of maintaining peace in the Pacific. Indeed, the very day that Ambassador Nomura called at the White House and received his warning, he drew from his pocket an instruction from his Government to the effect that the Prime Minister, Prince Konoye, felt strongly and earnestly about preserving peaceful relations with the United States and would be disposed to meet the President somewhere in the Pacific for the purpose of talking the matter out "in a peaceful spirit."

Subsequently, the Japanese project for a Pacific Conference was explored by exchanges of views between the two governments, over the merits of which students of diplomatic history will probably differ for years to come. These diplomatic exchanges continued for nearly two months—until the fall of the Konoye Cabinet in Tokyo on October 16, 1941. Whatever the justification for the position finally taken by President Roosevelt and Secretary Hull on the Japanese proposal, the methods they employed during this period were dilatory, and from start to finish they pursued the usual policy of secrecy. Numerous "leaks" in Washington, noncommittal releases from the Department of State, and rumors kept the American public in expectancy—and confusion. In fact, at one time, when it was openly said in newspaper circles that arrangements had been made for a meeting of President Roosevelt and Premier Konoye, this "rumor" was brushed aside humorously by the President's Secretary, Stephen Early, at the White House.

Although, during the tortuous exchanges of notes on the proposed conference in the Pacific, the American public remained in the dark with regard to the nature of the various offers and counteroffers, documents made available since December 7, 1941, have partly disclosed the nature of the tactics employed by President Roosevelt and Secretary Hull in conducting those exchanges. For example, in July, 1943, the State Department published *Peace and War, 1931–1941*, which contained many papers on relations with Japan; and in the same year it issued two bulky volumes, *Foreign Relations with Japan, 1931–1941*, with a prefatory note to the effect that additional documents were to come. In 1944, Joseph Grew, former American Ambassador at Tokyo, published his *Ten Years in Japan*, which illuminated the official documents released by the State Department. Additional evidence unearthed by the Congressional Committee on Pearl Harbor amplified the accounts of the Department and Ambassador Grew.

The strategy pursued by the President and the Secretary of State during these conversations on the Japanese Premier's proposal for a peace conference in the Pacific was, in brief, as follows. The President and the Secretary expressed to Japan a willingness to consider favorably the idea of a Pacific Conference, but insisted that the Premier should first agree upon certain principles in advance, with a view to assuring the success of the conference.

The Premier of Japan, on September 6, 1941, informed the American Ambassador in Tokyo that he subscribed fully to the four great principles of American policy laid down in Washington. Then President Roosevelt and Secretary Hull declared that this was not enough, that agreement on more principles and formulas was necessary, that the replies of the Japanese Government were still unsatisfactory; but they refrained from saying in precise language just what it was they demanded in detail as fixed conditions for accepting the Japanese invitation to a conference in the Pacific. To meet their obvious distrust of Japanese authorities and especially the Japanese militarists, Premier Konoye assured them that he had authority for bringing with him to the conference high army and naval officers as evidence that his commitments would have the support of the Army and the Navy of Japan. Still the President and the Secretary continued adamant in their tactics of prolonging the conversations as if they were merely playing for time, "babying the Japanese along."

It may be said that President Roosevelt and Secretary Hull thus chose a course well' within their discretion, and demonstrated wisdom in so doing. That militarists in the Japanese Government and outside had been engaged in barbaric practices in China for many years and were rattling the sabers in the autumn of 1941, was a matter of general knowledge in the United States. That the Roosevelt Administration had long been opposed to Japan's policies and measures was, at least, equally well known. Still, if keeping out of war in the Pacific was a serious issue for the United States, then the primary question for President Roosevelt and Secretary Hull was: Did the Japanese proposal offer an opportunity to effect a settlement in the Pacific and were the decisions they made in relation to it actually "looking" in the direction of peace?

Immediately pertinent to this question, and necessary to an informed judgment on it, is a report by Ambassador Grew to Secretary Hull and thus to the President, dated Tokyo, September 29, 1941, after discussions of the Japanese Conference proposal had been dragging along for more than a month. Mr. Grew had been the American Ambassador in Japan for about ten years. He was well acquainted with Japanese institutions, politics, party interests, and the bitter struggle between conciliatory citizens of Japan and the bellicose militarists. He and his secretaries were in intimate and constant touch with the Japanese Premier and Foreign Office from the beginning of the controversy over the proposed peace conference in the Pacific. To say that Mr. Grew had more firsthand knowledge about the possibilities of these negotiations looking in the direction of peace in the Pacific and about the probable outcome of a conference, if held, than did President Roosevelt and Secretary Hull is scarcely an overstatement. Hence, the advice given to them by their representative in the Japanese capital has an immediate bearing on how war came.

In his report to Washington, September 29, Ambassador Grew laid stress on the growing eagerness of the Japanese Government to bring about a peace conference with the President. He expressed the hope that "so propitious a period" be not permitted to slip by without laying a new foundation for a better order in Japan and her relations to the United States. Japan, he said, had joined the Italo-German Axis to obtain security against Russia and avoid the peril of being caught between the Soviet Union and the United States and was now attempting to get out of this dangerous position. The Ambassador considered that the time had arrived for the liberal elements to come to the top in Japan. He saw a good chance that Japan might fall into line if a program of world reconstruction could be followed as forecast by the joint declaration of President Roosevelt and Mr. Churchill at the Atlantic Conference. The United States, Mr. Grew thought, could choose one of two methods in dealing with Japan: progressive economic strangulation or constructive conciliation, "not so-called appeasement." If conciliation failed, he reasoned, the other method—coercion and war—would always be available. He believed that a failure of the United States to use the present opportunity in the interest of conciliation would result in adding to the chances of an armed conflict.

While admitting that there were risks in any course of dealings with Japan, Ambassador Grew offered "his carefully studied belief" that there would be substantial hope of preventing the Far Eastern situation from becoming worse, and perhaps of insuring "definitely constructive results, if an agreement along the lines of the preliminary discussions were brought to a head by the proposed meeting of the heads of the two Governments." The Ambassador then raised "the question whether the United States is not now given the opportunity to halt Japan's program without war, or an immediate risk of war, and further whether, through failure to use the present opportunity, the United States will not face a greatly increased risk of war. The Ambassador stated his firm belief in an affirmative answer to these two questions." Mr. Grew conceded that certain elements in Japan or the United States might so tend to inflame public opinion in the other country as to make war unavoidable; and he recalled the cases of the *Maine* and the *Panay*. But he solicitously advised President Roosevelt and Secretary Hull to accept the offer of the Japanese Premier to discuss the situation directly, especially since the Premier had taken important steps in showing evidences of good faith.

Aware that in negotiations with the Japanese Ambassador in Washington, President Roosevelt and Secretary Hull were insisting upon further explorations of the Japanese proposal and that more than a month had passed in these "exploratory" operations, Mr. Grew warned them against this procedure. He told them that if the United States expected or awaited "clear-cut commitments" which would satisfy the United States "both as to principle and as to concrete detail," the conversations would be drawn out indefinitely and unproductively "until the Konoye cabinet and its supporting elements desiring rapproachment with the United States will come to the conclusion that the outlook for an agreement is hopeless and that the United States Government is only playing for time." In this case, the Ambassador continued, the Konoye Government would be discredited. "The logical outcome of this will be the downfall of the Konoye cabinet and the formation of a military dictatorship which will lack either the disposition or the temperament to avoid colliding head-on with the United States."

If Premier Konoye was sincere in his intentions why could he not give President Roosevelt and Secretary Hull clear-cut commitments as to details before the conference? To this central question Ambassador Grew gave serious attention and provided for the President and the Secretary an answer based on his knowledge of the critical situation in Tokyo. Mr. Grew knew that a "liberal" government in Japan, or indeed any government inclined to keep peace with the United States, was beset by the militarist and chauvinist press, always engaged in frightening and inflaming the Japanese public by war-mongering. He knew also, what had recently been demonstrated many times, that the head and members of any such government were likely to be assassinated in cold blood by desperate agents of "patriotic" societies. He knew and so did Premier Konoye that Axis secret agents and Japanese enemies of peace with the United States were boring within the Konoye Government and watching with Argus eyes every message or communication sent from Tokyo to Washington. In other words, Premier Konoye could not be sure that any note he dispatched to Washington, no matter how guardedly, would escape the vigilance of his enemies on every side in Japan.

This situation Ambassador Grew went into at length in his report of September 29, 1941, to Secretary Hull and President Roosevelt. He had been in close and confidential communication with Premier Konoye. On the basis of very intimate knowledge, he informed them that the Japanese Government was ready to undertake commitments other than those set down in the communications which had already passed. He reported, if in cautious language as befitted a diplomat, that he had been told that "Prince Konoye is in a position in direct negotiations with President Roosevelt to offer him assurances which, because of their far-reaching character, will not fail to satisfy the United States." Mr. Grew added that he could not determine the truth of this statement, but he said definitely that while the Japanese Government could not overtly renounce its relations with the Axis Powers, it "actually has shown a readiness to reduce Japan's alliance adherence to a dead letter by its indication of willingness to enter formally into negotiations with the United States."

Thereupon Mr. Grew presented the alternatives as he saw them from his point of vantage in Tokyo. The Japanese military machine and army could be discredited by wholesale military defeat. That was one alternative. On the other hand the United States could place a "reasonable amount of confidence" in

the professed sincerity of intention and good faith of Prince Konoye and his supporters to mold Japan's future policy upon the basic principles they are ready to accept and then to adopt measures which gradually but loyally implement those principles, with it understood that the United States will implement its own commitments *pari passu* with the steps which Japan takes.

This was the alternative which the American Ambassador commended to President Roosevelt and Secretary Hull as "an attempt to produce a regeneration of Japanese thought and outlook through constructive conciliation, along the lines of American efforts at present."

As to the alternatives, Mr. Grew closed his plea by inquiring "whether the better part of wisdom and of statesmanship is not to bring such efforts to a head before the force of their initial impetus is lost, leaving it impossible to overcome an opposition which the Ambassador thinks will mount inevitably and steadily in Japan." In Mr. Grew's opinion it was evidently a question of now or never, though he ended by paying deference to "the much broader field of view of President Roosevelt and Secretary Hull" as compared with "the viewpoint of the American Embassy in Tokyo."

While the negotiations over the proposed meeting between President Roosevelt and Premier Konoye were still dragging along, the Japanese Foreign Minister, Toyoda, discussed with the British Ambassador in Tokyo, Sir Robert Craigie, various problems in the then delicate relations between Japan and the United States. At the same time, he asked Ambassador Grew to speak to Ambassador Craigie and later he learned that the British and American Ambassadors had held a conference on these questions. On October 3, 1941, Minister Toyoda sent to Ambassador Nomura in Washington information respecting the Japanese-British-American transactions in Tokyo and said to Ambassador Nomura: "Subsequently, according to absolutely unimpeachable sources, Ambassador Craigie cabled Foreign Secretary Eden and Ambassador Halifax, explaining the importance of having the United States and Japan come to an immediate agreement to hold a conference."

In a supplementary message to Ambassador Nomura, Tokyo furnished him with "the gist of Craigie's opinions" expressed in messages to Anthony Eden and Lord Halifax, with a warning to keep the information strictly secret. According to Minister Toyoda's summation, Ambassador Craigie presented the following views to his government in London and his colleague, Lord Halifax, in Washington. First, with the resignation of former Foreign Minister Yosuke Matsuoka "the chances of turning away from the Axis policy and toward the democracies, has been considerably enhanced." Second, to Japan the speeding up of the conference between President Roosevelt and Premier Konoye is important for the reason that undue delay would place the Konoye Cabinet in a precarious position owing to the opposition in Japan to a reversal of relations with the Axis. Third,

by pursuing a policy of stalling, the United States is arguing about every word and every phrase on the grounds that it is an essential preliminary to any kind of an agreement. It seems apparent that the United States does not comprehend the fact that by the nature of the Japanese and also on account of the domestic conditions in Japan, no delays can be countenanced. It would be very regrettable indeed if the best opportunity for the settlement of the Far Eastern problems since I assumed my post here, were to be lost in such a manner. . . . Both the U.S. Ambassador in Japan and I are firmly of the opinion that it would be a foolish policy if this superb opportunity is permitted to slip by assuming an unduly suspicious attitude.

Fourth, British retaliatory economic measures should be continued until "the Konoye principles actually materialize."

Nevertheless, President Roosevelt and Secretary Hull rejected the advice of their Ambassador in Japan and prolonged the "explorations" until the

Konoye Cabinet fell about two weeks later, October 16, 1941. Why? Records now available provide no answer. As far as the President was concerned, the question remains open, save for such inferences as may be drawn from collateral documents. Secretary Hull's answer is to be sought in many words spread over many pages, and, owing to the fact that he was the President's agent in the conduct of foreign affairs, his answer, by inference, may be treated as that of the Administration. When Secretary Hull's prolix and involved explanations as yet presented to the American public are all analyzed, compared, and tabulated, they amount to this: The Japanese had a long record of barbaric deeds; Prince Konoye was not much better, if any, than the bloodthirsty militarists; the promises and proposals of the Konoye Government were not to be trusted as offering any hope of peace to the "peace-loving nations of the world," as represented by the United States.

If this summation is regarded as too simple, then resort may be had to Secretary Hull's own summation. Although the state of Secretary Hull's health did not permit him to undergo a cross examination by any Republican members of the Congressional Committee on Pearl Harbor during its proceedings of 1945–46, he answered in his own way certain questions formulated by Senator Ferguson and submitted to him in writing on April 5, 1946.

In Questions 71 and 72, Senator Ferguson dealt with conversations relative to the Japanese proposal for negotiations looking to the maintenance of peace in the Pacific. Senator Ferguson referred to the message of the Japanese Foreign Minister on the resumption of conversations in mid-August transmitted to Washington with a covering note by Ambassador Grew. He quoted from the Ambassador's covering note in which he urged "with all the force at his command, for the sake of avoiding the obviously growing possibility of an utterly futile war between Japan and the United States, that this Japanese proposal be not turned aside without every prayerful consideration." Senator Ferguson also reminded Secretary Hull of Ambassador Grew's words that the proposal was "unprecedented" in Japanese history, and had been made with the approval of the Emperor and the highest authority of Japan. "That is correct, is it not?" The Senator asked.

Secretary Hull replied that there was no controversy about the contents of the documents in question and then said:

The President and I, together with our Far Eastern advisors, were looking at the situation with the benefit of all the worldwide information available to us in Washington. We judged that the Japanese Government had no serious expectation of reaching an understanding at the proposed meeting [in the Pacific] unless the American Government surrendered its basic position while Japan rigidly adhered to and went forward with its policy of aggression and conquest. We had fully tested out the Japanese Government by preliminary inquiries and found it adamant in its position.

In other words, the President and Secretary Hull regarded the Japanese proposal for a Pacific Conference as essentially dishonest, as if a kind of subterfuge to deceive the Government of the United States while Japan went on with aggression and conquest.

It is at present impossible to determine the parts played by President Roosevelt and Secretary Hull respectively in the final decision to reject the Konoye proposal, as it is in the case of their action on the memorandum of November 26, 1941. . . . According to Premier Konoye's Memoirs, the President was at first enthusiastic about the idea of a conference in the Pacific but Secretary Hull was at the outset cool and at length resolute in pursuing the course which, as Ambassador Grew had warned him in effect, would end in failure and war.

Nor is it possible now to discover whether, if the Pacific conference had been held, Premier Konoye could have carried out his intentions as communicated to the President and Secretary Hull. It is easy, of course, to take passages from Premier Konoye's Memoirs, and other fragmentary documents at present available, for the purpose of making an argument for or against American acceptance of his proposal; but, as Ambassador Grew informed the President and Secretary Hull at the time, the alternative of war would remain open to the United States if the conference had not fulfilled expectations. The "solution" of this insoluble "problem," however, lies outside the purposes and limitations of my inquiry. . . .

THE JAPANESE PROPOSAL OF A MODUS VIVENDI REJECTED IN FAVOR OF AN ULTIMATIVE NOTICE

Though the Konoye Cabinet in Tokyo had been succeeded by what was regarded as a "strong" government headed by General Hideki Tojo, supposed to be an irreconcilable militarist, the Japanese did not break off conversations "looking to the maintenance of peace in the Pacific." On the contrary, the Japanese Government early in November dispatched to Ambassador Nomura two proposals for new discussions to be taken up with President Roosevelt and Secretary Hull and sent a special agent, Saburo Kurusu, to assist the Ambassador in further explorations. The first of these proposals, called proposal "A," was plainly a document for bargaining; the second, proposal "B," was more conciliatory and had the signs of being the last offer the Japanese Government might make to the United States—"a last effort to prevent something happening." Was this move on the part of Japan just another evidence of what Secretary Hull called Japanese trickery, a desire to prolong negotiations and to deceive the Government of the United States?

On their face the two proposals, as finally presented to the State Department, might have been so regarded by Secretary Hull. But as a matter of fact, having previously broken the Japanese code, American Navy and Army Intelligence had intercepted, translated, and made available to the Administration, before either of the projects had been laid before Secretary Hull, the substance of the two documents as sent in code from Tokyo to Ambassador Nomura. It had done more. It had intercepted accompanying messages from Tokyo to the Ambassador which indicated, in the first place, that the Tojo Cabinet was anxious to reach some kind of settlement with the United States; and, in the next place, that the second proposal was, to use the language of the Japanese dispatch containing it, "advanced with the idea of making a last effort to prevent something from happening." If the opinion often expressed by Secretary Hull to the effect that the Japanese were chronic liars be accepted as correct, still it is hardly to be presumed that the Japanese Government was lying to its Ambassador when, in secret messages intended for his eyes alone, it informed him that a settlement was urgently desired in Tokyo and that proposal "B" was to be offered in a last effort to prevent something from happening—that is, doubtless, an open break and war.

In short, Secretary Hull knew in advance, on November 4, 1941, that the Japanese proposals were coming to him, that the Tokyo Government had expressed to Ambassador Nomura anxiety to reach some settlement with the United States, that it had fixed November 25 as a deadline, that failure to achieve a settlement or truce meant drastic action, if not war, on the part of the Japanese Government. On November 1, Secretary Hull had asked the Army and Navy whether they were ready to give support to new warnings to Japan, and expressed the opinion that there was no use to issue any additional warnings "if we can't back them up." On November 5, General Marshall and Admiral Stark addressed to President Roosevelt a memorandum in which they strongly objected to military action against Japan at the moment and urged the postponement of hostilities in order to allow the Army and Navy as much time as possible to effect better preparations for war. It was in this state of affairs that Secretary Hull undertook to deal with Ambassador Nomura when he presented a sketch of proposal "A," November 7, 1941.

As history long ago recorded, explorations of the Japanese proposal "A" came to nothing. On the afternoon of November 7, the day Ambassador Nomura laid the proposal before Secretary Hull, the President, at a meeting of his Cabinet, took a poll on the question "whether the people would back us up in case we struck at Japan down there and what the tactics should be." The vote was a solid yea. Such are the facts as recorded by Secretary Stimson in his *Diary* for his own eyes. He also added that Secretary Hull made a good presentation of the general situation and that he narrowed it down, following steps already taken to show "what needed to be done in the future." Secretary Stimson likewise noted that "the thing would have been much stronger if the Cabinet had known—and they did not know except in the case of Hull and the President—what the Army is doing with the big bombers and *how ready we are to pitch in*."

With reference to the conduct of foreign affairs, it is enlightening to compare the record of this Cabinet meeting as entered in Secretary Stimson's secret *Diary* with Secretary Hull's public statement describing the meaning to the Congressional Committee on Pearl Harbor in November, 1945. Mr. Hull then said that the President at the outset asked him whether he had anything on his mind and that he thereupon took about fifteen minutes in describing the dangers of the international situation. Mr. Hull stated that relations were extremely critical and that "we should be on the lookout for a military attack anywhere by Japan at any time." When he had finished, Mr. Hull continued, "the President went around the Cabinet. All concurred in my estimate of the dangers." The Cabinet agreed that some speeches should be delivered in order that "the country would, if possible, be better prepared for such a development." Four days later, November 11, 1941, Secretary Knox and Undersecretary Welles carried out the mandate. They served notice on the people of the United States. Secretary Knox called their attention to the dangers in the Pacific; and Mr. Welles informed them that "at any moment war may be forced upon us."

It was with this matured conviction secretly maintained in the Cabinet and the notice given to the public by Secretary Knox and Mr. Welles in circulation, that Secretary Hull began to explore proposition "B" with the Japanese Ambassador and Mr. Kurusu. This Japanese proposal, slightly modified as they presented it on November 20, embraced five principal points as follows:

1. Both the Governments of Japan and the United States undertake not to make any armed advancement into any of the regions in the Southeastern Asia and the Southern Pacific area excepting the part of French Indochina where the Japanese troops are stationed at present.

2. The Japanese Government undertakes to withdraw its troops now stationed in French Indochina upon either the restoration of peace between Japan and China or the establishment of an equitable peace in the Pacific Area.

In the meantime the Government of Japan declares that it is prepared to remove its troops now stationed in the southern part of French Indochina to the northern part of the said territory upon the conclusion of the present arrangement which shall later be embodied in the final agreement.

3. The Governments of Japan and the United States shall cooperate with a view to securing the acquisition of those goods and commodities which the two countries need in Netherlands East Indies.

4. The Governments of Japan and the United States mutually undertake to restore their commercial relations to those prevailing prior to the freezing of the assets.

The Government of the United States shall supply Japan a required quantity of oil.

5. The Government of the United States undertakes to refrain from such measures and actions as will be prejudicial to the endeavors for the restoration of general peace between Japan and China.

When President Roosevelt and Secretary Hull were called upon to make decisions with regard to the Japanese program for a kind of modus vivendi looking to a general settlement in the Pacific, they confronted a fateful choice and they knew it. From secret Japanese messages intercepted by the Army and Navy Intelligence, they had learned that this proposal was the final offering from the Japanese Government. They confronted the urgent appeal from General Marshall and Admiral Stark to postpone hostilties with Japan on the ground that the Army and Navy were not ready for war. Should at least a truce of some form be attempted if only to give the United States more time to prepare for war? The idea of a truce had been taken up by the President with Secretary Stimson as early as November 6, two days after the secret Japanese message on the negotiations had been intercepted. And Mr. Stimson had strongly objected to the idea.

Despite Secretary Stimson's objections, however, the President apparently decided that a truce or modus vivendi might and should be attempted; for he sent an undated note to Secretary Hull, giving his suggestions for the terms of such a temporary or preliminary adjustment with Japan. The President's note contained the following points:

6 Months

1. United States to resume economic relations—some oil and rice now—more later.

2. Japan to send no more troops to Indo-China or Manchurian border or any place South (Dutch, Brit. or Siam).

3. Japan to agree not to invoke tripartite pact even if the U.S. gets into European war.

4. U.S. to introduce Japs to Chinese to talk things over but U.S. to take no part in their conversation.

* * *

Later in Pacific agreements.

In addition to President Roosevelt's suggestions for a modus vivendi, Secretary Hull had for his consideration, in arriving at a decision, a long memorandum on the subject from his experts in the Far Eastern Division of the State Department. This document, dated November 11, 1941, contained a draft of principles and details to be applied in efforts to arrive at some kind of middle course in handling the now tense relations with Japan. The authors of the memorandum called Mr. Hull's attention to the difficulties involved in an attempt at the moment to reach a comprehensive settlement "covering the entire Pacific area," and then stated:

Such a prospect prompts the question whether it might not be possible to propose some tentative or transitional arrangement the very discussion of which might serve not only to continue the conversations pending the event of a more favorable situation, even if the proposal is not eventually agreed to, but also to provide the entering wedge toward a comprehensive settlement of the nature sought providing the proposal is accepted by Japan and provided further that China is able to obtain satisfactory terms from Japan.

While working at his reply to the "last effort" of Tokyo to reach an adjustment, Secretary Hull had, besides the President's proposals and the memorandum from the Far Eastern Division, a strong recommendation from the senior officers of the Far Eastern Division relative to a project for a Pacific settlement, not a mere truce. This recommendation from his specialists in Far Eastern affairs, dated November 19, grew out of an outline for "a proposed basis for agreement between the United States and Japan," prepared by the Secretary of the Treasury, Henry Morganthau, Jr. It took the form of a covering note to Secretary Hull initialed by Maxwell Hamilton, Chief of the Division. Mr. Hamilton pronounced the proposal offered by the Secretary of the Treasury "the most constructive I have seen," and added that all the senior officers in his Division concurred in his judgment. Therefore, he urged Secretary Hull to give it prompt and careful consideration and suggested a conference with General Marshall and Admiral Stark on the proposal.

During this period, as the testimony, documents, and exhibits procured by the Congressional Committee on Pearl Harbor abundantly demonstrate, hectic negotiations and conversations went on in Washington, with foreign ambassadors, ministers, and special agents, as well as American citizens and members of the Cabinet bringing pressures to bear on the President and Secretary Hull—some for war and others for peace. Insiders knew that the die was about to be cast, and some outsiders knew it too. If newspapers reflected the state of popular opinion, thousands of American citizens, utterly uninformed as to the nature of the inner transactions of the Administration, were aware of an approaching crisis. If they believed Undersecretary Welles' speech of November 11, they feared that war might at any moment be "forced upon us." Those who recalled the President's peace pledges of 1940, which still stood in the record, may have hoped that he could or would, in spite of the crisis, keep the country out of war.

It was amid complicated circumstances that Secretary Hull worked at the problem raised by the Japanese proposal for a truce or modus vivendi. He knew from intercepts of secret Japanese messages, that this was regarded in Tokyo as the "last effort" on the part of the Japanese Government. Should he make a blunt reply or resort to supreme diplomatic ingenuity in an attempt to keep conversations going in the hope of peace in the Pacific or at least postponing war for a time until the American Army and Navy were better equipped to fight it? He knew that on August 17, 1941, President Roosevelt had served a warning notice on Tokyo to the effect that in case of any further Japanese encroachments on their neighbors, the United States would take steps that meant war. He knew that during all the explorations since August, the position then taken had been firmly maintained, that the war plans for coöperation with Great Britain, the Netherlands, and Australia were all predicated upon joint action against Japan if she moved southward beyond definite boundary lines. Secretary Hull was well aware that General Marshall and Admiral Stark had been and were pressing for more time in which to prepare the Army and Navy for war. Was it not for him a matter of supreme statesmanship to prevent, if humanly possible, a two-front war for the United States—a war in the Pacific as well as the "shooting war" in the Atlantic?

As far as the documentary record goes, Secretary Hull for a few days at least considered a modus vivendi with Japan desirable and feasible. From November 22 to November 26, the Secretary, in consultation with the President and the highest military authorities, worked over proposals and plans for some kind of adjustment with Japan on the basis of the Japanese note of

November 20. In this connection the project was discussed with representatives of Great Britain, Australia, the Netherlands, and China. The principles of the final draft were approved by Secretary Stimson, who declared that it adequately safeguarded "American interests."

Alarmed lest the Government of the United States make something like a truce or temporary standstill with Japan, with a view to further negotiation actually looking to the maintenance of peace in the Pacific, Chinese diplomatic and special agents, supported by powerful American interests, made a storm over the proposed modus vivendi with Japan. In this operation, they were ably led by the Chinese Ambassador, Dr. Hu Shih, a liberal, wise in the ways of the West and the East, once well marked by the dread police of the Chiang Kai-shek Government, now serving it in the United States where "liberalism" was an asset. From day to day, hour to hour, the Chinese and their agents bombarded Secretary Hull so heavily with protests against any truce with Japan that the situation in Washington became almost hysterical.

This state of affairs was later described by Secretary Hull himself. The Secretary, in a subsequent statement relative to the pressures then brought to bear on him by the Chinese, declared that Chiang Kai-shek "has sent numerous hysterical cable messages to different cabinet officers and high officials in the Government other than the State Department, and sometimes even ignoring the President, intruding into a delicate and serious situation with no real idea of what the facts are." Secretary Hull further said that "Chiang Kai-shek had his brother-in-law, located here in Washington, disseminate damaging reports at times to the press and others, apparently with no particular purpose in mind." Besieged by Chinese agents in London, Prime Minister Churchill, instead of supporting his Ambassador in Washington, Lord Halifax, who was eager for a truce in the Pacific, intervened by sending a confusing message as if trying to support the Chinese side of the dispute with the Government of the United States.

Disturbed by the vacillations introduced by Mr. Churchcill's intrusion into American affairs, Secretary Hull exclaimed that

it would have been better if, when Churchill received Chiang Kai-shek's loud protest about our negotiations here with Japan, instead of passing the protest on to us without objection on his part, thereby qualifying and virtually killing what we knew were the individual views of the British Government toward these negotiations, he had sent a strong cable back to Chaing Kai-shek telling him to brace up and fight with the same zeal as the Japanese and the Germans are displaying instead of weakening and telling the Chinese people that all of the friendly countries were now striving primarily to protect themselves and to force an agreement between China and Japan, every Chinese should understand from such a procedure that the best possible course was being pursued and that this calls for resolute fighting until the undertaking is consummated by peace negotiations which Japan in due course would be obliged to enter into with China.

In other words, while the negotiations over the Japanese proposals for a modus vivendi were proceeding, Secretary Hull was disgusted with the operations of Chinese agents. He was convinced that the tentatives of the proposal should be explored and efforts be made to reach some kind of basis for further explorations in the direction of a settlement in the Far East. He was likewise convinced that in the proceedings along this line the real interests of China could be protected by the United States, indeed advanced, until, at least, the willingness of Japan to come to decent terms could be probed to the bottom. So, at least, it seems.

But for reasons which are nowhere explicit, despite the thousands of words on the subject that appear in the Pearl Harbor documents and testimony, Secretary Hull, after consulting President Roosevelt, suddenly and completely abandoned the project and on November 26, 1941, handed the Japanese Ambassador and Mr. Kurusu, the historic memorandum which the Japanese Government treated as an ultimatum. When the Japanese representatives in Washington read the document, Mr. Kurusu assured the Secretary that the Japanese Government, after examining it, would be likely to throw up its hands. When, the next morning, Secretary Stimson asked Secretary Hull what had been done about the modus vivendi project, the Secretary replied that "he had broken the whole matter off." He then added: "I have washed my hands of it and it is now in the hands of you and Knox—the Army and the Navy."

Roosevelt and Japan

BASIL RAUCH

THE THIRD ROUND: JAPAN

THE ARGENTIA discussions of the Azores and the Atlantic Charter did not provide Beard, Morgenstern [Pearl Harbor: *The Story of the Second War*] and the Minority of the Congressional Committee with the chief exhibit in their case against Roosevelt. They found that in the third round of discussions at the Conference, which dealt with the question of Japan. After the British staff officers failed to obtain a promise from the American officers that the United States would go to war if Japan attacked the territory of a country other than the United States—a repetition of their failures in the earlier talks at Washington and Singapore—Prime Minister Churchill attempted to obtain such a promise from Roosevelt.

Basil Rauch, *Roosevelt: From Munich to Pearl Harbor* (New York, 1950), 371–377; 434–454.

He proposed that the governments of the United States, Great Britain, and the Netherlands should make "parallel and simultaneous" declarations to Japan. The Soviet government should be informed and the question considered whether it should be asked to join in the parallel declaration. A draft of the declaration prepared by Cadogan read:

1. Any further encroachment by Japan in the Southwestern Pacific would produce a situation in which the United States [British, Netherlands] Government would be compelled to take counter measures even though these might lead to war between the United States [Great Britain, the Netherlands] and Japan.

2. If any third Power becomes the object of aggression by Japan in consequence of such counter measures or of their support of them, the President would have the intention to seek authority from Congress to give aid to such Power [His, Her Majesty's Government would give all possible aid to such Power].

Since the President already had authority from Congress to give Lend Lease aid to such a third power, the last clause was a strong hint that the President would ask Congress for a declaration of war, and the phrase to be used in the declarations of the other two governments, "give *all possible* aid," meant the same thing. The most likely event foreseen was a Japanese attack against the NEI. Britain expected to join in the defense of the rich islands, and Churchill's proposal was that the United States should warn Japan that it would in such a situation enter the war.

Churchill proposed this three- or four-power parallel declaration because, as he told Welles, he believed it was the only hope of preventing Japan from embarking on new aggressions which, unless the United States entered the war, would destroy British shipping in the Pacific and Indian Oceans and cut the lifeline between the British Dominions and the British Isles. If Japan were not restrained, or the United States did not enter the war following a Japanese attack against Great Britain, directly or indirectly through the NEI, the blow to the British cause might be decisive.

What Churchill proposed was, therefore, a united front to prevent Japan from defeating new victims one by one. He wished to face Japan with the certainty that if it attacked any one of the members of the united front, it would have to fight them all. It was an important British initiative to use the technique of collective security to prevent the war from spreading in the Far East.

No one among the Anglo-American leaders believed that Japan itself would in the end force war upon the three powers by attacking them all at once. The foolhardiness of that procedure placed it outside the calculations of Roosevelt and Churchill. This was proved by the nature of the Churchill proposal and the discussion that followed. The United States was thought to be the last power Japan would attack directly. Such a calculation was inevitable because it was the only procedure that made sense from the point of view of Japanese military interests and because Japan, like the other Axis governments, had so obviously pursued the "sensible" one-by-one strategy in its aggressions. It was the disunity of the peaceful nations that had made it possible for aggressor nations possessing a minority of world power to succeed in their designs. No reasonable person could be expected to foresee, prior to December 7, 1941, that in one blow the Axis would destroy the condition which alone made its victory possible. This is of supreme importance in the refutation of the isolationist thesis that Roosevelt "planned" Pearl Harbor.

The only event for which Churchill asked Roosevelt to plan was a Japanese attack on territory other than that of the United States. Because he proposed a plan based on the central conceptions of the policy of collective security, that an aggression against one peaceful nation is an aggression against all peaceful nations, and that the best way to prevent aggression is to face the potential aggressor with the certainty that it cannot attack one without fighting them all, the parallel declaration was bound to win a sympathetic hearing by Roosevelt. It presented him with the same choices he had faced again and again since he came to power, this time in the ultimate form of the ultimate sanction: war. The diplomatic sanction of the Stimson Doctrine he had inherited and sustained. The intermediate sanction of a discriminatory arms embargo against an aggressor, which he had tried and failed to make the policy of the United States prior to 1939, he had accomplished by August, 1941, and had reinforced with the unprecedented policy of Lend Lease aid to victims of aggression. In the Atlantic Charter he proposed eventual entry of the United States into a full-fledged system of collective security. But Churchill asked him to join immediately a united front of peaceful nations to prevent further spread of the war by invoking the ultimate sanction of collective security. It called for one of the crucial decisions of Roosevelt's career. To understand his decision, review of United States relations with Japan during preceding months is necessary.

Secretary Hull believed that in the fall of 1940 the United States caused Japan to postpone new aggressions. The Roosevelt administration advanced new economic sanctions against Japan when Japan joined the Axis military alliance, and carefully nourished the uncertainty of Japanese leaders regarding future American intentions. This, Hull believed, had kept Japan from seizing the greatest opportunity of its history when France and the Netherlands fell and Britain seemed about to fall.

During the winter, Foreign Minister Yosuke Matsuoka and other pro-Axis and militarist Japanese turned once more to belligerent assertions of Japanese ambitions. Hull on January 13, 1941, told the House Foreign Affairs Committee that the "new order" in Asia meant domination of nearly half the people of the world by one country and that such a program was of concern to every other nation. Matsuoka answered in a speech to the Japanese Diet a week later that he wanted the United States to agree to Japanese supremacy over the whole of the western Pacific and to end economic restrictions against Japan. Hull told the press next day:

We have threatened no one, invaded no one, and surrounded no one. We have freely offered and now freely offer cooperation in peaceful life to all who wish it.

This devotion to peace and friendly processes naturally warrants no implication of a desire to extend frontiers or assume hegemony. Our strategic line must depend primarily on the policies and courses of other nations.

JAPAN'S SECRET PROGRAM

Matsuoka's statement afforded a public glimpse of the secret program of the Japanese government, which was fully exposed after the war by the International Military Tribunal for the Far East. It was adopted in October, 1940, and designated three objectives: early successful settlement of the China Incident; a nonaggression pact with Russia; and incorporation of the countries of southeast Asia and the southwest Pacific, including Malaya, India, Australia, and New Zealand, in the Greater East Asia Co-Prosperity Sphere. Singapore and the Philippines were regarded as the keys. If they were won, all the rest would fall easily to Japan.

Action to achieve the third objective was planned on two fronts: diplomatic and military. Britain would be offered Japanese mediation in the European war in return for recognition of the Co-Prosperity Sphere, including surrender of Singapore. In February, 1941, the Japanese leaders told the Germans that a military attack against Singapore was planned. Military bases were to be secured in Indo-China and Thailand. The United States was to be offered Japanese recognition of "Philippine independence" in return for American recognition of the Co-Prosperity Sphere. In January, 1941, the Japanese Commander of the Combined Fleets approved and transmitted to Imperial General Headquarters a plan for a surprise attack on Pearl Harbor while the two countries were at peace. In May, 1941, the Japanese Navy began training for the attack.

Thus it is now clear that when Matsuoka told the Japanese Diet in January, 1941, that he wanted the United States to agree to Japanese supremacy in the western Pacific, he actually demanded American cooperation with Japan to achieve its conquests as the price of American immunity from Japanese attack against the United States.

In the innumerable American-Japanese conversations of 1941, the Roosevelt administration never refused to discuss a Japanese proposal, it never issued an ultimatum, and it never offered or agreed to proposals which signified appeasement, that is, which gave consent or support to Japanese conquests of territories of third countries. The administration gradually ended American economic support of the Japanese war machine, most decisively after Japan in July invaded southern Indo-China.

American isolationists argued that the Roosevelt administration should make an agreement with Japan, abandon economic sanctions, and "get out of Asia." They charged that the Roosevelt administration was responsible for the attack on Pearl Harbor because it did issue ultimatums to the Japanese government and encircled Japan with an alliance of the ABCD powers. The latter charge may be disposed of at the outset by reference to the fact that the first Anglo-American staff conference occurred no earlier than the formulation of the Japanese plan to attack Pearl Harbor. Besides, those conferences only considered defensive measures, while the Japanese planned aggression. . . .

JAPANESE FEAR OF RUSSIA

It should also be considered that Roosevelt's opinion, expressed at the Atlantic Conference, that war was inevitable, like any opinion, could be modified by developments. Japan's fear of Russia, reflected in its anxiety for a Roosevelt-Konoye meeting after the President delivered his warning and offer to renew conversations to Nomura on August 17, was such a development. The President had agreed in principle to the meeting, but had asked that Japan make a clear statement of its position before preparations began. He had gone so far as to name October 15 as a tentative date for the meeting. Nomura on August 23, before his government answered the President's statements of August 17, pleaded with Hull for an earlier date than October 15 for the Roosevelt-Konoye meeting. He said his government was afraid some agreements might be reached in the September American-Anglo-Russian conference in Moscow that would be "detrimental" to Japan. The Japanese regarded shipments of American supplies to Vladivostok as designed to build up Soviet strength in Siberia where it menaced Japan. Hull answered that American aid to Russia was directed exclusively against Germany, but added: "Of course, if Japan should project herself militarily into the Russo-German situation—which I hope she will not—an entirely different question will be presented."

Nomura thus represented Japanese fear of a Soviet-American rapprochement which would leave Japan exposed in the north greatly to the detriment of plans for southward invasions. He "contented himself with laughing very heartily" when Hull asked him whether he did not think the Russo-Japanese Neutrality Pact of April, 1941, gave Japan all the assurance of Russia's peaceful attitude Japan desired.

Japanese fear of Russia was reasonably assessed at face value by the American Chiefs of Staff. They made a report to the President on September 11, entitled "Joint Board Estimate of United States Over-all Production Requirements," which reveals that they saw Russia in the north checkmating Japanese moves to the south, and that they took for granted that the Japanese would be completely occupied between north and south without inviting completion of the circle in the east by the United States. For example, this important document states:

It is unlikely that Japan will simultaneously attempt a major effort to the Northward and to the Southward, because of her lack of equipment and raw materials.

All the more so, the Joint Board implied throughout the report, Japan would not simultaneously attempt a major effort to the eastward.

The Chiefs of Staff believed the United States should enter the war against Germany. But they believed that even that commitment would not weaken the United States in relation to Japan; on the contrary, they proposed that the United States should participate in the European war *"while holding Japan in check pending future developments."* Extreme limits of direct danger to the United States from Japan were defined as dependent, for one thing, upon results in Europe favorable to Japan. In that situation, *after* Hitler defeated Russia, Japan "might" engage in "submarine and raider action against United States naval forces and United States and British lines of communication in the Central and Eastern Pacific Ocean." In a situation even more favorable, that is, were Japan to defeat China and Russia and succeed in controlling Thailand, Malaya, and the NEI, it would work for peace for the purpose of organizing the "East Asia Co-Prosperity Sphere." In that event: "Almost inevitably the Philippine Islands would ultimately pass under Japanese hegemony."

This notable document pictured the United States as being capable, with Britain, Russia and China, of determining the sequence of events. The United States and its friends held the Axis powers in double pincers: Germany between Russia and Britain supported by the United States; Japan between Russia, China, Malaya-Australia and the NEI supported by the United States. Therefore the United States and its friends were regarded as capable of exercising the initiative in determining new developments of the global situation in such fashion as would close the double pincers. But the Joint Chiefs did not consider that Germany and Japan were equally able to picture the global situation as placing them in control of double pincers with which they could checkmate Russia in the east while destroying her in the west, break the British Empire in two, and attack the United States from the Pacific in order to undermine its campaign in the Atlantic.

For the immediate future it depended solely upon the question which side would in fact exercise the initiative to determine which side would wield the pincers. The American Chiefs of Staff believed the United States should join the war in Europe while holding Japan in check in the east: they wanted to wield the pincers. But they failed to estimate that if the United States did not *immediately* seize the initiative, the Axis would do so. Roosevelt consequently did not realize that the final moment for decision whether to break his antiwar pledge had arrived in September. He believed that moment would only arrive when Japan might play the strongest card it seemed to possess: attack northward or southward. His reasoning, that refusal to enter the European war made possible more effective American contributions to the defeat of Hitler, has been discussed in the previous chapter.

Either way, Roosevelt and his advisers believed to the end that Japan would at most only be able, and dare, to launch a limited offensive to the south *or* the north and that a Japanese offensive in either direction necessarily precluded a simultaneous offensive against the United States.

THE APPALLING PARADOX

Nothing in the report of September 11 suggests that the Joint Chiefs imagined Japan would dare to move into the central and eastern Pacific so long as Russia and Britain stood on its northern and southern flanks, that is, so long as Hitler had not subjugated them. The Joint Chiefs wanted the United States to enter the war in Europe, but they did not expect that to affect the current situation. Immediately following the proposal, the report stated: "Necessarily, only small Army contingents are now sufficiently equipped and trained for immediate participation in offensive operations." The military leaders saw United States entry into the war as having immediate effects chiefly upon morale in the armed forces and civilian production. When the Japanese chose their date for the attack on Pearl Harbor they *wrongly* judged that the condition named in the American Joint Chiefs of Staff report of September 11 had been met: but Hitler was *not* successful in Europe. America, the Japanese calculated, could be diverted to the Pacific and Britain cut off from the Far East to help Hitler finish off the British homeland. The American leaders, on the other hand, *rightly* judged that the condition prior to which the Japanese would not attack the United States had not been met, and the Russian counteroffensive on December 7 bore them out.

Thus may be understood the appalling paradox that Roosevelt and Hull were right in their belief that the United States was playing from strength in the final conversations with Japan even though the Japanese were actually planning the attack on Pearl Harbor. Each side set out to "baby along" the other, the Americans to postpone if not prevent Japanese aggression to the south or the north, the Japanese to prepare an attack on the United States as a "sanction" if appeasement could not be extorted from it. In the isolationist thesis attention is concentrated exclusively on the disaster at Pearl Harbor to prove that Roosevelt and Hull were victims—by implication, eager victims —of Japanese policy. But the outcome of the war is a better criterion by which to judge which side was the victim of Japanese policy.

THE JAPANESE STIFFEN THEIR TERMS

Playing from strength, Roosevelt and Hull were determined to avoid appeasement. The Japanese government answered Roosevelt's proposal on August 28. It insisted that the Roosevelt-Konoye meeting be held prior to any negotiations and as quickly as possible. In response to the President's request for a clear statement of its attitudes and plans, the Japanese government presented, besides usual protestations of peaceful intentions, several qualifications containing obvious escape clauses. It would not withdraw its troops from Indo-China until the China Incident was "settled," or a "just peace" was established in East Asia. It would take no military action against Russia so long as Russia "does not menace Japan or Manchoukuo." It would not use military force against a neighboring country "without provocation." How those phrases could be interpreted by the Japanese to claim American support for past and future aggressions was obvious from former Japanese practice. It was even made clear in the same communication, in a paragraph describing recent Japanese aggressions:

When a nation is obstructed in the path of natural and peaceful development, or when the means of its existence is threatened, not only is it imperative that that nation should take defensive measures, but it is also required to do so for the maintenance of a just peace. This was the motivating policy of the Japanese Government.

Then the Japanese made a charge, only slightly veiled, that, while Japan was defensive in its policy, it was the United States that was guilty of threatening weaker powers. This would make some "feel compelled to consider defensively their relations with the United States." The United States was furthermore warned to "avoid any action that might give rise to a fear of menace to Japan through collaboration with the Soviet Union." These assertions more than counterbalanced a statement that the Japanese action in Indo-China was not a "preparatory step for military advance into neighboring countries," and that this pledge would "suffice to clarify also Japan's intentions toward Thailand."

Roosevelt chose to respond as favorably as possible. He complimented Konoye, through Nomura, on the "spirit of his communication." He spoke encouragingly of a meeting with Konoye, but stated that he preferred Alaska as the scene rather than Hawaii. Nomura immediately afterwards suggested to Hull the date September 21–25. He hinted that Germany was inciting Japan against the United States.

President Roosevelt, according to Hull, "would have relished a meeting with Konoye, and at first he was excited at the prospect." But Hull insisted that agreement on essentials must be reached before the meeting, and the President "instantly agreed that it would be disastrous" to hold the meeting otherwise. Hull in his conversation with Nomura on August 28 made this condition known to him. A Roosevelt-Konoye meeting, he said, should have as its purpose "the ratification of essential points already agreed to in principle."

It may be observed here that this is valuable cautionary procedure in organizing a business meeting between heads of state. Bickering and risk of failure incident to any international negotiation is tolerable only if the officials engaged do not embody the ultimate sovereignty of their nations. Even between two governments so tightly bound in friendship and cooperation as Great Britain and the United States, preliminary agreement on essentials was necessary before Roosevelt and Churchill met at Argentia. This was the meaning of Roosevelt's instructions to Hopkins for his meeting with Churchill prior to the Conference: "Economic or territorial deals—NO. . . . No talk about war." Chamberlain had failed to obtain such preliminary agreement with Hitler before Munich. Roosevelt failed to obtain preliminary agreement with Stalin before Yalta.

The mistake was not made in 1941. Nomura himself admitted that with regard to Japanese troops in North China there would be "real difficulty." He accurately defined the difficulty. It arose because, as Hull noted:

it was the idea of the Japanese Government that we [the United States government] exercise our good offices in bringing the Chinese and Japanese together leaving China and Japan to reach a direct settlement among themselves whereas the United States Government desired to discuss with Japan the basic terms on which peace was to be concluded.

Coupled with Nomura's admission that Japanese troops in North China constitute a "real difficulty," this meant that Japan would insist on a "peace" with China that would leave Japan in military occupation of part of China, and the United States in entering an agreement with Japan at a Roosevelt-Konoye meeting must consent to Japanese imposition of such a "peace" on China.

Hull answered that in order to exercise good offices between Japan and China, the United States must have the confidence and friendship of the Chinese government before *and after* the event. Nomura thereupon proposed that the whole question of China should be ignored by Roosevelt and Konoye. Were there not, he asked Hull, other questions apart from China which could be disposed of "with a view to tiding over a critical situation?" The absurdity of this Nomura admitted by recalling that his government made withdrawal of its troops from Indo-China dependent on solution of the China Incident. Nomura ended the conversation with a statement that he recognized the reasonableness of Hull's position but had misgivings as to how far this government could go because of "internal political difficulties." Still he assured Hull that Konoye had great courage and was ready to assume great risks.

In followings days the Japanese begged for speedy arrangements and at the same time demanded preliminary actions by the United States government that far surpassed what the United States asked. Ambassador Grew in Tokyo was asked by Foreign Minister Toyoda to appeal to his government to take three steps without which Toyoda feared Konoye would meet "serious obstacles" in his efforts to bring about an understanding: 1) no delay in the Roosevelt-Konoye meeting; 2) give up sending tankers to Russia by the Pacific route at least pending the outcome of the meeting; 3) also pending the meeting, suspend the order freezing Japanese assets in the United States. Grew answered that he was "under no illusion" that his government would agree to the "preposterous requests" in points (2) and (3). And indeed this effort showed that the "moderate" Konoye government expected the United States to abandon aid to Russia and resume aid to Japan while the Japanese government should make no preliminary concessions and receive a blank check for the Roosevelt-Konoye meeting.

That it was a blank check the Japanese required is supported by evidence of Konoye himself in his memoirs, which were uncovered in 1945. There Konoye revealed that in August, 1941, when he told Army leaders of his desire to meet Roosevelt, the militarists made him promise that if Roosevelt failed to "understand" Japan, and was resolved to go on with his present policy, Konoye would quit the meeting determined to "make war on the United States."

Although this was not known by Hull at the time, it justified his suspicion that Japan would accept no agreement short of consent to the past and future program of the Japanese extremists. Points (2) and (3) of Toyoda's message to Grew repeated the pattern of the conversations earlier in the year: when the Japanese found the United States willing to discuss a given plan for agreement, they stiffened their terms. Furthermore, rumors in the American press raised an outcry against appeasement of Japan. This, if nothing else, imposed caution on the administration.

IDEAL PRINCIPLES AND THEIR PRACTICAL APPLICATION

Still Roosevelt and Hull did not close the door. On September 3, Nomura went to the White House for the answer to Konoye's letter of August 28. The President, in Secretary Hull's presence, assured Konoye that the United States government was prepared to proceed "as rapidly as possible" towards completion of arrangements for a meeting. But he had to take account of developments in the United States as well as Japan, and he could not avoid recognizing that some quarters in Japan raised obstacles to successful collaboration. Therefore he felt it necessary to suggest that:

we take precaution, toward ensuring that our proposed meeting shall prove a success, by endeavoring to enter immediately upon preliminary discussion of the fundamental and essential questions on which we seek agreement. The questions which I have in mind for such preliminary discussions involve *practical application* of the principles fundamental to achievement and maintenance of peace. . . .

The President also made an oral statement to Nomura reiterating the four fundamental principles originally offered by Hull on April 16. Adherence to courses in harmony with these principles, the President said, would bring Japan more benefit than any other course, and only upon the basis of such principles could an agreement be reached which would be effective. He attempted to pin down the vague assurances Japan had given on August 28:

The Government of the United States understands that [those assurances] exclude any policy which would seek political expansion or the acquisition of economic rights, advantages or preferences by force.

This oral statement also pinned down the practical matters at issue by referring Nomura to the "divergences of view" which "remained unreconciled" when the earlier round of conversations was interrupted in July. Pleas that the United States should "understand" the difficulty of the Japanese government in holding in check its populace and military leaders, Roosevelt answered as follows:

It goes without saying that each Government in reaching decisions on policy must take into account the internal situation in its own country and the attitude of public opinion therein. The Government of Japan will surely recognize that the Government of the United States could not enter into any agreement which would not be in harmony with the principles in which the American people—in fact all nations that prefer peaceful methods to methods of force—believe.

In conversation, Roosevelt and Hull repeatedly emphasized the necessity for Japan to state its position regarding three points at issue: evacuation of Japanese troops from China, nondiscrimination in commerce, and interpretation of Japanese obligations under the Axis alliance. Nomura said Konoye wanted to discuss these points at the meeting with Roosevelt. But it was made clear to Nomura that "several days should be consumed" by the Japanese government before the meeting in "clarifying and stating strongly" its position, and that the Japanese government should also work to educate and organize public opinion in support of the proposals for a peaceful settlement. Nomura was told that after the United States received assurances justifying a meeting, it would discuss the matter with the British, the Chinese, and the Dutch, because there was no other way to establish peace, confidence, and friendliness in the Pacific or to rebuild a suitable economic structure. This meant that Roosevelt would not dispose of the property of other governments in a bilateral agreement with Konoye—an elementary but necessary warning. Secretary Hull during following days gave assurance to the Chinese that the United States would not consider any arrangement that permitted the continuation of aggression in China.

The United States had now restated its position. It had dropped specific references to Indo-China and Thailand. Japanese invasion of southern Indo-China had disrupted the earlier conversations, and Roosevelt had offered neutralization as a solution of the status of those territories. Now in September the American administration by avoiding emphasis of the new aggression that had disrupted the conversations proved once more that it would erect no obstacle to a general settlement with Japan.

NEW ESCAPE CLAUSES

Confusion among the Japanese leaders followed the American offer of September 3. The next day Nomura handed Hull a statement containing a proposed draft agreement in terms quite vague, but he presently withdrew it because it was submitted "without the approval of the Japanese government." In Tokyo on the afternoon of September 5, Konoye invited Grew to a secret meeting that night, but then he withdrew the invitation.

On September 6, Nomura handed Hull a draft proposal from his government. It was riddled with escape clauses. Japan promised not to make any military advance against areas adjoining Indo-China or southward "without any justifiable reason." Another version read that Japan would make no advance to the north. Hull asked repeatedly for clarification but never received it. The interpretation and execution of the Axis alliance by Japan would be "independently decided." Japan would withdraw its armed forces from China in accordance with unspecified agreements between Japan and China. Japan would not restrict the economic activities of the United States in China "so long as pursued on an equitable basis." But the "reciprocal" undertakings of the United States contained no escape clauses. It would be required to stop aid to China; suspend military measures in the Far East and southwestern Pacific, that is, end the defense program in the Philippines, and stop aid to Australia, British possessions, and the NEI; resume exports to Japan, and discontinue the freezing order against Japanese funds, these acts to be reciprocated by Japan; and permit Japanese ships to use the Panama Canal.

Trade arrangements made crystal clear Japanese intentions in China. The United States and Japan would make reciprocal commitments to carry on trade in the southwestern Pacific area on a nondiscriminatory basis and help each other obtain raw materials there. But no such arrangement would be made regarding China: in that country Japan would not restrict United States economic activities "so long as pursued on an equitable basis." The United States had sufficient influence in the southwestern Pacific to obtain raw materials for Japan, therefore Japan installed no escape clause for their government for that area but asked for reciprocity. In China no reciprocity was offered, and the United States was asked to rely on Japanese judgment whether United States economic activities there were "equitable," with an obvious inference that Japan, after establishing "peace" with China, would be in control of all of that country.

The September 6 draft would make the United States help Japan consolidate positions in Asia already won by aggression and abandon present and future victims of Japanese imperialism. The American obligations would be inescapable, while Japanese obligations would be subject to Japanese interpretation of wide-open escape clauses. Furthermore, if the United States accepted this draft it would compromise the program of aid to Britain and Russia as well as abandon aid to China. Japan would exercise a right to decide whether the policy of the United States towards Germany was "offensive." Its demand that American shipments to Vladivostok be stopped had already indicated how this right would be exercised.

If interim shifts of front by the Japanese be disregarded, they had now offered the United States five draft proposals for agreement on the following dates: April 9, May 12, June 15, August 6, and September 6. After the first "unofficial" draft of April 9, each draft required more cooperation by the United States in Japanese aggression than the one preceding.

Hull decided that the Japanese proposals of September 6 "fell short by any possibility of acceptance." He saw only a remote chance of reaching agreement. His "major hope" was to postpone Japan's next advance, which would "probably" bring war in the Pacific. Foreign Minister Toyoda tried to transfer the conversations to Tokyo. Hull objected, but the Japanese nevertheless made important statements originally to Grew in Tokyo, and discrepancies between documents received in Washington from Grew and from Nomura added to the confusion. Several weeks passed before the confusion following Nomura's error in presenting the September 4 draft without approval of his government was straightened out.

On September 22, Toyoda handed Grew the text of basic terms of peace Japan proposed to establish with China. These terms were less acceptable than the list Japan had earlier proposed. In the new terms no limits were named for the "certain areas" of China in which Japan would continue to station troops after "peace." During the summer, Hull had signified willingness to eliminate the question of recognition of Manchuria from the agreement and leave it for later decision. Now Japan installed "Recognition of Manchoukuo" in its list of terms for peace with China. These terms, besides repetition of the former requirements that the Japanese puppet government in Nanking be "fused" with the government of Chiang Kai-shek, and the wide-open clause that economic activities of third powers in China would not be restricted by Japan "so long as they are pursued on an equitable basis," made the new terms more unacceptable than ever.

GREW PROPOSES "CONSTRUCTIVE CONCILIATION"

The most important comment, during the whole period, on the Roosevelt-Hull conduct of negotiations with Japan was made on September 29 by Ambassador Grew in a report to Secretary Hull. This report raised the question whether there was not a vista open to the Roosevelt administration located somewhere between the road of appeasement and the road of refusal to appease which might end in war. Grew asserted that such a vista existed. He called it "constructive conciliation," and located it between "the method of progressive economic strangulation" of Japan by American sanctions, and the method of "so-call appeasement." Grew rejected appeasement as a possible course. He saw the United States government as choosing "constructive conciliation" as evidenced by its continual willingness to negotiate any issues with Japan. He firmly believed the United States now had the opportunity to stop Japan's expansion without war or an immediate risk of war, and that failure to use the opportunity would face the United States with a greatly increased risk of war.

Grew warned Hull that Japan might deliberately decide on war with the United States in response to American action in the Pacific. He stressed that Japanese reactions could not be measured, nor Japanese actions predicted, by any Western measuring rod. Therein lay the danger of insisting on detailed and satisfactory preliminary commitments from Japan prior to a Roosevelt-Konoye meeting. Such insistence would cause the conversations to drag on until Japanese elements favorable to a rapprochement decided agreement was hopeless and that the United States was only playing for time. The abnormal sensitiveness of the Japanese would bring serious results, probably including "unbridled acts," and danger of war. Konoye would fall and a military dictatorship ready for a head-on collision with the United States would take over. Grew raised the question whether the consequences of a failure to hold the Roosevelt-Konoye meeting would not be worse than a failure of the meeting to achieve complete success. He considered that face value must be placed on confidential statements to him that the Japanese government could not "define its future assurances and commitments more specifically than hitherto stated," because Matsuoka in July, after retiring as Foreign Minister, had told the German Ambassador in detail the course of conversations with the United States, and it was feared that supporters of Matsuoka remaining in the Foreign Office would reveal to the Germans and to Japanese extremists any information that would make the position of the Konoye cabinet untenable.

Nevertheless Grew had been told that Konoye in direct negotiations with President Roosevelt could offer him assurances that "will not fail to satisfy the United States." The truth of this, Grew said, he could not determine. But he did not consider it unlikely because Japan had shown, by entering into formal negotiations with the United States, readiness, to make its adherence to the Axis alliance a dead letter.

In conclusion Grew gave his opinion that the United States would not reach its objective by insisting in preliminary conversations that Japan provide "the sort of clear-cut, specific commitments which appear in any final, formal convention or treaty." Confidence must be placed in the good faith of Konoye and his supporters

to mould Japan's future policy upon the basic principles they are ready to accept and then to adopt measures which gradually but loyally implement those principles, with it understood that the United States will implement its own commitments *pari passu* with the steps Japan takes. . . .

This was what Grew meant by "constructive conciliation," and it was, he asserted, the only alternative to wholesale military defeat of Japan. The Ambassador ended by deferring to "the much broader field of view of President Roosevelt and Secretary Hull," and he expressed "full awareness" that his own approach was "limited to the viewpoint of the American Embassy in Japan."

Secretary Hull makes no reference in his *Memoirs* to this significant report. It must engage the attention of anyone attempting to judge the Roosevelt-Hull policy. In the absence of comment by Hull, it may nevertheless be ventured to estimate his and Roosevelt's view of Grew's proposal on the basis of their known actions and general views. Hull in close contact with Roosevelt prepared a comprehensive statement to the Japanese government which he handed to Nomura on October 2. It amounted to an answer to Grew.

Grew's proposal for "constructive conciliation" was vitiated by a basic error of fact. Roosevelt and Hull did not refuse to hold the meeting with Konoye because, as Grew stated in his report, the Japanese failed to provide beforehand "the sort of clear-cut, specific commitments which appear in any final, formal convention or treaty," or because "moderates" in the Japanese government could not "define its future assurances and commitments more specifically than hitherto stated" for fear of pro-German officials. The Japanese government in its communications of September 6 and 22 had satisfied Roosevelt's and Hull's request for preliminary statements of its attitudes and purposes. Roosevelt and Hull refused to hold the meeting with Konoye for a quite different reason, namely, that *the Japanese proposals were unacceptable as a basis for agreement*. They meant nothing else than United States appeasement of Japan, which Grew himself had ruled out as a possible policy for the United States. In fact, they meant more than appeasement, they required United States cooperation with Japan in aggression.

Grew in his report emphasized Japan's agreement to American general principles for peace in the Pacific. He ignored the fact that the practical measures Japan proposed transformed those principles into their opposites. Grew asked Roosevelt and Hull to have faith that the Japanese government would adopt measures which would "gradually but loyally" implement those principles. But Konoye's first step in implementing them was to destroy them and ask the United States to help install opposite principles. If Roosevelt had met Konoye on the basis of the Japanese proposals, he himself would have been guilty of bad faith had he then refused to sign an agreement with Konoye to implement United States cooperation with Japan in aggression.

Postwar investigations of the International Military Tribunal for the Far East have brought to light documentary proof that Grew's belief that the Konoye government could be satisfied short of appeasement was mistaken. That government had adopted in October, 1940, and carried out step by step a program of aggression in which diplomacy was used merely as a weapon alternate to military action to achieve expansion.

A SET OF CONTRADICTIONS

Hull's worst suspicions of Japan were correct. In his communication to Nomura on October 2 he reiterated the four principles to which Japan claimed to subscribe. He specifically stated that the United States government had no purpose of discussing details. Rather it was the set of contradictions between principles avowed and applications proposed by the Japanese government that caused the difficulty. They were, he said, "a source of disappointment." He pointed them out one by one. He asked for further clarifications of the Japanese proposals:

From what the Japanese Government has so far indicated in regard to its purposes this Government derives the impression that the Japanese Government has in mind a program which would be circumscribed by the imposition of qualifications and exceptions to the actual application of those principles.

If this impression is correct, can the Japanese Government feel that a meeting between the responsible heads of government under such circumstances would be likely to contribute to the advancement of the high purposes which we have mutually had in mind?

Hull ended with strong assurances that the President hoped a meeting with
Konoye could be held.

WAKASUGI'S "MISTAKE"

Convincing evidence presently came from the Japanese themselves that it
was they who made impossible Grew's "constructive conciliation," that they
insisted upon appeasement as the only purpose of a Roosevelt-Konoye meeting. Japanese officials in Tokyo and Washington consumed many hours in
explaining to Americans that the October 2 statement mystified them because
Hull had not made known precisely what the United States would consider
proper bases for a Roosevelt-Konoye meeting. But Ambassador Nomura on
October 9 admitted in a conference with officials of the State Department
that he himself had noted "some contradictions" of the agreed-upon principles in the Japanese proposals for implementing them. He thereupon made
a frank justification of those contradictions:

> Mentioning that the Japanese public had suffered the sacrifices of four years
> of war, the Ambassador said that his Government would *necessarily* have to pre-
> sent to the Japanese people some *reward* for that sacrifice or some *attractive
> alternative gain.*

The Americans replied that Japan stood to gain more by following a "progressive and constructive program of peace in the entire Pacific than by any
other course," but the Japanese showed no comprehension of that alternative.

Nomura was no diplomat, and his inadvertencies of the sort quoted above
probably explain his virtual supersedure in November by Kurusu. But he had
only put into words what was apparent to Hull if not to Grew: that Japan
allowed the United States no alternative to appeasement.

Attempts of other Japanese officials, quite skilled in diplomacy, to plead
ignorance of American desires and mystification by the statement of October
2, also broke down. The Minister-Counselor of the Japanese Embassy, Wakasugi, had recently returned from Japan, and, on October 13, in conversation
with Under Secretary Welles, he at first repeated the refrain that the Japanese
government found it impossible to learn what "in reality" were the desires of
the United States. Then Wakasugi not only specified those desires with the
greatest clarity, but seemed to promise that the Japanese government would
satisfy them. He said the Japanese promise in the draft proposal not to undertake further aggressive action could be made without the qualification "save
for justifiable reasons," because that phrase "was entirely unnecessary and
could readily be withdrawn." He said the Japanese government would be
"entirely willing" to meet the American objection to omitting China from
the commitment in favor of commercial equality in the Pacific region.
Wakasugi asked whether the United States could not agree to leave to Japan
"discretion" in interpreting its obligations under the Axis alliance. He realized
a new Cabinet might interpret its obligations dfferently, but the present one
was the only Cabinet which could be set up that would desire to remain at

peace with the United States if the United States entered the European war. He said that the Japanese government was "willing to evacuate all of its troops from China." Welles thought he had misunderstood this last statement, but Wakasugi repeated it twice. Welles was furthermore assured that all the "controlling" Japanese Generals and Admirals fully supported the Japanese government in desiring to make a "comprehensive and satisfactory" agreement with the United States.

Wakasugi emphasized to Welles that he spoke "unofficially." But his statements on aggression, trade, and evacuation of China hit the precise points of the chief objections of Hull and Roosevelt to the Japanese proposals of September 6 and 22, and, since he had just returned from Japan, where he had presumably learned the views of his government, his statements to Welles on October 13 demolished the pretense that the Japanese did not understand what the United States "in reality" wanted.

Wakasugi said he believed his government must reach a final decision within twenty-four or forty-eight hours. Grew was informed of Wakasugi's remarkable statements to Welles. On October 15 he talked with the Japanese Vice Minister for Foreign Affairs "off the record," but, as Grew reported to Washington, "along lines largely parallel to" the Wakasugi-Welles conversation on October 13. A day later, October 16, the Konoye cabinet fell and the "Pearl Harbor" government took power with General Hideki Tojo as Premier and Shigenori Togo as Foreign Minister.

Wakasugi promptly changed front. He had appointments with Welles on October 16 and 17, and the Under Secretary took him to Hull for conversations on both days. According to Secretary Hull's memorandum, Wakasugi "sought to keep in harmony with his talks with Under Secretary Welles," but he actually hedged on the main points of evacuating China, nondiscrimination in the whole Pacific, and interpretation of the Axis alliance. The net result was to return the situation to the impasse preceding Wakasugi's strange statements to Welles on October 13. The tone of Hull's memorandum makes obvious the Secretary's impatience with Wakasugi's zigzag. If the October 13 "unofficial" statements meant anything, the new government of Tojo repudiated them. Hull wrote: "The upshot . . . left us with the view that the new Japanese Government would have to speak next and before we had further serious conversations with their representatives here."

The October 13 statements of Wakasugi might have been taken more seriously but for several circumstances. Toyoda had already told Grew on October 10 that because Ambassador Nomura seemed "very fatigued," a diplomat of wide experience would be sent to Washington to "assist" him. This was as much as to say that the existing Japanese delegation in Washington was repudiated. The fall of the Konoye Cabinet was already in sight. Japan was sending large new contingents of troops into Indo-China, building new air bases there, and displacing the Vichy French administrators with Japanese officials. This, as the Japanese government was told, constituted "a complete negation of the spirit and letter of the undertakings which the Japanese

Government expresses willingness to assume." Magic intercepts showed that Germany, after Roosevelt's September 11 "shoot on sight" order, applied extreme pressure on the Japanese government. One of Foreign Minister Toyoda's last acts was to send Nomura instructions, amounting to a weak version of German demands, that the United States be warned of trouble with Japan if the United States continued to "attack" the Axis powers.

In the light of these ominous events, Wakasugi's statements to Welles take on the appearance of a mistake arising from the confusion attendant upon the impending fall of Konoye. Far from working for agreement with the United States, the Konoye government in the main was attempting to stave off its overthrow by conceding to the demands of the militarists. The "mistake" is nevertheless an extremely valuable part of the record. First, it proves that the Japanese knew precisely what was necessary to bring about a Roosevelt-Konoye meeting and settlement with the United States. Second, the "mistake" and Japan's draft proposals prove that the Japanese consciously designed the escape clauses in the draft proposals to leave no room for Grew's policy of "constructive conciliation" short of American cooperation to help Japan win the fruits of aggression.

THE LAST CHANCE?

The coming to power of Tojo ended talk of a meeting between Roosevelt and the Japanese Premier. The administration in its efforts to maintain the secrecy of the negotiations, efforts insisted upon by the Japanese who feared the effects of publicity in rousing the militarists, had publicly denied that Prince Konoye had "invited" Roosevelt to a Pacific conference. It was true that the stage of issuing an invitation was never reached. Beard treats the administration's uncommunicativeness as part of its plot to deceive the public by maintaining false "appearances." In his exposition of the "realities" of the affair, Beard declares that Roosevelt and Hull not only pursued the "usual policy" of secrecy, but employed "dilatory" methods. Ambassador Grew's arguments in favor of "constructive conciliation" are Beard's chief evidence in support of his implication that Roosevelt and Hull wanted no reasonable settlement with Japan. But it is noteworthy that after carefully implanting in his reader's mind suspicion that Roosevelt and Hull deliberately rejected a reasonable opportunity for a settlement with Japan, Beard disclaims responsibility for arousing such suspicion by remarking that sufficient documents are not available for judgment. He admits that it is possible to find bases for argument *for*, as well as against Roosevelt's refusal to meet Konoye. Beard excuses his own failure to use the documents that are available because the " 'solution' of this insoluble 'problem' " lay outside the "purposes and limitations" of his book. After calling the Roosevelt-Konoye affair "momentous in the history of American relations with Japan," Beard's evasion of the problem, which would seem to be no more insoluble and is far more adequately documented than most of the problems he claims to solve, is disappointing.

Perhaps Beard had been discouraged by the statement in the Minority Report of the Pearl Harbor Joint Committee, that to go into the issue of the wisdom of the Roosevelt administration in its conduct of relations with Japan,

would involve the committee in the complexities of history extending back more than 50 years and in matters of opinion which cannot be settled by reference to anything as positive and definite as the Constitution, laws, and established administrative practices of the United States government.

Besides, the question was excluded by the terms of the Committee's instructions. But the Committee did not fail to develop information on the subject in order to "understand the questions involved." . . .

It cannot be admitted that with Konoye's fall the last chance of avoiding war with Japan disappeared. If the Roosevelt administration had been willing to support Japan's past and future program of aggression, the Tojo government would very likely have been happy to drop the plan to attack the United States, at least temporarily. The actions of Roosevelt and Hull lead one to assume that they believed the risk of new Japanese aggressions was preferable to a profoundly immoral Far Eastern Munich. History had proved that appeasement was not only immoral but also that aggressors could not be permanently appeased. The most that could have been accomplished by a Far Eastern Munich was to postpone a little longer new Japanese aggressions. This was no temptation for Roosevelt and Hull because it would be more than balanced by the degradation of the American and all free peoples, because it would violate the American commitment in the Lend Lease Act to aid peaceful nations against aggression, and because it was in any case politically impossible: the great majority of the American people long since had given up indifference to immorality in international relations.

The Decision to Drop the Bomb:

WAS IT JUSTIFIED?

It was clear to American strategists that the defeat of Japan would be achieved only after the Japanese homeland had been conquered. The Japanese would never surrender until a last stand was made on their own soil. To achieve victory, therefore, a campaign had to be launched against the home islands. Before that could be done, however, American forces had to dislodge the Japanese from their insular bases in the Pacific: the Solomons, New Guinea, and the Philippines in the Southwest Pacific; the Marshalls, Carolines, and Marianas in the Central Pacific. The fighting was tough and bloody. By the end of 1944, American air force units were engaged in a heavy bombardment of the homeland. By early 1945, the perimeter surrounding Japan was being narrowed—Okinawa and Iwo Jima were occupied: the former in June; the latter in March. The assault on Japan proper was being readied. At the conference of the Allied powers at Potsdam in July, 1945, the Allies gave Japan a final opportunity to surrender. She refused. Thereupon, President Truman decided to use the atomic bomb. The first one was dropped on Hiroshima on August 6, 1945; the second on Nagasaki three days later. On August 14, Prime Minister Suzuki yielded. Was the dropping of the bomb necessary for victory? Did it hasten the end of the war? Did it contribute to a more secure peace? Since that day in August, 1945, Americans have sought an answer to these questions.

Hanson W. Baldwin, one of the most widely read military critics and the military editor of The New York Times, answers with an emphatic No. The bomb was not necessary for victory, it did not greatly hasten the end of the war, and it did not help to promote a secure peace. Baldwin points out that at the time the bomb was dropped, Japan was practically finished. Her productive capacity had been so diminished that it could no longer supply the war machine. Food was short and raw materials were scarce. Her position was hopeless; the bomb was unnecessary. As for hastening the end of the war, the bomb may have brought victory closer, but only by a few days—not enough to justify so horrible a weapon. Finally, it deeply affected future relations between victor and vanquished. The Japanese would never forget American ruthlessness.

A different judgment is rendered by Herbert Feis, for many years a State Department official and the author of a series of historical works on World War II. While stating that in his view the bomb was not essential for victory, he makes it clear that the policy makers at the time considered it necessary. The leaders estimated that American losses would be in the millions if the Japanese were invaded, inasmuch as they expected a fierce, suicidal last-ditch stand from the Japanese. The bomb, they believed, was needed to save American lives. Feis does not think that any justification is really needed, however. During wartime a belligerent has the right to use any weapon that is not specifically banned. All the belligerents strove to perfect more destructive weapons, and any one of them would have used the atomic bomb had it been available. Indeed, he maintains that the peace may well have been enhanced by the bomb's use. It probably spurred the development of the United Nations in the sense that the need for international accord and organization appeared more urgent with such a mighty weapon at hand. It may also have helped to bridle extremists in the Soviet Union.

The Atomic Bomb—
The Penalty of Expediency

HANSON W. BALDWIN

THE UTILIZATION of the atomic bomb against a prostrate and defeated Japan in the closing days of the war exemplifies—even more graphically than any of the mistakes previously recounted—the narrow, astigmatic concentration of our planners upon one goal, and one alone: victory.

Nowhere in all of Mr. Stimson's forceful and eloquent apologia for the leveling of Hiroshima and Nagasaki is there any evidence of an ulterior vision; indeed, the entire effort of his famous Harper's article, reprinted and rearranged in his book, *On Active Service* is focused on proving that the bomb hastened the end of the war. But at what cost!

To accept the Stimson thesis that the atomic bomb should have been used as it was used, it is necessary first to accept the contention that the atomic bomb achieved or hastened victory, and second, and more important, that it helped to consolidate the peace or to further the political aims for which war was fought.

History can accept neither contention.

Let us examine the first. The atomic bomb was dropped in August. Long before that month started our forces were securely based in Okinawa, the Marianas and Iwo Jima; Germany had been defeated; our fleet had been cruising off the Japanese coast with impunity bombarding the shoreline; our submarines were operating in the Sea of Japan; even inter-island ferries had been attacked and sunk. Bombing, which started slowly in June, 1944, from China bases and from the Marianas in November, 1944, had been increased materially in 1945, and by August, 1945, more than 16,000 tons of bombs had ravaged Japanese cities. Food was short; mines and submarines and surface vessels and planes clamped an iron blockade around the main islands; raw materials were scarce. Blockade, bombing, and unsuccessful attempts at dispersion had reduced Japanese production capacity from 20 to 60 per cent. The enemy, in a military sense, was in a hopeless strategic position by the time the Potsdam demand for unconditional surrender was made on July 26.

Such, then, was the situation when we wiped out Hiroshima and Nagasaki.

Need we have done it? No one can, of course, be positive, but the answer is almost certainly negative.

The invasion of Japan, which Admiral Leahy had opposed as too wasteful of American blood, and in any case unnecessary, was scheduled (for the southern island of Kyushu) for Nov. 1, 1945, to be followed if necessary, in the spring of 1946, by a major landing on the main island of Honshu. We dropped the two atomic bombs in early August, almost two months before our first D-Day. The decision to drop them, after the Japanese rejection of the Potsdam ultimatum, was a pretty hasty one. It followed the recommendations of Secretary Stimson and an "Interim Committee" of distinguished officials and scientists, who had found "no acceptable alternative to direct military use."

But the weakness of this statement is inherent, for none was tried and "military use" of the bomb was undertaken despite strong opposition to this course by numerous scientists and Japanese experts, including former Ambassador Joseph Grew. Not only was the Potsdam ultimatum merely a restatement of the politically impossible—unconditional surrender—but it could hardly be construed as a direct warning of the atomic bomb and was not taken as such by anyone who did not know the bomb had been created. A technical demonstration of the bomb's power may well have been unfeasible, but certainly a far more definite warning could have been given; and it is hard to believe that a target objective in Japan with but sparse population could not have been found. The truth is we did not try; we gave no specific warning. There were almost two months before our scheduled invasion of Kyushu, in which American ingenuity could have found ways to bring home to the Japanese the impossibility of their position and the horrors of the weapon being held over them; yet we rushed to use the bomb as soon as unconditional surrender was rejected. Had we devised some demonstration or given a more specific warning than the Potsdam ultimatum, and had the Japanese still persisted in continued resistance after some weeks of our psychological offensive, we should perhaps have been justified in the bomb's use; at least, our hands would have been more clean.

But, in fact, our only warning to a Japan already militarily defeated, and in a hopeless situation, was the Potsdam demand for unconditional surrender issued on July 26, when we knew Japanese surrender attempts had started. Yet when the Japanese surrender was negotiated about two weeks later, after the bomb was dropped, our unconditional surrender demand was made conditional and we agreed, as Stimson had originally proposed we should do, to continuation of the Emperor upon his imperial throne.

We were, therefore, twice guilty. We dropped the bomb at a time when Japan already was negotiating for an end of the war but before those negotiations could come to fruition. We demanded unconditional surrender, then dropped the bomb and accepted conditional surrender, a sequence which indicates pretty clearly that the Japanese would have surrendered, even if the bomb had not been dropped, had the Potsdam Declaration included our promise to permit the Emperor to remain on his imperial throne.

What we now know of the condition of Japan, and of the days preceding her final surrender on Aug. 15, verifies these conclusions. It is clear, in retrospect (and was understood by some, notably Admiral Leahy, at the time), that Japan was militarily on her last legs. Yet our intelligence estimates greatly overstated her strength.

The background for surrender had been sketched in fully, well before the bombs were dropped, and the Strategic Bombing Survey declares that "interrogation of the highest Japanese officials, following V-J Day, indicated that Japan would have surrendered . . . even . . . if the atomic bombs had not been dropped." "Even before the large-scale bombing of Japan was initiated, the raw material base of Japanese industry was effectively undermined. An accelerated decline of armament production was inevitable."

Admiral Chester W. Nimitz, in a talk to the National Geographic Society on January 25, 1946, declared, "I am convinced that the complete impunity with which the Pacific Fleet pounded Japan at point-blank range was the decisive factor in forcing the Japanese to ask the Russians to approach us for peace proposals in July.

"Meanwhile, aircraft from our new fields in the Okinawa group were daily shuttling back and forth over Kyushu and Shokoku and B-29's of the Twentieth Air Force were fire-bombing major Japanese cities. The pace and the fury were mounting and the government of Japan, as its official spokesmen have now admitted, were looking for a way to end the war. At this point the Potsdam Ultimatum was delivered and the Japanese knew their choice.

"They were debating that choice when the atomic bomb fell on Hiroshima. They were debating that choice when our ships shelled installations within less than 100 miles of Tokyo. . . .

"The atomic bomb merely hastened a process already reaching an inevitable conclusion. . . ."

There can be no doubt that this conclusion of Admiral Nimitz will be the verdict of history. Militarily, we "killed" Japan in many different ways: by crushing defeats at sea and on land; by the strangulation of the blockade of which the principal instrument was the submarine; by bombing with conventional bombs. After the seizure of Okinawa—probably even before that—the blockade alone could have defeated Japan; was, indeed, defeating her. Admiral Leahy was right; invasion was not necessary.

By the time "intensive strategic bombing" of the home islands began in March, 1945, production of military supplies in Japan "was already 20 per cent below its peak." And this drop reached 50 per cent by July, 1945. Lack of steel and other minerals, and the inherent industrial weakness of Japan relative to her enemies, doomed the Japs. Japan was just too weak for the war she waged; her ambitions exceeded her capacity.

"Aircraft production from 1942 on (long before either blockade or bombing had become effective) never reached a level sufficient to allow the Japanese to obtain air superiority in any of the contested areas. . . .

"Production of weapons and ammunition for ground troops was not sufficient to keep line troops supplied, to fill the long sea lines, and to maintain adequate stocks in reserve. . . .

"Motor vehicles were never in sufficient supply. . . ."

In the words of a well known Japanese correspondent, Masuo Kato, who was in Washington for the Domei News Agency when the war started: "The thunderous arrival of the first atomic bomb at Hiroshima was only a *coup de grâce* for an empire already struggling in particularly agonizing death throes. The world's newest and most devastating of weapons had floated out of the summer sky to destroy a city at a stroke, but its arrival had small effect on the outcome of the war between Japan and the United Nations."

It is therefore clear today—and was clear to many even as early as the spring of 1945—that the military defeat of Japan was certain; the atomic bomb was not needed.

But if the bomb did not procure victory, did it hasten it?

This question cannot be answered with equal precision, particularly since the full story of the Japanese surrender attempts has not been compiled. But a brief chronology of known events indicates that the atomic bomb may have shortened the war by a few days—not more.

The day before Christmas, 1944 (two months *before* the Yalta conference), U.S. intelligence authorities in Washington received a report from a confidential agent in Japan that a peace party was emerging and that the Koiso cabinet would soon be succeeded by a cabinet headed by Admiral Baron Suzuki who would initiate surrender proceedings.

The Koiso cabinet *was* succeeded by a new government headed by Suzuki in early April, 1945, but even prior to this significant change, the Japanese— in February, 1945—had approached the Russians with a request that they act as intermediary in arranging a peace with the Western powers. The Russian Ambassador, Malik, in Tokyo, was the channel of the approach. The Russians, however, set their price of mediation so high that the Japanese temporarily dropped the matter. The United States was not officially informed of this approach until after the end of the war.

Prior to, coincident with, and after this February attempt, ill-defined peace approaches were made through the Japanese Ambassadors in Stockholm and Moscow, particularly Moscow. These approaches were so informal, and to some extent represented to such a degree the personal initiative of the two Ambassadors concerned, that they never came to a head.

But after a meeting with Stalin in Moscow on May 27, before the trial A-bomb was even tested in New Mexico, Harry Hopkins cabled President Truman that:

"1. Japan is doomed and the Japanese know it.

"2. Peace feelers are being put out by certain elements in Japan. . . ."

In April, 1945, as the United States was establishing a foothold on Okinawa, the Russians in effect denounced their neutrality agreement with Japan, and from then until July 12, the new cabinet was moving rapidly toward surrender attempts.

On July 12, fourteen days before we issued the Potsdam Proclamation, these attempts reached a clearly defined point. Prince Konoye was received by the Emperor on that day and ordered to Moscow as a peace plenipotentiary to "secure peace at any price." On July 13, Moscow was notified officially by the Japanese foreign office that the "Emperor was desirous of peace."

It was hoped that Moscow would inform the United States and Britain at the Potsdam conference of Japan's desire to discuss peace. But instead of an answer from the "Big Three," Ambassador Sato in Moscow was told by Molotov on August 8 of Russia's entry into the war against Japan, effective immediately.

However, since early May—well before this disappointing denouement to the most definite peace attempts the Japanese had yet made—the six-man Supreme War Direction Council in Japan had been discussing peace. On June 20, the Emperor told the (Supreme War Direction) Council that it "was necessary to have a plan to close the war at once as well as a plan to defend the home islands."

The Council was deadlocked three to three, and Premier Suzuki, to break the deadlock, had decided to summon a Gozenkaigi (a meeting of "Elder Statesmen," summoned only in hours of crises) at which the Emperor himself could make the decision for peace or further war. Suzuki knew his Emperor's mind; Hirohito had been convinced for some weeks that peace was the only answer to Japan's ordeal.

The first atomic bomb was dropped on Hiroshima on August 6; Russia entered the war on August 8; and the second atomic bomb was dropped on Nagasaki on August 9. The dropping of the first bomb, and the Russian entry into the war, gave Suzuki additional arguments for again putting the issue before the Supreme War Direction Council, and, on August 9, he won their approval for the Gozenkaigi. But neither the people of Japan nor their leaders were as impressed with the atomic bomb as were we. The public did not know until after the war what had happened to Hiroshima; and even so, they had endured fire raids against Tokyo which had caused more casualties than the atomic bomb and had devastated a greater area than that destroyed at Hiroshima. The Supreme War Direction Council was initially told that a fragment of the Hiroshima bomb indicated that it was made in Germany (!), that it appeared to be a conventional explosive of great power, and that there was only one bomb available. When the Gozenkaigi actually was held on August 14, five days after the second bomb was dropped, War Minister Anami and the chiefs of the Army and Navy General Staff—three members of the War Council who had been adamant for continuation of the war— were still in favor of continuing it; those who had wanted peace still wanted it. In other words, the bomb changed no opinions; the Emperor himself, who had already favored peace, broke the deadlock.

"If nobody else has any opinion to express," Hirohito said, "we would ·express our own. We demand that you will agree to it. We see only one way left for Japan to save herself. That is the reason we have made this determination to endure the unendurable and suffer the insufferable."

In the words of Harry F. Kern, managing editor of *Newsweek*, who had made a special study, with the assistance of *Newsweek* correspondents, of the events surrounding the Japanese surrender:

"I think it's fair to say that the principal effect of the atom bomb on the Japanese surrender was to provide Suzuki with the immediate excuse for setting in motion the chain of events which resulted in the surrender." (An "excuse" was necessary—as the attempted military coup, following the Gozen-kaigi of August 14, showed—if the leaders of the "peace party" were to avoid assassination at the hands of the rabid militarists of the "war party.")

"However, I think it is also a reasonable surmise that the Russian declaration of war would have served the same purpose, and that the dropping of the bomb was therefore unnecessary. In no case was the dropping of the bomb the reason for the Japanese surrender, and I don't think we can say that it acted as anything more than a catalyst in advancing the plans of Suzuki and his supporters."

Or, as the Strategic Bombing Survey puts it, "it is the Survey's opinion that certainly prior to December 31, 1945, and in all probability prior to November 1, 1945, Japan would have surrendered even if the atomic bombs had not been dropped, even if Russia had not entered the war, and even if no invasion had been planned or contemplated."

This seems, in the light of history, a reasonable judgment, and, in view of our available intelligence estimates, one that we could have then made. It is quite possible that the atomic bombs shortened the war by a day, a week, or a month or two—not more.

But at what a price! For whether or not the atomic bomb hastened victory, it is quite clear it has not won the peace.

Some may point to the comparative tranquility of Japan under MacArthur in the postwar period as due in part to the terror of American arms created by the bomb. This is scarcely so; Japan's seeming tranquility is a surface one which has been furthered by a single occupation authority and the nature of the Japanese people. But I venture to estimate that those who suffered at Hiroshima and Nagasaki will never forget it, and that we sowed there a whirl-wind of hate which we shall someday reap.

In estimating the effect of the use of the bomb upon the peace, we must remember, first, that we used the bomb for one purpose, and one only: not to secure a more equable peace, but to hasten victory. By using the bomb we have become identified, rightfully or wrongly, as inheritors of the mantle of Genghis Khan and all those of past history who have justified the use of utter ruthlessness in war.

It may well be argued, of course, that war—least of all modern war—knows no humanity, no rules, and no limitations, and that death by the atomic bomb is no worse than death by fire bombs or high explosives or gas or flame throwers. It is, of course, true that the atomic bomb is no worse qualitatively than other lethal weapons; it is merely quantitatively more powerful; other weapons cause death in fearful ways; the atomic bomb caused more deaths. We already had utilized fire raids, mass bombardment of cities, and flame throwers in the name of expediency and victory prior to August 6, even though many of our people had recoiled from such practices.

Even as late as June 1, 1945, Stimson "had sternly questioned his Air Forces leader, wanting to know whether the apparently indiscriminate bombings of Tokyo were absolutely necessary. Perhaps, as he [Stimson] later said, he was misled by the constant talk of 'precision bombing,' but he had believed that even air power could be limited in its use by the old concept of 'legitimate military targets.' Now in the conflagration bombings by massed B-29's, he was permitting a kind of total war he had always hated, and in recommending the use of the atomic bomb he was implicitly confessing that there could be no significant limits to the horror of modern war."

If we accept this confession—that there can be no limits set to modern war—we must also accept the bitter inheritance of Genghis Khan and the mantles of all the other ruthless despoilers of the past.

In reality, we took up where these great conquerors left off long before we dropped the atomic bomb. Americans, in their own eyes, are a naively idealistic people, with none of the crass ruthlessness so often exhibited by other nations. Yet in the eyes of others our record is very far from clean, nor can objective history palliate it. Rarely have we been found on the side of restricting horror; too often we have failed to support the feeble hands of those who would limit war. We did not ratify the Hague convention of 1899, outlawing the use of dumdum (expanding) bullets in war. We never ratified the Geneva Protocol of 1925, outlawing the use of biological agents and gas in war. At the time the war in the Pacific ended, pressure for the use of gas against Japanese island positions had reached the open discussion stage, and rationalization was leading surely to justification, an expedient justification since we had air superiority and the means to deluge the enemy with gas, while he had no similar way to reply. We condemned the Japanese for their alleged use of biological agents against the Chinese, yet in July and August, 1945, a shipload of U.S. biological agents for use in destruction of the Japanese rice crop was en route to the Marianas. And even before the war, our fundamental theory of air war, like the Trenchard school of Britain, coincided, or stemmed from, the Douchet doctrine of destructiveness: the bombardment of enemy cities and peoples.

Yet surely these methods—particularly the extension of unrestricted warfare to enemy civilians—defeated any peace aims we might have had, and had little appreciable effect in hastening military victory. For in any totalitarian state, the leaders rather than the peoples must be convinced of defeat, and the indiscriminate use of mass or area weapons, like biological agents and the atomic bomb, strike at the people, not the rulers. We cannot succeed, therefore, by such methods, in drawing that fine line between ruler and ruled that ought to be drawn in every war; we cannot hasten military victory by slaughtering the led; such methods only serve to bind the led closer to their leaders. Moreover, unrestricted warfare can never lay the groundwork for a more stable peace. Its heritage may be the salt-sown fields of Carthage, or the rubble and ruin of a Berlin or Tokyo or Hiroshima; but neither economically nor psychologically can unrestricted warfare—atomic warfare or biological warfare—lead anywhere save to eventual disaster.

During the last conflict we brought new horror to the meaning of war; the ruins of Germany and Japan, the flame-scarred tissues of the war-wounded attest our efficiency. And on August 6, 1945, that blinding flash above Hiroshima wrote a climax to an era of American expediency. On that date we joined the list of those who had introduced new and horrible weapons for the extermination of man; we joined the Germans who had first utilized gas, the Japanese with their biological agents, the Huns and the Mongols who had made destruction a fine art.

It is my contention that in the eyes of the world the atomic bomb has cost us dearly; we have lost morally; we no longer are the world's moral leader as in the days of the Wilsonian Fourteen Points. It is my contention that the unlimited destruction caused by our unlimited methods of waging war has caused us heavy economic losses in the forms of American tax subsidies to Germany and Japan. It is my contention that unrestricted warfare and unlimited aims cost us politically the winning of the peace.

But it is not only—and perhaps not chiefly—in public opinion or in the public pocketbook or even in public stability that we have suffered, but in our own souls. The American public is tending to accept the nefarious doctrine that the ends justify the means, the doctrine of exigency. What we have done to ourselves—and Hiroshima and Nagasaki were heavy blows to a weakening moral structure—can best be expressed in the words of the following editorial from the Bulletin of the Atomic Scientists:

In the first World War, American public opinion was shocked by the sinking of passenger-carrying ships by German submarines; in the second World War, American submarines sank all Japanese ships on sight, and even the revelation that one of these ships was carrying American prisoners of war, has brought no belated wave of indignation at home. The Germans began the terror bombing of cities. The American propaganda long stuck to the pretense that we bombed only "military objectives" (with "pin-point" accuracy). Probably, this was done out of consideration for public opinion; but this concern proved to be excessive. Public opinion in America as well as elsewhere has long since accepted terror bombing of whole cities as legitimate means of warfare. So conditioned, it was able to "take" the news of the destruction of Hiroshima and Nagasaki almost without qualms. Is it not legitimate to predict that if another war comes, no public indignation will meet an announcement of a successful use of psitaccosis virus, or of the wiping-out of enemy crops by chemicals, or poisoning of drinking water in the enemy's capital by radioactive poisons?

In mass fire and bomb raids on German and Japanese cities, America has won the leadership in this form of terror warfare; in the atomic bombardment of Hiroshima (arranged so as to inflict the maximum number of civilian casualties), we have compounded the terror of aerial war a thousandfold.

The use of the atomic bomb, therefore, cost us dearly; we are now branded with the mark of the beast. Its use may have hastened victory—though by very little—but it has cost us in peace and pre-eminent moral position we once occupied. Japan's economic troubles are in some degree the result of unnecessary devastation. We have embarked upon Total War with a vengeance; we have done our best to make it far more total. If we do not soon reverse this trend, if we do not cast about for means to limit and control war, if we do not abandon the doctrine of expediency, of unconditional surrender, of total victory, we shall someday ourselves become the victims of our own theories and practices.

Such mistakes as those outlined in these pages—the attempt to find total victory, to inflict absolute destruction, to use unlimited means, and to mistake military victory for political victory—have been heretofore in history the peculiar characteristics of totalitarian or dictator-led states. The long view, the greatest good of the greatest number, a desire for world tranquilization and peace, have never characterized absolute rulers.

One reflection from a prison cell by the German General Kleist ought to be emblazoned above every doorway in the Pentagon and in the State Department:

"The German mistake was to think that a military success would solve political problems. Indeed, under the Nazis we tend to reverse Clausewitz's dictum, and to regard peace as a continuation of war."

Comments and Conjectures on the Use of the Atomic Bomb against Japan

HERBERT FEIS

AT THE TIME of the event, only a group of contributing scientists protested the use of the atomic bomb against a vulnerable live target. The people of the nations allied against Japan were awed by the release of energy of the atom, but they looked upon its employment against the enemy as a natural

Reprinted from *Japan Subdued* by Herbert Feis by permission of Princeton University Press. Copyright 1961 by Princeton University Press, all rights reserved.

act of war. Such doubts as may have entered their minds were routed by the thought that if Germans or Japanese had developed this weapon they would surely have used it. Subsequently, however, as the blast and radiation effects of this new projectile were more fully appreciated, and as more and more powerful kinds were spawned in the factories of the United States and the Soviet Union, the precedent act has been regarded by many with rue.

In the evolving discussion, various related but separable questions have been commingled. The first of these, and by far the easiest to answer, is whether it was *essential* to use the bomb in order to compel the Japanese to surrender on our terms within a few months. It was not. That ought to have been obvious even at the time of decision, but to most of the men concerned with the decision, especially those in the army, it does not seem to have been. For their military histories had told the story of how the hopelessly beaten Confederate army had battled on, and they had witnessed the refusal of the German army to give up long after any chance of winning was gone, and how the German people had not only survived but rallied from the shattering attacks upon their cities. But now it is obvious. There can hardly be a well-grounded dissent from the conclusion reached by the members of the U.S. Strategic Bombing Survey after their inspection of the condition to which Japan had been reduced by the summer of 1945. From its studies of Japanese resources, military position, and ruling politics, the Survey estimated "that certainly prior to 31 December 1945, and in all probability prior to 1 November 1945, Japan would have surrendered even if the atomic bombs had not been dropped, even if Russia had not entered the war and even if no invasion had been planned or contemplated."

If, then, use of the bomb was not essential, was it justified—justified, that is, as the surest way, in combination with other measures, to bring about the earliest surrender? That is a harder question to answer, harder now than it seemed to be at the time of decision.

It may be contended with assurance supported by history that no justification for the use of the bomb is needed, since the accepted and ruling attitude sanctions the use of any and all weapons in war except any banned by explicit international agreement. Did not every one of the contending nations strive its utmost to invent and produce more effective weapons: faster planes of greater bomb capacity, new types of mines, rockets and buzz-bombs; and were not each and every one brought into action without ado or reproach? Almost all professional military men, and probably almost all men in uniform in 1945, would then have denied that any justification was needed, and would still dispose of the subject in this way. They might add, as well, that the decision to use the bomb was not really important; that the measures of permanent significance to mankind had been taken when physicists learned how to split the atom, and when the scientists and engineers and builders succeeded in embodying the energy of the fissured atom in a bomb; and that after these were achieved, it made little or no difference if this novel weapon was used against Japan, since it would certainly be used in the future time unless nations renounced war. Or if it were not, other equally dreadful threats would remain: chemical and biological ways of bringing death; and these were already in the secret arsenals of nations.

The source of restraint lies in fear of consequences; fear of the fact that the enemy will use the terrible weapon. This was, for example, why neither side used poison gas in the war. When humane feeling is allied to such fear it may command respect, and even those striving to win a war may recognize that "virtue it is to abstain even from that which is lawful."

Our right, legal and historical, to use the bomb may thus be well defended; but those who made the decision to use it were not much concerned over these considerations, taking them for granted. Their thoughts about its employment were governed by one reason which was deemed imperative: that by using the bomb, the agony of war might be ended most quickly and many lives be saved. It was believed that thousands, probably tens of thousands, of lives would have to be spent in the continuation of our air and sea bombardment and blockade, victims mainly of Japanese suicide planes.

In spite of its confidence in ultimate success, the assailant force felt vulnerable, because of grim and agonizing experience. Since the desperate kamikaze attack began, suicide planes had sunk 34 American ships, including 3 aircraft carriers, and damaged 285 (including 36 carriers of all sizes and sorts, 15 battleships, 15 cruisers, and 87 destroyers). During the Okinawa campaign alone 16 of our ships had been sunk, and 185 damaged (including 7 carriers, 10 battleships, and 5 cruisers).

It was reliably known that the Japanese were assembling thousands of planes, of all kinds and conditions, to fling against the invasion fleet and the troop-carrying ships.[1]

Thus if it proved necessary to carry out the plans for invasion, the losses might mount to hundreds of thousands. Our allies, it was reckoned, would suffer a corresponding loss of life—the men in the naval and air groups of the British Commonwealth, if they had to engage in amphibious operations in Southeast Asia; and the soldiers in the Red Army if they had to fight on until they smashed the Kwantung Army in its last stand in Southeastern Manchuria and Korea.

But the people who would have suffered most, if the war went on much

---

[1] According to Samuel Eliot Morison, in mid-August "Although 2550 kamikaze planes had been expended, there were 5350 of them still left, together with as many more ready for orthodox use and 7000 under repair or in storage; and 5000 young men were training for the Kamikaze Corps." Article in *Atlantic Monthly*, October 1960, "Why Japan Surrendered." This is a much higher estimate of actual usable Japanese air strength than others I have seen, but I leave the task of confirming or contradicting it to military historians who are better acquainted with all the Japanese records.

longer and if their country was invaded, were the Japanese. One American incendiary air raid on the Tokyo area in March 1945 did more damage and killed and injured more Japanese than at Hiroshima. Had the war continued, even greater groups of American bombing planes would have hovered over Japan, consuming their land and its people with blast and fire, leaving them no place to hide, no chance to rest, no hope of reprieve. A glance at the charts kept in the Headquarters of the U.S. Strategic Air Force at Guam, with its steeply ascending record of bombing flights during the summer of 1945 and scheduled for the next month or two, leaves visions of horror of which Hiroshima is only a local illustration.

The primary and sustaining aim from the start of the great exertion to make the bomb was military, and the impelling reason for the decision to use it was military—to end the war victoriously as soon as possible. The whole record bespeaks this fact, and leading participants in the decision had attested to its truth.

General Groves, the Commanding General of the Manhattan Project: "My mission as given to me by Secretary of War Stimson [in October 1942] was to produce this [the atomic bomb] at the earliest possible date so as to bring the war to a conclusion."

Truman: "I regarded the bomb as a military weapon and never had any doubt that it should be used."

Churchill: "The historic fact remains . . . that the decision whether or not to use the atomic bomb to compel the surrender of Japan was never even an issue. There was unanimous, automatic, unquestioned agreement around our table; nor did I ever hear the slightest suggestion that we should do otherwise."

Stimson: "Stimson believed, both at the time and later, that the dominant fact of 1945 was war, and that therefore, necessarily, the dominant objective was victory. If victory could be speeded by using the bomb, it should be used; if victory must be delayed in order to use the bomb, it should *not* be used. So far as he knew, this general view was fully shared by the President and all his associates."

Some of those men who concurred in the decision to use the bomb discerned other advantages and justifications. It may be also—but this is only conjecture—that Churchill and Truman and some of their colleagues conceived that besides bringing the war to a quick end, it would improve the chances of arranging a satisfactory peace. For would not the same dramatic proof of western power that shocked Japan into surrender impress the Russians also? Might it not influence them to be more restrained? Might it not make more effective the resistance of the western allies to excessive Soviet pretensions and ventures, such as the Soviet bids for a military base in the Black Sea Straits, and a part in the occupation and control Japan akin to that which it had in Germany? If these conjectures have any basis in actuality, they would provide another justification for using the bomb as a military weapon. We were not only subduing Japanese aggressors; we were perhaps monitoring the emergent Russian aggression.

Recognition of this tendency must not be distorted into an accusation that the American government engaged in what Soviet propagandists and historians have called "atomic blackmail." To the contrary, the American government remained intently desirous of preserving the friendly connection with the Soviet Union. It had rejected Churchill's proposal to face down the Soviet government in some climactic confrontation over the outward thrust of Soviet power. It showed throughout the Conference at Potsdam, which preceded the use of the bomb, a patient disposition to arrive at compromises with the Soviet government. In brief, the purposes of the men who determined American policy were directed toward achieving a stable international order by peaceful ways, not swayed by excited thought or wish of imposing our will on the rest of the world by keeping atomic bombs poised over their lives.

The train of inference about other confluent thoughts that may have figured in the minds of those who supported the decision to use the bomb may be carried further. The scientists who served on the Interim Committee, Conant and Bush and Compton, and others who were on the Scientific Panel, were gravely aware of the lasting significance of the achievement. Stimson, Chairman of the Interim Committee, sharing their perception of the bearing upon human destiny, was impelled, despite age and fatigue, to write memo after memo expounding his conviction that every effort must be exerted to get the nations to cooperate to prevent impending mutual destruction.

These first official parents of this new form of force verged toward the conclusion that the world had no alternative; renunciation of the resort to war would be the condition of human survival. But would the nations defer to that reality unless the horrifying power of this new weapon to destroy human life was proven indisputably? Proven by human sacrifice?

Connectedly, this course of reflection supported the conclusion that it was imperative that nations support the new international security organization that had been created in San Francisco. But would they submit to the necessary restraints unless convinced that if they did not, they would all be consumed together in the vengeful burst of atomic explosion? By convincing them that this was so by using the bomb against Japan, this new and awesome weapon could be the needed and longed-for procreator of a lastingly peaceful political order. Hiroshima could thus be regarded as an object lesson not of brutality but of the need to banish brutality henceforth. War could perhaps at long and final last be brought to condemn itself irretrievably.

As recounted, there had been a suggestion that before using the new weapon against an actual target, it could and should be introduced in some other way.

One group of scientists urged that its destructive power should be displayed to the world by dropping the bomb in some remote, uninhabited or cleared spot—an isolated island perhaps, or in the sea—with witnesses present. As told, their proposals were considered by Stimson and Marshall, by the Interim Committee, and by the Scientific Panel. All were judged impractical, ineffective, or risky.

The inquirer is compelled to rely on fragmentary individual explanations of the reasons which led to this adverse conclusion, and these differ. A basic fear of a failure in demonstration lingered. This was genuine despite various kinds of evidence—almost proof—that the bomb would produce an atomic explosion. It will be remembered that as early as December 1944 General Groves had reported that he, Groves, and by inference, his scientific advisers, were so confident that one of the two types (the gun type that was dropped on Hiroshima) would perform as conceived that a preliminary test before use was not deemed essential. This did not mean, however, that they were entirely sure, only that they thought the risk acceptable because of the length of time required to produce the U-235 consumed in the explosion.

The physicist, Smyth, who became the historian of the project, has recounted that "the end of June 1945 finds us expecting from day to day to hear of the explosion of the first atomic bomb devised by man. All the problems are believed to have been solved at least well enough to make a bomb practicable. A sustained neutron chain reaction resulting from nuclear fission has been demonstrated; the conditions necessary to cause such a reaction to occur explosively have been established and can be achieved. . . ."

One reason why fear of failure persisted was that all the preliminary tests of the detonating mechanism of the chain reaction had been in a stationary situation, either on the ground or from a fixed tower, as in the test of the plutonium, implosion-type bomb, in New Mexico. There were chances of human error or accident. What if the individuals entrusted with the task of turning the containing tube (in the U-235 gun type bomb that was the first available for use in Japan) into an atomic weapon faulted? Then no one was sure that they would work as well if the containing projectile was dropped from a swiftly-moving plane at high altitude. What might happen during its fall to earth? Or if some part of the mechanism of any one specimen was defective? Many precautions had been conceived and taken against each and every hazard; many rehearsals had trained mechanics and bombing crews to detect any causes of failure beforehand and to correct them. But still uncertainty remained about the outcome of the first trial.

Suppose an announced demonstration had failed, would the consequences have been serious? The President and Stimson, among others, thought so; they believed that it would sustain the belief of the Japanese that if they fought on they might secure an arranged peace, and so have prolonged the war. Moreover, a failure in demonstration might have aroused angry criticism throughout the United States and in Congress; and it could well have seemed foolish to responsible officials to incur these risks for a probably ineffectual effort to bring the war to an end as soon as possible by mere display of the bomb, no matter how dramatic.

Another reason was that the American government had so few of the new bombs. One was consumed by the New Mexico test; another was developed in time for use after July 31st; and it was reckoned that another could be assembled by August 6th, and, according to the anticipated schedule, no more would be available for use until about August 20th. By using all—two or three —with utmost effectiveness, the desired quick end of the war might well be brought about. If one were spent in a demonstration that went wrong for any reason, could the failure be justified to the men in uniform whose lives were in hazard every day the war went on?

Possibly as much in mind as either of these two reasons was the opinion that even if the demonstration went well, it could not be as quickly effective in ending the war as use against an actual target. Dropped in water there would be an immense displacement that would soon pass. Dropped on a barren stretch the appalling nature of this new weapon would not be fully displayed. The only visible effects left by detonation in New Mexico, after the great flash and bolt of thunderous sound, were a shallow depression in the ground, emptiness where the drop-tower had stood, and the fusion of the sand into glass where touched by the fire ball. Would such indications register its full meaning in human lives? It was concluded that this would follow only upon the actual, awful experience. Such precursory reasoning was in accord with Stimson's subsequent interpretation of why its use was so effective.

"But the atomic bomb was more than a weapon of terrible destruction; it was a psychological weapon. In March, 1945, our Air Forces had launched the first great incendiary raid on the Tokyo area. In this raid more damage was done and more casualties were inflicted than was the case at Hiroshima. Hundreds of bombs took part and hundreds of tons of incendiaries were dropped. Similar successive raids burned out a great part of the urban area of Japan, but the Japanese fought on. On August 6th one B-29 dropped a single atomic bomb on Hiroshima. Three days later a second bomb was dropped on Nagasaki and the war was over. So far as the Japanese could know, our ability to execute atomic attacks, if necessary by many planes at a time, was unlimited. As Dr. Karl Compton has said, 'it was not one atomic bomb, or two, which brought surrender; it was the experience of what an atomic bomb will actually do to a community, plus the dread of many more, that was effective.' "

These reasons, military, humane, political, for the use of the bomb against an actual target in Japan, are an acceptable and adequate justification for the action. But a cluster of worrisome queries remain which seem to me, despite the lapse of time, to retain ethical and historical interest.

Could the American government not have induced the desired quick surrender by informing the Japanese (and the whole world) of the results of the New Mexico test—informing them by words and pictures? The most promising time for such an effort would have been in connection with the issuance of the Potsdam Declaration; for by then the American air assaults and naval bombardments were spreading havoc everywhere, and most Japanese were aware they had no way of countering them, no clear idea of how to survive them. Suppose, to be more precise, the American government had published the reports on the test which were sent by General Groves for the President at Potsdam and the many official photographs of the explosion and of the mushroom cloud; might not that broadcast knowledge, prefaced by an explanation that the purpose was to spare the Japanese, have had enough shock effect to cause the Emperor to overrule the resistant Japanese military leaders? If not at once, may it not have done so if followed first by a demonstration in or near Japan and then by the Soviet entry into the war?

I think it quite possible, probable in fact, that such a combination of actions would have impelled the Japanese government to yield almost as soon as it did, or a few weeks later after the Red Army had smashed the Kwantung Army. But this is a disputable surmise about the results of a conceivable other course; a course set by considerations which seemed remote or unreal at the time, and may still be deemed so by others. Whether or not the surmise is sustainable, the spirit may still harbor regret that the meaning of the Potsdam Declaration was not illuminated by a candid revelation of the new weapon that would be used if Japan rejected this bid for surrender.

Another lingering query is whether the American government would not have been well advised explicitly to warn the Japanese in the selected target areas of what was in store for them, and to give them a good chance to flee or hide. Proposals that this be done gave way before a variety of objections. One was that if forewarning were followed by failure, the Japanese would discount all other vaunted indications of American power; that seems to me hardly to have been warranted. Two objections of another sort could not be dismissed; if the target was identified, would not the Japanese do their utmost to knock down the plane carrying the bomb? Even if they failed to do so, might not their attack cause the drop to go amiss? Was the government justified in exposing the crew of the plane to an avoidable danger and risking the loss of the bomb? The negative answer is easy to understand.

I will end this roving examination with one summary conclusion: the only score on which the American government can be fairly criticized is that it did not let the Japanese know the nature and destructive power of the new weapon to be used against them if the Potsdam Declaration was rejected.

By this time, however, all plans and determinations had been made for its use, without such a preliminary exposure. The test was on July 16th; it would not have been easy to assemble photographs and convincing accounts of it quickly. Therefore it might have been necessary to postpone for some time, perhaps until after the end of the conference at Potsdam, the issuance of the Declaration, thereby prolonging the period of assault and loss of life.

However, in retrospect, I believe that the risk should have been taken and the cost endured; for by doing this we might have been spared the need to use it. In the more likely event that the Japanese would not have heeded even the more explicit and ample warning, we as a people would be freer of any remorse, unjustified as it may be, at the historical necessity of enrolling Hiroshima and Nagasaki forever in the annals of history. But the mind, circling upon itself, may wonder whether, if the exterminating power of the bomb had not been actually displayed, the nations would have been impelled to make even as faltering an effort as they have made to agree on measures to save themselves from mutual extinction by this ultimate weapon.

14

Yalta:

SUCCESS *or* FAILURE ?

DURING *the course of the war the Allied powers—Great Britain, the United States, and the Soviet Union—met irregularly to coordinate military and diplomatic plans and policies. The most important of these conferences took place at Yalta in the Crimea from the fourth to the eleventh of February, 1945. At this conference Churchill, Roosevelt, and Stalin met to lay final plans for the destruction of Germany and to complete other arrangements regarding the war and the peace that was to follow. In a cordial and friendly spirit the three leaders agreed to another conference that was to meet in the United States on April 25, 1945, to establish a United Nations. In addition, some voting procedures for the United Nations were discussed and agreed upon. They pledged to support the right of the liberated peoples in Europe to choose their own forms of government in a democratic way, and agreed on procedures for the dismemberment and occupation of Germany and for extracting reparations from that country. Stalin was given a large area of eastern Poland in exchange for his willingness to see "free and unfettered" elections serve as the basis for a new Polish government. In return for the Soviet Union's entry into the war against Japan, she was given vast territories and great privileges in Asia, chiefly at China's expense and without China's prior approval.*

These agreements soon came in for much criticism. Some observers believed that Stalin had received substantially more than he gave, and placed the blame either on "softness to Communism" by certain American or on Roosevelt's incompetence. Other observers thought that the agreements were necessary and even desirable in the light of existing conditions.

William H. Chamberlin, author of numerous books on international affairs, an expert on Russia, and a journalist (presently an editorial contributor to The Wall Street Journal) *describes Yalta as a disaster, a sordid deal, and a violation of the basic human rights embodied in the Atlantic Charter. Stalin* got what he wanted in return for flimsy and in some cases worthless promises to join the new world organization, to respect democratic processes in the liberated areas, and to join the war against Japan. For these assurances China and Poland were betrayed. Chamberlin imputes this policy of appeasement to Roosevelt's physical and mental deterioration, to Stettinius's naivete and ignorance, and to the absence of a prepared agenda and a clearly defined purpose by the American delegation. His argument rests chiefly on the fact that the United States did not need Soviet military help in 1945 to defeat Germany or Japan.

Forrest C. Pogue, the biographer of George C. Marshall, and an important military historian who specializes in World War II, does not deny that the Soviet Union received handsome concessions at Yalta, mainly in Asia. He contends, however, that these were necessary in the light of conditions existing at the time. The agreements must be viewed in terms of the importance of the Soviet Union to the total war effort. Russia's entry into the war in 1941 took a tremendous strain off the Allies in Western Europe. Her assistance in 1945, was deemed indispensable. The Germans were by no means defeated—indeed, in December, 1944, they had launched a powerful drive in Belgium and were repulsed with great difficulty. In Asia the Japanese effort increased with even greater vigor and fanaticism than before and it appeared that only a large-scale assault on the Japanese homeland could end the war in the Pacific. In addition to Russia's military importance, her cooperation was necessary for Roosevelt's plans for world order. Without Soviet participation a United Nations would be meaningless. Necessity rather than appeasement directed the terms at Yalta.

The Munich Called Yalta

WILLIAM HENRY CHAMBERLIN

THE SECOND conference of the Big Three, held at Yalta in February 1945, represented the high point of Soviet diplomatic success and correspondingly the low point of American appeasement. This conference took place under circumstances which were very disadvantageous to the western powers.

Roosevelt's mental and physical condition had disquieted Stimson at the time when the Morgenthau Plan was being approved. It certainly did not improve as a result of the strenuous presidential campaign and the long trip to the Crimean resort.

There has been no authoritative uninhibited analysis of the state of the President's health during the war. But there is a good deal of reliable testimony of serious deterioration, especially during the last year of Mr. Roosevelt's life. And it was during this year that decisions of the most vital moral and political importance had to be taken.

Among the symptoms of the President's bad health were liability to severe debilitating colds, extreme haggardness of appearance, occasional blackouts of memory, and loss of capacity for mental concentration. An extremely high authority who may not be identified described Roosevelt's condition at three of the principal conferences as follows:

"The President looked physically tired at Casablanca; but his mind worked well. At Teheran there were signs of loss of memory. At Yalta he could neither think consecutively nor express himself coherently."

An official who was in frequent contact with Roosevelt during the last months of his life gave me the following account of getting essential state papers considered:

I would go to the President with perhaps a dozen documents requiring his approval or signature. By talking fast as soon as I opened the door of his study I could get action, perhaps, on three or four. Then the President would begin to talk about irrelevant matters, repeating stories and anecdotes I had often heard from him before and falling behind in his schedule of appointments. It was difficult and embarrassing to get away from him.

A similar impression was carried away by General Joseph Stilwell, who talked with Roosevelt after the Cairo and Teheran conferences and asked what American policy he should communicate to Chiang Kai-shek after re-

---

From William Henry Chamberlin, *America's Second Crusade* (Chicago: Henry Regnery Company, 1962) pp. 206–225, 230–231. Reprinted by permission of Henry Regnery Company.

turning to China. The reply was a long rambling monologue. The President told how his grandfather made a couple of million dollars out of China in the 1830's and "all through the Civil War". He expounded a plan for taking fifty or one hundred million American dollars and buying up Chinese paper money on the black market so as to check inflation. He talked about postwar airplanes and how much the Chinese should pay American engineers. And Stillwell never got his direction as to policy.

It is certainly no exaggeration to say that Roosevelt was physically and mentally far less fit than Churchill and Stalin during the period when American military power was at its height and the supreme decisions which confronted the national leaders in the last phase of the war had to be taken. Had Roosevelt been able to delegate power and had there been a strong and capable Secretary of State, some of the unfortunate consequences of the President's incapacitation might have been averted and softened.

But Roosevelt clung to power with hands that were too weak to use it effectively. After his death it required much searching of files and ransacking of the memories of the participants to reconstruct what had occurred and to find out just what the President had or had not agreed to.

When Hull laid down his office on account of bad health in November 1944, his successor was Edward Stettinius. The ignorance and naïveté of the latter in foreign affairs soon became a byword to his associates in government service and to foreign diplomats. Stettinius was much better qualified to be master of ceremonies at the high jinks of some fraternal organization than to direct American foreign policy at a critical period.

Stettinius shared Roosevelt's delusion that successful diplomacy was largely a matter of establishing friendly personal contacts. At the Dumbarton Oaks conference which shaped the preliminary draft of the United Nations charter Stettinius made himself ridiculous by cheerfully shouting "Hi, Alex" and "Hiya, Andrei" at his partners in the negotiations, the correct and pained Sir Alexander Cadogan and the sullen and bored Andrei Gromyko.

The appointment of Stettinius was due to the influence of Hopkins. The latter's star as court favorite, after a temporary eclipse, was again in the ascendant at the time of the Yalta Conference. Hopkins was a very sick man and had to spend most of his time at Yalta in bed.

Roosevelt went to Yalta with no prepared agenda and no clearly defined purpose, except to get along with Stalin at any price. He had been provided with a very complete file of studies and recommendations, drawn up by the State Department, before he boarded the heavy cruiser *Quincy*, which took him to Malta, where there was a break in the journey to the Crimea. But these were never looked at. The President suffered from a cold and from sinus trouble and his appearance "disturbed" James F. Byrnes, who accompanied him on this trip.

The conference at Yalta lasted a week, from February 4 until February 11,

1945. The principal subjects discussed were Poland, German boundaries and reparations, the occupation regime for Germany, the conditions of Soviet participation in the war against Japan, procedure and voting rights in the future United Nations organization.

At the price of a few promises which were soon to prove worthless in practice, Stalin got what he wanted in Poland: a frontier that assigned to the Soviet Union almost half of Poland's prewar territory and the abandonment by America and Great Britain of the Polish government-in-exile in London. Roosevelt made a feeble plea that Lwów and the adjacent oil fields be included in Poland. Churchill appealed to Stalin's sense of generosity. Neither achieved any success.

On the German question Churchill took a stand for moderation. Stalin recommended the western frontier of Poland should be extended to the Neisse River, bringing large tracts of ethnic German territory under Polish rule. Churchill suggested that it would be a pity to stuff the Polish goose so full of German food that he would die of indigestion.

The British Premier privately estimated to Byrnes that nine million Germans would be displaced by giving Poland a frontier on the Neisse River and that such a number could never be absorbed. It is the Neisse River that marks the Polish-German frontier in 1950, although the Yalta communiqué merely stated that "Poland must receive substantial accessions of territory in the North and West."

There was agreement in principle that Germany should be broken up into separate states. However, no positive decision was adopted. The matter was referred to the European Advisory Commission, composed of American, British, and Soviet representatives sitting in London. Here it died a natural death. The dismemberment of Germany was not discussed at the next major conference, at Potsdam.

The Soviet representatives at Yalta had large and fairly precise ideas as to what they wished to take from Germany as reparations. They wanted to remove physically 80 per cent of Germany's heavy industries and also to receive deliveries in kind for ten years. Churchill recalled the unsuccessful experience with reparations after the last war and spoke of "the spectre of an absolutely starving Germany". Ivan Maisky, Soviet spokesman on this question, proposed that reparations be fixed at the figure of twenty billion dollars, with the Soviet Union to receive at least half of this sum.

Roosevelt had little to suggest on this subject, except to remark that the United States would have no money to send into Germany for food, clothing, and housing. It was finally decided to leave the details to a reparations commission. There was no firm promise on America's part to support a Soviet claim for ten billion dollars in reparations, although the Soviet Government, with its usual tendency to lose nothing for want of asking for it, later tried to represent that there had been such a commitment.

If one considers the value of the territory lost by Germany in the East, the prodigious looting, organized and unorganized, carried out by the Red Army, and the system in the Soviet zone of occupation under which a large share of German industrial output is siphoned off for Soviet use, it is probable that Germany was stripped of assets considerably in excess of ten billion dollars in value.

The protocol on reparations mentioned "the use of labor" as a possible source of reparations. Roosevelt observed that "the United States cannot take man power as the Soviet Republic can." This gave implied American sanction to the large-scale exploitation of German war prisoners as slave labor in Britain and France, as well as in Russia, after the end of the war. The Morgenthau Plan, which Roosevelt and Churchill had approved at Quebec, recommended "forced German labor outside Germany" as a form of reparations.

Procedure in the United Nations was discussed at some length. The records show that Roosevelt and Churchill were as unwilling as Stalin to forego the right of veto in serious disputes, where the use of armed force was under discussion. There was a dispute, not settled at Yalta, as to whether the right of veto should apply to discussion of controversial matters. The Russians insisted that it should, the western representatives contended that it should not. Stalin conceded this minor point when Harry Hopkins visited Moscow in June 1945.

The Soviet Government received Roosevelt's consent to its proposal that Byelorussia and the Ukraine, two of the affiliated Soviet republics, should be granted individual votes in the United Nations Assembly. When Byrnes learned of this he raised vigorous objection, reminding Roosevelt that some of the opposition to America's entrance into the League of Nations was based on the argument that Britain would have five votes, one for each member of the Commonwealth. Roovelt then asked for and obtained Stalin's consent to an arrangement which would give the United States three votes in the Assembly. This compensation was never pressed for and did not go into effect.

In reason and logic there was no case for giving separate votes to the Ukraine and Byelorussia. If the Soviet Union was a loose federation of independent states, like the British Commonwealth, each of its sixteen constituent republics should have been entitled to a vote. If it was a centralized unitary state, it should have received only one vote. No one with an elementary knowledge of Soviet political realities could doubt that the Soviet Union belongs in the second category. It would cause no special shock or surprise to see Canada, South Africa, Australia, or India voting in opposition to Britain on some issues. It would be unthinkable for the Ukraine or Byelorussia to oppose the Soviet Union.

So far as the Assembly is concerned, Moscow's three votes have thus far been of little practical importance. The Assembly possesses little power and the Soviet satellites are in the minority. But, as Byrnes was to discover later during the arduous negotiation of the peace treaties with Italy, Hungary, Bulgaria, Rumania, and Finland, it was an advantage for the Soviet Union to start with three of the twenty-one votes of the participating nations in its pocket.

Contempt for the rights of smaller and weaker nations was conspicuous in the Soviet attitude at Yalta. At the first dinner Vishinsky declared that the Soviet Union would never agree to the right of the small nations to judge the acts of the great powers. Charles E. Bohlen, American State Department expert on Russia, replied that the American people were not likely to approve of any denial of the small nations' right. Vishinsky's comment was that the American people should "learn to obey their leaders."

Churchill, discussing the same subject with Stalin, quoted the proverb: "The eagle should permit the small birds to sing and not care wherefore they sang." Stalin's low opinion of France, as a country that had been knocked out early in the war, was reflected in his remark: "I cannot forget that in this war France opened the gates to the enemy."

What Stalin did forget, and what no one reminded him of, was that while France was fighting the Germans, the Soviet Government was enthusiastically collaborating with the Nazi dictatorship, sending messages of congratulation after every new victory of the Wehrmacht. French Communists, acting under Stalin's orders, certainly contributed more than other Frenchmen to "opening the gates to the enemy."

Stalin was only willing to grant France a zone of occupation on condition that this should be carved out of territory assigned to the United States and Great Britain. For a time he held out against giving France a place on the Allied Control Council for Germany. In the end he yielded to Roosevelt on this point. The President's attitude toward General de Gaulle had always been strained and chilly. But, in Hopkins's words, "Winston and Anthony [Eden] fought like tigers" for France. They enlisted the aid of Hopkins, who persuaded Roosevelt to use his influence, in this case successfully, with Stalin.

On the subject of Iran there was complete disagreement. That country had been jointly occupied by Russia and Britain since 1942. There had been an agreement at Teheran that all foreign troops should be withdrawn six months after the end of the war, but the Soviet Government was already displaying the balkiness about implementing this agreement which was to lead to a serious international crisis in 1946. The brief text of the final discussion at the meeting of foreign ministers on February 10 is worth quoting as a foretaste of Molotov's methods in negotiation:

Mr. Eden inquired whether Mr. Molotov had considered the British document on Iran.

Mr. Molotov stated that he had nothing to add to what he had said several days ago on the subject.

Mr. Eden inquired whether it would not be advisable to issue a communiqué on Iran.

Mr. Molotov stated that this would be inadvisable.

Mr. Stettinius urged that some reference be made that Iranian problems had been discussed and clarified during the Crimean Conference.

Mr. Molotov stated that he opposed this idea.

Mr. Eden suggested that it be stated that the declaration on Iran had been reaffirmed and re-examined during the present meeting.

Mr. Molotov opposed this suggestion.

In Yugoslavia, as in Poland, the Yalta Agreement provided a screen of fair words behind which the friends of the West were ruthlessly liquidated. It was decided to recommend that a new government be formed on the basis of agreement between Tito and Subasic. The antifascist Assembly of National Liberation (an organization of Tito's predominantly Communist followers) was to be enlarged by the addition of members of the last Yugoslav parliament who "had not compromised themselves by collaboration with the enemy." Legislative acts passed by the Assembly were to be subject to ratification by a constituent asstmbly.

All this sounded fair enough. What is meant in practice was that two non-Communists, Subasic and Grol, joined Tito's regime, the former as Foreign Minister, the latter as Vice-Premier. But their tenure of office was precarious and brief. Grol's newspaper was suppressed and he resigned from the government in August 1945, accusing the regime of a long series of violations of elementary political and civil liberties. Subasic followed his example soon afterwards and was placed under house arrest.

And Tito's constituent assembly was chosen under an electoral law "which rendered the very appearance of a candidate's name on the opposition list a danger to that candidate's life." The "new democracy", so very like the old fascism in psychology and methods, marched on to further victories. Yalta put the seal on the process which had begun at Teheran of betraying the East Europeans who preferred free institutions to communism. All that followed, or could follow, was a long series of futile diplomatic protests from Washington and London.

Another country was offered up as a sacrifice on the altar of appeasement at Yalta. This was China. Stalin had told Hull at Moscow and Roosevelt at Teheran that he would be on the side of the United States and Great Britain against Japan after the end of the war with Germany. At Yalta, with German military collapse clearly impending, the Soviet dictator set a price for his intervention in the Far East. The price was stiff. And it included items which it was not morally justifiable for the United States to accept. The Big Three agreed that

the former rights of Russia, violated by the treacherous attack of Japan in 1904, shall be restored, viz.:

(a) The southern part of Sakhalin as well as the islands adjacent to it shall be returned to the Soviet Union;

(b) The commercial port of Dairen shall be internationalized, the pre-eminent interest of the Soviet Union in this port being safeguarded and the lease of Port Arthur as a naval base of the Soviet Union restored.

(c) The Chinese Eastern Railway and the South Manchuria Railway, which provide an outlet to Dairen, shall be jointly operated by the establishment of a joint Soviet-Chinese company, it being understood that the pre-eminent interests of the Soviet Union shall be safeguarded and that China shall retain full sovereignty in Manchuria.

The Kurile Islands, a long chain of barren, volcanic islands extending into the North Pacific northeast of Japan proper, were to be handed over to the Soviet Union. The *status quo* was to be preserved in Outer Mongolia, a huge, sparsely populated, arid region which the Soviet Union took over without formal annexation in 1924.

South Sakhalin (which had belonged to Russia until 1905) and the Kurile Islands might be regarded as war booty, to be taken from Japan. And China had no prospect of upsetting *de facto* Soviet rule of Outer Mongolia by its own strength. But the concessions which Roosevelt and Churchill made to Stalin in Manchuria were of fateful importance for China's independence and territorial integrity.

Manchuria, because of its natural wealth in coal, iron, soya beans, and other resources, and because of the large investment of Japanese capital and technical skill, intensified after 1931, was the most industrially developed part of China. To give a strong foreign power control over its railways, a predominant interest in its chief port, Dairen, and a naval base at Port Arthur was to sign away China's sovereignty in Manchuria.

And this was done not only without consulting China but without informing China. The Chinese Government was prevented from even discussing Soviet claims in the future. For, at Stalin's insistence, the agreement to satisfy his annexationist claims was put in writing and contained this decisive assurance:

"The Heads of the three Great Powers have agreed that these claims of the Soviet Union shall be unquestioningly fulfilled after Japan has been defeated."

In the opinion of former Ambassador William C. Bullitt "no more unnecessary, disgraceful and potentially disastrous document has ever been signed by a President of the United States."

Severe as this judgment sounds, it has been borne out by the course of subsequent events. The Soviet intervention in the Far Eastern war was of no military benefit to the United States, because it took place only a few days before Japan surrendered. Politically this intervention was an unmitigated disaster.

During the Soviet occupation of Manchuria industrial equipment of an estimated value of two billion dollars was looted and carried off to Russia. This delayed for a long time any prospect of Chinese industrial self-sufficiency. As soon as Soviet troops occupied Manchuria, Chinese Communist forces, as if by a mysterious signal, began to converge on that area.

The Soviet military commanders shrewdly avoided direct, ostentatious co-operation with the Communists. After all, the Soviet Government had signed a treaty of friendship and alliance with the Nationalist Government of

China on August 14, 1945. One clause of this treaty prescribed that "the Soviet Government is ready to render China moral support and assistance with military equipment and other material resources, this support and assistance to be given fully to the National Government as the central government of China."

This treaty was to prove about as valuable to the cosignatory as the non-aggression pacts which the Soviet Government concluded with Poland, Finland, Latvia, Lithuania, and Estonia. There is no indication that the Soviet Government gave the slightest "moral" or material support to the Chinese Nationalist Government. But Manchuria became an arsenal for the Chinese Communists, who were able to equip themselves with Japanese arms, obligingly stacked up for them by the Soviet occupation forces.

Soviet control of Dairen was used to block the use of this important port by Nationalist troops. Manchiuria became the base from which the Chinese Communists could launch a campaign that led to the overrunning of almost all China.

Roosevelt's concessions at Yalta represented an abandonment of the historic policy of the United States in the Far East. This policy was in favor of the "open door", of equal commercial opportunity for all foreign nations, together with respect for Chinese independence. The American State Department had always been opposed to the "closed door" methods of Imperial Russia.

But at Yalta the "open door" was abandoned in a document that repeatedly referred to "the pre-eminent interests of the Soviet Union" in Manchuria. Those interests have now become pre-eminent in China. And the surrender of Manchuria to Stalin is not the least of the reasons for this development.

The Yalta concessions were a violation of the American pledge at Cairo that Manchuria should be restored to China. If New York State had been occupied by an enemy and was then handed back to the United States on condition that another alien power should have joint control of its railway systems, a predominant voice in the Port of New York Authority, and the right to maintain a naval base on Staten Island, most Americans would not feel that American sovereignty had been respected.

Whether considered from the standpoint of consistency with professed war aims or from the standpoint of serving American national interests, the record of Yalta is profoundly depressing. The large-scale alienation of Polish territory to the Soviet Union, of German territory to Poland, constituted an obvious and flagrant violation of the self-determination clauses of the Atlantic Charter. An offensive note of hypocrisy was added by inserting into the Yalta communiqué repeated professions of adherence to the Atlantic Charter.

The hopes of tens of millions of East Europeans for national independence and personal liberty were betrayed. The leaders of the Axis could scarcely have surpassed the cynicism of Roosevelt and Churchill in throwing over allies like Poland and China. The unwarranted concessions to Stalin in the

Far East opened a Pandora's Box of troubles for the United States, the end of which has not yet been seen.

There was not one positive, worth-while contribution to European revival and stability in the sordid deals of Yalta, only imperialist power politics at its worst. The vindictive peace settlement, far worse than that of Versailles, which was being prepared promised little for European reconstruction. Roosevelt not long before had piously declared that "the German people are not going to be enslaved, because the United Nations do not traffic in human slavery." But at Yalta he sanctioned the use of the slave labor of German war prisoners, a throwback to one of the most barbarous practices of antiquity.

The agreements, published and secret, concluded at Yalta are defended mainly on two grounds. It is contended that military necessity forced the President to comply with Stalin's demands in Eastern Europe and East Asia. It is also argued that the source of difficulties in postwar Europe is to be found, not in the Yalta agreements, but in the Soviet failure to abide by these agreements.

Neither of these justifications stands up under serious examination. America in February 1945 was close to the peak of its military power. The atomic bomb still lay a few months in the future. But the United States possessed the most powerful navy in the world, the greatest aircraft production in quantity and quality, an army that, with its British and other allies, had swept the Germans from North Africa, France, Belgium, and much of Italy.

The lumbering Soviet offensive in the East was dependent in no small degree on lend-lease American trucks and communication equipment. There was, therefore, no good reason for approaching Stalin with an inferiority complex or for consenting to a Polish settlement which sacrificed the friends of the West in that country and paved the way for the establishment of a Soviet puppet regime.

No doubt Stalin could have imposed such a regime by force. Only the Red Army in February 1945 was in a position to occupy Poland. How much better the outlook would have been if Churchill's repeated prodding for action in the Balkans had been heeded, if the Polish Army of General Anders, battle-hardened in Italy, had been able to reach Poland ahead of the Red Army!

But there would have been a great difference between a Soviet stooge regime set up by the naked force of the Red Army and one strengthened by the acquiescence and endorsement of the western powers. The former would have enjoyed no shred of moral authority. As it was, nationalist guerrilla resistance to the made-in-Moscow government was prolonged and embittered. Many thousands of lives were lost on both sides before the satellite regime, with a good deal of Russian military and police aid, clamped down its rule more or less effectively over the entire country. How much stronger this resistance would have been if the United States and Great Britain had continued to recognize the government-in-exile and insisted on adequate guarantees of free and fair elections!

There was equally little reason to give in to Stalin's Far Eastern demands. The desire to draw the Soviet Union into this war was fatuous, from the standpoint of America's interest in a truly independent China. Apparently Roosevelt was the victim of some extremely bad intelligence work. He was given to understand that the Kwantung Army, the Japanese occupation force in Manchuria, was a formidable fighting machine, which might be used to resist the American invasion of the Japanese home islands which was planned for the autumn.

But the Kwantung Army offered no serious resistance to the Soviet invasion in August. It had evidently been heavily depleted in numbers and lowered in fighting quality.

Apologists for the Yalta concessions maintain that Japan in February 1945 presented the aspect of a formidable, unbeaten enemy. Therefore, so the argument runs, Roosevelt was justified in paying a price for Soviet intervention, in the interest of ending the war quickly and saving American lives.

But Japanese resistance to American air and naval attacks on its own coasts was already negligible. American warships were able to cruise along the shores of Japan, bombarding at will. According to an account later published by Arthur Krock, of the *New York Times*, an Air Force general presented a report at Yalta pointing to the complete undermining of the Japanese capacity to resist. But the mistaken and misleading view that Japan still possessed powerful military and naval force prevailed.

Acceptance of this view by Roosevelt was especially unwarranted because two days before he left for Yalta Roosevelt received from General MacArthur a forty-page message outlining five unofficial Japanese peace overtures which amounted to an acceptance of unconditional surrender, with the sole reservation that the Emperor should be preserved. The other terms offered by the Japanese, who were responsible men, in touch with Emperor Hirohito, may be summarized as follows:

1. Complete surrender of all Japanese forces.

2. Surrender of all arms and munitions.

3. Occupation of the Japanese homeland and island possessions by Allied troops under American direction.

4. Japanese relinquishment of Manchuria, Korea, and Formosa, as well as all territory seized during the war.

5. Regulation of Japanese industry to halt present and future production of implements of war.

6. Turning over of any Japanese the United States might designate as war criminals.

7. Immediate release of all prisoners of war and internees in Japan and areas under Japanese control.

MacArthur recommended negotiations on the basis of the Japanese overtures. But Roosevelt brushed off this suggestion with the remark: "MacArthur is our greatest general and our poorest politician."

That the President, after receiving such a clear indication that Japan was on the verge of military collapse, should have felt it necessary to bribe Stalin into entering the Far Eastern war must surely be reckoned a major error of judgment, most charitably explained by Roosevelt's failing mental and physical powers.

Captain Ellis M. Zacharias, Navy expert on Japan whose broadcasts in fluent Japanese hastened the surrender, asserts that intelligence reports indicating Japanese impending willingness to surrender were available at the time of the Yalta Conference.

One such report, communicated in the utmost secrecy to an American intelligence officer in a neutral capital, predicted the resignation of General Koiso as Premier in favor of the pacific Admiral Suzuki. The Admiral, in turn, according to the report, would turn over power to the Imperial Prince Higashi Kuni, who would possess sufficient authority and prestige, backed by a command from the Emperor, to arrange the surrender.

I am convinced that had this document, later proven to be correct in every detail, been brought to the attention of President Roosevelt and his military advisers, the war might have been viewed in a different light, both Iwo Jima and Okinawa might have been avoided, and different decisions could have been reached at Yalta.

Zacharias also believes that if the Japanese had been given a precise definition of what America understood by unconditional surrender as late as June, or even at the end of July 1945, both Soviet intervention and the dropping of atomic bombs on Hiroshima and Nagasaki could have been averted.

Certainly there was a hopeful alternative to the policy, so disastrous in its results, of encouraging and bribing the Soviet Union to enter the Far Eastern picture. This was to aim at a quick peace with Japan, before the Soviet armies could have been transferred from the West to the East. There is every reason to believe that such a peace was attainable, if the Japanese had been assured of the right to keep the Emperor and perhaps given some assurance that their commercial interests in Manchuria and Korea would not be entirely wiped out.

There is little weight in the contention that the Yalta agreements, in themselves, were excellent, if the Soviet Government had only lived up to them. These agreements grossly violated the Atlantic Charter by assigning Polish territory to the Soviet Union and German territory to Poland without plebiscites. They violated the most elementary rules of humanity and civilized warfare by sanctioning slave labor as "reparations". And the whole historic basis of American foreign policy in the Far East was upset by the virtual invitation to Stalin to take over Japan's former exclusive and dominant role in Manchuria.

There was certainly no reason for self-congratulation on the part of any of the western representatives at Yalta. But human capacity for self-deception is strong. According to Robert E. Sherwood, "the mood of the American delegates, including Roosevelt and Hopkins, could be described as one of supreme exultation as they left Yalta." And Hopkins later told Sherwood:

We really believed in our hearts that this was the dawn of the new day we had all been praying for and talking about for so many years. We were absolutely certain that we had won the first great victory of the peace—and by "we", I mean *all* of us, the whole civilized human race. The Russians had proved that they could be reasonable and farseeing and there wasn't any doubt in the minds of the President or any of us that we could live with them and get along with them peacefully for as far into the future as any of us could imagine.

A chorus of hallelujahs went up from the less perspicacious politicians and publicists in the United States. Raymond Gram Swing perhaps took first prize for unqualified enthusiasm. He said: "No more appropriate news could be conceived to celebrate the birthday of Abraham Lincoln." William L. Shirer saw in Yalta "a landmark in human history." Senator Alben Barkley pronounced it "one of the most important steps ever taken to promote peace and happiness in the world." In the face of such authoritative declarations the suicides of scores of "unknown Polish soldiers" in Italy, desperate over the betrayal of their country, received little attention.

However, the honeymoon mood inspired by the first news of Yalta did not last long. The ink of the agreement was scarcely dry when there were two serious and flagrant violations: one in Rumania, one in Poland. It had been formally agreed at Yalta that the three big powers should "concert their policies in assisting the peoples liberated from the domination of Nazi Germany and the peoples of the former Axis satellite states to solve by democratic means their pressing political and economic problems." The three governments were "to jointly assist the peoples in these states in such matters as establishing conditions of internal peace and forming interim governmental authorities." And there was to be immediate consultation on "the measures necessary to discharge the joint responsibilities set forth in this declaration."

The Kremlin decided to get rid of the government of General Radescu, set up after Rumania had turned against Germany, and to replace it with a regime subservient to Moscow. Rejecting and ignoring repeated American proposals for three-power consultation on the question, the Soviet Government sent Deputy Foreign Minister Andrei Vishinsky to Bucharest on February 27. Vishinsky stormed and bullied until the young Rumanian King Michael dismissed Radescu and appointed the Soviet-designated Prime Minister, Petru Groza. The Soviet envoy's methods of persuasion varied from slamming a door in the royal palace so hard the plaster cracked to threatening the King that it would be impossible to guarantee the further existence of Rumania as an independent state if Groza were not appointed.

The King yielded and Rumania was started on the road to complete Communist dictatorship. When the American Ambassador in Moscow, Averell Harriman, proposed that a three-power committee be set up in Bucharest to implement the Yalta resolution on consultation, Molotov's rejection was prompt and blunt. This was typical of the Soviet attitude not only in Rumania, but in all countries under Red Army occupation.

Meanwhile the Soviet Government was delaying and sabotaging the creation of a new government in Poland. Stalin and Molotov interpreted the Yalta agreement on this point (the phrasing was loose and elastic) to mean that no Pole distasteful to the Provisional Government (made up of hand-picked Soviet candidates) should be eligible for membership in the new government.

And the Provisional Government authorities, backed up by Soviet military and police power, were rapidly making the Yalta promise of "free unfettered elections" an empty mockery. There were numerous arbitrary arrests. Freedom of the press was nonexistent. The historic Polish parties were dissolved and replaced by pro-Communist groups which stole their names. In order to conceal the reign of terror that was going on, foreigners were systematically excluded from Poland. There was a long delay even in admitting representatives of UNRRA, interested in working out a program to meet the country's urgent need for food, clothing, and other relief supplies.

Toward the end of March Churchill warned Roosevelt that the Yalta agreement on Poland was clearly breaking down. The President on March 27 informed Churchill that he too "had been watching with anxiety and concern the development of the Soviet attitude since Yalta." Along with this message he sent the draft of a proposed communication to Stalin.

This communication, sent to Moscow on April 1, was phrased in sharper terms than Roosevelt had been accustomed to use in exchanges with the Soviet dictator. Perhaps by this time the President had realized that personal charm and an avoidance of unpleasant subjects do not constitute an unfailing formula for diplomatic success.

Roosevelt in this telegram expressed concern over the development of events. He regretted the "lack of progress made in the carrying out, which the world expects, of the political decisions which we reached at Yalta, particularly those relating to the Polish question." The President emphasized that "any solution which would result in a thinly disguised continuation of the present government would be entirely unacceptable and would cause our people to regard the Yalta agreement as a failure."

Roosevelt urged that American and British representatives be permitted to visit Poland. If there was no successful co-operation in solving the Polish question, he warned, "all the difficulties and dangers to Allied unity will face us in an even more acute form." The President also referred to Rumania, suggesting that developments there fell within the terms of the Yalta declaration on liberated areas and requesting Stalin to examine personally the diplomatic exchanges which had taken place on this subject.

Stalin's reply, dispatched on April 7, offered no satisfaction. It contested Roosevelt's interpretation of Yalta and flatly refused to permit the sending of American and British observers to Poland—on the ground that the Poles would consider this an insult to their national dignity! Apparently Stalin felt no corresponding squeamish fear of insulting Polish national dignity by filling high posts in the Polish Army and police with Russian agents, some of whom could not even speak Polish.

Roosevelt and Churchill decided to send a new joint message to Stalin. While this was in preparation Roosevelt died. News of the treacherous arrest of fifteen Polish underground leaders could scarcely have strengthened his confidence in Stalin's good faith and good will. And even before the sharp exchanges on the Polish question, this confidence had been shaken by another incident.

About the middle of March there was a preliminary meeting in Berne of American, British, and German military representatives to arrange for the surrender of the German armies in Italy, under the command of Marshal Kesselring. The Soviet Government had been informed of this development, and Molotov had expressed a desire to send Red Army officers to take part in the discussions. The Chiefs of Staff informed Molotov that nothing would be done at Berne, except to make preparations for a further meeting at Allied headquarters in Caserta, in Italy. This elicited from Moscow a sharp reply, refusing to send military representatives and "insisting" that the "negotiations" be stopped.

Roosevelt personally assured Stalin that no negotiations had taken place and that the Soviet Government would be kept fully informed of further developments. Then Stalin sent a message which Roosevelt took to heart very deeply as an insult to his integrity and loyalty to the alliance. Stalin declared that Roosevelt had been misinformed by his military advisers. According to Red Army intelligence reports, Stalin continued, a deal had been struck with Kesselring. The front would be opened to the American Army and Germany would be granted easier peace terms in exchange.

These allegations are devoid of any shadow of probability. American policy toward Germany had been based on rigid adherence to the unconditional surrender formula and avoidance of any step that would have remotely suggested separate dealing with Germany.

Roosevelt's hurt feelings found reflection in a reply which expressed "deep resentment" over "the vile misrepresentations of Stalin's informers." The President intimated that these informers wished to destroy the friendly relations between the two countries.

The friction over the Polish and Rumanian issues and over Stalin's insinuations of American bad faith were shrouded in secrecy at the time. This friction is now a matter of record and seems to dispose of a favorite thesis of Soviet sympathizers. This is that American-Soviet relations were invariably smooth and friendly during Roosevelt's lifetime and only began to deteriorate after his death. The evidence indicates that this is not the case, that Roosevelt was hurt and offended by what he regarded as a betrayal of the Yalta assurances and, had he lived, would quite probably have shifted American policy more quickly than Truman felt able to do.

Two well-known American journalists who saw Roosevelt separately in the last weeks of his life agree that he was both discouraged and indignant over what he regarded as breach of faith and lack of cooperative spirit on the Soviet side. He was considering, according to their reports, a fundamental re-examination of American policy toward the Soviet Union.

What Roosevelt would have done, had he lived longer, is a matter of conjecture. He left an unhappy legacy in foreign relations to his successor, who was without personal knowledge and experience in this field. So secretive and personal had been Roosevelt's diplomacy that for some time it was impossible for the new Chief Executive to get a clear picture of what assurances had been given to foreign governments, of what diplomatic IOU's were outstanding. . . .

Roosevelt in the last weeks of his life was certainly shaken, if not altogether disillusioned, in his great expectations of Stalin's co-operation. But Harry Hopkins seems to have remained naive and self-deluded to the bitter end. On this point we have the testimony of a sketchy memorandum which he wrote in August 1945, shortly before his death.

We know or believe that Russia's interests, so far as we can anticipate them, do not afford an opportunity for a major difference with us in foreign affairs. We believe we are mutually dependent upon each other for economic reasons. We find the Russians as individuals easy to deal with. The Russians undoubtedly like the American people. They like the United States. . . .

The Soviet Union is made up of 180 million hardworking proud people. They are not an uncivilized people. They are a tenacious, determined people, who think just like [sic] you and I do.

The secretary of some branch of the Council of American-Soviet Friendship could scarcely have pronounced a judgment more dismally lacking in intelligent anticipation of the shape of things to come. And this man, as ignorant of foreign languages as of history and political and economic theory, was, after Roosevelt, the main architect of America's disastrous foreign policy.

There were trained and experienced foreign service officials who saw the situation far more realistically. Joseph C. Grew, Undersecretary of State during the first months of 1945, wrote his views on the growing Russian danger in a remarkably prescient memorandum in May 1945. Arthur Bliss Lane fought gallantly and consistently for justice to Poland. Loy Henderson and George Kennan never succumbed to the trend in favor of blindly trusting Stalin and appeasing him at any cost.

Unfortunately the judgments and recommendations of these trained experts were often brushed aside. Roosevelt preferred the opinions of his court favorites, inexperienced amateurs, dilettantes, wishful thinkers. It is, after all, not difficult to be a wishful thinker on a subject of which one has no real knowledge.

The war ended with the unconditional surrender of the Axis powers. But the realization of this vainglorious Casablanca slogan did not usher in the reign of assured peace, international justice, and all the humane virtues which the more imaginative evangelists of intervention had so confidently prophesied. What followed the world's worst war was the world's most dismal inability to achieve any kind of peace settlement. Indeed, five years after the end of the fighting there was no formal peace at all, only the shadow of another war. There is the measure of the failure of America's Second Crusade.

The Meaning of Yalta

FORREST C. POGUE

WHEN ON June 22, 1941, Hitler struck with some 164 divisions against the U.S.S.R., Churchill, an ancient and bitter foe of Communist Russia, declared: "If Hitler invaded Hell I would make at least a favourable reference to the Devil in the House of Commons." To the British people he said: "Any man or state who fights on against Nazidom will have our aid. Any man or state who marches with Hitler is our foe." In his conclusion, he sanctified the Russian cause in a way that he could never thereafter completely gainsay:

The Russian danger is, therefore, our danger, and the danger of the United States, just as the cause of any Russian fighting for his hearth and home is the cause of free men and free peoples in every quarter of the globe. Let us learn the lessons already taught by such cruel experience. Let us redouble our exertions, and strike with united strength while life and power remain.

To Britain, Russia's entry in the war meant immediate salvation and the ultimate defeat of Hitler. For the United States it meant the chance to re-establish the balance of power in Europe. At the beginning of October the still technically neutral Roosevelt agreed to extend lend-lease to the Soviet Union. His main desire was to help in the fight against Hitler, but it is likely that he also agreed with Joseph E. Davies' remark two weeks after Hitler attacked the U.S.S.R. that it was to our advantage "to have a friendly Russia at Japan's rear."

British and American relief at having the Soviet Union on their side restrained them from putting pressure on the U.S.S.R. when that country was

From Forrest C. Pogue, "The Struggle for a New Order," in *The Meaning of Yalta*, edited by John Snell (Baton Rouge: Lousiana State University Press, 1956) pp. 7-9; 14-34. Reprinted by permission of Louisiana State University Press.

desperate for aid. Churchill, who tried to get a settlement of Polish questions with Stalin in July, 1941, ultimately settled for a mere statement that the Nazi-Soviet Pact of 1939 had lost its validity. Later he explained that the Allies faced a dilemma from the start. Despite a strong sympathy for the Poles, in whose behalf Britain had gone to war in 1939, he felt that he could not force Britain's "new and sorely threatened ally to abandon, even on paper, regions on her frontiers which she had regarded for generations as vital to her security." For him there was no way out and the issue of Polish boundaries had to be postponed to "easier times." This dilemma was never completely resolved and its horns showed plainly in the Yalta settlement.

The United States became a full partner with Britain and the Soviet Union in December, 1941, when Japan struck at Pearl Harbor and Germany and Italy declared war on the United States in support of their Axis partner. Since 1945 some noted historians have held that Roosevelt provoked Japan to war, and they have implied that Japan was not aggressive. But among the American people who had watched Japan march across Manchuria and China and then, after the fall of France, into French Indochina, the reaction in December, 1941, was that Japanese military power must be destroyed if there was to be peace in the Pacific. The attack on Pearl Harbor, Clark Field, Bataan, and Corregidor, stories of the Death March, the menace of the Japanese advance on the Dutch East Indies and Australia all created an impression which was not effaced throughout the war. Even though the public might accept attack against the Germans first, the fundamental feeling was that ultimately "we must settle with the Japs." Americans might talk of vengeance against the Germans, but they felt a burning anger against the "treacherous" Japanese that was not completely satisfied until American troops stood on Japanese soil and hauled up the Stars and Stripes over Tokyo.

The Big Three were now in active partnership, although the U.S.S.R. did not declare war against Japan. For the moment the Americans and the British were content that their hard-pressed ally remain at peace with the Pacific foe. More than nine months before, British and American army and navy representatives had agreed that if the United States and Britain should find themselves at war with Germany and Japan, American operations in the Pacific would be conducted in such a manner as to facilitate the major attack against Germany. Shortly after the war began, the war plans division of the War Department prepared a report, drawn up in part by Brigadier General Dwight D. Eisenhower, which approved this strategy. For the moment, therefore, the emphasis was on British and American efforts to aid the Russians against Germany. The period in which Soviet aid against Japan would be needed was to come later. . . .

THE SEARCH FOR A LASTING PEACE

An important reason for American concessions at Yalta was to be Roosevelt's conviction, nurtured by Hull, that a successful world order could be built only with Soviet cooperation. The President did not initially visualize an organization like the old League of Nations, but from the very beginning of war in Europe he said that the United States would use its influence to seek a final peace which would eliminate the use of force as far as possible. Hull, who had strongly supported Wilson's League, concentrated his efforts on drafting a peace organization which the United States Congress and the Great Powers of the world would accept. Soon after the outbreak of war in Europe, he instituted studies of postwar problems. Under the chairmanship of Undersecretary of State Sumner Welles, the postwar peace organization became one of the State Department's chief projects. Hull established a committee of forty-five members, including representatives from Congress, the press, and labor and business organizations, and asked the Senate Foreign Relations Committee to select members of the major parties to study the draft proposals and suggest changes.

Great emphasis was also placed on the need for Russian collaboration in the establishment of the proposed world organization. The State Department's Subcommittee on Political Problems declared in a report of January, 1943, that "Russian co-operation on the principal international problems was essential and must be obtained." A short time later, Roosevelt, who had been discussing with Churchill the possible establishment of regional councils under a world organization, suggested a four-power arrangement by which the United States, Great Britain, the Soviet Union, and China would police the world until the other powers were disarmed. He thought that these powers had worked well together in prosecuting the war, that personal contacts among the heads of governments were effective, and that "the direct relationship among the chiefs of the four nations would result in efficient future management of the world." While he eventually changed this concept somewhat, the President never gave up his belief that the Big Four or the Big Three must continue to serve as the world "policemen" until the new order was completely established. At various conferences he tended to be impatient with the claims of the lesser powers. More than once in discussing the Poles, Roosevelt said that he would not have them disturbing the peace but would have just settlements worked out for them by the Great Powers. This idea foretold trouble when Roosevelt coupled it with the notion that he could work out any world problem by sitting down and talking to Churchill and Stalin.

The efforts of Hull and Roosevelt toward four-power co-operation bore fruit in the declaration by Great Britain, the United States, the U.S.S.R., and China at Moscow in October, 1943, that there should be organized as soon as practicable "a general international organization, based on the principle of sovereign equality of all peace-loving states, and open to membership by all such states, large and small, for the maintenance of international peace and security." On his return from the meeting, Hull told a joint session of Congress that, once the provisions of the Moscow Declaration were carried into effect, there would be no need "for spheres of influence, for alliances, for balance of power or any other of the special arrangements through which, in the unhappy past, the nations strove to safeguard their security or to promote their interests."

The passage of the Fulbright Resolution by the House of Representatives in September and of the Connally Resolution by the Senate in November, 1943, gave impetus to the movement to establish the postwar organization. The overwhelming majorities in favor of these resolutions for United States participation in an international organization indicated that Congress had changed since 1920 and, indeed, since 1940. At the beginning of February, 1944, the President approved the State Department's draft charter for a United Nations organization. Shortly afterwards, Secretary Hull invited the British and Soviet governments to exchange ideas on a future peace organization. In April Hull outlined his own view of the proposed international authority, emphasizing that there was no hope of "turning victory into enduring peace" unless the four major powers agreed to work together. "This," wrote Hull, "is the solid framework upon which all future policy and international organization must be built." "Without an enduring understanding between these four nations upon their fundamental purposes, interests, and obligations to one another," the Secretary of State continued, "all organizations to preserve peace are creations on paper and the path is wide open again for the rise of a new aggressor."

By late April the State Department decided that the Executive Council of the world organization should contain the four major Allied powers as permanent members plus other nonpermanent members elected by the Assembly. In an effort to settle an old question which had raised trouble in the League of Nations, the planners deliberately sought to protect the interests of the Great Powers by recommending that their concurring vote would be required on all decisions affecting (1) final terms of settlement of disputes, (2) the regulation of armaments and armed forces, (3) the maintenance of peace, and (4) enforcement measures. In this provision that the Council majority vote must include the concurrence of all permanent members was the idea of the veto, a provision of the United Nations Charter sometimes attributed to Soviet Russia and often blamed on the Yalta conference. Some of the members of the State Department committee even objected to the provision that a permanent member could not have its vote counted if it were a party to a dispute before the Council. As a result of their objection to any impairment of the right of veto, the matter was left open for later settlement. It is clear that the veto was one invention for which the Russians cannot claim sole credit; it had strong support in American and British circles before the meeting at Yalta.

In keeping with his policy of avoiding the mistakes which frustrated the work of the League, Hull submitted the finished draft of the State Department's peace organization recommendations to former Chief Justice Charles Evans Hughes, to Nathan Miller, former Republican governor of New York, and to John W. Davis, onetime Democratic candidate for President. All three made suggestions for improving the draft, but gave it their approval. At the Secretary of State's request, the Senate Foreign Relations Committee next named eight of its members to study the draft with him. The group included eight of the most distinguished members of the upper house: Tom Connally, Alben W. Barkley, Walter George, Guy Gillette, Robert M. LaFollette, Arthur H. Vandenberg, Warren Austin, and Wallace H. White. Hull, after outlining the steps which had been taken, said that the success of the organization would depend on keeping Russia "solidly in the international movement," having an informed public opinion, and preventing the organization from becoming a domestic political issue. Vandenberg, after studying the State Department's draft, found it striking in that it was "so conservative from a nationalist standpoint." Noting that there was no action looking toward the use of force if any one of the Big Four objected, he called it "anything but a wild-eyed internationalist dream of a world State." The Republican Senator's only misgiving was over the possibility that, if established before the peace treaty, the peace organization might have to uphold a bad peace: this point aside, Vandenberg was "deeply impressed (and surprised) to find Hull so carefully guarding our American veto in his scheme of things."

Some of the senators, unnamed by Hull, but apparently including Austin and White, thought the veto to be a serious defect. The Secretary of State replied: "The veto power is in the document primarily on account of the United States. It is a necessary safeguard in dealing with a new and untried world arrangement." Hull added that it was necessary to make the organization palatable to the Big Three, since there was no likelihood that any two of the three Great Powers would undertake another world organization with the third missing. On this point the Secretary added that the United States could not stop in the middle of the war and quarrel with the Soviet Union over peace terms, and could not serve her with ultimatums which might drive her into Hitler's arms.

The senators did not give Hull's draft a complete endorsement, but they told him to go ahead with his planning. Much of his energies in the summer of 1944 were spent in keeping the proposed peace organization out of the presidential campaign. At Hull's invitation the Republican candidate, Governor Thomas E. Dewey, sent his adviser on foreign affairs, John Foster Dulles, to discuss the draft. After three sessions, Dulles said that Dewey would go along with Hull's proposals. Later, the New York governor sent down three proposed amendments on procedure, two of which were adopted. It was believed that the third was adequately covered in the draft. After the close of the Dumbarton Oaks conference, Dulles wrote Hull that he and Dewey highly appreciated the results of that meeting. He added that while there were many imperfections and inadequacies, the main thing was that the organization had been brought into sight. "For this," he declared, "the world owes you much." Apparently he accepted the veto idea along with the other elements of the peace organization.

In an effort to get broad agreement by the four Great Powers on the draft of the postwar peace organization, conversations were carried on by representatives of the United States, Great Britain, and the U.S.S.R. at Dumbarton Oaks, in Washington, from August 21 to September 28, 1944, and between the United States, Great Britain, and China from September 29 to October 7, 1944. The United States, which had taken the lead in outlining the framework of the peace organization, played host to the delegates. Secretary Hull, who had already by his unceasing efforts established his claim to the title of "Father of the U.N." later bestowed on him by Roosevelt, continued to work as hard as his failing health permitted to eliminate differences at home and abroad which might interfere with the ultimate adoption of the peace organization. In the course of the discussions the title "United Nations," which had already appeared in some earlier drafts, was adopted as the title of the new organization. It appeared in the seventh draft of the text under the date of September 15, 1944.

The first differences between the Russians and the western Allies in the conference developed when the British delegation declared that the votes of parties to a dispute before the Security Council should not be counted. The Americans agreed, adding that this was a case in which even a permanent member of the Council could not impose its veto. They made clear that there was no disagreement on the requirement of unanimous consent by all permanent members on nonprocedural matters of peace and security. The Soviet representatives at once disagreed. A second point of disagreement developed on August 28 when Ambassador Andrei A. Gromyko declared that the sixteen Soviet Republics of the U.S.S.R. should be initial members of the new peace organization. This proposal was not entirely unexpected since the Russians had asked for extra seats on the War Crimes Commission in the previous December, and in February, 1944, had announced that the Soviet Republics were autonomous in matters of foreign affairs. President Roosevelt, on being informed of Gromyko's proposal, replied that the United States could "under no conditions accept such a proposal." Both he and members of the State Department delegation talked to the Russian ambassador, who said he would drop the point but that his government would probably raise the question again.

Fearing that the Russian proposal would endanger the success of the whole peace project, the Americans argued that the question of membership for the Soviet Republics should be postponed until after the organization was established. The President cabled Stalin at the end of August, expressing his doubts about Gromyko's suggestion, and received a reply indicating the Marshal's desire for an opportunity to explain the political importance of the proposal. So convinced was the White House of the danger of the Soviet proposition that knowledge of it was closely restricted. It was not known to the entire American delegation until mid-October.

During the first ten days of September, Hull and Under-secretary of State

Edward R. Stettinius discussed the voting formula with Roosevelt. The President and Secretary both instructed Stettinius to vote "no" on the Russian proposal for voting in procedural matters. In writing of this episode, Hull has noted: "Aside from this, there was no question in our minds, however, that the vote of the permanent members of the Council should be unanimous on questions involving security. This was the so-called veto power. We were no less resolute than the Russians in adhering to this principle. . . ." On the remaining, but key, exception Hull tried unsuccessfully to get Gromyko to withdraw his proposal for sixteen seats. Roosevelt intervened with the Soviet ambassador and urged Stalin by cable to agree to the American and British views. Despite these efforts, the Russians held firm and announced on September 13 that their government insisted on a complete veto for permanent members of the Council and that this position was final.

The American delegation, anxious to break the deadlock with the U.S.S.R., now began work on possible compromise solutions. One suggestion, that of empowering the Council to request, but not require, a major nation to refrain from voting on consideration of a matter to which it was a party, was dropped as insufficient. Next a compromise formula was brought forward which would differentiate between the degree of unanimity required on decisions involving the pacific settlement of disputes and other decisions made by the Security Council. This was not presented officially, but was set down as the maximum compromise the United States would make. Meanwhile, Marshal Stalin on September 15 cabled the President that the way to a solution might still be found in some special procedure for voting, but it was felt in Washington that this gave no real encouragement for a change in his basic position. Neither Roosevelt nor Churchill at this juncture appeared favorable to any compromise.

Differences developed between two groups in the American delegation at Dumbarton Oaks over the need of reaching a compromise. One group held that continued controversy would prejudice the success of the conference, impair military co-operation among the Great Powers, and "adversely affect the prospect of Russia's entering the war against Japan." The other group held that the danger of disagreement was exaggerated. Hull at this point called the delegation together and reminded them of the need for patience and friendliness toward the Russians. He felt in the long run that they would follow the course of international co-operation, since it was the only way in which they could advance their vital interests. The Secretary voiced his anxiety over the effects of the Russian proposals on the attitudes of the small nations, and indicated his concern over the effect on the postwar organization of a "walk out" by any major nation.

The Russians made Hull's position no easier by announcing a few days later, through Gromyko, that Russian agreement upon a date for calling a general conference of the United Nations would depend on British and American acceptance of the Soviet view on voting and on membership for the Soviet Republics. The other delegations made no comment at this point, but turned to the second phase of the conferences, in which they discussed the peace organization draft with the more agreeable Chinese.

Hull's anxiety over the effect of Russian abstention from a postwar peace organization was shared by an old champion of the League of Nations and an adviser of prime ministers and presidents, Marshal Jan Smuts of the Union of South Africa. Smuts was no friend of communism, but he wrote Churchill in September, 1944, when Russia was giving trouble at Dumbarton Oaks: "Should a World Organization be formed which does not include Russia she will become the power centre of another group. We shall then be heading towards a third World War." He also felt that it might be necessary to have Russian help in driving Japan from China. Churchill forwarded this message to Roosevelt, who replied: "I think we are all in full agreement with him as to the necessity of having the U.S.S.R. as a fully accepted and equal member of any association of the Great Powers formed for the purpose of preventing international war." In a significant statement, he added: "It should be possible to accomplish this by adjusting our differences through compromise by all the parties concerned, and this ought to tide things over for a few years until the child learns how to toddle."

In early October the President characterized as "absurd" the Soviet proposal to extend membership to all the Soviet Republics. China's ambassador was informed of the suggestion and was told that Roosevelt, Churchill, and Chiang Kai-shek would probably have to take up the matter with Stalin. Members of the Joint Steering Committee were warned to keep the Russian position secret inasmuch as "the whole civilized world would be shocked by such a proposal" if it were not handled properly. Gossip about the matter, it was feared, would lead to criticism of the Soviet Union and jeopardize the whole movement toward international organization.

The President on October 7, the last day of the Dumbarton Oaks conference, informed the delegates that the matter of voting and membership should be dealt with at the highest level. Soon after the conference adjourned, Roosevelt declared that there was no time to lose in pressing forward the formation of a world organization. "It is our objective," he added, "to establish the solid foundations of the peace organization without further delay, and without waiting for the end of hostilities." Stalin about a month later spoke of differences which existed between the Great Powers, but noted that the surprising thing was not the number of differences, but the fact that there were so few. "What matters," he asserted, "is not that there are differences, but that these differences do not transgress the bounds of what the interests of unity of the three great powers allow, and that in the long run they are resolved in accordance with the interests of that unity."

Six questions relating to the international organization were left open by the Dumbarton Oaks conference for future settlement by a conference of the heads of governments. In addition to voting and membership, these included territorial trusteeship, the statute of an international court, the location of the international organization, and the means of transition from the League of Nations to the new organization. Of these, voting and membership were most pressing. Both were to have a prominent place on the agenda at Yalta and are commonly associated with the mistakes of that conference.

YALTA AND THE WAR

Stettinius, Brynes, Sherwood, and others have blamed the President's "concessions" at Yalta on the exigencies, real or imagined, of the military situation just before and during the Crimea conference. It is useful to consider: (1) the extent to which Soviet contributions to the war conditioned the decisions of Roosevelt and Churchill at Yalta, (2) the extent to which the Russian military position in February, 1945, made it impossible for the West to impose conditions unacceptable to the U.S.S.R., and (3) the extent to which Russian help was necessary in the Far East.

THE GROWING POWER OF THE U.S.S.R.

From June, 1941, until the opening of the Allied attack on North Africa in November, 1942, the Soviet Union bore the brunt of German attacks virtually alone. The British, still reeling from the Battle of Britain and with their forces spread out in the Pacific, the Mediterranean, the Near East, and the home islands, found it impossible to meet Stalin's continued pleas for the opening of a second front in the Arctic and in France. When in September, 1941, Stalin asked the British to send twenty-five to thirty divisions to Archangel or across Iran to his southern front, Churchill had to refuse. Hitler then had more troops in France than the British had in the United Kingdom, and the Prime Minister replied that to put even two divisions into the Caucasus would take at least three months. Nor did the entry of the United States into the war immediately help the situation. With no more divisions in being than Stalin had on the Manchurian border, and with part of these not ready for combat, the United States was in no position to accept Stalin's invitation to fight on Russian soil.

The best the western Allies could offer the Russians in the spring of 1942 was a possible emergency landing in the Cherbourg Peninsula in France to take some pressure off the eastern front. But with only nine divisions available for this task, it seemed unlikely that such an attack would create much diversion from the German offensive. When Churchill journeyed to Moscow to explain that the main Allied offensive in 1942 would be in North Africa, he was bluntly told that it would be of little direct help to the U.S.S.R. When, a year later, the second front in western Europe had still not been opened, Stalin declared that he had not been aided by the fighting in the Mediterranean; in fact, he said, Hitler had transferred thirty-six more divisions from the west to the Russian front. In these circumstances the Prime Minister often hesitated to oppose strongly some of the territorial concessions demanded by the Soviet government.

When at last the second front was opened in Normandy in June, 1944, the U.S.S.R. had passed over from the defensive to the offensive. A few days after D Day, the Red army began a sweep into Rumania, Hungary, the Baltic states, and Poland, making clear to the world that a new force was now abroad in Europe. It does not detract from the great victories of the British and American forces in the west to state that their conquests were surpassed by those of the Russians. In the three months from June to September, when the forces under Eisenhower fought brilliantly against 700,000 Germans in the west, the much larger Soviet forces inflicted 900,000 casualties on Hitler's armies. When Churchill and American strategists reflected on this fact it became apparent to them that Britain's position would be diminished in the postwar world. The United States, with great manpower reserves and enormous industrial production, might sit down in the future on a basis of equality with the U.S.S.R., but it was clear that the British role would be reduced. And when Roosevelt spoke, as he often did, of taking his troops back home as soon as possible after the war, the Prime Minister felt much alone. However, as a historian and a generous ally, he gave due credit to the Russians in his address to the House of Commons in August, 1944, when he said flatly that the Russian Army had done "the main work of tearing the guts out of the German army."

There can be little doubt that Churchill's desire to build up the British position counted as much as his anti-Russian fears in his much publicized argument for additional operations in the Mediterranean. In June, 1944, as he argued against the launching of the attack against southern France, he angrily declared: "Let us at least have a chance to launch a decisive strategic stroke with what is entirely British and under British command. I am not going to give way about this for anybody. Alexander is to have his campaign." He also spoke of sending troops in Istria at the head of the Adriatic Sea and possibly on to Vienna. When these suggestions went unheeded, he turned from the military to the diplomatic field, seeking to obtain commitments from Stalin in October, 1944, which would guarantee a degree of British influence in eastern Europe. The fact that the Prime Minister took the initiative must have indicated to Stalin that the British now held an uncertain position and under sufficient pressure would retreat in future exchanges. And the agreement to divide the Balkans into spheres of influence was bound to weaken any moral stand Churchill might wish to take at a later conference.

REVERSES IN THE WEST

Western bargaining power at Yalta was limited by the realities of the military situation which then prevailed. Two German armies, containing a number of divisions shifted from the eastern front, hit General Eisenhower's First Army on December 16, 1944. In the week that followed, Hitler's forces took advantage of surprise, concentration, and bad flying weather to create the "Bulge," forcing American troops back to the Meuse. The attack upset an offensive which had just been launched by the First Army in the direction of the Roer River dams, and disrupted planning for an Allied spring campaign.

The German surprise punch intensified already existing shortages of riflemen and supplies. The British since late summer had been forced to break up some of their regular units to get infantry replacements; the French surplus manpower could not yet be used for lack of equipment. At Eisenhower's call for more men, the Joint Chiefs of Staff moved up the sailing date of all units assigned to the European theater and allocated two other divisions initially intended for the Pacific area. In addition, Washington ordered a "comb out" of all men in Panama, Alaska, and the American defense commands who were fit for infantry duty. Eisenhower started a drastic search for front-line men in his own rear echelon commands and asked if the Marines might be able to send 100,000 men. Among the troops rushed to the front there were many newly inducted eighteen-year-olds with little training. The Joint Chiefs of Staff notified the President that when the units already allocated had sailed, there would not be another division left in the United States. All these actions did not mean that the American position was desperate, but they did indicate that the United States was in no position to dispense with Soviet aid in Europe.

With the possibility that the Russian drive in the east was stalled for weeks or perhaps "for the duration," Eisenhower asked Washington on December 21 to determine Soviet intentions for operations in the coming months. A few days before, Ambassador Averell Harriman had asked about Stalin's intentions and had learned that a Soviet winter offensive would be launched. Unaware of this, Eisenhower reminded Marshall of the shift of German units from the Russian front to his own and stated that, if the trend continued, "it will affect the decisions which I have to make regarding future strategy in the west. . . . If, for instance, it is the Russian intention to launch a major offensive in the course of this or next month, knowledge of the fact would be of the utmost importance to me and I would condition my plans accordingly."

Eisenhower's request for information prompted the President to ask Marshal Stalin if he would receive SHAEF representatives to discuss the situation in western Europe and future plans, adding that the situation in Belguim was not bad but that it was necessary to see what came next. When the Soviet chief agreed, Eisenhower sent his deputy commander, his chief of operations, and his deputy chief of intelligence to Moscow. On January 15, soon after their arrival in Moscow, they were told that the Russian offensive had been opened three days earlier. Stalin declared that in view of Allied difficulties the attack, under preparation for more than a month, had been speeded up despite bad weather. He added that from 150 to 160 divisions had been thrown into an eight- to ten-week campaign with orders to reach the Oder. Stalin was not certain that he could keep the attack going until May, but he promised to stir up the Germans and prevent them from shifting from his front to the west. Even though his attack had come two weeks after the worst of the Ardennes offensive had been met by Allied troops, Stalin stressed his benevolent role in aiding Eisenhower. He remarked that it would be as foolish for him to stand aside while the Germans annihilated the western Allies as it was wise for the West to prevent the enemy from crushing the Soviet forces.

General Eisenhower, in outlining future operations, informed General Marshall on January 15 of the importance of a continued Russian offensive to the success of the Allied spring offensive. Asked whether or not the eighty-five divisions which would be available in the spring would be sufficient to defeat Germany, he said they might if the Soviet attack went well. Two weeks later Eisenhower reviewed his situation with Marshall at Marseilles when the Chief of Staff stopped briefly on his way to Malta, where he was to discuss military plans before proceeding to Yalta. At Malta a few days later, Eisenhower's chief of staff, Lieutenant General Walter Bedell Smith, told Stettinius there was an outside chance that the Russian advance might be at an end, and that there was a possibility that the Germans might retire to southwest Germany and conduct guerrilla warfare for months or even years. Thus, on the eve of the Yalta conference Marshall and his associates were convinced that Russian aid was essential to a successful and speedy culmination of the war in Europe.

It would be totally misleading to hold Eisenhower or his staff responsible for the Yalta concessions. It was Hitler's fault that Eisenhower needed a continued Russian offensive. Because of the Ardennes counteroffensive, it would be March 24 before the Anglo-American forces could cross the Rhine in force on all fronts. Meanwhile, Eisenhower's emphasis on the importance of the aid by a Russian force, plus General Bedell Smith's anxieties about the future course of Russian action, must have been considered by Roosevelt's military advisers when they suggested at Yalta that he get further Soviet help. Certainly, as far as Eisenhower was concerned, the need to co-ordinate his drive with that of the Russians was of paramount interest. However, his insistence on keeping Stalin informed of his plans drew down on him sharp words from Churchill and the British Chiefs of Staff.

THE RUSSIAN FRONT DURING THE YALTA CONFERENCE

The effect of the Russian initiative in the east was soon apparent. The Soviet offensive began on January 12, 1945. In two weeks the Red Army cut off some thirty German divisions in Latvia and it appeared that the enemy could not make a stand short of the Oder. On January 20 Hitler ordered Field Marshal Gerd von Rundstedt, commander-in-chief of the western front, to prepare to send the Sixth Panzer Army with four SS armored divisions and two Fuehrer brigades to the Russian front. Reichsfuehrer SS Heinrich Himmler was transferred from command of Army Group Oberrhein to Army Group Weichsel on the eastern front.

At the end of January, 1945, Marshal Konstantin K. Rokossovsky had moved northward from Warsaw to the Baltic and isolated East Prussia from the Reich. Marshal Ivan S. Konev forced his way westward across the south of Poland to the Oder and established several bridgeheads across it during the early days of February—in time for his action to be announced at the Yalta conference. Poland thus lay in the hands of the Russians or of the Lublin government, which the U.S.S.R. recognized as the government of the liberated area. In the area between Rokossovsky's and Konev's forces, Marshal Georgi K. Zhukov moved westward, sending powerful armored columns in the direction of Berlin. Advance units were within less than one hundred miles of the German capital while the Big Three debated the fate of Poland and Germany at Yalta. These were facts above which personal diplomacy could not rise.

THE WAR IN THE FAR EAST

Military needs in the Far East likewise demanded consideration by Churchill and Roosevelt in February, 1945. At the time of the Yalta conference, the Japanese had 2,000,000 to 2,500,000 men under arms in Japan, 1,000,000 in China, and 1,000,000 in Manchuria and Korea. The United States by the end of the war had sent approximately 1,459,000 army and air force men and 187,500 Marines into the Pacific, scattered from Australia to Alaska. "In general," as Admiral Ernest J. King, Chief of Naval Operations, put it at Yalta, "the forward line . . . included Attu, the Marianas, and Luzon." He added that American forces controlled the sea and air beyond that line and up to China, Formosa, the Ryukyus, and even to the coast of Japan itself. Luzon, he might have added, had been under attack for a month, and it was to be nearly five more months before Bataan was cleared and Corregidor was retaken. In this last six-month campaign to clear the Philippines, American forces were to suffer 60,000 casualties while killing 300,000 Japanese.

Between February 19, 1945, and March 16, 1945, two to six weeks after the completion of the Yalta conference and at a time when many experts later claimed the Japanese had been defeated by air and sea action, the Marine Corps took Iwo Jima, an island two and one-half miles wide by four and two-thirds miles long. In what has been called its bitterest battle, the Marine Corps killed some 20,000 Japanese at a cost of nearly 7,000 dead and some 20,000 wounded. Just as they were completing this operation, the "greatest sea-air battle in history" was launched against Okinawa by Admiral Richmond K. Turner and General Simon B. Buckner. In eighty-two days of struggle the Japanese force (including Okinawan conscripts) lost more than 100,000 dead. More than 7,800 planes were destroyed. But United States Army and Marine casualties numbered some 39,000, of whom 7,300, including General Buckner, were dead. Naval casualties afloat were 10,000 with 5,000 dead. Japanese planes sank 36 ships and damaged 368 others. American losses were the highest experienced in any campaign against the Japanese. Hanson Baldwin has summarized the results succinctly: "Never before, in so short a space, had the Navy lost so many; never before in land fighting had so much American blood been shed in so short a time in so small an area; probably never before in any three months of the war had the enemy suffered so hugely." Japan was by no means defeated in February, 1945, and Russian participation in the war against her seemed highly desirable to the West.

General Douglas MacArthur was among those who realized this and advocated Soviet entry into the war in the Pacific. On February 25, 1945, Rear Admiral Charles M. Cooke and Brigadier General G. A. Lincoln discussed these matters with the Pacific commander, and shortly afterward Lincoln took them up with General MacArthur and his chief of staff. In a memorandum written on February 25, Lincoln reported: "General MacArthur spoke of the strength of the opposition to be expeceted in invading the Japanese home islands. He declared that planning should start at once, that heavy fire power would be needed to cover the beachheads, and that as many Japanese divisions as possible should first be pinned down on the mainland, principally by Soviet forces."

It is understandable that the Pacific commander would want additional help at the time of his landings. Enemy conduct in opposing landings on Luzon, Iwo Jima, and Okinawa in the spring and summer of 1945 provided no grounds for the belief that opposition was getting lighter. American casualty figures in the Pacific jumped from an average of 3,200 per month to 12,750 per month in the first seven months of 1945. Apparently MacArthur's view of the value of a Russian attack did not lessen during the summer months. When news was brought him of the Soviet declaration of war, he declared on August 9, 1945: "I am delighted at the Russian declaration of war against Japan. This will make possible a great pincers movement that cannot fail to end in the destruction of the enemy."

All in all, the military backdrop for the Yalta negotiations, while more favorable to the West than it had been at any time since 1939, did not yet afford Roosevelt and Churchill the luxury of renouncing or foregoing Soviet military co-operation in Europe and Asia.

15

The Communist Victory in China:

WAS CHINA BETRAYED?

DURING *World War II, Marshal Stalin had, at various times, pledged to support Chiang Kai-shek's Nationalist regime in China. Simultaneously, however, he was secretly lending assistance to the Chinese Communists who, under Mao Tse-tung, were planning to oust Chiang and take over the country. Open warfare between the two Chinese factions erupted at the end of 1945, and the long, cruel Chinese civil war began. The United States did not have much choice in settling on a China policy. It could not mount a large-scale invasion to help Chiang, largely because American troops were in the process of demobilization and the public would not have been willing to see them back in uniform fighting halfway across the world. Nor could Washington have washed its hands of the whole affair—Chiang was an ally and the American people had a sympathy with China which precluded abandonment. The only alternative was to attempt to bring the warring factions together and have them establish a coalition government. This task was undertaken by General George C. Marshall on a special mission in 1945. Marshall achieved some success in calling a truce and in gaining the consent of both sides to work on a new constitution and a coalition government. But his triumph was short-lived. War soon broke out again. General Albert Wedemeyer on another mission in 1947 could accomplish nothing. Despite American military and economic aid to Chiang, Mao moved from victory to victory. In January, 1949, he captured Peking, in May Shanghai, Canton in October, and Chungking in November. On December 8, 1949, Chiang fled to Formosa. China was in Communist hands. How did it happen? Was the United States to blame? Could the United States have saved the Nationalist government?*

A large segment of the American people believed that China fell because important officials in the Department of State favored the Communists and withheld aid from Chiang. The veteran journalist John T. Flynn presents that view in the selection that follows. A severe critic of Franklin D. Roose-

velt, the New Deal, and Democratic foreign policy, Flynn lists four blunders which lost China to the Communists and imputes the mistakes to three men —Franklin D. Roosevelt, Dean Acheson, and George C. Marshall who were sold the idea by Communists and Communist sympathizers in the United States government that the Chinese Reds constituted the wave of the future while the Nationalists were hopeless fascists. Flynn recounts as errors in policy Marshall's insistence on a coalition government despite the fact that many persons considered this merely a prelude to Communist usurpation; Stillwell's appointment as commander in China despite the fact that he loathed Chiang and was, in Flynn's opinion, a dupe of pro-Communist foreign service officers in China; the allowing of Russia's entry into the war in Asia which, though needless, was urged by the "Red and pink-infested State Department"; and Marshall's threat that American help would be withheld from Chiang if he did not coalesce with Mao.

A substantially different interpretation is presented by John King Fairbank, an authority on Chinese history and a professor at Harvard. He maintains that the United States could not have prevented Communist domination of China. Indeed, China could not be controlled from the outside. The Communists were victorious because they were able to make the most of their revolutionary potentialities. They promised reform and social justice, and all the other benefits to be expected of a revolution. The Nationalists, on the other hand, met defeat because they were corrupt and demoralized. They collapsed economically, politically, morally, and militarily. Fairbank's reply to those who criticize the United States for not having extended to China the same type of aid as that given to Greece and Turkey is to point out the enormous differences in the size of the two areas. In a concluding section he comments on possible explanations for the prevalence of the "betrayal" theory.

The Blunders That Lost a Continent

JOHN T. FLYNN

As the war neared its end, it was clear that the "greatest whitewash in history" predicted by Senator LaFollette had been completed. We may assume that a few root facts are established by the evidence produced in the preceding pages. One is that our government had convinced itself that Russia and its Chinese dupes could be trusted as sincere partners in a peaceful world. The other is that our government, through a powerful propaganda drive in the press, books, the radio, movies and through government agencies had set out to sell this idea to the American people.

As a result of these two basic errors, a series of blunders were committed by our government which have resulted in the loss of China, in the possible loss of Japan and other Asiatic countries and in a war in Korea.

Where these fatal notions originated is difficult to say with certainty. But a few things are now clear. One is that Roosevelt adopted these ideas almost the moment they were presented to him. The other is that they were swallowed completely by General George Marshall and Secretary Dean Acheson. There is no doubt that these three men were willing and eager partners in the appeasement of Russia and the sacrifice of China, Korea and, in the end, perhaps all Asia.

BLUNDER NUMBER ONE

At the root of so many of the worst blunders in China was the decision of our government to force what it called "unity in China." We have already seen that this slogan was invented by the Soviet leaders in 1943 when they saw that German defeat was inevitable and they turned their attention to their suspended plans in Asia.

The Japanese occupied Manchuria and the entire Chinese coast. Chiang Kai-shek had a very large army, though poorly equipped. The Chinese Communists occupied just a few provinces at the North. Russia was then interested in checking further Japanese seizures in China. She was also interested in inserting her Communist leaders and armies in to the Nationalist government. This she called unity. It was a plausible slogan while Japan was in China. But in August 1945, when Japan surrendered and proceeded to evacu-

Quoted from *While You Slept* by John T. Flynn, published 1951 by The Devin-Adair Company, New York; copyright 1951 by John T. Flynn. Pp.157–178.

ate China, it lost its relevancy. As a matter of fact, the Chinese Communists and Russia, once Japan surrendered, were no longer interested in "unity in China" save on terms that would enable the Red politicians and Red soldiers to move into the government to disrupt it and, ultimately, take it over.

Those who are familiar with the history of Communist strategy and tactics know that the Communists have developed a highly effective method by which small, compact minorities can disrupt majority action. Chiang Kai-shek had been in this struggle against the Communists for years. He knew what we in America now know. We suffered a brief period of unity with a very small number of Communists in this country during the war. There is no one now—apparently not even Henry Wallace, their prize dupe—who has any illusions on that score any more. We who wanted Chiang Kai-shek to put the Communists in his government are now putting our American Communists in jail.

In spite of all this, Chiang Kai-shek was at all times willing, under the pressure we applied, to permit the Chinese Communists to come into the government as a political party, enjoying such influence as their numbers entitled them to have. But the Chinese Communists were never willing to come in as a political party, standing on their numerical strength. They wanted to march in intact and with their army intact. They did not want to unite with the government. They wanted to invade it.

Dr. Walter Judd, once a medical missionary in China and now a member of Congress, stated the proposal of a rational unity method in a Town Meeting of the Air Debate, December 27, 1945. He said that "if the Communists will agree to become a political party without an autonomous army and Chiang refuses to establish a democratic government with legal and equal status for all parties" then Chiang should be condemned. But "if he is willing to establish such a government and the Communists are unwilling to give up their separate army and administration and become a loyal opposition instead of an armed rebellion then their pretense is exposed."

Chiang did actually call a National Assembly which set in motion machinery to prepare and set up a constitution for a free republic in which all parties would be represented. The Communists made a show for a while of collaboration. But they were never serious in it and ultimately denounced the whole plan and refused to participate in the elections.

As a part of the whole Red program the most unrestrained abuse was hurled at Chiang Kai-shek in our newspapers, in our magazines, in those books and radio programs to which we referred in an earlier part of this book. Of course the Nationalist government had its defects. China is an old country, with no experience in representative government. It was painfully and disastrously emerging from its old feudal ways. There were selfish interests and extreme reactionary interests as well as extremely radical and visionary interests. Chiang sat at the center of all these contending elements seeking with an almost incredible patience to establish order in a republican government while all the time he was being opposed by a military force.

This was civil war, of course. General Marshall and our State Department demanded that Chiang end the civil war by surrendering to the rebels and bringing their army intact into his government. As we look at it now, that was the most monstrously crazy idea that ever entered the mind of a sane statesman. How does a government end a civil war? It can be done only by abdicating or by crushing the rebels. But Chiang was forbidden to attempt to crush the rebels by force on pain of being disarmed. General Marshall insisted that Chiang could trust the Communists. He now says he knew all along they were Communists. But he stated more than once to Americans in China that the charge was ridiculous—they were only "agrarian reformers." But Chiang knew, as everyone knows who was familiar with the strange, twisted morals of Communist associations, that they could not be trusted. Our State Department was to learn that late in the day. In 1950, after our policies had forced the defeat of Chiang and the establishment of the Chinese Soviet, the State Department wrote to Senator Knowland of California in answer to an inquiry, in which it repudiated every stupid claim it made for the Reds when it was coercing Chiang. It said:

"The Chinese leaders have betrayed their longstanding pledge of demobilization; instead are increasing manpower. Peiping has also broken its promises of social and economic improvement. In the great cities dependent on imported materials unemployment increases. The regime has not lightened the burdens of the people. They have increased them."

Yet, during the struggle we found our Communist sympathizers—writers, journalists, and some statesmen and State Department officials—regaling us with stories of the wonderful things the Communists were doing while calling on Chiang to do the same and, above all, to lower taxes, while we threatened that if the government dared to oppose the rebels with arms we would cut off their aid.

After the Chinese Republican government had been defeated—thanks to the State Department and General Marshall—and driven out of China, our State Department began to see some light. The so-called "agrarian reformers" had now become real Communists and, according to Secretary Acheson, "the Soviet government's largest and most important satellite."

Most impressive, Mr. Dean Rusk, Assistant Secretary of State in charge of the Far Eastern Division, said in a speech on May 18, 1951, what the government's critics had been saying all the time and for which they were denounced as "Fascists." Here we need quote only some sections of that speech:

"The independence of China is gravely threatened. In the Communist world there is room for only one master. . . . How many Chinese in one community after another are being destroyed because they love China more than they love Soviet Russia? The freedoms of the Chinese people are disappearing. Trial by mob, mass slaughter, banishment to forced labor in Manchuria and Siberia. . . ."

The peace and security of China are being driven by foreign masters into an adventure in foreign aggression."

Then comes this amazing statement:

"But one thing we can say: If the Chinese move to assert their freedom to work out their destiny in accordance with their own historical purposes, they can count on tremendous support from free peoples in other parts of the world."

This is indeed a nice time to talk of "support." When the Chinese tried to work out that destiny under Chiang Kai-shek they were told they would not get aid from us unless they took into their government the same collection of Communist assassins and tyrants who now govern China and who have shot down American boys in Korea. Mr. Rusk then makes this almost ridiculous statement: "We can tell our friends in China that the United States will not acquiesce in what is being forced on them." There is grim comedy for you —a very sour and bitter kind of comedy, however. And finally Assistant Secretary Rusk says:

"We do not recognize the authorities in Peiping for what they pretend to be. It is not the government of China. It does not pass the first test. It is not Chinese. . . . We recognize the Nationalist government of the Republic of China even though the territory under its control is severely restricted."

Restricted is hardly the word. It was driven out of China while we badgered, reviled and refused to aid it and has taken refuge in the small island of Formosa off the coast. Now, says Mr. Rusk, "we believe it more authoritatively represents the views of the great body of the people of China, particularly their demand for independence from foreign control." And then he concludes: "That government will *continue* to receive important aid and assistance from the United States." (Italics added.)

Confronted with this at the MacArthur hearings, Mr. Acheson said: "Mr. Rusk did not think he was stating any change in any policy established by the President and followed by the Department." For sheer, unadulterated gall, that is entitled to a prize.

BLUNDER NUMBER TWO

Even before his major intrusion into Chinese affairs, General Marshall made a grave mistake when he sent General Joseph W. Stilwell to China as military adviser to Chiang Kai-shek. Stilwell was an old soldier with many human and soldierly qualities. He knew something of China, where he had served for a spell. But he was utterly unconscious of its strange world of Communist dialectics and strategy. He was pathetically lacking in tact. He was, in fact, an irascible, intolerant and vitriolic partner. There was a gulf between this self-opinionated old warrior and the grave and reserved Oriental Generalissimo.

When Stilwell got to China in 1942, he flung himself into the struggle for the Burma Road then raging. In this he suffered a disastrous and, as he called it, "humiliating defeat." The China war, after that, for him was lost in the immensity of his own war against the Japs—to wipe out this stain on the fame of Joe Stilwell.

When he reached China he fell—as did everyone—into that busy, virulent cabal of State Department officials and news correspondents, almost all of whom had become the feverish protagonists of the "agrarian reformers" headed by Mao Tse-tung, and the bitter, busy critics of General Chiang Kai-shek. One of these China officials—John P. Davies, whom we have already met—was assigned to him as his adviser. Freda Utley, who was there, says that Agnes Smedley, an old and lyrical champion of the Chinese Red leaders, fascinated Stilwell. He and Chiang could agree on nothing. The Generalissimo resolutely refused to authorize another Burma expedition because he believed it hopeless unless he could get amphibious reinforcements. This ripened into a bitter feud on Stilwell's part. He poured out his scorn on the Generalissimo to the correspondents and State Department philosophers at his headquarters, who served as an admiring audience. Reports of Stilwell's unhappy relationships in China reached Roosevelt's ears. Harry Hopkins made a note at the time:

"The President indicated his strong dissatisfaction with the way the whole show was running in China. He stated that Stilwell obviously hated the Chinese and that his cablegrams are sarcastic about the Chinese and this feeling is undoubtedly known to the Generalissimo."

Roosevelt decided to bring Stilwell home, but Marshall defended him. Sherwood, Hopkin's biographer, wrote that Marshall had told him that his only serious disagreement with Hopkins was on the issue of Stilwell. Sherwood adds that "he was unquestionably a serious nuisance to Roosevelt and there were many times when he was on the verge of recalling him."

However, in spite of all this, Stilwell finally persuaded Chiang to launch another expedition into Burma. In addition, he persisted in his demand that he be made commander-in-chief of all Chiang's armies. In the midst of this situation, General Patrick J. Hurley arrived from Washington with a demand from the President, instigated by Marshall, that Stilwell be made commander-in-chief. Stilwell was an inveterate diarist and on September 12, 1944, he wrote triumphantly: "Chiang Kai-shek agrees to appoint Joseph W. Stilwell [as commander-in-chief] and give him his full confidence." But there was some delay and a few days later he confided to his diary: "We are in a battle with the Peanut." This was his name for Chiang. Finally, Stilwell received a cable from Roosevelt to Chiang to be delivered by Stilwell personally. Its contents have never been revealed. Hurley saw it and tried to dissuade Stilwell from delivering it. But Stilwell handed it to Chiang personally. He records the event in his diary:

"At long last . . . FDR has spoken plain words . . . with a firecracker in every sentence . . . "Get busy or else!" . . . I handed this bundle of paprika to the Peanut and then sank back with a sigh. The harpoon hit the little bugger right in the solar plexus and went right through him. It was a clear hit. But beyond turning green and losing the power of speech, he did not bat an eye."

Then he wrote a poem about it in his diary:

"I've waited long for vengeance—
      At last I've had my chance.
I've looked the Peanut in the eye
      And kicked him in the pants . . .

"The little bastard shivered
      And lost the power of speech.
His face turned green and quivered
      And he struggled not to screech . . .

"For all my weary battles
      For all my hours of woe
At last I've had my innings
      And laid the Peanut low."

But Stilwell reckoned without his host. A few weeks later he had to write in his diary: "The ax falls. Radio from George Marshall . . . I am recalled . . . so FDR has quit. Everybody at headquarters horrified." This meant the State Department and newspaper claque. But in Washington Marshall did not quit so easily. Admiral Leahy records what happened. The Generalissimo wrote Roosevelt that he "was willing and anxious to meet Roosevelt's wishes" that an American officer command all Chinese forces. But he insisted that "it must be one in whom I can repose confidence. . . . The officer must be capable of frank and sincere cooperation, and General Stilwell has shown himself conspicuously lacking in these indispensable qualifications." Admiral Leahy writes that Marshall even after this made an effort to dissuade Roosevelt but without success. Stilwell himself committed his sentiments to another poem about his downfall in unprintable English (though it appears in his posthumous papers) and disappeared from the scene.

BLUNDER NUMBER THREE

Probably the greatest blunder of all in Asia was Roosevelt's decision to get Stalin into the war against Japan. Had he known anything of Russian history he would have known that nothing could have kept Stalin out of that war if he could get the door opened. Actually, Stalin had expressed his intention of coming in a number of times. In 1943, he told Hull in Moscow that he would join in defeating Japan. He made the promise "without any strings to it" and without being asked and he told Hull he might inform Roosevelt. On another occasion he told our Ambassador to Russia, Averell Harriman, that "Japan was the historic enemy of Russia and her eventual defeat was essential to Russian interests" and that "eventually she would come in." On another occasion the Marshall told General Hurley that he would assist America against Japan, and in 1944 he again told Harriman he would come in "provided the United States would assist in building up the reserves for 60 divisions in Siberia" and, of course "provided the political aspects of Russia's participation had been clarified." Indeed, Secretary Acheson, testifying during the MacArthur inquiry, admitted that "Russian participation or intervention in Manchuria was something that nobody had any power to prevent."

Had Roosevelt known as much as his shirt-stuffers have ascribed to him, he would have known that above all things he must keep Stalin out of the Asiatic war. Stalin would wish to be in it if for no other reason than to collect his share of the victory. There were scores of men in America who knew this subject who could have told Roosevelt precisely what Russia wanted. However, if such men opened their mouths, as some did, they were promptly set upon as "Fascists."

So intent was Stalin on insulating Roosevelt from adverse advice that he managed to get him into a secret meeting at which Russia agreed to enter the war. Roosevelt, sick, weary, ignorant of Soviet history, was an easy mark. Stalin, on his side, knew precisely what Roosevelt wanted. There was the Silvermaster group in Washington which used Harry Dexter White, Assistant Secretary of the Treasury, as one of its most important agents. There was Alger Hiss, high in the Division of Political Affairs of the State Department. They knew all that was in Roosevelt's mind. And what they knew Stalin knew. I know it is difficult for Americans to believe such things, but this is no longer a matter of mere surmise. The proof is all in.

The normal American does not understand the ceaseless energy that drove the Russian leaders and their dupes in this country. Someone has said that the strength of communism lies in its relentless activity. There is an overpowering element of drama in its dreams, its burning passion for pushing those dreams, its relentless cruelty in method—murder, blood, violence, conspiracy, vengeance—all exalted from the level of evil into a lofty plane of flaming righteousness by the splendor of the great dream. It is precisely the same evil human disorder which has sent religious fanatics out with flame and sword and the rack to punish and exterminate heretics. It is a kind of malignant idealism ablaze with glorified mischief which goads the minds of its devotees into restless and hot activity. Thus, while the evil saints in the Kremlin and in Yenan, with their agents in Washington at the highest levels, plotted and contrived, our President, aflame with pure vanity, and the more or less normal and uninformed men around him were so many jumping jacks in Stalin's hands. Meantime, our native contemptuous know-it-alls, either through sheer ignorance or something worse, assured us that "the Communists have become a peasant party . . . The Soviet Union stands for democracy" (Owen Lattimore in *Solution in Asia*, p. 108) and "The Soviet Union cannot have any expansionist tendencies" (Edgar Snow in *Battle for Asia*, p. 300). And our rather foolish agents in Washington swallowed it all.

In an earlier chapter we outlined the history of Russia's long-time aims in Manchuria, Mongolia and Sinkiang. The game in Asia was a struggle between

Japan and Russia for the Kwantung Peninsula and Manchuria. Russia had stolen these things from China and Japar stole them from Russia. Stalin's plan was to come into the war as close to the moment of Japan's exhaustion as possible, walk into Manchuria, and steal back as much of it as he could get. Roosevelt agreed he should have Port Arthur, Dairen, the Kurile Islands, Sakhalin and control of the Manchurian Railroads. But Stalin had not the slightest intention of permitting the Chinese Nationalist government to recover Manchuria. So he arranged that, with Roosevelt's consent, he would have an army of 1,250,000 Soviet troops fully equipped by the United States and perched on the Manchurian border when the Japanese surrendered, ready to walk in, and take as much as they could. Did not Roosevelt realize that he would turn the rest over to the Chinese Communists? This he could do only if he could get into the Japanese war. And this, of course, he did.

At Yalta, Stalin knew precisely the condition of Japan. He was at peace with her. He had a huge embassy in Tokyo and consuls all over Japan. And we may be sure that he had plenty of secret agents there. He knew Japan was exhausted. He knew the day of reckoning was not far off. Actually on the eve of Yalta the Japanese Foreign Minister had suggested to the Russian Ambassador in Tokyo the possibility of arranging for a settlement. Stalin did not communicate this to his allies.

George Marshall, for some reason which leads him astray whenever he moves away from the field of military organization, convinced himself that Japan would fight to the last Jap—something no nation has ever done, though many have threatened. He insisted on preparing for a land invasion of Japan with an army of 2,000,000 men and with an appalling number of estimated casualties. And he insisted we had to have Russia in the war to win—to fight the immense Kwantung army which Japan had in Manchuria. He apparently did not know what he should have known and what others knew—that this army was sadly deteriorated by levies for use in other parts of the vast Pacific battleground. Admiral Nimitz and General MacArthur had assured Roosevelt at Hawaii just after Roosevelt's nomination for his fourth term that as soon as they took the Philippines and the Marianas, Japan would be hopelessly cut off from supplies and that she would have to surrender. But Marshall was adamant.

Admiral Leahy says that Marshall didn't seem to realize that the Navy had beaten Japan. Edward Stettinius said that he knew of the "immense pressure put on the President by our military leaders to bring Russia into the Far Eastern war." He said that, as early as 1943 at Cairo, Harry Hopkins appeared with a document from the military, urging that Russia be brought in because "with Russia as an ally against Japan the war can be terminated in less time and at less expense in life and resources." From a political view of the matter there could be no possible argument for letting Russia in. However, from a military viewpoint this was more reasonable in 1943. At Yalta, in 1945, it was preposterous. Yet Stettinius says that as soon as Roosevelt reached Yalta, General Marshall went into a secret session with him. No delegates knew anything of this. The actual agreement about Russia's entry was made later in a secret session between Stalin and Roosevelt only. When later Secretary Stettinius asked Roosevelt about this secret meeting, Roosevelt put him off with the statement that it was a military matter and had better remain on that level. Thus even the Secretary of State was not let into the secret. So far as I know, only Hiss knew of it. The agreements made at Yalta were drawn up by a committee representing Britain, Russia and the United States. It was composed of Sir Gladwyn Jebb, Andrei Gromyko and Alger Hiss. Who represented us?

Admiral Leahy wrote in his memoirs:

"I was of the firm opinion that our war against Japan had progressed to the point where I was convinced that her defeat was only a matter of time and attrition. Therefore we did not need Stalin's help to defeat our enemy in the Pacific. The Army did not agree with me, and Roosevelt was prepared to bargain with Stalin."

Admiral King, in a letter to a Senate Committee, said he "believed" Japan could and should have been defeated without an invasion of the home islands. He said, "When the President asked me about making concessions to Premier Stalin in order to get him to play ball, I replied that I would concede him only half of the island of Sakhalin, and that as a sop." In addition, General H. H. Arnold, head of the Air Force, said in his memoirs that he sent one of his officers to Yalta to inform Roosevelt that the Japs had already been brought to their knees and that no Russian aid was needed.

A point stressed by the Marshall apologists is that at the time of Yalta no one knew whether or not the atomic bomb would work. However, General Leslie R. Groves, who was head of the atomic bomb project, informed Senator Hickenlooper (New York *Times*, June 28, 1951) that before the Yalta conference Roosevelt had been told that the atomic bomb was a 99-per-cent certainty and that the first bomb would be ready in August 1945 and that it would be extremely powerful.

Marshall was Chief of Staff of the Army. Of course, as we now know, and shall see fully, it was the huge Communist army on the Siberian border, equipped by us at an enormous outlay, which marched into Manchuria five days before the Japanese surrendered, took Manchuria, enabled the Japanese to deliver their arms to the Chinese Communists and for the first time set them up in business as a powerful war machine. At the roots of all this was the fact that in the State Department there were no political experts on Russo-Asiatic and Communist history and techniques to guide the generals. Marshall was getting his briefing on that from our Red and pink-infested State Department.

Secretary Acheson denied on the witness stand that there were any men in the State Department who favored the Communists. Yet we know that up to 1947 there were over a hundred in the Department who were so bad that a loyalty board after investigating them forced them out as bad security risks. This, however, did not eliminate all of those who favored the Communists in

China as against the Nationalist government. We have seen the evidence of that, and many of these men remained in the Department. On the witness stand following Acheson, General Hurley, who had been sent to China as the personal envoy of President Roosevelt, was asked about this. He answered by producing a letter he wrote to President Truman in November 1945:

"It is no secret that the American policy in China did not have the support of all the career men in the Department. The professional foreign service men sided with the Chinese Communists' armed party and the imperialist bloc of nations whose policy it was to keep China divided against herself. Our professional diplomats continuously advised the Communists that my efforts in preventing the collapse of the Nationalist government did not represent the policy of the United States. These same professionals openly advised the Communist armed party to decline unification of the Chinese Communists Army with the Nationalist Army unless the Chinese Communists were given control."

Hurley added: "I requested the relief of the career men who were opposing the American policy in the Chinese theatre of war. These professional diplomats were returned to Washington and placed in the Far Eastern and Chinese divisions of the State Department as my supervisors. Some of these same career men whom I relieved have been assigned as advisers to the Supreme Commander in Asia."

The men named by Hurley for return to America were George Atcheson, Jr., Chargé d'Affaires of the American Embassy, John P. Davies, Jr., consul and later second secretary, Fulton Freeman and Arthur Ringwalt, secretaries, John Stewart Service, Raymond P. Ludden, Hungerford B. Howard, Edward E. Rice and Philip D. Sprouse. In proof of Hurley's statement that when they got back to Washington some of them became his supervisors, John Carter Vincent made Ringwalt chief of the China Division, with Edward E. Rice and Fulton Freeman as assistant chiefs. John Stewart Service was made head of the promotions and placement section of the Department. Atcheson was sent as an adviser to General MacArthur. Ludden, Howard and Sprouse were returned to China in the consular service.

BLUNDER NUMBER FOUR

We must now look at General Marshall's final crushing blow to the Chinese republic. Prior to the Japanese surrender General Hurley went to China as the President's envoy. He induced Chiang Kai-shek to invite the Communists to enter discussions looking toward an end of the civil war. A Political and Consultative Conference was arranged to which the Communists sent a large delegation. General Hurley then left China and General Marshall was sent as President Truman's envoy at the end of 1945.

Almost the first thing General Marshall did was to inform both parties that *if* they would work out a plan of unity the United States would aid with material and credits. Here was the clearly implied threat that if they did not the government of China would get no help from us. Under this pressure a joint statement was issued by Nationalist and Communist leaders providing for an end of all military action pending the negotiations. A representative of each side, with General Marshall as chairman, sat down to discuss the plan. But the truce did not last long. Of course the blame was put upon the Nationalist government. Nathaniel Peffer in the New York *Times* weekly magazine section said that the "Nationalists had scuttled the truce." This was untrue. When the truce was ordered the Communists held 57 counties. A year later they had 310—indicating that they had taken advantage of the truce to expand, which was a violation of the truce. The Bolton Congressional report has made up an impressive catalogue of the bridges, railway stations and other installations destroyed by the Communists during this time.

General Marshall, in pursuance of his threat to cut off all supplies to the government if they did not make terms with the Communists, now promptly imposed an embargo—and he himself later labeled it as such. All aid of all sorts to China was discontinued until the summer of 1947. The war ended August 14, 1945. In December 1946, President Truman admitted we had given no military aid since V-J Day. And now Marshall had cut it off until August 1947. Thus for two years China got no real aid from us.

John Carter Vincent, then head of the Far Eastern Division of the State Department, stated its philosophy thus.

"I believe it is unsound to invest private or public capital in countries where a government is wasting its substance on excessive armaments, where the factor of civil war exists, where tendencies toward government monopolization exclude American business or where undemocratic concepts of government are controlling."

Analyze this specious plea. This did not involve a question of investment. It was a question of whether we would aid the Chinese government to arm itself to fight a Communist rebellion. This was a question to be resolved on principles wholly unconnected with business investment. China was in a civil war, in which a movement guided, financed and armed by Communist Russia was undertaking by force to overthrow the government of China and to bring that immense country into the Communist world. The State Department now admits that Russia was trying to do this. The question arose—was it a wise course to enable the Chinese Nationalist government to crush the Chinese Red rebellion or should we permit that rebellion to succeed? The issues here would rest on certain great principles unconnected with any immediate investment considerations.

As for China wasting her substance on armaments, she had no armaments and depended on us to get them and we refused to give them to her. The point raised was that where a country is attacked by revolutionists it must "waste its substance on armaments." The alternative, of course, in that case is that it must surrender to the revolutionists. This was a dishonest statement. In 1950, the North Koreans attacked the South Koreans. The South Koreans resisted. Were they not then wasting their substance on armament? Should we aid a country like that? That statement was so patently a piece of special pleading for the Communists that this alone marks the spot where our State Department stood.

China having got no aid since V-J Day (August 14, 1945), we have General Marshall's testimony that from then on she got no further aid until 1947, when the embargo was lifted. Then, he said, until 1948 there was only one important commercial contract made by the Chinese government. As for arms and ammunition only one important purchase was made—130 million rounds of rifle ammunition. The Chinese government got also 150 C-46's. In 1948 they sought to buy additional surplus ammunition from the Marianas, but Mr. Acheson, in his testimony during the MacArthur inquiry, did not say it was ever delivered. Others, however, have pointed out that it was practically worthless.

Then, in April 1948, Congress passed the China Aid Act providing $125,-000,000 as a grant for military assistance. Acheson said all of this was delivered by the end of 1949. He refers to the White Paper for proof. But that lists only $60,000,000 of shipments to March 1949. Acheson attempted to pull the wool over the eyes of the Senate Committee with the bald statement that we had given China $2,000,000,000 since V-J Day. But that did not stand up under cross examination. He had to admit that we had actually sent $747,000,000 and that $335,000,000 of that was for transporting troops to accept the Japanese surrender. The most he could scratch up as aid by his statistics was $430,000,000. And he admits that after 1948 all shipments went to Formosa, to which the government was preparing to flee. It is patently ridiculous to have Acheson on one hand attempting to exaggerate the aid given to China, while one of his high-ranking subordinates offers a set of excuses in defense of our failure to send adequate aid.

When Secretary Acheson was testifying in the famous MacArthur hearings, Senator Owen Brewster of Maine produced the report of Colonel L. B. Moody, U. S. Army Ordnance Corps officer, who had made a study of China's military needs and supplies with one of our missions. Excerpts from this report speak for themselves. He stated:

1. The inevitable defeat of the Nationalist army was due to their deficit in items of infantry weapons and especially ammunition, and the Communist superiority in these items.

2. Military aid to the Chinese means infantry weapons and ammunition above all else and it is "precisely these items which the United States has consistently denied, delayed or limited. Only passing reference will be made to the billions of mouldy cigarettes, blown-up guns, and junk bombs and disabled vehicles from the Pacific Islands which have been totalled up with other real or alleged aid in various State Department, Communist and leftist statements to create the impression that we have furnished the Nationalist government with hundreds of millions or billions of useful fighting equipment."

Secretary Acheson had testified as to the ammunition left by the Marines when they debarked from China. Colonel Moody said that when they left, the items referred to gave them a six-day supply for their 30-calibre weapons. Colonel Moody's study estimated that of the total brought in from various Pacific bases, only three per cent was of required ground-force types and only two per cent of the useful air-force types and that not all of this was serviceable. He estimated that the total Chinese and American rifle and machine-gun ammunition produced in 1948 amounted to only some 63 days' supply in active operations.

Of course, the pretense that our government was supplying the Nationalists with ammunition while at the same time they were giving out publicly their reasons for not doing it exposes the whole mendacious argument. The simple truth, as we have seen, is that when the Japanese surrendered, the Chinese Nationalists army far outnumbered the Red revolutionary army. Then appeared Stalin's army of 1,250,000 men armed with American guns, planes, tanks and munitions and other supplies and the balance began to alter. Now the Chinese Communists had in their hands the immense quantities of munitions laid down by the Japanese in the North. After that the Russian army was on their northern border and able to provide them not merely with arms and munitions but with military advice.

That was the situation in 1945. Then in 1946 General Marshall cut off the arms and supplies to the Nationalist army. Supplies were not resumed again for nearly two years, by which time the balance had wholly shifted. Even then what we sent was a mere niggardly handout. The end of it was that the Communists captured one province after another and ultimately drove the Nationalist government out of China to the island of Formosa.

During this time—that is, from 1945 to 1946—General Marshall was Chief of Staff and from 1946 to 1947 the President's special envoy in China and after that Secretary of State. He, more than any other man, was responsible for this policy. Was it because he was a Communist? There is probably no one in the country further removed from that stain than General Marshall. Was it because he was stupid or ignorant? Of course, he is neither. But he was certainly ignorant—shockingly and pathetically ignorant—of the dark, subtle, amoral and shameless techniques of Communist revolutionary strategy. Floundering around in a world as strange to him as military strategy would be to me, he inevitably fell into the hands of the State Department men in Washington and in China.

Senator Walter George, of Georgia, a patient and considerate man, said to Acheson when he was a witness before the MacArthur hearings that in 1946, when Marshall came back from China, he (Senator George) asked Marshall if he did not conclude that the only way to bring about any stability in government in China was through a coalition or integration of the forces. Said Senator George: "General Marshall's reply to me based upon his testimony before the Foreign Relations Committee after he had been named Secretary of State, when he finally came back, was that he hardly knew what he thought at that time, that there was so much confusion in his own mind as to what he thought could be done or could not be done." Acheson answered that this accorded with his own recollection of what Marshall's attitude was.

I think we may say with safety that there was no such confusion in Stalin's mind. The simple truth—and Americans, particularly American public men, will do well to heed this—is that there is a highly developed, comprehensive and intricate political technology which has been developed by the Communist technicians for dealing with political pressures of every description. They are unknown to Americans, including most public men. They are so devious, so malignant, yet so intelligent, and so utterly foreign to the processes of the ordinary American mentality, that Americans generally refuse to believe them. There are men in this country who know of this dark art. They attempted to put up the warning signals during the war and after. But they were silenced with the cry of "Fascist." It was difficult for them to be heard—however well known they were. The magazines, the radio and even the book publishers closed their doors on them. It was a high crime and a form of treason to the Brave New World to tell the truths which I have outlined here and which now, when the hour is late, our people are beginning at least dimly to see.

United States Policy and the Nationalist Collapse

JOHN K. FAIRBANK

MY VIEW of this controversial question is that the American capacity to influence the Chinese scene in the 1940's has been exaggerated. I do not believe that a sub-continent of half a billion or more people, still largely imbedded in their own immemorial culture, inaccessible for the most part except by footpath or sampan, can be controlled from outside. It is noteworthy that the Chinese Communist Party, created expressly as a tool for foreign influence, followed the guidance of the Comintern in the 1920's only to disaster. It began its rise to power only after its alien creed had been adapted and Sinicized under Mao Tse-tung.

The outcome in 1949 showed, not that Soviet aid had been greater than American, but that the Chinese Communists had been able to mobilize and

Reprinted by permission of the publishers from John K. Fairbank *The United States and China*, New Edition Revised and Enlarged, Cambridge, Mass.: Harvard University Press, Copyright, 1948, 1958, by The President and Fellows of Harvard College. Pp. 262–275.

utilize the potentialities of revolution while the Nationalists had not. The Communist victory also showed that over a period of thirty years the American influence on China had not contributed to the organization of political power in an American fashion as effectively as the Soviet influence had contributed to its organization in a Soviet fashion. We had no Comintern. Behind our lack of a conspiratorial revolutionary apparatus lay the more general lack of any philosophy or method for forced-draft economic development and political collectivism. Considering the suffering that rapid modernization of any sort was bound to bring upon the Chinese people, we need not entirely regret our inability to be China's model for the brutal task of remaking and industrializing her ancient society in the shortest possible time.

My answer to the imponderable question, Could we have saved China from Communism? is: Not without an utterly different approach prior to 1944; not at all thereafter. By the time we began to try, it was already too late.

Now historians have a weakness for accepting what happened as inevitable in the context of "social trends and forces" alleged and abstracted after the fact. This annoys men of action, who are conscious of the random elements of chance and personality in history. The only way to appraise the American role in the Fall (or Liberation) of China is to study the official record in the State Department archives, as Herbert Feis has done so ably in his book, *The China Tangle*, and to try to relate it, as no one yet can do, to the experience of the Chinese people in the same period.

War's Frustrations. Japan's Pacific War after December 7, 1941, soon intensified Chungking's frustration: Chiang Kai-shek failed to get a coordinated allied strategy centered around himself. Britain failed to hold Singapore or the Burma Road. General Stilwell had hardly arrived to be Chiang's chief of staff when he was given the hopeless task of defending Burma. Burma fell, with much Anglo-Chinese-American recrimination, and he then set himself the grueling three-year task of reopening a land route to China across the North Burma jungle. Yet even after it and its accompanying pipeline were opened in early 1945, the incredible Hump airlift still carried more tonnage. Again, our 20th Bomber Command got five big airfields built near Chengtu in Szechwan, of rock crushed by Chinese corvée labor. Supplying their B-29's took more Hump tonnage in 1944 than was allocated to the Chinese armies. But they had hardly begun to bomb Japan before their base was shifted to the Marianas, supplied by sea and nearer Tokyo. Entering the war as the prospective allied base for defeating Japan, Free China found that job done by naval-air-power at sea and herself cut off, a low-priority sideshow. The American aim became merely to keep Free China in the war. The result was not defeat but neither was it victory.

These frustrations of warfare should not surprise us, in an era when we have bloodily extirpated Fascism only to be confronted by Communism. But many felt that the frustration rate in the China-Burma-India Theater was preternaturally high.

Chinese nationalism continued to suffer frustration after Japan's defeat.

Well before Pearl Harbor, in May 1941, we had offered to abandon extra-territoriality as soon as peace should come in China. In October 1942 we offered to negotiate immediately, and a new Sino-American treaty on equal terms was signed January 11, 1943. But within five months another agreement was made, freeing American troops in China from Chinese criminal jurisdiction. American bases, supply and transport services, radio networks, airlines and army post offices were soon operating on Chinese soil in greater volume and with greater license than Southwest China had ever seen under the unequal treaties. At war's end Shanghai streets for many months were filled with GI's and roistering sailors far beyond the memory of treaty-port days. This ill suited China's new great-power status. China's new-found sovereignty took on a quizzical character. Right-wing chauvinists, Communists, and patriotic liberals could unite in inveighing against GI incidents connected with wine, women, and jeeps.

AMERICAN AID AND MEDIATION

Our Wartime China Policy. From late 1943 American diplomats began to glimpse the inherent danger in KMT-CCP (Nationalist-Communist) rivalry —"civil war at some undetermined future date," which might hamstring the war effort and eventually let Russia back the Communists. The Americans aimed therefore (1) to avert civil war by encouraging a political settlement, which Chiang Kai-shek advocated as early as September 1943, and (2) to strengthen the Nationalist Government position, partly by building up its armies, partly by getting it to reform itself. Armies were built up but reform proved impossible, for reasons already indicated. The idea of a political settlement, however, was accepted by all parties at least verbally. KMT-CCP negotiations had been resumed early in 1943. American policy proceeded on three levels.

First, on the international stage we tried to make China a great power in form if not in substance. She was permanently excluded from the high command of the war at the Anglo-American conference at Quebec in August 1943, but was included along with the Soviet Union in the Moscow Declaration of great-power principles in October. The Anglo-American-Chinese Cairo Declaration of December 1943 promised to return to China all territories lost to Japan, and Roosevelt at the Teheran conference stood firm for China's great-power status on the future UN Security Council. But this conferring of great-power status on the Nationalist Government was an American accomplishment, not Chinese or, least of all, British or Soviet. It was seen at the time as a fine and friendly gesture toward a great and deserving people. History, however, may view it with disillusion as a doctrinaire effort at transpacific master-minding of Chinese history, trying with words from abroad to strengthen a regime already in decline at home. (Peking of course now calls it simply an imperialist plot.)

Second, our idealistic support of Chungking's international prestige accompanied a realistic military effort, which produced a modernized Nationalist army and airforce. Stilwell's successor, General Albert C. Wedemeyer, with a thousand American instructors and advisors, carried on the training and equipping of 39 divisions.

Third, we tried to heal the KMT-CCP breach. The U. S. Army's single-minded concern for defeating Japan led it to question the efficacy of having 200 to 400 thousand Nationalist troops blockade the Communist area. In June 1944 Vice-President Wallace visited Chungking to suggest that Nationalist and Communist forces both fight Japan rather than watch each other. He got Chiang to let an American Military Observer Mission stay in Yenan, whither Western journalists had already been admitted in May. This opened an interesting window on the Communist scene but it remained apparent that Chungking and Yenan were each more concerned about the other than about Japan. Japanese forces meanwhile by late 1944 had pushed south through the Hunan rice-bowl and west from Canton to seize the major Sino-American base at Kweilin. During this crisis Chiang had held out against Stilwell's appointment to over-all command in China, and forced his recall in October; he also held out against the projected arming and use of Communist forces in a unified Chinese war effort. Unity and reform both remained remote hopes, but Ambassador Patrick J. Hurley, with more bravado than finesse, continued to encourage a Nationalist-Communist *rapprochement*.

At Yalta in February 1945 Roosevelt tried to secure Stalin's future support of the Nationalist Government as the price of Russia's recovery of the Tsarist position in northeast Asia. This was made known to Chiang, whose concurrence we had promised to obtain, only in June; and ratified in a Sino-Soviet treaty only as Japan surrendered, on August 14. By that date Russia was already in possession of Manchuria.

Behind all the infinitely detailed complexities of this story looms a basic fact: the Soviet Union and the Chinese Communists had the military capability to expand into Manchuria and parts of North China, respectively, and they could hardly have been controlled merely by a token show of force. Soon the Communists were further strengthened with surrendered Japanese arms which they got through Soviet connivance in Manchuria.

With peace came a great American air-and-sea lift of half a million Nationalist forces back to the coastal centers, a Communist race overland to expand by taking Japanese surrenders in North China, and American repatriation of 1,200,000 enemy troops to Japan. Even as the United States began to relax and demobilize, the long foreseen civil war began in the rivalry over the occupied areas. This was a moment when the American people were least prepared, emotionally and intellectually, to face a Chinese crisis. We had no intention in the winter of 1945–46 of fighting another war in East Asia.

General Marshall's Mediation. It was against this background that George C. Marshall went to Chungking in December 1945. His first months there were a hopeful chapter of American diplomacy. His aim was a political settlement of the burgeoning civil war. The only statemanlike alternative to internecine warfare was to get the Chinese Communists into the political and military framework of a constitutional regime, in a position similar to that of Communist parties in Western Europe. The two contending parties would both be represented in a reorganized coalition government under Chiang; their armies would be merged and reduced, whereupon American aid would be forthcoming. In January 1946 the Political Consultative Conference in Chungking reached a political agreement. A cease-fire order was issued by both armies. In February a military merger was agreed to. Meanwhile an unprecedented tripartite agency, the Executive Headquarters, was set up in the modern halls of the Rockefeller hospital in Peiping to superintend the quelling of a subcontinental civil war. American planes took jeeps, radios, supplies, and truce teams, composed usually of an American colonel with Nationalist and Communist generals, to far-flung inaccessible spots where fighting was in progress. Fighting practically stopped.

This breath-taking achievement was a personal tribute to General Marshall. It involved a strenuous effort to remain neutral in China's internal political process, and simultaneously to uphold the supremacy of the recognized government without being used by it. The truce collapsed principally in Manchuria, which still remained beyond the effective cease-fire limits. Behind the renewal of civil war in 1946 lay an intransigent Nationalist confidence in their superior armament, a shrewd Communist calculation of the Nationalists' actual vulnerability, and also, I think, the Russians' determination to embark upon a cold war of force and fraud against their erstwhile allies. While Stalin showed little confidence in the Chinese Communists' being soon victorious over the Nationalists, his cold war with the West gave them stimulus and opportunity to bid for power.

Stated conversely, one main background factor was the aversion of the American people in 1945–46 to use their armed power in continued warfare if necessary to secure and maintain a satisfactory peace settlement. On the contrary, we had only a vague idea of the kind of peace we wanted in East Asia. Like any postwar democracy, we were intent on demobilization and normalcy. Our China policy-makers were confined within this sincere but disastrously inhibiting framework of assumptions.

Might the American mediation, after all, have been successful? In the unfolding of history it is hard to prove a might-have-been: neither Chinese party trusted the other, nor was ready to give up its hope of eventual country-wide control. They had rival armies and organizations, and bitter memories of two decades of killing and being killed. In its historical context, a more irrepressible conflict can hardly be imagined. In the long view it is easy to conclude that Marshall's effort was a forlorn hope.

Yet the Chinese people wanted peace, the United States had enormous prestige and power to bring to bear upon the scene, the Communists stood to gain from the agreements, the Kuomintang was heavily dependent upon us. Not the least of our problems was how to get a party dictatorship to pursue democratic reforms in order to head off a revolution. Actually we had a divided objective: to press the Kuomintang leaders into reform which would diminish their autocratic power and facilitate internal peace; at the same time to strengthen the Kuomintang-controlled regime as a step toward political stability in East Asia. We became involved in continuing to build the Kuomintang dictatorship up materially at the same time that we tried to get it to tear itself down politically. But we could not control Chiang and his generals, who preferred to do things their way. They relied on their new arms.

After General Marshall became secretary of state in 1947 and we checked Communist expansion with the Greek-Turkish aid program, some felt that we should have saved China in the same way. China was roughly 45 times bigger than Greece in territory and 85 times in population. To treat China like Greece might have required millions of American troops and billions of dollars and even so would probably have been a failure. General Marshall, of all people, best knew the magnitude of such a task. We had no alternative after 1947 but to abstain from intervention in the Chinese civil war. Whether we should have given greater aid to the Nationalists in this period has been much disputed. Responsible American generals say there was no lack of arms. Many disputants have overlooked the severe limitations of our capacity to affect the outcome by means of material aid from outside.

THE NATIONALIST DEBACLE

From 1946 to 1949 China saw one of the big wars of modern times. Nationalist forces totaled at the beginning about three million men, the Communists about one million. United States aid to China between V-J Day and early 1948 cost over two billion dollars, in addition to some billion and a half committed during World War II. By sheer weight of arms Nationalist forces spread out to major cities and, when eventually permitted by Russia, into Manchuria. An infinitude of factors undid them: the military under Chiang were out of civilian control, their postwar reorganization heightened the confusion, the sessile Whampoa clique discriminated against provincial commanders and armies, particularly those of Kwangsi. Their strategic doctrine was to hold strong positions defensively, their instinct was to hoard supplies and wait for others to move first, their field tactics were sometimes masterminded by the Generalissimo from a great distance. Corruption, demoralization, and desertion steadily depleted the Nationalist armies. The Communists pursued opposite tactics, maneuvering in the countryside, recruiting among the populace, destroying railroads, avoiding unfavorable terms of battle. They grew in numbers and armament, both from the Japanese Manchurian stocks already noted and from Nationalist defections, sales, and surrenders. By June 1948 they were roughly equal in numbers of men, rifles, and cannon. Late in 1947 they had cut off the Manchurian garrisons. In October 1948 they forced their surrender—a third of a million men. This set the stage for a showdown.

The balance of power had not shifted only at the front, where the Communists steadily built up their stock of American guns and supplies. The

Nationalist cause had also been degutted in the rear, in its city bases, by an economic collapse, indexed by inflation.

Bombing by an enemy, like flood, fire, earthquake, or other disasters of nature, though destructive, tends to increase public morale and community effort in the face of a common danger. Hyperinflation, on the other hand, impoverishes and demoralizes each salaried individual as it gradually destroys the regime's fiscal capacity and public confidence in it. Life under hyperinflation is a slow strangulation. Salaries and wages never keep up. Furniture, books, and clothing go for food. Gradual malnutrition produces skin diseases, stomach ailments, tuberculosis. The whole society sickens, and the responsibility is put on those in power. Nationalist military collapse when it came was headlined in America, the ten-year hyperinflation which preceded it was not.

Free China's price level had risen only moderately in 1937–1939. The Nationalist currency still circulated over the whole country; Japanese-puppet note issues began at Peking only in 1938 and at Nanking only in 1939. Thereafter the Japanese mounted a campaign to undermine Free China's price stability, and meanwhile Chungking steadily increased its expenditures, with income lagging far behind outlay. In 1941, when revenues provided only 15 per cent of expenditures, the Central Government finally took over the land tax in kind. Income from it and from government monopolies and indirect taxes still provided, temporarily, only 30 per cent of the budget. Government taxes, domestic loans, gold sales and bond drives proved ineffective in mopping up the public's excess purchasing power. The situation steadily deteriorated, prices doubling every few months or weeks. In September 1945 the volume of note issue was 465 times that of July 1937.

The end of World War II gave a brief respite as the Nationalist currency spread back over all China, but large government expenditures continued, to say nothing of the buying spree by civilians returning to the coastal cities. Hyperinflation was resumed. Prices doubled 67 times in the two and one-half years from January 1946 to August 1948. Counting on its military superiority to end the civil war quickly, Nanking let its foreign exchange reserve be gradually reduced to pay for consumer imports and industrial raw materials. Foreign exchange was at first not seriously rationed nor imports restricted, and so capital fled the country. Meanwhile the domestic currency began to be replaced by foreign dollars and gold.

In order to break the vicious circle a "currency reform" in August 1948 demonetized the old currency and replaced it by the "gold yuan." At the same time price ceilings were set and enforced by police methods, and private holdings of specie and foreign currencies were forcibly converted to the new currency, while new note issue still continued to finance the civil war. Thus the few resources remaining to the most anti-Communist element, the urban upper middle class, were tied to the "gold yuan"; when it collapsed in late 1948 (prices finally rose 85,000 times in six months), the last remnant of civilian support for the Nationalist cause went with it.

The great two-month-long battle of the Huai-Hai was fought in the old Nien area of the Huai River basin, south of the Lunghai Railway, 100 miles or so north of Nanking. Generalissimo Chiang against the best advice of his staff committed some 50 divisions, out of 200 still remaining, to form a strong-point on the plains around Hsuchow. He himself from Nanking directed their tactical movements down to the division level in battle. The Communists, however, not only controlled the villages but by reactivating the railways as they advanced were able to deploy large forces. By mid-November four Nationalist army groups, about 340,000 men, had been quickly cut off and encircled on the plain around Hsuchow. A relief force of 120,000 troops, including the best American-trained divisions, was similarly blocked and encircled south of there. When the Hsuchow armies broke out to effect a junction, taking along their American trucks and cannon and the armored corps of tanks, this "mobile fortress" was blocked in turn by deep trenches and soon ripped by American-made Nationalist-surrendered heavy artillery. By late December the 130,000 surviving Nationalist forces, out of 66 divisions committed, were squeezed into six square miles, surrounded by 300,000 Reds. They learned that Nanking proposed to destroy their treasured heavy equipment "by air bombardment—*in situ*," as Edmund Clubb (our last consul-general in Peiping) puts it; they surrendered on January 10, 1949. Of 550,000 Nationalists lost, the Communists claimed 327,000 surrendered.

Typical of the entire Nationalist fiasco were Chiang Kai-shek's unwise decision to fight on the Hsuchow plain instead of the Huai River and his refusal to give command to the Kwangsi general, Pai Ch'ung-hsi, an able tactician who knew the terrain. Jealous non-cooperation among the Whampoa commanders, nonuse of Nanking's monopoly of the air, inability to bring their American-made firepower to bear upon the enemy, every aspect of this great defeat underlines the old adage that armament alone cannot bring victory. Tientsin and Peking surrendered in January 1949. In April the Communists crossed the Yangtze, in May they entered Shanghai, in October Canton, in November Chungking.

The Nationalist debacle had been not only military but also economic, political, and moral. The chaos, disorders and dangers of 1948–49 turned city dwellers irrevocably against the Nationalist Government and therefore against American aid to it. Having backed that government increasingly since 1937, we could not in the Chinese view divest ourselves of responsibility for its evils even though our aid had been well-intended, often critical of those selfsame evils and consequently limited in scope and amount. Our top generals opposed Chiang's strategy, to no avail.

Our worst disaster, however, came from the widening gulf between Chinese and American public feeling—in the postwar years when ineptitude and corruption were thoroughly discrediting the Kuomintang in China, we were experiencing intensified alarm over Soviet expansionist aims and methods, particularly over the cynical duplicity and ruthless ambition of the Communist movement. As the experience and circumstances of daily life continued to diverge in China and America, Communism seemed increasingly to be the only way out for one people and the mortal enemy of the other.

THE FALL OF CHINA IN AMERICA

For a decade the American public had idealized Free China; increasingly the combination of the atomic age and the cold war had intensified their fear of Communism. To have Free China become Communist seemed a national disaster. Like the Great Depression, it became political ammunition against the party in office. Governor Dewey used it in the 1948 campaign. Soon the Hiss case, the Fuchs case, the fear of spies and conspiracies, capped by a major war against Communist China in Korea, among other complex factors, took the lid off the McCarthy era.

The open season on China specialists in 1951–52 was facilitated by several circumstances. The American corps of China specialists both in and outside the government had been a small group in the 1930's. Most of them knew one another professionally as Foreign Service officers, scholars, or journalists. They had nearly all been "associated" with one another, if only at social or professional gatherings. If one assumed that American aid was a determining factor in China's domestic affairs, that the Nationalists could have lost their military superiority only through treachery, that American policy-makers had been anti-Chiang and therefore pro-Communist, and that Communist conspiracy could be detected through a man's associations (a series of untrue non sequiturs accepted by many during the McCarthy era)—then it became a public duty (and a rich opportunity) to investigate.

The motives for pursuing investigations were quite various. They ranged from the conscientious concern of officers responsible for our security to the shrewd calculations of political opportunists. In the background was a mood of anti-intellectualism and insecurity in a nation of whodunit readers suddenly fascinated by the morbid thought that almost anybody who seemed innocent of conspiracy might therefore be guilty of it. Along with the Congressional investigations of the time came intensified security screenings in the executive branch and industry which still continue, in a defensive imitation of totalitarianism. (This defensiveness fits the overly-pessimistic thesis that the American liberal tradition has lost its creative capacity at home, in addition to being non-exportable to Asia.)

Among China specialists the opportunity to find guilt by association was enhanced by fortuitous circumstance. The Institute of Pacific Relations since 1925 had pursued a program of research and publication punctuated by private conferences of scholars, diplomats, and businessmen representing research bodies, like the Royal Institute of International Affairs in London, in eleven countries concerned with the Pacific area. The IPR had produced some 1200 publications—books, pamphlets, reports—many of high scholarly value. While avoiding expressions of opinion itself, it had also sought contact with persons of many views and its records had been preserved. The files of the American IPR were replete with references to China specialists high and low, as well as some Communists, pro-Communists, and numerous foreigners. By seizing and exploiting these files a senatorial sub-committee was able to make frequent headlines for almost a year, up to the eve of the Republican convention of 1952.

The committee's report claimed in sweeping terms to show an IPR conspiracy to influence State Department policy-makers under Democratic administrations in favor of the Chinese Communists. The 14 volumes of hearings disregarded almost entirely the IPR's conferences and publications and concentrated on dubious contacts and questionable or pro-Communist utterances, whether or not actually connected with the IPR. My personal view is that the investigation got the truth of the matter thoroughly mixed up with hearsay, evidence out of context and guilt by association. If this had been combined with executive powers and police measures, it might have resembled a totalitarian purge trial. It was based on the necessary legislators' right of investigation, but exploited the great American tradition of playing cops-and-robbers and dirty politics.

This personal impression is not the verdict of history, which has yet to be worked out by research. The only action resulting from the IPR hearings was the indictment of one of Senator McCarthy's numerous targets, Owen Lattimore, for perjury allegedly committed during a record-breaking 12 days of public questioning. A federal court threw out this indictment in 1955.

These hearings and those on General MacArthur's recall were only the visible top of the iceberg. They were paralleled by secret security investigations of Foreign Service officers and other government employees on a wide and continuing scale. The China specialists were generally transferred to other areas, some were dismissed and some resigned. John S. Service was cleared six times in succession by the State Department Loyalty Board but was eventually dismissed at the request of the Loyalty Review Board. In June 1957 as a result of a Supreme Court order he was reinstated.

To an observer outside the government, the chief results of all these China policy investigations seem to have been security-consciousness and conformity. Very little if any Communism, espionage, or treachery was uncovered but everyone was intimidated. Fearfulness has handicapped our officials ever since. The peoples abroad whom we seek as allies cannot be cleared for security; our representatives who seek friends there may endanger their own careers.

Matters so recent as our China policy and the conduct of our China specialists are hard to judge. One's personal picture of the scene is too narrow. In addition each observer must strike his own balance between cognate but frequently conflicting interests. How reconcile the demands of national security, on which our freedom depends, with the free functioning and freedom of contact of the individual, for whom the nation exists? How evaluate the threat of totalitarian subversion from abroad as against the danger of totalitarian tendencies at home? Each citizen must work on these questions for himself.

My own impression is that the American people responded to the cold war and the Chinese Communist victory more fearfully than creatively. The chief significance of McCarthy was that he was tolerated for so long by those Americans who approved his stated aims but not his methods and yet out of fear were willing to countenance his methods.

Fear was compounded by ignorance. After 1949 the score or more of American press correspondents formerly in China were excluded. The gigantic upheavals among the Chinese people, the metamorphosis of Chinese society, remained almost unknown in America.

Fear and ignorance lead only toward disaster. We need instead a great effort to find out about Communist China in every way and to compete creatively with the totalitarian approach to Chinese problems, at least in our thinking and when possible in action. Constructive action on a frontier of modernization suits us better than a conservative, security-conscious defensiveness. . . .